Fishes

David Starr Jordan

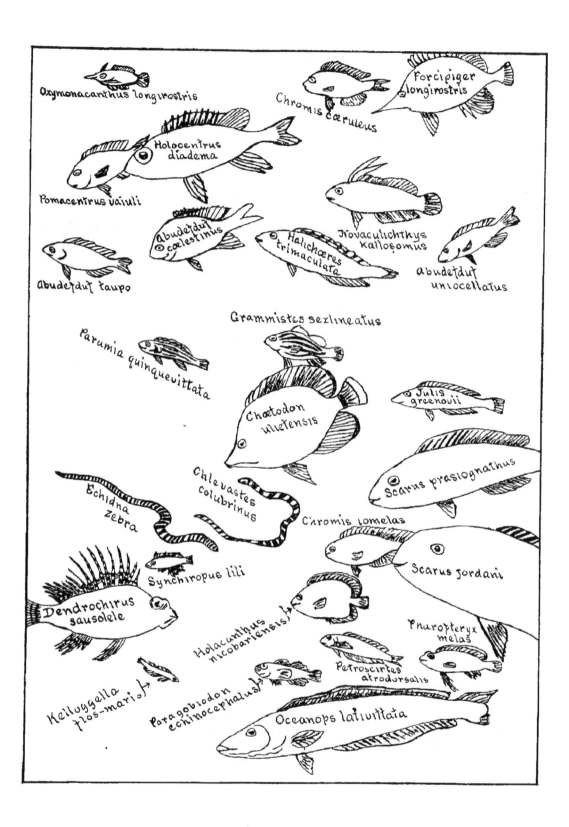

PREFATORY NOTE

This work contains virtually all the non-technical material contained in the author's "Guide to the Study of Fishes" It lacks the considerable portion relating to the structure and classification of fishes, which is intended rather for the technical student of ichthyology

The present volume contains substantially all which the author would have written had his original purpose been to cover the subject of fishes in a general natural history of animals. The fishes used as food and those sought by anglers in America are treated fully, and proportionate attention is paid to all the existing as well as all extinct families of fishes

Notwithstanding the relative absence of technical material in the present volume, the writer hopes that it may still be valuable to students of ichthyology, though his chief aim has been to make it interesting to nature-lovers and anglers, and instructive to all who open its pages.

DAVID STARR JORDAN.

June 15, 1907.

CONTENTS

CHAPTER I.

THE LIFE OF THE FISH (*Lepomis megalotis*)

CHAPTER II

THE EXTERIOR OF THE FISH

CHAPTER III.

THE DISSECTION OF THE FISH

CHAPTER IV

INSTINCTS, HABITS, AND ADAPTATIONS

CHAPTER V

ADAPTATIONS OF FISHES

Contents

CHAPTER VI

COLORS OF FISHES

CHAPTER VII

GEOGRAPHICAL DISTRIBUTION OF FISHES

CHAPTER VIII

BARRIERS TO DISPERSION OF RIVER FISHES

CHAPTER IX.

FISHES AS FOOD FOR MAN

CHAPTER X

THE MYTHOLOGY OF FISHES.

CHAPTER XI

THE COLLECTION OF FISHES

CHAPTER XII

THE LEPTOCARDII, OR LANCELETS

CHAPTER XIII

THE CYCLOSTOMES, OR LAMPREYS

CHAPTER XIV

THE CLASS ELASMOBRANCHII, OR SHARK-LIKE FISHES — TRUE SHARKS

Contents

Contents

CHAPTER XXI

THE GRAYLING AND THE SMELT

CHAPTER XXII

THE APODES, OR EEL-LIKE FISHES

CHAPTER XXIII

SERIES OSTARIOPHYSI

CHAPTER XXIV

THE NEMATOGNATHI, OR CATFISHES

CHAPTER XXV

THE SCYPHOPHORI, HAPLOMI, AND XENOMI

PAGE

CHAPTER XXVI

ACANTHOPTERYGII, SYNENTOGNATHI

CHAPTER XXVII

PERCESOCES AND RHEGNOPTERI

CHAPTER XXVIII

PHTHINOBRANCHII HEMIBRANCHII, LOPHOBRANCHII, AND HYPOSTOMIDES

CHAPTER XXIX

SALMOPERCÆ AND OTHER TRANSITIONAL GROUPS

CHAPTER XXX

BERYCOIDEI

Contents

CHAPTER XLI.

GOBIOIDEI, DISCOCEPHALI, AND TÆNIOSOMI

CHAPTER XLII

SUBORDER HETEROSOMATA

CHAPTER XLIII

SUBORDER JUGULARES

CHAPTER XLIV

THE BLENNIES BLENNIIDÆ

CHAPTER XLV

OPISTHOMI AND ANACANTHINI

CHAPTER XLVI

ORDER PEDICULATI THE ANGLERS

COLORED PLATES

CHAPTER I

THE LIFE OF THE FISH

A POPULAR ACCOUNT OF THE LIFE OF THE LONG-EARED
SUNFISH, *LEPOMIS MEGALOTIS*

WHAT is a Fish?—A fish is a back-boned animal which lives in the water and cannot ever live very long anywhere else. Its ancestors have always dwelt in water, and most likely its descendents will forever follow their example. So, as the water is a region very different from the fields or the woods, a fish in form and structure must be quite unlike all the beasts and birds that walk or creep or fly above ground, breathing air and being fitted to live in it. There are a great many kinds of animals called fishes, but in this all of them agree: all have some sort of a back-bone, all of them breathe their life long by means of gills, and none have fingers or toes with which to creep about on land.

The Long-eared Sunfish.—If we would understand a fish, we must first go and catch one. This is not very hard to do, for there are plenty of them in the little rushing brook or among the lilies of the pond. Let us take a small hook, put on it an angle-worm or a grasshopper,—no need to seek an elaborate artificial fly,—and we will go out to the old "swimming-hole" or the deep eddy at the root of the old stump where the stream has gnawed away the bank in changing its course. Here we will find fishes, and one of them will take the bait very soon. In one part of the country the first fish that bites will be different from the first one taken in some other. But as we are fishing in the United States, we will locate our brook in the centre of population of our country. This will be to the northwest of Cincin-

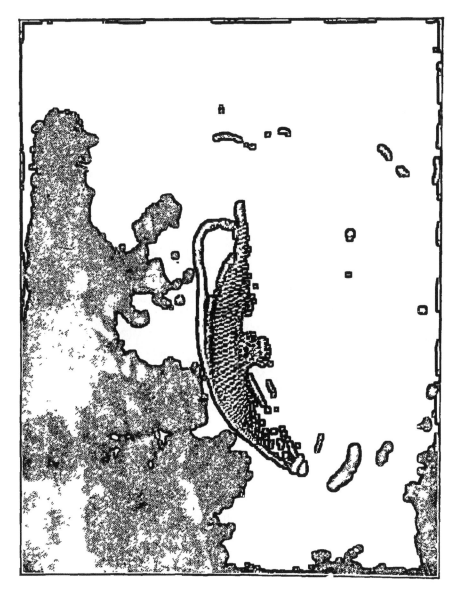

Fig. 1 —Long-eared Sunfish, *Lepomis megalotis* (Rafinesque) (From life by R. W. Shufeldt)—Page 2.

nati, among the low wooded hills from which clear brooks flow over gravelly bottoms toward the Ohio River   Here we will catch sunfishes of certain species, or maybe rock bass or catfish any of these will do for our purpose.   But one of our sunfishes is especially beautiful—mottled blue and golden and scarlet, with a long, black, ear-like appendage backward from his gill-covers— and this one we will keep and hold for our first lesson in fishes It is a small fish, not longer than your hand most likely, but it can take the bait as savagely as the best, swimming away with it with such force that you might think from the vigor of its pull that you have a pickerel or a bass   But when it comes out of the water you see a little, flapping, unhappy, living plate of

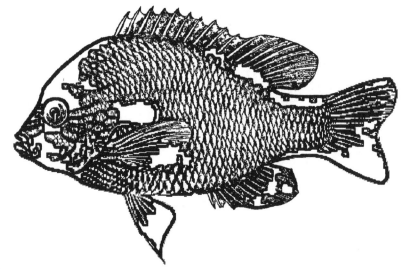

Fig 2 —Long-eared Sunfish, *Lepomis megalotis* (Rafinesque)   (From Clear Creek, Bloomington, Indiana) Family *Centrarchidæ*

brown and blue and orange, with fins wide-spread and eyes red with rage

Form of the Fish.—And now we have put the fish into a bucket of water, where it lies close to the bottom   Then we take it home and place it in an aquarium, and for the first time we have a chance to see what it is like   We see that its body is almost elliptical in outline, but with flat sides and shaped on the lower parts very much like a boat   This form we see is such as to enable it to part the water as it swims   We notice that its progress comes through the sculling motion of its broad, flat tail.

Face of a Fish.—When we look at the sunfish from the front we see that it has a sort of face, not unlike that of higher animals The big eyes, one on each side, stand out without eyelids, but the fish can move them at will, so that once in a while he seems to wink   There isn't much of a nose between the eyes, but the mouth is very evident, and the fish opens and shuts it as it breathes   We soon see that it breathes water, taking it in through the mouth and letting it flow over the gills, and then out through the opening behind the gill-covers

How the Fish Breathes—If we take another fish—for we shall not kill this one—we shall see that in its throat, behind the mouth-cavity, there are four rib-like bones on each side, above the beginning of the gullet   These are the gill-arches, and on each one of them there is a pair of rows of red fringes called the gills Into each of these fringes runs a blood-vessel   As the water passes over it the oxygen it contains is absorbed through the skin of the gill-fringe into the blood, which thus becomes puri-fied   In the same manner the impurities of the blood pass out into the water, and go out through the gill-openings behind The fish needs to breathe just as we do, though the apparatus of breathing is not the same   Just as the air becomes loaded with impurities when many people breathe it, so does the water in our jar or aquarium become foul if it is breathed over and over again by fishes   When a fish finds the water bad he comes to the sur-face to gulp air, but his gills are not well fitted to use undissolved air as a substitute for that contained in water   The rush of a stream through the air purifies the water, and so again does the growth of water plants, for these in the sunshine absorb and break up carbonic acid gas, and throw out oxygen into the water

Teeth of the Fish—On the inner side of the gill-arch we find some little projections which serve as strainers to the water These are called gill-rakers   In our sunfish they are short and thick, seeming not to amount to much but in a herring they are very long and numerous

Behind the gills, at the opening of the gullet, are some round-ish bones armed with short, thick teeth   These are called pharyn-geals   They form a sort of jaws in the throat, and they are useful in helping the little fish to crack shells   If we look at the mouth of our live fish, we shall find that when it breathes or bites it moves the lower jaw very much as a dog does   But it can move the upper jaw, too, a little, and that by pushing it out in a queer fashion, as though it were thrust out of a sheath and then drawn in   If we look at our dead fish, we shall see that the upper jaw divides in the middle and has two bones on each side   On one bone are rows of little teeth, while the other bone that lies behind it has no teeth at all   The lower jaw has little teeth like those of the upper jaw, and there is a patch of teeth on the roof of the mouth also   In some sunfishes there are three little patches, the vomer in the middle and the palatines on either side.

The tongue of the fish is flat and gristly   It cannot move it, scarce even taste its food with it, nor can it use it for making a noise   The unruly member of a fish is not its tongue, but its tail

How the Fish Sees.—To come back to the fish's eye again We say that it has no eyelids, and so, if it ever goes to sleep, it must keep its eyes wide open   The iris is brown or red   The pupil is round, and if we could cut open the eye we should see that the crystalline lens is almost a perfect sphere, much more convex than the lens in land animals   We shall learn that this is necessary for the fish to see under water   It takes a very convex lens or even one perfectly round to form images from rays of light passing through the water, because the lens is but little more dense than the water itself   This makes the fish near-sighted He cannot see clearly anything out of water or at a distance Thus he has learned that when, in water or out, he sees anything moving quickly it is probably something dangerous, and the thing for him to do is to swim away and hide as swiftly as possible

In front of the eye are the nostrils, on each side a pair of openings   But they lead not into tubes, but into a little cup lined with delicate pink tissues and the branching nerves of smell   The organ of smell in nearly all fishes is a closed sac, and the fish does not use the nostrils at all in breathing   But they can indicate the presence of anything in the water which is good to eat, and eating is about the only thing a fish cares for

Color of the Fish.—Behind the eye there are several bones on the side of the head which are more or less distinct from the skull itself   These are called membrane bones because they are formed of membrane which has become bony by the deposition

in it of salts of lime.   One of these is called the opercle, or
gill-cover, and before it, forming a right angle, is the preopercle, or false gill-cover.   On our sunfish we see that the
opercle ends behind in a long and narrow flap, which looks
like an ear.   This is black in color, with an edging of scarlet
as though a drop of blood had spread along its margin.
When the fish is in the water its back is dark greenish-looking,
like the weeds and the sticks in the bottom, so that we cannot
see it very plainly.   This is the way the fish looks to the fish-
hawks or herons in the air above it who may come to the stream
to look for fish.   Those fishes which from above look most like
the bottom can most readily hide and save themselves.   The
under side of the sunfish is paler, and most fishes have the belly
white.   Fishes with white bellies swim high in the water, and the
fishes who would catch them lie below.   To the fish in the water

Fig. 3.—Common Sunfish, *Eupomotis gibbosus* (Linnæus).   Natural size.   (From
life by R. W. Shufeldt.)

all outside the water looks white, and so the white-bellied fishes
are hard for other fishes to see, just as it is hard for us to see a
white rabbit bounding over the snow.

But to be known of his own kind is good for the sunfish, and we may imagine that the black ear-flap with its scarlet edge helps his mate and friends to find him out, where they swim on his own level near the bottom Such marks are called recognition-marks, and a great many fishes have them, but we have no certain knowledge as to their actual purpose

We are sure that the ear-flap is not an ear, however No fishes have any external ear, all their hearing apparatus being buried in the skull They cannot hear very much possibly a great jar or splash in the water may reach them, but whenever they hear any noise they swim off to a hiding-place, for any disturbance whatever in the water must arouse a fish's anxiety The color of the live sunfish is very brilliant Its body is covered with scales, hard and firm, making a close coat of mail, overlapping one another like shingles on a roof Over these is a thin skin in which are set little globules of bright-colored matter, green, brown, and black, with dashes of scarlet, blue, and white as well These give the fish its varied colors Some coloring matter is under the scales also, and this especially makes the back darker than the lower parts The bright colors of the sunfish change with its surroundings or with its feelings When it lies in wait under a dark log its colors are very dark When it rests above the white sands it is very pale When it is guarding its nest from some meddling perch its red shades flash out as it stands with fins spread, as though a water knight with lance at rest, looking its fiercest at the intruder

When the sunfish is taken out of the water its colors seem to fade In the aquarium it is generally paler, but it will sometimes brighten up when another of its own species is placed beside it A cause of this may lie in the nervous control of the muscles at the base of the scales When the scales lie very flat the color has one appearance When they rise a little the shade of color seems to change If you let fall some ink-drops between two panes of glass, then spread them apart or press them together, you will see changes in the color and size of the spots Of this nature is the apparent change in the colors of fishes under different conditions Where the fish feels at its best the colors are the richest. There are some fishes, too, in which the male grows very brilliant in the breeding season through the deposition of red, white, black,

or blue pigments, or coloring matter, on its scales or on its head
or fins, this pigment being absorbed when the mating season is
over   This is not true of the sunfish, who remains just about
the same at all seasons   The male and female are colored
alike and are not to be distinguished without dissection   If we
examine the scales, we shall find that these are marked with fine
lines and concentric striæ, and part of the apparent color is due
to the effect of the fine lines on the light   This gives the bluish
lustre or sheen which we can see in certain lights, although we
shall find no real blue pigment under it   The inner edge of each
scale is usually scalloped or crinkled, and the outer margin of
most of them has little prickly points which make the fish seem
rough when we pass our hand along his sides

The Lateral Line.—Along the side of the fish is a line of
peculiar scales which runs from the head to the tail.   This is

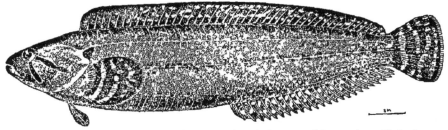

FIG 4 —*Ozorthe dictyogramma* (Herzenstein)   A Japanese blenny, from Hakodate
    showing increased number of lateral lines, a trait characteristic of many fishes of
    the north Pacific

called the lateral line   If we examine it carefully, we shall see
that each scale has a tube from which exudes a watery or
mucous fluid   Behind these tubes are nerves, and although not
much is known of the function of the tubes, we can be sure that
in some degree the lateral line is a sense-organ, perhaps aiding
the fish to feel sound-waves or other disturbances in the water

The Fins of the Fish.—The fish moves itself and directs its
course in the water by means of its fins   These are made up of
stiff or flexible rods growing out from the body and joined together by membrane   There are two kinds of these rays or rods
in the fins   One sort is without joints or branches, tapering to
a sharp point   The rays thus fashioned are called spines, and
they are in the sunfish stiff and sharp-pointed   The others,

known as soft rays, are made up of many little joints, and most of them branch and spread out brush-like at their tips   In the fin on the back the first ten of the rays are spines, the rest are soft rays   In the fin under the tail there are three spines, and in each fin at the breast there is one spine with five soft rays   In the other fins all the rays are soft

The fin on the back is called the dorsal fin, the fin at the end of the tail is the caudal fin, the fin just in front of this on the lower side is the anal fin   The fins, one on each side, just behind the gill-openings are called the pectoral fins   These correspond to the arms of man, the wings of birds, or the fore legs of a turtle or lizard   Below these, corresponding to the hind legs, is the pair of fins known as the ventral fins   If we examine the bones behind the gill-openings to which the pectoral fins are attached, we shall find that they correspond after a fashion to the shoulder-girdle of higher animals   But the shoulder-bone in the sunfish is joined to the back part of the skull, so that the fish has not any neck at all   In animals with necks the bones at the shoulder are placed at some distance behind the skull

If we examine the legs of a fish, the ventral fins, we shall find that, as in man, these are fastened to a bone inside called the pelvis   But the pelvis in the sunfish is small and it is placed far forward, so that it is joined to the tip of the "collar-bone" of the shoulder-girdle and pelvis attached together   The caudal fin gives most of the motion of a fish   The other fins are mostly used in maintaining equilibrium and direction   The pectoral fins are almost constantly in motion, and they may sometimes help in breathing by starting currents outside which draw water over the gills

The Skeleton of the Fish.—The skeleton of the fish, like that of man, is made up of the skull, the back-bone, the limbs, and their appendages   But in the fish the bones are relatively smaller, more numerous, and not so firm   The front end of the vertebral column is modified as a skull to contain the little brain which serves for all a fish's activities   To the skull are attached the jaws, the membrane bones, and the shoulder-girdle   The back-bone itself in the sunfish is made of about twenty-four pieces, or vertebræ   Each of these has a rounded central part, concave in front and behind   Above this is a channel through which the great spinal cord passes, and above and below are a certain number of processes or projecting points To some of these, through the medium of another set of sharp bones, the fins of the back are attached.   Along the sides of the body are the slender ribs

The Fish in Action.— The fish is, like any other animal, a machine to convert food into power   It devours other animals or plants, assimilates their substance, takes it over into itself, and through its movements uses up this substance again   The food of the sunfish is made up of worms, insects, and little fishes. To seize these it uses its mouth and teeth   To digest them it needs its alimentary canal, made of the stomach with its glands and intestines   If we cut the fish open, we shall find the stomach with its pyloric cæca, near it the large liver with its gallbladder, and on the other side the smaller spleen.   After the food is dissolved in the stomach and intestines the nutritious part is taken up by the walls of the alimentary canal, whence it passes into the blood

The blood is made pure in the gills, as we have already seen To send it to the gills the fish has need of a little pumping-engine, and this we shall find at work in the fish as in all higher animals This engine of stout muscle surrounding a cavity is called the heart   In most fishes it is close behind the gills   It contains one auricle and one ventricle only, not two of each as in man The auricle receives the impure blood from all parts of the body It passes it on to the ventricle, which, being thick-walled, is dark red in color   This passes the blood by convulsive action, or heart-beating, on to the gills   From these the blood is collected in arteries, and without again returning to the heart it flows all through the body   The blood in the fish flows sluggishly   The combustion of waste material goes on slowly, and so the blood is not made hot as it is in the higher beasts and birds   Fishes have relatively little blood, what there is is rather pale and cold and has no swift current

If we look about in the inside of a fish, we shall find close along the lower side of the back-bone, covering the great artery, the dark red kidneys   These strain out from the blood a certain class of impurities, poisons made from nerve or muscle waste which cannot be burned away by the oxygen of respiration.

The Air-bladder.—In the front part of the sunfish, just above the stomach, is a closed sac, filled with air   This is called the air-bladder, or swim-bladder   It helps the fish to maintain its place in the water   In bottom fishes it is almost always small, while fishes that rise and fall in the current generally have a large swim-bladder   The gas inside it is secreted from the blood, for the sunfish has no way of getting any air into it from the outside

But the primal purpose of the air-bladder was not to serve as a float   In very old-fashioned fishes it has a tube connecting it with the throat, and instead of being an empty sac it is a true lung made up of many lobes and parts and lined with little blood-vessels   Such fishes as the garpike and the bowfin have lung-like air-bladders and gulp air from the surface of the water

In the very little sunfish, when he is just hatched, the air-bladder has an air-duct, which, however, is soon lost, leaving only a closed sac   From all this we know that the air-bladder is the remains of what was once a lung, or additional arrangement for breathing   As the gills furnish oxygen enough, the lung of the common fish has fallen into disuse and thrifty Nature has used the parts and the space for another and a very different purpose   This will serve to help us to understand the swim-bladder and the way the fish came to acquire it as a substitute for a lung

The Brain of the Fish—The movements of the fish, like those of every other complex animal, are directed by a central nervous system, of which the principal part is in the head and is known as the brain   From the eye of the fish a large nerve goes to the brain to report what is in sight   Other nerves go from the nostrils, the ears, the skin, and every part which has any sort of capacity for feeling   These nerves carry their messages inward, and when they reach the brain they may be transformed into movement   The brain sends back messages to the muscles, directing them to contract   Their contraction moves the fins, and the fish is shoved along through the water   To scare the fish or to attract it to its food or to its mate is about the whole range of the effect that sight or touch has on the animal   These sensations changed into movement constitute what is called reflex action, performance without thinking of

Fig 5 —Common Sunfish. *Eupomotis gibbosus* (Linnæus)   Natural size   (From life by R W Shufeldt)—Page 12

what is being done   With a boy, many familiar actions may be equally reflex   The boy can also do many other things "of his own accord," that is, by conscious effort   He can choose among a great many possible actions   But a fish cannot   If he is scared, he must swim away, and he has no way to stop himself   If he is hungry, and most fishes are so all the time, he will spring at the bait   If he is thirsty, he will gasp, and there is nothing else for him to do   In other words, the activities of a fish are nearly all reflex, most of them being suggested and immediately directed by the influence of external things   Because its actions are all reflex the brain is very small, very primitive, and very simple, nothing more being needed for automatic movement   Small as the fish's skull-cavity is, the brain does not half fill it

The vacant space about the little brain is filled with a fatty fluid mass looking like white of egg, intended for its protection   Taking the dead sunfish (for the live one we shall look after carefully, giving him every day fresh water and a fresh worm or snail or bit of beef), if we cut off the upper part of the skull we shall see the separate parts of the brain, most of them lying in pairs, side by side, in the bottom of the brain-cavity   The largest pair is near the middle of the length of the brain, two nerve-masses (or ganglia), each one round and hollow   If we turn these over, we shall see that the nerves of the eye run into them   We know then that these nerve-masses receive the impressions of sight, and so they are called optic lobes   In front of the optic lobes are two smaller and more oblong nerve-masses   These constitute the cerebrum   This is the thinking part of the brain, and in man and in the higher animals it makes up the greater part of it, overlapping and hiding the other ganglia   But the fish has not much need for thinking and its fore-brain or cerebrum is very small   In front of these are two small, slim projections, one going to each nostril   These are the olfactory lobes which receive the sensation of smell   Behind the optic lobes is a single small lobe, not divided into two   This is the cerebellum and it has charge of certain powers of motion   Under the cerebellum is the medulla, below which the spinal cord begins   The rest of the spinal cord is threaded through the different vertebræ back to the tail, and at each joint it sends

out nerves of motion and receives nerves of sense   Everything
that is done by the fish, inside or outside, receives the attention
of the little branches of the great nerve-cord.

The Fish's Nest.—The sunfish in the spawning time will
build some sort of a nest of stones on the bottom of the eddy,
and then, when the eggs are laid, the male with flashing eye and
fins all spread will defend the place with a good deal of spirit
All this we call instinct   He fights as well the first time as
the last   The pressure of the eggs suggests nest-building to
the female   The presence of the eggs tells the male to defend
them   But the facts of the nest-building and nest protection are
not very well understood, and any boy who can watch them and
describe them truly will be able to add something to science.

CHAPTER II

THE EXTERIOR OF THE FISH

FORM of Body.—With a glance at the fish as a living organism and some knowledge of those structures which are to be readily seen without dissection, we are prepared to examine its anatomy in detail, and to note some of the variations which may be seen in different parts of the great group.

In general fishes are boat-shaped, adapted for swift progress through the water. They are longer than broad or deep and the greatest width is in front of the middle, leaving the compressed paddle-like tail as the chief organ of locomotion.

But to all these statements there are numerous exceptions. Some fishes depend for protection, not on swiftness, but on the thorny skin or a bony coat of mail. Some of these are almost globular in form, and their outline bears no resemblance to that

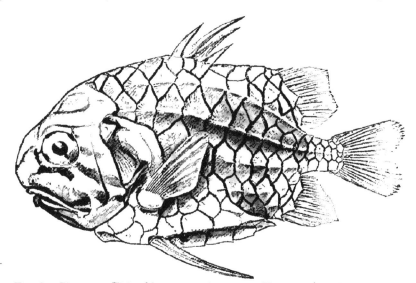

FIG. 6.—Pine-cone Fish, *Monocentris japonicus* (Houttuyn). Waka, Japan.

of a boat. The trunkfish (*Ostracion*) in a hard bony box has no need of rapid progress.

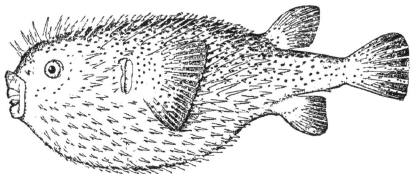

FIG 7 —Porcupine-fish, *Diodon hystrix* (Linnæus)   Tortugas Islands

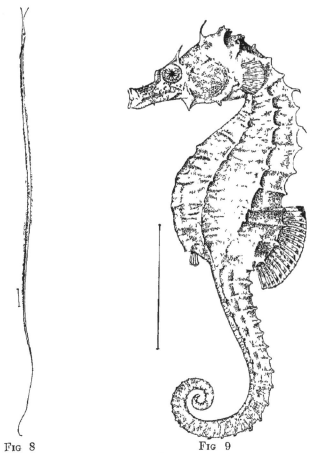

FIG 8   FIG 9

FIG 8 —Thread-eel, *Nemichthys avocetta* Jordan and Gilbert   Vancouver Island
FIG 9 —Sea-horse, *Hippocampus hudsonius* Dekay.   Virginia

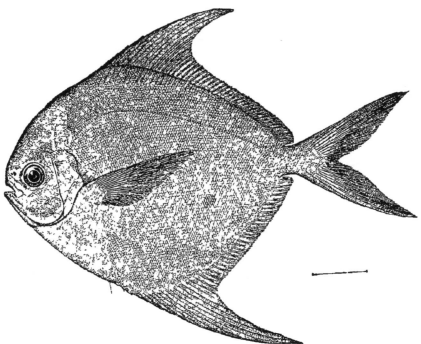

FIG 10 —Harvest-fish, *Peprilus paru* (Linnæus)   Virginia

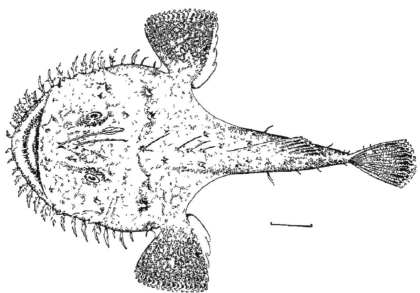

FIG 11 —Anko or Fishing-frog, *Lophius litulon* (Jordan)   Matsushima Bay, Japan
(The short line in all cases shows the degree of reduction, it represents an
inch of the fish's length)

The pine-cone fish (*Monocentris japonicus*) adds strong fin-spines to its bony box, and the porcupine fish (*Diodon hystrix*) is covered with long prickles which keep away all enemies

Among swift fishes, there are some in which the body is much deeper than long, as in *Antigonia* Certain sluggish fishes seem to be all head and tail, looking as though the body by some accident had been omitted These, like the headfish (*Mola mola*) are protected by a leathery skin Other fishes, as the eels, are extremely long and slender, and some carry this elongation to great extremes Usually the head is in a line with the axis of the body, but in some cases, as the sea-horse (*Hippocampus*), the head is placed at right angles to the axis, and the body itself is curved and cannot be straightened without injury The type of the swiftest fish is seen among the mackerels and tunnies, where every outline is such that a racing yacht might copy it

The body or head of the fish is said to be compressed when it is flattened sidewise, depressed when it is flattened vertically Thus the *Peprilus* (Fig 10) is said to be compressed, while the fishing-frog (*Lophius*) (Fig 11) has a depressed body and head Other terms as truncate (cut off short), attenuate (long-drawn out), robust, cuboid, filiform, and the like may be needed in descriptions

Measurement of the Fish.—As most fishes grow as long as they live, the actual length of a specimen has not much value for purposes of description The essential point is not actual length, but relative length The usual standard of measurement is the length from the tip of the snout to the base of the caudal fin With this length the greatest depth of the body, the greatest length of the head, and the length of individual parts may be compared Thus in the Rock Hind (*Epinephelus adscensionis*), fig 12, the head is contained $2\frac{3}{5}$ times in the length, while the greatest depth is contained three times

Thus, again, the length of the muzzle, the diameter of the eye, and other dimensions may be compared with the length of the head In the Rock Hind, fig 12, the eye is 5 in head, the snout is $4\frac{2}{3}$ in head, and the maxillary $2\frac{3}{8}$ Young fishes have the eye larger, the body slenderer, and the head larger in proportion than old fishes of the same kind The mouth grows larger with age, and is sometimes larger also in the male sex. The development of the fins often varies a good deal in some fishes with age, old fishes and male fishes having higher fins when

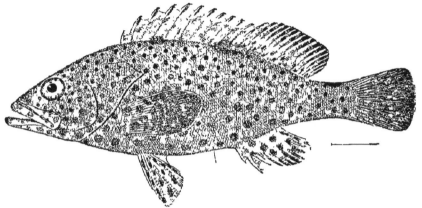

FIG 12 —Rock Hind or Cabra Mora of the West Indies, *Epinephelus adscensionis* (Osbeck)   Family *Serranidæ*

such differences exist   These variations are soon understood by the student of fishes and cause little doubt or confusion in the study of fishes

The Scales, or Exoskeleton.—The surface of the fish may be naked as in the catfish, or it may be covered with scales, prickles, shagreen, or bony plates   The hard covering of the skin, when present, is known as the exoskeleton, or outer skeleton   In the fish, the exoskeleton, whatever form it may assume, may be held to consist of modified scales, and this is usually obviously the case   The skin of the fish may be thick or thin, bony, horny, leathery, or papery, or it may have almost any intermediate character. When protected by scales the skin is usually thin and tender, when unprotected it may be ossified, as in the sea-horse, horny, as in the headfish, leathery, as in the catfish, or it may, as in the sea-snails, form a loose scarf readily detachable from the muscles below

The scales themselves may be broadly classified as ctenoid, cycloid, placoid, ganoid, or prickly

Ctenoid and Cycloid Scales —Normally formed scales are rounded in outline, marked by fine concentric rings, and crossed on the inner side by a few strong radiating ridges and folds

They usually cover the body more or less evenly and are imbricated like shingles on a roof, the free edge being turned backward   Such normal scales are of two types, ctenoid or cycloid   Ctenoid scales have a comb-edge of fine prickles or cilia, cycloid scales have the edges smooth   These two types are not very different, and the one readily passes into the other, both being sometimes seen on different parts of the same fish   In general, however, the more primitive representatives of the typical fishes, those with abdominal ventrals and without spines in the fins, have cycloid or smooth scales   Examples are the salmon, herring, minnow, and carp   Some of the more specialized spiny-rayed fishes, as the parrot-fishes, have, however, scales equally smooth, although somewhat different in structure   Sometimes, as in the eel, the cycloid scales may be reduced to mere rudiments buried in the skin

Ctenoid scales are beset on the free edge by little prickles or points, sometimes rising to the rank of spines, at other times soft and scarcely noticeable, when they are known as ciliate or eyelash-like   Such scales are possessed in general by the more specialized types of bony fishes, as the perch and bass, those with thoracic ventrals and spines in the fins

Placoid Scales —Placoid scales are ossified papillæ, minute, enamelled, and close-set, forming a fine shagreen   These are characteristic of the sharks, and in the most primitive sharks the teeth are evidently modifications of these primitive structures   Some other fishes have scales which appear shagreen-like to sight and feeling, but only the sharks have the peculiar structure to which Agassiz gave the name of placoid   The rough prickles of the filefishes and some sculpins are not placoid, but are reduced or modified ctenoid scales, scales narrowed and reduced to prickles

FIG 13 —Scales of *Acanthoessus bronni* (Agassiz) (After Dean)

Bony and Prickly Scales —Bony and prickly scales are found in great variety, and scarcely admit of description or classification   In general, prickly points on the skin are modifications of ctenoid scales   Ganoid scales are thickened and covered with bony enamel, much like that seen in teeth, otherwise essentially like cycloid scales. These are found in the garpike and in many genera of extinct Ganoid and Crossopterygian fishes In the line of descent the placoid scale preceded the ganoid, which in turn was followed by the cycloid and lastly by the ctenoid scale Bony scales in other types of fishes may have nothing structurally in common with ganoid scales or plates, however great may be the superficial resemblance

Fig 14 —Cycloid Scale

The distribution of scales on the body may vary exceedingly In some fishes the scales are arranged in very regular series, in others they are variously scattered over the body Some are scaly everywhere on head, body, and fins Others may have only a few lines or patches The scales may be everywhere alike, or they may in one part or another be greatly modified Sometimes they are transformed into feelers or tactile organs The number of scales is always one of the most valuable of the characters by which to distinguish species

Lateral Line.—The lateral line in most fishes consists of a series of modified scales, each one provided with a mucous tube extending along the side of the body from the head to the caudal fin The canal which pierces each scale is simple at its base, but its free edge is often branched or ramified In most spiny-rayed fishes it runs parallel with the outline of the back In most soft-rayed fishes it follows rather the outline of the belly It is subject to many variations In some large groups (*Gobiidæ, Pœciliidæ*) its surface structures are entirely wanting In scaleless fishes the mucous tube lies in the skin itself In some groups the lateral line has a peculiar position, as in the flyingfishes, where it forms a raised ridge bounding the belly In many cases the lateral line has branches of one sort or another It is often double or triple, and in some cases the whole back and sides of the fish are covered with lateral lines and their ramifications Sometimes peculiar sense-organs and occasionally eye-like luminous spots are developed in connection with the lateral line, enabling the fish to see in the black depths of the sea. These will be noticed in another chapter

The Lateral Line as a Mucous Channel —The more primitive

condition of the lateral line is seen in the sharks and chimæras, in which fishes it appears as a series of channels in or under the skin   These channels are filled with mucus, which exudes through occasional open pores   In many fishes the bones of the skull are cavernous, that is, provided with cavities filled

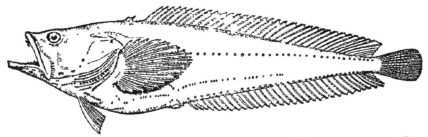

FIG 15 —Singing Fish (with many lateral lines), *Porichthys porosissimus* (Cuv and Val)   Gulf of Mexico

with mucus   Analogous to these cavities are the mucous channels which in primitive fishes constitute the lateral line

Function of the Lateral Line —The general function of the lateral line with its tubes and pores is still little understood   As the structures of the lateral line are well provided with nerves, it has been thought to be an organ of sense of some sort not yet understood   Its close relation to the ear is beyond question, the ear-sac being an outgrowth from it

"The original significance of the lateral line," according to Dr Dean,* "as yet remains undetermined   It appears intimately if not genetically related to the sense-organs of the head and gill region of the ancestral fish   In response to special aquatic needs, it may thence have extended farther and farther backward along the median line of the trunk, and in its later differentiation acquired its metameral characters"   In view of its peculiar nerve-supply, "the precise function of this entire system of organs becomes especially difficult to determine   Feeling, in its broadest sense, has safely been admitted as its possible use   Its close genetic relationship to the hearing organ suggests the kindred function of determining waves of vibration   These are transmitted in so favorable a way in the aquatic medium that from the side of theory a system of

* Fishes Recent and Fossil, p 52

hypersensitive end-organs may well have been established. The sensory tracts along the sides of the body are certainly well situated to determine the direction of the approach of friend, enemy, or prey "

The Fins of Fishes.—The organs of locomotion in the fishes are known as fins These are composed of bony or cartilaginous rods or rays connected by membranes The fins are divided into two groups, paired fins and vertical fins The pectoral fins, one on either side, correspond to the anterior limbs of the higher vertebrates The ventral fins below or behind them represent the hinder limbs Either or both pairs may be absent, but the ventrals are much more frequently abortive than the pectorals The insertion of the ventral fins may be abdominal, as in the sharks and the more generalized of the bony fishes, thoracic under the breast (the pelvis attached to the shoulder-girdle) or jugular, under the throat When the ventral fins are abdominal, the pectoral fins are usually placed very low The paired fins are not in general used for progression in the water, but serve rather to enable the fish to keep its equilibrium With the rays, however, the wing-like pectoral fins form the chief organ of locomotion.

The fin on the median line of the back is called the dorsal, that on the tail the caudal, and that on the lower median line the anal fin The dorsal is often divided into two fins or even three The anal is sometimes divided, and either dorsal or anal fin may have behind it detached single rays called finlets

The rays composing the fin may be either simple or branched The branched rays are always articulated, that is, crossed by numerous fine joints which render them flexible Simple rays are also sometimes articulate Rays thus jointed are known as soft rays, while those rays which are neither jointed nor branched are called spines A spine is usually stiff and sharp-pointed, but it may be neither, and some spines are very slender and flexible, the lack of branches or joints being the feature which distinguishes spine from soft ray

The anterior rays of the dorsal and anal fins are spinous in most fishes with thoracic ventrals The dorsal fin has usually about ten spines, the anal three, but as to this there is much variation in different groups When the dorsal is di-

vided all the rays of the first dorsal and usually the first ray of
the second are spines   The caudal fin has never true spines,
though at the base of its lobes are often rudimentary rays
which resemble spines   Most spineless fishes have such rudiments in front of their vertical fins   The pectoral, as a rule,
is without spines, although in the catfishes and some others a
single large spine may be developed   The ventrals when ab-
nominal are usually without spines   When thoracic each
usually, but not always, consists of one spine and five soft
rays   When jugular the number of soft rays may be reduced,
this being a phase of degeneration of the fin   In writing descriptions of fishes the number of spines may be indicated by
Roman numerals, those of the soft rays by Arabic   Thus
D XII–I, 17 means that the dorsal is divided, that the anterior portion consists of twelve spines, the posterior of one
spine and seventeen soft rays   In some fishes, as the catfish or
the salmon, there is a small fin on the back behind the dorsal
fin   This is known as the adipose fin, being formed of fatty
substance covered by skin   In a few catfishes, this adipose fin
develops a spine or soft rays

Muscles.—The movements of the fins are accomplished by
the muscles   These organs lie along the sides of the body,
forming the flesh of the fish   They are little specialized, and
not clearly differentiated as in the higher vertebrates

With the higher fishes there are several distinct systems of
muscles controlling the jaws, the gills, the eye, the different
fins, and the body itself   The largest of all is the great lateral
muscle, composed of flake-like segments (myocommas) which
correspond in general with the number of the vertebræ   In
general the muscles of the fish are white in color   In some
groups, especially of the mackerel family, they are deep red,
charged with animal oils   In the salmon they are orange-red,
a color also due to the presence of certain oils

In a few fishes muscular structures are modified into electric
organs   These will be discussed in a later chapter

CHAPTER III

THE DISSECTION OF THE FISH

THE Blue-green Sunfish.—The organs found in the abdominal cavity of the fish may be readily traced in a rapid dissection   Any of the bony fishes may be chosen, but for our purposes the sunfish will serve as well as any   The names and location of the principal organs are shown in the accompanying figure, from Kellogg's Zoology   It represents the blue-green sunfish, *Apomotis cyanellus*, from the Kansas River, but in these regards all the species of sunfishes are alike   We may first glance at the different organs as shown in the sequence of dissection, leaving a detailed account of each to the subsequent pages

The Viscera.—Opening the body cavity of the fish, as shown in the plate, we see below the back-bone a membranous sac closed and filled with air   This is the air-bladder, a rudiment of that structure which in higher vertebrates is developed as a lung   The alimentary canal passes through the abdominal cavity extending from the mouth through the pharynx and ending at the anus or vent   The stomach has the form of a blind sac, and at its termination are a number of tubular sacs, the pyloric cæca, which secrete a digestive fluid   Beyond the pylorus extends the intestine with one or two loops to the anus   Connected with the intestine anteriorly is the large red mass of the liver, with its gall-bladder, which serves as a reservoir for bile, the fluid the liver secretes   Farther back is another red glandular mass, the spleen

In front of the liver and separated from it by a membrane is the heart   This is of four parts.   The posterior part is a thin-walled reservoir, the sinus venosus, into which blood enters through the jugular vein from the head and through the cardinal vein from the kidney   From the sinus venosus it passes forward into a large thin-walled chamber, the auricle.

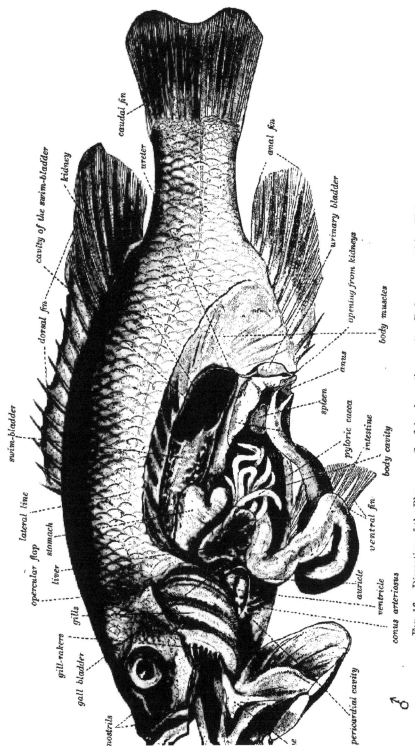

caudal fin

ureter

kidney

cavity of the swim-bladder

dorsal fin

swim-bladder

lateral line

opercular flap

stomach

liver

gills

gill-rakers

gall bladder

nostrils

anal fin

urinary bladder

opening from kidneys

body muscles

anus

spleen

pyloric caeca

intestine

body cavity

ventral fin

ventricle

auricle

conus arteriosus

pericardial cavity

♂

Fig. 16.—Dissection of the Blue-green Sunfish, *Apomotis cyanellus* Rafinesque. (After Kellogg.)—26.

Next it flows into the thick-walled ventricle, whence by the rhythmical construction of its walls it is forced into an arterial bulb which lies at the base of the ventral aorta, which carries it on to the gills After passing through the fine gill-filaments, it is returned to the dorsal aorta, a large blood-vessel which extends along the lower surface of the back-bone, giving out branches from time to time.

The kidneys in fishes constitute an irregular mass under the back-bone posteriorly They discharge their secretions through the ureter to a small urinary bladder, and thence into the urogenital sinus, a small opening behind the anus Into the same sinus are discharged the reproductive cells in both sexes

In the female sunfish the ovaries consist of two granular masses of yellowish tissue lying just below and behind the swimbladder In the spring they fill much of the body cavity and the many little eggs can be plainly seen When mature they are discharged through the oviduct to the urogenital sinus In some fishes there is no special oviduct and the eggs pass into the abdominal cavity before exclusion

In the male the reproductive organs have the same position as the ovaries in the female They are, however, much smaller in size and paler in color, while the minute spermatozoa appear milky rather than granular on casual examination A *vas deferens* leads from each of these organs into the urogenital sinus

The lancelets, lampreys, and hagfishes possess no genital ducts In the former the germ cells are shed into the atrial cavity, and from there find their way to the exterior either through the mouth or the atrial pore, in the latter they are shed directly into the body cavity, from which they escape through the abdominal pores In the sharks and skates the Wolffian duct in the male, in addition to its function as an excretory duct, serves also as a passage for the sperm, the testes having a direct connection with the kidneys. In these forms there is a pair of Mullerian ducts which serve as oviducts in the females, they extend the length of the body cavity, and at their anterior end have an opening which receives the eggs which have escaped from the ovary into the body cavity In some bony fishes as the eels and female salmon the germ cells are shed into the body cavity and escape through genital pores, which, however. may

not be homologous with abdominal pores. In most other bony
fishes the testes and ovaries are continued directly into ducts
which open to the outside

Organs of Nutrition.—The organs thus shown in dissection
we may now examine in detail

The mouth of the fish is the organ or series of structures first
concerned in nutrition   The teeth are outgrowths from the

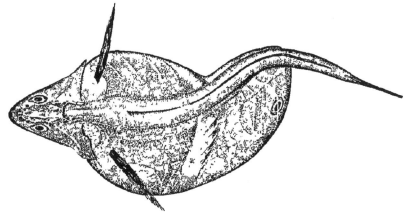

FIG 17.—Black Swallower, *Chiasmodon niger* Johnson, containing a fish larger
than itself   Le Have Bank

skin, primarily as modified papillæ, aiding the mouth in its various
functions of seizing, holding, cutting, or crushing the various kinds
of food material   Some fishes feed exclusively on plants, some
on plants and animals alike, some exclusively on animals, some
on the mud in which minute plants and animals occur   The
majority of fishes feed on other fishes, and without much regard
to species or condition   With the carnivorous fishes, to feed represents the chief activity of the organism   In proportion to the
voracity of the fish is usually the size of the mouth, the sharp-
ness of the teeth, and the length of the lower jaw

The most usual type of teeth among fishes is that of villiform
bands   Villiform teeth are short, slender, even, close-set, making
a rough velvety surface   When the teeth are larger and more
widely separated, they are called cardiform, like the teeth of a
wool-card   Granular teeth are small, blunt, and sand-like   Canine teeth are those projecting above the level of the others,
usually sharp, curved, and in some species barbed   Sometimes

the canines are in front   In some families the last tooth in either jaw may be a "posterior canine," serving to hold small animals in place while the anterior teeth crush them   Canine teeth are often depressible, having a hinge at base

Teeth very slender and brush-like are called setiform   Teeth with blunt tips are molar   These are usually enlarged and fitted for crushing shells   Flat teeth set in mosaic, as in many rays and in the pharyngeals of parrot-fishes, are said to be *paved* or tessellated   Knife-like teeth, occasionally with serrated edges, are found in many sharks   Many fishes have incisor-like teeth, some flattened and truncate like human teeth, as in the sheepshead, sometimes with serrated edges   Often these teeth are movable, implanted only in the skin of the lips   In other cases they are set fast in the jaw   Most species with movable teeth or teeth with serrated edges are herbivorous, while strong incisors may indicate the choice of snails and crabs as food   Two or more of these different types may be found in the same fish   The knife-like teeth of the sharks are progressively shed, new ones being constantly formed on the inner margins of the jaw, so that the teeth are marching to be lost over the edge of the jaw as soon as each has fulfilled its function   In general the more distinctly a species is a fish-eater, the sharper are the teeth   Usually fishes show little discrimination in their choice of food, often they devour the young of their own species as readily as any other   The digestive process is rapid, and most fishes rapidly increase in size in the process of development   When food ceases to be abundant the fishes grow more slowly   For this reason the same species will grow to a larger size in large streams than in small ones, in lakes than in brooks   In most cases there is no absolute limit to growth, the species growing as long as it lives   But while some species endure many years, others are certainly very short-

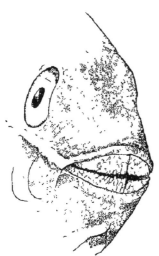

Fig 18 —Jaws of a Parrot-fish, *Sparisoma aurofrenatum* (Val) Cuba

lived, and some may be even annual, dying after spawning, perhaps at the end of the first season

Teeth are wholly absent in several groups of fishes They are, however, usually present on the premaxillary, dentary, and pharyngeal bones In the higher forms, the vomer, palatines, and gill-rakers are rarely without teeth, and in many cases the pterygoids, sphenoids, and the bones of the tongue are similarly armed

No salivary glands or palatine velum are developed in fishes The tongue is always bony or gristly and immovable Sometimes taste-buds are developed on it, and sometimes these are found on the barbels outside the mouth

The Alimentary Canal.—The mouth-cavity opens through the pharynx between the upper and lower pharyngeal bones into the

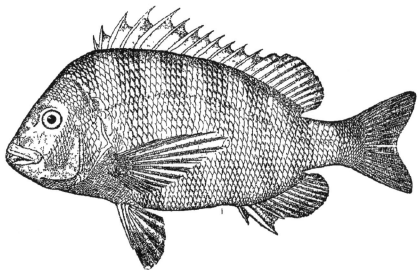

FIG 19 —Sheepshead (with incisor teeth), *Archosargus probatocephalus* (Walbaum) Beaufort, N C

oesophagus, whence the food passes into the stomach The intestinal tract is in general divided into four portions—oesophagus, stomach, small and large intestines But these divisions of the intestines are not always recognizable, and in the very lowest forms, as in the lancelet, the stomach is a simple straight tube without subdivision

In the lampreys there is a distinction only of the oesophagus with many longitudinal folds and the intestine with but one. In the bony fishes the stomach is an enlarged area, either siphon-shaped, with an opening at either end, or else forming a blind sac with the openings for entrance (cardiac) and exit (pyloric) close together at the anterior end. In the various kinds of mollets (*Mugil*) and in the hickory shad (*Dorosoma*), fishes which feed on minute vegetation mixed with mud, the stomach becomes enlarged to a muscular gizzard, like that of a fowl Attached near the pylorus and pouring their secretions into the duodenum or small intestine are the *pyloric cæca* These are tubular sacs secreting a pale fluid and often almost as long as the stomach or as wide as the intestine These may be very numerous as in the salmon, in which case they are likely to become coalescent at base, or they be few or altogether wanting

Besides these appendages which are wanting in the higher vertebrates, a pancreas is also found in the sharks and many other fishes. This is a glandular mass behind the stomach, its duct leading into the duodenum and often coalescent with the bile duct from the liver The liver in the lancelet is a long diverticulum of the intestine In the true fishes it becomes a large gland of irregular form, and usually but not always provided with a gall-bladder as in the higher vertebrates Its secretions usually pass through a *ductus cholodechus* to the duodenum

The *spleen*, a dark-red lymphatic gland, is found attached to the stomach in all fish-like vertebrates except the lancelet

The lining membrane of the abdominal cavity is known as the *peritoneum*, and the membrane sustaining the intestines from the dorsal side, as in the higher vertebrates, is called the *mesentery*. In many species the peritoneum is jet black, while in related forms it may be pale in color. It is more likely to be black in fishes from deep water and in fishes which feed on plants.

The Spiral Valve.—In the sharks or skates the rectum or large intestine is peculiarly modified, being provided with a spiral valve, with sometimes as many as forty gyrations A spiral valve is also present in the more ancient types of the true fishes as dipnoans, crossopterygians, and ganoids This valve greatly increases the surface of the intestine, doing away with the necessity for length In the bowfin (*Amia*) and the garpike (*Lepi-*

sosteus) the valve is reduced to a rudiment of three or four convolutions near the end of the intestine. In the sharks and skates the intestine opens into a cloaca, which contains also the urogenital openings. In all fishes the latter lie behind the orifice of the intestine. In the bony fishes and the ganoids there is no cloaca.

Length of the Intestine.—In all fishes, as in the higher vertebrates, the length of the alimentary canal is coordinated with the food of the fish. In those which feed upon plants the intes-

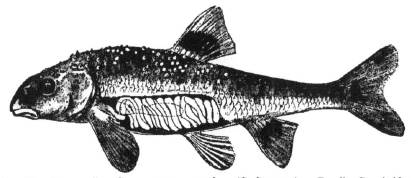

Fig. 20.—Stone-roller, *Campostoma anomalum* (Rafinesque). Family *Cyprinidœ*. Showing nuptial tubercles and intestines coiled about the air-bladder.

tine is very long and much convoluted, while in those which feed on other fishes it is always relatively short. In the stone-roller, a fresh-water minnow (*Campostoma*) found in the Mississippi Valley, the excessively long intestines filled with vegetable matter are wound spool-fashion about the large air-bladder. In all other fishes the air-bladder lies on the dorsal side of the intestinal canal.

Fig. 21.—Skeleton of the Cow-fish, *Lactophrys tricornis* (Linnæus).

The Eggs of Fishes.—The great majority of fishes are oviparous, the eggs being fertilized after deposition. The eggs are laid in gravel or sand or other places suitable for the species, and the milt containing the sperm-cells of the male is discharged over or among them in the water. A very small quantity of the sperm-fluid may impregnate a large number of eggs. But one sperm-cell can enter a particular egg. In a number of families the species are ovoviviparous, the eggs being hatched in the ovary or in a dilated part of the oviduct, the latter resembling a real uterus. In some sharks there is a structure analogous to

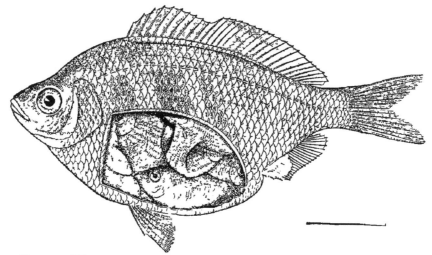

Fig. 22.—White Surf-fish, viviparous, with young, *Cymatogaster aggregatus*
Gibbons   San Francisco

the placenta of higher animals, but not of the same structure or origin. In the case of viviparous fishes actual copulation takes place and there is usually a modification of some organ to effect transfer of the sperm-cells. This is the purpose of the sword-shaped anal fin in many top-minnows (*Pœciliidæ*), the fin itself being placed in advance of its usual position. In the surf-fishes (*Embiotocidæ*) the structure of part of the anal fin is modified, although it is not used as an intromittent organ. In the Elasmobranchs, as already stated, large organs of cartilage (claspers) are developed from the ventral fins.

In some viviparous fishes, as in the rockfishes (*Sebastodes*) and rosefishes (*Sebastes*), the young are very minute at birth.

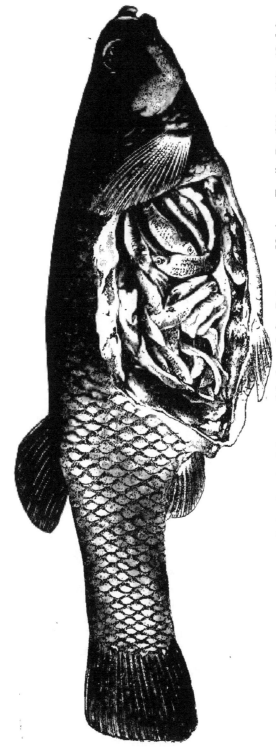

Fig. 23.—*Goodea luitpoldi* (Steindachner). A viviparous fish from Lake Patzcuaro, Mexico. Family *Pœciliidæ*. (After Meek.)

34

In others, as the surf-fishes (*Embiotocidæ*), they are relatively large and few in number   In the viviparous sharks, which constitute the majority of the species of living sharks, the young are large at birth and prepared to take care of themselves

The eggs of fishes vary very much in size and form   In

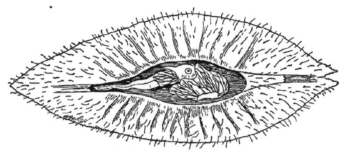

FIG. 24 —Egg of *Callorhynchus antorcticus*, the Bottle-nosed Chimæra   (After Parker and Haswell)

those sharks and rays which lay eggs the ova are deposited in a horny egg-case, in color and texture suggesting the kelp in which they are laid   The eggs of the bull-head sharks (*Heterodontus*) are spirally twisted, those of the cat-sharks (*Scyliorhinidæ*) are quadrate with long filaments at the angles.   Those of rays are wheelbarrow-shaped with four "handles"   One egg-case

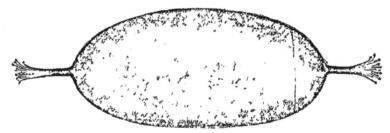

FIG. 25 —Egg of the Hagfish, *Myxine limosa* Girard, showing threads for attachment   (After Dean)

of a ray may sometimes contain several eggs and develop several young   The eggs of lancelets are small, but those of the hagfishes are large, ovate, with fibres at each side, each with a triple hook at tip   The chimæra has also large egg-cases, oblong in form.

In the higher fishes the eggs are spherical, large or small according to the species, and varying in the firmness of their outer walls   All contain food-yolk from which the embryo in its earlier stages is fed   The eggs of the eel (*Anguilla*) are micro-

scopic   According to Gunther 25,000 eggs have been counted in the herring, 155,000 in the lumpfish, 3,500,000 in the halibut, 635,200 in the sturgeon, and 9,344,000 in the cod   Smaller numbers are found in fishes with large ova   The red salmon has about 3500 eggs, the king salmon about 5200   Where an oviduct is present the eggs are often poured out in glutinous masses, as in the bass   When, as in the salmon, there is no oviduct, the eggs lie separate and do not cohere together   It is only with the latter class of fishes, those in which the eggs remain distinct, that artificial impregnation and hatching is practicable   In this re-

Fig 26 —Egg of Port Jackson Shark, *Heterodontus philippi* (Lacépède) (After Parker and Haswell)

gard the value of the salmon and trout is predominant   In some fishes, especially those of elongate form, as the needle-fish (*Tylosurus*), the ovary of but one side is developed

Protection of the Young.—In most fishes the parents take no care of their eggs or young   In some catfishes (*Platystacus*) the eggs adhere to the under surface of the female   In the sea-horses and pipefishes a pouch is formed in the skin, usually underneath the tail of the male   Into this the eggs are thrust, and here the young fishes hatch out, remaining until large enough to take care of themselves   In certain sea catfishes (*Galeichthys*) the male carries the eggs in his mouth, thus protecting them from the attacks of other fishes   In numerous cases the male constructs a rough nest, which he defends against all intruders, against the female as well as against outside enemies   The nest-building habit is especially developed in the sticklebacks (*Gasterosteida*), a group in which the male fish, though a pygmy in size, is very fierce in disposition

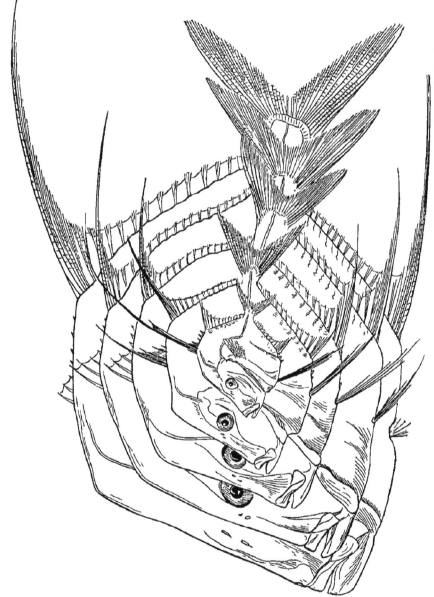

FIG 27 —Development of the Horsehead-fish, *Selene vomer* (Linnæus). Family *Carangidæ* (After Lutken)

37

CHAPTER IV

INSTINCTS, HABITS, AND ADAPTATIONS

THE Habits of Fishes.—The habits of fishes can hardly be summarized in any simple mode of classification In the usual course of fish-life the egg is laid in the early spring, in water shallower than that in which the parents spend their lives In most cases it is hatched as the water grows warmer The eggs of the members of the salmon and cod families are, however, mostly hatched in cooling waters The young fish gathers with others of its species in little schools, feeds on smaller fishes of other species or of its own, grows and changes until maturity, deposits its eggs, and the cycle of life begins again, while the old fish ultimately dies or is devoured

Irritability of Animals.—All animals, of whatever degree of organization, show in life the quality of irritability or response to external stimulus Contact with external things produces some effect on each of them, and this effect is something more than the mere mechanical effect on the matter of which the animal is composed In the one-celled animals the functions of response to external stimulus are not localized They are the property of any part of the protoplasm of the body In the higher or many-celled animals each of these functions is specialized and localized A certain set of cells is set apart for each function, and each organ or series of cells is released from all functions save its own

Nerve-cells and Fibres.—In the development of the individual animal certain cells from the primitive external layer or ectoblast of the embryo are set apart to preside over the relations of the creature to its environment These cells are highly specialized, and while some of them are highly sensitive, others are adapted for carrying or transmitting the stimuli received by the sensitive cells, and still others have the function of receiving sense-impressions and of translating them into impulses of motion   The nerve-cells are receivers of impressions   These are gathered together in nerve-masses or ganglia, the largest of these being known as the brain, the ganglia in general being known as nerve-centres   The nerves are of two classes   The one class, called sensory nerves, extends from the skin or other organ of sensation to the nerve-centre   The nerves of the other class, motor nerves, carry impulses to motion

The Brain, or Sensorium.—The brain or other nerve-centre sits in darkness, surrounded by a bony protecting box   To this main nerve-centre, or *sensorium*, come the nerves from all parts of the body that have sensation, the external skin as well as the special organs of sight, hearing, taste, and smell   With these come nerves bearing sensations of pain, temperature, muscular effort—all kinds of sensation which the brain can receive   These nerves are the sole sources of knowledge to any animal organism. Whatever idea its brain may contain must be built up through these nerve-impressions   The aggregate of these impressions constitute the world as the organism knows it   All sensation is related to action   If an organism is not to act, it cannot feel, and the intensity of its feeling is related to its power to act

Reflex Action—These impressions brought to the brain by the sensory nerves represent in some degree the facts in the animal's environment   They teach something as to its food or its safety   The power of locomotion is characteristic of animals   If they move, their actions must depend on the indications carried to the nerve-centre from the outside, if they feed on living organisms, they must seek their food, if, as in many cases, other living organisms prey on them, they must bestir themselves to escape   The impulse of hunger on the one hand and of fear on the other are elemental   The sensorium receives an impression that food exists in a certain direction   At once an impulse to motion is sent out from it to the muscles necessary to move the body in that direction   In the higher animals these movements are more rapid and more exact   This is because organs of sense, muscles, nerve-fibres, and the nerve-cells are all alike highly specialized   In the fish the sensation is slow, the muscular response sluggish, but the method remains the same.   This is simple reflex action, an impulse from the

environment carried to the brain and then unconsciously reflected back as motion   The impulse of fear is of the same
nature.   Reflex action is in general unconscious, but with animals, as with man, it shades by degrees into conscious action,
and into volition or action "done on purpose"

Instinct.—Different animals show differences in method or
degree of response to external influences   Fishes will pursue
their prey, flee from a threatening motion, or disgorge sand or
gravel swallowed with their food   Such peculiarities of different forms of life constitute the basis of instinct

Instinct is automatic obedience to the demands of conditions
external to the nervous system   As these conditions vary with
each kind of animal, so must the demands vary, and from this
arises the great variety actually seen in the instincts of different
animals   As the demands of life become complex, so do the instincts   The greater the stress of environment, the more perfect
the automatism, for impulses to safe action are necessarily adequate to the duty they have to perform   If the instinct were
inadequate, the species would have become extinct   The fact
that its individuals persist shows that they are provided with
the instincts necessary to that end   Instinct differs from other
allied forms of response to external condition in being hereditary,
continuous from generation to generation   This sufficiently distinguishes it from reason, but the line between instinct and reason
and other forms of reflex action cannot be sharply drawn

It is not necessary to consider here the question of the origin
of instincts   Some writers regard them as "inherited habits,"
while others, with apparent justice, doubt if mere habits or
voluntary actions repeated till they become a "second nature"
ever leave a trace upon heredity   Such investigators regard
instinct as the natural survival of those methods of automatic
response which were most useful to the life of the animal, the
individual having less effective methods of reflex action perish-
ing, leaving no posterity

Classification of Instincts. —The instincts of fishes may be
roughly classified as to their relation to the individual into
egoistic and altruistic instincts.

Egoistic instincts are those which concern chiefly the individual animal itself   To this class belong the instincts of feed-

ing, those of self-defense and of strife, the instincts of play, the climatic instincts, and environmental instincts, those which direct the animal's mode of life

Altruistic instincts are those which relate to parenthood and those which are concerned with the mass of individuals of the same species   The latter may be called the social instincts In the former class, the instincts of parenthood, may be included the instinct of courtship, reproduction, home-making, nest-building, and care for the young   Most of these are feebly developed among fishes

The instincts of feeding are primitively simple, growing complex through complex conditions   The fish seizes its prey by direct motion, but the conditions of life modify this simple action to a very great degree

The instinct of self-defense is even more varied in its manifestations   It may show itself either in the impulse to make war on an intruder or in the desire to flee from its enemies Among carnivorous forms fierceness of demeanor serves at once in attack and in defense

Herbivorous fishes, as a rule, make little direct resistance to their enemies, depending rather on swiftness of movement, or in some cases on simple insignificance   To the latter cause the abundance of minnows, anchovies, and other small or feeble fishes may be attributed, for all are the prey of carnivorous fishes, which they far exceed in number

The instincts of courtship relate chiefly to the male, the female being more or less passive   Among many fishes the male makes himself conspicuous in the breeding season, spreading his fins, intensifying his pigmented colors through muscular tension, all this supposedly to attract the attention of the female   That this purpose is actually accomplished by such display is not, however, easily proved   In the little brooks in spring, male minnows can be found with warts on the nose or head, with crimson pigment on the fins, or blue pigment on the back, or jet-black pigment all over the head, or with varied combination of all these   Their instinct is to display all these to the best advantage, even though the conspicuous hues lead to their own destruction

The movements of many migratory animals are mainly controlled by the impulse to reproduce   Some pelagic fishes, especially flying fishes and fishes allied to the mackerel, swim long distances to a region favorable for a deposition of spawn   Some species are known only in the waters they make their breeding homes, the individuals being scattered through the wide seas at other times   Many fresh-water fishes, as trout, suckers, etc , forsake the large streams in the spring, ascending the small brooks

Fig 28 —Jaws of *Nemichthys arocetta* Jordan and Gilbert

where they can rear their young in greater safety   Still others, known as anadromous fishes, feed and mature in the sea, but ascend the rivers as the impulse of reproduction grows strong An account of these is given in a subsequent paragraph

Variability of Instincts —When we study instincts of animals with care and in detail, we find that their regularity is much less than has been supposed   There is as much variation in regard to instinct among individuals as there is with regard to other characters of the species   Some power of choice is found in almost every operation of instinct   Even the most machine-like instinct shows some degree of adaptability to new conditions   On the other hand, in no animal does reason show entire freedom from automatism or reflex action   "The fundamental identity of instinct with intelligence," says Dr Charles O Whitman, "is shown in their dependence upon the same structural mechanism (the brain and nerves) and in their responsive adaptability "

Adaptation to Environment.—In general food-securing structures are connected with the mouth, or, as in the anglers, are hung as lures above it, spines of offense and defense, electric organs, poison-glands, and the like are used in self-protection, the bright nuptial colors and adornments of the breeding season are doubtfully classed as useful in rivalry, the egg-sacs, nests, and other structures or habits may serve to defend the ~ing, while skinny flaps, sand or weed-like markings, and many other features of mimicry serve as concessions to the environment.

Each kind of fishes has its own ways of life, fitted to the conditions of environment. Some species lie on the bottom, flat, as a flounder, or prone on their lower fins, as a darter or a stone-roller. Some swim freely in the depths, others at the surface of the depths. Some leap out of the water from time to time, as the mullet (*Mugil*) or the tarpon (*Tarpon atlanticus*).

Flight of Fishes.—Some fishes called the flying-fishes sail through the air with a grasshopper-like motion that closely imitates true flight. The long pectoral fins, wing-like in form, cannot, however, be flapped by the fish, the muscles serving

Fig. 29.—Catalina Flying Fish, *Cypsilurus californicus* (Cooper). Santa Barbara.

only to expand or fold them. These fishes live in the open sea or open channel, swimming in large schools. The small species fly for a few feet only, the large ones for more than an eighth of a mile. These may rise five to twenty feet above the water.

The flight of one of the largest flying fishes (*Cypsilurus californicus*) has been carefully studied by Dr. Charles H. Gilbert and the writer. The movements of the fish in the water are extremely rapid. The sole motive power is the action under the water of the strong tail. No force can be acquired while the fish is in the air. On rising from the water the movements

of the tail are continued until the whole body is out of the water
When the tail is in motion the pectorals seem in a state of rapid
vibration This is not produced by muscular action on the
fins themselves It is the body of the fish which vibrates, the
pectorals projecting farthest having the greatest amplitude of
movement While the tail is in the water the ventral fins are
folded When the action of the tail ceases the pectorals and
ventrals are spread out wide and held at rest They are not
used as true wings, but are held out firmly, acting as parachutes,
enabling the body to skim through the air When the fish
begins to fall the tail touches the water As soon as it is in the
water it begins its motion, and the body with the pectorals
again begins to vibrate The fish may, by skimming the water,
regain motion once or twice, but it finally falls into the water
with a splash While in the air it suggests a large dragon-fly

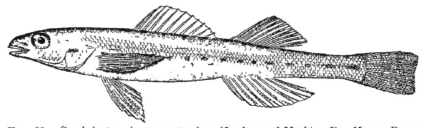

Fig 30 —Sand-darter, *Ammocrypta clara* (Jordan and Meek) Des Moines River

The motion is very swift at first in a straight line, but is later
deflected in a curve, the direction bearing little or no relation
to that of the wind When a vessel passes through a school
of these fishes, they spring up before it, moving in all directions,
as grasshoppers in a meadow

Quiescent Fishes —Some fishes, as the lancelet, lie buried in
the sand all their lives Others, as the sand-darter (*Ammocrypta
pellucida*) and the hinalea (*Julis gaimard*), bury themselves in
the sand at intervals or to escape from their enemies Some live
in the cavities of tunicates or sponges or holothurians or corals
or oysters, often passing their whole lives inside the cavity of
one animal Many others hide themselves in the interstices of
kelp or seaweeds Some eels coil themselves in the crevices of
rocks or coral masses, striking at their prey like snakes Some
sea-horses cling by their tails to gulfweed or sea-wrack Many

little fishes (*Gobiomorus, Carangus, Psenes*) cluster under the stinging tentacles of the Portuguese man-of-war or under ordinary jellyfishes   In the tide-pools, whether rock, coral, or mud, in all regions multitudes of little fishes abound   As these localities are neglected by most collectors, they have proved of late years a most prolific source of new species

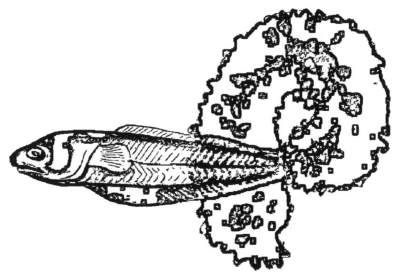

FIG 31 —Pearl-fish, *Fierasfer acus* (Linnæus), issuing from a *Holothurian* Coast of Italy   (After Emery)

The tide-pools of Cuba, Key West, Cape Flattery, Sitka, Una-laska, Monterey, San Diego, Mazatlan, Hilo, Kailua and Waianæ in Hawaii, Apia and Pago-Pago in Samoa, the present writer has found peculiarly rich in rock-loving forms   Even richer are the pools of the promontories of Japan, Hakodate. Head, Misaki, Awa, Izu, Waka, and Kagoshima, where a whole new fish fauna unknown to collectors in markets and sandy bays has been brought to light   Some of these rock-fishes are left buried in the rock weeds as the tide flows, lying quietly until it returns   Others cling to the rocks by ventral suckers, while still others depend for their safety on their powers of leaping or on their quickness of their movements in the water Those of the latter class are often brilliantly colored, but the others mimic closely the algæ or the rocks   Some fishes live in the sea only, some prefer brackish water   Some are found only in the rivers, and a few pass more or less indiscriminately from one kind of water to another.

Migratory Fishes.—The movements of migratory fishes are mainly controlled by the impulse of reproduction. Some pelagic

fishes, especially those of the mackerel and flying-fish families, swim long distances to a region favorable for the deposition of spawn. Others pursue for equal distances the schools of menhaden or other fishes which serve as their prey. Some species are known mainly in the waters they make their breeding homes, as in Cuba, Southern California, Hawaii, or Japan, the individuals being scattered at other times through the wide seas.

Anadromous Fishes. — Many fresh-water fishes, as trout and suckers, forsake the large streams in the spring, ascending the small brooks where their young can be reared in greater safety. Still others, known as *anadromous* fishes, feed and mature in the sea, but ascend the rivers as the impulse of reproduction grows

FIG. 32. — Portuguese Man-of-war Fish, *Gobiomorus gronovii*. Family *Stromateidæ*.

strong. Among such fishes are the salmon, shad, alewife, sturgeon, and striped bass in American waters. The most remarkable case of the anadromous instinct is found in the king salmon or quinnat (*Oncorhynchus tschawytscha*) of the Pacific Coast. This great fish spawns in November, at the age of four years and an average weight of twenty-two pounds. In the Columbia River it begins running with the spring freshets in March and April. It spends the whole summer, without feeding, in the ascent of the river. By autumn the individuals have reached the mountain streams of Idaho, greatly changed in appearance,

discolored, worn, and distorted   The male is humpbacked, with
sunken scales, and greatly enlarged, hooked, bent, or twisted
jaws, with enlarged dog-like teeth   On reaching the spawning
beds, which may be a thousand miles from the sea in the
Columbia, over two thousand in the Yukon, the female deposits her eggs in the gravel of some shallow brook   The
male covers them and scrapes the gravel over them.   Then both
male and female drift tail foremost helplessly down the stream,
none, so far as certainly known, ever survives the reproductive
act   The same habits are found in the five other species of
salmon in the Pacific, but in most cases the individuals do not
start so early nor run so far   The blue-back salmon or redfish,
however, does not fall far short in these regards   The salmon
of the Atlantic has a similar habit, but the distance traveled is
everywhere much less, and most of the hook-jawed males drop
down to the sea and survive to repeat the acts of reproduction

Catadromous fishes, as the true eel (*Anguilla*), reverse this
order, feeding in the rivers and brackish estuaries, apparently
finding their usual spawning-ground in the sea

Pugnacity of Fishes.—Some fishes are very pugnacious, always ready for a quarrel with their own kind   The sticklebacks show this disposition, especially the males   In Hawaii the
natives take advantage of this trait to catch the Uu (*Myripristis*

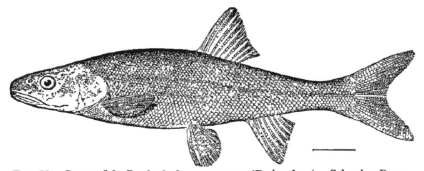

Fig. 33 —Squaw-fish, *Ptychocheilus oregonensis* (Richardson)   Columbia River

murdjan), a bright crimson-colored fish found in those waters
The species lives in crevices in lava rocks   Catching a live one,
the fishermen suspend it by a string in front of the rocks   It
remains there with spread fins and flashing scales, and the others
come out to fight it, when all are drawn to the surface by a

concealed net   Another decoy is substituted and the trick
is repeated until the showy and quarrelsome fishes are all
secured

In Siam the fighting-fish (*Betta pugnax*) is widely noted   The
following account of this fish is given by Cantor *

"When the fish is in a state of quiet, its dull colors present nothing remarkable, but if two be brought together, or if
one sees its own image in a looking-glass, the little creature
becomes suddenly excited, the raised fins and the whole body
shine with metallic colors of dazzling beauty, while the projected gill membrane, waving like a black frill round the throat,
adds something of grotesqueness to the general appearance   In
this state it makes repeated darts at its real or reflected antag-
onist   But both, when taken out of each other's sight, instantly
become quiet   The fishes were kept in glasses of water, fed
with larvæ of mosquitoes, and had thus lived for many months
The Siamese are as infatuated with the combats of these fish
as the Malays are with their cock-fights, and stake on the issue
considerable sums, and sometimes their own persons and families   The license to exhibit fish-fights is farmed, and brings a
considerable annual revenue to the king of Siam   The species
abounds in the rivulets at the foot of the hills of Penang   The
inhabitants name it 'Pla-kat,' or the 'fighting-fish', but the
kind kept especially for fighting is an artificial variety cultivated for the purpose "

A related species is the equally famous tree-climber of India
(*Anabas scandens*)   In 1797 Lieutenant Daldorf describes his
capture of an *Anabas*, five feet above the water, on the bark of
a palm-tree   In the effort to do this, the fish held on to the
bark by its preopercular spines, bent its tail, inserted its anal
spines, then pushing forward, repeated the operation

* Cantor, Catal Malayan Fishes, 1850, p 87   Bowring, Siam, p 155, gives
a similar account of the battles of these fishes

FIG. 34.—Tide-pools of Misaki. The Misaki Biological Station, from the north side.

49

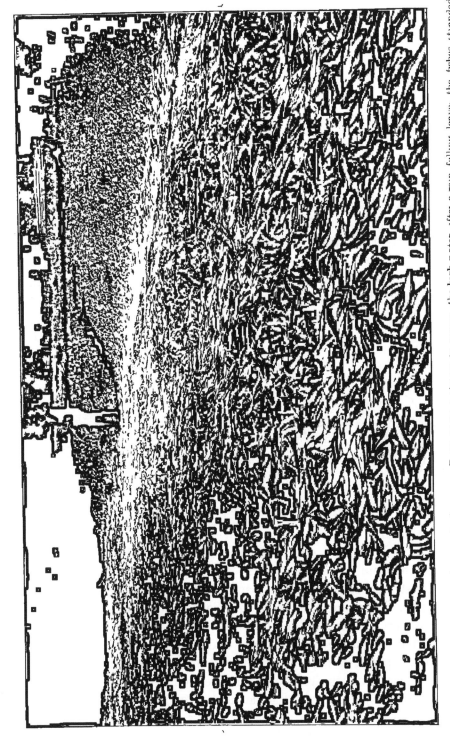

Fig 34a —Squaw fish *Ptychocheilus grandis* Agassiz   Running up a stream to spawn, the high water, after a rain, falling leaves the fishes stranded   Kelsey Creek, Clear Lake, California, April 29, 1899   (Photograph by O E Meddaugh)—Page 50

CHAPTER V

ADAPTATIONS OF FISHES

SPINES of the Catfishes.—The catfishes or horned pouts (*Siluridæ*) have a strong spine in the pectoral fin, one or both edges of this being jagged or serrated. This spine fits into a peculiar joint and by means of a slight downward or forward twist can be set immovably It can then be broken more easily than it can be depressed A slight turn in the opposite direction releases the joint, a fact known to the fish and readily learned by the boy The sharp spine inflicts a jagged wound

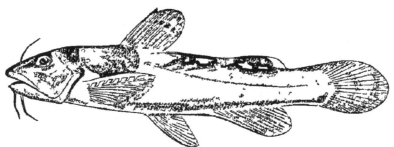

FIG 35 —Mad-tom, *Schilbeodes furiosus* Jordan and Meek Showing the poisoned pectoral spine Family *Siluridæ* Neuse River

Pelicans which have swallowed the catfish have been known to die of the wounds inflicted by the fish's spine When the catfish was first introduced into the Sacramento, according to Mr Will S Green, it caused the death of many of the native "Sacramento perch" (*Archoplites interruptus*) This perch (or rather bass) fed on the young catfish, and the latter erecting their pectoral spines in turn caused the death of the perch by tearing the walls of its stomach In like manner the sharp dorsal and ventral spines of the sticklebacks have been known to cause the death of fishes who swallow them, and even of ducks In Puget Sound the stickleback is often known as salmon-killer.

51

Certain small catfishes known as stone-cats and mad-toms (*Noturus, Schilbeodes*), found in the rivers of the Southern and Middle Western States, are provided with special organs of offense. At the base of the pectoral spine, which is sometimes very jagged, is a structure supposed by Professor Cope to be a poison gland the nature of which has not yet been fully ascertained. The wounds made by these spines are exceedingly painful like those made by the sting of a wasp. They are, however, apparently not dangerous.

Venomous Spines.—Many species of scorpion-fishes (*Scorpæna, Synanceia, Pelor, Pterois,* etc.), found in warm seas, as well as the European weavers (*Trachinus*), secrete poison

Fig. 36—Black Nohu, or Poison-fish, *Emmydrichthys vulcanus* Jordan. A species with stinging spines, showing resemblance to lumps of lava among which it lives. Family *Scorpænidæ*. From Tahiti.

from under the skin of each dorsal spine. The wounds made by these spines are very exasperating, but are not often dangerous. In some cases the glands producing these poisons form an oblong bag excreting a milky juice, and placed on the base of the spine.

In *Thalassophryne*, a genus of toad-fishes of tropical America, is found the most perfect system of poison organs known among fishes. The spinous armature of the opercle and the two spines of the first dorsal fin constitute the weapons. The details are known from the dissections of Dr. Günther. According to his* observations, the opercle in *Thalassophryne* "is very narrow,

* Günther, Introd. to the Study of Fishes, p. 192.

vertically styliform and very mobile   It is armed behind with a spine eight lines long and of the same form as the hollow venom-fang of a snake, being perforated at its base and at its extremity   A sac covering the base of the spine discharges its contents through the apertures and the canal in the interior of the spine   The structure of the dorsal spines is similar   There are no secretory glands imbedded in the membranes of the sacs and the fluid must be secreted by their mucous membrane   The sacs are without an external muscular layer and situated immediately below the thick, loose skin which envelops the spines at their extremity   The ejection of the poison into a living animal, therefore, can only be effected as in *Synanceia*, by the pressure to which the sac is subjected the moment the spine enters another body "

The Lancet of the Surgeon-fish.—Some fishes defend themselves by lashing their enemies with their tails   In the tangs, or surgeon-fishes (*Teuthis*), the tail is provided with a formidable weapon,

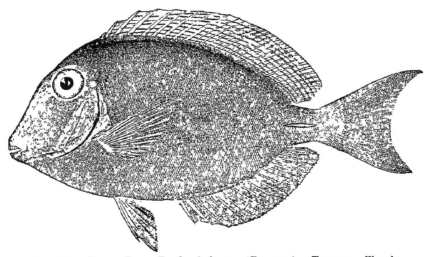

FIG 37 —Brown Tang, *Teuthis bahianus* (Ranzani)   Tortugas Florida

a knife-like spine, with the sharp edge directed forward   This spine when not in use slips forward into a sheath   The fish, when alive, cannot be handled without danger of a severe cut

In the related genera, this lancet is very much more blunt and immovable, degenerating at last into the rough spines of *Balistapus* or the hair-like prickles of *Monacanthus*

Spines of the Sting-ray. — In all the large group of sting-rays the tail is provided with one or more large, stiff, barbed spines, which are used with great force by the animal, and are capable of piercing the leathery skin of the sting-ray itself. There is no evidence that these spines bear any specific poison, but the ragged wounds they make are always dangerous and often end in gangrene   It is possible that the mucus on the surface of the spine acts as a poison on the lacerated tissues, rendering the wound something very different from a simple cut

Protection Through Poisonous Flesh of Fishes. — In certain groups of fishes a strange form of self-protection is acquired by

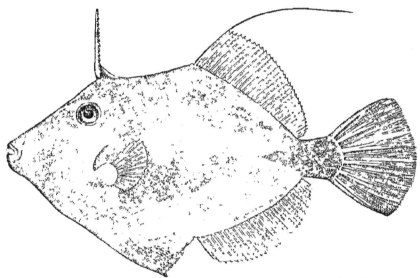

FIG 38 —Common Filefish, *Stephanolepis hispidus* (Linnæus)   Virginia

the presence in the body of poisonous alkaloids, by means of which the enemies of the species are destroyed in the death of the individual devoured

Such alkaloids are present in the globefishes (*Tetraodontidæ*), the filefishes (*Monacanthus*), and in some related forms, while members of other groups (*Batrachoididæ*) are under suspicion in this regard   The alkaloids produce a disease known as ciguatera, characterized by paralysis and gastric derangements Severe cases of ciguatera with men, as well as with lower animals, may end fatally in a short time

The flesh of the filefishes (*Stephanolepis tomentosus*), which the writer has tested, is very meager and bitter, having a decidedly offensive taste It is suspected, probably justly, of being poisonous In the globefishes the flesh is always more or less poisonous, that of *Tetraodon hispidus*, called muki-muki, or death-fish, in Hawaii, is reputed as excessively so The poisonous fishes have been lately studied in detail by Dr Jacques Pellegrin, of the Museum d'Histoire Naturelle at Paris He shows that any species of fish may be poisonous under certain circumstances, that under certain conditions certain species are poisonous, and that certain kinds are poisonous more or less at

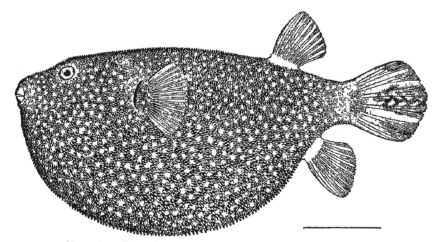

FIG. 39.—*Tetraodon meleagris* (Lacépède) Riu Kiu Islands

all times The following account is condensed from Dr Pellegrin's observations

The flesh of fishes soon undergoes decomposition in hot climates The consumption of decayed fish may produce serious disorders, usually with symptoms of diarrhœa or eruption of the skin There is in this case no specific poison, but the formation of leucomaines through the influence of bacteria This may take place with other kinds of flesh, and is known as botulism, or allantiasis For this disease, as produced by the flesh of fishes, Dr Pellegrin suggests the name of ichthyosism It is especially severe in certain very oily fishes, as the tunny, the anchovy, or the salmon The flesh of these and other fishes occasionally produces similar disorders through mere indigestion In this case the flesh undergoes decay in the stomach

In certain groups (wrasse-fishes, parrot-fishes, etc) in the tropics, individual fishes are sometimes rendered poisonous by feeding on poisonous mussels, holothurians, or possibly polyps, species which at certain times, and especially in their spawning season, develops alkaloids which themselves may cause cigua-tera   In this case it is usually the very old or large fishes which are liable to be infected   In some markets numerous species are excluded as suspicious for this reason.   Such a list is in use in the fish-market of Havana, where the sale of certain species, elsewhere healthful, or at the most suspected, was rigidly

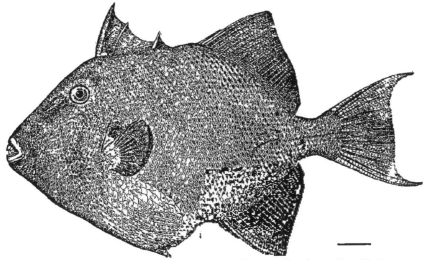

Fig 40 —The Trigger-fish, *Balistes carolinensis* Gmelin   New York

prohibited under the Spanish régime.   A list of these suspicious fishes has been given by Prof Poey

In many of the eels the serum of the blood is poisonous, but its venom is destroyed by the gastric juice, so that the flesh may be eaten with impunity, unless decay has set in   To eat too much of the tropical morays is to invite gastric troubles, but no true ciguatera   The true ciguatera is produced by a specific poisonous alkaloid   This is most developed in the globefishes or puffers (*Tetraodon, Spheroides, Tropidichthys*, etc) It is present in the filefishes (*Monacanthus, Alutera*, etc), prob-ably in some toadfishes (*Batrachoides*, etc), and similar com-pounds are found in the flesh of sharks and especially in sharks' livers.

These alkaloids are most developed in the ovaries and testes, and in the spawning season   They are also found in the liver and sometimes elsewhere in the body   In many species otherwise innocuous, purgative alkaloids are developed in or about the eggs   Serious illness has been caused by eating the roe of the pike and the barbel   The poison is less virulent in the species which ascend the rivers   It is also much less developed in cooler waters   For this reason ciguatera is almost confined to the tropics.   In Havana, Manila, and other tropical ports it is of frequent occurrence, while northward it is practically unknown as a disease requiring a special name or treatment   On the coast of Alaska, about Prince William Sound and Cook Inlet,

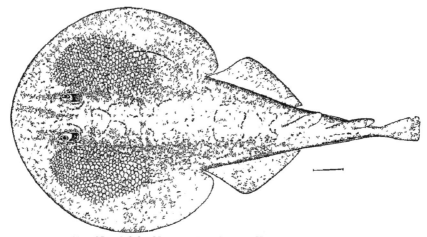

Fig 41 —Numbfish, *Narcine brasiliensis* Henle, showing *electric cells*
Pensacola, Florida

a fatal disease resembling ciguatera has been occasionally produced by the eating of clams

The purpose of the alkaloids producing ciguatera is considered by Dr Pellegrin as protective, saving the species by the poisoning of its enemies   The sickness caused by the specific poison must be separated from that produced by ptomaines and leucomaines in decaying flesh or in the oil diffused through it   Poisonous bacteria may be destroyed by cooking, but the alkaloids which cause ciguatera are unaltered by heat.

It is claimed in tropical regions that the germs of the bubonic plague may be carried through the mediation of fishes which feed on sewage   It is suggested by Dr Charles B. Ash-

mead that leprosy may be so carried   It is further suggested
that the custom of eating the flesh of fishes raw almost universal in Japan, Hawaii, and other regions may be responsible
for the spread of certain contagious diseases, in which the fish
acts as an intermediate host, much as certain mosquitoes spread
the germs of malaria and yellow fever

Electric Fishes.—Several species of fishes possess the power
to inflict electric shocks not unlike those of the Leyden jar.
This is useful in stunning their prey and especially in confounding their enemies   In most cases these electric organs are
evidently developed from muscular substance   Their action,
which is largely voluntary, is in its nature like muscular action.
The power is soon exhausted and must be restored by rest and
food   The effects of artificial stimulation and of poisons are
parallel with the effect of similar agents on muscles

In the electric rays or torpedos (*Narcobatidæ*) the electric
organs are large honeycomb-like structures, "vertical hexag-

Fic 42 —Electric Catfish *Torpedo electricus* (Gmelin)   Congo River.
(After Boulenger)

onal prisms," upwards of 400 of them, at the base of the pectoral fins   Each prism is filled "with a clear trembling jelly-like
substance "   These fishes give a shock which is communicable
through a metallic conductor, as an iron spear or the handle of
a knife   It produces a peculiar and disagreeable sensation not
at all dangerous   It is said that this living battery shows all
the known qualities of magnetism, rendering the needle mag-
netic, decomposing chemical compounds, etc   In the Nile is
an electric catfish (*Torpedo electricus*) having similar powers.
Its electric organ extends over the whole body, being thickest
below   It consists of rhomboidal cells of a firm gelatinous
substance

The electric eel (*Electrophorus electricus*), the most powerful of electric fishes, is not an eel, but allied rather to the sucker or carp. It is, however, eel-like in form and lives in rivers of Brazil and Guiana. The electric organs are in two pairs, one on the back of the tail, the other on the anal fin. These are made up of an enormous number of minute cells. In the electric eel, as in the other electric fishes, the nerves supplying these organs are much larger than those passing from the spinal cord for any other purpose. In all these cases closely related species show no trace of the electric powers.

Dr. Gilbert has described the electric powers of species of star-gazer (*Astroscopus y-græcum* and *A. zephyreus*), the electric cells lying under the naked skin of the top of the head. Electric power is ascribed to a species of cusk (*Urophycis regius*), but this perhaps needs verification.

Photophores or Luminous Organs.—Many fishes, chiefly of the deep seas, develop organs for producing light. These are known as luminous organs, phosphorescent organs, or photophores. These are independently developed in four entirely unrelated groups of fishes. This difference in origin is accompanied

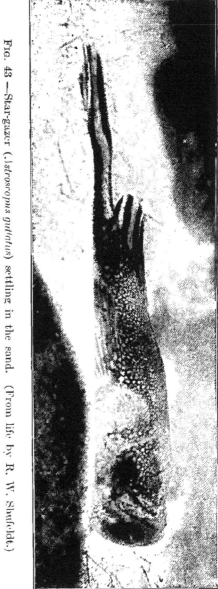

FIG. 43.—Star-gazer (*Astroscopus guttatus*) settling in the sand. (From life by R. W. Shufeldt.)

by corresponding difference in structure. The best-known type is found in the Iniomi, including the lantern-fishes and their many relatives. These may have luminous spots, differentiated areas round or oblong which shine star-like in the dark. These are usually symmetrically placed on the sides of

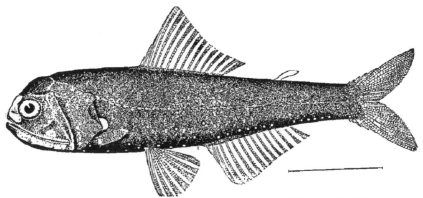

Fig. 44.—Headlight Fish, _Ethoprora lucida_ Goode and Bean. Gulf Stream.

the body. They may have also luminous glands or diffuse areas which are luminous, but which do not show the specialized structure of the phosphorescent spots. These glands of similar nature to the spots are mostly on the head or tail. In one

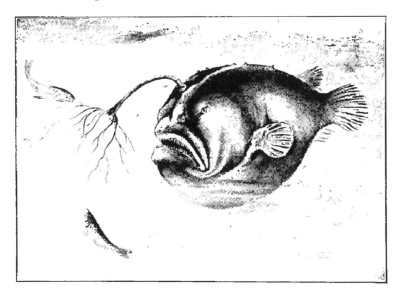

Fig. 45.—_Corynolophus reinhardti_ (Lütken), showing luminous bulb (modified after Lütken). Family _Ceratiidæ_. Deep sea off Greenland.

genus, _Æthoprora_, the luminous snout is compared to the head-light of an engine.

Entirely different are the photophores in the midshipman or singing-fish (*Porichthys*), a genus of toad-fishes or *Batrachoididæ*. This species lives near the shore and the luminous spots are outgrowths from pores of the lateral line.

In one of the anglers (*Corynolophus reinhardti*) the complex bait is said to be luminous, and luminous areas are said to occur on the belly of a very small shark of the deep seas of

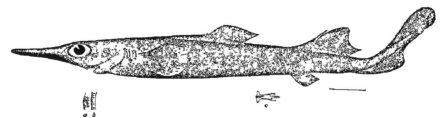

FIG. 46 —*Etmopterus lucifer* Jordan and Snyder. Misaki, Japan

Japan (*Etmopterus lucifer*). This phenomenon is now the subject of study by one of the numerous pupils of Dr Mitsukuri. The structures in *Corynolophus* are practically unknown.

Photophores in Iniomous Fishes —In the *Iniomi* the luminous organs have been the subject of an elaborate paper by Dr R von Lendenfeld (Deep-sea Fishes of the Challenger. Appendix B) These he divides into ocellar organs of regular form or luminous spots, and irregular glandular organs or luminous areas. The ocellar spots may be on the scales of the lateral line or on other definite areas. They may be raised above the surface or sunk below it. They may be simple, with or without black pigment, or they may have within them a reflecting surface. They are best shown in the *Myctophidæ* and *Stomiatidæ*, but are found in numerous other families in nearly all soft-rayed fishes of the deep sea.

The glandular areas may be placed on the lower jaw, on the barbels, under the gill cover, on the suborbital or preorbital, on the tail, or they may be irregularly scattered. Those about the eye have usually the reflecting membrane.

In all these structures, according to Dr von Lendenfeld, the whole or part of the organ is glandular. The glandular part is at the base and the other structures are added distally. The primitive organ was a gland which produced luminous slime

To this in the process of specialization greater complexity has been added

The luminous organs of some fishes resemble the supposed original structure of the primitive photophore, though of course these cannot actually represent it   The simplest type of photophore now found is in *Astronesthes*, in the form of irregular glandular luminous patches on the surface of the skin

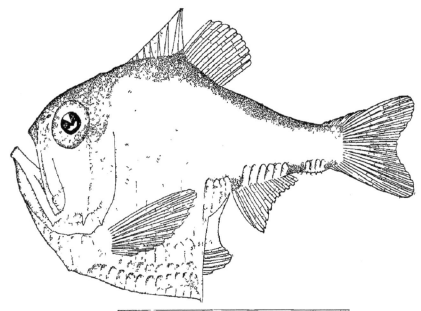

Fig 47 —*Argyropelecus olfersi* Cuvier   Gulf Stream

There is no homology between the luminous organs of any insect and those of any fish

Photophores of Porichthys —Entirely distinct in their origin are the luminous spots in the midshipman (*Porichthys notatus*), a shore fish of California   These have been described in detail by Dr Charles Wilson Greene (late of Stanford University, now of the University of Missouri) in the *Journal of Morphology*, xv , p 667   These are found on various parts of the body in connection with the mucous pores of the lateral lines and about the mucous pores of the head   The skin in *Porichthys* is naked, and the photophores arise from a modification of its epidermis Each is spherical, shining white, and consists of four parts—the lens, the gland, the reflector, and the pigment As to its function Prof Greene observes

"I have kept specimens of *Porichthys* in aquaria at the Hopkins Seaside Laboratory, and have made numerous observations on them with an effort to secure ocular proof of the phosphorescence of the living active fish The fish was observed in the dark when quiet and when violently excited, but, with a single exception, only negative results were obtained Once a phosphorescent glow of scarcely perceptible intensity was observed when the fish was pressed against the side of the aquarium Then this is a shore fish and quite common, and one might suppose that so striking a phenomenon as it would present if these organs were phosphorescent in a small degree would be observed by ichthyologists in the field, or by fishermen, but diligent inquiry reveals no such evidence

"Notwithstanding the fact that *Porichthys* has been observed to voluntarily exhibit only the trace of phosphorescence mentioned above, still the organs which it possesses in such numbers are beyond doubt true phosphorescent organs, as the following observations will demonstrate A live fish put into an aquarium of sea-water made alkaline with ammonia water exhibited a most brilliant glow along the location of the well-developed organs Not only did the lines of organs shine forth, but the individual organs themselves were distinguishable The glow appeared after about five minutes, remained prominent for a few minutes, and then for twenty minutes gradually became weaker until it was scarcely perceptible Rubbing the hand over the organs was followed always by a distinct increase in the phosphorescence Pieces of the fish containing the organs taken five and six hours after the death of the animal became luminous upon treatment with ammonia water

"Electrical stimulation of the live fish was also tried with good success The interrupted current from an induction coil was used, one electrode being fixed on the head over the brain or on the exposed spinal cord near the brain, and the other moved around on different parts of the body No results followed relatively weak stimulation of the fish, although such currents produced violent contractions of the muscular system

of the body. But when a current strong enough to be quite
painful to the hands while handling the electrodes was used
then stimulation of the fish called forth a brilliant glow of light
apparently from every well-developed photophore   All the
lines on the ventral and lateral surfaces of the body glowed
with a beautiful light, and continued to do so while the stimulation lasted   The single well-developed organ just back of
and below the eye was especially prominent   No luminosity
was observed in the region of the dorsal organs previously described as rudimentary in structure   I was also able to produce

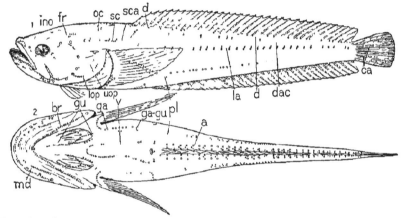

FIG 48 —Luminous organs and lateral line of Midshipman, *Porichthys notatus*
Girard   Family *Batrachoididæ*   Monterey, California   (After Greene)

the same effect by galvanic stimulation, rapidly making and
breaking the current by hand

"The light produced in *Porichthys* was, as near as could be
determined by direct observation, a white light   When produced by electric stimulation it did not suddenly reach its
maximal intensity, but came in quite gradually and disappeared
in the same way when the stimulation ceased   The light was
not a strong one, only strong enough to enable one to quite
easily distinguish the apparatus used in the experiment

"An important fact brought out by the above experiment is
that an electrical stimulation strong enough to most violently
stimulate the nervous system, as shown by the violent contractions of the muscular system, may still be too weak to
produce phosphorescence   This fact gives a physiological con-

firmation of the morphological result stated above that no specific nerves are distributed to the phosphorescent organs

"I can explain the action of the electrical current in these experiments only on the supposition that it produces its effect by direct action on the gland

"The experiments just related were all tried on specimens of the fish taken from under the rocks where they were guarding

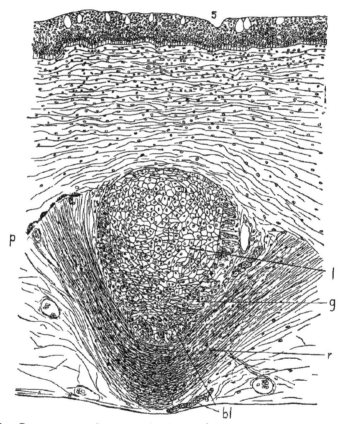

Fig 49 —Cross-section of a ventral phosphorescent organ of the Midshipman, *Porichthys notatus* Girard   *l*, lens, *gl*, gland, *r*, reflector, *bl*, blood, *p*, pigment   (After Greene)

the young brood   Two specimens, however, taken by hooks from the deeper water of Monterey Bay, could not be made to show phosphorescence either by electrical stimulation or by treatment with ammonia.   These specimens did not have the high development of the system of mucous cells of the skin exhibited by the nesting fish.   My observations were, how-

ever, not numerous enough to more than suggest the possibility
of a seasonal high development of the phosphorescent organs.

" Two of the most important parts of the organ have to do
with the physical manipulation of light—the reflector and the
lens, respectively   The property of the reflector needs no discussion other than to call attention to its enormous development   The lens cells are composed of a highly refractive substance, and the part as a whole gives every evidence of light
refraction and condensation   The form of the lens gives a
theoretical condensation of light at a very short focus.   That
such is in reality the case, I have proved conclusively by examination of fresh material.   If the fresh fish be exposed to direct

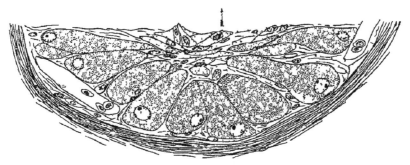

FIG 50—Section of the deeper portion of phosphorescent organ of *Porichthys
notatus*, highly magnified   (After Greene)

sunlight, there is a reflected spot of intense light from each
phosphorescent organ   This spot is constant in position with
reference to the sun in whatever position the fish be turned
and is lost if the lens be dissected away and only the reflector
left   With needles and a simple microscope it is comparatively
easy to free the lens from the surrounding tissue and to examine
it directly   When thus freed and examined in normal saline, I
have found by rough estimates that it condenses sunlight to a
bright point a distance back of the lens of from one-fourth to
one-half its diameter   I regret that I have been unable to make
precise physical developments

" The literature on the histological structure of known phosphorescent organs of fishes is rather meager and unsatisfactory.
Von Lendenfeld describes twelve classes of phosphorescent
organs from deep-sea fishes collected by the *Challenger* expe-

dition   All of these, however, are greater or less modifications of one type   This type includes, according to von Lendenfeld's views, three essential parts, *i c*, a gland, phosphorescent cells, and a local ganglion.   These parts may have added a reflector, a pigment layer, or both, and all these may be simple or compounded in various ways, giving rise to the twelve classes. Blood-vessels and nerves are distributed to the glandular portion   Of the twelve classes direct ocular proof is given for one, i e, ocellar organs of *Myctophum* which were observed by Willemoes-Suhm at night to shine 'like a star in the net'   Von Lendenfeld says that the gland produces a secretion, and he supposes the light or phosphorescence to be produced either by the 'burning or consuming' of this secretion by the phosphorescent cells, or else by some substance produced by the phosphorescent cells   Furthermore, he says that the phosphorescent cells act at the 'will of the fish' and are excited to action by the local ganglion

" Some of these statements and conclusions seem insufficiently grounded, as, for example, the supposed action of the phosphorescent cells, and especially the control of the ganglion over them   In the first place, the relation between the ganglion and the central nervous system in the forms described by von Lendenfeld is very obscure, and the structure described as a ganglion, to judge from the figures and the text descriptions, may be wrongly identified   At least it is scarcely safe to ascribe ganglionic function to a group of adult cells so poorly preserved that only nuclei are to be distinguished   In the second place, no structural character is shown to belong to the 'phosphorescent cells' by which they may take part in the process ascribed to them *

" The action of the organs described by him may be explained on other grounds, and entirely independent of the so-called 'ganglion cells' and of the 'phosphorescent cells '

---

* The cells which von Lendenfeld designates 'phosphorescent cells' have as their peculiar characteristic a large, oval, highly refracting body imbedded in the protoplasm of the larger end of the clavate cells   These cells have nothing in common with the structure of the cells of the firefly known to be phosphorescent in nature   In fact the true phosphorescent cells are more probably the 'gland-cells' found in ten of the twelve classes of organs which he describes

" Phosphorescence as applied to the production of light by a
living animal is, according to our present ideas, a chemical action,
an oxidation process   The necessary conditions for producing it
are two—an oxidizable substance that is luminous on oxidation, i e , a photogenic substance on the one hand, and the presence of free oxygen on the other   Every phosphorescent organ
must have a mechanism for producing these two conditions,
all other factors are only secondary and accessory   If the
gland of a firefly can produce a substance that is oxidizable
and luminous on oxidation, as shown as far back as 1828 by
Faraday and confirmed and extended recently by Watasé, it is
conceivable, indeed probable, that phosphorescence in *Myctophum*
and other deep-sea forms is produced in the same direct way,
that is, by direct oxidation of the secretion of the gland found
in each of at least ten of the twelve groups of organs described
by von Lendenfeld   Free oxygen may be supplied directly
from the blood in the capillaries distributed to the gland
which he describes   The possibility of the regulation of the
supply of blood carrying oxygen is analogous to what takes
place in the firefly and is wholly adequate to account for any
'flashes of light' 'at the will of the fish '

" In the phosphorescent organs of *Porichthys* the only part
the function of which cannot be explained on physical grounds
is the group of cells called the gland   If the large granular
cells of this portion of the structure produce a secretion, as seems
probable from the character of the cells and their behavior
toward reagents, and this substance be oxidizable and luminous
in the presence of free oxygen, i e , photogenic, then we have
the conditions necessary for a light-producing organ   The
numerous capillaries distributed to the gland will supply free
oxygen sufficient to meet the needs of the case   Light produced in the gland is ultimately all projected to the exterior,
either directly from the luminous points in the gland or reflected
outward by the reflector, the lens condensing all the rays into
a definite pencil or slightly diverging cone   This explanation
of the light-producing process rests on the assumption of a
secretion product with certain specific characters   But comparing the organ with structures known to produce such a substance, i e , the glands of the firefly or the photospheres of Eu-

phausia, it seems to me the assumption is not less certain than the assumption that twelve structures resembling each other in certain particulars have a common function to that proved for one only of the twelve

" I am inclined to the belief that whatever regulation of the action of the phosphorescent organ occurs is controlled by the regulation of the supply of free oxygen by the blood-stream flowing through the organ, but, however this may be, the essential fact remains that the organs in *Porichthys* are true phosphorescent organs" (GREENE)

Other species of *Porichthys* with similar photophores occur in Texas, Guiana, Panama, and Chile   The name midshipman alludes to these shining spots, compared to buttons

Globefishes.—The globefishes (*Tetraodon*, etc) and the porcupine-fishes have the surface defended by spines   These fishes have an additional safeguard through the instinct to swallow air   When one of these fishes is seriously disturbed it rises to

FIG 51 —Sucking-fish or Pegador, *Leptecheneis naucrates* (Linnæus). Virginia

the surface, gulps air into a capacious sac, and then floats belly upward on the surface   It is thus protected from other fishes, although easily taken by man   The same habit appears in some of the frog-fishes (*Antennarius*) and in the Swell sharks (*Cephaloscyllium*)

The writer once hauled out a netful of globefishes (*Tetraodon hispidus*) from a Hawaiian lagoon   As they lay on the bank a dog came up and sniffed at them   As his nose touched them they swelled themselves up with air, becoming visibly two or three times as large as before   It is not often that the lower animals show surprise at natural phenomena, but the attitude of the dog left no question as to his feeling

Remoras.—The different species of Remora, or shark-suckers, fasten themselves to the surface of sharks or other fishes and are carried about by them often to great distances   These fishes attach themselves by a large sucking-disk on the top of the head, which is a modified spinous dorsal fin   They do not harm the shark, except possibly to retard its motion   If the shark is caught and drawn out of the water, these fishes often instantly let go and plunge into the sea, swimming away with great celerity

Sucking-disks of Clingfishes. — Other fishes have sucking-disks differently made, by which they cling to rocks   In the gobies the united ventrals have some adhesive power   The blind goby (*Typhlogobius californiensis*) is said to adhere to rocks in dark holes by the ventral fins   In most gobies the adhesive power is slight   In the sea-snails (*Liparididæ*) and lumpfishes (*Cyclopteridæ*) the united ventral fins are modified into an

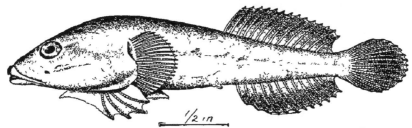

FIG 52 —Clingfish, *Caularchus mæandricus* (Girard)   Monterey, California

elaborate circular sucking-disk   In the clingfishes (*Gobiesocidæ*) the sucking-disk lies between the ventral fins and is made in part of modified folds of the naked skin   Some fishes creep over the bottom, exploring it with their sensitive barbels, as the gurnard, surmullet, and goatfish   The suckers (*Catostomus*) test the bottom with their thick, sensitive lips, either puckered or papillose, feeding by suction

Lampreys and Hagfishes.—The lampreys suck the blood of other fishes to which they fasten themselves by their disk-like mouth armed with rasping teeth

The hagfishes (*Myxine, Eptatretus*) alone among fishes are truly parasitic   These fishes, worm-like in form, have round mouths, armed with strong hooked teeth   They fasten themselves at the throats of large fishes, work their way into the muscle without tearing the skin, and finally once inside devour all the muscles of the fish, leaving the skin unbroken and the viscera undisturbed   These fishes become living hulks before they die. If lifted out of the water, the slimy hagfish at once slips out and swims quickly away. In gill-nets in Monterey Bay great mischief is done by hagfish (*Polistotrema stouti*). It is a curious fact that large numbers of hagfish eggs are taken from the stomachs of the male hagfish, which seems to be

FIG 53 —Hagfish, *Polistotrema stouti* (Lockington)

almost the only enemy of his own species, keeping the numbers in check

The Swordfishes.—In the swordfish and its relatives, the sail-fish and the spearfish, the bones of the anterior part of the head are grown together, making an efficient organ of attack. The sword of the swordfish, the most powerful of these fishes, has been known to pierce the long planks of boats, and it is supposed that the animal sometimes attacks the whale. But stories of this sort lack verification

The Paddle-fishes.—In the paddle-fishes (*Polyodon spatula* and *Psephurus gladius*) the snout is spread out forming a broad paddle or spatula. This the animal uses to stir up the mud on the bottoms of rivers, the small organisms contained in mud constituting food. Similar paddle-like projections are developed in certain deep-water Chimæras (*Harriotta, Rhino-chimæra*), and in the deep-sea shark, *Mitsukurina*

The Sawfishes.—A certain genus of rays (*Pristis*, the saw-fish) and a genus of sharks (*Pristiophorus*, the saw-shark), possess a similar spatula-shaped snout. But in these fishes the snout is provided on either side with enamelled teeth set in sockets and standing at right angles with the snout. The animal swims through schools of sardines and anchovies, strikes

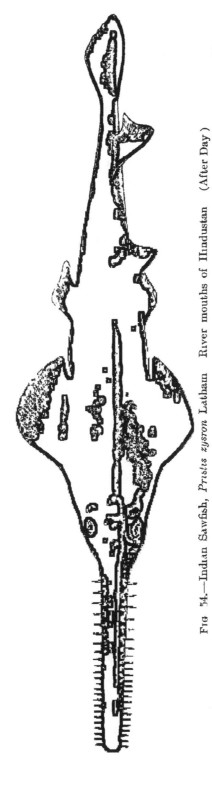

FIG 54.—Indian Sawfish, *Pristis zysron* Latham   River mouths of Hindustan   (After Day)

72

right and left with this saw, destroying the small fishes, who
thus become an easy prey.   These fishes live in estuaries and
river mouths, *Pristis* in tropical America and Guinea, *Pristiophorus* in Japan and Australia.   In the mythology of science, the

Fig. 55.—Saw-shark, *Pristiophorus japonicus* Günther.   Specimen from
Nagasaki.

sawfish attacks the whale, but in fact the two animals never
come within miles of each other, and the sawfish is an object of
danger only to the tender fishes, the small fry of the sea.

Peculiarties of Jaws and Teeth.—The jaws of fishes are subject to a great variety of modifications.   In some the bones are
joined by distensible ligaments and the fish can swallow other
fishes larger than itself.   In other cases the jaws are excessively
small and toothless, at the end of a long tube, so ineffective in
appearance that it is a marvel that the fish can swallow anything at all.

In the thread-eels (*Nemichthys*) the jaws are so recurved
that they cannot possibly meet, and in their great length seem
worse than useless.

In some species the knife-like canines of the lower jaw pierce
through the substance of the upper.

In four different and wholly unrelated groups of fishes the
teeth are grown fast together, forming a horny beak like that of
the parrot.   These are the Chimæras, the globefishes (*Tetroadon*),
and their relatives, the parrot-fishes (*Scarus*, etc.), and the
stone-wall perch (*Oplegnathus*).   The structure of the beak
varies considerably in these four cases, in accord with the difference in the origin of its structures.   In the globefishes the

jaw-bones are fused together, and in the Chimæras they are solidly joined to the cranium itself

The Angler-fishes.—In the large group of angler-fishes the first spine of the dorsal fin is modified into a sort of bait to attract smaller fishes into the capacious mouth below. This structure is typical in the fishing-frog (*Lophius*), where the fleshy tip of this spine hangs over the great mouth, the huge fish lying on the bottom apparently inanimate as a stone. In other related fishes this spine has different forms, being often reduced to a vestige, of little value as a lure, but retained in accordance with the law of heredity. In a deep-sea angler the bait is enlarged, provided with fleshy streamers and a luminous body which serves to attract small fishes in the depths

The forms and uses of this spine in this group constitute a very suggestive chapter in the study of specialization and ultimate degradation, when the special function is not needed or becomes ineffective

Similar phases of excessive development and final degradation may be found in almost every group in which abnormal stress has been laid on a particular organ. Thus the ventral fins, made into a large sucking-disk in *Liparis*, are lost altogether in *Paraliparis*. The very large poisoned spines of *Pterois* become very short in *Aploactis*, the high dorsal spines of *Citula* are lost in *Alectis*, and sometimes a very large organ dwindles to a very small one within the limits of the same genus. An example of this is seen in the poisoned pectoral spines of *Schilbeodes*

The Unsymmetrical Eyes of Flounders.—In the two great families of flounders and soles the head is unsymmetrically formed, the cranium being twisted and both eyes placed on the same side. The body is strongly compressed, and the side possessing the eyes is uppermost in all the actions of the fish. This upper side, whether right or left, is colored, while the eyeless side is white or very nearly so

It is well known that in the very young flounder the body rests upright in the water. After a little there is a tendency to turn to one side and the lower eye begins its migration to the other side, the interorbital bones or part of them moving before

it. In most flounders the eye seems to move over the surface
of the head, before the dorsal fin, or across the axil of its first
ray.   In the tropical genus *Platophrys* the movement of the eye
is most easily followed, as the species reach a larger size than
do most flounders before the change takes place.   The larva,
while symmetrical, is in all cases transparent.

In a recent study of the migration of the eye in the winter

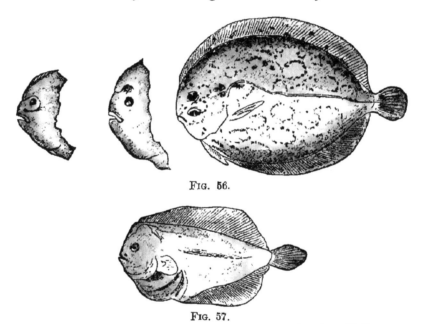

Fig. 56.

Fig. 57.

Figs. 56, 57.—Larval stages of *Platophrys podas*, a flounder of the Mediterranean,
showing the migration of the eye.   (After Emery.)

flounder (*Pseudopleuronectes americanus*) Mr. Stephen R. Williams reaches the following conclusions:

1. The young of *Limanda ferruginea* (the rusty dab) are
probably in the larval stage at the same time as those of *Pseudopleuronectes americanus* (the winter flounder).

2. The recently hatched fish are symmetrical, except for the
relative positions of the two optic nerves.

3. The first observed occurrence in preparation for metamorphosis in *P. americanus* is the rapid resorption of the part
of the supraorbital cartilage bar which lies in the path of the
eye.

4. Correlated with this is an increase in distance between

the eyes and the brain, caused by the growth of the facial cartilages.

5. The migrating eye moves through an arc of about 120 degrees.

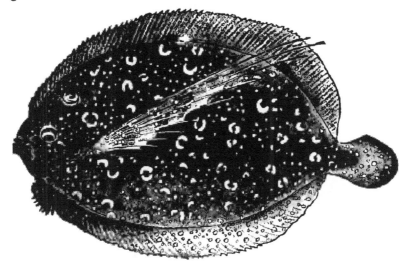

FIG. 58.—*Platophrys lunatus* (Linnæus), the Wide-eyed Flounder. Family *Pleuronectidæ*. Cuba. (From nature by Mrs. H. C. Nash.)

6. The greater part of this rotation (three-fourths of it in *P. americanus*) is a rapid process, taking not more than three days.

7. The anterior ethmoidal region is not so strongly influenced by the twisting as the ocular region.

8. The location of the olfactory nerves (in the adult) shows that the morphological midline follows the interorbital septum.

FIG. 59. — Young Flounder, just hatched, with symmetrical eyes. (After S. R. Williams.)

9. The cartilage mass lying in the front part of the orbit of the adult eye is a separate anterior structure in the larva.

10. With unimportant differences, the process of metamorphosis in the sinistral fish is parallel to that in the dextral fish.

11. The original location of the eye is indicated in the adult by the direction first taken, as they leave the brain, by those cranial nerves having to do with the transposed eye.

12. The only well-marked asymmetry in the adult brain is due to the much larger size of the olfactory nerve and lobe of the ocular side.

13. There is a perfect chiasma.

14. The optic nerve of the migrating eye is always anterior to that of the other eye.

"The why of the peculiar metamorphosis of the *Pleuronectidæ* is an unsolved problem. The presence or absence of a swim-bladder can have nothing to do with the change of habit of the young flatfish, for *P. americanus* must lose its air-bladder before metamorphosis begins, since sections showed no

Fig. 60.—Larval Flounder, *Pseudopleuronectes americanus*. (After S. R. Williams.)

Fig. 61.—Larval Flounder, *Pseudopleuronectes americanus*. (After S. R. Williams.)

evidence of it, whereas in *Lophopsetta maculata*, 'the window-pane flounder,' the air-sac can often be seen by the naked eye up to the time when the fish assumes the adult coloration, and long after it has assumed the adult form.

"Cunningham has suggested that the weight of the fish acting upon the lower eye after the turning would press it toward the upper side out of the way. But in all probability the planktonic larva rests on the sea-bottom little if at all before metamorphosing. Those taken by Mr. Williams into the laboratory showed in resting no preference for either side until the eye was near the midline.

FIG 62 —Japanese Sea-horse, *Hippocampus mohnikei* Bleeker. Misaki, Japan.

CHAPTER VI

THE COLORS OF FISHES

PIGMENTATION.—The colors of fishes are in general produced by oil sacs or pigment cells beneath the epidermis or in some cases beneath the scales Certain metallic shades, silvery blue or iridescent, are produced, not by actual pigment, but, as among insects, by the deflection of light from the polished skin or the striated surfaces of the scales Certain fine striations give an iridescent appearance through the interference of light

The pigmentary colors may be divided into two general classes, ground coloration and ornamentation or markings Of these the ground color is most subject to individual or local variation, although usually within narrow limits, while the markings are more subject to change with age or sex On the other hand, they are more distinctive of the species itself

Protective Coloration.— The ground coloration most usual among fishes is protective in its nature In a majority of fishes the back is olivaceous or gray, either plain or mottled, and the belly white To birds looking down into the water, the back is colored like the water itself or like the bottom below it To fishes in search of prey from below, the belly is colored like the surface of the water or the atmosphere above it In any case the darker colored upper surface casts its shadow over the paler lower parts

In shallow waters or in rivers the bottom is not uniformly colored The fish, especially if it be one which swims close to the bottom, is better protected if the olivaceous surface is marked by darker cross streaks and blotches These give the fish a color resemblance to the weeds about it or to the sand and stones on which it lies As a rule, no fish which lies on the bottom is ever quite uniformly colored.

In the open seas, where the water seems very blue, blue

colors, and especially metallic shades, take the place of olivaceous gray or green.   As we descend into deep water, especially in the warm seas, red pigment takes the place of olive   At a moderate depth a large percentage of the fishes are of various shades of red. Several of the large groupers of the West Indies are represented by two color forms, a shore form in which the prevailing shade is olive-green, and a deeper-water form which is crimson   In several cases an inter-

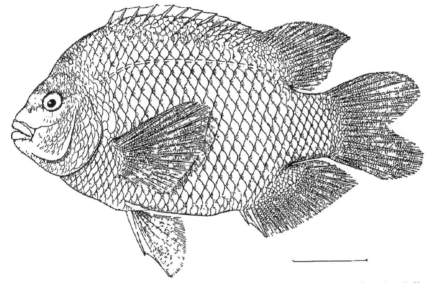

Fig 63 —Garibaldi (scarlet in color), *Hypsypops rubicunda* (Girard)   La Jolla, San Diego, California

mediate-color form also exists which is lemon-yellow   On the coast of California is a band-shaped blenny (*Apodichthys flavidus*) which appears in three colors, according to its surroundings, blood-red, grass-green, and olive-yellow   The red coloration is also essentially protective, for the region inhabited by such forms is the zone of the rose-red algæ. In the arctic waters, and in lakes where rose-red algæ are not found, the red-ground coloration is almost unknown, although red may appear in markings or in nuptial colors   It is possible that the red, both of fishes and algæ, in deeper water is related to the effect of water on the waves of light, but whether this should make fishes red or violet has never been clearly under-

1 HALICHŒRES TRIMACULATUS (QUOY & GAIMARD)
2 HALICHŒRES DÆDALMA (JORDAN & SEALE)
3 HALICHŒRES OPERCULARIS (GÜNTHER)

FISHES OF THE CORAL REEFS, SAMOA. FAMILY LABRIDÆ

stood   It is true also that where the red in fishes ceases violet-black begins.

In the greater depths, from 500 to 4000 fathoms, the ground color in most fishes becomes deep black or violet-black, sometimes with silvery luster reflected from the scales, but more usually dull and lusterless.   This shade may be also protective   In these depths the sun's rays scarcely penetrate, and the fish and the water are of the same apparent shade, for black coloration is here the mere absence of light

In general, the markings of various sorts grow less distinct with the increase of depth   Bright-red fishes of the depths are usually uniform red   The violet-black fishes of the oceanic abysses show no markings whatever (luminous glands excepted), and in deep waters there are no nuptial or sexual differences in color

Ground colors other than olive-green, gray, brown, or silvery rarely appear among fresh-water fishes   Marine fishes in the tropics sometimes show as ground color bright blue, grass-green, crimson, orange-yellow, or black, but these showy colors are almost confined to fishes of the coral reefs, where they are often associated with elaborate systems of markings

Protective Markings —The markings of fishes are of almost every conceivable character   They may be roughly grouped as protective coloration, sexual coloration, nuptial coloration, recognition colors, and ornamentation, if we may use the latter term for brilliant hues which serve no obvious purpose to the fish itself

Examples of protective markings may be seen everywhere   The flounder which lies on the sand has its upper surface covered with sand-like blotches, and these again will vary according to the kind of sand it imitates   It may be true sand or crushed coral or the detritus of lava, in any case perfectly imitated

Equally closely will the markings on a fish correspond with rock surroundings   With granite rocks we find an elaborate series of granitic markings, with coral rocks another series of shades, and if red corals be present, red shades of like appearance are found on the fish   Still another kind of mark indicates rock pools lined with the red calcareous algæ called corallina   Black species are found in lava masses, grass-green ones

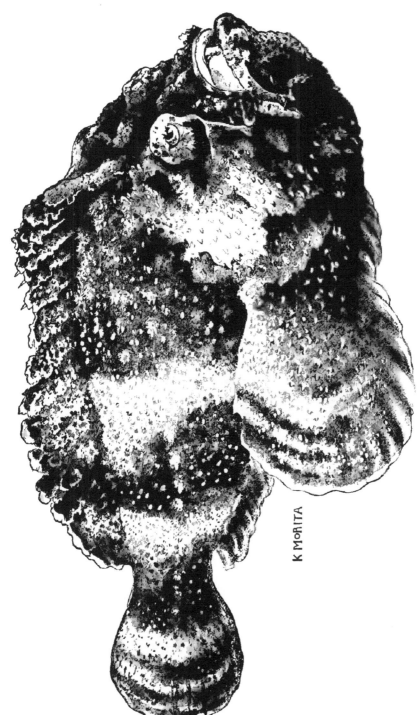

K MORITA

FIG. 64.—Gofu, or Poison Fish, *Synanceia verrucosa* (Linnæus). Family *Scorpænidæ*. Specimen from Apia, Samoa, showing resemblance to coral masses, in the clefts of which it lives.

82

among the fronds of ulva, and olive-green among Sargassum
or fucus, the markings and often the form corresponding to the
nature of the algæ in which the species makes its home.

Sexual Coloration. — In many groups of fishes the sexes are
differently colored. In some cases bright-red, blue, or black
markings characterize the male, the female having similar
marks, but less distinct, and the bright colors replaced by olive,

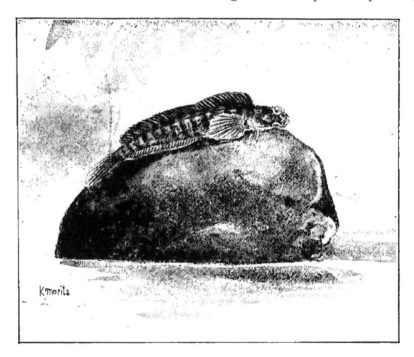

Fig. 65.—Lizard-skipper, *Alticus saliens* (Forster). A blenny which lies out of
water on lava-rocks, leaping from one to another with great agility. From
nature; specimen from Point Distress, Tutuila Island, Samoa. (About one-
half size.)

brown, or gray. In a few cases, however, the female has marks
of a totally different nature, and scarcely less bright than those
of the male.

Nuptial Coloration. — Nuptial colors are those which appear
on the male in the breeding season only, the pigment afterwards vanishing, leaving the sexes essentially alike. Such
colors are found on most of the minnows and dace (*Cyprinidæ*)
of the rivers and to a less degree in some other fresh-water
fishes, as the darters (*Etheostominæ*) and the trout. In the

minnows of many species the male in spring has the skin charged
with bright pigment, red, black, or bright silvery, for the most
part, the black most often on the head, the red on the head
and body, and the silvery on the tips of the fins   At the same
time other markings are intensified, and in many species the
head and sometimes the body and fins are covered with warty
excrescences   These shades are most distinct on the most vigor-

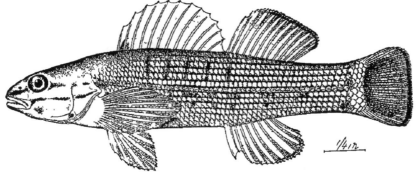

Fig 66 —Blue-breasted Darter, *Etheostoma camurum* (Cope), the most brilliantly
colored of American river-fishes   Cumberland Gap, Tennessee

ous males, and disappear with the warty excrescences after the
fertilization of the eggs

Nuptial colors do not often appear among marine fishes, and
in but few families are the sexes distinguishable by differences
in coloration

Recognition-marks.—Under the head of "recognition-marks"
may be grouped a great variety of special markings, which may
be conceived to aid the representatives of a given species to
recognize each other   That they actually serve this purpose is
a matter of theory, but the theory is plausible, and these markings have much in common with the white tail feathers, scarlet
crests, colored wing patches, and other markings regarded as
recognition marks among birds

Among these are ocelli, black- or blue-ringed with white or
yellow, on various parts of the body, black spots on the dorsal
fin, black spots below or behind the eye, black, red, blue, or
yellow spots variously placed, cross-bars of red or black or green,
with or without pale edges, a blood-red fin or a fin of shining
blue among pale ones, a white edge to the tail, a yellow, blue,
or red streamer to the dorsal fin, a black tip to the pectoral

1 ABUDEFDUF LEUCOPOMUS (CUVIER & VALENCIENNES)

or ventral; a hidden spot of emerald in the mouth or in the axil, an almost endless variety of sharply defined markings, not directly protective, which serve as recognition-marks, if not to the fish itself, certainly to the naturalist who studies it

These marks shade off into an equally great variety for which we can devise no better name than "ornamentation" Some fishes are simply covered with brilliant spots or bars or reticulations, their nature and variety baffling description, while no useful purpose seems to be served by them, unless we stretch still more widely the convenient theory of recognition-marks

In many cases the markings change with age, certain bands, stripes, or ocelli being characteristic of the young and gradually disappearing In such cases the same marks will be found permanent in some related species of less differentiated coloration In such cases it is safe to regard them as ancestral.

In case of markings on the fins and of elaborate ornamentation in general, it is best defined in the oldest and most vigorous individuals, becoming intensified by degrees The most brilliantly colored fishes are found about the coral reefs Here may be found species of which the ground color is the most intense blue, others are crimson, grass-green, lemon-yellow, jet-black, and each with a great variety of contrasted markings The frontispiece of this volume shows a series of such fishes drawn from nature from specimens taken in pools of the great coral reef of Apia in Samoa These colors are not protective The coral masses are mostly plain gray, and the fishes which lie on the bottom are plain gray also Nothing could be more brilliant or varied than the hues of the free-swimming fishes What their cause or purpose may be, it is impossible to say It is certain that their intense activity and the ease with which they can seek shelter in the coral masses enable them to defy their enemies Nature seems to riot in bright colors where her creatures are not destroyed by their presence

Intensity of Coloration —In general, coloration is most intense and varied in certain families of the tropical shores, and especially about coral reefs But in brilliancy of individual markings some fresh-water fishes are scarcely less notable, especially the darters (*Etheostominæ*) and sunfishes (*Centrarchidæ*) of the streams of eastern North America The bright hues of these fresh-water fishes are, however, more or less concealed in the water by the olivaceous markings and dark blotches of the upper parts

Coral-reef Fishes.—The brilliantly colored fishes of the tropical reefs seem, as already stated, to have no need of protective coloration They save themselves from their enemies in most cases by excessive alertness and activity (*Chætodon, Pomacentrus*), or else by burying themselves in coral sand (*Julis gaimard*), a habit more frequent than has been suspected. Every large mass of branching coral is full of lurking fishes, some of them often most brilliantly colored

Fading of Pigments in Spirits.—In the preservation of specimens most red and blue pigments fade to whitish, and it requires considerable care to interpret the traces which may be left of red bands or blue markings Yet some blue pigments are absolutely permanent, and occasionally blood-red pigments persist through all conditions Black pigment seldom changes in spirits, and olivaceous markings simply fade a little without material alteration It is an important part of the work of the systematic ichthyologist to learn to interpret the traces of the faded pigment left on specimens he may have occasion to examine In such cases it is more important to trace the markings than to restore the ground color, as the ground color is at once more variable with individuals and more constant in large groups

Variation in Pattern.—Occasionally, however, a species is found in which, other characters being constant, both ground color and markings are subject to a remarkable range of variation In such cases the actual unity of the species is open to serious question The most remarkable case of such variation known is found in a West Indian fish, the vaca, which bears the incongruous name of *Hypoplectrus unicolor* In the typical vaca the body is orange with black marks and blue lines, the fins checkered with orange and blue In a second form the body is violet, barred with black, the head with blue spots and bands In another form the blue on the head is wanting In still another the body is yellow and black, with blue on the head only In others the fins are plain orange, without checks, and the body yellow, with or without blue stripes and spots, and

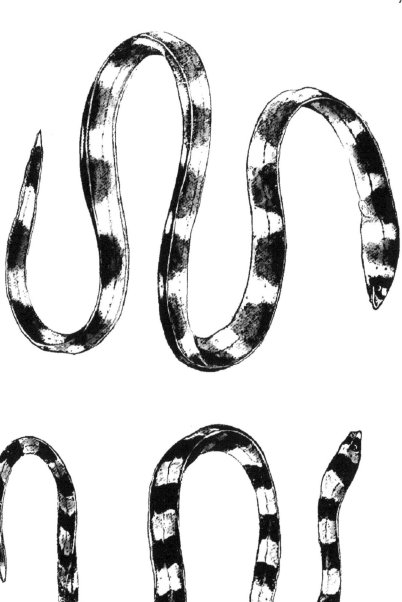

FIG. 67.—Snake-eels, *Leiuranus semicinctus* (Lay and Bennett), and *Chlevastes colubrinus* (Boddaert), from Riu Kiu Islands, Japan.

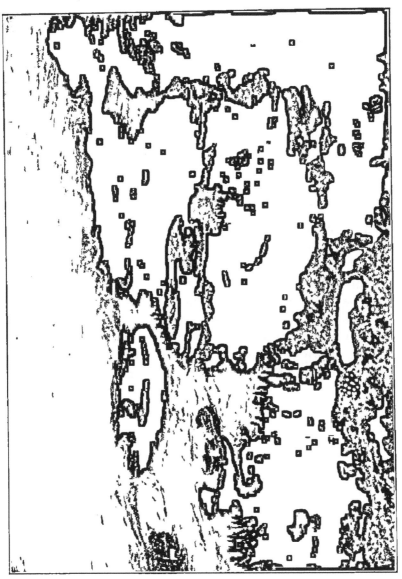

Fig 68 —Coral Reef at Apia.

sometimes with spots of black or violet   In still others the body
may be pink or brown, or violet-black, the fins all yellow, part
black or all black   Finally, there are forms deep indigo-blue in
color everywhere, with cross bands of indigo-black, and these
again may have bars of deeper blue on the head or may lack
these altogether   I find no difference among these fishes except in color, and no way of accounting for the differences in
this regard

Certain species of puffer (*Tetraodon setosus*, of Panama, and
Tetraodon nigropunctatus, of Polynesia) show similar remarkable variations, being dark gray with white spots, but varying
to indigo-blue, lemon-yellow, or sometimes having coarse blotches
of either   Lemon-yellow varieties of several species are known,
and these may be due to a failure of pigment, a sort of semi-
albinism   True albinos, individuals wholly without pigment, are
rare among fishes   In some cases the markings, commonly
black, will be replaced by a deep crimson which does not fade
in alcohol   This change happens most frequently among the
Scorpænidæ   An example of this is shown on colored plate
facing page 644   The Japanese okose or poison-fish (*Inimicus*)
is black and gray about lava-rocks.   In deeper water among
red algæ it is bright crimson, the color not fading in spirits, the
markings remaining the same.   In still deeper water it is lemon-
yellow

CHAPTER VII

THE GEOGRAPHICAL DISTRIBUTION OF FISHES

ZOOGEOGRAPHY —Under the head of distribution we consider the facts of the actual location of species of organisms on the surface of the earth and the laws by which their location is governed   This constitutes the subject-matter of the science of zoogeography   In physical geography we may prepare maps of the earth or of any part of it, these bringing to prominence the physical features of its surface   Such maps show here a sea, there a plateau, here a mountain chain, there a desert, a prairie, a peninsula, or an island   In political geography the maps show their physical features of the earth as related to the people who inhabit them and the states or powers which receive or claim their allegiance   In zoogeography the realms of the earth are considered in relation to the species or tribes of animals which inhabit them   Thus series of maps could be drawn representing those parts of North America in which catfishes or trout or sunfishes are found in the streams   In like manner the distribution of any particular fish as the muskallonge or the yellow perch could be shown on the map   The details of such a map are very instructive, and their consideration at once raises a series of questions as to the cause behind each fact   In science it must be supposed that no fact is arbitrary or meaningless   In the case of fishes the details of the method of diffusion of species afford matters of deep interest   These are considered in a subsequent chapter

The dispersion of animals may be described as a matter of space and time, the movement being continuous but modified by barriers and other codnitions of environment   The tendency of recent studies in zoogeography has been to consider the facts of present distribution as the result of conditions in the past, thus correlating our present knowledge with the past relations of land and water as shown through paleontology Dr A E Ortmann well observes that "Any division of the earth's surface into zoogeographical regions which starts exclusively from the present distribution of animals without considering its origin must always be unsatisfactory" We must therefore consider the coast-lines and barriers of Tertiary and earlier times as well as those of to-day to understand the present distribution of fishes

General Laws of Distribution —The general laws governing the distribution of all animals are reducible to three very simple propositions

Each species of animal is found in every part of the earth having conditions suitable for its maintenance, unless

(*a*) Its individuals have been unable to reach this region through barriers of some sort, or,

(*b*) Having reached it, the species is unable to maintain itself, through lack of capacity for adaptation, through severity of competition with other forms, or through destructive conditions of environment, or else,

(*c*) Having entered and maintained itself, it has become so altered in the process of adaptation as to become a species distinct from the original type

Species Absent through Barriers —The absence from the Japanese fauna of most European or American species comes under the first head   The pike has never reached the Japanese lakes, though the shade of the-lotus leaf in the many clear ponds would suit its habits exactly   The grunt * and porgies † of our West Indian waters have failed to cross the ocean and therefore have no descendants in Europe or Asia

Species Absent through Failure to Maintain Foothold —Of species under (*b*), those who have crossed the seas and not found lodgement, we have, in the nature of things, no record   Of the existence of multitudes of estrays we have abundant evidence In the Gulf Stream off Cape Cod are every year taken many young fishes belonging to species at home in the Bahamas and which find no permanent place in the New England fauna   In

---

* *Hæmulon*   † *Calamus*

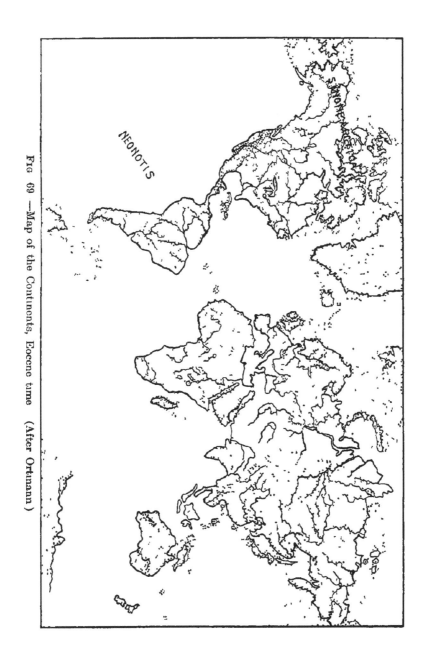

Fig 69 —Map of the Continents, Eocene time   (After Ortmann)

like fashion, young fishes from the tropics drift northward in the Kuro Shiwo to the coasts of Japan, but never finding a permanent breeding-place and never joining the ranks of the Japanese fishes But to this there have been, and will be, occasional exceptions. Now and then one among thousands finds permanent lodgement, and by such means a species from another region will be added to the fauna The rest disappear and leave no trace A knowledge of these currents and their influence is eventual to any detailed study of the dispersion of fishes

The occurrence of the young of many shore fishes of the Hawaiian Islands as drifting plankton at a considerable distance from the shores has been lately discovered by Dr Gilbert Each island is, in a sense, a "sphere of influence," affecting the fauna of neighboring regions

Species Changed through Natural Selection —In the third class, that of species changed in the process of adaptation, most insular forms belong As a matter of fact, at some time or another almost every species must be in this category, for isolation is a source of the most potent elements in the initiation and intensification of the minor differences which separate related species It is not the preservation of the most useful features, but of those which actually existed in the ancestral individuals, which distinguish such species Natural selection must include not only the process of the survival of the fittest, but also the results of the survival of the existing This means the preservation through heredity of the traits not of the species alone, but those of the actual individuals set apart to be the first in the line of descent in a new environment In hosts of cases the persistence of characters rests not on any special usefulness or fitness, but on the fact that individuals possessing these characters have, at one time or another, invaded a certain area and populated it The principle of utility explains survivals among competing structures It rarely accounts for qualities associated with geographical distribution

Extinction of Species — The extinction of species may be noted here in connection with their extension of range Prof. Herbert Osborn has recognized five different types of elimination

1 That extinction which comes from modification or progressive evolution, a relegation to the past as the result of a transmutation into more advanced forms   2 Extinction from changes of physical environment which outrun the powers of adaptation   3 The extinction which results from competition   4 The extinction from extreme specialization and limitation to special conditions the loss of which means extinction   5 Extinction as a result of exhaustion   As an illustration of No 1, we may take almost any species which has a cognate species on the further side of some barrier or in the tertiary seas   Thus the trout of the Twin Lakes in Colorado has acquired its present characters in the place of those brought into the lake by its actual ancestors   No 2 is illustrated by the disappearance of East Indian types (*Zanclus*, *Platax*, *Toxotes*, etc) in Italy at the end of the Eocene, perhaps for climatic reasons   Extinction through competition is shown in the gradual disappearance of the Sacramento perch (*Archoplitis interruptius*) after the invasion of the river by catfish and carp   From extreme specializaion certain forms have doubtless disappeared, but no certain case of this kind has been pointed out among fishes, unless this be the cause of the disappearance of the Devonian mailed *Ostracophores* and *Arthrodires*   It is not likely that any group of fishes has perished through exhaustion of the stock of vigor

Barriers Checking Movement of Marine Fishes —The limits of the distribution of individual species or genera must be found in some sort of barrier, past or present   The chief barriers which limit marine fishes are the presence of land, the presence of great oceans, the differences of temperature arising from differences in latitude, the nature of the sea bottom, and the direction of oceanic currents   That which is a barrier to one species may be an agent in distribution to another   The common shore fishes would perish in deep waters almost as surely as on land, while the open Pacific is a broad highway to the albacore or the swordfish

Again, that which is a barrier to rapid distribution may become an agent in the slow extension of the range of a species   The great continent of Asia is undoubtedly one of the greatest of barriers to the wide movement of species of fish, yet its long shore-line enables species to creep, as it were, from bay to bay, or from rock to rock, till, in many cases, the same species is found in the Red Sea and in the tide-pools or sand-reaches of Japan   In the North Pacific, the presence of a range of half-submerged volcanoes, known as the Aleutian and the Kurile Islands, has greatly aided the slow movement of the fishes of the tide-pools and the kelp   To a school of mackerel or of flying-fishes these rough islands with their narrow channels might form an insuperable barrier

Temperature the Central Fact in Distribution.—It has long been recognized that the matter of temperature is the central fact in all problems of geographical distribution. Few species in any group freely cross the frost-line, and except as borne by

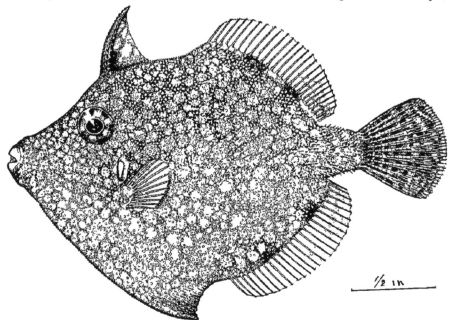

Fig 70 —Japanese file-fish, *Rudarius ercodes* Jordan and Snyder   Wakanoura, Japan   Family *Monacanthidæ*

oceanic currents, not many extend their range far into waters colder than those in which the species is distinctively at home Knowing the average temperature of the water in a given region we know in general the types of fishes which must inhabit it. It is the similarity in temperature and physical conditions which chiefly explains the resemblance of the Japanese fauna to that of the Mediterranean or the Antilles   This fact alone must explain the resemblance of the Arctic and Antarctic faunæ, there being in no case a barrier in the sea that may not some time be crossed   Like forms lodge in like places

Agency of Ocean Currents —We may consider again for a moment the movements of the great currents in the Pacific as agencies in the distribution of species

A great current sets to the eastward, crossing the ocean just south of the equator   It extends past Samoa and passes on nearly to the coast of Mexico, touching the Galapagos Islands, Clipperton Island, and especially the Revillagigedos   This may account for the number of Polynesian species found on these islands, about which they are freely mixed with immigrants from the mainland of Mexico

From the Revillagigedos * the current moves northward and westward, passing the Hawaiian Islands and thence onward to the Ladrones   The absence in Hawaii of most of the characteristic fishes of Polynesia and Micronesia may be in part due to the long detour made by these currents, as the conditions of life in these groups of islands are not very different   Northeast of Hawaii is a great spiral current, moving with the hands of the watch, forming what is called Fleurieu's Whirlpool   This does not reach the coast of California   This fact may help to account for the almost complete distinction in the shore fishes of Hawaii and California †

No other group of islands in the tropics has a fish fauna so isolated as that of Hawaii   The genera are largely the ordinary tropical types   The species are largely peculiar to these islands

The westward current from Hawaii reaches Luzon and Formosa   It is deflected to the northward and, joining a northward current from Celebes, it forms the Kuro Shiwo or Black Stream of Japan, which strews its tropical species in the rock pools along the Japanese promontories as far as Tokio   Then, turning into the open sea, it passes northward to the Aleutian Islands, across to Sitka   Thence it moves southward as a cold

---

* Clarion Island and Socorro Island

† A few Mexican shore fishes, *Chætodon humeralis, Galeichthys dasycephalus, Hypsoblennius parvipinnis,* have been wrongly accredited to Hawaii by some misplacement of labels

current, bearing Ochotsk-Alaskan types southward as far as the Santa Barbara Islands, to which region it is accompanied by species of Aleutian origin A cold return current seems to extend southward in Japan, along the east shore perhaps as far as Matsushima A similar current in the sea to the west of Japan extends still further to the southward, to Noto, or beyond

It is, of course, not necessary that the movements of a species in an oceanic current should coincide with the direction of the current Young fishes, or fresh-water fishes, would be borne along with the water Those that dwell within floating bodies of seaweed would go whither the waters carry the drifting mass But free-swimming fishes, as the mackerel or flying-fishes, might as readily choose the reverse direction To a free-swimming fish the temperature of the water would be the only consideration It is thus evident that a current which to certain forms would prove a barrier to distribution, to others would be a mere convenience in movement

In comparing the Japanese fauna with that of Australia, we find some trace of both these conditions Certain forms are perhaps excluded by cross-currents, while certain others seem to have been influenced only by the warmth of the water A few Australian types on the coast of Chile seem to have been carried over by the cross-currents of the South Atlantic

It is fair to say that the part taken by oceanic currents in the distribution of shore fishes is far from completely demonstrated The evidence that they assist in such distribution is, in brief, as follows

1 The young of shore fishes often swim at the surface

2 The young of very many tropical fishes drift northward in the Gulf Stream and the Japanese Kuro Shiwo

3 The faunal isolation of Hawaii may be correlated with the direction of the oceanic currents

Centers of Distribution.—We may assume, in regard to any species, that it has had its origin in or near that region in which it is most abundant and characteristic Such an assumption must involve a very large percentage of error or of doubt, but in considering the mass of species, it may represent essential truth In the same fashion we may regard a genus as being autochthonous or first developed in the region where it shows

the greatest range or variety of species   Those regions where
the greatest number of genera are thus autochthonous may be
regarded as centers of distribution   So far as the marine fishes
are concerned, the most important of these supposed centers are
found in the Pacific Ocean   First of these in importance is the
East-Indian Archipelago, with the neighboring shores of India
Next would come the Arctic Pacific and its bounding islands,
from Japan to British Columbia   Third in importance in this
regard is Australia   Important centers are found in temperate
Japan, in California, the Panama region, and in New Zealand,
Chili, and Patagonia   The fauna of Polynesia is almost entirely
derived from the Indies, and the shore fauna of the Red Sea,
the Bay of Bengal, and Madagascar, so far as genera are concerned, seems to be not really separable from the Indian fauna
generally

I know of but six genera which may be regarded as autochthonous in the Red Sea, and nearly all of these are of doubtful

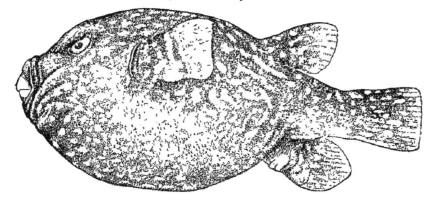

Fig 71 —Globe-fish, *Tetraodon setosus* Rosa Smith   Clarion Island, Mexico

value or of uncertain relation   The many peculiar genera described by Dr Alcock, from the dredgings of the *Investigator*
in the Bay of Bengal, belong to the bathybial or deep-water
series, and will all, doubtless, prove to be forms of wide distribution

In the Atlantic, the chief center of distribution is the West
Indies, the second is the Mediterranean   On the shores to the
northward or southward of these regions occasional genera have

found their origin. This is true especially of the New England region, the North Sea, the Gulf of Guinea, and the coast of Argentina The fish fauna of the North Atlantic is derived mainly from the North Pacific, the differences lying mainly in the relative paucity of the North Atlantic But in certain groups common to the two regions the migration must have been in the opposite direction, exceptions that prove the rule

Distribution of Marine Fishes —The distribution of marine fishes must be indicated in a different way from that of the fresh-water forms The barriers which limit their range furnish also their means of dispersion In some cases proximity overbalances the influence of temperature, with most forms questions of temperature are all-important

Pelagic Fishes —Before consideration of the coast-lines we may glance at the differences in vertical distribution Many species, especially those in groups allied to the mackerel family, are pelagic—that is, inhabiting the open sea and ranging widely within limits of temperature In this series some species are practically cosmopolitan In other cases the genera are so Each school or group of individuals has its breeding place, and from the isolation of breeding districts new species may be conceived to arise The pelagic types have reached a species of equilibrium in distribution Each type may be found where suitable conditions exist, and the distribution of species throws little light on questions of distribution of shore fishes Yet among these species are all degrees of localization The pelagic fishes shade into the shore fishes on the one hand and into the deep-sea fishes on the other

Bassalian Fishes —The vast group of bassalian or deep-sea fishes includes those forms which live below the line of adequate light These too are localized in their distribution, and to a much greater extent than was formerly supposed Yet as they dwell below the influence of the sun's rays, zones and surface temperatures are nearly alike to them, and the same forms may be found in the Arctic or under the equator Their differences in distribution are largely vertical, some living at greater depths than others, and they shade off by degrees from bathybial into semi-bathybial, and finally into ordinary pelagic and ordinary shore types Apparently all of the bassalian fishes are derived from littoral types, the changes in structure being due to degeneration of the osseous and muscular systems and of structures not needed in deep-sea life

The fishes of the great depths are soft in substance, some of them blind, some of them with very large eyes, all black in color, and very many are provided with luminous spots or areas A large body of species of fishes are semi-bathybial, inhabiting depths of 20 to 100 fathoms, showing many of the characters of shore fishes, but far more widely distributed   Many of the remarkable cases of wide distribution of type belong to this class   In moderate depths red colors are very common, corresponding to the zone of red algæ, and the colors in both

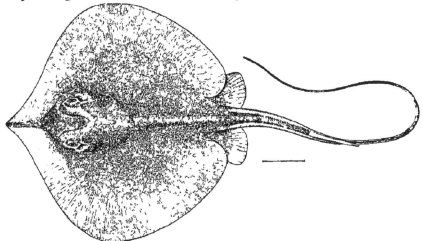

Fig 72 —Sting-ray, *Dasyatis sabina* Le Sueur   Galveston

cases are perhaps determined from the fact that the red rays of light are the least refrangible

A certain number of species are both marine and fresh water, inhabiting estuaries and brackish waters, while some more strictly marine ascend the rivers to spawn   In none of these cases can any hard and fast line be drawn, and some groups which are shore fishes in one region will be represented by semi-bathybial or fluviatile forms in another *

* The dragonets (*Callionymus*) are shore fishes of the shallowest waters in Europe and Asia, but inhabit considerable depths in tropical America   The sea robins (*Prionotus*) are shore fishes in Massachusetts, semi-bathybial fishes at Panama   Often Arctic shore fishes become sem bathybial in the Temperate Zone, living in water of a given temperature   A long period of cold weather will sometimes bring such to the surface

Littoral Fishes —The shore fishes are in general the most highly specialized in their respective groups, because exposed to the greatest variety of selecting conditions and of competition   Their distribution in space is more definite than that of, the pelagic and bassalian types, and they may be more definitely assigned to geographical areas

Distribution of Littoral Fishes by Coast-lines. — Their distribution is best indicated, not by realms or areas, but as forming four parallel series corresponding to the four great north and south continental outlines   Each of these series may be represented as beginning at the north in the Arctic fauna, practically identical in each of the four series, actually identical in the two Pacific series   Passing southward, forms are arranged according to temperature   One by one in each series, the Arctic types disappear, subarctic, temperate, and semi-tropical types take their places, giving way in turn to south-temperate and Antarctic forms   The distribution of these is modified by barriers and by currents, yet though genera and species may be different, each isotherm is represented in each series by certain general types of fishes

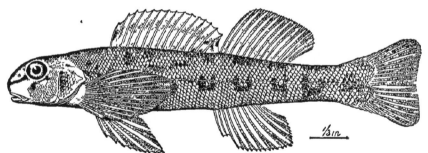

FIG 73 —Green-sided Darter, *Diplesion blennioides* Rafinesque   Clinch River. Family *Percidæ*

Passing southward the two American series, the East Atlantic and the East Pacific, pass on gradually through temperate to Antarctic types   These are analogous to those of the Arctic, and in a few cases they are generally identical   The West Pacific (East Asian) series is not a continuous line on account of the presence of Australia, the East Indies, and Polynesia   The irregularities of these regions make a number of subseries, which break up the simplicity expressed in the idea of four parallel series. Yet the fauna of Polynesia is strictly East Indian, modified by the omission or alteration of species, and that of Australia is Indian at the north, and changes to the southward much as that of Africa does.   In its marine fishes, it does not constitute a distinct "realm"   The East Atlantic (Europe-African) series follows the same general lines of change as that of the West Atlantic   It extends, however, only to the South Temperate Zone, developing no Antarctic elements   The relative shortness of Africa explains in large degree, as already shown, the similarity between the tropical elements in the two Old-World series, as the similarity in tropical elements in the two American series must be due to a former depression of the connecting Isthmus   The practical unity of the Arctic marine fauna needs no explanation in view of the present shore lines of the Arctic Ocean

Minor Faunal Areas.—The minor faunal areas of shore fishes may be grouped as follows

East Atlantic	East Pacific	West Pacific.
Icelandic,	Arctic,	Arctic,
British,	Aleutian,	Aleutian,
Mediterranean,	Sitkan,	Kurile,
Guinean,	Californian,	Hokkaido,
Cape	San Diegan,	Nippon,
	Sinaloan,	Chinese,
West Atlantic.	Panamanian,	East Indian,
Greenlandic,	Peruvian,	Polynesian,
New England,	Revillagigedan,	Hawaiian,
Virginian,	Galapagan,	Indian,
Austroriparian,	Chilian,	Arabian,
Floridian,	Patagonian	Madagascarian,
Antillæan,		Cape,
Caribbean,		North Australian,
Brazilian,		Tasmanian,
Argentinan,		New Zealand,
Patagonian.		Antarctic

Equatorial Fishes Most Specialized. — In general, the different types are most highly specialized in equatorial waters The processes of specific change, through natural selection or other causes, if other causes exist, take place most rapidly there and produce most far-reaching modification As elsewhere stated, the coral reefs of the tropics are the centers of fish-life, the cities in fish-economy The fresh waters, the arctic waters, the deep sea and the open sea represent forms of ichthyic backwoods, regions where change goes on more slowly, and in them we find survivals of archaic or generalized types For this reason the study in detail of the distribution of marine fishes of equatorial regions is in the highest degree instructive

Realms of Distribution of Fresh-water Fishes.—If we consider the fresh-water fishes alone we may divide the land areas of the earth into districts and zones not differing fundamentally with those marked out for mammals and birds The river basin, bounded by its shores and the sea at its mouth, shows many resemblances, from the point of view of a fish, to an island considered as the home of an animal It is evident that with fishes the differences in latitude outweigh those of continental areas, and a primary division into Old World and New World would not be tenable

The chief areas of distribution of fresh-water fishes we may indicate as follows, following essentially the grouping proposed by Dr. Gunther *

Northern Zone.—With Dr Gunther we may recognize first the *Northern Zone*, characterized familiarly by the presence of sturgeon, salmon, trout, white-fish, pike, lamprey, stickleback, and other species of which the genera and often the species are identical in Europe, Siberia, Canada, Alaska, and most of the United States, Japan, and China This is subject to crossdivision into two great districts, the first Europe-Asiatic, the second North American These two agree very closely to the northward, but diverge widely to the southward, developing a variety of specialized genera and species, and both of them passing finally by degrees into the Equatorial Zone

Still another line of division is made by the Ural Mountains in the Old World and by the Rocky Mountains in the New In both cases the Eastern region is vastly richer in genera and species, as well as in autochthonous forms, than the Western The reason for this lies in the vastly greater extent of the river

* " Introduction to the Study of Fishes "

basins of China and the Eastern United States, as compared with those of Europe or the Californian region

Minor divisions are those which separate the Great Lake region from the streams tributary to the Gulf of Mexico, and in Asia, those which separate China from tributaries of the Caspian, the Black, and the Mediterranean

Equatorial Zone.—The Equatorial Zone is roughly indicated by the tropics of Cancer and Capricorn   Its essential feature is that of the temperature, and the peculiarities of its divisions are caused by barriers of sea or mountains

Dr. Gunther finds the best line of separation into two divisions to lie in the presence or absence of the great group of dace or minnows,* to which nearly half of the species of fresh-water fishes the world over belong   The entire group, now spread everywhere except in the Arctic, South America, Australia, and the islands of the Pacific, seems to have had its origin in India, from which region its genera have radiated in every direction

The Cyprinoid division of the Equatorial Zone forms two districts, the Indian and the African   The Acyprinoid division includes South America, south of Mexico, and all the islands of the tropical Pacific lying to the east of Wallace's line   This line, separating Borneo from Celebes and Bali from Lompoe, marks in the Pacific the western limit of Cyprinoid fishes, as well as that of monkeys and other important groups of land animals   This line, recognized as very important in the distribution of land animals, coincides in general with the ocean current between Celebes and Papua, which is one of the sources of the Kuro Shiwo

In Australia, Hawaii, and Polynesia generally, the fresh-water fishes are derived from marine types by modification of one sort or another   In no case, so far as I know, in any island to the eastward of Borneo, is found any species derived from fresh-water families of either the Eastern or the Western Continent   Of course, minor subdivisions in these districts are formed by the contour lines of river basins   The fishes of the Nile differ from those of the Niger or the Congo, or of the streams of Mada-

* Cyprinidæ

gascar or Cape Colony, but in all these regions the essential character of the fish fauna remains the same

Southern Zone.—The third great region, the Southern Zone, is scantily supplied with fresh-water fishes, and the few it possesses are chiefly derived from modifications of the marine fauna or from the Equatorial Zone to the north   Three districts are recognized—Tasmania, New Zealand, and Patagonia

CHAPTER VIII

BARRIERS TO DISPERSION OF RIVER FISHES

THE Process of Natural Selection. — We can say, in general, that in all waters not absolutely uninhabitable there are fishes   The processes of natural selection have given to each kind of river or lake species of fishes adapted to the conditions of life which obtain there   There is no condition of water, of bottom, of depth, of speed of current, but finds some species with characters adjusted to it   These adjustments are, for the most part, of long standing, and the fauna of any single stream has as a rule been produced by immigration from other regions or from other streams   Each species has an ascertainable range of distribution, and within this range we may be reasonably certain to find it in any suitable waters

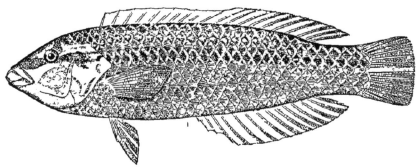

FIG 74 —Slippery-dick or Doncella, *Halichœres bivittatus* Bloch, a fish of the coral reefs, Key West   Family *Labridœ*

But every species has beyond question some sort of limit to its distribution, some sort of barrier which it has never passed in all the years of its existence   That this is true becomes evident when we compare the fish fauna of widely separated rivers   Thus the Sacramento, Connecticut, Rio Grande, and

106

St. John's Rivers have not a single species in common, and with one or two exceptions, not a species is common to any two of them None of these * has any species peculiar to itself, and each shares a large part of its fish fauna with the water-basin next to it It is probably true that the faunas of no two distinct hydrographic basins are wholly identical, while on the other hand there are very few species confined to a single one The supposed cases of this character, some twenty in number, occur chiefly in the streams of the South Atlantic States and of Arizona All of these need, however, the confirmation of further exploration It is certain that in no case has an entire river fauna† originated independently from the divergence into separate species of the descendants of a single type

The existence of boundaries to the range of species implies, therefore, the existence of barriers to their diffusion We may now consider these barriers and in the same connection the degree to which they may be overcome

Local Barriers.—Least important to these are the barriers which may exist within the limits of any single basin, and which tend to prevent a free diffusion through its waters of species inhabiting any portion of it In streams flowing southward, or across different parallels of latitude, the difference in climate becomes a matter of importance The distribution of species is governed very largely by the temperature of the water Each species has its range in this respect,—the free-swimming fishes, notably the trout, being most affected by it, the mud-loving or bottom fishes, like the catfishes, least The latter can reach the cool bottoms in hot weather, or the warm bottoms in cold weather, thus keeping their own temperature more even than that of the surface of the water Although water communication is perfectly free for most of the length of the Mississippi, there is a material difference between the faunæ of the stream in Minnesota and in Louisiana This difference is caused chiefly by the difference in temperature occupying the difference in latitude That a similar difference in longitude, with free

* Except possibly the Sacramento
† Unless the fauna of certain cave streams in the United States and Cuba be regarded as forming an exception

water communication, has no appreciable importance, is shown
by the almost absolute identity of the fish faunæ of Lake Winne-
bago and Lake Champlain   While many large fishes range
freely up and down the Mississippi, a majority of the species
do not do so, and the fauna of the upper Mississippi has more
in common with that of the tributaries of Lake Michigan than
it has with that of the Red River or the Arkansas   The influence of climate is again shown in the paucity of the fauna
of the cold waters of Lake Superior, as compared with that
of Lake Michigan   The majority of our species cannot endure
the cold   In general, therefore, cold or Northern waters contain fewer species than Southern waters do, though the number of individuals of any one kind may be greater   This is
shown in all waters, fresh or salt   The fisheries of the Northern
seas are more extensive than those of the tropics   There are
more fishes there, but they are far less varied in kind   The
writer once caught seventy-five species of fishes in a single

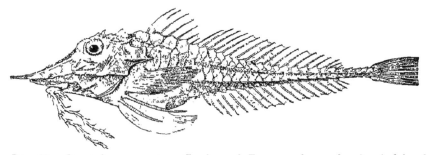

F IG 75 —*Peristedion miniatum* Goode and Bean, a deep-red colored fish of
the depths of the Gulf Stream

haul of the seine at Key West, while on Cape Cod he obtained
with the same net but forty-five species in the course of a week's
work   Thus it comes that the angler, contented with many
fishes of few kinds, goes to Northern streams to fish, while the
naturalist goes to the South

But in most streams the difference in latitude is insignificant,
and the chief differences in temperature come from differences
in elevation, or from the distance of the waters from the colder
source   Often the lowland waters are so different in character
as to produce a marked change in the quality of their fauna
These lowland waters may form a barrier to the free movements

of upland fishes, but that this barrier is not impassable is
shown by the identity of the fishes in the streams * of the uplands
of middle Tennessee with those of the Holston and French
Broad   Again, streams of the Ozark Mountains, similar in
character to the rivers of East Tennessee, have an essentially
similar fish fauna, although between the Ozarks and the Cumberland range lies an area of lowland bayous, into which such
fishes are never known to penetrate   We can, however, imagine that these upland fishes may be sometimes swept down
from one side or the other into the Mississippi, from which
they might ascend on the other side   But such transfers certainly do not often happen   This is apparent from the fact
that the two faunas † are not quite identical, and in some cases
the same species are represented by perceptibly different varieties on one side and the other   The time of the commingling of
these faunæ is perhaps now past, and it may have occurred
only when the climate of the intervening regions was colder
than at present

The effect of waterfalls and cascades as a barrier to the diffusion of most species is self-evident, but the importance of
such obstacles is less, in the course of time, than might be expected   In one way or another very many species have passed
these barriers   The falls of the Cumberland limit the range of
most of the larger fishes of the river, but the streams above it
have their quota of darters and minnows   It is evident that
the past history of the stream must enter as a factor into this
discussion, but this past history it is not always possible to
trace   Dams or artificial waterfalls now check the free movement of many species, especially those of migratory habits,
while conversely, numerous other species have extended their
range through the agency of canals ‡   .

* For example, Elk River, Duck River, etc

† There are three species of darters (*Cottogaster copelandi* Jordan, *Hadropterus evides* Jordan and Copeland, *Hadropterus scierus* Swain) which are now
known only from the Ozark region or beyond and from the uplands of Indiana,
not yet having been found at any point between Indiana and Missouri   These
constitute perhaps isolated colonies, now separated from the parent stock
in Arkansas by the prairie districts of Illinois, a region at present uninhabitable
for these fishes   But the non-occurrence of these species over the intervening
areas needs confirmation, as do most similar cases of anomalous distribution

‡ Thus, *Dorosoma cepedianum* Le Sueur and *Pomolobus chrysochloris* Rafinesque have found their way into Lake Michigan through canals

Every year fishes are swept down the rivers by the winter's floods, and in the spring, as the spawning season approaches, almost every species is found working its way up the stream In some cases, notably the Quinnat salmon * and the blueback salmon,† the length of these migrations is surprisingly great To some species rapids and shallows have proved a sufficient barrier, and other kinds have been kept back by unfavorable conditions of various sorts   Streams whose waters are always charged with silt or sediment, as the Missouri, Arkansas, or Brazos, do not invite fishes, and even the occasional floods of red mud such as disfigure otherwise clear streams, like the Red River or the Colorado (of Texas), are unfavorable   Extremely unfavorable also is the condition which obtains in many rivers of the Southwest, as, for example, the Red River, the Sabine, and the Trinity, which are full from bank to bank in winter and spring, and which dwindle to mere rivulets in the autumn droughts

Favorable Waters have Most Species.—In general, those streams which have conditions most favorable to fish life will be found to contain the greatest number of species   Such streams invite immigration, and in them the struggle for existence is individual against individual, species against species, and not a mere struggle with hard conditions of life   Some of the conditions most favorable to the existence in any stream of a large number of species of fishes are the following, the most important of which is the one mentioned first   Connection with a large hydrographic basin, a warm climate, clear water, a moderate current, a bottom of gravel (preferably covered by a growth of weeds), little fluctuation during the year in the volume of the stream or in the character of the water

Limestone streams usually yield more species than streams flowing over sandstone, and either more than the streams of regions having metamorphic rocks   Sandy bottoms usually are not favorable to fishes   In general, glacial drift makes a suitable river bottom, but the higher temperature usual in regions beyond the limits of the drift gives to certain Southern streams conditions still more favorable   These conditions are all well

---

* *Oncorhynchus tschawytscha* Walbaum
† *Oncorhynchus nerka* Walbaum

realized in the Washita River in Arkansas, and in various tributaries of the Tennessee, Cumberland, and Ohio, and in these,
among American streams, the greatest number of species has
been recorded

The isolation and the low temperature of the rivers of New
England have given to them a very scanty fish fauna as compared with the rivers of the South and West   This fact has
been noticed by Professor Agassiz, who has called New England
a "zoological island " *

In spite of the fact that barriers of every sort are sometimes crossed by fresh-water fishes, we must still regard the
matter of freedom of water communication as the essential one
in determining the range of most species   The larger the river
basin, the greater the variety of conditions likely to be offered
in it, and the greater the number of its species   In case of the
divergence of new forms by the processes called "natural selection," the greater the number of such forms which may have
spread through its waters, the more extended any river basin,
the greater are the chances that any given species may sometimes find its way into it, hence the greater the number of
species that actually occur in it, and, freedom of movement
being assumed, the greater the number of species to be found
in any one of its affluents

Of the six hundred species of fishes found in the rivers of the
United States, about two hundred have been recorded from
the basin of the Mississippi   From fifty to one hundred of
these species can be found in any one of the tributary streams
of the size, say, of the Housatonic River or the Charles   In
the Connecticut River there are but about eighteen species permanently resident, and the number found in the streams of
Texas is not much larger, the best known of these, the Rio
Colorado, having yielded but twenty-four species

The waters of the Great Basin are not rich in fishes, the

* "In this isolated region of North America, in this zoological island of
New England, as we may call it, we find neither Lepidosteus, nor Amia, nor
Polyodon, nor Amblodon (*Aplodinotus*), nor Grystes (*Micropterus*), nor Centrarchus, nor Pomoxis, nor Ambloplites, nor Callurus (*Chænobryttus*), nor Carpiodes,
nor Hyodon, nor indeed any of the characteristic forms of North American
fishes so common everywhere else with the exception of two Pomotis (*Lepomis*),
one Boleosoma, and a few Catostomus "—AGASSIZ, *Amer Journ Sci Arts*, 1854.

species now found being evidently an overflow from the Snake River when in late glacial times it drained Lake Bonneville. This postglacial lake once filled the present basin of the Great Salt Lake and Utah Lake, its outlet flowing northwest from Ogden into Snake River   The same fishes are now found in the upper Snake River and the basins of Utah Lake and of Sevier Lake.   In the same fashion Lake Lahontan once occupied the basin of Nevada, the Humboldt and Carson sinks, with Pyramid Lake   Its drainage fell also into the Snake River, and its former limits are shown in the present range of species. These have almost nothing in common with the group of species inhabiting the former drainage of Lake Bonneville   Another postglacial body of water, Lake Idaho, once united the lakes of Southeastern Oregon   The fauna of Lake Idaho, and of the lakes Malheur, Warner, Goose, etc , which have replaced it, is also isolated and distinctive.   The number of species now known from this region of these ancient lobes is about 125   This list is composed almost entirely of a few genera of suckers,* minnows,† and trout ‡   None of the catfishes, perch, darters, or sunfishes, moon-eyes, pike, killifishes, and none of the ordinary Eastern types of minnows § have passed the barrier of the Rocky Mountains

West of the Sierra Nevada the fauna is still more scanty, only about seventy species being enumerated   This fauna, except for certain immigrants‖ from the sea, is of the same general character as that of the Great Basin, though most of the species are different   This latter fact would indicate a considerable change, or "evolution," since the contents of the two faunæ were last mingled   There is a considerable difference between the fauna of the Columbia and that of the Sacramento   The species which these two basins have in common are chiefly those which at times pass out into the sea.   The rivers of Alaska contain but few species, barely a dozen in all, most of these being found also in Siberia and Kamchatka.   In the scanti-

* *Catostomus, Pantosteus, Chasmistes*
† *Gila, Ptychocheilus*, etc
‡ *Salmo clarkii* and its varieties
§ Genera *Notropis, Chrosomus*, etc
‖ As the fresh-water surf-fish (*Hysterocarpus traski*) and the species of salmon

Fig. 70 —Ancient Outlet of Lake Bonneville, Great Salt Lake, in Idaho. (Photograph by Prof. J. M. Aldrich.)

113

ness of its faunal list, the Yukon agrees with the Mackenzie River, and with Arctic rivers generally

There can be no doubt that the general tendency is for each species to extend its range more and more widely until all localities suitable for its growth are included   The various agencies of dispersal which have existed in the past are still in operation   There is apparently no limit to their action   It is probable that new "colonies" of one species or another may be planted each year in waters not heretofore inhabited by such species   But such colonies become permanent only where the conditions are so favorable that the species can hold its own in the struggle for food and subsistence   That the various modifications in the habitat of certain species have been caused by human agencies is of course too well known to need discussion here

Watersheds.—We may next consider the question of watersheds, or barriers which separate one river basin from another

Of such barriers in the United States, the most important and most effective is unquestionably that of the main chain of the Rocky Mountains   This is due in part to its great height, still more to its great breadth, and most of all, perhaps, to the fact that it is nowhere broken by the passage of a river   But two species—the red-throated or Rocky Mountain trout * and the Rocky Mountain whitefish†—are found on both sides of it, at least within the limits of the United States, while many genera, and even several families, find in it either an eastern or a western limit to their range   In a few instances representative species, probably modifications or separated branches of the same stock, occur on opposite sides of the range, but there are not many cases of correspondence even thus close   The two faunas are practically distinct   Even the widely distributed red-spotted or "dolly varden" trout ‡ of the Columbia River and its affluents does not cross to the east side of the mountains, nor does the Montana grayling § ever make its way to the West   In Northern Mexico, however, numerous Eastern river fishes have crossed the main chain of the Sierra Madre

* *Salmo clarki* Richardson   ‡ *Salvelinus malma* (Walbaum)
† *Coregonus williamsoni* Girard   § *Thymallus tricolor* Cope

How Fishes Cross Watersheds. — It is easy to account for this separation of the faunæ, but how shall we explain the almost universal diffusion of the whitefish and the trout in suitable waters on both sides of the dividing ridge? We may notice that these two are the species which ascend highest in the mountains, the whitefish inhabiting the mountain pools and lakes, the trout ascending all brooks and rapids in search of their fountainheads In many cases the ultimate dividing ridge is not very broad, and we may imagine that at some time spawn or even young fishes may have been carried across by birds or other animals, or by man, or more likely by the dash of some summer whirlwind Once carried across in favorable circumstances, the species might survive and spread

The following is an example of how such transfer of species may be accomplished, which shows that we need not be left to draw on the imagination to invent possible means of transit.

The Suletind. — There are few watersheds in the world better defined than the mountain range which forms the "backbone" of Norway I lately climbed a peak in this range, the Suletind From its summit I could look down into the valleys of the Lara and the Bagna, flowing in opposite directions to opposite sides of the peninsula To the north of the Suletind is a large double lake called the Sletningenvand The maps show this lake to be one of the chief sources of the westward-flowing river Lara. This lake is in August swollen by the melting of the snows, and at the time of my visit it was visibly the source of both these rivers From its southeastern side flowed a large brook into the valley of the Bagna, and from its southwestern corner, equally distinctly, came the waters which fed the Lara This lake, like similar mountain ponds in all northern countries, abounds in trout, and these trout certainly have for part of the year an uninterrupted line of water communication from the Sognefjord on the west of Norway to the Christianiafjord on the southeast,—from the North Sea to the Baltic. Part of the year the lake has probably but a single outlet through the Lara. A higher temperature would entirely cut off the flow into the Bagna, and a still higher one might dry up the lake altogether. This Sletningenvand, with its two outlets on the summit of a sharp watershed, may serve to show us how other lakes, permanent or temporary, may elsewhere have acted as agencies for the transfer of fishes   We can also see how it might be that certain mountain fishes should be so transferred while the fishes of the upland waters may be left behind   In some such way as this we may imagine that various species of fishes have attained their present wide range in the Rocky Mountain region, and in similar manner perhaps the Eastern brook trout * and some other mountain species †　may have been carried across the Alleghanies

The Cassiquiare.—Professor John C Branner calls my attention to a marshy upland which separates the valley of the La Plata from that of the Amazon, and which permits the free movement of fishes from the Paraguay River to the Tapajos   It is well known that through the Cassiquiare River the Rio Negro, another branch of the Amazon, is joined to the Orinoco River   It is thus evident that almost all the waters of eastern South America form a single basin, so far as the fishes are concerned

As to the method of transfer of the trout from the Columbia to the Missouri, we are not now left in doubt

Two-Ocean Pass.—To this day, as the present writer and later Evermann and Jenkins ‡ have shown, the Yellowstone and Snake Rivers are connected by two streams crossing the main divide of the Rocky Mountains from the Yellowstone to the Snake across Two-Ocean Pass

Prof Evermann has described the locality as follows

"Two-Ocean Pass is a high mountain meadow, about 8,200 feet above the sea and situated just south of the Yellowstone National Park. in longitude 110° 10′ W, latitude 44° 3′ N. It is surrounded on all sides by rather high mountains except where the narrow valleys of Atlantic and Pacific creeks open

---

* *Salvelinus fontinalis* Mitchill

† *Notropis rubricroceus* Cope, *Rhinichthys atronasus* Mitchill, etc

‡ Evermann, A Reconnoissance of the Streams and Lakes of Western Montana and Northwestern Wyoming, in Bull U S Fish Comm, XI, 1891, 24–28, pls i and ii, Jordan, The Story of a Strange Land, in Pop Sci Monthly, Feb, 1892, 447–458, Evermann, Two-Ocean Pass, in Proc Ind Ac Sci, 1892, 29–34, pl i, Evermann, Two-Ocean Pass, in Pop Sci Monthly, June, 1895, with plate

out from it Running back among the mountains to the northward are two small canyons down which come two small streams
On the opposite is another canyon down which comes another
small stream The extreme length of the meadow from east
to west is about a mile, while the width from north to south
is not much less The larger of the streams coming in from
the north is Pacific Creek, which, after winding along the western
side of the meadow, turns abruptly westward, leaving the meadow
through a narrow gorge Receiving numerous small affluents,
Pacific Creek soon becomes a good-sized stream, which finally
unites with Buffalo Creek a few miles above where the latter
stream flows into Snake River

"Atlantic Creek was found to have two forks entering the
pass At the north end of the meadow is a small wooded canyon
down which flows the North Folk. This stream hugs the border of the flat very closely The South Fork comes down the
canyon on the south side, skirting the brow of the hill a little
less closely than does the North Fork. The two, coming together near the middle of the eastern border of the meadow,
form Atlantic Creek, which after a course of a few miles flows
into the Upper Yellowstone But the remarkable phenomena
exhibited here remain to be described

"Each fork of Atlantic Creek, just after entering the
meadow, divides as if to flow around an island, but the stream
toward the meadow, instead of returning to the portion from
which it had parted, continues its westerly course across the
meadow Just before reaching the western border the two
streams unite and then pour their combined waters into Pacific
Creek, thus are Atlantic and Pacific creeks united and a continuous waterway from the Columbia via Two-Ocean Pass to
the Gulf of Mexico is established

"Pacific Creek is a stream of good size long before it enters
the pass, and its course through the meadow is in a definite
channel, but not so with Atlantic Creek The west bank of
each fork is low and the stream is liable to break through anywhere and thus send part of its water across to Pacific Creek
It is probably true that one or two branches always connect
the two creeks under ordinary conditions, and that following
heavy rains or when the snows are melting, a much greater

portion of the water of Atlantic Creek crosses the meadow to the other side

"Besides the channels already mentioned, there are several more or less distinct ones that were dry at the time of our visit. As already stated, the pass is a nearly level meadow covered with a heavy growth of grass and many small willows one to three feet high   While it is somewhat marshy in places it has nothing of the nature of a lake about it.   Of course, during

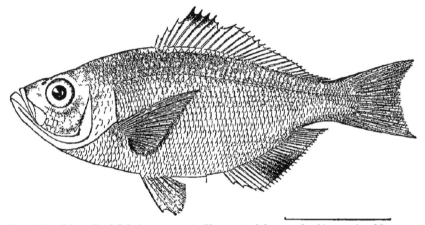

FIG 77 —Silver Surf-fish (viviparous), *Hypocritichthys analis* (Agassiz)   Monterey.

wet weather the small springs at the borders of the meadow would be stronger, but the important facts are that there is no lake or even marsh there and that neither Atlantic nor Pacific Creek has its rise in the meadow   Atlantic Creek, in fact, comes into the pass as two good-sized streams from opposite directions and leaves it by at least four channels, thus making an island of a considerable portion of the meadow. And it is certain that there is, under ordinary circumstances, a continuous waterway through Two-Ocean Pass of such a character as to permit fishes to pass easily and readily from Snake River over to the Yellowstone, or in the opposite direction   Indeed, it is quite possible, barring certain falls in the Snake River, for a fish so inclined, to start at the mouth of the Columbia, travel up that great river to its principal tributary, the Snake, thence on through the long, tortuous course of that stream, and, under the shadows of the Grand Teton, enter the cold waters of Pacific Creek, by which it could journey on up to the very crest of the great continental divide,—to Two-Ocean Pass, through this pass it may have a choice of two routes to Atlantic Creek, in which the downstream journey is begun Soon it reaches the Yellowstone, down which it continues to Yellowstone Lake, then through the lower Yellowstone out into the turbid waters of the Missouri, for many hundred miles it may continue down this mighty river before reaching the Father of Waters, which will finally carry it to the Gulf of Mexico—a wonderful journey of nearly 6,000 miles, by far the longest possible fresh-water journey in the world

"We found trout in Pacific Creek at every point where we examined it In Two-Ocean Pass we found trout in each of the streams and in such positions as would have permitted them to pass easily from one side of the divide to the other We also found trout in Atlantic Creek below the pass, and in the upper Yellowstone they were abundant Thus it is certain that there is no obstruction, even in dry weather, to prevent the passage of trout from the Snake River to Yellowstone Lake, it is quite evident that trout do pass over in this way, and it is almost certain that Yellowstone Lake was stocked with trout from the west via Two-Ocean Pass "—-EVERMANN

Mountain Chains. — The Sierra Nevada constitutes also a very important barrier to the diffusion of species This is, however, broken by the passage of the Columbia River, and many species thus find their way across it That the waters to the west of it are not unfavorable for the growth of Eastern fishes is shown by the fact of the rapid spread of the common Eastern catfish,* or horned pout, when transported from the Schuylkill to the Sacramento The catfish is now one of the important food fishes of the San Francisco markets, and with the Chinaman its patron, it has gone from California to Hawaii The Chinese catfish, described by Bleeker as *Ameiurus cantonensis*, was doubtless carried home by some Chinaman returning from San Francisco In like fashion the small-mouthed black bass is now frequent in California streams, as is also the blue-green sunfish, *Apomotis cyanellus*, introduced as food for the bass.

---

* *Ameiurus nebulosus* Le Sueur *Ameiurus catus* Linnæus

The mountain mass of Mount Shasta is, as already stated, a considerable barrier to the range of fishes, though a number of species find their way around it through the sea   The lower and irregular ridges of the Coast Range are of small importance in this regard, as the streams of their east slope reach the sea on the west through San Francisco Bay.   Yet the San Joaquin contains a few species not yet recorded from the smaller rivers of southwestern California

The main chain of the Alleghanies forms a barrier of importance separating the rich fish fauna of the Tennessee and Ohio basins from the scantier faunæ of the Atlantic streams   Yet this barrier is crossed by many more species than is the case with either the Rocky Mountains or the Sierra Nevada   It is lower, narrower, and much more broken,—as in New York, in Pennsylvania, and in Georgia there are several streams which pass through it or around it   The much greater age of the Alleghany chain, as compared with the Rocky Mountains, seems not to be an element of any importance in this connection   Of the fish which cross this chain, the most prominent is the brook trout,* which is found in all suitable waters from Hudson's Bay to the head of the Chattahoochee

Upland Fishes.—A few other species are locally found in the head waters of certain streams on opposite sides of the range   An example of this is the little red "fallfish,"† found only in the mountain tributaries of the Savannah and the Tennessee   We may suppose the same agencies to have assisted these species that we have imagined in the case of the Rocky Mountain trout, and such agencies were doubtless more operative in the times immediately following the glacial epoch than they are now. Prof Cope calls attention also to the numerous caverns existing in these mountains as a sufficient medium for the transfer of many species   I doubt whether the main chains of the Blue Ridge or the Great Smoky can be crossed in that way, though such channels are not rare in the subcarboniferous limestones of the Cumberland range   In the brooks at the head waters of the Roanoke River about Alleghany Springs in Virginia, fishes of the Tennessee Basin are found, instead of those characteristic

* *Salvelinus fontinalis*
† *Notropis rubricroceus* Cope

of the lower Roanoke. In this case it is likely that we have to consider the results of local erosion   Probably the divide has been so shifted that some small stream with its fishes has been cut off from the Holston and transferred to the Roanoke

The passage of species from stream to stream along the Atlantic slope deserves a moment's notice.   It is under present conditions impossible for any mountain or upland fish, as the trout or the miller's thumb,* to cross from the Potomac River to the James, or from the Neuse to the Santee, by descending to the lower courses of the rivers, and thence passing along either through the swamps or by way of the sea   The lower courses of these streams, warm and muddy, are uninhabitable by such fishes   Such transfers are, however, possible farther north   From the rivers of Canada and from many rivers of New England the trout does descend to the sea and into the sea, and farther north the whitefish does this also   Thus these fishes readily pass from one river basin to another.   As this is the case now everywhere in the North, it may have been the case farther south in the time of the glacial cold   We may, I think, imagine a condition of things in which the snow-fields of the Alleghany chain might have played some part in aiding the diffusion of cold-loving fishes   A permanent snow-field on the Blue Ridge in western North Carolina might render almost any stream in the Carolinas suitable for trout, from its source to its mouth   An increased volume of colder water might carry the trout of the head streams of the Catawba and the Savannah as far down as the sea   We can even imagine that the trout reached these streams in the first place through such agencies, though of this there is no positive evidence   For the presence of trout in the upper Chattahoochee we must account in some other way

It is noteworthy that the upland fishes are nearly the same in all these streams until we reach the southern limit of possible glacial influence   South of western North Carolina the faunæ of the different river basins appear to be more distinct from one another   Certain ripple-loving types are represented by closely related but unquestionably different species in each

---

* *Cottus ictalops* Rafinesque

river basin, and it would appear that a thorough mingling of
the upland species in these rivers has never taken place

The best examples of this are the following   In the Santee
basin are found *Notropis pyrrhomelas, Notropis niveus,* and *Notropis chloristius,* in the Altamaha, *Notropis xœnurus* and *Notropis callisemus;* in the Chattahoochee, *Notropis hypselopterus* and
Notropis eurystomus; in the Alabama, *Notropis cœruleus, Notropis trichroistius,* and *Notropis callistius*   In the Alabama, Es-
cambia, Pearl, and numerous other rivers is found *Notropis cercostigma*   This species descends to the sea in the cool streams of
the pine woods   Its range is wider than that of the others, and
in the rivers of Texas it reappears in the form of a scarcely distinct variety, *Notropis venustus.*   In the Tennessee and Cumberland, and in the rivers of the Ozark range, is *Notropis galacturus;*
and in the upper Arkansas *Notropis camurus,*—all distinct species
of the same general type   Northward, in all the streams from
the Potomac to the Oswego, and westward to the Des Moines and
the Arkansas, occurs a single species of this type, *Notropis
whipplei,* varying eastward into *Notropis analostanus*   But this
species is not known from any of the streams inhabited by any
of the other species mentioned, although very likely it is the
parent stock of them all

Lowland Fishes.—With the lowland species of the Southern
rivers it is different.   Few of these are confined within narrow
limits   The streams of the whole South Atlantic and Gulf
Coast flow into shallow bays, mostly bounded by sand-spits or
sand-bars which the rivers themselves have brought down.   In
these bays the waters are often neither fresh nor salt, or, rather,
they are alternately fresh and salt, the former condition being
that of the winter and spring   Many species descend into these
bays, thus finding every facility for transfer from river to river.
There is a continuous inland passage in fresh or brackish waters,
traversable by such fishes, from Chesapeake Bay nearly to
Cape Fear, and similar conditions exist on the coasts of Louisiana, Texas, and much of Florida   In Perdido Bay I have found
fresh-water minnows * and silversides† living together with
marine gobies‡ and salt-water eels §   Fresh-water alligator

* *Notropis cercostigma, Notropis xœnocephalus*   ‡ *Gobiosoma molestum*
† *Labidesthes sicculus*   § *Myrophis punctatus*

gars* and marine sharks compete for the garbage thrown over from the Pensacola wharves   In Lake Pontchartrain the fauna is a remarkable mixture of fresh-water fishes from the Mississippi and marine fishes from the Gulf   Channel-cats, sharks, sea-crabs, sunfishes, and mullets can all be found there together   It is therefore to be expected that the lowland fauna of all the rivers of the Gulf States would closely resemble that of the lower Mississippi, and this, in fact, is the case

The streams of southern Florida and those of southwestern Texas offer some peculiarities connected with their warmer climate   The Florida streams contain a few peculiar fishes,† while the rivers of Texas, with the same general fauna as those farther north, have also a few distinctly tropical types,‡ immigrants from the lowlands of Mexico

Cuban Fishes.—The fresh waters of Cuba are inhabited by fishes unlike those found in the United States   Some of these are evidently indigenous, derived in the waters they now inhabit directly from marine forms   Two of these are eyeless species,§ inhabiting streams in the caverns   They have no relatives in the fresh waters of any other region, the blind fishes ‖ of our caves being of a wholly different type   Some of the Cuban fishes are common to the fresh waters of the other West Indies   Of Northern types, only one, the alligator gar,¶ is found in Cuba, and this is evidently a filibuster immigrant from the coasts of Florida

Swampy Watersheds. — The low and irregular watershed which separates the tributaries of Lake Michigan and Lake Erie from those of the Ohio is of little importance in determining the range of species   Many of the distinctively Northern fishes are found in the headwaters of the Wabash and the Scioto   The considerable difference in the general fauna of the Ohio Valley as compared with that of the streams of Michigan is due to the higher temperature of the former region, rather than

---

* *Lepisosteus tristœchus*

† *Jordanella, Rivulus, Heterandria*, etc

‡ *Heros, Tetragonopterus*

§ *Lucifuga* and *Stygicola*, fishes allied to the cusk, and belonging to the family of *Brotulidœ*

‖ *Amblyopsis, Typhlichthys*

¶ *Lepisosteus tristœchus*

to any existing barriers between the river and the Great Lakes.
In northern Indiana the watershed is often swampy, and in
many places large ponds exist in the early spring

At times of heavy rains many species will move through considerable distances by means of temporary ponds and brooks.
Fishes that have thus emigrated often reach places ordinarily
inaccessible, and people finding them in such localities often
imagine that they have "rained down" Once, near Indian-
apolis, after a heavy shower, I found in a furrow in a corn-field
a small pike,* some half a mile from the creek in which he
should belong The fish was swimming along in a temporary
brook, apparently wholly unconscious that he was not in his
native stream Migratory fishes, which ascend small streams to
spawn, are especially likely to be transferred in this way By
some such means any of the watersheds in Ohio, Indiana, or
Illinois may be passed

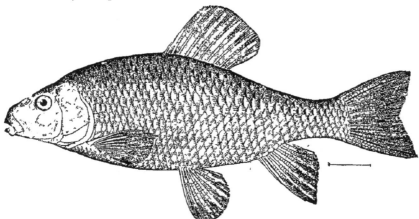

Fig 78 —Creekfish or Chub-sucker, *Erimyzon sucetta* (Lacépède). Nipisink
Lake, Illinois Family *Catostomidæ*

It is certain that the limits of Lake Erie and Lake Michigan
were once more extended than now It is reasonably probable that some of the territory now drained by the Wabash
and the Illinois was once covered by the waters of Lake Michigan The cisco† of Lake Tippecanoe, Lake Geneva, and the
lakes of the Oconomowoc chain is evidently a modified descendant of the so-called lake herring‡ Its origin most likely

* *Esox vermiculatus* Le Sueur   † *Argyrosomus sisco* Jordan
‡ *Argyrosomus artedi* Le Sueur

dates from the time when these small deep lakes of Indiana and Wisconsin were connected with Lake Michigan The changes in habits which the cisco has undergone are considerable The changes in external characters are but trifling The presence of the cisco in these lakes and its periodical disappearance—that is, retreat into deep water when not in the breeding season—have given rise to much nonsensical discussion as to whether any or all of these lakes are still joined to Lake Michigan by subterranean channels Several of the larger fishes, properly characteristic of the Great Lake region,* are occasionally taken in the Ohio River, where they are usually recognized as rare stragglers The difference in physical conditions is probably the sole cause of their scarcity in the Ohio basin

The Great Basin of Utah.—The similarity of the fishes in the different streams and lakes of the Great Basin is doubtless to be attributed to the general mingling of their waters which took place during and after the Glacial Epoch Since that period the climate in that region has grown hotter and drier, until the overflow of the various lakes into the Columbia basin through the Snake River has long since ceased These lakes have become isolated from each other, and many of them have become salt or alkaline and therefore uninhabitable In some of these lakes certain species may now have become extinct which still remain in others In some cases, perhaps, the differences in surroundings may have caused divergence into distinct species of what was once one parent stock The suckers in Lake Tahoe † and those in Utah Lake are certainly now different from each other and from those in the Columbia The trout ‡ in the same waters can be regarded as more or less tangible species, while the whitefishes§ show no differences at all The differences in the present faunas of Lake Tahoe and Utah Lake must be chiefly due to influences which have acted since the Glacial Epoch, when the whole Utah Basin was part of the drainage of the Columbia

Arctic Species in Lakes.—Connected perhaps with changes

---

* As *Lota maculosa, Percopsis guttata, Esox masquinongy*

† *Catostomus tahoensis*, in Lake Tahoe, *Catostomus macrocheilus* and *discobolus*, in the Columbia, *Catostomus fecundus, Catostomus ardens, Chasmistes liorus* and *Pantosteus generosus*, in Utah Lake.

‡ *Salmo henshawi* and *virginalis*.

§ *Coregonus williamsoni*

due to glacial influences is the presence in the deep waters of the Great Lakes of certain marine types,* as shown by the explorations of Professor Sidney I Smith and others   One of these is a genus of fishes,† of which the nearest allies now inhabit the Arctic Seas   In his review of the fish fauna of Finland,‡ Professor A J. Malmgren finds a number of Arctic species in the waters of Finland which are not found either in the North Sea or in the southern portions of the Baltic   These fishes are said to "agree with their 'forefathers' in the Glacial Ocean in every point, but remain comparatively smaller, leaner, almost starved " Professor Lovén§ also has shown that numerous small animals of marine origin are found in the deep lakes of Sweden and Finland as well as in the Gulf of Bothnia   These anomalies of distribution are explained by Lovén and Malmgren on the supposition of the former continuity of the Baltic through the Gulf of Bothnia with the Glacial Ocean   During the second half of the Glacial Period, according to Lovén, "the greater part of Finland and of the middle of Sweden was submerged, and the Baltic was a great gulf of the Glacial Ocean, and not connected with the German Ocean   By the gradual elevation of the Scandinavian Continent, the Baltic became disconnected from the Glacial Ocean and the Great Lakes separated from the Baltic   In consequence of the gradual change of the salt water into fresh, the marine fauna became gradually extinct, with the exception of the glacial forms mentioned above "

It is possible that the presence of marine types in our Great Lakes is to be regarded as due to some depression of the land which would connect their waters with those of the Gulf of St. Lawrence   On this point, however, our data are still incomplete.

To certain species of upland or mountain fishes the depression of the Mississippi basin itself forms a barrier which cannot be passed   The black-spotted trout,‖ very closely related species

---

* Species of *Mysis* and other genera of Crustaceans, similar to species described by Sars and others, in lakes of Sweden and Finland

† *Triglopsis thompsoni* Girard, a near ally of the marine species *Oncocottus quadricornis* L

‡ Kritisk Ofversigt af Finlands Fisk-Fauna, Helsingfors, 1863

§ See Günther, Zoological Record for 1864, p 137

‖ *Salmo fario* L , in Europe, *Salmo labrax* Pallas, etc , in Asia, *Salmo gairdneri* Richardson, in streams of the Pacific Coast, *Salmo perryi*, in Japan,

of which abound in all waters of northern Asia, Europe, and western North America, has nowhere crossed the basin of the Mississippi, although one of its species finds no difficulty in passing Bering Strait   The trout and whitefish of the Rocky Mountain region are all species different from those of the Great Lakes or the streams of the Alleghany system.   To the grayling, the trout, the whitefish, the pike, and to arctic and subarctic species generally, Bering Strait has evidently proved no serious obstacle to diffusion, and it is not unlikely that much of the close resemblance of the fresh-water faunæ of northern Europe, Asia, and North America is due to this fact   To attempt to decide from which side the first migration came in regard to each group of fishes might be interesting, but without a wider range of facts than is now in our possession, most such attempts, based on guesswork, would have little value   The interlocking of the fish faunas of Asia and North America presents, however, a number of interesting problems, for migrations in both directions have doubtless taken place

Causes of Dispersion Still in Operation.—One might go on indefinitely with the discussion of special cases, each more or less interesting or suggestive in itself, but the general conclusion is in all cases the same   The present distribution of fishes is the result of the long-continued action of forces still in operation   The species have entered our waters in many invasions from the Old World or from the sea   Each species has been subjected to the various influences implied in the term "natural selection," and under varying conditions its representatives have undergone many different modifications   Each of the six hundred fresh-water species we now know in the United States may be conceived as making every year inroads on territory occupied by other species   If these colonies are able to hold their own in the struggle for possession, they will multiply in the new conditions, and the range of the species becomes widened   If the surroundings are different, new species or varieties may be formed with time, and these new forms may again invade the territory of the parent species.   Again, colony after colony of species

---

Salmo clarki Richardson, throughout the Rocky Mountain range to the Mexican boundary and the headwaters of the Kansas, Platte, and Missouri

after species may be destroyed by other species or by uncongenial surroundings.

The ultimate result of centuries on centuries of the restlessness of individuals is seen in the facts of geographical distribution Only in the most general way can the history of any species be traced, but could we know it all, it would be as long and as eventful a story as the history of the colonization and settlement of North America by immigrants from Europe But by the fishes each river in America has been a hundred times discovered, its colonization a hundred times attempted   In these efforts there is no co-operation   Every individual is for himself, every struggle a struggle of life and death, for each fish is a cannibal, and to each species each member of every other species is an alien and a savage

CHAPTER IX

FISHES AS FOOD FOR MAN

THE Flesh of Fishes.—Among all races of men, fishes are freely eaten as food, either raw, as preferred by the Japanese and Hawaiians, or else as cooked, salted, dried, or otherwise preserved

The flesh of most fishes is white, flaky, readily digestible, and with an agreeable flavor Some, as the salmon, are charged with oil, which aids to give an orange hue known as salmon color Others have colorless oil which may be of various consistencies. Some have dark-red flesh, which usually contains a heavy oil which becomes acrid when stale Some fishes, as the sharks, have tough, coarse flesh Some have flesh which is watery and coarse Some are watery and tasteless, some dry and tasteless Some, otherwise excellent, have the muscular area, which constitutes the chief edible part of the fish, filled with small bones

Relative Rank of Food-fishes—The writer has tested most of the noted food-fishes of the Northern Hemisphere When

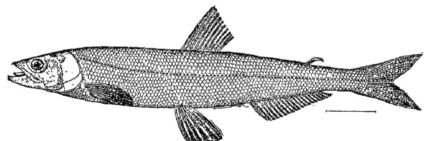

Fig 79.—Eulachon, or Ulchen *Thaleichthys pretiosus* Girard Columbia River Family *Argentinidæ.*

properly cooked (for he is no judge of raw fish) he would place first in the ranks as a food-fish the eulachon, or candle-fish (*Thaleichthys pacificus*).

This little smelt, about a foot long, ascends the Columbia
River, Frazer River, and streams of southern Alaska in the
spring in great numbers for the purpose of spawning. Its flesh
is white, very delicate, charged with a white and very agree-

FIG. 80.—Ayu, or Japanese Samlet, *Plecoglossus altivelis* Schlegel. Tanagawa,
Tokyo, Japan.

able oil, readily digested, and with a sort of fragrance peculiar
to the species.

Next to this he is inclined to place the ayu (*Plecoglossus
altivelis*), a sort of dwarf salmon which runs in similar fashion
in the rivers of Japan and Formosa. The ayu is about as large

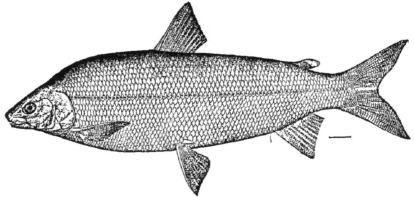

FIG. 81.—Whitefish, *Coregonus clupeiformis* Mitchill. Ecorse, Mich.

as the eulachon and has similar flesh, but with little oil and no
fragrance.

Very near the first among sea-fishes must come the pampano

(*Trachinotus carolinus*) of the Gulf of Mexico, with firm, white, finely flavored flesh

The red surmullet of Europe (*Mullus barbatus*) has been long famed for its delicate flesh, and may perhaps be placed next   Two related species in Polynesia, the munu and the

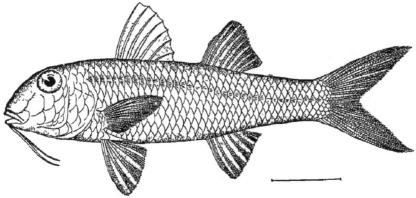

FIG 82 —Golden Surmullet, *Mullus auratus* Jordan & Gilbert.
Woods Hole, Mass

kumu (*Pseudupeneus bifasciatus* and *Pseudupeneus porphyreus*), are scarcely inferior to it

Side by side with these belongs the whitefish of the Great Lakes (*Coregonus clupeiformis*)   Its flesh, delicate, slightly

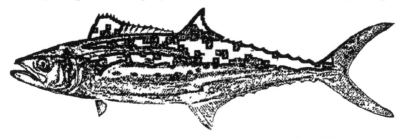

FIG 83 —Spanish Mackerel, *Scomberomorus maculatus* Mitchill.
Family *Scombridæ*   Key West

gelatinous, moderately oily, is extremely agreeable   Sir John Richardson records the fact that one can eat the flesh of this fish longer than any other without the feeling of cloying   The salmon cannot be placed in the front rank, because, however excellent, the stomach soon becomes tired of it   The Spanish mackerel (*Scomberomorus maculatus*), with flesh at once rich and delicate, the great opah (*Lampris luna*), still richer and still

FIG. 84.—Opah, or Moonfish, *Lampris luna* (Gmelin). Specimen in Honolulu market weighing 317½ lbs. (Photograph by E. L. Berndt.)—Page 132.

more delicate, the bluefish (*Pomatomus saltatrix*) similar but a little coarser, the ulua (*Carangus sem*), the finest large food-fish of the South Seas, the dainty California poppy-fish, miscalled "Pampano" (*Palometa simillima*), and the kingfish firm and

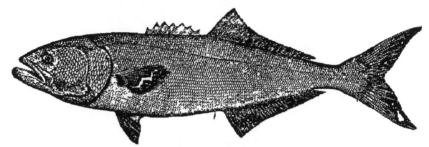

FIG 85 —Bluefish, *Pomatomus saltatrix* (L) New York

well-flavored (*Scomberomorus cavalla*), represent the best of the fishes allied to the mackerel

The shad (*Alosa sapidissima*), with its sweet, tender, finely oily flesh, stands also near the front among food-fishes, but it sins above all others in the matter of small bones   The weak-fish (*Cynoscion nobilis*) and numerous relatives rank first among

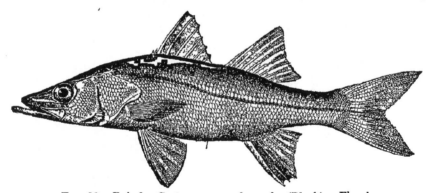

FIG 86 —Robalo, *Centropomus undecimalis* (Bloch)   Florida

those with tender, white, savorous flesh   Among the bass and perch-like fishes, common consent places near the first the striped bass (*Roccus lineatus*), the bass of Europe (*Dicentrarchus labrax*), the susuki of Japan (*Lateolabrax japonicus*), the red tai of Japan (*Pagrus major* and *P. cardinalis*), the sheep's-head (*Archosargus probatocephalus*), the mutton-fish or Pargo Criollo of Cuba (*Lutianus analis*), the European porgy (*Pagrus pagrus*), the robalo (*Centropomus undecimalis*), the uku (*Aprion vires-cens*) of Hawaii, the spadefish (*Chætodipterus faber*), and the black bass (*Micropterus dolomieu*).

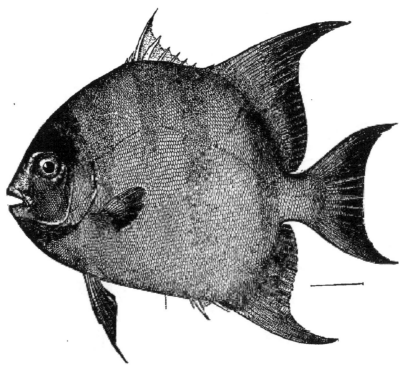

FIG. 87.—Spadefish, *Chætodipterus faber* (L.). Virginia.

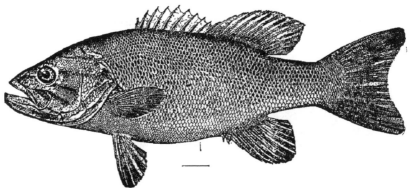

FIG. 88.—Small-mouthed Black Bass, *Micropterus dolomieu* (Lacépède). Potomac River.

The various kinds of trout have been made famous the world over. All are attractive in form and color; all are gamy; all have the most charming of scenic surroundings, and, finally, all are excellent as food, not in the first rank perhaps, but well above the second Notable among these are the European

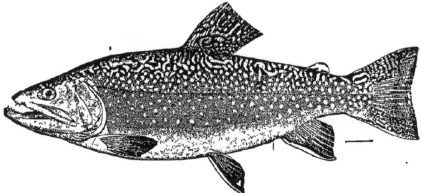

FIG. 89.—Speckled Trout (male), *Salvelinus fontinalis* (Mitchill) New York

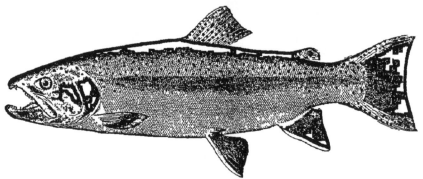

FIG 90 —Rainbow Trout, *Salmo irideus* Gibbons Sacramento River, California

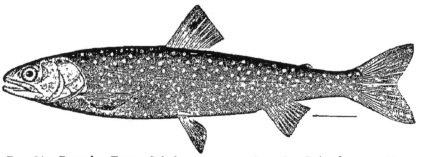

FIG 91.—Rangeley Trout, *Salvelinus oquassa* (Girard) Lake Oquassa, Maine

charr (*Salvelinus alpinus*), the American speckled trout or charr (*Salvelinus fontinalis*), the Dolly Varden or malma (*Salvelinus malma*), and the oquassa trout (*Salvelinus oquassa*) Scarcely

less attractive are the true trout, the brown trout, or forelle
(*Salmo fario*), in Europe, the rainbow-trout (*Salmo irideus*),

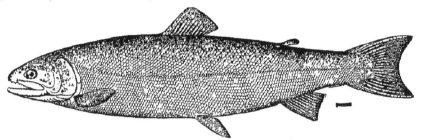

Fig. 92 —Steelhead Trout, *Salmo gairdneri* Richardson   Columbia River

the steelhead (*Salmo gairdneri*), the cut-throat trout (*Salmo
clarkii*), and the Tahoe trout (*Salmo henshawi*), in America,

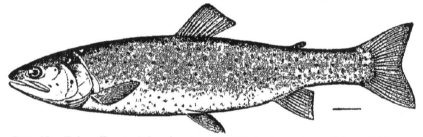

Fig 93 —Tahoe Trout, *Salmo henshawi* Gill & Jordan.   Lake Tahoe, California

and the yamabe (*Salmo perryi*) of Japan   Not least of all
these is the flower of fishes, the grayling (*Thymallus*), of different species in different parts of the world

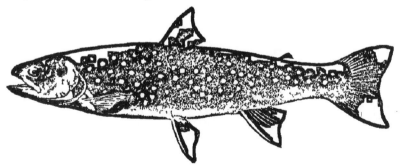

Fig 94 —The Dolly Varden Trout, *Salvelinus malma* (Walbaum).   Lake Pend
d'Oreille, Idaho   (After Evermann)

Other most excellent food-fishes are the eel (*Anguilla* species),
the pike (*Esox lucius*), the muskallonge (*Esox masquinongy*),
the sole of Europe (*Solea solea*), the sardine (*Sardinella pilchar-*

dus), the atka-fish (*Pleurogrammus monopterygius*) of Bering Sea, the pescado blanco of Lake Chapala (*Chirostoma estor* and other species), the Hawaiian mullet (*Mugil cephalus*), the channel

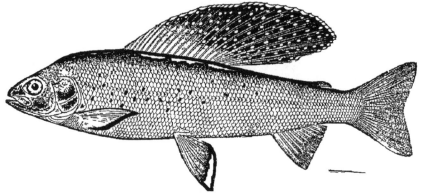

Fig 95 —Alaska Grayling, *Thymallus signifer* Richardson   Nulato, Alaska

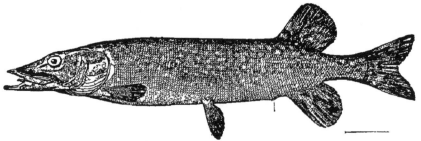

Fig 96 —Pike, *Esox lucius* L   Ecorse, Mich.

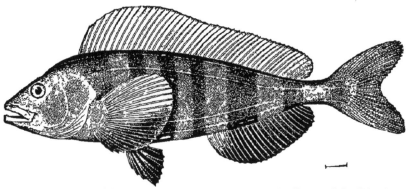

Fig 97 —Atka-fish, *Pleurogrammus monopterygius* (Pallas)   Atka Island

catfish (*Ictalurus punctatus*), the turbot (*Scophthalmus maximus*), the barracuda (*Sphyræna*), and the young of various sardines and herring, known as whitebait. Of large fishes, probably the swordfish (*Xiphias gladius*), the halibut (*Hippoglossus hippoglossus*), and the king-salmon, or quinnat (*Oncorhynchus tschawytscha*), may be placed first. Those people who feed on raw fish

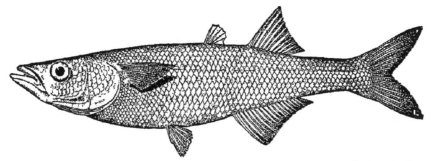

FIG 98 —Pescado blanco, *Chirostoma humboldtianum* (Val). Lake Chalco, City of Mexico

prefer in general the large parrot-fishes (as *Pseudoscarus jordani* in Hawaii), or else the young of mullet and similar species

Abundance of Food-fishes.—In general, the economical value of any species depends not on its toothsomeness, but on its abundance and the ease with which it may be caught and pre-

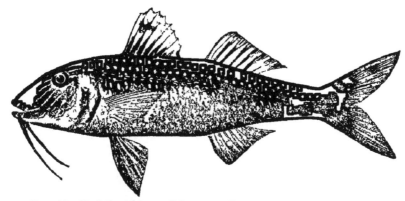

FIG 99—Red Goatfish, or Salmonete, *Pseudupeneus maculatus* Bloch. Family *Mullidæ* (Surmullets).

served   It is said that more individuals of the herring (*Clupea harengus* in the Atlantic, *Clupea pallasi* in the Pacific) exist than of any other species   The herring is a good food-fish and whenever it runs it is freely sought   According to Bjornson, wherever the school of herring touches the coast of Norway, there a village springs up, and this is true in Scotland, Newfoundland, and from Killisnoo in Alaska to Otaru in Japan, and to Strielok in Siberia. Goode estimates the herring product of the North Atlantic at 1,500,000,000 pounds annually   In 1881 Professor Huxley used these words·

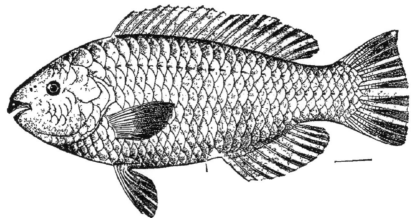

FIG 100.—Great Parrot-fish, or Guacamaia, *Pseudoscarus guacamaia* Bloch & Schneider   Florida

"It is said that 2,500,000,000 or thereabout of herrings are every year taken out of the North Sea and the Atlantic Suppose we assume the number to be 2,000,000,000 so as to be quite safe.   It is a large number undoubtedly, but what does

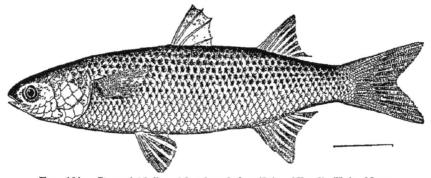

FIG, 101 —Striped Mullet, *Mugil cephalus* (L).   Wood's Hole, Mass

it come to?   Not more than that of the herrings which may be contained in one shoal, if it covers half a dozen square miles, and shoals of much larger size are on record   It is safe to say that scattered through the North Sea and the Atlantic, at one and the same time, there must be scores of shoals, any one of which would go a long way toward supplying the whole of man's consumption of herrings "

The codfish (*Gadus callarias* in the Atlantic, *Gadus macro-*

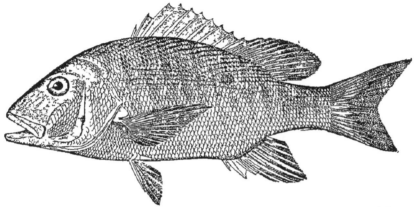

FIG 102 —Mutton-snapper, or Pargo criollo, *Lutianus analis* (Cuv & Val) Key West

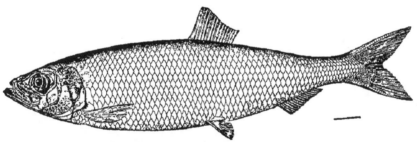

FIG 103 —Herring, *Clupea harengus* L　New York

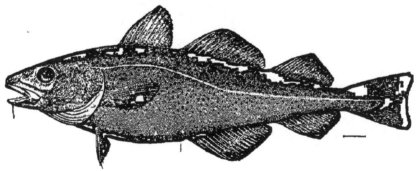

FIG 104 —Codfish, *Gadus callarias* L　Eastport, Maine

cephalus in the Pacific) likewise swarms in all the northern seas, takes the hook readily, and is better food when salted and dried than it is when fresh

Next in economic importance probably stands the mackerel of the Atlantic (*Scomber scombrus*), a rich, oily fish which bears salting better than most.

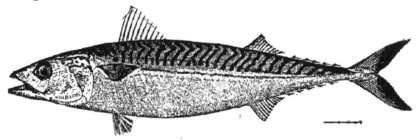

Fig. 105.—Mackerel, *Scomber scombrus* L. New York.

Not less important is the great king-salmon, or quinnat (*Oncorhynchus tschawytscha*), and the still more valuable blue-back salmon, or red-fish (*Oncorhynchus nerka*).

Fig. 106.—Halibut, *Hippoglossus hippoglossus* (Linnæus). St. Paul Island, Bering Sea. (Photograph by U. S. Fur Seal Commission.)

The salmon of the Atlantic (*Salmo salar*), the various species of sturgeon (*Acipenser*), the sardines (*Sardinella*), the halibut (*Hippoglossus*), are also food-fishes of great importance.

Variety of Tropical Fishes.—In the tropics no one species is represented by enormous numbers of individuals as is the case in colder regions. On the other hand, the number of species regarded as food-fishes is much greater in any given port. In Havana, about 350 different species are sold as food in the markets, and an equal number are found in Honolulu. Upward of 600 different species appear in the markets of Japan. In England, on the contrary, about 50 species make up the list of fishes commonly used as food. Yet the number of individual fishes is probably not greater about Japan or Hawaii than in a similar stretch of British coast.

Economic Fisheries.—Volumes have been written on the economic value of the different species of fishes, and it is not the purpose of the present work to summarize their contents.

Fig. 107.—Fishing for Ayu with Cormorants in the Tanagawa, near Tokyo.
(After photograph by J. O. Snyder by Sekko Shimada.)

Equally voluminous is the literature on the subject of catching fishes. It ranges in quality from the quaint wisdom of the "Compleat Angler" and the delicate wit of "Little Rivers" to elaborate discussions of the most economic and effective forms and methods, of the beam-trawl, the purse-seine, and the codfish hook   In general, fishes are caught in four ways—by baited hooks, by spears, by traps, and by nets   Special local methods, such as the use of the tamed cormorant * in the catching of the ayu, by the Japanese fishermen at Gifu, may be set aside for the moment, and all general methods of fishing come under one of these four classes.   Of these methods, the hook, the spear, the seine, the beam-trawl, the gill-net, the purse-net, the sweep-net,, the trap and the weir are the most important   The use of the hook is again extremely varied   In the deep sea long, sunken lines are sometimes used for codfish, each baited with many hooks   For pelagic fish, a baited hook is drawn swiftly over the surface, with a "spoon" attached which looks like a living fish.   In the rivers a line is attached to a pole, and when fish are caught for pleasure or for the joy of being in the woods, recreation rises to the dignity of angling   Angling may be accomplished with a hook baited with an earthworm, a grasshopper, a living fish, or the larva of some insect   The angler of to-day, however, prefers the artificial fly, as being more workmanlike and also more effective than bait-fishing   The man who fishes, not for the good company of the woods and brooks, but to get as many fish as possible to eat or sell, is not an angler but a pot-fisher   The man who kills all the trout he can, to boast of his skill or fortune, is technically known as a trout-hog   Ethically, it is better to lie about your great catches of fine fishes than to make them   For most anglers, also, it is more easy

Fisheries.—With the multiplicity of apparatus for fishing, there is the greatest variety in the boats which may be used   The fishing-fleet of any port of the world is a most interesting

* The cormorant is tamed for this purpose   A harness is placed about its wings and a ring about the lower part of its neck   Two or three birds may be driven by a boy in a shallow stream, a small net behind him to drive the fish down the river   In a large river like that of Gifu, where the cormorants are most used, the fishermen hold the birds from the boats and fish after dark by torchlight   The bird takes a great interest in the work, darts at the fishes with great eagerness, and fills its throat and gular pouch as far down as the ring   Then the boy takes him out of the water, holds him by the leg and shakes the fishes out into a basket   When the fishing is over the ayu are preserved, the ring is taken off from the bird's neck, and the zako or minnows are thrown to him for his share   These he devours greedily

object, as are also the fishermen with their quaint garb, plain speech, and their strange songs and calls with the hauling in of the net.

For much information on the fishing apparatus in use in

Fig. 108.—Fishing for Ayu in the Tanagawa, Japan. Emptying the pouch of the cormorant. (Photograph by J. O. Snyder.)

America the reader is referred to the Reports of the Fisheries in the Tenth Census, in 1880, under the editorship of Dr. George Brown Goode. In these reports Goode, Stearns, Earle, Gilbert, Bean, and the present writer have treated very fully of all economic relations of the American fishes. In an admirable work entitled "American Fishes," Dr. Goode, with the fine literary touch of which he was master, has fully discoursed of the game- and food-fishes of America with especial reference to the habits and methods of capture of each   To these sources, to Jordan and Evermann's " Food and Game Fishes of North America," and to many other works of similar purport in other lands, the reader is referred for an account of the economic and the human side of fish and fisheries

Angling.—It is no part of the purpose of this work to describe the methods or materials of angling, still less to sing its praises as a means of physical or moral regeneration   We may perhaps find room for a first and a last word on the subject, the one the classic from the pen of the angler of the brooks of Staffordshire, and the other the fresh expression of a Stanford student setting out for streams such as Walton never knew, the Purissima, the Stanislaus, or perchance his home streams, the Provo or the Bear

" And let me tell you, this kind of fishing with a dead rod, and laying night-hooks, are like putting money to use ; for they both work for the owners when they do nothing but sleep, or eat, or rejoice, as you know we have done this last hour, and sat as quietly and as free from cares under this sycamore as Virgil's Tityrus and his Meliboeus did under their broad beech-tree   No life, my honest scholar,—no life so happy and so pleasant as the life of a well-governed angler, for when the lawyer is swallowed up with business and the statesman is preventing or contriving plots, then we sit on the cowslip-banks, hear the birds sing, and possess ourselves in as much quietness as these silent silver streams which we now see glide so quietly by us   Indeed, my good scholar, we may say of angling, as Dr Boteler said of strawberries, 'Doubtless God could have made a better berry, but doubtless God never did', and so, if I might be judge, 'God never made a more calm, quiet, innocent recreation than angling.'

" I'll tell you, scholar, when I sat last on this primrose-bank, and looked down these meadows, I thought of them as Charles the Emperor did of Florence, 'That they were too pleasant to be looked on but only on holidays '

" Gentle Izaak! He has been dead these many years, but his disciples are still faithful   When the cares of business lie heavy and the sound of wheels jarring on cobbled streets grows painful, one's fingers itch for the rod, one would away to the quiet brook among the pines, where one has fished so often. Every man who has ever got the love of the stream in his blood feels often this longing

"It comes to me each year with the first breath of spring. There is something in the sweetness of the air, the growing things, the 'robin in the greening grass' that voices it. Duties that have before held in their performance something of pleasure become irksome, and practical thoughts of the day's work are replaced by dreamy pictures of a tent by the side of a mountain stream—close enough to hear the water's singing in the night Two light bamboo rods rest against the tent-pole, and a little column of smoke rising straight up through the branches marks the supper fire Jack is preparing the evening meal, and, as I dream, there comes to me the odor of crisply browned trout and sputtering bacon—was ever odor more delicious? I dare say that had the good Charles Lamb smelled it as I have, his 'Dissertation on Roast Pig' would never have been written But then Charles Lamb never went a-fishing as we do here in the west—we who have the mountains and the fresh air so boundlessly

"And neither did Izaak Walton for that matter He who is sponsor for all that is gentle in angling missed much that is best in the sport by living too early He did not experience the exquisite pleasure of wading down mountain streams in supposedly water-proof boots and feeling the water trickling in coolingly, nor did he know the joy of casting a gaudy fly far ahead with a four-ounce rod, letting it drift, insect-like, over that black hole by the tree stump, and then feeling the sea-weed line slip through his fingers to the *whirr* of the reel And, at the end of the day, supper over, he did not squat around a big camp-fire and light his pipe, the silent darkness of the mountains gathering round, and a basketful of willow-packed trout hung in the clump of pines by the tent Izaak's idea of fishing did not comprehend such joy With a can of worms and a crude hook, he passed the day by quiet streams, threading the worms on his hook and thinking kindly of all things The day's meditations over, he went back to the village, and, mayhap, joined a few kindred souls over a tankard of ale at the sign of the Red Lobster. But he missed the mountains, the water rushing past his tent, the bacon and trout, the camp-

Fig. 109 —Fishing for Tai, Tokyo Bay. (Photograph by J. O. Snyder.)

fire—the physical exaltation of it all. His kind of fishing was angling purely, while modern Waltons, as a rule, eschew the worm.

"To my mind, there is no real sport in any kind of fishing except fly-fishing   This sitting on the bank of a muddy stream with your bait sunk, waiting for a bite, may be conducive to gentleness and patience of spirit, but it has not the joy of action in which a healthy man revels   How much more sport is it to clamber over fallen logs that stretch far out a-stream, to wade slipping over boulders and let your fly drop caressingly on ripples and swirling eddies and still holes!   It is worth all the work to see the gleam of a silver side as a half-pounder rises, and, with a flop, takes the fly excitedly to the bottom   And then the nervous thrill as, with a deft turn of the wrist, you hook him securely—whoever has felt that thrill cannot forget it   It will come back to him in his law office when he should be thinking of other things, and with it will come a longing for that dear remembered stream and the old days   That is the hold trout-fishing takes on a man

"It is spring now and I feel the old longing myself, as I always do when life comes into the air and the smell of new growth is sweet   I got my rod out to-day, put it together, and have been looking over my flies   If I cannot use them, I can at least muse over days of the past and dream of those to come."   (WALDEMAR YOUNG)

CHAPTER X

THE MYTHOLOGY OF FISHES

THE **Mermaid.**—A word may be said of the fishes which have no existence in fact and yet appear in popular literature or in superstition

The mermaid, half woman and half fish, has been one of the most tenacious among these, and the manufacture of their dried bodies from the head, shoulders, and ribs of a monkey sealed to the body of a fish has long been a profitable industry in the Orient. The sea-lion, the dugong, and other marine mammals have been mistaken for mermaids, for their faces seen at a distance and their movements at rest are not inhuman, and their limbs and movements in the water are fishlike.

In China, small mermaids are very often made and sold to the curious The head and torso of a monkey are fastened ingeniously to the body and tail of a fish It is said that Linnæus was once forced to leave a town in Holland for questioning the genuineness of one of these mermaids, the property of some high official. These monsters are still manufactured for the " curio-trade "

The Monk-fish.—Many strange fishes were described in the Middle Ages, the interest usually centering in some supposed relation of their appearance with the affairs of men Some of these find their way into Rondelet's excellent book, " Histoire Entière des Poissons," in 1558 Two of these with the accompanying plate of one we here reproduce Other myths less interesting grew out of careless, misprinted, or confused accounts on the part of naturalists and travelers

" In our times in Norway a sea-monster has been taken after a great storm, to which all that saw it at once gave the name of monk; for it had a man's face, rude and ungracious, the head shorn and smooth.   On the shoulders, like the cloak of a monk, were two long fins instead of arms, and the end of the body was finished by a long tail   The picture I present was given me by the very illustrious lady, Margaret de Valois, Queen of Navarre,

Fig 110 —"*Le monstre marin en habit de Moine*"   (After Rondelet)

who received it from a gentleman who gave a similar one to the emperor, Charles V , then in Spain   This gentleman said that he had seen the monster as the portrait shows it in Norway, thrown by the waves and tempests on the beach at a place called Dieze, near the town called Denelopoch. I have seen a similar picture at Rome not differing in mien   Among the sea-beasts, Pliny mentions a sea-mare and a Triton as among the creatures not imaginary   Pausanias also mentions a Triton."

Rondelet further says:

The Bishop-fish —"I have seen a portrait of another sea-monster at Rome, whither it had been sent with letters that affirmed for certain that in 1531 one had seen this monster in a bishop's garb, as here portrayed, in Poland   Carried to the king of that country, it made certain signs that it had a great desire to return to the sea   Being taken thither it threw itself instantly into the water "

The Sea-serpent.—A myth of especial persistency is that of the sea-serpent   Most of the stories of this creature are seaman's yarns, sometimes based on a fragment of wreck, a long strip of kelp, the power of suggestion or the incitement of alcohol   But certain of these tales relate to real fishes   The sea-serpent with an uprearing red mane like that of a horse is the oarfish (*Regalecus*), a long, slender, fragile fish compressed like a ribbon and reaching a length of 25 feet We here present a photograph of an oarfish (*Regalecus rus-selli*) stranded on the Cali-

Fig 111—"*Le monstre marin en habit d' Évéque*"   (After Rondelet)

fornia coast at Newport in Orange County, California   A figure of a European species (*Regalecus glesne*) is also given showing the fish in its uninjured condition   Another reputed sea-serpent is the frilled shark (*Chlamydoselachus anguineus*), which has been occasionally noticed by seamen.   The struggles of the great killer (*Orca orca*) with the whales it attacks and destroys has also given rise to stories of the whale struggling in the embrace of some huge sea-monster   This description is correct, but the mammal is a monster itself, a relative of the whale and not a reptile.

Fig. 112.—Oarfish, *Regalecus russelli*, on the beach at Newport, Orange Co., Cal. (Photograph by C. P. Remsberg.)

152

It is often hard to account for some of the stories of the sea-serpent   A gentleman of unquestioned intelligence and sincerity lately dercribed to the writer a sea-serpent he had seen at short range, 100 feet long, swimming at the surface, and with a head as large as a barrel.   I do not know what he saw, but I do know that memory sometimes plays strange freaks

Little venomous snakes with flattened tails (*Platyurus, Pelamis*) are found in the salt bays in many tropical regions of the Pacifie (Gulf of California, Panama, East Indies, Japan), but these are not the conventional sea-serpents

Certain slender fishes, as the thread-eel (*Nemichthys*) and the wolf-eel (*Anarrhichthys*), have been brought to naturalists as young sea-serpents, but these of course are genuine fishes

Whatever the nature of the sea-serpent may be, this much is certain, that while many may be seen, none will ever be caught   The great swimming reptiles of the sea vanished at the end of Mesozoic time, and as living creatures will never be known of man

As a record of the Mythology of Science, we may add the following remarks of Rafinesque on the imaginary garpike (*Litholepis adamantinus*), of which a specimen was painted for him by the wonderful brush of Audubon:

"This fish may be reckoned the wonder of the Ohio   It is only found as far up as the falls, and probably lives also in the Mississippi   I have seen it, but only at a distance, and have been shown some of its singular scales   Wonderful stories are related concerning this fish, but I have principally relied upon the description and picture given me by Mr. Audubon   Its length is from 4 to 10 feet   One was caught which weighed 400 pounds   It lies sometimes asleep or motionless on the surface of the water, and may be mistaken for a log or snag   It is impossible to take it in any other way than with the seine or a very strong hook, the prongs of the gig cannot pierce the scales, which are as hard as flint, and even proof against lead balls!   Its flesh is not good to eat   It is a voracious fish   Its vulgar names are diamond-fish (owing to its scales being cut like diamonds), devil-fish, jackfish, garjack, etc   The snout is large, convex above, very obtuse, the eyes small and black; nostrils small, round before the eyes, mouth beneath the eyes, transversal with large angular teeth   Pectoral and abdominal fins trapezoidal   Dorsal and anal fins equal, longitudinal, with many rays. Th: whole body covered with large stone scales, lying in oblique rows, they are conical, pentagonal pentædral, with equal sides, from half an inch to one inch in diameter, brown at first but becoming the color of turtle-shell when dry. They strike fire with steel and are ball-proof!"   .

Fig. 113.—Glesnæs Oarfish, *Regalecus glesne* Ascanius. Newcastle, England. (After Day.)

155

FIG. 114.—Thread-eel, *Nemicthys avocetta* Jordan & Gilbert. Puget Sound.

CHAPTER XI

THE COLLECTION OF FISHES

HOW **to Secure Fishes.**—In collecting fishes three things are vitally necessary—a keen eye, some skill in adapting means to ends, and some willingness to take pains in the preservation of material

In coming into a new district the collector should try to preserve the first specimen of every species he sees It may not come up again. He should watch carefully for specimens which look just a little different from their fellows, especially for those which are duller, less striking, or with lower fins. Many species have remained unnoticed through generations of collectors who have chosen the handsomest or most ornate specimens In some groups with striking peculiarities, as the trunk-fishes, practically all the species were known to Linnæus No collector could pass them by. On the other hand, new gobies or blennies can be picked up almost every day in the lesser known parts of the world. For these overlooked forms—herrings, anchovies, sculpins, blennies, gobies, scorpion-fishes—the competent collector should be always on the watch If any specimen looks different from the rest, take it at once and find out the reason why.

In most regions the chief dependence of the collector is on the markets and these should be watched most critically By paying a little more for unusual, neglected, or useless fish, the supply of these will rise to the demand The word passed along among the people of Onomichi in Japan, that "Ebisu the fish-god was in the village" and would pay more for okose (poison scorpion-fishes) and umiuma (sea-horses) than real fishes were worth soon brought (in 1900) all sorts of okose and umiuma into the market when they were formerly left neglected on the beach Thus with a little ingenuity the markets in any country can be greatly extended.

The collector can, if he thinks best, use all kinds of fishing tackle for himself. In Japan he can use the "dabonawa" long lines, and secure the fishes which were otherwise dredged by the *Challenger* and *Albatross* If dredges or trawls are at his hand he can hire them and use them for scientific purposes He should neglect no kind of bottom, no conditions of fish life which he can reach

Especially important is the fauna of the tide-pools, neglected by almost all collectors As the tide goes down, especially on rocky capes which project into the sea, myriads of little fishes will remain in the rock-pools, the algæ, and the clefts of rock In regions like California, where the rocks are buried with kelp, blennies will lie in the kelp as quiescent as the branches of the algæ themselves until the flow of water returns

A sharp three-tined fork will help in spearing them   The water in pools can be poisoned on the coast of Mexico with the milky juice of the "hava" tree, a tree which yields strychnine In default of this, pools can be poisoned by chloride of lime, sulphate of copper, or, if small enough, by formalin   Of all poisons the commercial chloride of lime seems to be most effective   By such means the contents of the pool can be secured and the next tide carries away the poison   The water in pools can be bailed out, or, better, emptied by a siphon made of small garden-hose or rubber tubing   On rocky shores, dynamite can be used to advantage if the collector or his assistant dare risk it and if the laws of the country do no prevent

Most effective in rock-pool work is the help of the small boy. In all lands the collector will do well to take him into his pay and confidence   Of the hundred or more new species of rock-pool fishes lately secured by the writer in Japan, fully two-thirds were obtained by the Japanese boys. Equally effective is the "muchacho" on the coasts of Mexico.

Masses of coral, sponges, tunicates, and other porous or hollow organisms often contain small fishes and should be carefully examined   On the coral reefs the breaking up of large masses is often most remunerative

The importance of securing the young of pelagic fishes by tow-nets and otherwise cannot be too strongly emphasized.

How to Preserve Fishes.—Fishes must be permanently preserved in alcohol Dried skins are far from satisfactory, except as a choice of difficulties in the case of large species

Dr Gunther thus describes the process of skinning fishes

"Scaly fishes are skinned thus With a strong pair of scissors an incision is made along the median line of the abdomen from the foremost part of the throat, passing on one side of the base of the ventral and anal fins to the root of the caudal fin, the cut being continued upward to the back of the tail close to the base of the caudal The skin of one side of the fish is then severed with the scalpel from the underlying muscles to the median line of the back, the bones which support the dorsal and caudal are cut through, so that these fins remain attached to the skin The removal of the skin of the opposite side is easy More difficult is the preparation of the head and scapulary region The two halves of the scapular arch which have been severed from each other by the first incision are pressed toward the right and left, and the spine is severed behind the head, so that now only the head and shoulder bones remain attached to the skin These parts have to be cleaned from the inside, all soft parts, the branchial and hyoid apparatus, and all smaller bones being cut away with the scissors or scraped off with the scalpel In many fishes which are provided with a characteristic dental apparatus in the pharynx (Labroids, Cyprinoids), the pharyngeal bones ought to be preserved and tied with a thread to their specimen The skin being now prepared so far, its entire inner surface as well as the inner side of the head are rubbed with arsenical soap, cotton-wool or some other soft material is inserted into any cavities or hollows, and finally a thin layer of the same material is placed between the two flaps of the skin The specimen is then dried under a slight weight to keep it from shrinking

"The scales of some fishes, as for instance of many kinds of herrings, are so delicate and deciduous that the mere handling causes them to rub off easily Such fishes may be covered with thin-paper (tissue paper is the best) which is allowed to dry on them before skinning There is no need for removing the paper before the specimen has reached its destination

"Scaleless fishes, as siluroids and sturgeons, are skinned in the same manner, but the skin can be rolled up over the head; such skins can also be preserved in spirits, in which case the traveler may save to himself the trouble of cleaning the head

"Some sharks are known to attain to a length of thirty feet, and some rays to a width of twenty feet The preservation of such gigantic specimens is much to be recommended, and although the difficulties of preserving fishes increase with their size, the operation is facilitated, because the skins of all sharks and rays can easily be preserved in salt and strong brine Sharks are skinned much in the same way as ordinary fishes In rays an incision is made not only from the snout to the end of the fleshy part of the tail, but also a second across the widest part of the body When the skin is removed from the fish, it is placed into a cask with strong brine mixed with alum, the head occupying the upper part of the cask, this is necessary, because this part is most likely to show signs of decomposition, and therefore most requires supervision When the preserving fluid has become decidedly weaker from the extracted blood and water, it is thrown away and replaced by fresh brine After a week's or fortnight's soaking the skin is taken out of the cask to allow the fluid to drain off, its inner side is covered with a thin layer of salt, and after being rolled up (the head being inside) it is packed in a cask the bottom of which is covered with salt, all the interstices and the top are likewise filled with salt The cask must be perfectly water-tight "

Value of Formalin —In the field it is much better to use formalin (formaldehyde) in preference to alcohol. This is an antiseptic fluid dissolved in water, and it at once arrests decay, leaving the specimen as though preserved in water. If left too long in formalin fishes swell, the bones are softened, and the specimens become brittle or even worthless But for ordinary purposes (except use as skeleton) no harm arises from two or three months' saturation in formalin The commercial formalin can be mixed with about twenty parts of water On the whole it is better to have the solution too weak rather than too strong Too much formalin makes the specimens stiff, swollen, and intractable, besides too soon destroying the color

Formalin has the advantage, in collecting, of cheapness and of ease in transportation, as a single small bottle will make a large amount of the fluid. The specimens also require much less attention. An incision should be made in the (right) side of the abdomen to let in the fluid The specimen can then be placed in formalin When saturated, in the course of the day, it can be wrapped in a cloth, packed in an empty petroleum can, and at once shipped The wide use of petroleum in all parts of the world is a great boon to the naturalist

Before preservation, the fishes should be washed, to remove slime and dirt. They should have an incision to let the fluid into the body cavity and an injection with a syringe is a useful help to saturation, especially with large fishes Even decaying fishes can be saved with formalin

Records of Fishes.—The collector should mark localities most carefully with tin tags and note-book records if possible He should, so far as possible keep records of life colors, and water-color sketches are of great assistance in this matter. In spirits or formalin the life colors soon fade, although the pattern of marking is usually preserved or at least indicated A mixture of formalin and alcohol is favorable to the preservation of markings

In the museum all specimens should be removed at once from formalin to alcohol No substitute for alcohol as a permanent preservative has been found The spirits derived from wine, grain, or sugar is much preferable to the poisonous methyl or wood alcohol

In placing specimens directly into alcohol, care should be taken not to crowd them too much The fish yields water which dilutes the spirit For the same reason, spirits too dilute are ineffective On the other hand, delicate fishes put into very strong alcohol are likely to shrivel, a condition which may prevent an accurate study of their fins or other structures It is usually necessary to change a fish from the first alcohol used as a bath into stronger alcohol in the course of a few days, the time depending on the closeness with which fishes are packed In the tropics, fishes in alcohol often require attention within a few hours In formalin there is much less difficulty with tropical fishes

Fishes intended for skeletons should never be placed in formalin A softening of the bones which prevents future exact studies of the bones is sure to take place   Generally alcohol or other spirits (arrack, brandy, cognac, rum, sake "vino") can be tested with a match   If sufficiently concentrated to be ignited, they can be safely used for preservation of fishes   The best test is that of the hydrometer   Spirits for permanent use should show on the hydrometer 40 to 60 above proof   Decaying specimens show it by color and smell and the collector should be alive to their condition   One rotting fish may endanger many others   With alcohol it is necessary to take especial pains to ensure immediate saturation Deep cuts should be made into the muscles of large fishes as well as into the body cavity   Sometimes a small distilling apparatus is useful to redistil impure or dilute alcohol   The use of formalin avoids this necessity

Small fishes should not be packed with large ones, small bottles are very desirable for their preservation   All spinous or scaly fishes should be so wrapped in cotton muslin as to prevent all friction

Eternal Vigilance —The methods of treating individual groups of fishes and of handling them under different climatic and other conditions are matters to be learned by experience Eternal vigilance is the price of a good collection, as it is said to be of some other good things   Mechanical collecting—picking up the thing got without effort and putting it in alcohol without further thought—rarely serves any useful end in science The best collectors are usually the best naturalists   The collections made by the men who are to study them and who are competent to do so are the ones which most help the progress of ichthyology   The student of a group of fishes misses half the collection teaches if he has made no part of it himself.

CHAPTER XII

THE LEPTOCARDII, OR LANCELETS

THE Lancelet.—The lancelet is a vertebrate reduced to its very lowest terms   The essential organs of vertebrate life are there, but each one in its simplest form unspecialized and with structure and function feebly differentiated.   The skeleton consists of a cartilaginous notochord inclosed in a membranous sheath   There is no skull   No limbs, no conspicuous processes, and no vertebræ are present   The heart is simply a long contractile tube, hence the name *Leptocardii* (from λεπτός, slender, καρδία, heart)   The blood is colorless. There is a hepatic portal circulation   There is no brain, the spinal cord tapering in front as behind   The water for respiration passes through very many gill-slits from the pharynx into the atrium, from which it is excluded through the atripore in front of the vent   A large chamber, called the atrium, extends almost the length of the body along the ventral and lateral regions   It communicates with the pharynx through the gill-slits and with the exterior through a small opening in front of the vent, the atripore.   The atrium is not found in forms above the lancelets

The reproductive organs consist of a series of pairs of segmentally arranged gonads   The excretory organs consist of a series of tubules in the region of the pharynx, connecting the body-cavity with the atrium   The mouth is a lengthwise slit without jaws, and on either side is a row of fringes   From this feature comes the name *Cirrosiomi*, from cirrus, a fringe of hair, and στόμα, mouth   The body is lanceolate in form, sharp at either end.   From this fact arises a third name, *Amphioxus*, from αμφί, both, ὀξύς, sharp   Dorsal and anal fins are developed as folds of the skin supported by very slender rays

There are no other fins   The alimentary canal is straight, and is differentiated into pharynx and intestine, the liver is a blind sac arising from the anterior end of the intestine   A pigment spot in the wall of the spinal cord has been interpreted as an eye   Above the snout is a supposed olfactory pit which some have thought to be connected with the pineal structure   The muscular impressions along the sides are very distinct and it is chiefly by means of the variation in numbers of these that the species can be distinguished   Thus in the common lancelet of Europe, *Branchiostoma lanceolatum*, the muscular bands are $35 + 14 + 12 = 61$ In the common species of the Eastern coasts of America, *Branchiostoma caribæum*, these are $35 + 14 + 9 = 58$, while in the California lancelet, *Branchiostoma californiense*, these are $44 + 16 + 9 = 69$

Habits of Lancelets —Lancelets are slender translucent worm-like creatures, varying from half an inch (*Asymmetron lucayanum*) to four inches (*Branchiostoma californiense*) in length They live buried in sand in shallow waters along the coasts of warm seas.   One species, *Amphioxides pelagicus*, has been taken at the depth of 1000 fathoms, but whether at the bottom or floating near the surface is not known   The species are very tenacious of life and will endure considerable mutilation   Some of them are found on almost every coast in semi-tropical and tropical regions

Species of Lancelets.—The Mediterranean species ranges northward to the south of England   Others are found as far north as Chesapeake Bay, San Diego, and Misaki in Japan, where is found a species called *Branchiostoma belcheri*   The sands at the mouth of San Diego Bay are noted as producing the largest of the species of lancelets, *Branchiostoma californiense*   From the Bahamas comes the smallest, the type of a distinct genus, *Asymmetron lucayanum*, distinguished among other things by a projecting tail   Other supposed genera are *Amphioxides* (*pelagicus*), dredged in the deep sea off Hawaii and supposed to be pelagic, the mouth without cirri, *Epigonichthys* (*cultellus*), from the East Indies, and *Heteropleuron* (*bassanum*), from Bass Straits, Australia   These little animals are of great interest to anatomists as giving the clue to the primitive structure of vertebrates   While possibly these have diverged widely from their actual common ancestry with the fishes, they must approach near to these in many ways   Their simplicity is largely primitive, not, as in the Tunicates, the result of subsequent degradation

The lancelets, less than a dozen species in all, constitute a single family, *Branchiostomidæ*   The principal genus, *Branchiostoma*, is usually called *Amphioxus* by anatomists   But while

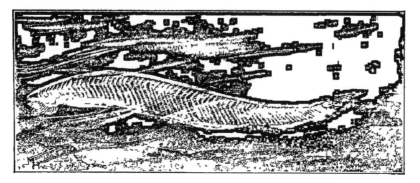

Fig 115 —California Lancelet, *Branchiostoma californiense* Gill
(From San Diego)

the name *Amphioxus*, like lancelet, is convenient in vernacular use, it has no standing in systematic nomenclature   The name *Branchiostoma* was given to lancelets from Naples in 1834, by Costa, while that of *Amphioxus*, given to specimens from Cornwall, dates from Yarrell's work on the British fishes in 1836 The name Amphioxus may be pleasanter or shorter or more familiar or more correctly descriptive than *Branchiostoma*, but if so the fact cannot be considered in science as affecting the duty of priority

The name *Acraniata* (without skull) is often used for the lower Chordates taken collectively, and it is sometimes applied to the lancelets alone   It refers to those chordate forms which have no skull nor brain, as distinguished from the *Craniota*, or forms with a distinct brain having a bony or cartilaginous capsule for its protection

Origin of Lancelets.—It is doubtless true, as Dr. Willey suggests, that the Vertebrates became separated from their worm-like ancestry through "the concentration of the central nervous system along the dorsal side of the body and its conversion into a hollow tube " Besides this trait two others are common to all of them, the presence of the gill-slits and that of the noto-chord The gill-slits may have served primarily to relieve the stomach of water, as in the lowest forms they enter directly into the body-cavity The primitive function of the notochord is still far from clear, but its ultimate use of its structures in affording protection and in furnishing a fulcrum for the muscles and limbs is of the greatest importance in the processes of life.

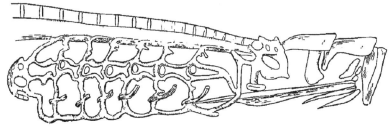

FIG 116 —Gill-basket of Lamprey.

CHAPTER XIII

THE CYCLOSTOMES, OR LAMPREYS

THE **Lampreys.**—Passing upward from the lancelets and setting aside the descending series of Tunicates, we have a long step indeed to the next class of fish-like vertebrates. During the period this great gap represents in time we have the development of brain, skull, heart, and other differentiated organs replacing the simple structures found in the lancelet

The presence of brain without limbs and without coat-of-mail distinguishes the class of *Cyclostomes*, or lampreys (κυκλός, round, στόμα, mouth) This group is also known as *Marsipobranchi* (μαρσίπιον, pouch, βράγχος, gill), *Dermopteri* (δερμα, skin, πτερόν, fin), and *Myzontes* (μυζάω, to suck) It includes the forms known as lampreys, slime-eels, and hagfishes

Structure of the Lamprey.—Comparing a Cyclostome with a lancelet we may see many evidences of specialization in structure The Cyclostome has a distinct head with a cranium formed of a continuous body of cartilage modified to contain a fish-like brain, a cartilaginous skeleton of which the cranium is evidently a differentiated part The vertebræ are undeveloped, the notochord being surrounded by its membranes, without bony or cartilaginous segments The gills have the form of fixed sacs, six to fourteen in number, on each side, arranged in a cartilaginous structure known as "branchial basket" (fig 116), the elements (f which are not clearly homologous with the gill-arches of the true fishes Fish-like eyes are developed on the sides of the head. There is a median nostril associated with a pituitary pouch, which pierces the skull floor An ear-capsule is developed. The brain s composed of paired ganglia in general appearance resembling the brain of the true fish, but the detailed homology of its different parts offers considerable uncertainty   The heart is modified to form two pulsating cavities, auricle and ventricle   The folds of the dorsal and anal fins are distinct, supported by slender rays

The mouth is a roundish disk, with rasping teeth over its surface and with sharper and stronger teeth on the tongue. The intestine is straight and simple   The kidney is represented by a highly primitive pronephros and no trace exists of an air-bladder or lung   The skin is smooth and naked, sometimes secreting an excessive quantity of slime

From the true fishes the Cyclostomes differ in the total absence cf limbs and of shoulder and pelvic girdles, as well as of jaws   It has been thought by some writers that the limbs were ancestrally present and lost through degeneration, as in the eels   Dr Ayers, following Huxley, finds evidence of the ancestral existence of a lower jaw   The majority of observers, however, regard the absence of limbs and jaws in Cyclostomes as a primitive character, although numerous other features of the modern hagfish and lamprey may have resulted from degeneration   There is no clear evidence that the class of Cyclostomes, as now known to us, has any great antiquity, and its members may be all degenerate offshoots from types of greater complexity of structure

Supposed Extinct Cyclostomes — No fossil Cyclostomes are known   The strange forms called Conodontes, thought for a time to be teeth of lampreys, are probably teeth of worms, or perhaps appendages of Trilobites   The singular fossil, *Palæospondylus*, once supposed to be a lamprey, it is certain belongs to some higher order

Orders of Cyclostomes.—The known Cyclostomes are naturally divided into two orders, the *Hyperotreta*, or hagfishes, and the *Hyperoartia*, or lampreys   These two orders are very distinct from each other   While the two groups agree in the general form of the body, they differ in almost every detail, and there is much pertinence in Lankester's suggestions that each should stand as a separate class   The ancestral forms of each, as well as the intervening types if such ever existed, are left unrecorded in the rocks

The Hyperotreta, or Hagfishes.—The *Hyperotreta* (ὑπζρόα, palate; τρετός, perforate), or hagfishes, have the nostril highly developed, a tube-like cylinder with cartilaginous rings penetrating the palate. In these the eyes are little developed and the species are parasitic on other fishes In *Polistotrema stouti*, the hagfish of the coast of California, is parasitic on large fishes, rockfishes, or flounders. It usually fastens itself at the throat or isthmus of its host and sometimes at the eyes Thence it works very rapidly to the inside of the body It there devours all the muscular part of the fish without breaking the skin or the peritoneum, leaving the fish a living hulk of head, skin, and bones It is especially destructive to fishes taken in gill-nets The voracity of the Chilean species *Polistotrema dombeyi* is equally remarkable Dr Federico T Delfin finds that in seven hours a hagfish of this species will devour eighteen times its own weight of fish-flesh The intestinal canal is a simple tube, through which most of the food passes undigested. The eggs are large, each in a yellowish horny case, at one end of which are barbed threads by which they cling together and to kelp or other objects In the California hagfish, *Polistotrema stouti*, great numbers of these eggs have been found in the stomachs of the males

Similar habits are possessed by all the species in the two families, *Myxinidæ* and *Eptatretidæ*. In the *Myxinidæ* the

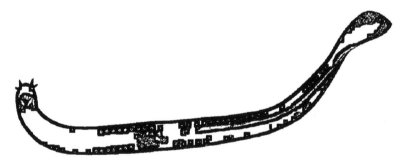

Fig 117 —California Hagfish, *Polistotrema stouti* Lockington.

gill-openings are apparently single on each side, the six gills being internal and leading by six separate ducts to each of the six branchial sacs The skin is excessively slimy, the extensible tongue is armed with two cone-like series of strong teeth. About the mouth are eight barbels

Of *Myxine*, numerous species are known—*Myxine glutinosa*, in the north of Europe, *Myxine limosa*, of the West Atlantic; *Myxine australis*, and several others about Cape Horn, and *Myxine garmani* in Japan   All live in deep waters and none have been fully studied   It has been claimed that the hagfish is male when young, many individuals gradually changing to female, but this conclusion lacks verification and is doubtless without foundation

In the *Eptatretidæ* the gill-openings, six to fourteen in number, are externally separate, each with its own branchial sac as in the lampreys

The species of the genus *Eptatretus* (*Bdellostoma*, *Heptatrema*, and *Homea*, all later names for the same group) are found only in the Pacific, in California, Chile, Patagonia, South Africa, and Japan.   In general appearance and habits these agree with the species of *Myxine*   The species with ten to fourteen gill-openings (*dombeyi stouti*) are sometimes set off as a distinct genus (*Polistotrema*), but in other regards the species differ little, and frequent individual variations occur   *Eptatretus burgeri* is found in Japan and *Eptatretus forsteri* in Australia

The Hyperoartia, or Lampreys.—In the order *Hyperoartia*, or lampreys, the single nostril is a blind sac which does not penetrate the palate   The seven gill-openings lead each to a separate sac, the skin is not especially covered with mucus, the eyes are well developed in the adult, and the mouth is a round disk armed with rasp-like teeth, the comb-like teeth on the tongue being less developed than in the hagfishes   The intestine in the lampreys has a spiral valve   The eggs are small and are usually laid in brooks away from the sea, and in most cases the adult lamprey dies after spawning   According to Thoreau, "it is thought by fishermen that they never return, but waste away and die, clinging to rocks and stumps of trees for an indefinite period, a tragic feature in the scenery of the river-bottoms worthy to be remembered with Shakespeare's description of the sea-floor " This account is not far from the truth, as recent studies have shown

The lampreys of the northern regions constitute the family of *Petromyzonidæ*   The larger species (*Petromyzon*, *Entosphenus*) live in the sea, ascending rivers to spawn, and often becoming

land-locked and reduced in size by living in rivers only. Such
land-locked marine lampreys (*Petromyzon marinus unico'or*) breed
in Cayuga Lake and other lakes in New York   The marine forms
reach a length of three feet   Smaller lampreys of other genera
six inches to eighteen inches in length remain all their lives in
the rivers, ascending the little brooks in the spring, clinging to
stones and clods of earth till their eggs are deposited   These
are found throughout northern Europe, northern Asia, and
the colder parts of North America, belonging to the genera
Lampetra and *Ichthyomyzon*   Other and more aberrant genera
from Chile and Australia are *Geotria* and *Mordacia*, the latter
forming a distinct family, *Mordacidæ*   In *Geotria*, a large and
peculiar gular pouch is developed at the throat   In *Macroph-
thalmia chilensis* from Chile the eyes are large and conspicuous

Food of Lampreys.—The lampreys feed on the blood and flesh
of fishes   They attach themselves to the sides of the various
species, rasp off the flesh with their teeth, sucking the blood
till the fish weakens and dies   Preparations made by students
of Professor Jacob Reighard in the University of Michigan show
clearly that the lamprey stomach contains muscular tissue as well
as the blood of fishes   The river species do a great deal of mis-

Fig 118 —Lamprey, *Petromyzon marinus* L   Wood's Hole, Mass.

chief, a fact which has been the subject of a valuable investigation by Professor H A Surface, who has also considered the
methods available for their destruction   The flesh of the lamprey is wholesome, and the larger species, especially the great
sea lamprey of the Atlantic, *Petromyzon marinus*, are valued as
food.   The small species, according to Prof. Gage, never feed on
fishes

Metamorphosis of Lampreys.—All lampreys, so far as known,
pass through a distinct metamorphosis.   The young, known as
the *Ammocœtes* form, are slender, eyeless, and with the mouth

narrow and toothless   From Professor Surface's paper on "The Removal of Lampreys from the Interior Waters of New York" we have the following extracts (slightly condensed)

"In the latter part of the fall the young lampreys, *Petromyzon marinus unicolor*, the variety land-locked in the lakes of Central New York, metamorphose and assume the form of the adult   They are now about six or eight inches long   The externally segmented condition of the body disappears   The

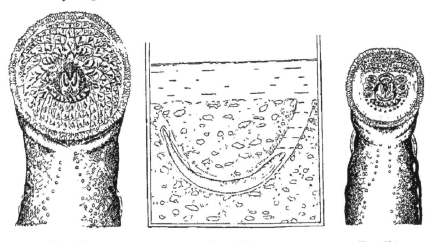

FIG 119   FIG 120   FIG 121

FIG 119 —*Petromyzon marinus unicolor* (De Kay)   Mouth of Lake Lamprey, Cayuga Lake   (After Gage)
FIG 120 —*Lampetra wilderi* Jordan & Evermann   Larval brook lamprey in its burrow in a glass filled with sand   (After Gage)
FIG 121 —*Lampetra wilderi* Jordan & Evermann   Mouth of Brook Lamprey, Cayuga Lake   (After Gage)

eyes appear to grow out through the skin and become plainly visible and functional   The mouth is no longer filled with vertical membranous sheets to act as a sieve, but it contains nearly one hundred and fifty sharp and chitinous teeth, arranged in rows that are more or less concentric and at the same time presenting the appearance of circular radiation   These teeth are very strong, with sharp points, and in structure each has the appearance of a hollow cone of chitin placed over another cone or papilla   A little below the center of the mouth is the oral opening, which is circular and contains a flattened tongue which bears finer teeth of chitin set closely together and arranged in two interrupted (appearing as four) curved rows extending up and down from the ventral toward the dorsal side of the mouth Around the mouth is a circle of soft membrane final'y surrounded by a margin of fimbriæ or small fringe This completes the apparatus with which the lamprey attaches itself to its victims, takes its food, carries stones, builds and tears down its nest, seizes its mate, holds itself in position in a strong current, and climbs over falls

Mischief Done by Lampreys.—" The most common economic feature in the entire life history of these animals is their feeding habits in this (spawning) stage, their food now consisting wholly of the blood (and flesh) of fishes A lamprey is able to strike its suctorial mouth against a fish, and in an instant becomes so firmly attached that it is very rarely indeed that the efforts of the fish will avail to rid itself of its persecutor When a lamprey attaches itself to a person's hand in the aquarium, it can only be freed by lifting it from the water As a rule it will drop the instant it is exposed to the open air, although often it will remain attached for some time even in the open air, or may attach itself to an object while out of water

" Nearly all lampreys that are attached to fish when they are caught in nets will escape through the meshes of the nets, but some are occasionally brought ashore and may hang on to their victim with bulldog pertinacity

" The fishes that are mostly attacked are of the soft-rayed species, having cycloid scales, the spiny-rayed species with ctenoid scales being most nearly immune from their attacks We think there may be three reasons for this 1st, the fishes of the latter group are generally more alert and more active than those of the former, and may be able more readily to dart away from such enemies, 2d, their scales are thicker and stronger and appear to be more firmly imbedded in the skin, consequently it is more difficult for the lampreys to hold on and cut through the heavier coat-of-mail to obtain the blood of the victim, 3d, since the fishes of the second group are wholly carnivorous and in fact almost exclusively fish-eating when adult, in every body of water they are more rare than those of the first group, which are more nearly omnivorous According to the laws and requirements of nature the fishes of the first group must be more abundant, as they become the food for those of the second, and it is on account of their greater abundance that the lampreys' attacks on them are more observed

" There is no doubt that the bullhead, or horned pout (*Ameiurus nebulosus*), is by far the greatest sufferer from lamprey attacks in Cayuga Lake   This may be due in part to the sluggish habits of the fish, which render it an easy victim, but it is more likely due to the fact that this fish has no scales and the lamprey has nothing to do but to pierce the thick skin and find its feast of blood ready for it   There is no doubt of the excellency of the bullhead as a food-fish and of its increasing favor with mankind   It is at present the most important food- and market-fish of the State (New York), being caught by bushels in the early part of June when preparing to spawn   As we have observed at times more than ninety·per cent of the catch attacked by lampreys, it can readily be seen how very serious are the attacks of this terrible parasite which is surely devastating our lakes and streams

Migration or " Running " of Lampreys.—" After thus feeding to an unusual extent, their reproductive elements (gonads) become mature and their alimentary canals commence to atrophy This duct finally becomes so occluded that from formerly being large enough to admit a lead-pencil of average size when forced through it, later not even liquids can pass through, and it becomes nearly a thread closely surrounded by the crowding reproductive organs   When these changes commence to ensue, the lampreys turn their heads against the current and set out on their long journeys to the sites that are favorable for spawning, which here may be from two to eight miles from the lake In this migration they are true to their instincts and habits of laziness in being carried about, as they make use of any available object, such as a fish, boat, etc , that is going in their direction, fastening to it with their suctorial mouths and being borne along at their ease   During this season it is not infrequent that as the Cornell crews come in from practice and lift their shells from the water, they find lampreys clinging to the bottoms of the boats, sometimes as many as fifty at one time They are likely to crowd up all streams flowing into the lake, inspecting the bed of the stream as they go   They do not stop until they reach favorable spawning sites, and if they

Fig. 122.—Oregon Lamprey, *Entosphenus tridentatus*, ascending a brook. (Modified from a photograph by Dr. H. M. Smith. Published by Prof. H. A. Surface.) Willamette River, Oregon.

Fig. 123.—Catfishes, *Ameiurus nebulosus* Le Sueur, destroyed by lampreys (*Petromyzon marinus unicolor* De Kay). Cayuga Lake, N. Y. (Modified from photograph by Prof. H. A. Surface.)

176

find unsurmountable obstacles in their way, such as vertical
falls or dams, they turn around and go down-stream until they
find another, up which they go This is proved every spring
by the number of adult lampreys which are seen temporarily
in Fall Creek and Cascadilla Creek. In each of these streams,
about a mile from its mouth, there is a vertical fall over
thirty feet in height which the lampreys cannot surmount, and
in fact they have never been seen attempting to do so After
clinging with their mouths to the stones at the foot of the
falls for a few days, they work their way down-stream, care-

FIG 124 —Kamchatka Lamprey, *Lampetra camtschatica* (Tilesius) Kamchatka

fully inspecting all the bottom for suitable spawning sites
They do not spawn in these streams because there are too many
rocks and no sand, but finally enter the only stream (the Cayuga
Lake inlet) in which they find suitable and accessible spawning sites

"The three-toothed lampreys (*Entosphenus tridentatus*) of
the West Coast climb low falls or rapids by a series of leaps,
holding with their mouths to rest, then jumping and striking
again and holding, thus leap by leap gaining the entire distance

"The lampreys here have never been known to show any
tendency or ability to climb, probably because there are no
rapids or mere low falls in the streams up which they would
run In fact, as the inlet is the only stream entering Cayuga
Lake in this region which presents suitable spawning conditions and no obstructions, it can be seen at once that all the
lampreys must spawn in this stream and its tributaries

"In 'running' they move almost entirely at night, and if
they do not reach a suitable spawning site by daylight, they
will cling to roots or stones during the day and complete their
journey the next night This has been proven by the positive

observation of individuals Of the specimens that run up early in the season, about four-fifths are males Thus the males do not exactly precede the females, because we have found the latter sex represented in the stream as early in the season as the former, but in the earlier part of the season the number of the males certainly greatly predominates This proportion of males gradually decreases, until in the middle of the spawning season the sexes are about equally represented, and toward the latter part of the season the females continue to come until they in turn show the greater numbers Thus it appears very evident in general that the reproductive instinct impels the most of the males to seek the spawning ground before the most of the females do However, it should be said that neither the males nor the females show all of the entirely sexually mature features when they first run up-stream in the beginning of the season, but later they are perfectly mature and 'ripe' in every regard when they first appear in the stream When they migrate, they stop at the site that seems to suit their fancy, many stopping near the lake, others pushing on four or five miles farther up-stream We have noted, however, that later in the season the lower courses become more crowded, showing that the late comers do not attempt to push up-stream as far as those that came earlier Also it thus follows, from what was just said about late-running females, that in the latter part of the season the lower spawning beds are especially crowded with females In fact, during the early part of the month of June we have found, not more than half a mile above the lowest spawning bed, as many as five females on a spawning nest with but one male, and in that immediate vicinity many nests indeed were found at that time with two or three females and but one male

" Having arrived at a shoal which seems to present suitable conditions for a spawning nest, the individual or pair commences at once to move stones with its mouth from the centre to the margin of an area one or two feet in diameter When many stones are thus placed, especially at the upper edge, and they are cleaned quite free of sediment and algæ, both by being moved and by being fanned with the tail, and when the proper condition of sand is found in the bottom of the basin thus formed, it is ready to be used as a spawning bed or nest A great many nests are commenced and deserted This has been left as a mystery in publications on the subject, but we are well convinced that it is because the lampreys do not find the requisites or proper conditions of bottom to supply all their needs and fulfill all conditions for ideal sites

CHAPTER XIV

THE CLASS ELASMOBRANCHII OR SHARK-LIKE FISHES.—TRUE SHARKS

THE Sharks.—The gap between the lancelets and the lampreys is a very wide one Assuming the primitive nature of both groups, this gap must represent the period necessary for the evolution of brain, skull, and elaborate sense organs The interspace between the lampreys and the nearest fish-like forms which follow them in an ascending scale is not less remarkable Between the lamprey and the shark we have the development of paired fins with their basal attachments of shoulder-girdle and pelvis, the formation of a lower jaw, the relegation of the teeth to the borders of the mouth, the development of separate vertebræ along the line of the notochord, the development of the gill-arches, and of an external covering of enameled points or placoid scales

These traits of progress separate the Elasmobranchs from all lower vertebrates For those animals which possess them, the class name of *Pisces* or fishes has been adopted by numerous authors If this term is to be retained for technical purposes, it should be applied to the aquatic vertebrates above the lampreys and lancelets We may, however, regard fish as a popular term only, rather than to restrict the name to members of a class called *Pisces*. From the bony fishes, on the other hand, the sharks are distinguished by the much less specialization of the skeleton, both as regards form and substance, by the lack of membrane bones, of air-bladder, and of true scales, and by various peculiarities of the skeleton itself The upper jaw, for example, is formed not of maxillary and premaxillary, but of elements which in the lower fishes would be regarded as belonging to the palatine and pterygoid series The lower jaw is formed not of several pieces, but of a cartilage called Meckel's cartilage, which in higher fishes precedes the development of a separate dentary bone These structures are sometimes called primary jaws, as distinguished from secondary jaws or true jaws developed in addition to those bones in the *Actinopteri* or typical fishes In the sharks the shoulder-girdle is attached, not to the skull, but to a vertebra at some distance behind it, leaving a distinct neck, such as is possessed or retained by the vertebrate higher than fishes The shoulder-girdle itself is a continuous arch of cartilage, joining its fellow at the breast of the fish Other peculiar traits will be mentioned later

Characters of Elasmobranchs —The essential character of the Elasmobranchs as a whole are these The skeleton is cartilaginous, the skull without sutures, and the notochord more or less fully replaced or inclosed by vertebral segments The jaws are peculiar in structure, as are also the teeth, which are usually highly specialized and found on the jaws only There are no membrane bones, the shoulder-girdle is well developed, each half of one piece of cartilage, and the ventral fins, with the pelvic-girdle, are always present, always many-rayed, and abdominal in position The skin is covered with placoid scales, or shagreen, or with bony bucklers, or else it is naked It is never provided with imbricated scales The tail is diphycercal, heterocercal, or else it degenerates into a whip-like organ, a form which has been called leptocercal The gill-arches are 5, 6, or 7 in number, with often an accessory gill-slit or spiracle. The ventral fins in the males (except perhaps in certain primitive forms) are provided with elaborate cartilaginous appendages or claspers The brain is elongate, its parts well separated, the optic nerves interlacing The heart has a contractile arterial cone containing several rows of valves, the intestine has a spiral valve, the eggs are large, hatched within the body, or else deposited in a leathery case

Classification of Elasmobranchs.—The group of sharks and their allies, rays, and Chimæras, is usually known collective y as *Elasmobranchii* (ἐλάσμος, blade or plate, βράγχος, gill) Other names applied to all or a part of this group are these *Selachii* (σελαχός, a cartilage, the name also used by the Greeks for the gristle-fishes or sharks), *Plagiostomi* (πλαγιός, oblique, στόμα, mouth), *Chondropterygu* (χόνδρος, cartilage, πτερίζ, fin), and *Antacea* (ἀντακαίος, sturgeon)   They represent the most primitive known type of jaw-bearing vertebrates, or *Gnathostomi* (γνάθος, jaw, στόμα, mouth), the Chordates without jaws being sometimes called collectively *Agnatha* (ἀ-γνάθος, without jaws)   These higher types of fishes have been also called collectively *Lyrifera*, the form of the two shoulder-girdles taken together being compared to that of a lyre   Through shark-like forms all the higher vertebrates must probably trace their descent   Sharks' teeth and fin-spines are found in all rocks from the Upper Silurian deposits to the present time, and while the majority of the genera are now extinct, the class has had a vigorous representation in all the seas, later Palæozoic, Mesozoic, and Cenozoic, as well as in recent times

Most of the Elasmobranchs are large, coarse-fleshed, active animals feeding on fishes, hunting down their prey through superior strength and activity   But to this there are many exceptions, and the highly specialized modern shark of the type of the mackerel-shark or man-eater is by no means a fair type of the whole great class, some of the earliest types being diminutive, feeble, and toothless

Subclasses of Elasmobranchs —With the very earliest recognizable remains it is clear that the Elasmobranchs are already divided into two great divisions, the sharks and the *Chimæras*   These groups we may call subclasses, the *Selachii* and the *Holocephali*, or Chismopnea

The *Selachii*, or sharks and rays, have the skull hyostylic, that is, with the quadrate bone grown fast to the palate which forms the upper jaw, the hyomandibular, acting as suspensorium to the lower jaw, being articulated directly to it

The palato-quadrate apparatus, the front of which forms the upper jaw in the shark, is not fused to the cranium, although it is sometimes articulated with it   There are as many external gill-slits as there are gill-arches (5, 6, or 7), and the gills are adnate to the flesh of their own arches, without free tips   The cerebral hemispheres are grown together   The teeth are separated and usually strongly specialized, being primitively modified from the prickles or other defences of the skin   There is no frontal holder or bony hook on the forehead of the male.

The subclass *Holocephali*, or *Chimæras*, differ from the sharks in all this series of characters, and its separation as a distinct group goes back to the Devonian or even farther, the earliest known sharks having little more in common with Chimæras than the modern forms have

The Selachii.—There have been many efforts to divide the sharks and rays into natural orders   Most writers have contented themselves with placing the sharks in one order (*Squali* or *Galei* or *Pleurotremi*) having the gill-openings on the side, and the rays in another (*Rajæ*, *Batoidei*, *Hypotrema*) having the gill-openings underneath   Of far more importance than this superficial character of adaptation are the distinctions drawn from the skeleton   Dr Gill has used the attachment of the palato-quadrate apparatus as the basis of a classification   The *Opistharthri* (*Hexanchidæ*) have this structure articulated with the postorbital part of the skull   In the *Prosarthri* (*Heterodon'idæ*) it is articulated with the preorbital part of the skull, while in the other sharks (*Anarthri*) it is not articulated at all   But these characters do not appear to be always important   *Chlamydoselachus*, for example, differs in this regard from *Heptranchias*, which in other respects it closely resembles   Yet, .n general, the groups thus characterized are undoubtedly natural ones

The sharks are among the earliest fishes to appear in the rocks, and from primitive sharks all the higher groups of fishes are descended   The earliest known and lowest in

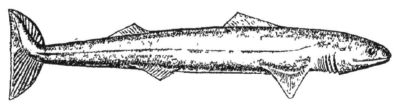

FIG 125 —*Cladoselache fyleri* (Newberry), restored   Middle Devonian of Ohio
(After Dean)

structure constitute the order *Pleuropterygii* (*Cladoselachidæ*), typified by *Cladoselache fyleri* from the middle Devonian of Ohio

Order Notidani.—We may recognize as a distinct order a primitive group of recent sharks, a group of forms finding its natural place somewhere between the *Cladoselachidæ* and *Heterodontidæ*, both of which groups long preceded it in geological time

It has been lately announced that a rudimentary sixth gill-arch exists in *Heterodontus* This would show the close affinity of these two primitive groups, *Notidani* and *Cestraciontes*, and the latter should be removed from the *Asterospondyli*. The presence of five species in the *Squalidæ* perhaps indicates affinity with *Heterodontus* The fact that *Cestraciontes* were the only sharks living in the Triassic, soon followed by *Notidani* and later by squaloid and galeoid sharks, seems to be significant

The name *Notidani* (*Notidanus*, νωτιδάνος, dry back, an old name of one of the genera) may be retained for this group, which corresponds to the *Diplospondyli* of Hasse, the *Opistharthri* of Gill, and the *Protoselachii* of Parker and Haswell The *Notidani* are characterized by the primitive structure of the spinal column, which is without calcareous matter, the centra being imperfectly developed There are six or seven branchial arches, and in the typical forms not in *Chlamydoselachus*) the palato-quadrate or upper jaw articulates with the postorbital

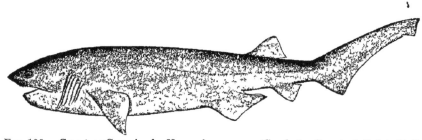

Fig 126 —Griset or Cow-shark, *Hexanchus griseus* (Gmelin) Currituck Inlet, N C

region of the skull The teeth are of primitive character, of different forms in the same jaw, each with many cusps The fins are without spines, the pectoral fin having the three basal cartilages (mesopterygium with propterygium and metapterygium) as usual among sharks

The few living forms are of high interest The extinct species are numerous, but not very different from the living species.

Family Hexanchidæ.—The majority of the living Notidanoid sharks belong to the family of *Hexanchidæ* These sharks have six or seven gill-openings, one dorsal fin, and a relatively simple organization The bodies are moderately elongate, not eel-shaped, and the palato-quadrate articulates with the post-orbital part of the skull The six or eight species are found sparsely in the warm seas. The two genera, *Hexanchus*, with six, and *Heptranchias*, with seven vertebræ, are found in the Mediterranean The European species are *Hexanchus griseus*, the cow-shark, and *Heptranchias cinereus* The former crosses to the West Indies In California, *Heptranchias maculatus*

FIG 127 —Teeth of *Heptranchias indicus* Gmelin

and *Hexanchus cornuus* are occasionally taken, while *Heptranchias deani* is the well known Aburazame or oil shark of Japan *Heptranchias indicus*, a similar species, is found in India

Fossil *Hexanchidæ* exist in large numbers, all of them referred by Woodward to the genus *Notidanus* (which is a later name than *Hexanchus* and *Heptranchias* and intended to include both these genera), differing chiefly in the number of gil-openings, a character not ascertainable in the fossils None of these, however, appear before Cretaceous time, a fact which may indicate that the simplicity of structure in *Hexanchus* and *Heptranchias* is a result of degeneration and not altogether a mark of primitive simplicity The group is apparently much younger than the Cestraciontes and little older than the Lamnoids, or the Squaloid groups   *Heptranchias microdon* is common in English Cretaceous rocks, and *Heptranchias primigenius* and other species are found in the Eocene

Family Chlamydoselachidæ —Very great interest is attached to the recent discovery by Samuel Garman of the frilled shark, *Chlamydosclachus anguineus*, the sole living representative of the *Chlamydoselachidæ*

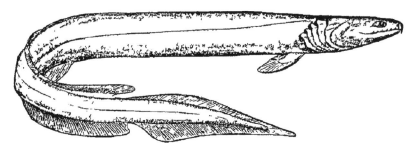

Fig 128 —Frill-shark, *Chlamydoselachus anguineus* Garman   From Misaki, Japan   (After Gunther)

This shark was first found on the coast of Japan, where it is rather common in deep water   It has since been taken off Madeira and off the coast of Norway   It is a long, slender, eel-shaped shark with six gill-openings and the palato-quadrate not articulated to the cranium   The notochord is mainly persistent, in part replaced by feeble cyclospondylic vertebral centra   Each gill-opening is bordered by a broad frill of skin There is but one dorsal fin   The teeth closely resemble those of *Dittodus* or *Didymodus* and other extinct *Ichthyotomi*   The teeth have broad, backwardly extended bases overlapping, the crown consisting of three slender curved cusps, separated by rudimentary denticles   Teeth of a fossil species, *Chlamydosclachus lawleyi*, are recorded by J W Davis from the Pliocene of Tuscany

Order Asterospondyli.—The order of *Asterospondyli* comprises the typical sharks, those in which the individual vertebræ are well developed, the calcareous lamellæ arranged so as to radiate, star-fashion, from the central axis   All these sharks possess two dorsal fins and one anal fin, the pectoral fin is normally developed, with the three basal cartilages, there are five gill-openings, and the tail is heterocercal

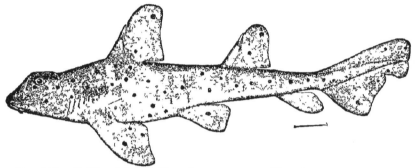

Fig 129 —Bullhead-shark, *Heterodontus francisci* (Girard)   San Pedro, Cal

Suborder Cestraciontes.—The most ancient types may be set off as a distinct suborder under the name of *Cestraciontes* or *Prosarthii*.

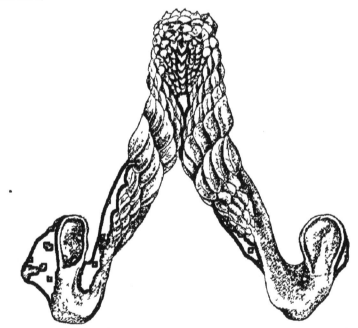

Fig 130 —Lower jaw of *Heterodontus philippi*   From Australia   Family *Heterodontidæ*   (After Zittel)

These forms find their nearest allies in the *Notidani*, which they resemble to some extent in dentition and in having the palato-quadrate articulated to the skull although fastened farther forward than in the *Notidani*   Each of the two dorsal fins has a strong spine

Family Heterodontidæ. — Among recent species this group contains only the family of *Heterodontidæ*, the bullhead sharks, or Port Jackson sharks   In this family the head is high, with usually projecting eyebrows, the lateral teeth are pad-like, ridged or rounded, arranged in many rows, different from the

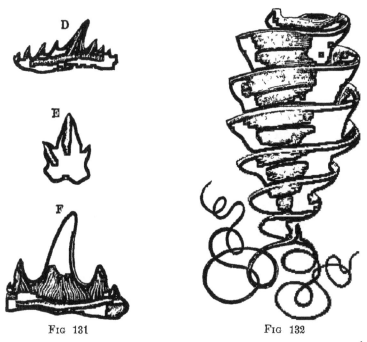

FIG 131   FIG 132

FIG 131 —Teeth of Cestraciont Sharks   (After Woodward)   *d, Synechodus dubrisianus* Mackie,   *e, Heterodontus canaliculatus* Egerton,   *f, Hybodus striatulus* Agassiz   (After Woodward)

FIG 132 —Egg of Port Jackson Shark, *Heterodontus philippi* (Lacépède)   (After Parker & Haswell)

pointed anterior teeth, the fins are large, the coloration is strongly marked, and the large egg-cases are spirally twisted   All have five gill-openings   The living species of *Heterodontidæ* are found only in the Pacific, the Port Jackson shark of Australia, *Heterodontus philippi*, being longest known   Other species are *Heterodontus francisci*, common in California, *Heterodontus japonicus*, in Japan, and *Heterodontus zebra*, in China   These small and harmless sharks at once attract attention by their peculiar forms   In the American species the jaws are less

contracted than in the Asiastic species, called *Heterodontus.*
For this reason Dr Gill has separated the former under the
name of *Gyropleurodus* The differences are, however, of slight
value The genus *Heterodontus* first appears in the Jurassic,
where a number of species are known, one of the earliest
being *Heterodontus falcifer.*

The discussion of the long array of fossil *Heterodontidæ* and
allied families may be here omitted It is an interesting fact
that the only sharks known to exist in the Triassic period
belong to this family from which all recent sharks are descended

Very lately the discovery has been made that in sharks of
this group a rudiment of a sixth gill-segment exists This
demonstrates a close relation to the *Notidani*

Suborder Galei.—The great body of recent sharks belong to
the suborder *Galei*, or *Eusclachii*, characterized by the asterospondylous vertebræ, each having a star-shaped nucleus, and
by the fact that the palato-quadrate apparatus or upper jaw
is not articulated with the skull The sharks of this suborder
are the most highly specialized of the group, the strongest and
largest and, in general, the most active and voracious They
are of three types and naturally group themselves about the
three central families *Scylliorhinidæ, Lamnidæ,* and *Carchariidæ*
(*Galeorhinidæ*)

The *Asterospondyli* are less ancient than the preceding groups,
but the modern families were well differentiated in Mesozoic
times

Among the *Galei* the dentition is less complex than with
the ancient forms, although the individual teeth are more
highly specialized The teeth are usually adapted for biting,
often with knife-like or serrated edges, only the outer teeth
are in function, as they are gradually lost, the inner teeth are
moved outward, gradually taking the place of these

We may place first, as most primitive, the forms without
nictitating membrane

Family Scylliorhinidæ. — The most primitive of the modern
families is doubtless that of the *Scylliorhinidæ*, or cat-sharks
This group includes sharks with the dorsal fins both behind
the ventrals, the tail not keeled and not bent upward, the
spiracles present, and the teeth small and close-set The species

are small and mostly spotted, found in the warm seas   All
of them lay their eggs in large cases, oblong, and with long
filaments or strings at the corners   The cat-sharks, or rous-
settes, *Scylliorhinus canicula* and *Catulus stellaris*, abound in
the Mediterranean   Their skin is used as shagreen or sand-
paper in polishing furniture   The species of swell-sharks
(*Cephaloscylium*) (*C uter*, in California, *C ventriosus*, in Chile,
C laticeps, in Australia, *C umbratile*, in Japan) are short,
wide-bodied sharks, which have the habit of filling the capacious
stomach with air, then floating belly upward like a globe-fish
Other species are found in the depths of the sea   *Scylliorhinus*, *Catulus*, and numerous other genera are found fossil
The earliest is *Palæoscyllium*, in the Jurassic, not very different from *Scylliorhinus*, but the fins are described as more
nearly like those of *Ginglymostoma*

Close to the *Scylliorhinidæ* is the Asiatic family, *Hemi-
scyllidæ*, which differs in being ovoviviparous, the young,
according to Mr Edgar R Waite, hatched within the body
The general appearance is that of the *Scylliorhinidæ*, the body
being elongate   *Chiloscyllium* is a well-known genus with several species in the East Indies   *Chiloscyllium modestum* is the
dogfish of the Australian fishermen   The *Orectolobidæ* are thick-
set sharks, with large heads provided with fleshy fringes   *Orectolobus barbatus* (*Crossorhinus* of authors) abounds from Japan
to Australia

Another family, *Ginglymostomidæ*, differs mainly in the
form of the tail, which is long and bent abruptly upward at
its base   These large sharks, known as nurse-sharks, are found
in the warm seas   *Ginglymostoma cirrhatum* is the common
species with *Orectolobus Stegostoma tigrinum*, of the Indian
seas and north to Japan, one of several genera called tiger-
sharks, is remarkable for its handsome spotted coloration
The extinct genus *Pseudogaleus* (*voltai*) is said to connect the
Scylliorhinidæ with the *Carcharioid* sharks

The Lamnoid or Mackerel Sharks.—The most active and most
ferocious of the sharks, as well as the largest and some of the
most sluggish, belong to a group of families known collectively
as Lamnoid, because of a general resemblance to the mackerel-

shark, or *Lamna*, as distinguished from the blue sharks and white sharks allied to *Carcharias* (*Carcharhinus*)

The Lamnoid sharks agree with the cat-sharks in the absence of nictitating membrane or third eyelid, but differ in the anterior insertion of the first dorsal fin, which is before the ventrals   Some of these sharks have the most highly specialized teeth to be found among fishes, most effective as knives or as scissors   Still others have the most highly specialized tails, either long and flail-like, or short, broad, and muscular, fitting the animal for swifter progression than is possible for any other sharks   The Lamnoid families are especially numerous as fossils, their teeth abounding in all suitable rock deposits from Mesozoic times till now   Among the Lamnoid sharks numerous families must be recognized

The most primitive is perhaps that of the *Odontaspididæ* (called *Carchariida* by some recent authors), now chiefly extinct, with the tail unequal and not keeled, and the teeth slender and sharp, often with smaller cusps at their base   *Odontaspis* and its relatives of the same genus are numerous, from the Cretaceous onward, and three species are still extant, small sharks of a voracious habit, living on sandy shores   *Odontaspis littoralis* (also known as *Carcharias littoralis*) is the common sand-shark of our Atlantic coast   *Odontaspis taurus* is a similar form in the Mediterranean

Family Mitsukurinidæ, the Goblin-sharks — Closely allied to *Odontaspis* is the small family of *Mitsukurinidæ*, of which a single living species is known   The teeth are like those of *Odontaspis*, but the appearance is very different

The goblin-shark, or Tenguzame, *Mitsukurina owstoni*, is a very large shark rarely taken in the Kuro Shiwo, or warm " Black Current" of Japan   It is characterized by the development of the snout into a long flat blade, extending far beyond the mouth, much as in *Polyodon* and in certain Chimæras   Several specimens are now known, all taken by Capt Alan Owston of Yokohoma in Sagami Bay, Japan   The original specimen, a young shark just born, was presented by him to Professor Kakichi Mitsukuri of the University of Tokyo   From this our figure was taken   The largest specimen now known is in the United States National Museum and is fourteen feet in

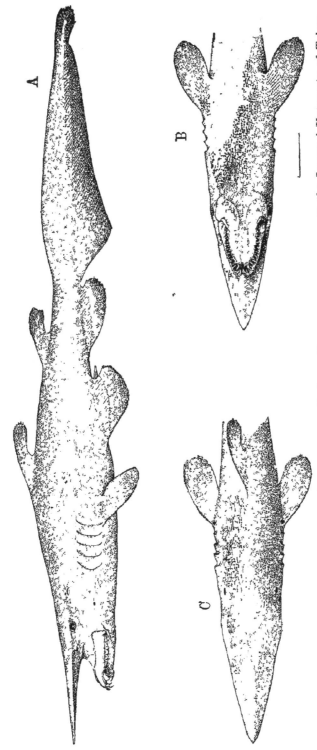

Fig 133—Goblin shark (Tenguzame), *Mitsukurina owstoni* Jordan From a young specimen in the Imperial University of Tokyo

192

length   In the Upper Cretaceous is a very similar genus, *Scapanorhynchus* (*lewisi*, etc), which Professor Woodward thinks may be even generically identical with *Mitsukurina*, though there is considerable difference in the form of the still longer rostral plate, and the species of *Scapanorhynchus* differ among themselves in this regard

Mitsukurina, with *Heterodontus*, *Heptranchias*, and *Chlamydoselache*, is a very remarkable survival of a very ancient form

FIG 134 —*Scapanorhynchus lewisi* Davis   Family *Mitsukurinidæ*   Under side of snout   (After Woodward)

It is an interesting fact that the center of abundance of all these relics of ancient life is in the Black Current, or Gulf Stream, of Japan

Family Alopiidæ, or Thresher Sharks.—The related family of *Alopiidæ* contains probably but one recent species, the great fox-shark, or thresher, found in all warm seas   In this species, *Alopias vulpes*, the tail is as long as the rest of the body and bent upward from the base   The snout is very short, and the teeth are small and close-set   The species reaches a length of about twenty-five feet   It is not especially ferocious, and the current stories of its attacks on whales probably arise from a mistake of the observers, who have taken the great killer, *Orca*, for a shark   The killer is a mammal, allied to the porpoise   It attacks the whale with great ferocity, clinging to its flesh by its strong teeth   The whale rolls over and over, throwing the killer into the air, and sailors report it as a thresher As a matter of fact the thresher very rarely if ever attacks any animal except small fish   It is said to use its tail in rounding up and destroying schools of herring and sardines   Fossil teeth of thresher-sharks of some species are found from the Miocene.

Family Pseudotriakidæ.—The *Pseudotriakidæ* consist of two species   One of these is *Pseudotriakis microdon*, a large shark

with a long low tail, long and low dorsal fin, and small teeth
It has been only twice taken, off Portugal and off Long Island.
The other, the mute shark, *Pseudotriakis acrales*, a large shark
with the body as soft as a rag, is in the museum of Stanford
University, having been taken by Mr Owston off Misaki

Family Lamnidæ.—To the family of *Lamnidæ* proper belong
the swiftest, strongest, and most voracious of all sharks   The
chief distinction lies in the lunate tail, which has a keel on
either side at base, as in the mackerels   This
form is especially favorable for swift swimming, and it has been independently developed in the mackerel-sharks, as in the
mackerels, in the interest of speed in movement.

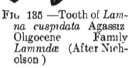

The porbeagle, *Lamna cornubica*, known
as salmon-shark in Alaska, has long been
noted for its murderous voracity   About
Kadiak Island it destroys schools of
salmon, and along the coasts of Japan, and
especially of Europe and across to New

FIG 135 —Tooth of *Lam-
na cuspidata* Agassiz
Oligocene   Family
Lamnidæ (After Nich-
olson)

England, it makes its evil presence felt among the fishermen
Numerous fossil species of *Lamna* occur, known by the long
knife-like flexuous teeth, each having one or two small cusps
at its base.

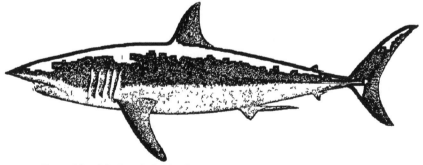

FIG 136 —Mackerel-shark, *Isuropsis dekayi* Gill   Pensacola, Fla

In the closely related genus, *Isurus*, the mackerel-sharks,
this cusp is wanting, while in *Isuropsis* the dorsal fin is set
farther back   In each of these genera the species reach a
length of 20 to 25 feet   Each is strong, swift, and voracious

Isurus oxyrhynchus occurs in the Mediterranean, *Isuropsis dekayi*, in the Gulf of Mexico, and *Isuropsis glauca*, from Hawaii and Japan westward to the Red Sea

Man-eating Sharks —Equally swift and vastly stronger than these mackerel-sharks is the man-eater, or great white shark, *Carcharodon carcharias* This shark, found occasionally in all warm seas, reaches a length of over thirty feet and has been known to devour men   According to Linnæus, it is the animal which swallowed the prophet Jonah " Jonam Prophetum," he observes, "ut veteris Herculem trinoctem, in hujus ventriculo tridui spateo bæsisse, verosimile est "

FIG 137 —Tooth of *Isurus hastalis* (Agassiz) Miocene Family *Lamnidæ* (After Nicholson)

It is beyond comparison the most voracious of fish-like animals   Near Soquel, California, the writer obtained a specimen in 1880, with a young sea-lion (*Zalophus*) in its stomach. It has been taken on the coasts of Europe, New England, Carolina, California, Hawaii, and Japan, its distribution evidently girdling the globe   The genus *Carcharodon* is known at once by its broad, evenly triangular, knife-like teeth, with finely serrated edges, and without notch or cusp of any kind   But one species is now living   Fossil teeth are found from the Eocene   One of these, *Carcharodon megalodon* (Fig 138), from fish-guano deposits in South Carolina and elsewhere, has teeth nearly six inches long The animal could not have been less than ninety feet in length. These huge sharks can be but recently extinct, as their teeth have been dredged from the sea-bottom by the *Challenger* in the mid-Pacific

Fossil teeth of *Lamna* and *Isurus* as well as of *Carcharodon* are found in great abundance in Cretaceous and Tertiary rocks Among the earlier species are forms which connect these genera very closely

The fossil genus *Otodus* must belong to the *Lamnidæ*   Its massive teeth with entire edges and blunt cusps at base are common in Cretaceous and Tertiary deposits   The teeth are formed much as in *Lamna*, but are blunter, heavier, and much less effective as instruments of destruction   The extinct genus *Corax* is also placed here by Woodward

Family Cetorhinidæ, or Basking Sharks.—The largest of all living sharks is the great basking shark (*Cetorhinus maximus*), constituting the family of *Cetorhinidæ*. This is the largest of all fishes, reaching a length of thirty-six feet and an enormous

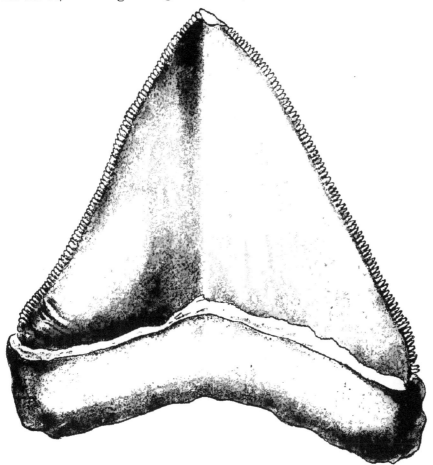

FIG. 138.—*Carcharodon megalodon* Charlesworth.   Miocene.   Family *Lamnidæ*
(After Zittel.)

weight. It is a dull and sluggish animal of the northern seas, almost as inert as a sawlog, often floating slowly southward in pairs in the spring and caught occasionally by whalers for its liver. When caught, its huge flabby head spreads out wide on the ground, its weight in connection with the great size of the mouth-cavity rendering it shapeless. Although so clumsy and without spirit, it is said that a blow with its tail will crush

an ordinary whaleboat   The basking shark is known on all
northern coasts, but has most frequently been taken in the
North Sea, and about Monterey Bay in California   From this
locality specimens have been sent to the chief museums of
Europe.   In its external characters the basking shark has much
in common with the man-eater   Its body is, however, rela-

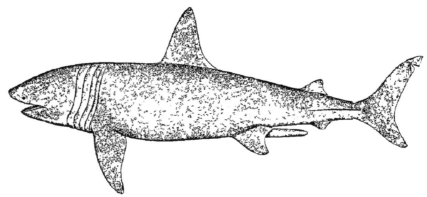

Fig 139 —Basking Shark, *Cetorhinus maximus* (Gunner)   France

tively clumsy forward, its fins are lower, and its gill-openings
are much broader, almost meeting under the throat   The
great difference lies in the teeth, which in *Cetorhinus* are very
small and weak, about 200 in each row   The basking shark,
also called elephant-shark and bone-shark, does not pursue its
prey, but feeds on small creatures to be taken without effort
Fossil teeth of *Cetorhinus* have been found from the Cretaceous, as also fossil gill-rakers, structures which in this shark
are so long as to suggest whalebone

Family Rhineodontidæ. — The whale-sharks, *Rhineodontidæ*,
are likewise sluggish monsters with feeble teeth and keeled
tails   From *Cetorhinus* they differ mainly in having the last
gill-opening above the pectorals   There is probably but one
species, *Rhineodon typicus*, of the tropical Pacific, straying northward to Florida, Lower California, and Japan

The Carcharioid Sharks, or Requins.—The largest family of recent sharks is that of *Carchariidæ* (often called *Galeorhinidæ*,
or *Galeidæ*), a modern offshoot from the Lamnoid type, and
especially characterized by the presence of a third eyelid, the
nictitating membrane, which can be drawn across the eye from

below   The heterocercal tail has no keel, the end is bent upward, both dorsal fins are present, and the first is well in front of the ventral fins, the last gill-opening over the base of the pectoral, the head normally formed, these sharks are ovoviviparous, the young being hatched in a sort of uterus, with or without placental attachment

Some of these sharks are small, blunt-toothed, and innocuous. Others reach a very large size and are surpassed in voracity only by the various *Lamnidæ*

The genera *Cynias* and *Mustelus*, comprising the soft-mouthed or hound-sharks, have the teeth flat and paved, while well-developed spiracles are present   These small, harmless sharks abound on almost all coasts in warm regions, and are largely used as food by those who do not object to the harsh odor of

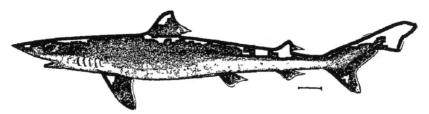

Fig 140.—Soup-fin Shark, *Galeus zyopterus* (Jordan & Gilbert)   Monterey.

shark's flesh   The best-known species is *Cynias canis* of the Atlantic   By a regular gradation of intermediate forms, through such genera as *Rhinotriacis* and *Triakis* with tricuspid teeth, we reach the large sharp-toothed members of this family   *Galeus* (or *Galeorhinus*) includes large sharks having spiracles, no pit at the root of the tail, and with large, coarsely serrated teeth   One species, the soup-fin shark (*Galeus zyopterus*), is found on the coast of California, where its fins are highly valued by the Chinese, selling at from one to two dollars for each set   The delicate fin-rays are the part used, these dissolving into a finely flavored gelatine   The liver of this and other species is used in making a coarse oil, like that taken from the dogfish   Other species of *Galeus* are found in other regions, *Galeus galeus* being known in England as tope, *Galeus japonicus* abounding in Japan

Galeocerdo differs mainly in having a pit at the root of the tail   Its species, large, voracious, and tiger-spotted, are found in warm seas and known as tiger-sharks (*Galeocerdo maculatus* in the Atlantic, *Galeocerdo tigrinus* in the Pacific)

The species of *Carcharias* (*Carcharhinus* of Blainville) lack the spiracles These species are very numerous, voracious, armed with sharp teeth, broad or narrow, and finely serrated on both edges Some of these sharks reach a length of thirty feet. They are very destructive to other fishes, and often to fishery apparatus as well They are sometimes sought as food, more often for the oil in their livers, but, as a rule, they are rarely caught except as a measure for getting rid of them Of the many species the best known is the broad-headed *Carcharias lamia*, or cub-shark, of the Atlantic This the writer has taken with a great hook and chain from the wharves at Key West These great sharks swim about harbors in the tropics, acting as

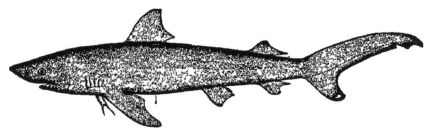

FIG 141.—Cub-shark, *Carcharias lamia* Rafinesque Florida.

scavengers and occasionally seizing arm or leg of those who venture within their reach One species (*Carcharias nicaraguensis*) is found in Lake Nicaragua, the only fresh-water shark known, although some run up the brackish mouth of the Ganges and into Lake Pontchartrain *Carcharias japonicus* abounds in Japan

A closely related genus is *Prionace*, its species *Prionace glauca*, the great blue shark, being slender and swift, with the dorsal farther back than in *Carcharias* Of the remaining genera the most important is *Scoliodon*, small sharks with oblique teeth which have no serrature One of these, *Scoliodon terræ-novæ*, is the common sharp-nosed shark of our Carolina coast Fossil teeth representing nearly all of these genera are common in Tertiary rocks

Probably allied to the *Carchariidæ* is the genus *Corax*, containing large extinct sharks of the Cretaceous with broad-triangular scrrate teeth, very massive in substance, and without denticles   As only the teeth are known, the actual relations of the several species of *Corax* are not certainly known, and they may belong to the *Lamnidæ*

Family Sphyrnidæ, or Hammer-head Sharks.—The *Sphyrnidæ*, or hammer-headed sharks, are exactly like the *Carcharidæ* except that the sides of the head are produced, so as to give it the shape of a hammer or of a kidney, the eye being on the produced outer edge

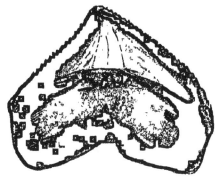

Fig 142 —Teeth of *Corax pristodontus*

The species are few, but mostly widely distributed, rather large, voracious sharks with small sharp teeth

The true hammer-head, *Sphyrna zygæna*, Fig 143, is common from the Mediterranean to Cape Cod, California, Hawaii, and Japan   The singular form of its head is one of the most extraordinary modifications shown among fishes   The bonnet-head (*Sphyrna tiburo*) has the head kidney-shaped or crescent-shaped It is a smaller fish, but much the same in distribution and habits Intermediate forms occur, so that with all the actual differences we must place the *Sphyrnidæ* all in one genus   Fossil hammerheads occur in the Miocene, but their teeth are scarcely different from those of *Carcharias   Sphyrna prisca*, described by Agassiz, is the primeval species

The Order of Tectospondyli.—The sharks and rays having no anal fin and with the calcareous lamellæ arranged in one or more rings around a central axis constitute a natural group to which, following Woodward, we may apply the name of *Tectospondyli*   The *Cyclospondyli* (*Squalidæ*, etc) with one ring only of calcareous lamellæ may be included in this order, as also the rays, which have tectospondylous vertebræ and differ from the sharks as a group only in having the gill-openings relegated to the lower side by the expansion of the pectoral fins   The group of rays and Hasse's order of *Cyclospondyli* we may consider each as a suborder of *Tectospondyli*   The origin

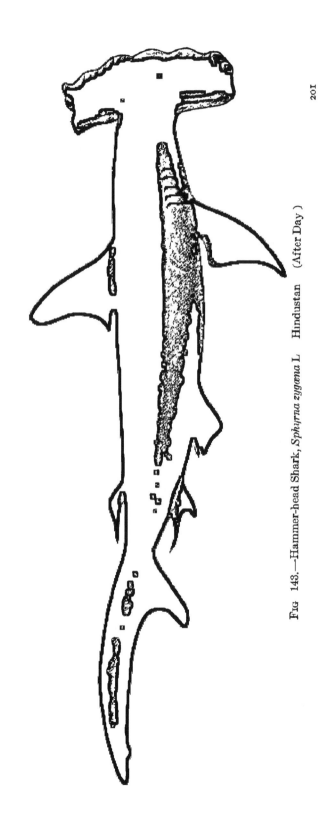

Fig 143.—Hammer-head Shark, *Sphyrna zygaena* L   Hindustan   (After Day)

of this group is probably to be found in or near the *Cestraciontes*, as the strong dorsal spines of the *Squalidæ* resemble those of the *Heterodontidæ*.

Suborder Cyclospondyli.—In this group the vertebræ have the calcareous lamellæ arranged in a single ring about the central axis   The anal fin, as in all the tectospondylous sharks and rays, is wanting   In all the asterospondylous sharks, as in the *Ichthyotomi, Acanthodei*, and *Chimæras*, this fin is present   It is present in almost all of the bony fishes   All the species have spiracles, and in all are two dorsal fins   None have the nictitating membrane, and in all the eggs are hatched internally   Within the group there is considerable variety of form and structure   As above stated, we have a perfect gradation among *Tectospondyli* from true sharks, with the gill-openings lateral, to rays, which have the gill-opening on the ventral side, the great expansion of the pectoral fins, a character of relatively recent acquisition, having crowded the gill-openings from their usual position

Family Squalidæ—The largest and most primitive family of *Cyclospondyli* is that of the *Squalidæ*, collectively known as dogfishes or skittle-dogs   In the *Squalidæ* each dorsal fin has a stout spine in front, the caudal is bent upward and not keeled, and the teeth are small and varied in form, usually not all alike in the same jaw

The genus *Squalus* includes the dogfishes, small, greedy sharks abundant in almost all cool seas and in some tropical

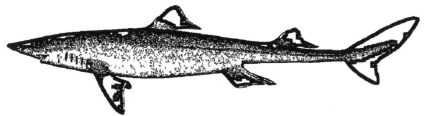

Fig. 144 —Dogfish, *Squalus acanthias* L   Gloucester, Mass

waters   They are known by the stout spines in the dorsal fins and by their sharp, squarish cutting teeth   They are largely sought by fishermen for the oil in their livers, which is used to adulterate better oils   Sometimes 20,000 have been taken in one

haul of the net   They are very destructive to herrings and other
food-fishes   Usually the fishermen cut out the liver, throwing
the shark overboard to die or to be cast on the beach   In
northern Europe and New England *Squalus acanthias* is abundant   *Squalus sucklii* replaces it in the waters about Puget
Sound, and *Squalus mitsukurii* in Japan and Hawaii   Still
others are found in Chile and Australia.   The species of *Squalus*
live near shore and have the gray color usual among sharks
Allied forms perhaps hardly different from *Squalus* are found in
the Cretaceous rocks and have been described as *Centrophoroides*
Other genera related to *Squalus* live in greater depths, from 100
to 600 fathoms, and these are violet-black   Some of the deep-
water forms are the smallest of all sharks, scarcely exceeding a

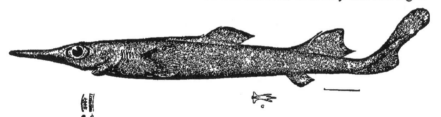

Fig. 145 —*Etmopterus lucifer* Jordan & Snyder   Misaki, Japan

foot in length.   *Etmopterus spinax* lives in the Mediterranean,
and teeth of a similar species occur in the Italian Pliocene
rocks   *Etmopterus lucifer,** a deep-water species of Japan, has a
brilliant luminous glandular area along the sides of the belly
Other small species of deeper waters belong to the genera
Centrophorus, Centroscymnus, and *Deania*   In some of these
species the scales are highly specialized, pedunculate, or having
the form of serrated leaves   Some species are Arctic, the others
are most abundant about Misaki in Japan and the Madeira
Islands, two regions especially rich in semibathybial types
Allied to the *Squalidæ* is the small family of *Oxynotidæ* with
short bodies and strong dorsal spine   *Oxynotus centrina* is found
in the Mediterranean, and its teeth occur in the Miocene

   Family Dalatiidæ.—The *Dalatiidæ,* or scymnoid sharks, differ
from the *Squalidæ* almost solely in the absence of dorsal spines
The smaller species belonging to *Dalatias* (*Scymnorhinus,* or
Scymnus), *Dalatias licha,* etc , are very much like the dog-

* Dr Peter Schmidt has made a sketch of this little shark at night from a
living example, using its own light

fishes. They are, however, nowhere very common   The teeth of *Dalatias major* exist in Miocene rocks   In the genus *Somniosus* the species are of very much greater size, *Somniosus microcephalus* attaining the length of about twenty-five feet This species, known as the sleeper-shark or Greenland shark, lives in all cold seas and is an especial enemy of the whale, from which it bites large masses of flesh with a ferocity hardly to be expected from its clumsy appearance   From its habit of feeding on fish-offal, it is known in New England as "gurry-shark"   Its small quadrate teeth are very much like those of the dogfish, their tips so turned aside as to form a cutting edge   The species is stout in form and sluggish in movement.   It is taken for its liver in the north Atlantic on both coasts in Puget Sound and Bering Sea, and I have seen it in the markets of Tokyo   In Alaska it abounds about the salmon canneries feeding on the refuse

Family Echinorhinidæ—The bramble-sharks, *Echinorhinidæ*, differ in the posterior insertion of the very small dorsal fins, and in the presence of scattered round tubercles, like the thorns of a bramble instead of shagreen   The single species, *Echinorhinus spinosus* reaches a large size   It is rather scarce on the coasts of Europe, and was once taken on Cape Cod   The teeth of an extinct species, *Echinorhinus richardi*, are found in the Pliocene

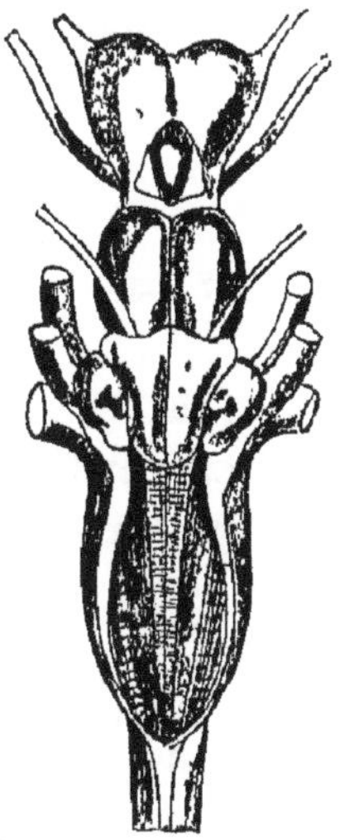

Suborder Rhinæ.—The suborder *Rhinæ* includes those sharks having the vertebræ tectospondylous, that is, with two or more series of calcified lamellæ, as on the rays   They are transitional forms, as near the rays as the sharks, although having the gill-openings rather lateral than inferior, the great pectoral fins being separated by a notch from the head

The principal family is that of the angelfishes, or monkfishes (*Squatinidæ*)   In this group the body is depressed and flat like that of a ray   The greatly enlarged pectorals form a sort of shoulder in front alongside of the

Fig 146 —Brain of Monkfish, *Squatina squatina* L (After Duméril)

gill-openings, which has suggested the bend of the angel's wing

The dorsals are small and far back, the tail is slender with small fins, all these being characters shared by the rays. But one genus is now extant, widely diffused in warm seas. The species if really distinct are all very close to the European *Squatina squatina.* This is a moderate-sized shark of sluggish habit feeding on crabs and shells, which it crushes with its small, pointed, nail-shaped teeth. Numerous fossil species of *Squatina* are found from the Triassic and Cretaceous, *Squatina alifera* being the best known.

Family Pristiophoridæ, or Sawsharks. — Another highly aberrant family is that of the sawsharks, *Pristiophoridæ.* These are small sharks, much like the *Dalatiidæ* in appearance, but with the snout produced into a long flat blade, on either side of which is a

Fig. 147. —Sawshark, *Pristiophorus japonicus* Günther. Specimen from Nagasaki.

row of rather small sharp enameled teeth. These teeth are smaller and sharper than in the sawfish (*Pristis*), and the whole animal is much smaller than its analogue among the rays. This saw must be an effective weapon among the schools of herring and anchovies on which the sawsharks feed. The true teeth are small, sharp, and close-set. The few species of sawsharks are marine, inhabiting the shores of eastern Asia and Australia. *Pristiophorus japonicus* is found rather sparsely along the shores of Japan. The vertebræ in this group are also tectospondylous. Both the *Squatina* and *Pristiophorus* represent a perfect transition from the sharks and rays. We regard them as sharks only because the gill-openings are on the side, not

crowded downward to the under side of the body-disk As
fossil, *Pristiophorus* is known only from a few detached vertebræ found in Germany.

Suborder Batoidei, or Rays.—The suborder of *Batoidei, Rajæ,*
or *Hypotrema,* including the skates and rays, is a direct modern
offshoot from the ancestors of tectospondylous sharks, its characters all specialized in the direction of life on the bottom with
a food of shells, crabs, and other creatures less active than fishes

The single tangible distinctive character of the rays as a
whole lies in the position of the gill-openings, which are directly
below the disk and not on the side of the neck in all the sharks
This difference in position is produced by the anterior encroach-
ment of the large pectoral fins, which are more or less attached to
the side of the head   By this arrangement, which aids in giving
the body the form of a flat disk, the gill-openings are limited
and forced downward   In the *Squatinidæ* (angel-fishes) and
the *Pristiophoridæ* (sawsharks) the gill-openings have an intermediate position, and these families might well be referred to
the *Batoidei,* with which group they agree in the tectospondylous vertebræ

Other characters of the rays, appearing progressively, are
the widening of the disk, through the greater and greater development of the fins, the reduction of the tail, which in the
more specialized forms becomes a long whip, the reduction, more
and more posterior insertion, and the final loss of the dorsal
fins, which are always without spine, the reduction of the teeth
to a tessellated pavement, then finally to flat plates and the
retention of the large spiracle   Through this spiracle the rays
breathe while lying on the bottom, thus avoiding the danger of
introducing sand into their gills, as would be done if they
breathed through the mouth   In common with the cyclospondylous sharks, all the rays lack the anal fin   The rays rarely
descend to great depths in the sea   The different members
have varying relations, but the group most naturally divides
into thick-tailed rays or skates (*Sarcura*) and whip-tailed rays
or sting-rays (*Masticura*)   The former are much nearer to the
sharks and also appear earliest in geological times

Pristididæ, or Sawfishes.—The sawfishes, *Pristididæ,* are long,
shark-like rays of large size, having, like the sawsharks, the

snout prolonged into a very long and strong flat blade, with a series of strong enameled teeth implanted in sockets along either side of it   These teeth are much larger and much less sharp than in the sawsharks, but they are certainly homologous with these, and the two groups must have a common descent, distinct from that of the other rays   Doubtless when taxonomy is a more refined art they will constitute a small suborder together   This character of enameled teeth on the snout would seem of more importance than the position of the gill-openings or even the flattening and expansion of the body   The true teeth in the sawfishes are blunt and close-set, pavement-like as befitting a ray   (See Fig. 54)

The sawfishes are found chiefly in river-mouths of tropical America and West Africa. *Pristis pectinatus* in the West

Fig 148 —Sawfish, *Pristis pectinatus* Latham   Pensacola, Fla.

Indies; *Pristis zephyreus* in western Mexico, and *Pristis pectinatus* in the Senegal.   They reach a length of ten to twenty feet, and with their saws they make great havoc among the schools of mullets and sardines on which they feed   The stories of their attacks on the whale are without foundation   The writer has never found any of the species in the open sea   They live chiefly in the brackish water of estuaries and river-mouths

Fossil teeth of sawfishes occur in abundance in the Eocene   Still older are vertebræ from the Upper Cretaceous at Maestricht   In *Propristis schweinfurthi* the tooth-sockets are not yet calcified   In *Sclerorhynchus atavus*, from the Upper Cretaceous, the teeth are complex in form, with a "crimped" or stellate base and a sharp, backward-directed enameled crown

Rhinobatidæ, or Guitar-fishes. — The *Rhinobatidæ* (guitar-fishes) are long-bodied, shovel-nosed rays, with strong tails, they are ovoviviparous, hatching the eggs within the body   The body, like that of the shark or sawfish, is covered with nearly uniform shagreen   The numerous species abound in all warm seas, they are olive-gray in color and feed on small animals of the sea-bottoms The length of the snout differs considerably in different species, but in all the body is relatively long and strong Most of the species belong to *Rhinobatus* The best-known American species are *Rhinobatus lentiginosus* of Florida and *Rhinobatus productus* of California The names guitar-fish, fiddler-fish, etc, refer to the form of the body Numerous fossil species, allied to the recent forms, occur from the Jurassic Species much like *Rhinobatus* occur in the Cretaceous and Eocene *Tamiobatis vetustus*, lately described by Dr Eastman from a skull found in the Devonian of eastern Kentucky, the oldest ray-like fish yet known, is doubtless the type of a distinct family, *Tamiobatidæ* It is more likely a shark however than a ray, although the skull has a flattened ray-like form

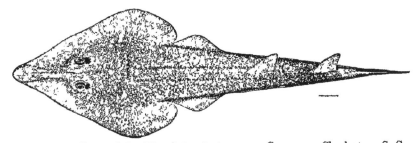

FIG 149 —Guitar-fish, *Rhinobatus lentiginosus* Garman   Charleston, S C

Closely related to the *Rhinobatidæ* are the *Rhinidæ* (*Ramphobatidæ*), a small family of large rays shaped like the guitar-fishes and found on the coast of Asia *Rhina ancylostoma* extends northward to Japan

In the extinct family of *Astrodermidæ*, allied to the *Rhinobatidæ*, the tail has two smooth spines and the skin is covered with tubercles In *Belemnobatis sismondæ* the tubercles are conical, in *Astrodermus platypterus* they are stellate

Rajidæ, or Skates.—The *Rajidæ*, skates, or rays, inhabit the colder waters of the globe and are represented by a large number of living species In this family the tail is stout, with two-rayed dorsal fins and sometimes a caudal fin The skin is variously armed with spines, there being always in the male two series of specialized spinous hooks on the outer edge of the pectoral fin There is no serrated spine or "sting," and in all the species the eggs are laid in leathery cases, which are "wheelbarrow-shaped," with a projecting tube at each of the four angles   The size of this egg-case depends on the size of the species, ranging from three to about eight inches in length   In some species more than one egg is included in the same case

Most of the species belong to the typical genus *Raja*, and these are especially numerous on the coasts of all northern regions, where they are largely used as food   The flesh, although rather coarse and not well flavored, can be improved by hot butter, and as "raie au beurre noir" is appreciated by the epicure   The rays of all have small rounded teeth, set in a close pavement

Some of the species, known on our coasts as "barn-door skates," reach a length of four or five feet   Among these are *Raja lævis* and *Raja ocellata* on our Atlantic coast, *Raja binocu-*

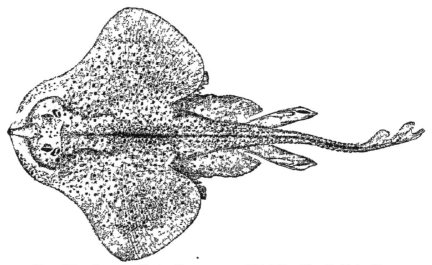

Fig 150 —Common Skate, *Raja erinacea* Mitchill   Wood's Hole, Mass

lata in California, and *Raja tengu* in Japan   The small tobacco-box skate, brown with black spots, abundant on the New England coast, is *Raja erinacea*   The corresponding species in California is *Raja inornata*, and in Japan *Raja kenojei*   Numerous other species, *Raja batis, clavata, circularis, fullonica,* etc , occur on the coasts of Europe   Some species are variegated in color, with eye-like spots or jet-black marblings   Still, others, living in deep waters, are jet-black with the body very soft and limp   For these Garman has proposed the generic name *Mala-corhinus*, a name which may come into general use when the species are better known   In the deep seas rays are found even under the equator   In the south-temperate zone the species are mostly generically distinct, *Psammobatis* being a typical form, differing from *Raja*   *Discobatus sinensis*, common in China and Japan, is a shagreen-covered form, looking like a *Rhinobatus*   It is, however, a true ray, laying its eggs in egg-cases, and with the pectorals extending on the snout. Fossil *Rajdæ*, known by the teeth and bony tubercles, are found from the Cretaceous onward   They belong to *Raja* and to the extinct genera *Dynatobatis*, *Oncobatis*, and *Acanthobatis* The genus *Arthropterus* (*rileyi*), from the Lias, known from a large pectoral fin, with distinct cylindrical-jointed rays, may have been one of the *Rajdæ*, or perhaps the type of a distinct family, *Arthropteridæ*.

Narcobatidæ, or Torpedoes —The torpedoes, or electric rays (*Narcobatidæ*), are characterized by the soft, perfectly smooth

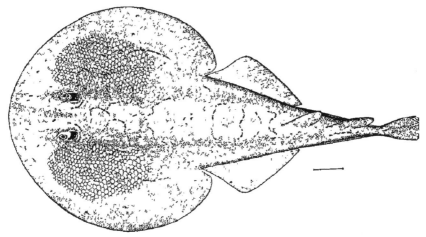

Fig 151.—Numbfish, *Narcine brasiliensis* Henle, showing electric cells
Pensacola, Fla

skin, by the stout tail with rayed fins, and by the ovoviviparous habit, the eggs being hatched internally   In all the species is developed an elaborate electric organ, muscular in its origin and composed of many hexagonal cells, each filled with soft fluid   These cells are arranged under the skin about the back of the head and at the base of the pectoral fin, and are capable of benumbing an enemy by means of a severe electric shock. The exercise of this power soon exhausts the animal, and a certain amount of rest is essential to recovery

The torpedoes, also known as crampfishes or numbfishes, are peculiarly soft to the touch and rather limp, the substance consisting largely of watery or fatty tissues They are found in all warm seas They are not often abundant, and as food they have not much value

Perhaps the largest species is *Tetronarce occidentalis*, the crampfish of our Atlantic coast, black in color, and said sometimes to weigh 200 pounds In California *Tetronarce californica* reaches a length of three feet and is very rarely taken, in warm sandy bays *Tetronarce nobiliana* in Europe is much like these two American species In the European species, *Narcobatus torpedo*, the spiracles are fringed and the animal is of smaller size To *Narcine* belong the smaller numbfish, or "entemedor," of tropical America These have the spiracles close behind the eyes, not at a distance as in *Narcobatus* and *Tetronarce* *Narcine brasiliensis* is found throughout the West Indies, and *Narcine entemedor* in the Gulf of California *Astrape*, a genus with but one dorsal fin, is common in southern Japan. Fossil *Narcobatus* and *Astrape* occur in the Eocene, one specimen of the former nearly five feet long Vertebræ of *Astrape* occur in Prussia in the amber-beds

Petalodontidæ. — Near the *Squatinidæ*, between the sharks and the rays, Woodward places the large extinct family of

Fig 152 —Teeth of *Janassa lingueformis* Attley Carboniferous Family *Petalodontidæ* (After Nicholson)

Petalodontidæ, with coarsely paved teeth each of which is elongate with a central ridge and one or more strong roots at base The best-known genera are *Janassa* and *Petalodus*, widely distributed in Carboniferous time *Janassa* is a broad flat shark, or, perhaps, a skate, covered with smooth shagreen The large pectoral fins are grown to the head, the rather large ventral fins are separated from them. The tail is small,

and the fins, as in the rays, are without spines   The teeth
bear some resemblance to those of *Myliobatis*   *Janassa* is found
in the coal-measures of Europe
and America, and other genera
extend upward from the Subcarboniferous limestones, disappearing near the end of Carboniferous time   *Petalodus* is
equally common, but known
only from the teeth   Other

Fig 153 —*Polyrhizodus radicans* Agassiz   Family *Petalodontidæ*   Carboniferous of Ireland   (After McCoy)

widely distributed genera are *Ctenoptychius* and *Polyrhizodus*

These forms may be intermediate between the skates and
the sting-rays   In dentition they resemble most the latter

Similar to these is the extinct family of *Pristodontidæ* with
one large tooth in each jaw, the one hollowed out to meet the
other   It is supposed that but two teeth existed in life, but
that is not certain   Nothing is known of the rest of the body
in *Pristodus*, the only genus of the group

Dasyatidæ, or Sting-rays.—In the section *Masticura* the tail
is slender, mostly whip-like, without rayed dorsal or caudal
fins, and it is usually armed with a very long spine with saw-
teeth projecting backward   In the typical forms this is a
very effective weapon, being wielded with great force and making
a jagged wound which in man rarely heals without danger of
blood-poisoning   There is no specific poison, but the slime
and the loose cuticle of the spine serve to aggravate the irregular cut   I have seen one sting-ray thrust this spine through
the body of another lying near it in a boat   Occasionally two
or three of these spines are present   In the more specialized
forms of sting-rays this spine loses its importance   It becomes very small and not functional, and is then occasionally
or even generally absent in individuals

The common sting-rays, those in which the caudal spine
is most developed, belong to the family of *Dasyatidæ*   This
group is characterized by the small skate-like teeth and by
the non-extension of the pectoral rays on the head   The skin is
smooth or more or less rough   These animals lie flat on the sandy
bottoms in nearly all seas, feeding on crabs and shellfish   All
hatch the eggs within the body   The genus *Urolophus* has a

rounded disk, and a stout, short tail with a caudal fin It has a strong spine, and for its size is the most dangerous of the sting-rays *Urolophus halleri*, the California species, was named for a young man who was stung by the species at the time of its first discovery at San Diego in 1863 *Urolophus jamaicensis* abounds in the West Indies, *Urolophus mundus* at Panama, and *Urolophus fuscus* in Japan None of the species reach Europe The true sting-ray (stingaree, or clam-cracker), *Dasyatis*, is more widely diffused and the species are very closely related In these species the body is angular and the tail whip-like Some

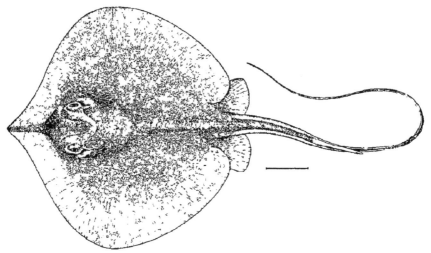

Fig 154 —Sting-ray, *Dasyatis sabina* Le Sueur Galveston

of the species reach a length of ten or twelve feet None have any economic value, and all are disliked by fishermen *Dasyatis pastinaca* is common in Europe, *Dasyatis centrura* along our Atlantic coast, *Dasyatis sabina* ascends the rivers of Florida, and *Dasyatis dipterura* abounds in the bay of San Diego Other species are found in tropical America, while still others (*Dasyatis akajei*, *kuhlii*, *zugei*, etc) swarm in Japan and across India to Zanzibar

Pteroplatea, the butterfly-ray, has the disk very much broader than long, and the trivial tail is very short, its little spine more often lost than present Different species of this genus circle the globe *Pteroplatea maclura*, on our Atlantic coast, *Pteroplatea marmorata*, in California, *Pteroplatea japonica*, in Japan, and *Pteroplatea altavela*, in Europe   They are all very much alike, olive, with the brown upper surface pleasingly mottled and spotted

Sting-rays of various types, *Tæniura, Urolophus*, etc., occur as fossils from the Eocene onward   A complete skeleton called *Xiphotrygon acutidens*, distinguished from *Dasyatis* by its sharp teeth, is described by Cope from the Eocene of Twin Creek in Wyoming   Vertebræ of *Urolophus* are found in German Eocene *Cyclobatis* (*oligodactylus*), allied to *Urolophus*, with a few long pectoral rays greatly produced, extending over the tail and forming a rayed wreath-like projection over the snout, is known from the Lower Cretaceous

Myliobatidæ — The eagle-rays, *Myliobatidæ*, have the pectoral fins extended to the snout, where they form a sort of rayed pad   The teeth are very large, flat, and laid in mosaic   The whip-like tail is much like that in the *Dasyatidæ*, but the spine is usually smaller   The eagle-like appearance is suggested by the form of the skull   The eyes are on the side of the head with heavy eyebrows above them   The species are destructive to clams and oysters, crushing them with their strong flat teeth.

In *Aëtobatus* the teeth are very large, forming but one row   The species *Aetobatus narinari* is showily colored, brown with yellow spots, the body very angular, with long whip-like tail   It is found from Brazil to Hawaii and is rather common

In *Myliobatis* the teeth are in several series   The species are many, and found in all warm seas   *Myliobatis aquila* is the eagle-ray of Europe, *Myliobatis californicus* is the batfish of California, and *Myliobatis tobijei* takes its place in Japan

In *Rhinoptera* the snout is notched and cross-notched in front so that it appears as if ending in four lobes at the tip   These "cow-nosed rays," or "whipparees," root up the soft bottoms of shallow bays in their search for clams, much as a drove of hogs would do it   The common American species is *Rhinopterus bonasus   Rhinoptera steindachneri* lives in the Gulf of California

Teeth and spines of all these genera are common as fossils from the Eocene onwards, as well as many of the extinct genus, *Ptychodus*, with cyclospondylous vertebræ   *Ptychodus mammillaris, rugosus*, and *decurrens* are characteristic of the Cretaceous of England   *Myliobatis dixoni* is common in the European Eocene, as is also *Myliobatis toliapicus* and *Aetobatis*

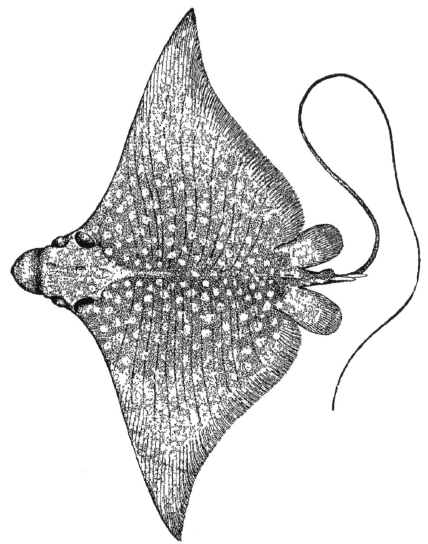

FIG 155 —Eagle-ray, *Aetobatis narinari* (Euphrasen)   Cedar Keys, Fla.

irregularis   Apocopodon seruacus is known from the Cretaceous of Brazil

Family Psammodontidæ. — The *Psammodontidæ* are known only from the teeth, large, flat, or rounded and finely dotted or roughened on the upper surface, as the name *Psammodus* (ψάμμος,

sand, ὀδούς, tooth) would indicate   The way in which the
jaws lie indicates that these teeth belonged to rays rather than
sharks   Numerous species have been described, mostly from
the Subcarboniferous limestones   *Archæobatis gigas*, perhaps,
as its name would indicate, the primeval skate, is from the
Subcarboniferous limestone of Greencastle, Indiana   Teeth
of numerous species of *Psammodus* and *Copodus* are found in

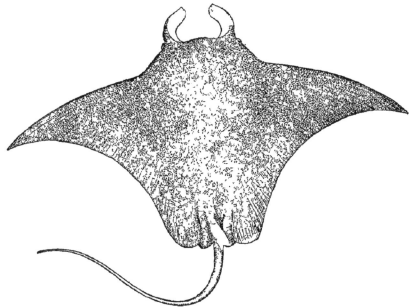

FIG 156 —Devil-ray or Sea-devil, *Manta birostris* (Walbaum)   Florida

many rocks of Carboniferous age   *Psammodus rugosus* common in Carboniferous rocks of Europe

Family Mobulidæ.—The sea-devils, *Mobulidæ*, are the mightiest
of all the rays, characterized by the development of the anterior
lobe of the pectorals as a pair of cephalic fins   These stand
up like horns or ears on the upper part of the head   The teeth
are small and flat, tubercular, and the whip-like tail is with
or without spine   The species are few, little known, and inordinately large, reaching a width of more than twenty feet
and a weight, according to Risso, of 1250 pounds   When harpooned it is said that they will drag a large boat with great
swiftness   The manta, or sea-devil, of tropical America is

Manta birostris. It is said to be much dreaded by the pearl-fishers, who fear that it will devour them "after enveloping them in its vast wings" It is not likely, however, that the manta devours anything larger than the pearl-oyster itself *Manta hamiltoni* is a name given to a sea-devil of the Gulf of California The European species *Mobula edentula* reaches a similarly enormous size, and *Mobula hypostoma* has been scantily described from Jamaica and Brazil *Mobula japonica* occurs in Japan A foetus in my possession from a huge specimen taken at Misaki is nearly a foot across In *Mobula (Cephaloptera)* there are teeth in both jaws, in *Manta (Ceratoptera)* in the lower jaw only • In *Ceratobatis* from Jamaica (*C robertsi*) there are teeth in the upper jaw only Otherwise the species of the three genera are much alike, and from their huge size are little known and rarely seen in collections. Of *Mobulidæ* no extinct species are known.

CHAPTER XV

THE HOLOCEPHALI, OR CHIMÆRAS

THE Chimæras. — Very early in geological times, certainly as early as the middle Silurian, the type of *Chimæras* diverged from that of the sharks   Hasse derives them directly from his hypothetical primitive *Polyospondyli*, by way of the *Acanthodei* and *Ichthyotomi*   In any event the point of divergence must be placed very early in the evolution of sharks, and this suggestion is as likely as any other   The chief character of Chimæras is found in the autostylic skull, which is quite different from the hyostylic skull of the sharks   In the sharks and in all higher fishes the mandible is joined to the skull by a suspensorium of bones or cartilages (quadrate, symplectic, and hyomandibular bones in the Teleost fishes)   To this arrangement the name hyostylic is given   In the Chimæra there is no suspensorium, the mandible being directly attached to the cranium, of which the hyomandibular and quadrate elements form an integral part, this arrangement being called autostylic   The palato-quadrate apparatus, of which the upper jaw is the anterior part, is immovably fused with the cranium, instead of being articulated with it   This fact gives the name to the subclass *Holocephali* (ὅλος, whole or solid, κεφαλή, head)   Other characters are found in the incomplete character of the back-bone, which consists of a scarcely segmented notochord differing from the most primitive condition imagined only in being surrounded by calcareous rings, no lime entering into the composition of the notochord itself   The tail is diphycercal and usually prolonged in a filament (leptocercal)   The shoulder-girdle, as in the sharks, is free from the skull   The pectoral fins are short and broad, without segmented axis or archipterygium and without recognizable analogue of the three large cartilages seen in the sharks, the propterygium, mesopterygium, and metapterygium   In the mouth, instead of teeth, are developed flat, bony plates called tritors or grinders, set endwise in the front of the jaws   The gills are fringe-like, free at the tips as in ordinary fishes, and there is a single external opening for them all as in true fishes, and they are covered with a flap of skin   These structures are, however, quite different from those of the true fishes and are doubtless independently developed   There is no spiracle   The skin is smooth or rough. In the living forms and most of the extinct species there is a strong spine in the dorsal fin   The ventral fin in the male has complex, usually trifid, claspers, and an analogous organ, the cephalic holder, is developed on the front of the head, in the adult male   This is a bony hook with a brush of glistening enameled teeth at the end   The eggs are large, and laid in oblong or elliptical egg-cases, provided with silky filaments The eggs are fertilized after they are extruded   Mucous channels and lateral line are highly developed, being most complex about the head   The brain is essentially shark-like, the optic nerves form a chiasma, and the central hemispheres are large

The teeth of the Chimæras are thus described by Woodward, vol 2, pp 36, 37

"In all the known families of Chimæroids, the dentition consists of a few large plates of vascular dentine, of which certain areas ('tritors') are specially hardened by the deposition of calcareous salts within and around groups of medullary canals, which rise at right angles to the functional surface   In most cases there is a single pair of such plates in the lower jaw, meeting at the symphysis, while two pairs are arranged to oppose these above   As a whole, the dentition thus closely resembles that of the typical Dipnoi (as has often been pointed out), and the upper teeth may be provisionally named palatine and vomerine until further discoveries shall have revealed their precise homologies   The structures are sometimes described as 'jaws,' and regarded as dentaries, maxillæ, and premaxillæ, but the presence of a permanent pulp under each tooth is conclusive proof of their bearing no relation to the familiar membrane-bones thus named in higher fishes "

Relationship of Chimæras.—As to the origin of the Chimæras and their relation to the sharks, Dr Dean has this recent ("The Devonian Lamprey") and interesting word

"The Holocephali have always been a doubtful group, anatomy and palæontology contributing but imperfect evidence as to their position in the gnathostome phylum   Their embryology, however, is still undescribed, except in a brief note by T J Parker, and it is reasonably looked to to contribute evidence as to their line of descent   The problem of the relationships of the Chimæroids has long been of especial interest to me, and it has led me to obtain embryonic material of a Pacific species of one of these forms   It may be of interest in this connection to state that the embryology of this form gives the clearest evidence that the wide separation of the Selachii and Holocephali is not tenable   The entire plan of development in *Chimæra colliei* is clearly like that of a shark   The ovulation is closely like that of certain of the rays and sharks the eggs are large, the segmentation is distinctly shark-like, the circular blastoderm overgrows the yolk in an elasmobranchian manner   The early embryos are shark-like, and the later ones have, as T J Parker has shown, external gills, and I note further that these arise, precisely as in shark-embryos, from the posterior margin of the gill-bar   A spiracle also is present A further and most interesting developmental feature is the fact that the autostylism in *Chimæra* is purely of secondary nature and is at the most of ordinal value   It is found that in a larva of *Chimæra* measuring 45 mm in length, the palato-quadrate cartilage is still separated from the skull by a wide fissure   This becomes gradually reduced by the confluence of the palato-quadrate cartilage with the skull, the fusion taking place at both the anterior and posterior ends of the mesal rim of the cartilage   The remains of the fissure are still well marked in the young *Chimæra*, four inches in length, and a rudiment of it is present in the adult skull as a passage-way for a nerve   Regarding the dentition   it may also be noted in the present connection that the growth of the dental plates in *Chimæra* suggests distinctly elasmobranchian conditions   Thus on the roof of the mouth the palatine plates are early represented by a series of small more or less conical elements which resemble outwardly, at least, the 'anlagen' of the pavement teeth in cestraciont sharks "

Family Chimæridæ.—The existing Chimæras are known also as spookfishes, ratfishes, and elephant-fishes   These are divided by Garman into three families, and in the principal family, the *Chimæridæ*, the snout is blunt, the skin without plates, and the dorsal fin is provided with a long spine   The flat tritors

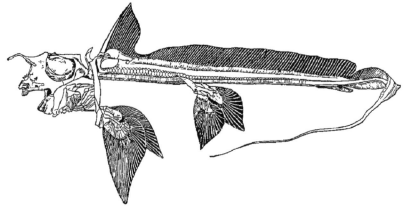

FIG 157 —Skeleton of *Chimæra monstrosa* Linnæus   (After Dean)

vary in the different genera   The single genus represented among living fishes is *Chimæra*, found in cold seas and in the oceanic depths   The best-known species, *Chimæra colliei*, the elephant-fish, or chimæra of California, abounds in shallow waters of ten to twenty fathoms from Sitka to San Diego. It is a harmless fish. useless except for the oil in its liver, and of special interest to anatomists as the only member of the family to be found when desired for dissection   This species was first found at Monterey by Mr Collie, naturalist of Captain Beechey's ship, the *Blossom*   It is brown in color, with whitish spots, and reaches a length of 2½ feet   As a shallow-water form, with certain differences in the claspers and in the tail, *Chimæra colliei* is sometimes placed in a distinct genus, *Hydrolagus*   Other species inhabit much greater depths and have the tail produced into a long filament   Of these, *Chimæra monstrosa*, the sea-cat of the north Atlantic, has been longer known than any other Chimæra   *Chimæra affinis* has been dredged in the Gulf Stream and off Portugal   *Chimæra phantasma* and *Chimæra mitsukurii* are frequently taken in Japan, and the huge jet-black *Chimæra purpurascens* in Hawaii and Japan   None of these species are valued as food, but all impress the spectator with their curious forms

The fossil *Chimæridæ*, although numerous from Triassic times and referred to several genera, are known chiefly by their teeth with occasional fin-spines, frontal holders, or impressions of parts of the skeleton   The earliest of chimæroid remains has

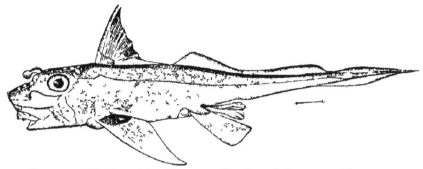

Fɪɢ. 158 —Elephant-fish, *Chimæra collei* Lay & Bennett   Monterey

been described by Dr Charles D Walcott * from Ordovician or Lower Silurian rocks at Cañon City, Colorado   Of the species called *Dictyorhabdus priscus*, only parts supposed to be the sheath of the notochord have been preserved   Dr Dean thinks this more likely to be part of the axis of a cephalopod shell The definitely known *Chimæridæ* are mainly confined to the rocks of the Mesozoic and subsequent eras   *Ischyodus priscus* (*avitus*) of the lower Jura resembles a modern chimæra *Granodus oweni* is another extinct chimæra, and numerous fin-spines, teeth, and other fragments in the Cretaceous and Eocene of America and Europe are referred to *Edaphodon*   A species of *Chimæra* has been recorded from the Pliocene of Tuscany, and one of *Calorhynchus* from the greensand of New Zealand   Other American Cretaceous genera of chimæroids are *Myognathus, Bryactinus, Isotænia, Leptomylus* and *Sphagepœa* Dental plates called *Rhynchodus* are found in the Devonian

Rhinochimæridæ.—The most degenerate of existing chimæras belong to the family of *Rhinochimæridæ*, characterized by the long flat soft blade in which the snout terminates   This struc-

* Bulletin Geol Soc America, 1892

ture resembles that seen in the deep-sea shark, *Mitsukurina*, and in *Polyodon* In *Rhinochimæra pacifica* of Japan the teeth in each jaw form but a single plate In *Harriotta raleighana*, of the Gulf Stream, they are more nearly as in *Chimæra*. Both are bathybial fishes, soft in texture, and found in great depths The family of *Callorhynchidæ*, or Antarctic Chimæras, includes the bottle-nosed Chimæra (*Callorhynchus callorhynchus*) of the Patagonian region In this species the snout is also produced, a portion being turned backward below in front of the mouth, forming a sensory pad well supplied with nerves

Ostracophori.—In natural sequence the class or subclass of *Ostracophores* follows the sharks and Chimæras

As all the *Ostracophori* are now extinct, we may here pass them by without further discussion, referring the reader to the full treatment in the "Guide to the Study of Fishes" These are most extraordinary creatures, jawless, apparently limbless, and enveloped in most cases anteriorly in a coat of mail In typical forms the head is very broad, bony, and horseshoe-shaped, attached to a slender body, often scaly, with small fins and ending in a heterocercal tail What the mouth was like can only be guessed, but no trace of jaws has yet been found in connection with it The most remarkable distinctive character is found in the absence of jaws and limbs in connection with the bony armature The latter is, however, sometimes obsolete. The back-bone, as usual in primitive fishes, is developed as a persistent notochord imperfectly segmented The entire absence of jaw structures, as well as the character of the armature, at once separates them widely from the mailed *Arthrodires* of a later period. But it is by no means certain that these structures were not represented by soft cartilage, of which no traces have been preserved in the specimens known

CHAPTER XVI

THE CROSSOPTERYGII

CLASS Teleostomi —We may unite the remaining groups of fishes into a single class, for which the name *Teleostomi* ($\tau\epsilon\lambda\epsilon\acute{o}\varsigma$, true, $\sigma\tau\acute{o}\mu\alpha$, mouth), proposed by Bonaparte in 1838, may be retained The fishes of this class are characterized by the presence of a suspensorium to the mandible, by the existence of membrane-bones (opercles, suborbitals, etc) on the head, by a single gill-opening leading to gill-arches bearing filamentous gills, and by the absence of claspers on the ventral fins The skeleton is at least partly ossified in all the *Teleostomi* More important as a primary character, distinguishing these fishes from the sharks, is the presence typically and primitively of the air-bladder This is at first a lung, arising as a diverticulum from the ventral side of the œsophagus, but in later forms it becomes dorsal and is, by degrees, degraded into a swim-bladder, and in very many forms it is altogether lost with age

This group comprises the vast majority of recent fishes, as well as a large percentage of those known only as fossils In these the condition of the lung can be only guessed

The *Teleostomi* are doubtless derived from sharks, their relationship being possibly nearest to the *Ichthyotomi* or to the primitive *Chimæras* The Dipnoans among *Teleostomi* retain the shark-like condition of the upper jaw, made of palatal elements, which may be, as in the *Chimæra*, fused with the cranium In the lower forms also the primitive diphycercal or protocercal form of tail is retained, as also the archipterygium or jointed axis of the paired fins, fringed with rays on one or both sides.

We may divide the Teleostomes, or true fishes, into three subclasses the *Crossopterygii*, or fringe-fins, the *Dipneusti*, or lung-fishes, *Actinopteri*, or ray-fins, including the *Ganoidei* and the *Teleostei*, or bony fishes Of these many recent writers are disposed to consider the *Crossopterygii* as most primitive, and to derive from it by separate lines each of the remaining subclasses, as well as the higher vertebrates The *Ganoidei* and *Teleostei* (constituting the *Actinopteri*) are very closely related, the ancient group passing by almost imperceptible degrees into the modern group of bony fishes

Subclass Crossopterygii. — The earliest Teleostomes known belong to the subclass or group called after Huxley, *Crossopterygii* (κρόσσος, fringe, πτερύξ, fin) A prominent character of the group lies in the retention of the jointed pectoral fin or archipterygium, its axis fringed by a series of soft rays This character it shares with the *Ichthyotomi* among sharks, and with the *Dipneusti* From the latter it differs in the hyostylic cranium, the lower jaw being suspended from the hyomandibular, and by the presence of distinct premaxillary and maxillary elements in the upper jaw In these characters it agrees with the ordinary fishes In the living Crossopterygians the air-bladder is lung-like, attached by a duct to the ventral side of the œsophagus The lung-sac, though specialized in structure, is simple, not cellular as in the Dipnoans The skeleton is more or less perfectly ossified Outside the cartilaginous skull is a bony coat of mail The skin is covered with firm scales or bony plates, the tail is diphycercal, straight, and ending in a point, the shoulder-girdle attached to the cranium is cartilaginous but overlaid with bony plates, and the branchiostigals are represented by a pair of gular plates

In the single family represented among living fishes the heart has a muscular arterial bulb with many series of valves on its inner edge, and the large air-bladder is divided into two lobes, having the functions of a lung, though not cellular as in the lung-fishes

The fossil types are very closely allied to the lung-fishes, and the two groups have no doubt a common origin in Silurian times It is now usually considered that the Crossopterygian is more primitive than the lung-fish, though at the same time more nearly related to the Ganoids, and through them to the ordinary fishes

Origin of Amphibians—From the primitive *Crossopterygii* the step to the ancestral *Amphibia*, which are likewise mailed and semi-aquatic, seems a very short one   It is true that most writers until recently have regarded certain Dipneustans as the *Dipteridæ* as representing the parents of the Amphibians But the weight of recent authority, Gill, Pollard, Boulenger, Dollo, and others, seems to place the point of separation of the higher vertebrates with the Crossopterygians, and to regard the lobate pectoral member of *Polypterus* as a possible source of the five-fingered arm of the frog   This view is still, however, extremely hypothetical and there is still much to be said in favor of the theory of the origin of Amphibia from Dipnoans and in

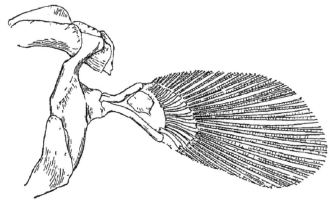

Fig 159.—Shoulder-girdle of *Polypterus bichir*   Specimen from the White Nile

favor of the view that the Dipnoans are also ancestors of the Crossopterygians

In the true Amphibians the lungs are better developed than in the Crossopterygian or Dipnoan, although the lungs are finally lost in certain salamanders which breathe through epithelial cells   The gills lose, among the Amphibia, their primitive importance, although in *Proteus anguineus* of Austria and *Necturus maculosus*, the American "mud-puppy" or water-dog, these persist through life   The archipterygium, or primitive fin, gives place to the chiropterygium or fingered arm   In this the basal segment of the archipterygium gives place to the humerus, the diverging segments seen in the most specialized type of archipterygium (*Polypterus*) become perhaps radius and ulna, the intermediate quadrate mass of cartilage possibly becoming carpal bones, and from these spring the joints called metacarpals and phalanges In the Amphibians and all higher forms the shoulder-girdle retains its primitive insertion at a distance from the head, and the posterior limbs remain abdominal

The Amphibians are therefore primarily fishes with fingers and toes instead of the fringe-fins of their ancestors Their relations are really with the fishes, as indicated by Huxley, who unites the amphibians and fishes in a primary group, *Ichthyopsida*, while reptiles and birds form the contrasting group of *Sauropsida*

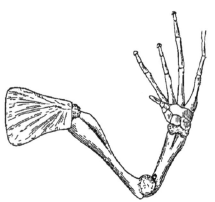

FIG 160 —Arm of a frog

The reptiles differ from the Amphibians through acceleration of development, passing through the gill-bearing stages within the egg The birds bear feathers instead of scales, and the mammals nourish their young by means of glandular secretions Through a reptile-amphibian ancestry the birds and mammals may trace back their descent from palæozoic Crossopterygians In the very young embryo of all higher vertebrates traces of double-breathing persist in all species, in the form of rudimentary gill-slits

The Fins of Crossopterygians —Dollo and Boulenger regard the heterocercal tail as a primitive form, the diphycercal form being a result of degradation, connected with its less extensive use as an organ of propulsion Most writers who adopt the theory of Gegenbaur that the archipterygium is the primitive form of the pectoral fin are likely, however, to consider the diphycercal tail found associated with it in the *Ichthyotomi, Dipneusti, Crossopterygii* as the more primitive form of the tail From this form the heterocercal tail of the higher sharks and

Ganoids may be derived, this giving way in the process of development to the imperfectly homocercal tail of the salmon, the homocercal tail of the perch, and the isocercal tail of the codfish and its allies, the gephyrocercal and the leptocercal tail, tapering or whip-like, representing various stages of degeneration Boulenger draws a distinction between the protocercal

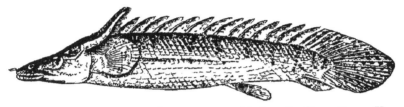

FIG 161 —*Polypterus congicus*, a Crossopterygian fish from the Congo River Young, with external gills (After Boulenger)

tail, the one primitively straight, and the diphycercal tail modified, like the homocercal tail, from an heterocercal ancestry

Orders of Crossopterygians —Cope and Woodward divide the *Crossopterygia* into four orders or suborders, *Haplistia*, *Rhipidistia*, *Actinistia*, and *Cladistia* To the latter belong the existing species, or the family of *Polypteridæ*, alone Boulenger unites the three extinct orders into one, which he calls *Osteolepida* In all three of these the pectorals are narrow with a single basal bone, and the nostrils, as in the Dipneustans, are below the snout The differences are apparently such as to justify Cope's division into three orders

Haplistia.—In the *Haplistia* the notochord is persistent, and the basal bones of dorsal and anal fins are in regular series, much fewer in number than the fin-rays The single family *Tarrassiidæ* is represented by *Tarrasius problematicus*, found by Traquair in Scotland This is regarded as the lowest of the Crossopterygians, a small fish of the Lower Carboniferous, the head mailed, the body with small bony scales

Rhipidistia —In the *Rhipidistia* the basal bones of the median fins ("axonosts and baseosts") are found in a single piece, not separate as in the *Haplistia* Four families are recognized, *Holoptychiidæ*, *Megalichthyidæ*, *Osteolepidæ*, and *Onychodontidæ*, the first of these being considered as the nearest approach of the Crossopterygians to the Dipnoans

The *Holoptychidæ* have the pectoral fins acute, the scales cycloid, enameled, and the teeth very complex *Holoptychius nobilissimus* is a very large fish from the Devonian *Glyptolepis leptopterus* from the Lower Devonian is also a notable species *Dendrodus* from the Devonian is known from detached teeth.

In the Ordovician rocks of Cañon City, Colorado, Dr Walcott finds numerous bony scales with folded surfaces and stellate ornamentation, and which he refers with some doubt to a Crossopterygian fish of the family *Holoptychidæ* This fish he

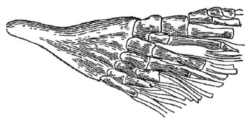

FIG 162 —Basal bone of dorsal fin, *Holoptychius leptopterus* (Agassiz)
(After Woodward)

names *Eriptychius americanus* If this identification proves correct, it will carry back the appearance of Crossopterygian fishes, the earliest of the Teleostome forms, to the beginning of the Silurian, these Cañon City shales being the oldest rocks in which remains of fishes are known to occur In the same rocks are found plates of Ostracophores and other fragments still more doubtful It is certain that our records in palæontology fall far short of disclosing the earliest sharks, as well as the earliest remains of Ostracophores, Arthrodires, or even Ganoids

Megalichthyidæ —The *Megalichthyidæ* (wrongly called " *Rhizodontidæ* ") have the pectoral fins obtuse, the teeth relatively simple, and the scales cycloid, enameled There are numerous species in the Carboniferous rocks, largely known from fragments or from teeth *Megalichthys, Strepsodus, Rhizodopsis, Gyroptychius, Tristichopterus, Eusthenopteron, Cricodus,* and *Sauripterus* are the genera, *Rhizodopsis sauroides* from the coal-measures of England being the best-known species

The *Osteolepidæ* differ from the *Megalichthyidæ* mainly in the presence of enameled rhomboid scales, as in *Polypterus* and

Lepisosteus In *Glyptopomus* these scales are sculptured, in
the others smooth   In *Osteolepis, Thursius, Diplopterus,* and
Glyptopomus a pineal foramen is present on the top of the head
This is wanting in *Parabatrachus* (*Megalichthys* of authors).
In *Osteolepis, Thursius,* and *Parabatrachus* the tail is heterocercal,

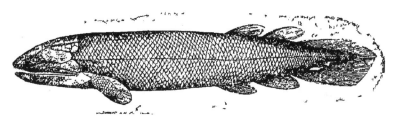

FIG 163 —*Gyroptychius microlepidotus* Agassiz   Devonian   Family *Megalichthyidæ*   (After Pander)

while in *Diplopterus* and *Glyptopomus* it is diphycercal   *Osteolepis macrolepidotus* and numerous other species occur in the
Lower Devonian   *Diplopterus agassizu* is common in the same
horizon   *Megalichthys hibberti* is found in the coal-measures,
and *Glyptopomus minimus* in the Upper Devonian   *Palæosteus*
is another genus recently described

The *Onychodontidæ* are known from a few fragments of
Onychodus sigmoides from the Lower Devonian of Ohio and
Onychodus anglicus from England

Order Actinistia —In the *Actinistia* there is a single fin-ray
to each basal bone, the axonosts of each ray fused in a single

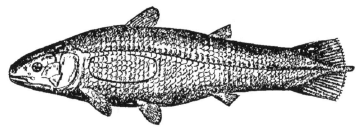

FIG 164 —*Cœlacanthus elegans* Newberry   From the Ohio Carboniferous, showing
air-bladder   (After Dean)

piece   The notochord is persistent, causing the back-bone
in fossils to appear hollow, the cartilaginous material leaving
no trace in the rocks   The genera and species are numerous,
ranging from the Subcarboniferous to the Upper Cretaceous,
many of them belonging to *Cœlacanthus,* the chief genus of the

single family *Cœlacanthidæ*. In *Cœlacanthus* the fin-rays are without denticles *Cœlacanthus granulatus* is found in the European Permian *Cœlacanthus elegans* of the coal-measures is found in America also In *Undina* the anterior fin-rays are marked with tubercles. *Undina penicillata* and *Undina gulo* from the Triassic are well-preserved species In *Macropoma* (*lewesiensis*) the fin-rays are robust, long, and little articulated

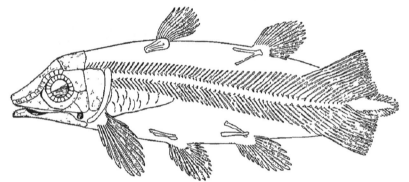

FIG 165 —*Undina gulo* Egerton, Lias Family *Cœlacanthidæ* (After Woodward)

Other genera are *Heptanema*, *Coccoderma*, *Libys*, *Diplurus*, and *Graphiurus* *Diplurus longicaudatus* was found by Newberry in the Triassic of New Jersey and Connecticut

Order Cladistia.—In the *Cladistia* the axis of the pectoral limb is fan-shaped, made of two diversified bones joined by cartilage The notochord is restricted and replaced by ossified vertebræ The axonosts of the dorsal and anal are in regular series, each bearing a fin-ray The order contains the single family *Polypteridæ* In this group the pectoral fin is formed differently from that of the other Crossopterygians, being broad, its base of two diverging bones with cartilage between. This structure, more specialized than in any other of the Crossopterygians or *Dipneusti*, has been regarded by Gill and others, as above stated, as the origin of the fingered hand (chiropterygium) of the frogs and higher vertebrates The base of the diverging bones has been identified as the antecedent of the humerus, the bones themselves as radius and ulna, while the intervening non-ossified cartilage breaks up into carpal bones, from which metacarpals and digits ultimately diverge This hypothesis is open to considerable doubt

The nostrils, as in true fishes, are superior. The body in these fishes is covered with rhombic enameled scales, as in the garpike, the head is similarly mailed, but, in distinction from the garpike, the anterior rays of the dorsal are developed as isolated spines

The young have a bushy external gill with a broad scaly base The air-bladder is double, not cellular, with a large air-duct joining the ventral surface of the œsophagus The intestine has a spiral valve

The cranium, according to Boulenger ("Poissons du Bassin du Congo," p 11), is remarkable for its generalized form, this character forming a trait of union between the Ganoids and the primitive *Amphibia* or *Stegocephali* Without considering *Polypterus*, it is not possible to interpret the homologies of the cranium of the amphibians and the sharks

The jaws are similar to those of the vertebrates higher than fishes Tooth-bearing premaxillaries and dentaries are solidly joined at the front of the cranium, and united by a suture to the toothed maxillaries which form most of the edge of the mouth Each half of the lower jaw consists of four elements, covering Meckel's cartilage, which is ossified at the symphysis These are the articular, angular, dentary, and splenial (coronoid) Most of these bones are armed with teeth The palato-suspensory consists of hyomandibular, quadrate, ecto-

FIG 166 — Lower jaw ot *Polypterus bichir*, from below

pterygoid, entopterygoid, metapterygoid, and palatine elements, the pterygoid elements bearing teeth In *Erpetoichthys* only the opercle is distinct among the gill-covers In *Polypterus* there is a subopercle also, the suborbital chain is represented by two small bones

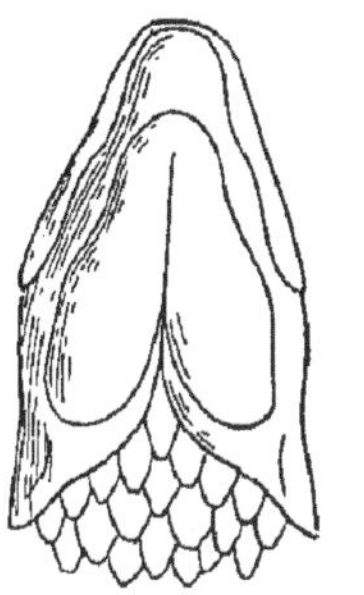

The gill-arches are four, but without lower pharyngeals The teeth are conic and pointed, and in structure, according to Agassiz, they differ largely from those of bony fishes, approaching the teeth of reptiles

The external gill of the young, first discovered by Steindachner in 1869, consists of a fleshy axis bordered above and below by secondary branches, themselves fringed In form and structure this resembles the external gills of amphibians

It is inserted, not on the gill-arches, but on the hyoid arch. Its origin is from the external skin It can therefore not be compared morphologically with the gills of other fishes, nor with the pseudobranchiæ, but rather with the external gills of larval sharks The vertebræ are very numerous and bi-

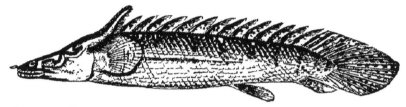

FIG 167 —*Polypterus congicus*, a Crossopterygian fish from the Congo River Young, with external gills. (After Boulenger)

concave as in ordinary fishes Each of the peculiar dorsal spines is primitively a single spine, not a finlet of several pieces, as some have suggested The enameled, rhomboid scales are in movable oblique whorls, each scale interlocked with its neighbors

The shoulder-girdle, suspended from the cranium by post-temporal and supraclavicle, is covered by bony plates To the small hypercoracoid and hypocoracoid the pectoral fin is attached Its basal bones may be compared to those of the sharks, mesopterygium, propterygium, and metapterygium, which may with less certainty be again called humerus, radius,

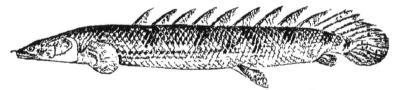

FIG 168 —*Polypterus delhezi* Boulenger Congo River

and ulna These are covered by flesh and by small imbricated scales The air-bladder resembles the lungs of terrestrial vertebrates It consists of two cylindrical sacs, that on the right the longer, then uniting in front to form a short tube, which enters the œsophagus from below with a slit-like glottis Unlike the lung of the *Dipneusti*, this air-bladder is not cellular, and it receives only arterial blood Its function is to assist the respiration by gills without replacing it

The Polypteridæ.—All the *Polypteridæ* are natives of Africa. Two genera are known, no species having been found fossil Of *Polypterus*, Boulenger, the latest authority, recognizes nine species six in the Congo, *Polypterus congicus*, *P delhezi*, *P ornatipinnis*, *P weeksi*, *P palmas*, and *P retropinnis*, one, *P. lapradei*, in the Niger, and two in the Nile, *Polypterus bichir* and *P endlicheri* Of these the only one known until very recently was *Polypterus bichir* of the Nile

These fishes in many respects resemble the garpike in habits They live close on the mud in the bottom of sluggish waters, moving the pectorals fan-fashion If the water is foul, they rise to the surface to gulp air, a part of which escapes through the gill-openings, after which they descend like a flash In the breeding season these fishes are very active, depositing their eggs in districts flooded in the spring The eggs are very numerous, grass-green, and of the size of eggs of millet The flesh is excellent as food

The genus *Erpetoichthys* contains a single species, *Erpetoichthys calabaricus*,* found also in the Senegal and Congo This

FIG 169.—*Erpetoichthys calabaricus* Smith Senegambia (After Dean.)

species is very slender, almost eel-like, extremely agile, and, as usual in wriggling or undulating fishes, it has lost its ventral fin It lives in shallow waters among interlaced roots of palms When disturbed it swims like a snake

* This genus was first called *Erpetoichthys*, but the name was afterwards changed by its author, J A Smith, to *Calamoichthys*, because there is an earlier genus *Erpichthys* among blennies, and a *Herpetoichthys* among eels But these two names, both wrongly spelled for *Herpetichthys*, are sufficiently different, and the earlier name should be retained 'A name in science is a name without necessary meaning" and without necessarily correct spelling Furthermore, if names are spelled differently, they are different, whatever their meaning The efforts of ornithologists, notably those of Dr Coues, to spell correctly improperly formed generic names have shown that to do so consistently would throw nomenclature into utter confusion It is well that generic names of classic origin should be correctly formed It is vastly more important that they should be stable Stability is the sole function of the law of priority

CHAPTER XVII

SUBCLASS DIPNEUSTI,* OR LUNG-FISHES

THE **Lung-fishes.** — The group of Dipneusti, or lung-fishes, is characterized by the presence of paired fins consisting of a jointed axis with or without rays The skull is autostylic, the upper jaw being made as in the Chimæra of palatal elements joined to the quadrate and fused with the cranium without premaxillary or maxillary The dentary bones are little developed The air-bladder is cellular, used as a lung in all the living species, its duct attached to the

Fig 170 —Shoulder-girdle of *Neoceratodus forsteri* Gunther   (After Zittel)

ventral side of the œsophagus The heart has many valves in the muscular arterial bulb The intestine has a spiral valve The teeth are usually of large plates of dentine covered with enamel, and are present on the pterygo-palatine and splenial bones The nostrils are concealed, when the mouth is closed, under a fold of the upper lip The scales are cycloid, mostly not enameled

The lung-fishes, or *Dipneusti* ($\delta i\varsigma$, two, $\pi\nu\epsilon\hat{\imath}\nu$, to breathe), arise, with the Crossopterygians, from the vast darkness of

---

* This group has been usually known as *Dipnoi*, a name chosen by Johannes Muller in 1845 But the latter term was first taken by Leuckart in 1821 as a name for Amphibians before any of the living *Dipneusti* were known We therefore follow Boulenger in the use of the name *Dipneusti*, suggested by Hæckel in 1866 The name Dipnoan may, however, be retained as a vernacular equivalent of *Dipneusti*

235

Palæozoic time, their origin with that or through that of the
latter to be traced to the Ichthyotomi or other primitive sharks
These two groups are separated from all the more primitive
fish-like vertebrates by the presence of lungs   In its origin
the lung or air-bladder arises as a diverticulum from the alimentary canal, used by the earliest fishes as a breathing-sac,
the respiratory functions lost in the progress of further divergence   Nothing of the nature of lung or air-bladder is
found in lancelet, lamprey, or shark   In none of the remaining
groups of fishes is it wholly wanting at all stages of development, although often lost in the adult   Among fishes it is most
completely functional in the *Dipneusti*, and it passes through
all stages of degeneration and atrophy in the more specialized
bony fishes

In the *Dipneusti*, or Dipnoans, as in the Crossopterygians
and the higher vertebrates, the trachea, or air-duct, arises, as
above stated, from the ventral side of the œsophagus   In the
more specialized fishes, yet to be considered, it is transferred
to the dorsal side, thus avoiding a turn in passing around the
œsophagus itself   From the sharks these forms are further
distinguished by the presence of membrane-bones about the
head   From the *Actinopteri* (Ganoids and Teleosts) Dipnoans
and Crossopterygians are again distinguished by the presence
of the fringe-fin, or archipterygium, as the form of the paired
limbs   From the Crossopterygians the Dipnoans are most
readily distinguished by the absence of maxillary and premaxillary, the characteristic structures of the jaw of the true
fish   The upper jaw in the Dipnoan is formed of palatal elements attached directly to the skull, and the lower jaw contains no true dentary bones   The skull in the Dipnoans, as
in the *Chimæra*, is autostylic, the mandible articulating directly
with the palatal apparatus, the front of which forms the upper
jaw and of which the pterygoid, hyomandibular and quadrate
elements form an immovable part   The shoulder-girdle, as
in the shark, is a single cartilage, but it supports a pair of superficial membrane-bones

In all the Dipnoans the trunk is covered with imbricated
cycloid scales and no bony plates, although sometimes the
scales are firm and enameled   The head has a roof of well-

developed bony plates made of ossified skin and not corresponding with the membrane-bones of higher fishes The fish-
like membrane-bones, opercles, branchiostegals, etc , are not
yet differentiated The teeth have the form of grinding-plates
on the pterygoid areas of the palate, being distinctly shark-like
in structure The paired fins are developed as archipterygia,
often without rays, and the pelvic arch consists of a single
cartilage, the two sides symmetrical and connected in front
There is but one external gill-opening leading to the gill-arches,
which, as in ordinary fishes, are fringe-like, attached at one
end In the young, as with the embryo shark, there is a bushy
external gill, which looks not unlike the archipterygium pectoral fin itself, although its rays are of different texture In
early forms, as in the Ganoids, the scales were bony and enameled, but in some recent forms deep sunken in the skin The
claspers have disappeared, the nostrils, as in the frog, open
into the pharynx, the heart is three-chambered, the arterial
bulb with many valves, and the cellular structure of the skin
and of other tissues is essentially as in the Amphibian

The developed lung, fitted for breathing air, which seems
the most important of all these characters, can, of course, be
traced only in the recent forms, although its existence in all
others can be safely predicated Besides the development
of the lung we may notice the gradual forward movement
of the shoulder-girdle, which in most of the Teleostomous
fishes is attached to the head In bony fishes generally
there is no distinct neck, as the post-temporal, the highest
bone of the shoulder-girdle, is articulated directly with the
skull In some specialized forms (*Balistes, Tetraodon*) it is
even immovably fused with it In a few groups (*Apodes,
Opisthomi, Heteromi*, etc) this connection ancestrally possessed
is lost through atrophy and the slipping backward of the
shoulder-girdle leaves again a distinct neck In the Amphibians and all higher vertebrates the shoulder-girdle is distinct from the skull, and the possession of a flexible neck is
an important feature of their structure In all these higher
forms the posterior limbs remain abdominal, as in the sharks
and the primitive and soft-rayed fishes generally In these
the pelvis or pelvic elements are attached toward the middle

of the body, giving a distinct back as well as neck. In the
spiny-rayed fishes the "back" as well as the neck disappears,
the pelvic elements being attached to the shoulder-girdle, and
in a few extreme forms (as *Ophidion*) the pelvis is fastened at
the chin

Classification of Dipnoans.—By Woodward the *Dipneusti* are
divided into two classes, the *Sirenoidei* and the *Arthrodira*
We follow Dean in regarding the latter as representative of a
distinct class, leaving the *Sirenoidei*, with the *Ctenodipterini*,
to constitute the subclass of *Dipneusti* The *Sirenoidei* are
divided by Gill into two orders, the *Monopneumona*, with one
lung, and the *Diplopneumona*, with the lung divided To the
latter order the *Lepidosirenidæ* belong To the former the
Ceratodontidæ, and presumably the extinct families also belong,
although nothing is known of their lung structures Zittel
and Hay adopt the names of *Ctenodipterini* and *Sirenoidei* for
these orders, the former being further characterized by the very
fine fin-rays, more numerous than their supports

Order Ctenodipterini — In this order the cranial roof-bones
are small and numerous, and the rays of the median fins are
very slender, much more numerous than their supports, which
are inserted directly on the vertebral arches

In the *Uronemidæ* the upper dentition comprises a cluster
of small, blunt, conical denticles on the palatine bones, the
lower dentition consists of similar denticles on the splenial
bone The vertical fins are continuous and the tail diphycercal.
There is a jugular plate, as in *Amia* The few species are found
in the Carboniferous, *Uronemus lobatus* being the best-known
species

In *Dipteridæ* there is a pair of dental plates on the palatines,
and an opposing pair on the splenials below Jugular plates
are present, and the tail is usually distinctly heterocercal

In *Phaneropleuron* there is a distinct anal fin shorter than
the very long dorsal, *Phaneropleuron andersoni* is known from
Scotland, and *Scaumenacia curta* is found at Scaumenac Bay
in the Upper Devonian of Canada

In *Dipterus* there are no marginal teeth, and the tail is
heterocercal, not diphycercal, as in the other Dipnoans generally Numerous species of *Dipterus* occur in Devonian rocks

In these the jugular plate is present, as in *Uronemus* *Dipterus valenciennesi* is the best-known European species *Dipterus nelsoni* and numerous other species are found in the Chemung and other groups of Devonian rocks in America

In the *Ctenodontidæ* the tail is diphycercal, and no jugular plates are present in the known specimens   In *Ctenodus* and *Sagenodus* there is no jugular plate and there are no marginal teeth   The numerous species of *Ctenodus* and *Sagenodus* belong

FIG 171 —*Phaneropleuron andersoni* Huxley, restored, Devonian   (After Dean)

chiefly to the Carboniferous age   *Ctenodus wagneri* is found in the Cleveland shale of the Ohio Devonian   *Sagenodus occidentalis*, one of the many American species, belongs to the coal-measures of Illinois

As regards the succession of the *Dipneusti*, Dr Dollo regards *Dipterus* as the most primitive, *Scaumenacia*, *Uronemus*, *Ctenodus*, *Ceratodus*, *Protopterus*, and *Lepidosiren* following in order   The last-named genus he thinks marks the terminus of the group, neither Ganoids nor Amphibians being derived from any Dipnoans

Order Sirenoidei. — The living families of *Dipneusti* differ from these extinct types in having the cranial roof-bones reduced in number   There are no jugular plates and no marginal teeth in the jaws   The tail is diphycercal in all, ending in a long point, and the body is covered with cycloid scales   To these forms the name *Sirenoidei* was applied by Johannes Muller

Family Ceratodontidæ. — The *Ceratodontidæ* have the teeth above and below developed as triangular plates, set obliquely each with several cusps on the outer margin   Nearly all the species, representing the genera *Ceratodus*, *Gosfordia*, and *Conchopoma*, are now extinct, the single genus *Neoceratodus* still existing in Australian rivers   Numerous fragments of *Ceratodus* are found in Mesozoic rocks in Europe, Colorado, and

India, *Ceratodus latissimus*, figured by Agassiz in 1838, being the best-known species

The abundance of the fossil teeth of *Ceratodus* renders the discovery of a living representative of the same type a matter of great interest

In 1870 the Barramunda of the rivers of Queensland was described

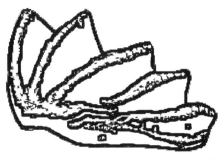

FIG 172 —Teeth of *Ceratodus runcinatus* Plie-ninger Carboniferous (After Zittel)

by Krefft, who recognized its relationship to *Ceratodus* and gave it the name of *Ceratodus forsteri* Later, generic differences were noticed, and it was separated as a distinct group by Castelnau in 1876, under the name of *Neoceratodus* (later called *Epiceratodus* by Teller) *Neoceratodus forsteri* and a second species, *Neoceratodus miolepis*, have been since very fully discussed by Dr Gunther and Dr Krefft

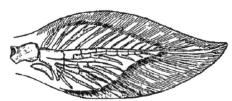

FIG 174 —Archipterygium of *Neoceratodus forsteri* Günther

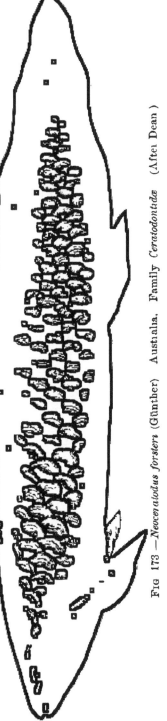

FIG 173 —*Neoceratodus forsteri* (Günther) Australia. Family *Ceratodontidæ* (After Dean)

They are known in Queensland as *Barramunda* They inhabit the
rivers known as Burnett, Dawson, and Mary, reaching a length
of six feet, and being locally much valued as food   From the
salmon-colored flesh, they are known to the settlers in Queensland as "salmon" According to Dr Gunther, "the Barramunda is said to be in the habit of going on land, or at least
on mud-flats, and this assertion appears to be borne out by
the fact that it is provided with a lung   However, it is much
more probable that it rises now and then to the surface of the
water in order to fill its lung with air, and then descends again
until the air is so much deoxygenized as to render a renewal
of it necessary   It is also said to make a grunting noise which
may be heard at night for some distance   This noise is probably produced by the passage of the air through the œsophagus
when it is expelled for the purpose of renewal   As the Barramunda has perfectly developed gills besides the lung, we can
hardly doubt that, when it is in water of normal composition
and sufficiently pure to yield the necessary supply of oxygen,
these organs are sufficient for the purpose of breathing, and
that the respiratory function rests with them alone   But
when the fish is compelled to sojourn in thick muddy water
charged with gases, which are the
products of decomposing organic
matter (and this must be the case
very frequently during the droughts
which annually exhaust the creeks
of tropical Australia), it commences
to breathe air with its lung in the
way indicated above   If the medium
in which it happens to be is perfectly
unfit for breathing, the gills cease to
have any function, if only in a less
degree, the gills may still continue
to assist in respiration   The Barramunda, in fact, can breathe by either
gills or lung alone or by both simultaneously   It is not probable that

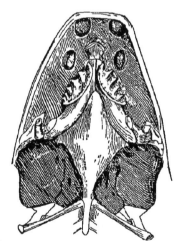

FIG 175 —Upper jaw of *Neoceratodus forsteri* Gunther (After
Zittel)

it lives freely out of water, its limbs being much too flexible
for supporting the heavy and unwieldy body and too feeble

generally to be of much use in locomotion on land. However, it is quite possible that it is occasionally compelled to leave the water, although we cannot believe that it can exist without it in a lively condition for any length of time

"Of its propagation or development we know nothing except that it deposits a great number of eggs of the size of those of a newt, and enveloped in a gelatinous case We may infer that the young are provided with external gills, as in *Protopterus* and *Polypterus*

"The discovery of *Ceratodus* does not date farther back

Fig 176 —Lower jaw of *Neoceratodus forsteri* Gunther (After Günther)

than the year 1870, and proved to be of the greatest interest, not only on account of the relation of this creature to the other living *Dipneusti* and *Ganoidei*, but also because it threw fresh light on those singular fossil teeth which are found in strata of Triassic and Jurassic formations in various parts of Europe, India, and America These teeth, of which there is a great variety with regard to general shape and size, are sometimes two inches long, much longer than broad, depressed, with a flat or slightly undulated, always

Lepidosirenidæ.—The family *Lepidosirenidæ*, representing the suborder *Diploneumona*, is represented by two genera of mud-fishes found in streams of Africa and South America *Lepidosiren paradoxa* was discovered by Natterer in 1837 in tributaries of the Amazon   It was long of great rarity in

Fig. 177 —Adult male of *Lepidosiren paradoxa* Fitzinger   (After Kerr)

collections, but quite recently large numbers have been obtained, and Dr J Graham Kerr of the University of Cambridge has given a very useful account of its structure and development.   From his memoir we condense the following record of its habits as seen in the swamps in a region known as Gran Chaco, which lies under the Tropic of Capricorn These swamps in the rainy season have a depth of from two to four feet, becoming entirely dry in the southern winter (June, July).

Kerr on the Habits of Lepidosiren.—The loalach, as the *Lepidosiren* is locally called, is normally sluggish, wriggling slowly about at the bottom of the swamp, using its hind limbs in irregular alternation as it clambers through the dense vegetation. More rapid movement is brought about by lateral strokes of the large and powerful posterior end of the body. It burrows with great facility, gliding through the mud, for which form of movement the shape of the head, with the

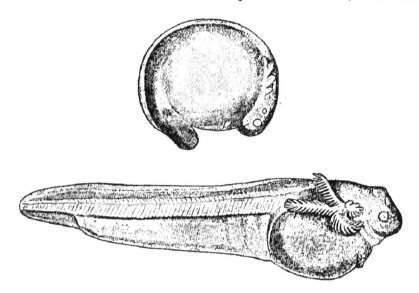

Fig. 178 —Embryo (3 days before hatching) and larva (13 days after hatching) of *Lepidosiren paradoxa* Fitzinger. (After Kerr.)

upper lip overlapping the lower and the external nostril placed within the lower lip, is admirably adapted. It feeds on plants, algæ, and leaves of flower-plants. The gills are small and quite unable to supply its respiratory needs, and the animal must rise to the surface at intervals, like a frog. It breathes with its lungs as continuously and rhythmically as a mammal, the air being inhaled through the mouth. The animal makes no vocal sound, the older observation that it utters a cry like that of a cat being doubtless erroneous. Its strongest sense is that of smell. In darkness it grows paler in color, the black chromatophores shrinking in absence of light and enlarging in the sunshine   In injured animals this reaction becomes much less, as they remain pale even in daylight.

In the rainy season when food is abundant the Lepidosiren eats voraciously and stores great quantities of orange-colored fat in the tissues between the muscles   In the dry season it ceases to feed, or, as the Indians put it, it feeds on water.   When the water disappears the Lepidosiren burrows down into the mud, closing its gill-openings, but breathing through the mouth   As the mud stiffens it retreats to the lower part of its burrow,

Fig 179 —Larva of *Lepidosiren paradoxa* 30 days after hatching   (After Kerr)

where it lies with its tail folded over its face, the body surrounded by a mucous secretion.   In its burrow there remains an opening which is closed by a lid of mud.   At the end of the

Fig 180 —Larva of *Lepidosiren paradoxa* 40 days after hatching   (After Kerr)

dry season this lid is pushed aside, and the animal comes out when the water is deep enough   When the waters rise the presence of Lepidosirens can be found only by a faint quivering

Fig 181 —Larva of *Lepidosiren paradoxa* 3 months after hatching   (After Kerr)

movement of the grass in the bottom of the swamp   When taken the body is found to be as slippery as an eel and as muscular   The eggs are laid in underground burrows in the black

peat. Their galleries run horizontally and are usually two feet
long by eight inches wide. After the eggs are laid the male
remains curled up in the nest with them. In the spawning
season an elaborate brush is developed in connection with the
ventral fins.

Protopterus, a second genus, is found in the rivers of Africa,
with three species, *P. annectens*, *P. dolloi*, and *P. æthiopicus*.

The genus has five gill-clefts, instead of four as in *Lepidosiren*.
It retains its external gills rather longer than the latter, and
its limbs are better developed. The habits of *Protopterus* are
essentially like those of *Lepidosiren*, and the two types have
developed along parallel lines doubtless from a common ancestry.
No fossil *Lepidosirenidæ* are known.

FIG. 182.—*Protopterus dolloi* Boulenger. Congo River. Family *Lepidosirenidæ*.

Arthrodires. — The large group of *Arthrodires* consists of
mailed and helmeted fishes with distinct jaws and other characters separating them widely from the *Ostracophores*. In the
latest view, that of Woodward and Eastman, these fishes con-

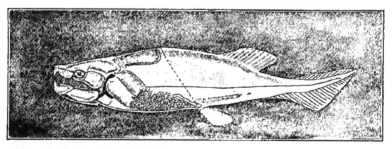

FIG. 183.—An Arthrodire, *Dinichthys intermedius* Newberry, restored. Devonian.

stitute an order of Dipnoans. As they are all extinct, the
reader is referred to the " Guide to the Study of Fishes " for
further discussion.

Cycliæ.—The hypothetical suborder, *Cycliæ*, based on the
extinct genus *Palæospondylus*, may be similarly treated.

CHAPTER XVIII

THE GANOIDS

SUBCLASS **Actinopteri.** — In our glance over the taxonomy of the earlier Chordates, or fish-like vertebrates, we have detached from the main stem one after another a long series of archaic or primitive types We have first set off those with rudimentary notochord, then those with retrogressive development who lose the notochord, then those without skull or brain, then those without limbs or lower jaws The residue assume the fish-like form of body, but still show great differences among themselves We have then detached those without membrane-bones, or trace of lung or air-bladder We next part company with those having the air-bladder a veritable lung, and those with an ancient type of paired fins, a jointed axis fringed with rays, and those having the palate still forming the upper jaw We have finally left only those having fish-jaws, fish-fins, and in general the structure of the modern fish For all these in all their variety, as a class or subclass, the name *Actinopteri*, or *Actinopterygii*, suggested by Professor Cope, is now generally adopted The shorter form, *Actinopteri*, being equally correct is certainly preferable This term ($\alpha\kappa\tau\iota\varsigma$, ray, $\pi\tau\epsilon\rho\acute{o}\nu$ or $\pi\tau\epsilon\rho\acute{v}\xi$, fin) refers to the structure of the paired fins In all these fishes the bones supporting the fin-rays are highly specialized and at the same time concealed by the general integument of the body In general two bones connect the pectoral fin with the shoulder-girdle The hypercoracoid is a flat square bone, usually perforated by a foramen Lying below it and parallel with it is the irregularly formed hypocoracoid Attached to them is a row of bones, the actinosts, or pterygials, short, often hour-glass-shaped, which actually support the fin-rays In the more specialized forms, or Teleosts, the actinosts are few (four to six) in number, but in the more primitive types, or Ganoids, they may remain numerous, a reminiscence of the condition seen in the Crossopterygians, and especially in *Polypterus* Other variations may

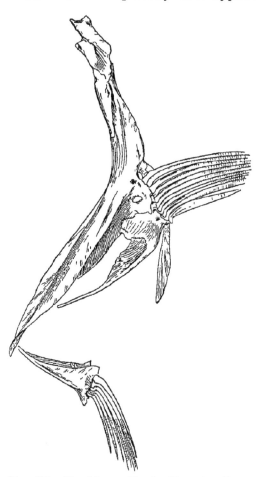

occur, the two coracoids sometimes are imperfect or specially modified, the upper sometimes without a foramen, and the actinosts may be distorted in form or position.

The Series Ganoidei.— Among the lower *Actinopteri* many archaic traits still persist, and in its earlier representatives the group approaches closely to the *Crossopterygii*, although no forms actually intermediate are known either living or fossil The great group of *Actinopteri* may be divided into two series or subclasses, the *Ganoidei*, or *Chrondrostei*, containing those forms, mostly extinct, which retain archaic traits of one sort or another, and the *Teleostei*, or bony fishes, in which most of the

Fig 184 —Shoulder-girdle of a Flounder, *Paralichthys californicus* (Ayres)

primitive characters have disappeared Doubtless all of the *Teleostei* are descended from a ganoid ancestry

Even among the *Ganoidei*, as the term is here restricted, there remains a very great variety of form and structure The fossil and existing forms do not form continuous series, but represent the tips and remains of many diverging branches perhaps from some Crossopterygian central stock The group constitutes at least three distinct orders and, as a whole, does not admit of

perfect definition In most but not all of the species the tail
is distinctly and obviously heterocercal, the lack of symmetry
of the tail in some Teleosts being confined to the bones and not
evident without dissection Most of the Ganoids have the
skeleton still cartilaginous, and in some it remains in a very
primitive condition Usually the Ganoids have an armature
of bony plates, diamond-shaped, with an enamel like that
developed on the teeth In all of them the pectoral fin has
numerous basal bones or actinosts All of them have the air-
bladder highly developed, usually cellular and functional as a
lung, but connecting with the dorsal side of the gullet, not with
the ventral side as in the Dipnoans In all living forms there
is a more or less perfect optic chiasma These ancient forms
retain also the many valves of the arterial bulb and the spiral
valve of the intestines found in the more archaic types of fishes
But traces of some or all of these structures are found in some
bony fishes, and their presence in the Ganoids by no means
justifies the union of the Ganoids with the sharks, Dipnoans,
and Crossopterygians to form a great primary class, *Palæich-
thyes*, as proposed by Dr Gunther Almost every form of body
may be found among the Ganoids In the Mesozoic seas these
fishes were scarcely less varied and perhaps scarcely less abundant
than the Teleosts in the seas of to-day They far exceed the
Crossopterygians in number and variety of forms Transitional
forms connecting the two groups are thus far not recognized So
far as fossils show, the characteristic actinopterous fin with its
reduced and altered basal bones appeared at once without intervening gradations

The name *Ganoidei* ($\gamma\acute{\alpha}\nu o s$, brightness, $\epsilon\hat{\iota}\delta o s$, resemblance),
alluding to the enameled plates, was first given by Agassiz to
those forms, mostly extinct, which were covered with bony scales
or hard plates of one sort or another As the term was originally
defined, mailed catfishes, sea-horses, *Agonidæ*, *Arthrodires*,
Ostracophores, and other wholly unrelated types were included
with the garpikes and sturgeons as Ganoids Most of these
intruding forms among living fishes were eliminated by Johannes
Muller, who recognized the various archaic characters common
to the existing forms after the removal of the mailed Teleosts
Still later Huxley separated the Crossopterygians as a distinct

group, while others have shown that the *Ostracophori* and *Arthro-dira* should be placed far from the garpike in systematic classification. Cope, Woodward, Hay, and others have dropped the name Ganoid altogether as productive of confusion through the many meanings attached to it Others have kept it as a convenient group name for the orders of archaic *Actinopteri* For these varied and more or less divergent forms it seems convenient to retain it As an adjective "ganoid" is sometimes used as descriptive of bony plates or enameled scales, some-in the sense of archaic, as applied to fishes

Classification of Ganoids. — The subdivision of the series of Ganoidei into orders offers great difficulty from the fact of the varying relationships of the members of the group and the fact that the great majority of the species are known only from broken skeletons preserved in the rocks It is apparently easy to separate those with cartilaginous skeletons from those with these bones more or less ossified It is also easy to separate those with bony scales or plates from those having the scales cycloid But the one type of skeleton grades into the other, and there is a bony basis even to the thinnest of scales found in this group Among the multitude of names and divisions proposed we may recognize six orders, for which the names *Lysopteri, Chondrostei, Selachostomi, Pycnodonti, Lepidostei,* and *Halecomorphi* are not inappropriate Each of these seems to represent a distinct offshoot from the first primitive group

Order Lysopteri.—In the most primitive order, called *Lysopteri* (λυσός, loose, πτερόν, fin) by Cope, *Heterocerci* by Zittel and Eastman, and the "ascending series of Chondrostei" by Woodward, we find the nearest approach to the Chondropterygians In this order the arches of the vertebræ are more or less ossified, the body is more or less short and deep, covered with bony dermal plates The opercular apparatus is well developed, with numerous branchiostegals Infraclavicles are present, and the fins provided with fulcra Dorsal and anal fins are present, with rays more numerous than their supports, ventral fin with basal supports which are imperfectly ossified, caudal fin mostly heterocercal, the scales mostly rhombic in form All the members of this group are now extinct

The Palæoniscidæ.—The numerous genera of this order are referred to three families, the *Palæoniscidæ, Platysomidæ*, and *Dictyopygidæ*, a fourth family, *Dorypteridæ*, of uncertain relations, being also tentatively recognized The family of *Palæoniscidæ* is the most primitive, ranging from the Devonian to the Lias, and some of them seem to have entered fresh waters in the time of the coal-measures These fishes have the body elongate and provided with one short dorsal fin The tail is heterocercal and the body covered with rhombic plates Fulcra or rudimentary spine-like scales are developed on the upper edge of the caudal fin in most recent Ganoids, and often the back has a median row of undeveloped scales A multitude of species and genera are recorded A typical form is the genus *Palæoniscum,*[*] with many species represented in the rocks of various parts of the world. The longest known species is *Palæoniscum frieslebenense* from the Permian of Germany and England. *Palæoniscum magnum*, sixteen inches long, occurs

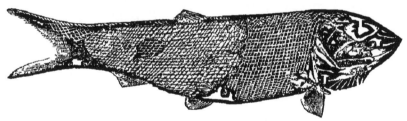

Fig 185 —*Palæoniscum frieslebenense* Blainville   Family *Palæoniscidæ*
(After Zittel)

in the Permian of Germany From *Canobius*, the most primitive genus, to *Coccolepis*, the most modern, is a continuous series, the suspensorium of the lower jaw becoming more oblique, the basal bones of the dorsal fewer, the dorsal extending farther forward, and the scales more completely imbricate Other prominent genera are *Amblypterus, Eurylepis, Cheirolepis, Rhadinichthys, Pygopterus, Elonichthys, Ærolepis, Gyrolepis, Myriolepis, Oxygnathus, Centrolepis*, and *Holurus*.

The Platysomidæ. — The *Platysomidæ* are different in form, the body being deep and compressed, often diamond-shaped,

[*] This word is usually written *Palæoniscus*, but Blainville, its author (1818), chose the neuter form

with very long dorsal and anal fins   In other respects they are very similar to the *Palæoniscidæ*, the osteology being the same The *Palæoniscidæ* were rapacious fishes with sharp teeth, the *Platysomidæ* less active, and, from the blunter teeth, probably feeding on small animals, as crabs and snails

The rhombic enameled scales are highly specialized and held together as a coat of mail by peg-and-socket joints   The most extreme form is *Platysomus*, with the body very deep. *Platysomus gibbosus* and other species occur in the Permian rocks of Germany   *Cheirodus* is similar to *Platysomus*, but without ventral fins   *Eurynotus*, the most primitive genus, is remarkable for its large pectoral fins   *Eurynotus crenatus* occurs

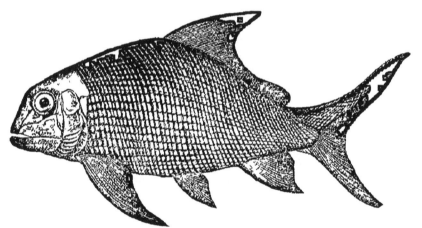

Fig 186 —*Eurynotus crenatus* Agassiz, restored   Carboniferous   Family *Platysomidæ*   (After Traquair)

in the Subcarboniferous of Scotland   Other genera are *Mesolepis*, *Globulodus*, *Wardichthys*, and *Cheirodopsis*

Some of the *Platysomidæ* have the interneural spines projecting through the skin before the dorsal fin   This condition is found also in certain bony fishes allied to the *Carangidæ*

The Dorypteridæ.—*Dorypterus hoffmani*, the type of the singular Palæozoic family of *Dorypteridæ*, with thoracic or subjugular many-rayed ventrals, is Stromateus-like to all appearance, with distinct resemblances to certain Scombroid forms, but with a heterocercal tail like a ganoid, imperfectly ossified back-bone, and other very archaic characters   The body is apparently scaleless, unlike the true *Platysomidæ*, in which the scales are highly developed A second species, *Dorypterus alihausi*, also from the German copper shales, has been described

This species has lower fins *mani*, but may be the adult *Dorypterus* is regarded by cialized offshoot from the many-rayed ventrals and the body and fins suggest affinity

Dictyopygidæ.—In the *Dic-dæ*), the body is gracefully pressed, the heterocercal tail turned upwards, the teeth hooked, and the bony plates this group two genera are taining numerous species In *terus* Redfield, not of Agassiz)

than *Dorypterus hoff-* of the same type Woodward as a spe- *Platysomidæ* The general form of the with the *Lampridæ tyopygidæ* (*Catopteri-* elongate, less com- is short and abruptly are sharp and usually well developed Of recognized, each con- *Redfieldius* (=*Catop-* the dorsal is inserted

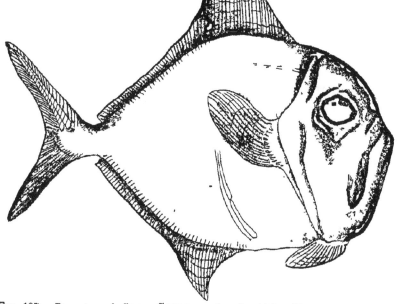

Fig 187 —*Dorypterus hoffmani* Germar, restored   (After Hancock and Howse)

behind the anal, while in *Dictyopyge* this is not the case   *Red-fieldius gracilis* and other species are found in the Triassic of the Connecticut River   *Dictyopyge macrura* is found in the same region, and *Dictyopyge catoptera* and other species in Europe.

Order Chondrostei.—The order *Chondrostei* (χόνδρος, cartilage, ὀστέον, bone), as accepted by Woodward, is characterized by the persistence of the notochord in greater or less degree, the endoskeleton remaining cartilaginous   In all, the axonosts and baseosts of the median fins are arranged in simple regular series and the rays are more numerous than the supporting elements   The shoulder-girdle has a pair of infraclavicular plates   The pelvic fins have well-developed baseosts   The branchiostegals are few or wanting   In the living forms, and probably in all others, a matter which can never be ascertained, the optic nerves are not decussating, but form an optic chiasma, and the intestine is provided with a spiral valve   In all the species there is one dorsal and one anal fin, separate from the caudal   The teeth are small or wanting, the body naked or covered with bony plates, the caudal fin is usually heterocercal, and on the tail are rhombic plates   To this order, as thus defined, about half of the extinct Ganoids belong, as well as the modern degenerate forms known as sturgeons and perhaps the paddle-fishes, which are apparently derived from fishes with rhombic enameled scales   The species extend from the Upper Carboniferous to the present time, being most numerous in the Triassic

At this point in Woodward's system diverges a descending series, characterized as a whole by imperfect squamation and elongate form, this leading through the synthetic type of *Chondrosteidæ* to the modern sturgeon and paddle-fish, which are regarded as degenerate types

The family of *Saurorhynchidæ* contains pike-like forms, with long jaws, and long conical teeth set wide apart   The tail is not heterocercal, but short-diphycercal, the bones of the head are covered with enamel, and those of the roof of the skull form a continuous shield   The opercular apparatus is much reduced, and there are no branchiostegals   The fins are all small, without fulcra, and the skin has isolated longitudinal series of bony scutes, but is not covered with continuous scales   The principal genus is *Saurorhynchus* (=*Belonorhynchus*, the former being the earlier name) from the Triassic   *Saurorhynchus acutus* from the English Triassic is the best known species

The family of *Chondrosteidæ* includes the Triassic precursors

of the sturgeons   The general form is that of the sturgeon,
but the body is scaleless except on the upper caudal lobe, and
there are no plates on the median line of the skull   The opercle and subopercle are present, the jaws are toothless, and there
are a few well-developed caudal rays   The caudal has large
fulcra   The single well-known species of this group, *Chondrosteus
acipenseroides*, is found in the Triassic rocks of England and
reaches a length of about three feet   It much resembles a
modern sturgeon, though differing in several technical respects
Chondrosteus pachyurus is based on the tail of a species of much
larger size and *Gyrosteus mirabilis*, also of the English Triassic,

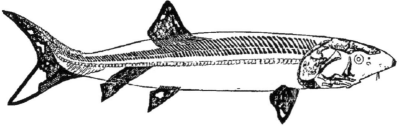

FIG 188 —*Chondrosteus acipenseroides* Egerton   Family *Chondrosteidæ*
(After Woodward)

is known from fragments of fishes which must have been 18
to 20 feet in length
    The sturgeons constitute the recent family of *Acipenseridæ*,
characterized by the prolonged snout and toothless jaws and
the presence of four barbels below the snout . In the *Acipenseridæ* there are no branchiostegals and a median series of plates
is present on the head   The body is armed with five rows of
large bony bucklers,—each often with a hooked spine, sharpest
in the young   Besides these, rhombic plates are developed
on the tail, besides large fulcra   The sturgeons are the youngest
of the Ganoids, not occurring before the Lower Eocene, one
species, *Acipenser toliapicus* occurring in the London clay
About thirty living species of sturgeon are known, referred
to three genera   *Acipenser*, found throughout the Northern
Hemisphere, *Scaphirhynchus*, in the Mississippi Valley, and
Kessleria (later called *Pseudoscaphirhynchus*), in Central Asia
alone   Most of the species belong to the genus *Acipenser*, which
abounds in all the rivers and seas in which salmon are found.
Some of the smaller species spend their lives in the rivers, ascend-

ing smaller streams to spawn   Other sturgeons are marine,
ascending fresh waters only for a moderate distance in the
spawning season   They range in length from 2½ to 30 feet

All are used as food, although the flesh is rather coarse
and beefy   From their large size and abundance they possess
great economic value   The eggs of some species are prepared
as caviar

The sturgeons are sluggish, clumsy, bottom-feeding fish.
The mouth, underneath the long snout, is very protractile,
sucker-like, and without teeth   Before it on the under side
of the snout are four long feelers   Ordinarily the sturgeon feeds
on mud and snails with other small creatures, but I have seen

FIG 189 —Common Sturgeon, *Acipenser sturio* Mitchill   Potomac River

large numbers of Eulachon (*Thaleichthys*) in the stomach of
the Columbia River sturgeon (*Acipenser transmontanus*)   This
fish and the Eulachon run in the Columbia at the same time,
and the sucker-mouth of a large sturgeon will draw into it numbers of small fishes who may be unsuspiciously engaged in
depositing their spawn   In the spawning season in June these
clumsy fishes will often leap wholly out of the water in their
play   The sturgeons have a rough skin besides five series of
bony plates which change much with age and which in very
old examples are sometimes lost or absorbed in the skin   The
common sturgeon of the Atlantic on both shores is *Acipenser
sturio   Acipenser huso* and numerous other species are found
in Russia and Siberia   The great sturgeon of the Columbia
is *Acipenser transmontanus*, and the great sturgeon of Japan
Acipenser kikuchii   Smaller species are found farther south,
as in the Mediterranean and along the the Carolina coast   Other
small species abound in rivers and lakes   *Acipenser rubicundus*
is found throughout the Great Lake region and the Mississippi
Valley, never entering the sea   It is four to six feet long, and
at Sandusky, Ohio, in one season 14,000 sturgeons were taken

in the pound nets. A similar species, *Acipenser mikado*, is abundant and valuable in the streams of northern Japan

FIG 190 —Lake Sturgeon, *Acipenser rubicundus* Le Sueur. Ecorse, Mich

In the genus *Acipenser* the snout is sharp and conical, and the shark-like spiracle is still retained

The shovel-nosed sturgeon (*Scaphirhynchus platyrhynchus*) has lost the spiracles, the tail is more slender, its surface wholly bony, and the snout is broad and shaped like a shovel. The single species of *Scaphirhynchus* abounds in the Mississippi

FIG 191 —Shovel-nosed Sturgeon *Scaphirhynchus platyrhynchus* (Rafinesque) Ohio River

Valley, a fish more interesting to the naturalist than to the fisherman It is the smallest of our sturgeons, often taken in the nets in large numbers

In *Scaphyrhynchus* the tail is covered by a continuous coat of mail In *Kessleria* * *jedtschenkoi*, *rossikowi*, and other Asiatic species the tail is not mailed

Order Selachostomi· the Paddle-fishes. — Another type of Ganoids, allied to the sturgeons, perhaps still further degenerate, is that of the paddle-fishes, called by Cope *Selachostomi* (σέλαχος, shark, στόμα, mouth) This group consists of a single family, *Polyodontidæ*, having apparently little in common with the other Ganoids, and in appearance still more suggestive of the sharks The common name of paddle-fishes is derived from the long flat blade in which the snout terminates This extends far beyond the mouth, is more or less sensitive, and is

---

* These species have also been named *Pseudoscaphirhynchus* *Kessleria* is the earlier name, left undefined by its describer, although the type was indicated

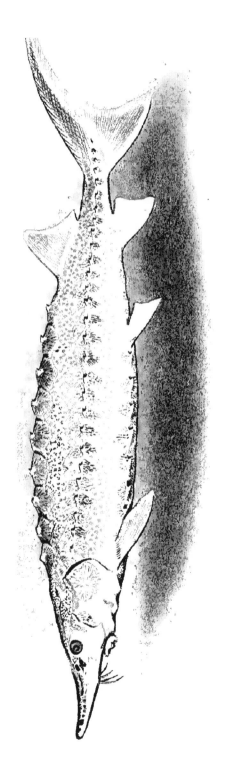

STURGEON (ACIPENSER STURIO)

used to stir up the mud in which are found the minute organisms on which the fish feeds   Under the paddle are four very minute

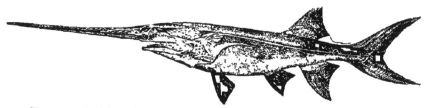

Fig 192 —Paddle-fish, *Polyodon spathula* (Walbaum)   Ohio River

barbels corresponding to those of the sturgeons   The vernacular names of spoonbill, duckbill cat, and shovel-fish are also derived from the form of the snout   The skin is nearly smooth, the tail is heterocercal, the teeth are very small, and a long fleshy flap covers the gill-opening   The very long and slender gill-rakers

Fig 193 —Paddle-fish *Polyodon spathula* (Walbaum)   Ohio River

serve to strain the food (worms, leeches, water-beetles, crustaceans, and algæ) from the muddy waters from which they are taken   The most important part of this diet consists of Entomostracans   The single American species, *Polyodon spathula*, abounds through the Mississippi Valley in all the larger streams   It reaches a length of three or four feet   It is often taken in the nets, but the coarse tough flesh, like that of our inferior catfish, is not much esteemed   In the great rivers of China, the Yangtse and the Hoang Ho, is a second species,

Fig 194 —*Psephurus gladius* Gunther   Yangtse River   (After Gunther)

Psephurus gladius, with narrower snout, fewer gill-rakers, and much coarser fulcra on the tail   The habits, so far as known, are much the same

Crossopholis magnicaudatus of the Green River Eocene shales is a primitive member of the *Polyodontidæ*   Its rostral blade is shorter than that of *Polyodon*, and the body is covered with small thin scales, each in the form of a small grooved disk with several posterior denticulations, arranged in oblique series but not in contact The scales are quadrate in form, and more widely separated anteriorly than posteriorly As in *Polyodon*, the teeth are minute and there are no branchiostegals The squamation of this fish shows that *Polyodon* as well as *Acipenser* may have sprung from a type having rhombic scales The tail of a Cretaceous fish, *Pholidurus disjectus* from the Cretaceous of Europe, has been referred with doubt to this family of *Polyodontidæ*.

Order Pycnodonti —In the extinct order *Pycnodonti*, as recognized by Dr O P Hay, the notochord is persistent and without ossification, the body is very deep, the teeth are always

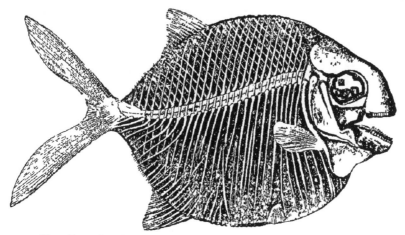

FIG 195—*Gyrodus hexagonus* Agassiz Family *Pycnodontidæ*
Lithographic Shales

blunt, the opercular apparatus is reduced, the dorsal fin many-rayed, and the fins without fulcra The scales are rhombic, but are sometimes wanting, at least on the tail Many genera and species of *Pycnodontidæ* are described, mostly from Triassic and Jurassic rocks of Europe Leading European genera are *Pycnodus*, *Typodus* (*Mesodon*), *Gyrodus*, and *Palæobalistum* The numerous American species belong to *Typodus*, *Cœlodus*, *Pycnodus*, *Hadrodus*, and *Uranoplosus* These forms have no affinity with *Balistes*, although there is some resemblance in appearance, which has suggested the name of *Palæobalistum*.

Woodward places these fishes with the *Semionotidæ* and *Halecomorphi* in his suborder of *Protospondyli*. It seems preferable, however, to consider them as forming a distinct order.

Order Lepidostei.—We may place, following Eastman's edition of Zittel, the allies and predecessors of the garpike in a single order, for which Huxley's name *Lepidostei* may well be used. In this group the notochord is persistent, and the vertebræ are in various degrees of ossification and of different forms. The

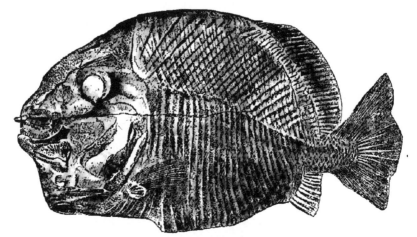

Fig. 196.—*Mesturus verrucosus* Wagner. Family *Pycnodontidæ*. (After Woodward.)

opercles are usually complete, the branchiostegals present, and there is often a gular plate. There is no infraclavicle and the jaws have sharp teeth. The fins have fulcra, and the supports of the fins agree in number with the rays. The tail is more or less heterocercal. The scales are rhombic, arranged in oblique series, which are often united above and below with peg-and-socket articulations. This group contains among recent fishes only the garpikes (*Lepisosteus*).

Family Lepisosteidæ.—The family of *Lepisosteidæ*, constituting the suborder *Ginglymodi* (γιγγλυμός, hinge), is characterized especially by the form of the vertebræ.

These are opisthocœlian, convex in front and concave behind, as in reptiles, being connected by ball-and-socket joints. The tail is moderately heterocercal, less so than in the *Halecomorphi*, and the body is covered with very hard, diamond-shaped, enameled scales in structure similar to that of the teeth A number of peculiar characters are shown by these fishes, some of them having often been regarded as reptilian traits Notable features are the elongate, crocodile-like jaws, the upper the longer, and both armed with strong teeth The mandible is without presymphysial bone The fins are small with large fulcra, and the scales are nearly uniform in size

All the species belong to a single family, *Lepisosteidæ*, which includes the modern garpikes and their immediate relatives, some of which occur in the early Tertiary These voracious fishes are characterized by long and slender cylindrical bodies, with enameled scales and mailed heads and heterocercal tail The teeth are sharp and unequal The skeleton is well ossified, and the animal itself is extremely voracious The vertebræ, reptile-like, are opisthocœlian, that is, convex in front, concave behind, forming ball-and-socket joints In almost all other fishes they are amphicœlian or double-concave, the interspace filled with gelatinous substance The recent species, and perhaps all the extinct species also, belong to the single genus *Lepisosteus* (more correctly, but also more recently, spelled *Lepidosteus*) Of existing forms there are not many species, three to five at the most, and they swarm in the lakes, bayous, and sluggish streams from Lake Champlain to Cuba and along the coast to Central America The best known of the species is the long-nosed garpike, *Lepisosteus osseus*, which is found throughout most of the Great Lake region and the Mississippi Valley, and in which the long and slender jaws are much longer than the rest of the head The garpike frequents quiet waters and is apparently of sleepy habit It often lies quiet for a long time, carried around and around by the eddies It does not readily take the hook and seldom feeds in the aquarium It feeds on crayfishes and small fishes, to which it is exceedingly destructive, as its bad reputation indicates Fishermen everywhere destroy it without mercy Its flesh is rank and tough and unfit even for dogs

In the young garpike the caudal fin appears as a second dorsal and anal, the filamentous tip of the tail passing through and beyond it

The short-nosed garpike, *Lepisosteus platystomus*, is generally common throughout the Mississippi Valley It has a short broad snout like the alligator gar, but seldom exceeds three feet in length In size, color, and habits it agrees closely with the common gar, differing only in the form of the snout. The form is subject to much variation, and it is possible that two or more species have been confounded

The great alligator-gar, *Lepisosteus tristœchus*, reaches a length of twenty feet or more, and is a notable inhabitant of the streams about the Gulf of Mexico Its snout is broad and relatively wide, and its teeth are very strong It is very destructive to all sorts of food-fishes Its flesh is worthless, and its enameled scales resist a spear or sometimes even shot

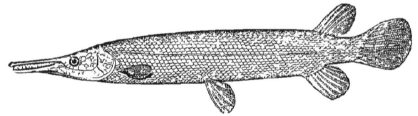

FIG 197.—Alligator-gar, *Lepisosteus tristœchus* (Bloch) Cuba

It breathes air to a certain extent by its lungs, but soon dies in foul water, not having the tenacity of life seen in *Amia*

Order Halecomorphi.—To this order belong the allies, living or extinct, of the bowfin (*Amia*), having for the most part cycloid scales and vertebræ approaching those of ordinary fishes The resemblance to the *Isospondyli*, or herring group, is indicated in the name (Halec, a herring, μορφή, form) The notochord is persistent, the vertebræ variously ossified The opercles are always complete The branchiostegals are broad and there is always a gular plate The teeth are pointed, usually strong There is no infraclavicle Fulcra are present or absent The supports of the dorsal and anal are equal in number to the rays Tail heterocercal Scales thin, mostly cycloid, but bony at base, not jointed with each other Mandible complex, with well-developed splenial rising into a coronoid process, which is completed by a distinct coronoid bone Pectoral fin with more than five actinosts, scales ganoid or cycloid In the living forms the air-bladder is connected with the œsophagus through life, optic chiasma present, intestine with a spiral valve

The Bowfins· Amiidæ.—The *Amiidæ* have the vertebræ more complete The dorsal fin is many-rayed and is without distinct fulcra The diamond-shaped enameled scales disappear, giving place to cycloid scales, which gradually become thin and membranous in structure A median gular plate is developed between the branchiostegals The tail is moderately heterocercal, and the head covered with a bony coat of mail

The family of *Amiidæ* contains a single recent species, *Amia calva*, the only living member of the order *Haleconiorphi*. The bowfin, or grindle, is a remarkable fish abounding in the lakes and swamps of the Mississippi Valley, the Great Lake region, and southward to Virginia, where it is known by the imposing but unexplained title of John A Grindle In the Great Lakes it is usually called "dogfish," because even the dogs will not eat it, and "lawyer," because, according to Dr Kirtland, "it will bite at anything and is good for nothing when caught "

The bowfin reaches a length of two and one half feet, the male being smaller than the female and marked by an ocellated black spot on the tail Both sexes are dark mottled green in

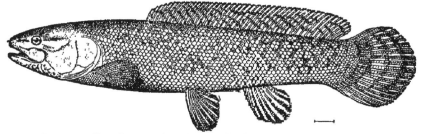

Fig 198 —Bowfin (female), *Amia calva* Linnæus Lake Michigan

color The flesh of the species is very watery, pasty, much of the substance evaporating when exposed to the air. It is ill-flavored, and is not often used as food. The species is very voracious and extremely tenacious of life Its well-developed lung enables it to breathe even when out of the water, and it will live in the air longer than any other fish of American waters, longer even than the horned pout (*Amciurus*) or the mud-minnow (*Umbra*) As a game fish the grindle is one of the very best, if the angler does not care·for the flesh of what he catches, it being one of the hardest fighters that ever took the hook

The *Amiidæ* retain many of the Ganoid characters, though approaching more nearly than any other of the Ganoids to the modern herring tribe   For this reason the name *Halecomorphi* (shad-formed) was given to this order by Professor Cope   The gular plate found in Amia and other Ganoids reappears in the herring-like family of *Elopidæ*, which includes the tarpon and the ten-pounder.

CHAPTER XIX

ISOSPONDYLI

THE Subclass Teleostei, or Bony Fishes —The fishes which still remain for discussion constitute the great subclass or series of *Teleostei* (τελεός, true, ὀστέον, bone), or bony fishes   They lack wholly or partly the Ganoid traits, or show them only in the embryo   The tail is slightly, if at all, heterocercal, the actinosts of the pectoral fins are few and large, rarely over five in number, except among the eels, the fulcra disappear, the air-bladder is no longer cellular, except in very rare cases, nor does it assist in respiration   The optic nerves are separate, one running to each eye without crossing   the skeleton is almost entirely bony, the notochord usually disappearing entirely with age, the valves in the arterial bulb are reduced in number, and the spiral valve of the intestines disappears   Traces of each of the Ganoid traits may persist somewhere in some group, but as a whole we see a distinct specialization and a distinct movement toward the fish type, with the loss of characters distinctive of sharks, Dipnoans, and Ganoids   In a general way the skeleton of all Teleosts corresponds with that of the striped bass, and the visceral anatomy is in all cases sufficiently like that of the sunfish (Fig 16)

The mesocoracoid or præcoracoid arch, found in all Ganoids, persists in the less specialized types of bony fishes, although no trace of it is found in the perch-like forms   With all this, there is developed among the bony fishes an infinite variety in details of structure   For this reason the *Teleostei* must be broken into many orders, and these orders are very different in value and in degrees of distinctness, the various groups being joined by numerous and puzzling intergradations

264

Order Isospondyli.—Of the various subordinate groups of bony fishes, there can be no question as to which is most primitive in structure, or as to which stands nearest the orders of Ganoids   Earliest of the bony fishes in geological time is the order of *Isospondyli* (ἴσος, equal, σπόνδυλος, vertebra), contain- the allies, recent or fossil, of the herring and the trout   This order contains those soft-rayed fishes in which the ventral fins are abdominal, a mesocoracoid or precoracoid arch is de- veloped, and the anterior vertebræ are unmodified and essen- tially similar to the others   The orbitosphenoid is present in all typical forms   In certain forms of doubtful affinity (*Iniomi*) the mesocoracoid is wanting or lost in degeneration   Through the *Isospondyli* all the families of fishes yet to be considered are apparently descended, their ancestors being Ganoid fishes and, still farther back, the Crossopterygians

Woodward gives this definition of the *Isospondyli*   ' Noto- chord varying in persistence, the vertebral centra usually com- plete, but none coalesced, tail homocercal, but hæmal supports not much expanded or fused   Symplectic bone present, mandible simple, each dentary consisting only of two elements (dentary and articulo-angular), with rare rudiments of a splenoid on the inner side   Pectoral arch suspended from the cranium, pre- coracoid (mesocoracoid) arch present, infraclavicular plates wanting   Pelvic (ventral) fins abdominal   Scales ganoid only in the less specialized families   In the living forms air-bladder connected with the œsophagus in the adult, optic nerves decus- sating (without chiasma), and intestine either wanting spiral valve or with an incomplete representative of it "

The Classification of the Bony Fishes.—The classification of fishes has been greatly complicated by the variety of names applied to groups which are substantially but not quite identical one with another   The difference in these schemes of classi- fication lies in the point of view   In all cases a single character must be brought to the front, such characters never stand quite alone, and to lay emphasis on another character is to make an alteration large or small in the name or in the bounda- ries of a class or order   Thus the *Ostariophysi* with the *Iso- spondyli, Haplomi*, and a few minor groups make up the great division of the *Abdominales*   These are fishes in which the

ventral fins are abdominal, that is, inserted backward, so that
the pelvis is free from the clavicle, the two sets of limbs being
attached to different parts of the skeleton   Most of the abdominal fishes are also soft-rayed fishes, that is, without con-
secutive spines in the dorsal and anal fins, and they show a number
of other archaic peculiarities   The Malacopterygians ($\mu\alpha\lambda\alpha\kappa\acute{o}s$,
soft, $\pi\tau\epsilon\rho\acute{v}\xi$, fin) of Cuvier therefore correspond very nearly
to the *Abdominales*   But they are not quite the same, as the
spiny-rayed barracudas and mullets have abdominal ventrals,
and many unquestioned thoracic or jugular fishes, as the sea-
snails and brotulids, have lost, through degeneration, all of their
fin-spines

In nearly but not quite all of the Abdominal fishes the
slender tube connecting the air-bladder with the œsophagus
persists through life   This character defines Muller's order
of *Physostomi* ($\phi v\sigma\acute{o}s$, bladder, $\sigma\tau\acute{o}\mu\alpha$, mouth), as opposed to
his *Physoclysti* ($\phi v\sigma\acute{o}s$, bladder, $\kappa\lambda\epsilon\tilde{\iota}\sigma\tau\acute{o}s$, closed), in which this
tube is present in the embryo or larva only   Thus the *Thoracices*
and *Jugulares*, or fishes having the ventrals thoracic or jugular,
together correspond almost exactly to the Acanthopterygians,
($\alpha\kappa\alpha\nu\theta\alpha$, spine, $\pi\tau\epsilon\rho\acute{v}\xi$, fin), or spiny-rayed fishes of Cuvier, or to
the *Physoclysti* of Muller   The Malacopterygians, the *Abdomi-
nales*, and the *Physostomi* are in the same way practically
identical groups   As the spiny-rayed fishes have mostly ctenoid
scales, and the soft-rayed fishes cycloid scales, the *Physostomi*
correspond roughly to Agassiz's *Cycloidei*, and the *Physoclysti*
to his *Ctenoidei*

But in none of these cases is the correspondence perfectly
exact, and in any system of classification we must choose characters for primary divisions so ancient and therefore so permanent as to leave no room for exceptions   The extraordinary
difficulty of doing this, with the presence of most puzzling
intergradations, has led Dr Gill to suggest that the great body
of bony fishes, soft-rayed and spiny-rayed, abdominal, thoracic,
and jugular alike, be placed in a single great order which he
calls *Teleocephali* ($\tau\epsilon\lambda\epsilon\acute{o}s$, perfect, $\kappa\epsilon\phi\alpha\lambda\acute{\eta}$, head)   The aberrant
forms with defective skull and membrane-bones he would sepa-
rate as minor offshoots from this great mass with the name
of separate orders   But while the divisions of *Teleocephali*

are not strongly differentiated, their distinctive characters are real, ancient, and important, while those of the aberrant groups, called orders by Gill (as *Plectognathi, Pediculati, Hemibranchii*), are relatively modern and superficial, which is one reason why they are more easily defined There seems to us no special advantage in the retention of a central order *Teleocephali*, from which the divergent branches are separated as distinct orders.

While our knowledge of the osteology and embryology of most of the families of fishes is very incomplete, it is evident that the relationships of the groups cannot be shown in any linear series or by any conceivable arrangement of orders and suborders The living teleost fishes have sprung from many lines of descent, their relationships are extremely diverse, and their differences are of every possible degree of value The ordinary schemes have magnified the value of a few common characters, at the same time neglecting other differences of equal value No system of arrangement which throws these fishes into large groups can ever be definite or permanent

Relationships of Isospondyli —For our purposes we may divide the physostomous fishes as understood by Müller into several orders, the most primitive, the most generalized, and economically the most important being the order of *Isospondyli* This order contains those bony fishes which have the anterior vertebræ unaltered (as distinguished from the *Ostariophysi*), the skull relatively complete, or at least not eel-like, the mesocoracoid typically developed, but atrophied in deep-sea forms and finally lost, the orbitosphenoid present In all the species the ventral fins are abdominal and normally composed of more than six rays, the air-duct is developed The scales are chiefly cycloid and the fins are without true spines In many ways the order is more primitive than *Nematognathi, Plectospondyli*, or *Apodes* It is certain that it began earlier in geological time than any of these On the other hand, the *Isospondyli* are closely connected through the *Berycoidei* with the highly specialized fishes The continuity of the natural series is therefore interrupted by the interposition of the side branches of Ostariophysans and eels before considering the *Haplomi* and the other transitional forms The forms called *Iniomi*, which lack the mesocoracoid and the orbitosphenoid, have been lately transferred to the *Haplomi* by Boulenger   This arrangement is probably a step in advance

Ganoid traits are present in certain families of *Isospondyli* Among these are the gular plate (found in *Amia* and the *Elopidæ*), doubtless derived from the similar structure in earlier Ganoids, additional valves in the arterial bulb in the cellular air-bladder of *Notopterus* and *Osteoglossum*, the spiral intestinal valve in *Churocentridæ*, and the ganoid scales of the extinct *Leptolepidæ*.

The Clupeoidea —The *Isospondyli* are divisible into numerous families, which may be grouped roughly under three subdivisions, *Clupeoidea*, the herring-like forms, the *Salmonoidea*, the trout-like forms, and the *Iniomi*, or lantern-fishes, and their allies   The last-named group should probably be removed from the order of *Isospondyli*.   In the *Clupeoidea*, the allies of the great family of the herring, the shoulder-girdle is normally developed, retaining the mesocoracoid arch on its inner edge, and through the post-temporal is articulated above with the cranium   The fishes in this group lack the adipose fin which is characteristic of most of the higher or salmon-like families

The Leptolepidæ.—Most primitive of the *Isospondyli* is the extinct family of *Leptolepidæ*, closely allied to the Ganoid families of *Pholidophoridæ* and *Oligopleuridæ*   It is composed of graceful,

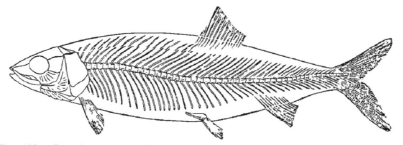

Fig 199 —*Lept lepis dubius* Blainville, Lithographic Stone   (After Woodward)

herring-like fishes, with the bones of the head thin but covered with enamel, and the scales thin but firm and enameled on their free portion   There are no fulcra and there is no lateral line The vertebræ are well developed, but always pierced by the notochord   The genera are *Lycoptera, Leptolepis, Æthalion,* and *Thrissops*   In *Lycoptera* of the Jurassic of China the vertebral centra are feebly developed, and the dorsal fin short and posterior. In *Leptolepis* the anal is short and placed behind the dorsal. There are many species, mostly from the Triassic and lithographic shales of Europe, one being found in the Cretaceous. *Leptolepis coryphænoides* and *Leptolepis dubius* arc among the more common species. *Æthalion (knorri)* differs in the form of the jaws. In *Thrissops* the anal fin is long and opposite the dorsal. *Thrissops salmonea* is found in the lithographic stone, *Thrissops exigua* in the Cretaceous. In all these early forms there is a hard casque over the brain-cavity, as in the living types, *Amia* and *Osteoglossum*.

The Elopidæ.—The family of *Elopidæ* contains large fishes herring-like in form and structure, but having a flat membrane-

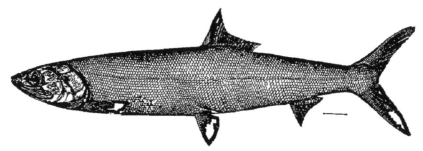

Fig 200.—Ten-pounder, *Elops saurus* L. An ally of the earliest bony fishes Virginia

bone or gular plate between the branches of the lower jaw, as in the Ganoid genus *Amia*. The living species are few, abounding in the tropical seas, important for their size and numbers,

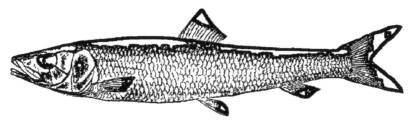

Fig 201.—A primitive Herring-like fish, *Holcolepis lewesiensis*, Mantell, restored Family *Elopidæ* English Chalk (After Woodward)

though not valued as food-fishes save to those who, like the Hawaiians and Japanese, eat fishes raw. These people prefer for that purpose the white-meated or soft-fleshed forms like *Elops* or *Scarus* to those which yield a better flavor when cooked

The ten-pounder (*Elops saurus*), pike-like in form but with very weak teeth, is found in tropical America *Elops machnata*, the jackmariddle, the awaawa of the Hawaiians, abounding in the Pacific, is scarcely if at all different

The tarpon, called also grande écaille, silver-king, and sabalo (*Tarpon atlanticus*), is a favorite game-fish along the coasts of Florida and Carolina   It takes the hook with great spirit, and

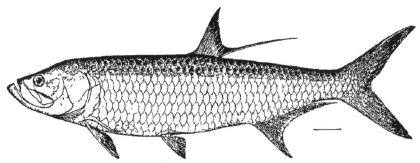

Fig 202 —Tarpon or Grande Écaille, *Tarpon atlanticus* Cuv & Val   Florida

as it reaches a length of six feet or more it affords much excitement to the successful angler   The very large scales are much used in ornamental work

A similar species of smaller size, also with the last ray of the dorsal very much produced, is *Megalops cyprinoides* of the East Indies   Other species occur in the South Seas

Numerous fossil genera related to *Elops* are found in the Cretaceous and Tertiary rocks   *Holcolepis lewesiensis* (wrongly called *Osmeroides*) is the best-known European species   Numerous species are referred to *Elopopsis*   *Megalops prisca* and species of *Elops* also occur in the London Eocene

In all these the large parietals meet along the median line of the skull   In the closely related family of *Spaniodontidæ* the parietals are small and do not meet   All the species of this group, united by Woodward with the *Elopidæ*, are extinct These fishes preceded the *Elopidæ* in the Cretaceous period Leading genera are *Thrissopater* and *Spaniodon*, the latter armed with large teeth. *Spaniodon blondeli* is from the Cretaceous of Mount Lebanon Many other species are found in the European and American Cretaceous rocks, but are known from imperfect specimens only

Sardinius, an American Cretaceous fossil herring, may stand near *Spaniodon Rhacolepis buccalis* and *Notelops brama* are found in Brazil, beautifully preserved in concretions of calcareous mud supposed to be of Cretaceous age

The extinct family of *Pachyrhizodontidæ* is perhaps allied to the *Elopidæ*. Numerous species of *Pachyrhizodus* are found in the Cretaceous of southern England and of Kansas

The Albulidæ.—The *Albulidæ*, or lady-fishes, characterized by the blunt and rounded teeth, are found in most warm seas

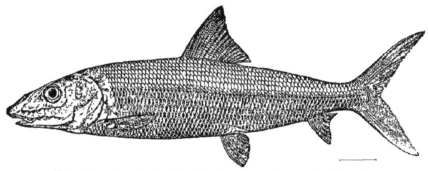

FIG 203 —The Lady-fish, *Albula vulpes* (Linnæus) Florida

Albula vulpes is a brilliantly silvery fish, little valued as food The metamorphosis which the lava undergoes is very remarkable It is probably, however, more or less typical of the changes which take place with soft-rayed fishes generally, though more strongly marked in *Albula* and in certain eels than in most related forms Fossils allied to *Albula, Albula oweni, Chanoides macropomus* are found in the Eocene of Europe, *Syntegmodus altus* in the Cretaceous of Kansas In *Chanoides*, the most primitive genus, the teeth are much fewer than in *Albula Plethodus* and *Thryptodus*, with peculiar dental plates on the roof and floor of the mouth, probably constitute a distinct family, *Thryptodontidæ* The species are found in European and American rocks, but are known from imperfect specimens only.

The Chanidæ.—The *Chanidæ*, or milkfishes, constitute another small archaic type, found in the tropical Pacific They are large, brilliantly silvery, toothless fishes, looking like enormous dace, swift in the water, and very abundant in the Gulf of

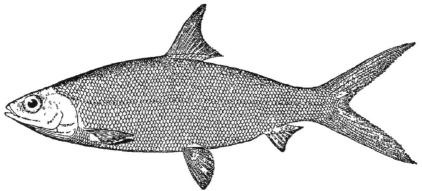

Fig 204 —Milkfish, *Chanos chanos* (L)   Mazatlan

California, Polynesia, and India The single living species is the *Awa*, or milkfish, *Chanos chanos*, largely used as food in Hawaii Species of *Prochanos* and *Chanos* occur in the Cretaceous, Eocene, and Miocene Allied to *Chanos* is the Cretaceous genus *Ancylostylos* (*gibbus*), probably the type of a distinct family, toothless and with many-rayed dorsal

The Hiodontidæ.—The *Hiodontidæ*, or mooneyes, inhabit the rivers of the central portion of the United States and Canada.

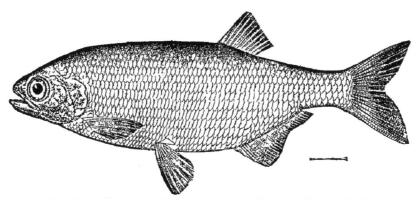

Fig 205 —Mooneye, *Hiodon tergisus* Le Sueur   Ecorse, Mich

They are shad-like fishes with brilliantly silvery scales and very strong sharp teeth, those on the tongue especially long They are very handsome fishes and take the hook with spirit, but the flesh is rather tasteless and full of small bones, much like that of the milkfish The commonest species is *Hiodon tergisus*. No fossil *Hiodontidæ* are known

The Pterothrissidæ.—The *Pterothrissidæ* are sea-fishes like *Albula*, but more slender and with a long dorsal fin They live

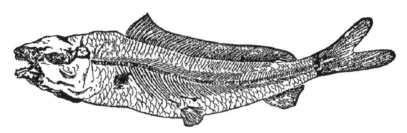

Fig 206 —*Istieus grandis* Agassiz Family *Pterothrissidæ* (After Zittel)

in deep or cold waters along the coasts of Japan, where they are known as gisu The single species is *Pterothrissus gissu* The fossil genus *Istieus*, from the Upper Cretaceous, probably belongs near the *Pterothrissidæ* *Istieus grandis* is the best-known

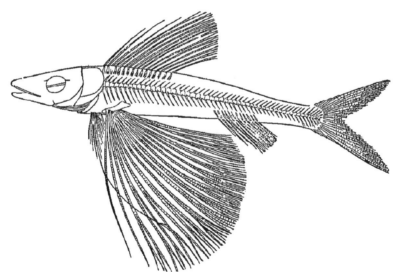

Fig 207 —*Chirothrix libanicus* Pictet & Humbert Cretaceous of Mt Lebanon
(After Woodward)

species. Another ancient family, now represented by a single species, is that of the *Chirocentridæ*, of which the living type is *Chirocentrus dorab*, a long, slender, much compressed herring-like fish, with a saw-edge on the belly, found in the East Indies, in which region *Chirocentrus polyodon* occurs as a fossil. Numerous fossil genera related to *Chirocentrus* are enumerated by Woodward, most of them to be referred to the related family of *Ichthyodectidæ (Saurodontidæ)*. Of these, *Portheus, Ichthyodectes, Saurocephalus (Saurodon)*, and *Gillicus* are represented by numerous species, some of them fishes of immense size and great voracity. *Portheus molossus*, found in the Cretaceous of Nebraska, is remarkable for its very strong teeth. Species of other genera are represented by numerous species in the Cretaceous of both the Rocky Mountain region and of Europe.

The Ctenothrissidæ.—A related family, *Ctenothrissidæ*, is represented solely by extinct Cretaceous species. In this group

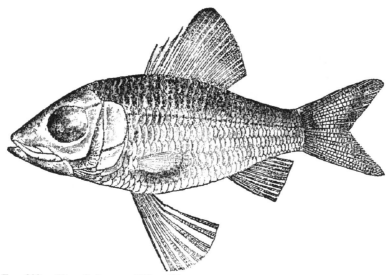

Fɪɢ. 208.—*Ctenothrissa vexillifera* Pictet, restored. Mt. Lebanon Cretaceous. (After Woodward.)

the body is robust with large scales, ctenoid in *Ctenothrissa*, cycloid in *Aulolepis*. The fins are large, the belly not serrated, and the teeth feeble. *Ctenothrissa vexillifera* is from Mount Lebanon. Other species occur in the European chalk. In the small family of *Phractolæmidæ* the interopercle, according to Boulenger, is enormously developed.

The Notopteridæ.—The *Notopteridæ* is another small family in the rivers of Africa and the East Indies. The body ends in a long and tapering fin, and, as usual in fishes which swim by body undulations, the ventral fins are lost   The belly is doubly serrate   The air-bladder is highly complex in structure, being divided into several compartments and terminating in two horns anteriorly and posteriorly, the anterior horns being in direct communication with the auditory organ   A fossil *Notopterus*, *N primævus*, is found in the same region

The Clupeidæ.—The great herring family, or *Clupeidæ*, comprises fishes with oblong or herring-shaped body, cycloid scales, and feeble dentition   From related families it is separated by the absence of lateral line and the division of the maxillary into three pieces   In most of the genera the belly ends in a serrated edge, though in the true herring this is not very evident,

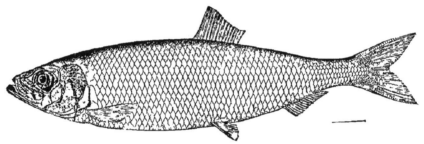

Fig 209 --Herring, *Clupea harengus* L   New York

and in some the belly has a blunt edge   Some of the species live in rivers, some ascend from the sea for the purpose of spawning   The majority are confined to the ocean   Among all the genera, the one most abundant in individuals is that of *Clupea*, the herring   Throughout the North Atlantic are immense schools of *Clupea harengus*   In the North Pacific on both shores another herring, *Clupea pallasi*, is equally abundant, and with the same market it would be equally valuable   As salted, dried, or smoked fish the herring is found throughout the civilized world, and its spawning and feeding-grounds have determined the location of cities.

The genus *Clupea*, of northern distribution, has the vertebræ in increased number (56), and there are weak teeth on the vomer. Several other genera are very closely related, but ranging farther south they have, with other characters, fewer (46 to 50) vertebræ The alewife, or branch-herring (*Pomolobus pseudoharengus*), ascends the rivers to spawn and has become land-locked in the lakes of New York   The skipjack of the Gulf of Mexico, *Pomolobus chrysochloris*, becomes very fat in the sea   The species becomes land-locked in the Ohio River, where it thrives as to numbers, but remains lean and almost useless as food   The glut-herring, *Pomolobus æstivalis*, and the sprat, *Pomolobus sprattus*, of Europe are related forms

Very near also to the herring is the shad (*Alosa sapidissima*) of the eastern coasts of America, and its inferior relatives, the

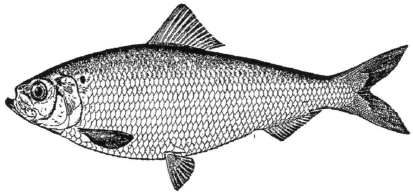

FIG 210 —Alewife, *Pomolobus pseudoharengus* (Wilson)   Potomac River

shad of the Gulf of Mexico (*Alosa alabamæ*), the Ohio River shad (*Alosa ohiensis*), very lately discovered, the Allice shad (*Alosa alosa*) of Europe, and the Thwaite shad (*Alosa finta*) In the genus *Alosa* the cheek region is very deep, giving the head a form different from that seen in the herring

The American shad is the best food-fish in the family, peculiarly delicate in flavor when broiled, but, to a greater degree than occurs in any other good food-fish, its flesh is crowded with small bones   The shad has been successfully introduced into the waters of California, where it abounds from Puget Sound to Point Concepcion, ascending the rivers to spawn in May as in its native region, the Atlantic coast

The genus *Sardinella* includes species of rich flesh and feeble skeleton, excellent when broiled, when they may be eaten bones and all   This condition favors their preservation in oil as "sardines"   All the species are alike excellent for this purpose   The sardine of Europe is the *Sardinella pilchardus*, known in England as the pilchard   The "Sardina de España" of

Cuba is *Sardinella pseudohispanica*, the sardine of California, *Sardinella cærulea Sardinella sagax* abounds in Chile, and *Sardinella melanosticta* is the valued sardine of Japan

In the tropical Pacific occur other valued species, largely belonging to the genus *Kowala* The genus *Harengula* contains small species with very large, firm scales which do not fall when touched, as is generally the case with the sardines Most common of these is *Harengula sardina* of the West Indies Similar species occur in southern Europe and in Japan

In *Opisthonema*, the thread-herring, the last dorsal ray is much produced, as in the gizzard-shad and the tarpon The two species known are abundant, but of little commercial importance Of greater value are the menhaden, or the moss-bunker, *Brevoortia tyrannus*, inhabiting the sandy coasts from New England southward It is a coarse and bony fish, rarely

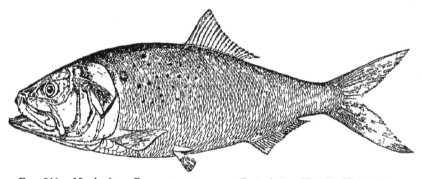

Fig 211 —Menhaden, *Brevoortia tyrannus* (Latrobe). Wood's Hole, Mass.

eaten when adult, although the young in oil makes acceptable sardines It is used chiefly for oil, the annual yield exceeding in value that of whale-oil The refuse is used as manure, a purpose for which the fishes are often taken without preparation, being carried directly to the cornfields From its abundance this species of inferior flesh exceeds in commercial value almost all other American fishes excepting the cod, the herring, and the quinnat salmon

One of the most complete of fish biographies is that of Dr G Brown Goode on the "Natural and Economic History of Menhaden"

Numerous other herring-like forms, usually with compressed bodies, dry and bony flesh, and serrated bellies, abound in the tropics and are largely salted and dried by the Chinese   Among these are *Ilisha elongata* of the Chinese coast   Related forms occur in Mexico and Brazil

The round herrings, small herrings which have no serrations on the belly, are referred by Dr Gill to the family of *Dussumieridæ*   These are mostly small tropical fishes used as food or bait   One of these, the Kobini-Iwashi of Japan (*Stolephorus japonicus*), with a very bright silver band on the side, has considerable commercial importance   Very small herrings of this type in the West Indies constitute the genus *Jenkinsia*, named for Dr. Oliver P Jenkins, the first to study seriously the fishes of Hawaii. Other species constitute the widely distributed genera *Etrumeus* and *Dussumieria*. *Etrumeus sardina* is the round herring of the Virginia coast   *Etrumeus micropus* is the Etrumei-Iwashi of Japan and Hawaii

Fossil herring are plentiful and exist in considerable variety, even among the *Clupeidæ* as at present restricted   *Histothrissa*

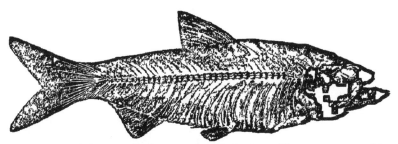

Fig 212 —A fossil Herring, *Diplomystus humilis* Leidy   (From a specimen obtained at Green River Wyo) The scutes along the back lost in the specimen Family *Clupeidæ*

of the Cretaceous seems to be allied to *Dussumieria* and *Stolephorus*   Another genus, from the Cretaceous of Palestine, *Pseudoberyx* (*syriacus*, etc), having pectinated scales, should perhaps constitute a distinct subfamily, but the general structure is like that of the herring   More evidently herring-like is *Scombroclupea* (*macrophthalma*). The genus *Diplomystus*, with enlarged scales along the back, is abundantly represented in the Eocene shales of Green River, Wyoming   Species of similar appearance, usually but wrongly referred to the same genus, occur on the coasts of Peru, Chile, and New South Wales A specimen of *Diplomystus humilis* from Green River is here figured. Numerous herring, referred to *Clupea*, but belonging rather to *Pomolobus*, or other non-Arctic genera, have been described from the Eocene and later rocks

Several American fossil herring-like fishes, of the genus *Leptosomus*, as *Leptosomus percrassus*, are found in the Cretaceous of South Dakota

Fossil species doubtfully referred to *Dorosoma*, but perhaps allied rather to the thread-herring (*Opisthonema*), being herrings with a prolonged dorsal ray, are recorded from the early Tertiary of Europe Among these is *Opisthonema doljeanum* from Austria.

The Dorosomatidæ — The gizzard-shad, *Dorosomatidæ*, are closely related to the *Clupeidæ*, differing in the small contracted toothless mouth and reduced maxillary. The species are deep-bodied, shad-like fishes of the rivers and estuaries of eastern America and eastern Asia. They feed on mud, and the stomach is thickened and muscular like that of a fowl As the stomach has the size and form of a hickory-nut, the common American

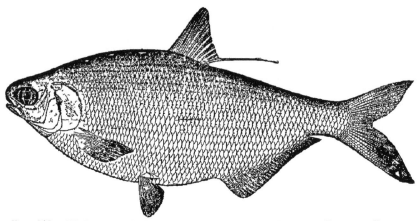

FIG. 213 —Hickory-shad, *Dorosoma cepedianum* (Le Sueur) Potomac River

species is often called hickory-shad The gizzard-shad are all very poor food-fish, bony and little valued, the flesh full of small bones The belly is always serrated In three of the four genera of *Dorosomatidæ* the last dorsal ray is much produced and whip-like The long and slender gill-rakers serve as strainers for the mud in which these fishes find their vegetable and animal food *Dorosoma cepedianum*, the common hickory-shad or gizzard-shad, is found in brackish river-mouths and ponds from Long Island to Texas, and throughout the Mississippi Valley in all the large rivers   Through the canals it has entered Lake Michigan   The Konoshiro, *Clupanodon thrissa*, is equally common in China and Japan

The Engraulididæ.—The anchovies (*Engraulididæ*) are dwarf herrings with the snout projecting beyond the very wide mouth They are small in size and weak in muscle, found in all warm seas, and making a large part of the food of the larger fish. The genus *Engraulis* includes the anchovy of Europe, *Engraulis encrasicholus*, with similar species in California, Chile, Japan, and Australia   In this genus the vertebræ are numerous, the bones feeble, and the flesh tender and oily.   The species of *Engraulis* are preserved in oil, often with spices, or are made into fish-paste, which is valued as a relish   The genus *Anchovia* replaces *Engraulis* in the tropics   The vertebræ are fewer, the

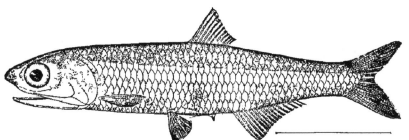

Fig 214.—A Silver Anchovy, *Anchovia perthecata* (Goode & Bean)   Tampa

bones firm and stiff, and the flesh generally dry   Except as food for larger fish, these have little value, although existing in immense schools   Most of the species have a bright silvery band along the side.   The most familiar of the very numerous species is the silver anchovy, *Anchovia browni*, which abounds in sandy bays from Cape Cod to Brazil   Several other genera occur farther southward, as well as in Asia, but *Engraulis* only is found in Europe   Fossil anchovies called *Engraulis* are recorded from the Tertiary of Europe

Gonorhynchidæ—To the *Isospondyli* belongs the small primitive family of *Gonorhynchidæ*, elongate fishes with small mouth, feeble teeth, no air-bladder, small scales of peculiar structure covering the head, weak dentition, the dorsal fin small, and

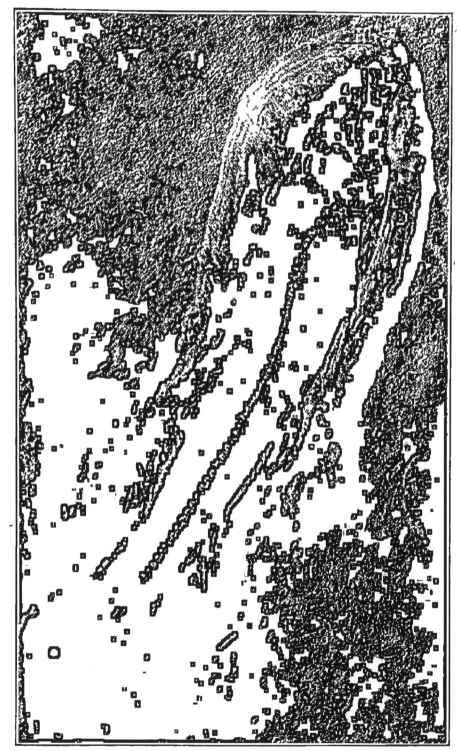

FIG 215 —*Notogoneus osculus* Cope Green River Eocene Family *Gonorhynchdia*

posterior without spines The mesocoracoid is present as in ordinary *Isospondyli* *Gonorhynchus abbreviatus* occurs in Japan, and *Gonorhynchus gonorhynchus* is found in Australia and about the Cape of Good Hope Numerous fossil species occur *Charitosomus lineolatus* and other species are found in the Cretaceous of Mount Lebanon and elsewhere Species without teeth from the Oligocene of Europe and America are referred to the genus *Notogoneus* *Notogoneus osculus* occurs in the Eocene fresh-water deposits at Green River, Wyoming It bears a very strong resemblance in form to an ordinary sucker (*Catostomus*), for which reason it was once described by the name of *Protocatostomus* The living *Gonorhynchidæ* are all strictly marine

In the small family of *Cromeriidæ* the head and body are naked.

The Osteoglossidæ.—Still less closely related to the herring is the family of *Osteoglossidæ*, huge pike-like fishes of the tropical rivers, armed with hard bony scales formed of pieces like mosaic. The largest of all fresh-water fishes is *Arapaima gigas* of the Amazon region, which reaches a length of fifteen feet and a weight of 400 pounds It has naturally considerable commercial importance, as have species of *Osteoglossum*, coarse river-fishes which occur in Brazil, Egypt, and the East Indies. *Heterotis nilotica* is a large fish of the Nile In some or all of these the air-bladder is cellular or lung-like, like that of a Ganoid

Allied to the *Osteoglossidæ* is *Phareodus* (*Dapedoglossus*), a group of large shad-like fossil fishes, with large scales of peculiar mosaic texture and with a bony casque on the head, found in fresh-water deposits of the Green River Eocene In the perfect specimens of *Phareodus* (or *Dapedoglossus*) *testis* the first ray of the pectoral is much enlarged and serrated on its inner edge, a character which may separate these fishes as a family from the true *Osteoglossidæ* It does not, however, appear in Cope's figures, none of his specimens having the pectorals perfect In these fishes the teeth are very strong and sharp, the scales are very large and thin, looking like the scales of a parrot-fish, the long dorsal is opposite to the anal and similar to it, and the caudal is truncate. The end of the vertebral column is turned upward

Other species are *Phareodus acutus*, known from the jaws; *P. encaustus* is known from a mass of thick scales with reticulate or mosaic-like surface, much as in *Osteoglossum*, and *P. æquipennis* from a small example, perhaps immature.

Fig. 216.—*Phareodus testis* (Cope). From a specimen 20 inches long collected at Fossil, Wyo., in the Museum of the Univ. of Wyoming. (Photograph by Prof. Wilbur C Knight.)

Phareodus testis is frequently found well preserved in the shales at Fossil Station, to the northwestward of Green River. Whether all these species possess the peculiar structure of the scales, and whether all belong to one genus, is uncertain.

In Eocene shales of England occurs *Brychætus muelleri*, a species closely related to *Phareodus*, but the scales smaller and without the characteristic reticulate or mosaic structure seen in *Phareodus encaustus*.

The Pantodontidæ.—The bony casque of *Osteoglossum* is found again in the *Pantodontidæ*, consisting of one species, *Pantodon buchholzi*, a small fish of the brooks of West Africa.

As in the *Osteoglossidæ* and in the *Siluridæ*, the subopercle is wanting in *Pantodon*.

The *Alepocephalidæ* are deep-sea herring-like fishes very soft in texture and black in color, taken in the oceanic abysses. Some species may be found in almost all seas below the depth

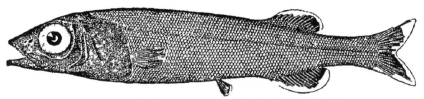

Fig 217 —*Alepocephalus agassizii* Goode & Bean   Gulf Stream

of half a mile   *Alepocephalus rostratus* of the Mediterranean has been long known, but most of the other genera, *Talismania, Mitchillina, Conocara*, etc , are of very recent discovery, having been brought to the surface by the deep-sea dredging of the *Challenger*, the *Albatross*, the *Blake*, the *Travailleur*, the *Talisman*, the *Investigator*, the *Hirondelle*, and the *Violante*

CHAPTER XX

SALMONIDÆ

THE Salmon Family.—The series or suborder *Salmonoidea*, or allies of the salmon and trout, are characterized as a whole by the presence of the adipose fin, a structure also retained in Characins and catfishes, which have no evident affinity with the trout, and in the lantern-fishes, lizard-fishes, and trout-perches, in which the affinity is very remote Probably these groups all have a common descent from some primitive fish having an adipose fin, or at least a fleshy fold on the back.

Of all the families of fishes, the one most interesting from almost every point of view is that of the *Salmonidæ*, the salmon family. As now restricted, it is not one of the largest families, as it comprises less than a hundred species, but in beauty, activity, gaminess, quality as food, and even in size of individuals, different members of the group stand easily with the first among fishes The following are the chief external characteristics which are common to the members of the family

Body oblong or moderately elongate, covered with cycloid, in scales of varying size Head naked Mouth terminal or somewhat inferior, varying considerably among the different species, those having the mouth largest usually having also the strongest teeth Maxillary provided with a supplemental bone, and forming the lateral margin of the upper jaw Pseudobranchiæ present Gill-rakers varying with the species Opercula complete No barbels Dorsal fin of moderate length, placed near the middle of the length of the body Adipose fin well developed Caudal fin forked Anal fin moderate or rather long Ventral fins nearly median in position Pectoral fins inserted low Lateral line present Outline of belly rounded Vertebræ in large number, usually about sixty

The stomach in all the *Salmonidæ* is siphonal, and at the pylorus are many (15 to 200) comparatively large pyloric cœca. The air-bladder is large The eggs are usually much larger than in fishes generally, and the ovaries are without special duct, the ova falling into the cavity of the abdomen before exclusion The large size of the eggs, their lack of adhesiveness, and the readiness with which they may be impregnated, render the *Salmonidæ* peculiarly adapted for artificial culture

The *Salmonidæ* are peculiar to the north temperate and Arctic regions, and within this range they are almost equally abundant wherever suitable waters occur Some of the species, especially the larger ones, are marine and anadromous, living and growing in the sea, and ascending fresh waters to spawn. Still others live in running brooks, entering lakes or the sea when occasion serves, but not habitually doing so Still others are lake fishes, approaching the shore or entering brooks in the spawning season, at other times retiring to waters of considerable depth Some of them are active, voracious, and gamy, while others are comparatively defenseless and will not take the hook They are divisible into ten easily recognized genera *Coregonus, Argyrosomus, Brachymystax, Stenodus, Oncorhynchus, Salmo, Hucho, Cristivomer, Salvelinus,* and *Plecoglossus*

Fragments of fossil trout, very imperfectly known, are recorded chiefly from Pleistocene deposits of Idaho, under the name of *Rhabdofario lacustris* We have also received from Dr John C Merriam, from ferruginous sands of the same region, several fragments of jaws of salmon, in the hook-nosed condition, with enlarged teeth, showing that the present salmon-runs have been in operation for many thousands of years Most other fragments hitherto referred to *Salmonidæ* belong to some other kind of fish

Coregonus, the Whitefish.—The genus *Coregonus*, which includes the various species known in America as lake whitefish, is distinguishable in general by the small size of its mouth, the weakness of its teeth, and the large size of its scales. The teeth, especially, are either reduced to slight asperities, or else are altogether wanting The species reach a length of one to three feet With scarcely an exception they inhabit clear lakes.

and rarely enter streams except to spawn. In far northern regions they often descend to the sea, but in the latitude of the United States this is never possible for them, as they are unable to endure warm or impure water. They seldom take the hook, and rarely feed on other fishes Numerous local varieties characterize the lakes of Scandinavia, Scotland, and Arctic Asia and America Largest and most desirable of all these as a food-fish is the common whitefish of the Great Lakes (*Coregonus clupeiformis*), with its allies or variants in the Mackenzie and Yukon.

The species of *Coregonus* differ from each other in the form and size of the mouth, in the form of the body, and in the development of the gill-rakers

Coregonus oxyrhynchus—the *Schnabel* of Holland, Germany, and Scandinavia—has the mouth very small, the sharp snout projecting far beyond it. No species similar to this is found in America

The Rocky Mountain whitefish (*Coregonus williamsoni*) has also a small mouth and projecting snout, but the latter is blunter

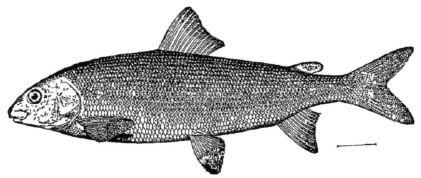

FIG 218 —Rocky Mountain Whitefish, *Coregonus williamsoni* Girard

and much shorter than in *C oxyrhynchus* This is a small species abounding everywhere in the clear lakes and streams of the Rocky Mountains and the Sierra Nevada, from Colorado to Vancouver Island. It is a handsome fish and excellent as food

Closely allied to *Coregonus williamsoni* is the pilot-fish, shad-waiter, roundfish, or Menomonee whitefish (*Coregonus quadrilateralis*). This species is found in the Great Lakes, the Adirondack region, the lakes of New Hampshire, and thence northwestward to the Yukon, abounding in cold deep waters, its range apparently nowhere coinciding with that of *Coregonus williamsoni*

The common whitefish (*Coregonus clupeiformis*) is the largest in size of the species of *Coregonus*, and is unquestionably the finest as an article of food.   It varies considerably in appearance with age and condition, but in general it is proportionately much deeper than any of the other small-mouthed *Coregoni* The adult fishes develop a considerable fleshy hump at the

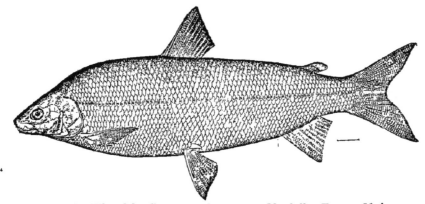

FIG 219 —Whitefish, *Coregonus clupeiformis* Mitchill   Ecorse, Mich

shoulders, which causes the head, which is very small, to appear disproportionately so   The whitefish spawns in November and December, on rocky shoals in the Great Lakes   Its food was ascertained by Dr P R Hoy to consist chiefly of deep-water crustaceans, with a few mollusks, and larvæ of water insects   "The whitefish," writes Mr James W Milner, "has been known since the time of the earliest explorers as pre-eminently a fine-flavored fish   In fact there are few table-fishes its equal   To be appreciated in its fullest excellence it should be taken fresh from the lake and broiled   Father Marquette, Charlevoix, Sir John Richardson—explorers who for months at a time had to depend upon the whitefish for their staple article of food—bore testimony to the fact that they never lost their relish for it, and deemed it a special excellence that the appetite never became cloyed with it "   The range of the whitefish extends from the lakes of New York and New England northward to the Arctic Circle   The "Otsego bass" of Otsego

Lake in New York, celebrated by De Witt Clinton, is a local form of the ordinary whitefish.

Allied to the American whitefish, but smaller in size, is the Lavaret, Weissfisch, Adelfisch, or Weissfelchen (*Coregonus lavaretus*), of the mountain lakes of Switzerland, Germany, and Sweden *Coregonus kennicotti*, the muksun, and *Coregonus nelsoni*, the humpback whitefish, are found in northern Alaska and in the Yukon Several other related species occur in northern Europe and Siberia

Another American species is the Sault whitefish, Lake Whiting or Musquaw River whitefish (*Coregonus labradoricus*) Its teeth are stronger, especially on the tongue, than in any of our other species, and its body is slenderer than that of the whitefish It is found in the upper Great Lakes, in the Adirondack region, in Lake Winnipeseogee, and in the lakes of Maine and New Brunswick It is said to rise to the fly in the Canadian lakes This species runs up the St Mary's River, from Lake Huron to Lake Superior, in July and August Great numbers are snared or speared by the Indians at this season at the Sault Ste Marie

In the breeding season the scales are sometimes thickened or covered with small warts, as in the male *Cyprinidæ*

Argyrosomus, the Lake Herring—In the genus *Argyrosomus* the mouth is larger, the premaxillary not set vertical, but extending forward on its lower edge, and the body is more elongate and more evenly elliptical The species are more active and predaceous than those of *Coregonus* and are, on the whole, inferior as food

The smallest and handsomest of the American whitefish is the cisco of Lake Michigan (*Argyrosomus hoyi*) It is a slender fish, rarely exceeding ten inches in length, and its scales have the brilliant silvery luster of the mooneye and the lady-fish

The lake herring, or cisco (*Argyrosomus artedi*), is, next to the whitefish, the most important of the American species It is more elongate than the others, and has a comparatively large mouth, with projecting under-jaw It is correspondingly more voracious, and often takes the hook During the spawning season of the whitefish the lake herring feeds on the ova of the latter, thereby doing a great amount of mischief. As food this species is fair, but much inferior to the whitefish. Its geographical distribution is essentially the same, but to a greater degree it frequents shoal waters   In the small lakes around Lake Michigan, in Indiana and Wisconsin (Tippecanoe, Geneva, Oconomowoc, etc), the cisco has long been established, and in these waters its habits have undergone some change, as has also its external appearance   It has been recorded as a distinct species, *Argyrosomus sisco,* and its excellence as a game-fish has been long appreciated by the angler   These lake ciscoes remain for most of the year in the depths of the lake, coming to the surface only in search of certain insects, and to shallow water only in the spawning season   This periodical disappearance of the cisco has led to much foolish discussion as to the probability of their returning by an underground passage to Lake

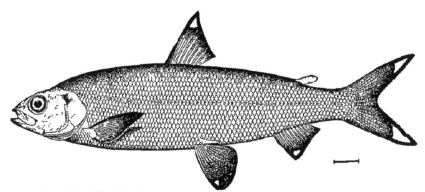

Fig 220 —Bluefin Cisco, *Argyrosomus nigripinnis* Gill   Sheboygan

Michigan during the periods of their absence   One author, confounding "cisco" with "siscowet," has assumed that this underground passage leads to Lake Superior, and that the cisco is identical with the fat lake trout which bears the latter name   The name "lake herring" alludes to the superficial resemblance which this species possesses to the marine herring, a fish of quite a different family

Closely allied to the lake herring is the bluefin of Lake Michigan and of certain lakes in New York (*Argyrosomus nigripinnis*), a fine large species inhabiting deep waters, and recognizable by the blue-black color of its lower fins   In the lakes of central New York are found two other species, the so-called lake smelt (*Argyrosomus osmeriformis*) and the long-jaw (*Argyrosomus prognathus*) *Argyrosomus lucidus* is abundant in Great Bear Lake In Alaska and Siberia are still other species of the cisco type (*Argyrosomus laurettæ, A pusillus, A. alascanus*); and in Europe very similar species are the Scotch vendace (*Argyrosomus vandesius*) and the Scandinavian Lok-Sild (lake herring), as well as others less perfectly known.

The Tullibee, or "mongrel whitefish" (*Argyrosomus tullibee*), has a deep body, like the shad, with the large mouth of the ciscoes It is found in the Great Lake region and northward, and very little is known of its habits A similar species (*Argyrosomus cyprinoides*) is recorded from Siberia—a region which is peculiarly suited for the growth of the *Coregoni*, but in which the species have never received much study

Brachymystax and Stenodus, the Inconnus.—Another little-known form, intermediate between the whitefish and the salmon,

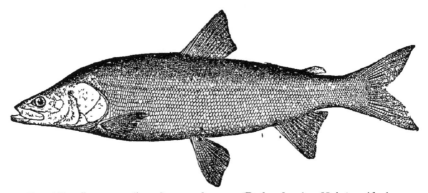

Fig 221 —Inconnu, *Stenodus mackenziei* (Richardson)   Nulato, Alaska

is *Brachymystax lenock*, a large fish of the mountain streams of Siberia. Only the skins brought home by Pallas a century ago are yet known. According to Pallas, it sometimes reaches a weight of eighty pounds

Still another genus, intermediate between the whitefish and the salmon, is *Stenodus*, distinguished by its elongate body, feeble teeth, and projecting lower jaw   The Inconnu, or Mackenzie River salmon, known on the Yukon as "charr" (*Stenodus mackenziei*), belongs to this genus   It reaches a weight of twenty pounds or more, and in the far north is a food-fish of good quality. It runs in the Yukon as far as White Horse Rapids. Not much is recorded of its habits, and few specimens exist in museums. A species of *Stenodus* called *Stenodus leucichihys* inhabits the Volga, Obi, Lena, and other northern rivers, but as yet little is definitely known of the species

Oncorhynchus, the Quinnat Salmon.—The genus *Oncorhynchus* contains the salmon of the Pacific They are in fact, as well as in name, the king salmon The genus is closely related to *Salmo*, with which it agrees in general as to the structure of its vomer, and from which it differs in the increased number of anal rays, branchiostegals, pyloric cœca, and gill-rakers The character most convenient for distinguishing *Oncorhynchus*, young or old, from all the species of *Salmo*, is the number of developed rays in the anal fin These in *Oncorhynchus* are thirteen to twenty, in *Salmo* nine to twelve

The species of *Oncorhynchus* have long been known as anadromous salmon, confined to the North Pacific The species were first made known nearly one hundred and fifty years ago by that most exact of early observers, Steller, who, almost simultaneously with Krascheninnikov, another early investigator, described and distinguished them with perfect accuracy under their Russian vernacular names These Russian names were, in 1792, adopted by Walbaum as specific names in giving to these animals a scientific nomenclature Five species of *Oncorhynchus* are well known on both shores of the North Pacific, besides one other in Japan These have been greatly misunderstood by early observers on account of the extraordinary changes due to differences in surroundings, in sex, and in age, and in conditions connected with the process of reproduction

There are five species of salmon (*Oncorhynchus*) in the waters of the North Pacific, all found on both sides, besides one other which is known only from the waters of Japan These species may be called (1) the quinnat, or king-salmon, (2) the blueback salmon, or redfish, (3) the silver salmon, (4) the dog-salmon, (5) the humpback salmon, and (6) the masu, or (1) *Oncorhynchus tschawytscha*, (2) *Oncorhynchus neika*, (3) *Oncorhynchus milktschitsch*, (4) *Oncorhynchus keta*, (5) *Oncorhynchus gorbuscha*, (6) *Oncorhynchus masou* All these species save the last are now known to occur in the waters of Kamchatka, as well as in those of Alaska and Oregon These species, in all their varied conditions, may usually be distinguished by the characters given below. Other differences of form, color, and appearance are absolutely valueless for distinction, unless specimens of the same age, sex, and condition are compared

The quinnat salmon (*Oncorhynchus tschawytscha*),* called quinnat, tyee, chinook, or king-salmon, has an average weight of 22 pounds, but individuals weighing 70 to 100 pounds are occasionally taken It has about 16 anal rays, 15 to 19 branchiostegals, 23 (9 + 14) gill-rakers on the anterior gill-arch, and 140 to 185 pyloric cœca The scales are comparatively large, there being from 130 to 155 in a longitudinal series In the spring the body is silvery, the back, dorsal fin, and caudal fin having more or less of round black spots, and the sides of the head having a peculiar tin-colored metallic luster. In the fall

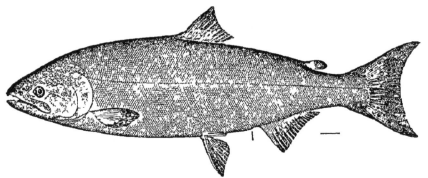

Fig 222.—Quinnat Salmon (female), *Oncorhynchus tschawytscha* (Walbaum)
Columbia River

the color is often black or dirty red, and the species can then be distinguished from the dog-salmon by its larger size and by its technical characters The flesh is rich and salmon-red, becoming suddenly pale as the spawning season draws near

The blue-back salmon (*Oncorhynchus nerka*),† also called red salmon, sukkegh, or sockeye, usually weighs from 5 to 8 pounds It has about 14 developed anal rays, 14 branchioste-

---

* For valuable accounts of the habits of this species the reader is referred to papers by the late Cloudsley Rutter, ichthyologist of the *Albatross*, in the publications of the United States Fish Commission, the *Popular Science Monthly*, and the *Overland Monthly*

† For valuable records of the natural history of this species the reader is referred to various papers by Dr Barton Warren Evermann in the Bulletins of the United States Fish Commission and elsewhere

gals, and 75 to 95 pyloric cœca   The gill-rakers are more numerous than in any other salmon, the number being usually about

FIG 223 —King-salmon grilse, *Oncorhynchus tschauytscha* (Walbaum)
(Photograph by Cloudsley Rutter)

39 (16 + 23)   The scales are larger, there being 130 to 140 in
the lateral line   In the spring the form is plumply rounded,
and the color is a clear bright blue above, silvery below, and
everywhere immaculate   Young fishes often show a few round
black spots, which disappear when they enter the sea.   Fall
specimens in the lakes are bright crimson in color, the head clear
olive-green, and they become in a high degree hook-nosed and
slab-sided, and bear little resemblance to the spring run   Young
spawning male grilse follow the changes which take place in the
adult, although often not more than half a pound in weight

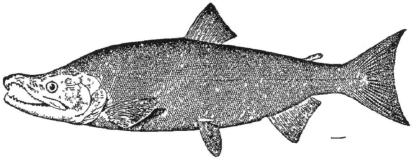

FIG 224 —Male Red Salmon in September, *Oncorhynchus nerka* (Walbaum).
Payette Lake, Idaho

These little fishes often appear in mountain lakes, but whether
they are landlocked or have come up from the sea is still un-

settled These dwarf forms, called kokos by the Indians and benimasu in Japan, form the subspecies *Oncorhynchus nerka kennerlyi* The flesh in this species is firmer than that of any other and very red, of good flavor, though drier and less rich than the king-salmon.

The silver salmon, or coho (*Oncorhynchus milktschitsch*, or *kisutch*), reaches a weight of 5 to 8 pounds It has 13 developed rays in the anal, 13 branchiostegals, 23 (10 + 13) gill-rakers, and 45 to 80 pyloric cœca There are about 127 scales in the lateral line The scales are thin and all except those of the lateral line readily fall off This feature distinguishes the species readily from the red salmon In color it is silvery in spring, greenish above, and with a few faint black spots on the upper parts only In the fall the males are mostly of a dirty red The flesh in this species is of excellent flavor, but pale in color, and hence less valued than that of the quinnat and the red salmon.

The dog-salmon, calico salmon, or chum, called saké in Japan (*Oncorhynchus keta*), reaches an average weight of about 7 to 10 pounds It has about 14 anal rays, 14 branchiostegals, 24 (9 + 15) gill-rakers, and 140 to 185 pyloric cœca There are about 150 scales in the lateral line In spring it is dirty silvery, immaculate, or sprinkled with small black specks, the fins dusky, the sides with faint traces of gridiron-like bars In the fall the male is brick-red or blackish, and its jaws are greatly distorted The pale flesh is well flavored when fresh, but pale and mushy in texture and muddy in taste when canned It is said to take salt well, and great numbers of salt dog-salmon are consumed in Japan

The humpback salmon, or pink salmon (*Oncorhynchus gorbuscha*), is the smallest of the American species, weighing from 3 to 5 pounds It has usually 15 anal rays, 12 branchiostegals, 28 (13 + 15) gill-rakers, and about 180 pyloric cœca Its scales are much smaller than in any other salmon, there being 180 to 240 in the lateral line In color it is bluish above, silvery below, the posterior and upper parts with many round black spots, the caudal fin always having a few large black spots oblong in form The males in fall are dirty red, and are more extravagantly distorted than in any other of the *Salmonidæ*

The flesh is softer than in the other species; it is pale in color, and, while of fair flavor when fresh, is distinctly inferior when canned

The masu, or yezomasu (*Oncorhynchus masou*), is very similar to the humpback, the scales a little larger, the caudal without

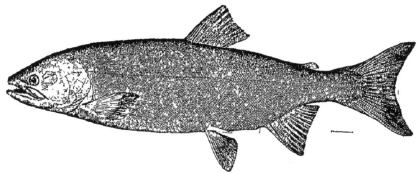

Fig 225 —Humpback Salmon (female), *Oncorhynchus gorbuscha* (Walbaum) Cook's Inlet.

black spots, the back usually immaculate It is one of the smaller salmon, and is fairly abundant in the streams of Hokkaido, the island formerly known as Yezo

Of these species the blue-back or red salmon predominates in Frazer River and in most of the small rivers of Alaska, includ-

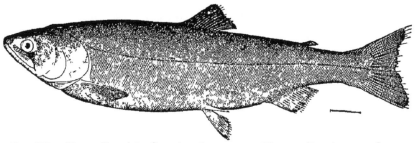

Fig 226 —Masu (female), *Oncorhynchus masou* (Brevoort) Aomori, Japan

ing all those which flow from lakes The greatest salmon rivers of the world are the Nushegak and Karluk in Alaska, with the Columbia River, Frazer River, and Sacramento River farther south The red and the silver salmon predominate in Puget Sound, the quinnat in the Columbia and the Sacramento, and the silver salmon in most of the smaller streams along the coast All the species occur, however, from the Columbia northward, but the blue-back is not found in the Sacramento. Only the quinnat and the dog-salmon have been noticed south of San Francisco In Japan *keta* is by far the most abundant species of salmon It is known as saké, and largely salted and sold in the markets *Nerka* is known in Japan only as landlocked in Lake Akan in northern Hokkaido *Milktschitsch* is generally common, and with *masou* is known as masu, or small salmon, as distinguished from the large salmon, or saké *Tschawytscha* and *gorbuscha* are unknown in Japan *Masou* has not been found elsewhere

The quinnat and blue-back salmon, the "noble salmon," habitually "run" in the spring, the others in the fall The usual order of running in the rivers is as follows *tschawytscha, nerka, milktschitsch, gorbuscha, keta* Those which run first go farthest In the Yukon the quinnat runs as far as Caribou Crossing and Lake Bennett, 2250 miles The red salmon runs to "Forty-Mile," which is nearly 1800 miles. Both ascend to the head of the Columbia, Fraser, Nass, Skeena, Stikeen, and Taku rivers The quinnat runs practically only in the streams of large size, fed with melting snows; the red salmon only in streams which pass through lakes It spawns only in small streams at the head of a lake The other species spawn in almost any fresh water and only close to the sea

The economic value of the spring-running salmon is far greater than that of the other species, because they can be captured in numbers when at their best, while the others are usually taken only after deterioration

The habits of the salmon in the ocean are not easily studied Quinnat and silver salmon of all sizes are taken with the seine at almost any season in Puget Sound and among the islands of Alaska This would indicate that these species do not go far from the shore The silver salmon certainly does not The quinnat pursues the schools of herring It takes the hook freely in Monterey Bay, both near the shore and at a distance of six to eight miles out We have reason to believe that these two species do not necessarily seek great depths, but probably remain not very far from the mouth of the rivers in which they were spawned The blue-back or red salmon certainly seeks deeper water, as it is seldom or never taken with the seine along shore, and it is known to enter the Strait of Fuca in

July, just before the running season, therefore coming in from the open sea   The great majority of the quinnat salmon, and probaby all the blue-back salmon, enter the rivers in the spring The run of the quinnat begins generally at the last of March, it lasts, with various modifications and interruptions, until the actual spawning season in November, the greatest run being in early June in Alaska, in July in the Columbia,   The run begins earliest in the northernmost rivers, and in the longest streams, the time of running and the proportionate amount in each of the subordinate runs varying with each different river   In general the runs are slack in the summer and increase with the first high water of autumn   By the last of August only straggling blue-backs can be found in the lower course of any stream, but both in the Columbia and in the Sacramento the quinnat runs in considerable numbers at least till October. In the Sacramento the run is greatest in the fall, and more run in the summer than in spring   In the Sacramento and the smaller rivers southward there is a winter run, beginning in December   The spring quinnat salmon ascends only those rivers which are fed by the melting snows from the mountains and which have sufficient volume to send their waters well out to sea   Those salmon which run in the spring are chiefly adults (supposed to be at least three years old)   Their milt and spawn are no more developed than at the same time in others of the same species which have not yet entered the rivers   It would appear that the contact with cold fresh water, when in the ocean, in some way causes them to run towards it, and to run before there is any special influence to that end exerted by the development of the organs of generation   High water on any of these rivers in the spring is always followed by an increased run of salmon   The salmon-canners think—and this is probably true—that salmon which would not have run till later are brought up by the contact with the cold water   The cause of this effect of cold fresh water is not understood   We may call it an instinct of the salmon, which is another way of expressing our ignorance   In general it seems to be true that in those rivers and during those years when the spring run is greatest the fall run is least to be depended on

The blue-back salmon runs chiefly in July and early August,

beginning in late June in Chilcoot River, where some were found actually spawning July 15, beginning after the middle of July in Frazer River

As the season advances, smaller and younger salmon of these species (quinnat and blue-back) enter the rivers to spawn, and in the fall these young specimens are very numerous We have thus far failed to notice any gradations in size or appearance of these young fish by which their ages could be ascertained It is, however, probable that some of both sexes reproduce at the age of one year In Frazer River, in the fall, quinnat male grilse of every size, from eight inches upwards, were running, the milt fully developed, but usually not showing the hooked jaws and dark colors of the older males Females less than eighteen inches in length were not seen All of either sex, large and small, then in the river had the ovaries or milt developed Little blue-backs of every size, down to six inches, are also found in the upper Columbia in the fall, with their organs of generation fully developed Nineteen-twentieths of these young fish are males, and some of them have the hooked jaws and red color of the old males Apparently all these young fishes, like the old ones, die after spawning

The average weight of the adult quinnat in the Columbia, in the spring, is twenty-two pounds, in the Sacramento, about sixteen Individuals weighing from forty to sixty pounds are frequently found in both rivers, and some as high as eighty or even one hundred pounds are recorded, especially in Alaska, where the species tends to run larger It is questionable whether these large fishes are those which, of the same age, have grown more rapidly, those which are older, but have for some reason failed to spawn, or those which have survived one or more spawing seasons All these origins may be possible in individual cases There is, however, no positive evidence that any salmon of the Pacific survives the spawning season

Those fish which enter the rivers in the spring continue their ascent till death or the spawning season overtakes them Doubtless not one of them ever returns to the ocean, and a large proportion fail to spawn They are known to ascend the Sacramento to its extreme head-waters, about four hundred miles. In the Columbia they ascend as far as the Bitter Root and Sawtooth mountains of Idaho, and their extreme limit is not known. This is a distance of nearly a thousand miles In the Yukon a few ascend to Caribou Crossing and Lake Bennett, 2250 miles. At these great distances, when the fish have reached the spawning grounds, besides the usual changes of the breeding season their bodies are covered with bruises, on which patches of white fungus (*Saprolegnia*) develop The fins become mutilated, their eyes are often injured or destroyed, parasitic worms gather in their gills, they become extremely emaciated, their flesh becomes white from the loss of oil, and as soon as the spawning act is accomplished, and sometimes before, *all* of them die The ascent of the Cascades and the Dalles of the Columbia causes the injury or death of a great many salmon

When the salmon enter the river they refuse to take bait, and their stomachs are always found empty and contracted.

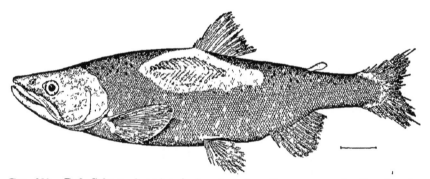

Fig 227 —Red Salmon (mutilated dwarf male, after spawning), *Oncorhynchus nerka* (Walbaum) Alturas Lake, Idaho

In the rivers they do not feed, and when they reach the spawning grounds their stomachs, pyloric cœca and all, are said to be no larger than one's finger They will sometimes take the fly, or a hook baited with salmon-roe, in the clear waters of the upper tributaries, but this is apparently solely out of annoyance, snapping at the meddling line Only the quinnat and blue-back (there called redfish) have been found at any great distance from the sea, and these (as adult fishes) only in late summer and fall

The spawning season is probably about the same for all the species It varies for each of the different rivers, and for different parts of the same river It doubtless extends from July to

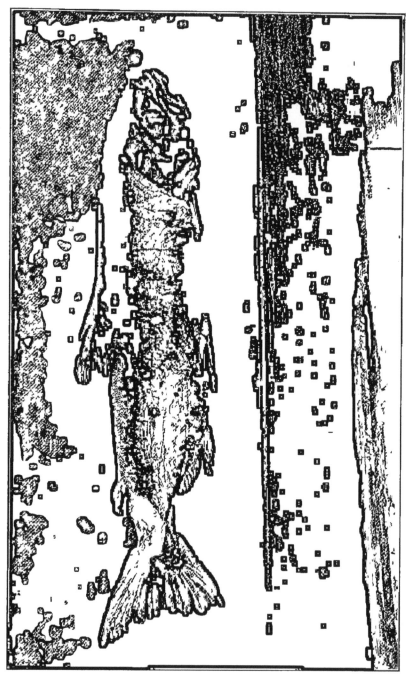

FIG. 228—Young Male Qunnat Salmon, *Oncorhynchus tschawytscha*, dying after spawning Sacramento River (Photograph by Cloudsley Rutter)

December, and takes place usually as soon as the temperature
of the water falls to 54°   The manner of spawning is probably
similar for all the species   In the quinnat the fishes pair off,
the male, with tail and snout, excavates a broad, shallow "nest"
in the gravelly bed of the stream, in rapid water, at a depth
of one to four feet and the female deposits her eggs in it
They then float down the stream tail foremost, the only
fashion in which salmon descend to the sea   As already
stated, in the head-waters of the large streams, unquestionably,
all die, it is the belief of the writer that none ever survive
The young hatch in sixty days, and most of them return to
the ocean during the high water of the spring   They enter the
river as adults at the age of about four years

The salmon of all kinds in the spring are silvery, spotted
or not according to the species, and with the mouth about equally
symmetrical in both sexes   As the spawning season approaches
the female loses her silvery color, becomes more slimy, the
scales on the back partly sink into the skin, and the flesh changes
from salmon-red and becomes variously paler, from the loss of
oil, the degree of paleness varying much with individuals and
with inhabitants of different rivers   In the Sacramento the
flesh of the quinnat, in either spring or fall, is rarely pale   In
the Columbia a few with pale flesh are sometimes taken in
spring, and an increasing number from July on   In Frazer
River the fall run of the quinnat is nearly worthless for canning
purposes, because so many are "white-meated"   In the spring
very few are "white-meated", but the number increases towards
fall, when there is every variation, some having red streaks
running through them, others being red toward the head and
pale toward the tail   The red and pale ones cannot be distinguished externally, and the color is dependent on neither
age nor sex   There is said to be no difference in the taste, but
there is little market for canned salmon not of the conventional
orange-color

As the season advances the difference between the males
and females becomes more and more marked, and keeps pace
with the development of the milt, as is shown by dissection
The males have (1) the premaxillaries and the tip of the lower
jaw more and more prolonged, both of the jaws becoming finally

strongly and often extravagantly hooked, so that either they shut by the side of each other like shears, or else the mouth cannot be closed   (2) The front teeth become very long and canine-like, their growth proceeding very rapidly, until they are often half an inch long   (3) The teeth on the vomer and tongue often disappear. (4) The body grows more compressed and deeper at the shoulders, so that a very distinct hump is formed; this is more developed in the humpback salmon, but is found in all. (5) The scales disappear, especially on the back, by the growth of spongy skin   (6) The color changes from silvery to various shades of black and red, or blotchy, according to the species   The blue-back turns rosy-red, the head bright olive, the dog-salmon a dull red with blackish bars, and the quinnat generally blackish   The distorted males are

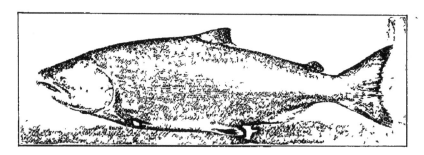

Fig 229 —Quinnat Salmon, *Oncorhynchus tschawytscha* (Walbaum)
Monterey Bay   (Photograph by C Rutter)

commonly considered worthless, rejected by the canners and salmon-salters, but preserved by the Indians   These changes are due solely to influences connected with the growth of the reproductive organs   They are not in any way due to the action of fresh water   They take place at about the same time in the adult males of all species, whether in the ocean or in the rivers   At the time of the spring runs all are symmetrical   In the fall all males, of whatever species, are more or less distorted   Among the dog-salmon, which run only in the fall, the males are hook-jawed and red-blotched when they first enter the Strait of Fuca from the outside   The humpback, taken in salt water about Seattle, have the same peculiarities   The male is slab-sided, hook-billed, and distorted, and is rejected by the canners No hook-jawed females of any species have been seen

On first entering a stream the salmon swim about as if playing They always head towards the current, and this appearance of playing may be simply due to facing the moving tide. Afterwards they enter the deepest parts of the stream and swim straight up, with few interruptions Their rate of travel at Sacramento is estimated by Stone at about two miles per day, on the Columbia at about three miles per day Those which enter the Columbia in the spring and ascend to the mountain rivers of Idaho must go at a more rapid rate than this, as they must make an average of nearly four miles per day

As already stated, the economic value of any species depends in great part on its being a "spring salmon" It is not generally possible to capture salmon of any species in large numbers until they have entered the estuaries or rivers, and the spring salmon enter the large rivers long before the growth of the organs of reproduction has reduced the richness of the flesh The fall salmon cannot be taken in quantity until their flesh has deteriorated, hence the dog-salmon is practically almost worthless except to the Indians, and the humpback salmon was regarded as little better until comparatively recently, when it has been placed on the market in cans as "Pink Salmon" It sells for about half the price of the red salmon and one-third that of the quinnat. The red salmon is smaller than the quinnat but, outside the Sacramento and the Columbia, far more abundant, and at present it exceeds the quinnat in economic value The pack of red salmon in Alaska amounted in 1902 to over two million cases (48 pounds each), worth wholesale about $4 00 per case, or about $8,000,000 The other species in Alaska yield about one million cases, the total wholesale value of the pack for 1902 being $8,667,673 The aggregate value of the quinnat is considerably less, but either species far exceed in value all other fishes of the Pacific taken together The silver salmon is found in the inland waters of Puget Sound for a considerable time before the fall rains cause the fall runs, and it may be taken in large numbers with seines before the season for entering the rivers

The fall salmon of all species, but especially of the dog-salmon, ascend streams but a short distance before spawning. They seem to be in great anxiety to find fresh water, and many of them work their way up little brooks only a few inches deep, where they perish miserably, floundering about on the stones. Every stream of whatever kind, from San Francisco to Bering Sea, has more or less of these fall salmon

The absence of the fine spring salmon in the streams of Japan is the cause of the relative unimportance of the river fisheries of the northern island of Japan, Hokkaido It is not likely that either the quinnat or the red salmon can be introduced into these rivers, as they have no snow-fed streams, and few of them pass through lakes which are not shut off by waterfalls For the same reason neither of these species is likely to become naturalized in the waters of our Eastern States, though it is worth while to bring the red salmon to the St. Lawrence The silver salmon, already abundant in Japan, should thrive in the rivers and bays of New England

The Parent-stream Theory. — It has been generally accepted as unquestioned by packers and fishermen that salmon return to spawn to the very stream in which they were hatched As early as 1880 the present writer placed on record his opinion that this theory was unsound In a general way most salmon return to the parent stream, because when in the sea the parent stream is the one most easily reached The channels and runways which directed their course to the sea may influence their return trip in the same fashion. When the salmon is mature it seeks fresh water. Other things being equal, about the same number will run each year in the same channel With all this, we find some curious facts Certain streams will have a run of exceptionally large or exceptionally small red salmon The time of the run bears some relation to the length of the stream: those who have farthest to go start earliest The time of running bears also a relation to the temperature of the spawning grounds· where the waters cool off earliest the fish run soonest

The supposed evidence in favor of the parent-stream theory may be considered under three heads * (1) Distinctive runs in

* See an excellent article by H S Davis in the *Pacific Fisherman* for July, 1903

various streams   (2) Return of marked salmon.   (3) Introduction of salmon into new streams followed by their return

Under the first head it is often asserted of fishermen that they can distinguish the salmon of different streams   Thus the Lynn Canal red salmon are larger than those in most waters, and it is claimed that those of Chilcoot Inlet are larger than those of the sister stream at Chilcat   The red salmon of Red Fish Bay on Baranof Island are said to be much smaller than usual, and those of the neighboring Necker Bay are not more than one-third the ordinary size   Those of a small rapid stream near Nass River are more wiry than those of the neighboring large stream.   The same claim is made for the different streams of Puget Sound, each one having its characteristic run.   In all this there is some truth and perhaps some exaggeration   I have noticed that the Chilcoot fish seem deeper in body than those at Chilcat.   The red salmon becomes compressed before spawning, and the Chilcoot fishes having a short run spawn earlier than the Chilcat fishes, which have many miles to go, the water being perhaps warmer at the mouth of the river   Perhaps some localities may meet the nervous reactions of small fishes, while not attracting the large ones   Mr H S Davis well observes that "until a constant difference has been demonstrated by a careful examination of large numbers of fish from each stream taken *at the same time*, but little weight can be attached to arguments of this nature "

It is doubtless true as a general proposition that nearly all salmon return to the region in which they were spawned   Most of them apparently never go far away from the mouth of the stream or the bay into which it flows   It is true that salmon are occasionally taken well out at sea, and it is certain that the red-salmon runs of Puget Sound come from outside the Straits of Fuca   There is, however, evidence that they rarely go so far as that   When seeking shore they do not reach the original channels

In 1880 the writer, studying the salmon of the Columbia, used the following words, which he has not had occasion to change

"It is the prevailing impression that the salmon have some special instinct which leads them to return to spawn in the

same spawning grounds where they were originally hatched.
We fail to find any evidence of this in the case of the Pacific-
coast salmon, and we do not believe it to be true   It seems
more probable that the young salmon hatched in any river
mostly remain in the ocean within a radius of twenty, thirty,
or forty miles of its mouth   These, in their movements about
in the ocean, may come into contact with the cold waters of
their parent rivers, or perhaps of any other river, at a considerable distance from the shore   In the case of the quinnat and
the blue-back their 'instinct' seems to lead them to ascend
these fresh waters, and in a majority of cases these waters will
be those in which the fishes in question were originally spawned.
Later in the season the growth of the reproductive organs leads
them to approach the shore and search for fresh waters, and
still the chances are that they may find the original stream
But undoubtedly many fall salmon ascend, or try to ascend,
streams in which no salmon was ever hatched   In little brooks
about Puget Sound, where the water is not three inches deep,
are often found dead or dying salmon which have entered them
for the purpose of spawning   It is said of the Russian River
and other California rivers that their mouths, in the time of
low water in summer, generally become entirely closed by sand-
bars, and that the salmon, in their eagerness to ascend them,
frequently fling themselves entirely out of water on the beach
But this does not prove that the salmon are guided by a marvelous geographical instinct which leads them to their parent
river in spite of the fact that the river cannot be found   The
waters of Russian River soak through these sand-bars, and
the salmon instinct, we think, leads them merely to search for
fresh waters   This matter is much in need of further investigation, at present, however, we find no reason to believe that
the salmon enter the Rogue River simply because they were
spawned there, or that a salmon hatched in the Clackamas
River is more likely, on that account, to return to the Clackamas than to go up the Cowlitz or the Des Chûtes ''

Attempts have been made to settle this question by marking
the fry. But this is a very difficult matter indeed   Almost
the only structure which can be safely mutilated is the adipose
fin, and this is often nipped off by sticklebacks and other med-

dling fish   The following experiments have been tried, according to Mr Davis

In March, 1896, 5000 king-salmon fry were marked by cutting off the adipose fin, then set free in the Clackamas River Nearly 400 of these marked fish are said to have been taken in the Columbia in 1898, and a few more in 1899   In addition a few were taken in 1898, 1899, and 1900 in the Sacramento River, but in much less numbers than in the Columbia   In the Columbia most were taken at the mouth of the river, where nearly all of the fishing was done, but a few were in the original stream, the Clackamas   It is stated that the fry thus set free in the Clackamas came from eggs obtained in the Sacramento— a matter which has, however, no bearing on the present case

In the Kalama hatchery on the Columbia River, Washington, 2000 fry of the quinnat or king-salmon were marked in 1899 by a V-shaped notch in the caudal fin   Numerous fishes thus marked were taken in the lower Columbia in 1901 and 1902 A few were taken at the Kalama hatchery, but some also at the hatcheries on Wind River and Clackamas River   At the hatchery on Chehalis River six or seven were taken, the stream not being a tributary of the Columbia, but flowing into Shoalwater Bay   None were noticed in the Sacramento   The evidence shows that the most who are hatched in a large stream tend to return to it, and that in general most salmon return to the parent region   There is no evidence that a salmon hatched in one branch of a river tends to return there rather than to any other   Experiments of Messrs Rutter and Spaulding in marking adult fish at Karluk would indicate that they roam rather widely about the island before spawning   An adult spawning fish, marked and set free at Karluk, was taken soon after on the opposite side of the island of Kadiak

The introduction of salmon into new streams may throw some light on this question   In 1897 and 1898 3,000,000 young quinnat-salmon fry were set free in Papermill Creek near Olema, California   This is a small stream flowing into the head of Tomales Bay, and it had never previously had a run of salmon In 1900, and especially in 1901, large quinnat salmon appeared in considerable numbers in this stream   One specimen weighing about sixteen pounds was sent to the present writer for identification These fishes certainly returned to the parent stream, although this stream was one not at all fitted for their purpose

But this may be accounted for by the topography of the bay Tomales Bay is a long and narrow channel, about twenty miles long and from one to five in width, isolated from other rivers and with but one tributary stream Probably the salmon had not wandered far from it, some may not have left it at all In any event, a large number certainly came back to the same place

That the salmon rarely go far away is fairly attested Schools of king-salmon play in Monterey Bay, and chase the herring about in the channels of southeastern Alaska A few years since Captain J F Moser, in charge of the *Albatross*, set gill-nets for salmon at various places in the sea off the Oregon and Washington coast, catching none except in the bays

Mr Davis gives an account of the liberation of salmon in Chinook River, which flows into the Columbia at Baker's Bay

"It is a small, sluggish stream and has never been frequented by Chinook salmon, although considerable numbers of silver and dog salmon enter it late in the fall A few years ago the State established a hatchery on this stream, and since 1898 between 1,000,000 and 2,000,000 Chinook fry have been turned out here annually The fish are taken from the pound-nets in Baker's Bay, towed into the river in crates and then liberated above the dike, which prevents their return to the Columbia When ripe the salmon ascend to the hatchery, some two or three miles farther up the river, where they are spawned

"The superintendent of the hatchery, Mr Hansen, informs me that in 1902, during November and December, quite a number of Chinook salmon ascended the Chinook River About 150 salmon of both sexes were taken in a trap located in the river about four miles from its mouth At first thought it would appear that these were probably fish which, when fry, had been liberated in the river, but unfortunately there is no proof that this was the case According to Mr Hansen, the season of 1902 was remarkable in that the salmon ran inshore in large schools, a thing which they had not done before for years It is possible that the fish, being forced in close to the shore, came in contact with the current from the Chinook River, which, since the stream is small and sluggish, would not be felt far from shore Once brought under the influence of the current from the river, the salmon would naturally ascend that stream, whether they had been hatched there or not "

The general conclusion, apparently warranted by the facts at hand, is that salmon, for the most part, do not go to a great distance from the stream in which they are hatched, that most of them return to the streams of the same region, a majority to the parent stream, but that there is no evidence that they choose the parental spawning grounds in preference to any other, and none that they will prefer an undesirable stream to a favorable one for the reason that they happen to have been hatched in the former

The Jadgeska Hatchery.—Mr John C Callbreath of Wrangel, Alaska, has long conducted a very interesting but very costly experiment in this line About 1890 he established himself in a small stream called Jadgeska on the west coast of Etolin Island, tributary to McHenry Inlet, Clarence Straits This stream led from a lake, and in it a few thousand red salmon spawned, besides multitudes of silver salmon, dog-salmon, and humpback salmon Making a dam across the stream, he helped the red salmon over it, destroying all of the inferior kinds which entered the stream He also established a hatchery for the red salmon, turning loose many fry yearly for ten or twelve years This was done in the expectation that all the salmon hatched would return to Jadgeska in about four years By destroying all individuals of other species attempting to run, it was expected that they would become extinct so far as the stream is concerned

The result of this experiment has been disappointment After twelve years or more there has been no increase of red salmon in the stream, and no decrease of humpbacks and other humbler forms of salmon Mr Callbreath draws the conclusion that salmon run at a much greater age than has been supposed—at the age of sixteen years, perhaps, instead of four. A far more probable conclusion is that his salmon have joined other bands bound for more suitable streams It is indeed claimed that since the establishment of Callbreath's hatchery on Etolin Island there has been a notable increase of the salmon run in the various streams of Prince of Wales Island on the opposite side of Clarence Straits But this statement, while largely current among the cannerymen, and not improbable, needs verification

We shall await with much interest the return of the thousands of salmon hatched in 1902 in Naha stream. We may venture the prophecy that while a large percentage will return to Loring, many others will enter Yes Bay, Karta Bay, Moira Sound, and other red-salmon waters along the line of their return from Dixon Entrance or the open sea

Salmon-packing.—The canning of salmon, that is, the packing of the flesh in tin cases, hermetically sealed after boiling, was begun on the Columbia River by the Hume Brothers in 1866 In 1874 canneries were established on the Sacramento River, in 1876 on Puget Sound and on Frazer River, and in 1878 in Alaska At first only the quinnat salmon was packed, afterwards the red salmon and the silver salmon, and finally the humpback, known commercially as pink salmon In most cases the flesh is packed in one-pound tins, forty-eight of which constitute a case The wholesale price in 1903 was for quinnat salmon $5 60 per case, red salmon $4 00, silver salmon $2 60, humpback salmon $2.00, and dog-salmon $1 50 It costs in round numbers $2 00 to pack a case of salmon. The very low price of the inferior brands is due to overproduction.

The output of the salmon fishery of the Pacific coast amounts to about fifteen millions per year, that of Alaska constituting seven to nine millions of this amount Of this amount the red salmon constitutes somewhat more than half, the quinnat about four-fifths of the rest

In almost all salmon streams there is evidence of considerable diminution in numbers, although the evidence is sometimes conflicting. In Alaska this has been due to the vicious custom, now done away with, of barricading the streams so that the fish could not reach the spawning grounds, but might be all taken with the net In the Columbia River the reduction in numbers is mainly due to stationary traps and salmon-wheels, which leave the fish relatively little chance to reach the spawning grounds. In years of high water doubtless many salmon run in the spring which might otherwise have waited until fall

The key to the situation lies in the artificial propagation of salmon by means of well-ordered hatcheries   By this means the fisheries of the Sacramento have been fully restored, those of the Columbia approximately maintained, and a hopeful beginning has been made in hatching red salmon in Alaska

The preservation of salmon and trout depends rather on artificial hatching than on protection

Salmo, the Trout and Atlantc Salmon.—The genus *Salmo* comprises those forms of salmon which have been longest known   As in related genera, the mouth is large, and the jaws, palatines, and tongue are armed with strong teeth   The vomer is flat, its shaft not depressed below the level of the head or chevron (the anterior end)   There are a few teeth on the chevron, and behind it, on the shaft, there is either a double series of teeth or an irregular single series   These teeth in the true salmon disappear with age, but in the others (the black-spotted trout) they are persistent   The scales are silvery and moderate or small in size   There are 9 to 11 developed rays in the anal fin   The caudal fin is truncate, or variously concave or forked   There are usually 40 to 70 pyloric cœca, 11 or 12 branchiostegals, and about 20 (8 + 12) gill-rakers   The sexual peculiarities are in general less marked than in *Oncorhynchus*, they are also greater in the anadromous species than in those which inhabit fresh waters   In general the male in the breeding season is redder, its jaws are prolonged, the front teeth enlarged, the lower jaw turned upwards at the end, and the upper jaw notched, or sometimes even perforated, by the tip of the lower   All the species of *Salmo* (like those of *Oncorhynchus*) are more or less spotted with black   Unlike the species of *Oncorhynchus*, the species of *Salmo* feed more or less while in fresh water, and the individuals for the most part do not die after spawning, although many old males do thus perish

The Atlantic Salmon.—The large species of *Salmo*, called salmon by English-speaking people (*Salmo salar, Salmo trutta*), are marine and anadromous, taking the place in the North Atlantic occupied in the North Pacific by the species of *Onco-*

rhynchus Two others more or less similar in character occur in Japan and Kamchatka The others (trout), forming the subgenus *Salar*, are non-migratory, or at least irregularly or imperfectly anadromous The true or black-spotted trout abound in all streams of northern Europe, northern Asia, and in that part of North America which lies *west* of the Mississippi Valley The black-spotted trout are entirely wanting in eastern America—a remarkable fact in geographical distribution, perhaps explained only on the hypothesis of the comparatively recent and Eurasiatic origin of the group, which, we may suppose, has not yet had opportunity to extend its range across the plains, unsuitable for salmon life, which separate the upper Missouri from the Great Lakes

The salmon (*Salmo salar*) is the only black-spotted salmonoid found in American waters tributary to the Atlantic In Europe, where other species similarly colored occur, the species may be best distinguished by the fact that the teeth on the shaft of the vomer mostly disappear with age From the only other species positively known, the salmon trout (*Salmo trutta*), which shares this character, the true salmon may be distinguished by the presence of but eleven scales between the adipose fin and the lateral line, while *Salmo trutta* has about fourteen The scales are comparatively large in the salmon, there being about one hundred and twenty-five in the lateral line The caudal fin, which is forked in the young, becomes, as in other species of salmon, more or less truncate with age The pyloric cœca are fifty to sixty in number

The color in adults, according to Dr Day, is "superiorly of a steel-blue, becoming lighter on the sides and beneath Mostly a few rounded or X-shaped spots scattered above the lateral line and upper half of the head, being more numerous in the female than in the male Dorsal, caudal, and pectoral fins dusky, ventrals and anal white, the former grayish internally Prior to entering fresh waters these fish are of a brilliant steel-blue along the back, which becomes changed to a muddy tinge when they enter rivers After these fish have passed into the fresh waters for the purpose of breeding, numerous orange streaks appear in the cheeks of the male, and also spots or even marks of the same, and likewise of a red color, on the body

It is now termed a 'redfish'   The female, however, is dark
in color and known as 'blackfish'   'Smolts' (young river fish)
are bluish along the upper half of the body, silvery along the
sides, due to a layer of silvery scales being formed over the
trout-like colors, while they have darker fins than the yearling
'ping,' but similar bands and spots, which can be seen (as
in the parr) if the example be held in certain positions of light
'Parr' (fishes of the year) have two or three black spots only
on the opercle, and black spots and also orange ones along the
upper half of the body, and no dark ones below the lateral line,
although there may be orange ones which can be seen in its
course   Along the side of the body are a series (12 to 15) of
transverse bluish bands, wider than the ground color and crossing
the lateral line, while in the upper half of the body the darker
color of the back forms an arch over each of these bands, a
row of spots along the middle of the rayed dorsal fin, and the
adipose orange-tipped ''

The dusky cross-shades found in the young salmon or parr
are characteristic of the young of salmon, trout, grayling, and
nearly all the other *Salmonidæ*

The salmon of the Atlantic is, as already stated, an anadromous fish, spending most of its life in the sea, and entering the
streams in the fall for the purpose of reproduction   The time
of running varies much in different streams and also in different
countries   As with the Pacific species, these salmon are not
easily discouraged in their progress, leaping cascades and other
obstructions, or, if these prove impassable, dying after repeated
fruitless attempts

The young salmon, known as the "parr," is hatched in the
spring.   It usually remains about two years in the rivers, descending at about the third spring to the sea, when it is known
as "smolt"   In the sea it grows much more rapidly, and becomes
more silvery in color, and is known as "grilse."   The grilse
rapidly develop into the adult salmon, and some of them, as in
the case with the grilse of the Pacific salmon, are capable of
reproduction

After spawning the salmon are very lean and unwholesome
in appearance, as in fact   They are then known as "kelts"
The Atlantic salmon does not ascend rivers to any such dis-

tances as those traversed by the quinnat and the blue-back.
Its kelts, therefore, for the most part survive the act of spawning Dr. Day thinks that they feed upon the young salmon in the
rivers, and that, therefore, the destruction of the kelts might
increase the supply of salmon.

As a food-fish the Atlantic salmon is very similar to the
quinnat salmon, neither better nor worse, so far as I can see,
when equally fresh In both the flesh is rich and finely flavored,
but the appetite of man becomes cloyed with salmon-flesh sooner
than with that of whitefish, smelt, or charr. In size the Atlantic salmon does not fall far short of the quinnat. The average
weight of the adult is probably less than fifteen pounds The
largest one of which I find a record was taken on the coast of
Ireland in 1881, and weighed 84¾ pounds.

The salmon is found in Europe between the latitude of 45°
and 75°. In the United States it is now rarely seen south of
Cape Cod, although formerly the Hudson and numerous other
rivers were salmon-streams Overfishing, obstructions in the
rivers, and pollution of the water by manufactories and by
city sewage are agencies against which the salmon cannot cope

Seven species of salmon (as distinguished from trout) are
recognized by Dr Gunther in Europe, and three in America.
The landlocked forms, abundant in Norway, Sweden, and
Maine, which cannot, or at least do not, descend to the sea, are
regarded by him as distinct species "The question," observes
Dr Gunther, "whether any of the migratory species can be
retained by artificial means in fresh water, and finally accom-
modate themselves to a permanent sojourn therein, must be
negatived for the present." On this point I think that the
balance of evidence leads to a different conclusion These
fresh-water forms (*Sebago* and *Ouananiche*) are actually salmon
which have become landlocked. I have compared numerous
specimens of the common landlocked salmon (*Salmo salar
sebago*) of the lakes of Maine and New Brunswick with land-
locked salmon (*Salmo salar hardini*) from the lakes of Sweden,
and with numerous migratory salmon, both from America and
Europe I see no reason for regarding them as specifically
distinct The differences are very trivial in kind, and not
greater than would be expected on the hypothesis of recent

adaptation of the salmon to lake life. We have therefore on our Atlantic coast but one species of salmon, *Salmo salar* The landlocked form of the lakes of Maine is *Salmo salar sebago* The *Ouananiche* of Lake St John and the Saguenay, beloved of anglers, is *Salmo salar ouananiche*

The Ouananiche.—Dr Henry Van Dyke writes thus of the *Ouananiche*. "But the prince of the pool was the fighting *Ouananiche*, the little salmon of St John Here let me chant thy praise, thou noblest and most high-minded fish, the cleanest feeder, the merriest liver, the loftiest leaper, and the bravest warrior of all creatures that swim! Thy cousin, the trout, in his purple and gold with crimson spots, wears a more splendid armor than thy russet and silver mottled with black, but thine is the kinglier nature.

"The old salmon of the sea who begat thee long ago in these inland waters became a backslider, descending again to the ocean, and grew gross and heavy with coarse feeding But thou, unsalted salmon of the foaming floods, not landlocked as men call thee, but choosing of thine own free will to dwell on a loftier level in the pure, swift current of a living stream, hath grown in grace and risen to a better life

"Thou art not to be measured by quantity but by quality, and thy five pounds of pure vigor will outweigh a score of pounds of flesh less vitalized by spirit Thou feedest on the flies of the air, and thy food is transformed into an aerial passion for flight, as thou springest across the pool, vaulting toward the sky Thine eyes have grown large and keen by piercing through the foam, and the feathered hook that can deceive thee must be deftly tied and delicately cast Thy tail and fins, by cease-less conflict with the rapids, have broadened and strengthened, so that they can flash thy slender body like a living arrow up the fall As Launcelot among the knights, so art thou among the fish, the plain-armored hero, the sunburnt champion of all the water-folk "

Dr Francis Day, who has very thoroughly studied these fishes, takes, in his memoir on "The Fishes of Great Britain and Ireland," and in other papers, a similar view in regard to the European species Omitting the species with permanent teeth on the shaft of the vomer (subgenus *Salar*), he finds among the salmon proper only two species, *Salmo salar* and *Salmo trutta* The latter species, the sea-trout or salmon-trout of England and the estuaries of northern Europe, is similar to the salmon in many respects, but has rather smaller scales, there being fourteen in an oblique series between the adipose fin and the lateral line It is not so strong a fish as the salmon, nor does it reach so large a size Although naturally anadromous, like the true salmon, landlocked forms of the salmon-trout are not uncommon These have been usually regarded as different species, while aberrant or intermediate individuals are usually regarded as hybrids The salmon-trout of Europe have many analogies with the steelhead of the Pacific

The present writer has examined many thousands of American *Salmonidæ*, both of *Oncorhynchus* and *Salmo* While many variations have come to his attention, and he has been compelled more than once to modify his views as to specific distinctions, he has never yet seen an individual which he had the slightest reason to regard as a "hybrid" It is certainly illogical to conclude that every specimen which does not correspond to our closet-formed definition of its species must therefore be a "hybrid" with some other There is no evidence worth mentioning, known to me, of extensive hybridization in a state of nature in any group of fishes This matter is much in need of further study, for what is true of the species in one region, in this regard, may not be true of others Dr Gunther observes

' Johnson, a correspondent of Willughby, had already expressed his belief that the different salmonoids interbreed, and this view has since been shared by many who have observed these fishes in nature Hybrids between the sewin (*Salmo trutta cambricus*) and the river-trout (*Salmo fario*) were numerous in the Rhymney and other rivers of South Wales before salmonoids were almost exterminated by the pollutions allowed to pass into these streams, and so variable in their characters that the passage from one species to the other could be demonstrated in an almost unbroken series, which might induce some naturalists to regard both species as identical Abundant evidence of a similar character has accumulated, showing the frequent occurrence of hybrids between *Salmo fario* and *S trutta* In some rivers the conditions appear

to be more favorable to hybridism than in others in which
hybrids are of comparatively rare occurrence Hybrids between the salmon and other species are very scarce everywhere "

Very similar to the European *Salmo trutta* is the trout of Japan
(*Salmo perryi*), the young called yamabe, the adult kawamasu,
or river-salmon This species abounds everywhere in Japan,
the young being the common trout of the brooks, black-spotted
and crossed by parr-marks, the adult reaching a weight of ten
or twelve pounds in the larger rivers and descending to the sea.
In Kamchatka is another large, black-spotted, salmon-like
species properly to be called a salmon-trout This is *Salmo
mykiss*, a name very wrongly applied to the cutthroat trout of
the Columbia

The black-spotted trout, forming the subgenus *Salar*, differ
from *Salmo salar* and *Salmo trutta* in the greater development of the vomerine teeth, which are persistent throughout
life, in a long double series on the shaft of the vomer About
seven species are laboriously distinguished by Dr Gunther
in the waters of western Europe Most of these are regarded
by Dr Day as varieties of *Salmo fario* The latter species,
the common river-trout or lake-trout of Europe, is found throughout northern and central Europe, wherever suitable waters
occur. It is abundant, gamy, takes the hook readily, and is
excellent as food It is more hardy than the different species
of charr, although from an æsthetic point of view it must be
regarded as inferior to all of the *Salvelini* The largest river-
trout recorded by Dr Day weighed twenty-one pounds Such
large individuals are usually found in lakes in the north, well
stocked with smaller fishes on which trout may feed Farther south, where the surroundings are less favorable to trout-
life, they become mature at a length of less than a foot, and a
weight of a few ounces These excessive variations in the size
of individuals have received too little notice from students of
Salmonidæ Similar variations occur in all the non-migratory
species of *Salmo* and of *Salvelinus* Numerous river-trout have
been recorded from northern Asia, but as yet nothing can be
definitely stated as to the number of species actually existing.

The Black-spotted Trout.—In North America only the region west of the Mississippi Valley, the streams of southeastern

Alaska, and the valley of Mackenzie River have species of black-spotted trout There are few of these north of Sitka in Alaska, although black-spotted trout are occasionally taken on Kadiak and about Bristol Bay, and none east of the Rocky Mountain region If we are to follow the usage of the names "salmon" and "trout" which prevails in England, we should say that, in America, it is only these western regions which have any trout at all. Of the number of species (about twenty-five in all) which have been indicated by authors, certainly not more than about 8 to 10 can possibly be regarded as distinct species The other names are either useless synonyms, or else they have been applied to local varieties which pass by degrees into the ordinary types.

The Trout of Western America.—In the western part of America are found more than a score of forms of trout of the genus *Salmo*, all closely related and difficult to distinguish There are representatives in the headwaters of the Rio Grande, Arkansas, South Platte, Missouri, and Colorado rivers, also in the Great Salt Lake basin, throughout the Columbia basin, in all suitable waters from southern California and Chihuahua to Sitka, and even to Bristol Bay, similar forms again appearing in Kamchatka and Japan

Among the various more or less tangible species that may be recognized, three distinct series appear These have been termed the cutthroat-trout series (allies of *Salmo clarkii*), the rainbow-trout series (allies of *Salmo irideus*), and the steelhead series (allies of *Salmo rivularis*, a species more usually but wrongly called *Salmo gairdneri*)

The steelhead, or *rivularis* series, is found in the coastwise streams of California and in the streams of Oregon and Washington, below the great Shoshone Falls of Snake River, and northward in Alaska along the mainland as far as Skaguay The steelhead-trout reach a large size (10 to 20 pounds) They spend a large part of their life in the sea In all the true steelheads the head is relatively very short, its length being contained about five times in the distance from tip of snout to base of caudal fin The scales in the steelhead are always rather small, about 150 in a linear series, and there is no red under the throat The spots on the dorsal fin are fewer in the steelhead (4 to 6 rows) than in the other American trout

The rainbow forms are chiefly confined to the streams of California and Oregon   In these the scales are large (about 135 in a lengthwise series) and the head is relatively large, forming nearly one-fourth of the length to base of caudal   These enter the sea only when in the small coastwise streams   Usually they have no red under the throat   The cutthroat forms are found from Humboldt Bay northward as far as Sitka, in the coastwise streams of northern California, Oregon, Washington, and Alaska, and all the clear streams on both sides of the Rocky Mountains, and in the Great Basin and the headwaters of the Colorado   The cutthroat-trout have the scales small, about 180, and there is always a bright dash of orange-red on each side concealed beneath the branches of the lower jaw   Along the western slope of the Sierra Nevada there are also forms of trout with the general appearance of rainbow-trout and evidently belonging to that species, but with scales intermediate in number (in McCloud River), var *shasta*, or with scales as small as in the typical cutthroat (Kern River), var *gilberti*   In these small-scaled forms more or less red appears below the lower jaw, and they are doubtless what they appear to be, really intermediate between *clarkii* and *irideus*, although certainly nearest the latter   A similar series of forms occurs in the Columbia basin, the upper Snake being inhabited by *clarkii* and the lower Snake by *clarkii* and *rivularis*, together with a medley of forms apparently intermediate

It seems probable that the American trout originated in Asia, extended its range to southeast Alaska, thence southward to the Fraser and Columbia, thence to the Yellowstone and the Missouri *via* Two-Ocean Pass, from the Snake River to the Great Basins of Utah and Nevada, from the Missouri southward to the Platte and the Arkansas, thence from the Platte to the Rio Grande and the Colorado, and then from Oregon southward coastwise and along the Sierras to northern Mexico, thence northward and coastwise, the sea-running forms passing from stream to stream

Of the American species the rainbow trout of California (*Salmo irideus*) most nearly approaches the European *Salmo fario*   It has the scales comparatively large, although rather smaller than in *Salmo fario*, the usual number in a longitudinal series being about 135. The mouth is smaller than in other American trout, the maxillary, except in old males, rarely extending beyond the eye The caudal fin is well forked, becoming in very old fishes more nearly truncate The head is relatively large, about four times in the total length The size of the head forms the best distinctive character The color, as in all the other species, is bluish, the sides silvery in the males, with a red lateral band, and reddish and dusky blotches The head, back, and upper fins are sprinkled with round black spots, which are very variable in number, those on the dorsal usually in about nine rows In specimens taken

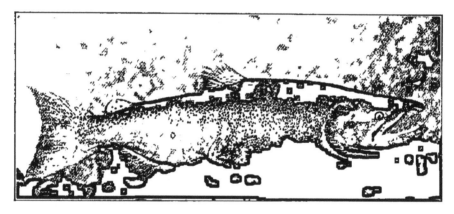

FIG 230 — Rainbow Trout (male), *Salmo irideus shasta* Jordan (Photograph by Cloudsley Rutter)

in the sea this species, like most other trout in similar conditions, is bright silvery, and sometimes immaculate This species is especially characteristic of the waters of California It abounds in every clear brook, from the Mexican line northward to Mount Shasta, or beyond, the species passing in the Columbia region by degrees into the species or form known as *Salmo masoni*, the Oregon rainbow trout, a small rainbow trout common in the forest streams of Oregon, with smaller mouth and fewer spots on the dorsal No true rainbow trout have been anywhere obtained to the eastward of the Cascade Range or of the Sierra Nevada, except as artificially planted in the Truckee River The species varies much in size, specimens from northern California often reach a weight of six pounds, while in the streams above Tia Juana in Lower California the southernmost locality from which I have obtained trout, they seldom exceed a length of six inches   Although not usually an anadromous species, the rainbow trout frequently moves about in the rivers, and it often enters the sea, large sea-run specimens being often taken for steelheads   Several attempts have been made to introduce it in Eastern streams, but it appears to seek the sea when it is lost   It is apparently more hardy and less greedy than the American charr, or brook-trout (*Salvelinus*

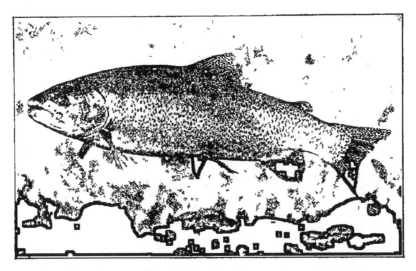

Fig 231 —Rainbow Trout (female), *Salmo irideus shasta* Jordan
(Photograph by Cloudsley Rutter)

fontinalis)   On the other hand, it is distinctly inferior to the latter in beauty and in gaminess.

In the Kings and Kern rivers of California occurs a beautiful trout, *Salmo gilberti,* a variant of *Salmo irideus,* but with smaller scales   In isolated streams with a bottom of red granite at the head-waters of the Kern are three species called "golden trout," all small and all brilliantly colored, each of the species being independently derived from *Salmo gilberti,* the special traits fixed through isolation.   These species are *Salmo aguabonita* Jordan, of the South Fork of the Kern, *Salmo roosevelti* Evermann of Volcano Creek, and *Salmo whitei* Evermann of Soda Creek   These rank with the most beautiful of all the many forms of trout, in which group their coloration is quite unique

In beauty of color, gracefulness of form and movement

KERN RIVER TROUT

SALMO GILBERTI (JORDAN)

(DRAWN FROM LIFE BY CHARLES B. HUDSON FROM A SPECIMEN 18¾ INCHES LONG)

sprightliness when in the water, reckless dash with which it springs from the water to meet the descending fly ere it strikes the surface, and the mad and repeated leaps from the water when hooked, the rainbow trout must ever hold a very high rank "The gamest fish we have ever seen," writes Dr Evermann, "was a 16-inch rainbow taken on a fly in a small spring branch tributary of Williamson River in southern Oregon It was in a broad and deep pool of exceedingly clear water. As the angler from behind a clump of willows made the cast the trout bounded from the water and met the fly in the air a foot or more above the surface, missing it, he dropped upon the water, only to turn about and strike viciously a second time at the fly just as it touched the surface, though he again missed the fly, the hook caught him in the lower jaw from the outside, and then began a fight which would delight the heart of any angler His first effort was to reach the bottom of the pool, then, doubling upon the line, he made three jumps from the water in quick succession, clearing the surface in each instance from one to four feet, and every time doing his utmost to free himself from the hook by shaking his head as vigorously as a dog shakes a rat Then he would rush wildly about in the large pool, now attempting to go down over the riffle below the pool, now trying the opposite direction, and often striving to hide under one or the other of the banks It was easy to handle the fish when the dash was made up or down stream or for the opposite side, but when he turned about and made a rush for the protection of the overhanging bank upon which the angler stood it was not easy to keep the line taut Movements such as these were frequently repeated, and two more leaps were made But finally he was worn out after as honest a fight as trout ever made "

"The rainbow takes the fly so readily that there is no reason for resorting to grasshoppers, salmon-eggs, or other bait It is a fish whose gameness will satisfy the most exacting of expert anglers and whose readiness to take any proper line will please the most impatient of inexperienced amateurs "

The steelhead (*Salmo rivularis*) is a large trout, reaching twelve to twenty pounds in weight, found abundantly in river estuaries and sometimes in lakes from Lynn Canal to Santa

Barbara The spent fish abound in the rivers in spring at the time of the salmon-run The species is rarely canned, but is valued for shipment in cold storage Its bones are much more firm than those of the salmon—a trait unfavorable for canning purposes The flesh when not spent after spawning is excellent The steelhead does not die after spawning, as all the Pacific salmon do

It is thought by some anglers that the young fish hatched in the brooks from eggs of the steelhead remain in mountain streams from six to thirty-six months, going down to the sea with the high waters of spring, after which they return to spawn as typical steelhead trout I now regard this view as unfounded In my experience the rainbow and the steelhead are always distinguishable the steelhead abounds where the rain-

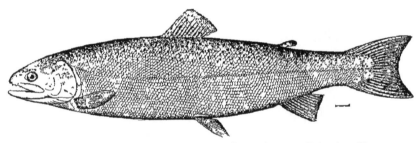

Fig 232 —Steelhead Trout, *Salmo rivularis* Ayres Columbia River

bow trout is unknown, the scales in the steelhead are always smaller (about 155) than in typical rainbow trout, finally, the small size of the head in the steelhead is always distinctive

The Kamloops trout, described by the writer from the upper Columbia, seems to be a typical steelhead as found well up the rivers away from the sea Derived from the steelhead, but apparently quite distinct from it, are three very noble trout, all confined so far as yet known to Lake Crescent in northwestern Washington These are the crescent trout, *Salmo crescentis*, the Beardslee trout, *Salmo beardsleei*, and the long-headed trout, *Salmo bathœcetor* The first two, discovered by Admiral L A. Beardslee, are trout of peculiar attractiveness and excellence The third is a deep-water form, never rising to the surface, and caught only on set lines Its origin is still uncertain, and it may be derived from some type other than the steelhead

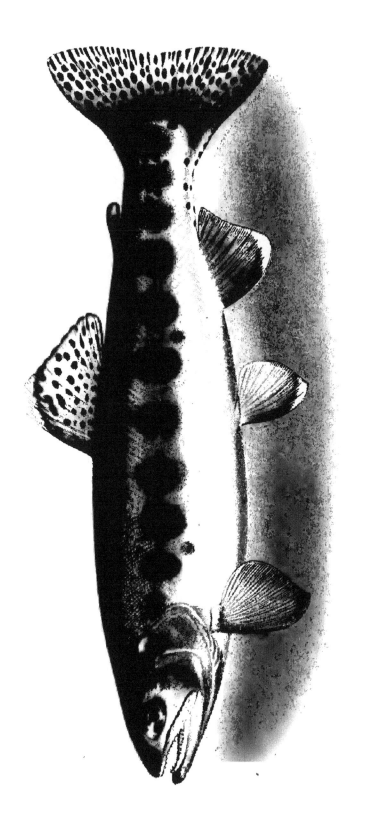

GOLDEN TROUT OF VOLCANO CREEK

SALMO ROOSEVELTI EVERMANN

(DRAWN FROM LIFE BY CHARLES B. HUDSON FROM THE TYPE, A SPECIMEN 11½ INCHES LONG)

Cutthroat or Red-throated Trout. — This species has much smaller scales than the rainbow trout or steelhead, the usual number in a longitudinal series being 160 to 170 Its head is longer (about four times in length to base of caudal) Its mouth is proportionately larger, and there is always a narrow band of small teeth on the hyoid bone at the base of the tongue These teeth are always wanting in *Salmo irideus* and *rivularis* in which species the rim of the tongue only has teeth The color in *Salmo clarkii* is, as in other species, exceedingly variable In life there is always a deep-red blotch on the throat, between the branches of the lower jaw and the membrane connecting them This is not found in other species, or is reduced to a narrow strip or·pinkish shade It seems to be constant in all varieties of *Salmo clarkii*, at all ages, thus furnishing a good distinctive character. It is the sign manual of the Sioux Indians, and the anglers have already accepted from this mark the name of cutthroat-trout The cutthroat-trout of some species is found in every suitable river and lake in the great basin of Utah, in the streams of Colorado, Wyoming, and Montana, on both sides of the Rocky Mountains It is also found throughout Oregon, Washington, Idaho, British Columbia, the coastwise islands of southeastern Alaska (Baranof, etc), to Kadiak and Bristol Bay, probably no stream or lake suitable for trout-life being without it In California the species seems to be comparatively rare, and its range rarely extending south of Cape Mendocino Large sea-run individuals analogous to the steelheads are sometimes found in the mouth of the Sacramento In Washington and Alaska this species regularly enters the sea In Puget Sound it is a common fish These sea-run individuals are more silvery and less spotted than those found in the mountain streams and lakes The size of *Salmo clarkii* is subject to much variation Ordinarily four to six pounds is a large size, but in certain favored waters, as Lake Tahoe, and the fjords of southeastern Alaska, specimens from twenty to thirty pounds are occasionally taken

Those species or individuals dwelling in lakes of considerable size, where the water is of such temperature and depth as insures an ample food-supply, will reach a large size, while those in a restricted environment, where both the water and food are limited, will be small directly in proportion to these environing restrictions   The trout of the Klamath Lakes, for example, reach a weight of at least 17 pounds, while in Fish Lake in Idaho mature trout do not exceed 8 to 9¼ inches in total length or one-fourth pound in weight   In small creeks in the Sawtooth Mountains and elsewhere they reach maturity at a length of 5 or 6 inches, and are often spoken of as brook-trout and with the impression that they are a species different from the larger ones found in the lakes and larger streams   But as all sorts and gradations between these extreme forms may be found in the intervening and connecting waters, the differences are not even of sub-specific significance

Dr Evermann observes. "The various forms of cutthroat-trout vary greatly in game qualities, even the same subspecies in different waters, in different parts of its habitat, or at different

Fig 233   Fig 234

Fig 233 —Head of adult Trout-worm, *Dibothrium cordiceps* Leidy, a parasite of *Salmo clarku*   From intestine of white pelican, Yellowstone Lake   (After Linton)

Fig 234 —Median segments of *Dibothrium cordiceps*

seasons, will vary greatly in this regard   In general, however, it is perhaps a fair statement to say that the cutthroat-trout are regarded by anglers as being inferior in gaminess to the Eastern brook-trout   But while this is true, it must not by any means be inferred that it is without game qualities, for it is really a fish which possesses those qualities in a very high degree   Its vigor and voraciousness are determined largely, of course, by the character of the stream or lake in which it lives.   The individuals which dwell in cold streams about cascades and seething rapids will show marvelous strength and will make a fight which is rarely equaled by its Eastern cousin, while in warmer and larger streams and lakes they may be very sluggish and show but little fight   Yet this is by no means always true. In the Klamath Lakes, where the trout grow very large and

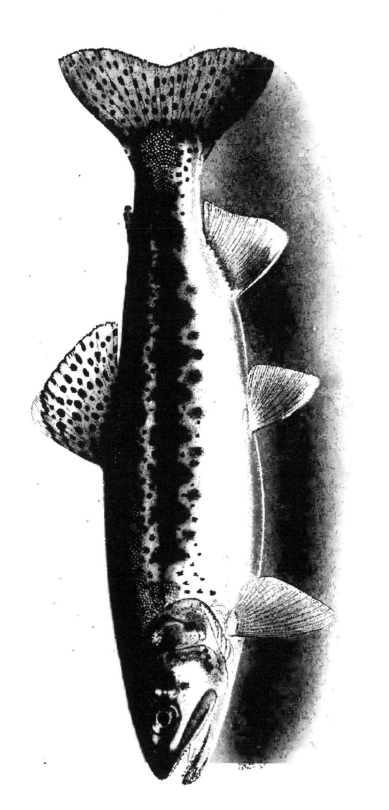

GOLDEN TROUT OF SODA CREEK

SALMO WHITEI EVERMANN

(DRAWN FROM LIFE BY CHARLES B. HUDSON FROM THE TYPE, A SPECIMEN 7¾ INCHES LONG)

where they are often very logy, one is occasionally hooked which tries to the utmost the skill of the angler to prevent his tackle from being smashed and at the same time save the fish "

Of the various forms derived from *Salmo clarkii* some mere varieties, some distinct species, the following are among the most marked

Salmo henshawi, the trout of Lake Tahoe and its tributaries and outlet, Truckee River, found in fact also in the Humboldt

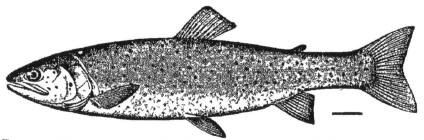

FIG 235 —Tahoe Trout, *Salmo henshawi* Gill & Jordan   Lake Tahoe, California

and the Carson and throughout the basin of the former glacial lake called Lake Lahontan   This is a distinct species from *Salmo clarkii* and must be regarded as the finest of all the cut-throat-trout   It is readily known by its spotted belly, the black spots being evenly scattered over the whole surface of the body, above and below   This is an excellent game-fish, and from Lake Tahoe and Pyramid Lake it is brought in large numbers to the markets of San Francisco   In the depths of Lake Tahoe, which is the finest mountain lake of the Sierra Nevada, occurs a very large variety which spawns in the lake, *Salmo henshawi tahoensis*   This reaches a weight of twenty-eight pounds

In the Great Basin of Utah is found a fine trout, very close to the ordinary cutthroat of the Columbia, from which it is derived   This is known as *Salmo clarkii virginalis*   In Utah Lake it reaches a large size

In Waha Lake in Washington, a lake without outlet, is found a small trout with peculiar markings called *Salmo clarkii bouvieri*

In the head-waters of the Platte and Arkansas rivers is the small green-back trout, green or brown, with red throat-patch and large black spots　This is *Salmo clarkii stomias*, and it is especially fine in St Vrain's River and the streams of Estes Park

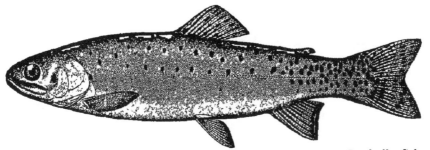

Fig 236 —Green-back Trout, *Salmo stomias* Cope　Arkansas River, Leadville, Colo

In Twin Lakes, a pair of glacial lakes tributary of the Arkansas near Leadville, is found *Salmo clarkii macdonaldi*, the yellow-finned trout, a large and very handsome species living in deep water, and with the fins golden yellow. This approaches the Colorado trout, *Salmo clarkii pleuriticus*, and it may be derived

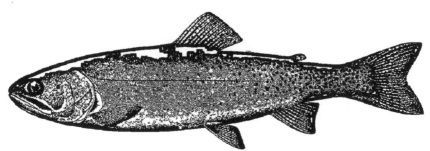

Fig 237 —Yellow-fin Trout of Twin Lakes, *Salmo macdonaldi* Jordan & Evermann
Twin Lakes, Colo

from the latter, although it occurs in the same waters as the very different green-back trout, or *Salmo clarkii stomias*

Two fine trout derived from *Salmo clarkii* have been lately discovered by Dr Daniel G Elliot in Lake Southerland, a mountain lake near Lake Crescent, but not connected with it, the two separated from the sea by high waterfalls　These have been described by Dr Seth E Meek as *Salmo jordani*, the "spotted trout" of Lake Southerland, and *Salmo declivifrons*, the "salmon-trout"　These seem to be distinct forms or subspecies produced through isolation

The Rio Grande trout (*Salmo clarku spilurus*) is a large and profusely spotted trout, found in the head-waters of the Rio

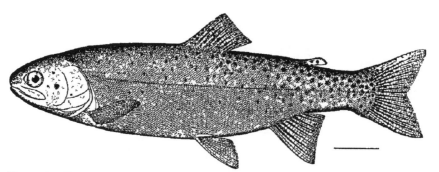

FIG 238 — Rio Grande Trout, *Salmo clarku spilurus* Cope   Del Norte, Colo

Grande, the mountain streams of the Great Basin of Utah, and as far south as the northern part of Chihuahua   Its scales are still smaller than those of the ordinary cutthroat-trout, and the black spots are chiefly confined to the tail.   Closely related to

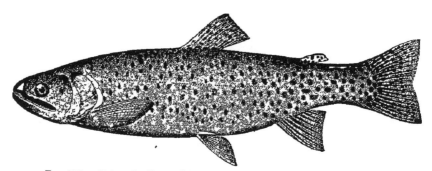

FIG 239 — Colorado River Trout, *Salmo clarku pleuriticus* Cope
Trapper's Lake, Colo

it is the trout of the Colorado Basin, *Salmo clarku pleuriticus*, a large and handsome trout with very small scales, much sought by anglers in western Colorado, and abounding in all suitable streams throughout the Colorado Basin

Hucho, the Huchen. — The genus *Hucho* has been framed for the Huchen or Rothfisch (*Hucho hucho*) of the Danube, a very large trout, differing from the genus *Salmo* in having no teeth on the shaft of the vomer, and from the *Salvelini* at least in form and coloration   The huchen is a long and slender, somewhat pike-like fish, with depressed snout and strong teeth.

The color is silvery, sprinkled with small black dots   It reaches a size little inferior to that of the salmon, and it is said to be an excellent food-fish   In northern Japan is a similar species,

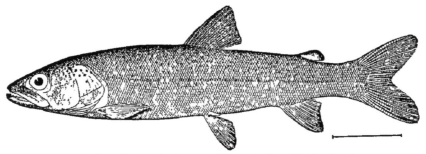

FIG 240 —Ito, *Hucho blackistoni* (Hilgendorf)   Hokkaido, Japan

Hucho blackistoni, locally known as Ito, a large and handsome trout with very slender body, reaching a length of 2½ feet.   It is well worthy of introduction into American and European waters

Salvelinus, the Charr —The genus *Salvelinus* comprises the finest of the *Salmonidæ,* from the point of view of the angler or the artist   In England the species are known as charr or char, in contradistinction to the black-spotted species of *Salmo,* which are called trout.   The former name has unfortunately been lost in America, where the name "trout" is given indiscriminately to both groups, and, still worse, to numerous other fishes (*Micropterus, Hexagrammos, Cynoscion, Agonostomus*) wholly unlike the *Salmonidæ* in all respects   It is sometimes said that "the American brook-trout is no trout, nothing but a charr," almost as though "charr" were a word of reproach Nothing higher, however, can be said of a salmonoid than that it is a "charr"   The technical character of the genus *Salvelinus* lies in the form of its vomer.   This is deeper than in *Salmo,* and when the flesh is removed the bone is found to be somewhat boat-shaped above, and with the shaft depressed and out of the line of the head of the vomer   Only the head or chevron is armed with teeth, and the shaft is covered by skin

In color all the charrs differ from the salmon and trout The body in all is covered with round spots which are paler than the ground color, and crimson or gray   The lower fins are usually edged with bright colors The sexual differences are not great. The scales, in general, are smaller than in other *Salmonidæ*, and they are imbedded in the skin to such a degree as to escape the notice of casual observers and even of most anglers.

> "One trout scale in the scales I'd lay
> (If trout had scales), and 'twill outweigh
> The wrong side of the balances "—LOWELL

The charrs inhabit, in general, only the clearest and coldest of mountain streams and lakes, or bays of similar temperature They are not migratory, or only to a limited extent   In northern regions they descend to the sea, where they grow much more rapidly and assume a nearly uniform silvery-gray color   The different species are found in all suitable waters throughout the northern parts of both continents, except in the Rocky Mountains and Great Basin, where only the black-spotted trout occur   The number of species of charr is very uncertain, as, both in America and Europe, trivial variations and individual peculiarities have been raised to the rank of species.   More types, however, seem to be represented in America than in Europe

The only really well-authenticated species of charr in European waters is the red charr, salbling, or ombre chevalier (*Salve-*

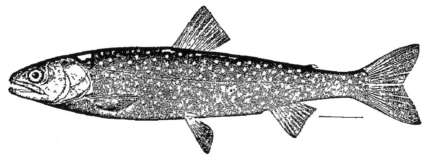

FIG 241 —Rangeley Trout, *Salvelinus oquassa* (Girard)   Lake Oquassa, Maine

linus alpinus)   This species is found in cold, clear streams in Switzerland, Germany, and throughout Scandinavia and the British Islands   Compared with the American charr or brook-trout, it is a slenderer fish, with smaller mouth, longer fins, and smaller red spots, which are confined to the sides of the

body It is a "gregarious and deep-swimming fish, shy of
taking the bait and feeding largely at night-time It appears
to require very pure and mostly deep water for its residence"
It is less tenacious of life than the trout It reaches a weight of
from one to five pounds, probably rarely exceeding the latter
in size The various charr described from Siberia are far too
little known to be enumerated here

Of the American charr the one most resembling the European
species is the Rangeley Lake trout (*Salvelinus oquassa*). The
exquisite little fish is known in the United States only from
the Rangeley chain of lakes in western Maine This is very
close to the Greenland charr, *Salvelinus stagnalis*, a beautiful
species of the far north The Rangeley trout is much slenderer
than the common brook-trout, with much smaller head and
smaller mouth In life it is dark blue above, and the deep-red
spots are confined to the sides of the body The species rarely
exceeds the length of a foot in the Rangeley Lakes, but in some
other waters it reaches a much larger size So far as is known
it keeps itself in the depths of the lake until its spawning season
approaches, in October, when it ascends the stream to spawn

Still other species of this type are the Sunapee trout,
Salvelinus aureolus, a beautiful charr almost identical with the

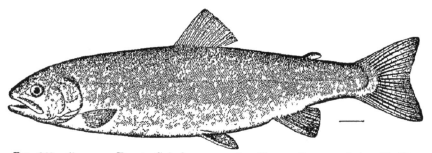

Fig 242 —Sunapee Trout, *Salvelinus aureolus* Bean Sunapee Lake, N H

European species, found in numerous ponds and lakes of eastern
New Hampshire and neighboring parts of Maine Mr Garman
regards this trout as the offspring of an importation of the ombre
chevalier and not as a native species, and in this view he may
be correct *Salvelinus alipes* of the far north may be the same
species Another remarkable form is the Lac de Marbre trout
of Canada, *Salvelinus marstoni* of Garman

In Arctic regions another species, called *Salvelinus naresi*, is very close to *Salvelinus oquassa* and may be the same

Another beautiful little charr, allied to *Salvelinus stagnalis*, is the Floeberg charr (*Salvelinus arcturus*) This species has been brought from Victoria Lake and Floeberg Beach, in the

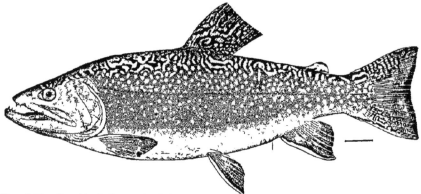

Fig 243 —Speckled Trout (male), *Salvelinus fontinalis* (Mitchill)   New York.

extreme northern part of Arctic America, the northernmost point whence any salmonoid has been obtained

The American charr, or, as it is usually called, the brook-trout (*Salvelinus fontinalis*), although one of the most beautiful of fishes, is perhaps the least graceful of all the genuine charrs It is technically distinguished by the somewhat heavy head and large mouth, the maxillary bone reaching more or less beyond the eye   There are no teeth on the hyoid bone, traces at least of such teeth being found in nearly all other species   Its color is somewhat different from that of the others, the red spots being large and the black more or less mottled and barred with darker olive   The dorsal and caudal fins are likewise barred or mottled, while in the other species they are generally uniform in color   The brook-trout is found only in streams east of the Mississippi and Saskatchewan   It occurs in all suitable streams of the Alleghany region and the Great Lake system, from the Chattahoochee River in northern Georgia northward at least to Labrador and Hudson Bay, the northern limits of its range being as yet not well ascertained   It varies greatly in size, according to its surroundings, those found in lakes being larger than those resident in small brooks   Those found

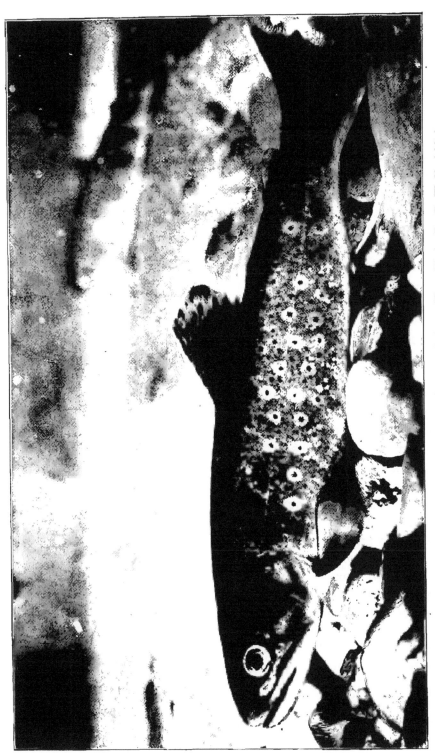

FIG. 244.—Brook Trout, *Salvelinus fontinalis* (Mitchill), natural size.   (From life by Dr. R. W. Shufeldt.)

334

farthest south, in the head-waters of the Chattahoochee, Savannah, Catawba, and French Broad, rarely pass the dimensions of fingerlings. The largest specimens are recorded from the sea along the Canadian coast. These frequently reach a weight of ten pounds, and from their marine and migratory habits, they have been regarded as forming a distinct variety (*Salvelinus fontinalis immaculatus*), but this form is merely a sea-run brook-trout. The largest fresh-water specimens rarely exceed seven pounds in weight. Some unusually large brook-trout have been taken in the Rangeley Lakes, the largest known to me having a reputed weight of eleven pounds. The brook-trout is the favorite game-fish of American waters, preeminent in wariness, in beauty, and in delicacy of flesh. It inhabits all clear and cold waters within its range, the large lakes and the smallest ponds, the tiniest brooks and the largest rivers, and when it can do so without soiling its aristocratic gills on the way, it descends to the sea and grows large and fat on the animals of the ocean. Although a bold biter it is a wary fish, and it often requires much skill to capture it. It can be caught, too, with artificial or natural flies, minnows, crickets, worms, grasshoppers, grubs, the spawn of other fish, or even the eyes or cut pieces of other trout. It spawns in the fall, from September to late in November. It begins to reproduce at the age of two years, then having a length of about six inches. In spring-time the trout delight in rapids and swiftly running water, and in the hot months of midsummer they resort to deep, cool, and shaded pools. Later, at the approach of the spawning season, they gather around the mouths of cool, gravelly brooks, whither they resort to make their beds *

The trout are rapidly disappearing from our streams through the agency of the manufacturer and the summer boarder. In the words of an excellent angler, the late Myron W. Reed of Denver "This is the last generation of trout-fishers. The children will not be able to find any. Already there are well-trodden paths by every stream in Maine, in New York, and in Michigan. I know of but one river in North America by the side of which you will find no paper collar or other evidence of civilization. It is the Nameless River. Not that trout will

* Hallock

cease to be   They will be hatched by machinery and raised in ponds, and fattened on chopped liver, and grow flabby and lose their spots   The trout of the restaurant will not cease to be   He is no more like the trout of the wild river than the fat and songless reedbird is like the bobolink   Gross feeding and easy pond-life enervate and deprave him   The trout that the children will know only by legend is the gold-sprinkled, living arrow of the white water, able to zigzag up the cataract, able to loiter in the rapids, whose dainty meat is the glancing butterfly ''

The brook-trout adapts itself readily to cultivation in artificial ponds   It has been successfully transported to Europe, and it is already abundant in certain streams in England, in California, and elsewhere

In Dublin Pond, New Hampshire, is a gray variety without red spots, called *Salvelinus agassizi*

The "Dolly Varden" trout, or malma (*Salvelinus malma*), is very similar to the brook-trout, closely resembling it in size, form, color, and habits.   It is found always to the westward of the Rocky Mountains, in the streams of northern California, Oregon,

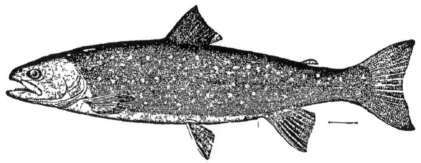

Fig 245 —Malma Trout, or "Dolly Varden," *Salvelinus malma* (Walbaum)
Cook Inlet, Alaska

Washington, and British Columbia, Alaska, and Kamtchatka, as far as the Kurile Islands   It abounds in the sea in the northward, and specimens of ten to twelve pounds weight are not uncommon in Puget Sound and especially in Alaska   The Dolly Varden trout is, in general, slenderer and less compressed than the Eastern brook-trout   The red spots are found on the back of the fish as well as on the sides, and the back and upper fins are without the blackish marblings and blotches seen in

Salvelinus fontinalis In value as food, in beauty, and in gaminess *Salvelinus malma* is very similar to its Eastern cousin.

In Alaska the Dolly Varden, locally known as salmon-trout, is very destructive to the eggs of the salmon, and countless numbers are taken in the salmon-nets of Alaska and thrown away as useless by the canners In every coastwise stream of Alaska

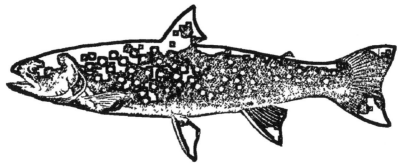

Fig 246 —The Dolly Varden Trout, *Salvelinus malma* (Walbaum) Lake Pend d'Oreille, Idaho (After Evermann)

the water fairly "boils" with these trout They are, however, not found in the Yukon In northern Japan occurs *Salvelinus pluvius*, the iwana, a species very similar to the Dolly Varden, but not so large or so brightly colored In the Kurile region and Kamtchatka is another large charr, *Salvelinus kundscha*, with the spots large and cream-color instead of crimson

Cristivomer, the Great Lake Trout.—Allied to the true charrs, but now placed by us in a different genus, *Cristivomer*, is the

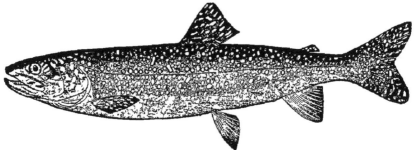

Fig 247 —Great Lake Trout, *Cristivomer namaycush* (Walbaum). Lake Michigan

Great Lake trout, otherwise known as Mackinaw trout, longe, or togue (*Cristivomer namaycush*) Technically this fish differs from the true charrs in having on its vomer a raised crest behind the chevron and free from the shaft   This crest is armed with strong teeth.   There are also large hooked teeth on the hyoid bone, and the teeth generally are proportionately stronger than in most of the other species   The Great Lake trout is grayish in color, light or dark according to its surroundings, and the body is covered with round paler spots, which are gray instead of red The dorsal and caudal fins are marked with darker reticulations, somewhat as in the brook-trout.   This noble species is found in all the larger lakes from New England and New York to Wisconsin, Montana, the Mackenzie River, and in all the lakes tributary to the Yukon in Alaska   We have taken examples from Lake Bennett, Lake Tagish, Summit Lake (White Pass), and have seen specimens from Lake La Hache in British Columbia   It reaches a much larger size than any *Salvelinus*, specimens of from fifteen to twenty pounds weight being not uncommon, while it occasionally attains a weight of fifty to eighty pounds   As a food-fish it ranks high, although it may be regarded as somewhat inferior to the brook-trout or the whitefish Compared with other salmonoids, the Great Lake trout is a sluggish, heavy, and ravenous fish   It has been known to eat raw potato, liver, and corn-cobs,—refuse thrown from passing steamers According to Herbert, "a coarse, heavy, stiff rod, and a powerful oiled hempen or flaxen line, on a winch, with a heavy sinker, a cod-hook, baited with any kind of flesh, fish, or fowl,—is the most successful, if not the most orthodox or scientific, mode of capturing him   His great size and immense strength alone give him value as a fish of game, but when hooked he pulls strongly and fights hard, though he is a boring, deep fighter, and seldom if ever leaps out of the water, like the true salmon or brook-trout "

In the depths of Lake Superior is a variety of the Great Lake trout known as the Siscowet (*Cristivomer namaycush siskawitz*), remarkable for its extraordinary fatness of flesh   The cause of this difference lies probably in some peculiarity of food as yet unascertained

The Ayu, or Sweetfish — The ayu, or sweetfish, of Japan, *Plecoglossus altivelis*, resembles a small trout in form, habits, and scaling   Its teeth are, however, totally different, being arranged on serrated plates on the sides of the jaws, and the tongue marked with similar folds   The ayu abounds in all clear streams of Japan and Formosa. It runs up from the sea like a salmon. It reaches the length of about a foot. The

Fig. 248 —Ayu, or Japanese Samlet, *Plecoglossus altivelis* Schlegel. Tamagawa, Tokyo, Japan.

flesh is very fine and delicate, scarcely surpassed by that of any other fish whatsoever. It should be introduced into clear short streams throughout the temperate zones.

In the river at Gifu in Japan and in some other streams the ayu is fished for on a large scale by means of tamed cormorants. This is usually done from boats in the night by the light of torches.

Cormorant-fishing.—The following account of cormorant-fishing is taken, by the kind permission of Mr. Caspar W. Whitney, from an article contributed by the writer to *Outing*, April, 1902:

Tamagawa means Jewel River, and no water could be clearer. It rises somewhere up in the delectable mountains to the eastward of Musashi, among the mysterious pines and green-brown fir-trees, and it flows across the plains bordered by rice-fields and mulberry orchards to the misty bay of Tokyo. It is, therefore, a river of Japan, and along its shores are quaint old temples, each guarding its section of primitive forest, picturesque bridges, huddling villages, and torii, or gates through which the gods may pass.

The stream itself is none too large—a boy may wade it—but it runs on a wide bed, which it will need in flood-time, when the snow melts in the mountains. And this broad flood-bed is filled with gravel, with straggling willows, showy day-lilies, orange amaryllis, and the little sky-blue spider-flower, which the Japanese call chocho, or butterfly-weed

In the Tamagawa are many fishes. shining minnows in the white ripples, dark catfishes in the pools and eddies, and little sculpins and gobies lurking under the stones Trout dart through its upper waters, and at times salmon run up from the sea

But the one fish of all its fishes is the ayu This is a sort of dwarf salmon, running in the spring and spawning in the rivers just as a salmon does But it is smaller than any salmon, not larger than a smelt, and its flesh is white and tender, and so very delicate in its taste and odor that one who tastes it crisply fried or broiled feels that he has never tasted real fish before In all its anatomy the ayu is a salmon, a dwarf of its kind, one which our ancestors in England would have called a "samlet" Its scientific name is *Plecoglossus altivelis Plecoglossus* means plaited tongue, and *altivelis*, having a high sail, for the skin of the tongue is plaited or folded in a curious way, and the dorsal fin is higher than that of the salmon, and one poetically inclined might, if he likes, call it a sail The teeth of the ayu are very peculiar, for they constitute a series of saw-edged folds or plaits along the sides of the jaws, quite different from those of any other fish whatsoever.

In size the ayu is not more than a foot to fifteen inches long It is like a trout in build, and its scales are just as small. It is light yellowish or olive in color, growing silvery below Behind its gills is a bar of bright shining yellow, and its adipose fin is edged with scarlet The fins are yellow, and the dorsal fin shaded with black, while the anal fin is dashed with pale red

So much for the river and the ayu. It is time for us to go afishing It is easy enough to find the place, for it is not more than ten miles out of Tokyo, on a fine old farm just by the ancient Temple of Tachikawa, with its famous inscribed stone, given by the emperor of China

At the farmhouse, commodious and hospitable, likewise clean and charming after the fashion of Japan, we send for the boy who brings our fishing-tackle

They come waddling into the yard, the three birds with which we are to do our fishing   Black cormorants they are, each with a white spot behind its eye, and a hoarse voice, come of standing in the water, with which it says *y-eugh* whenever a stranger makes a friendly overture   The cormorants answer to the name of Ou, which in Japanese is something like the only word the cormorants can say   The boy puts them in a box together and we set off across the drifted gravel to the Tamagawa   Arrived at the stream, the boy takes the three cormorants out of the box and adjusts their fishing-harness   This consists of a tight ring about the bottom of the neck, of a loop under each wing, and a directing line

Two other boys take a low net   They drag it down the stream, driving the little fishes—ayu, zakko, hae, and all the rest—before it   The boy with the cormorants goes in advance. The three birds are eager as pointer dogs, and apparently full of perfect enjoyment   To the right and left they plunge with lightning strokes, each dip bringing up a shining fish   When the bird's neck is full of fishes down to the level of the shoulders, the boy draws him in, grabs him by the leg, and shakes him unceremoniously over a basket until all the fishes have flopped out.

The cormorants watch the sorting of the fish with eager eyes and much repeating of *y-eugh*, the only word they know. The ayu are not for them, and some of the kajikas and hazés were prizes of science   But zakko (the dace) and hae (the minnow) were made for the cormorant.   The boy picks out the chubs and minnows and throws them to one bird and then another   Each catches his share on the fly, swallows it at one gulp, for the ring is off his neck by this time, and then says *y-eugh*, which means that he likes the fun, and when we are ready will be glad to try again   And no doubt they have tried it many times since, for there are plenty of fishes in the Jewel River, zakko and hae as well as ayu

Fossil Salmonidæ.—Fossil salmonidæ are rare and known chiefly from detached scales, the bones in this family being very brittle and easily destroyed   Nothing is added to our knowledge of the origin of these fishes from such fossils

A large fossil trout or salmon, called *Rhabdofario lacustris,* has been brought from the Pliocene at Catherine's Creek, Idaho. It is known from the skull only *Thaumaturus luxatus,* from the Miocene of Bohemia, shows the print of the adipose fin As already stated, some fragments of the hooked jaws of salmon, from pleistocene deposits in Idaho, are in the museum of the University of California.

CHAPTER XXI

THE GRAYLING AND THE SMELT

THE Grayling, or **Thymallidæ** — The small family of *Thymallidæ*, or grayling, is composed of finely organized fishes allied to the trout, but differing in having the frontal bones meeting on the middle line of the skull, thus excluding the frontals from contact with the supraoccipital The anterior half of the very high dorsal is made up of unbranched simple rays There is but one genus, *Thymallus*, comprising very noble game-fishes characteristic of sub-arctic streams

The grayling, *Thymallus*, of Europe, is termed by Saint Ambrose "the flower of fishes" The teeth on the tongue,

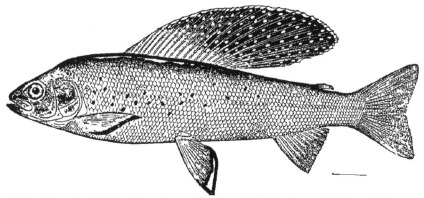

Fig 249 —Alaska Grayling, *Thymallus signifer* Richardson Nulato, Alaska

found in all the trout and salmon, are obsolete in the grayling The chief distinctive peculiarity of the genus *Thymallus* is the great development of the dorsal fin, which has more rays (20 to 24) than are found in any of the *Salmonidæ*, and the fin is also higher All the species are gaily colored, the dorsal fin especially being marked with purplish or greenish bands

343

and bright rose-colored spots, while the body is mostly purplish gray, often with spots of black   Most of the species rarely exceed a foot in length, but northward they grow larger   Grayling weighing five pounds have been taken in England, and according to Dr Day they are said in Lapland to reach a weight of eight or nine pounds   The grayling in all countries frequent clear, cold brooks, and rarely, if ever, enter the sea, or even the larger lakes   They congregate in small shoals in the streams, and prefer those which have a succession of pools and shallows, with a sandy or gravelly rather than rocky bottom   The grayling spawns on the shallows in April or May (in England) It is non-migratory in its habits, depositing its ova in the neighborhood of its usual haunts   The ova are far more delicate and easily killed than those of the trout or charr   The grayling and the trout often inhabit the same waters, but not altogether in harmony   It is said that the grayling devours the eggs of the trout   It is certain that the trout feed on the young grayling   As a food-fish, the grayling of course ranks high, and it is beloved by the sportsman   They are considered gamy fishes, although less strong than the brook-trout, and perhaps less wary   The five or six known species of grayling are very closely related, and are doubtless comparatively recent offshoots from a common stock, which has now spread itself widely through the northern regions

The common grayling of Europe (*Thymallus thymallus*) is found throughout northern Europe, and as far south as the mountains of Hungary and northern Italy   The name *Thymallus* was given by the ancients, because the fish, when fresh, was said to have the odor of water-thyme   Grayling belonging to this or other species are found in the waters of Russia and Siberia

The American grayling (*Thymallus signifer*) is widely distributed in British America and Alaska   In the Yukon it is very abundant, rising readily to the fly   In several streams in northern Michigan, Au Sable River, and Jordan River in the southern peninsula, and Otter Creek near Keweenaw in the northern peninsula, occurs a dwarfish variety or species with shorter and lower dorsal fins, known to anglers as the Michigan grayling (*Thymallus tricolor*)   This form has a longer head, rather smaller scales, and the dorsal fin rather lower than in the northern form (*signifer*), but the constancy of these characters in specimens from intermediate localities is yet to be proved Another very similar form, called *Thymallus montanus*, occurs in the Gallatin, Madison, and other rivers of Western Montana tributary to the Missouri It is locally still abundant and one of the finest of game-fishes It is probable that the grayling once had a wider range to the southward than now, and that so far as the waters of the United States are concerned it is tending toward extinction This tendency is, of course, being

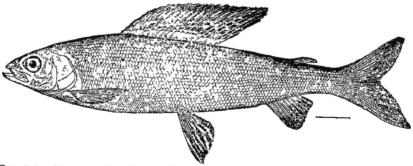

FIG 250 - Michigan Grayling, *Thymallus tricolor* Cope Au Sable River, Mich

accelerated in Michigan by lumbermen and anglers The colonies of grayling in Michigan and Montana are probably remains of a post-glacial fauna

The Argentinidæ.—The family of *Argentinidæ*, or smelt, is very closely related to the *Salmonidæ*, representing a dwarf series of similar type The chief essential difference lies in the form of the stomach, which is a blind sac, the two openings near together, and about the second or pyloric opening there are few if any pyloric cæca In all the *Salmonidæ* the stomach has the form of a siphon, and about the pylorus there are very many pyloric cæca The smelt have the adipose fin and the general structure of the salmon All the species are small in size, and most of them are strictly marine, though some of them ascend the rivers to spawn, just as salmon do, but not going very far A few kinds become land-locked in ponds Most of the species are confined to the north temperate zone, and a few sink into the deep seas All that are sufficiently abundant furnish excellent food, the flesh being extremely delicate and often charged with a fragrant oil easy of digestion

The best-known genus, *Osmerus*, includes the smelt, or spirling (éperlan), of Europe, and its relatives, all excellent food-fishes, although quickly spoiling in warm weather *Osmerus eperlanus* is the European species, *Osmerus mordax* of our eastern coast is very much like it, as is also the rainbow-smelt, *Osmerus dentex* of Japan and Alaska A larger smelt, *Osmerus albatrossis*, occurs on the coast of Alaska, and a small and feeble one, *Osmerus thaleichthys*, mixed with other small or delicate fishes, is the whitebait of the San Francisco restaurants The whitebait of the London epicure is made up of the young of herrings and sprats of different species The still more delicate whitebait of the Hong Kong hotels is the icefish, *Salanx chinensis*.

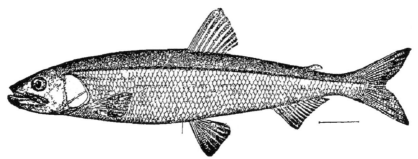

FIG 251 —Smelt, *Osmerus mordax* (Mitchill) Wood's Hole, Mass

Retropinna retropinna, so called from the backward insertion of its dorsal, is the excellent smelt of the rivers of New Zealand All the other species belong to northern waters *Mesopus*, the surf-smelt, has a smaller mouth than *Osmerus* and inhabits the North Pacific The California species, *Mesopus pretiosus*, of Neah Bay has, according to James G Swan, "the belly covered with a coating of yellow fat which imparts an oily appearance to the water where the fish has been cleansed or washed and makes them the very perfection of pan-fish " This species spawns in late summer along the surf-line According to Mr Swan the water seems to be filled with them "They come in with the flood-tide, and when a wave breaks upon the beach they crowd up into the very foam, and as the surf recedes many will be seen flapping on the sand and shingle, but invariably returning with the undertow to deeper water " The Quillute Indians of Washington believe that "the first surf-smelts that appear must not be sold or given away to be taken to another place, nor must they be cut transversely, but split open with a mussel-shell "

The surf-smelt is marine, as is also a similar species, *Mesopus japonicus*, in Japan. *Mesopus olidus*, the pond-smelt of Alaska, Kamchatka, and Northern Japan, spawns in fresh-water ponds

Still more excellent as a food-fish than even these exquisite species is the famous eulachon, or candle-fish (*Thaleichthys pacificus*). The Chinook name, usually written eulachon, is perhaps more accurately represented as ulchen This little fish has the form of a smelt and reaches the length of nearly a foot In the spring it ascends in enormous numbers all the

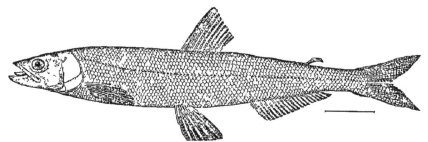

FIG 252 —Eulachon, or Ulchen *Thaleichthys pretiosus* Girard Columbia River Family *Argentinidæ*

rivers north of the Columbia, as far as Skaguay, for a short distance for the purpose of spawning These runs take place usually in advance of the salmon-runs Various predatory fishes and sea-birds persecute the eulachon during its runs, and even the stomachs of the sturgeons are often found full of the little fishes, which they have taken in by their sucker-like mouths At the time of the runs the eulachon are extremely fat, so much so that it is said that when dried and a wick drawn through the body they may be used as candles On Nass River, in British Columbia, a stream in which their run is greatest, there is a factory for the manufacture of eulachon-oil from them This delicate oil is proposed as a substitute for cod-liver oil in medicine Whatever may be its merits in this regard, it has the disadvantage in respect to salability of being semi-solid or lard-like at ordinary temperatures, requiring melting to make it flow as oil The eulachon is a favorite

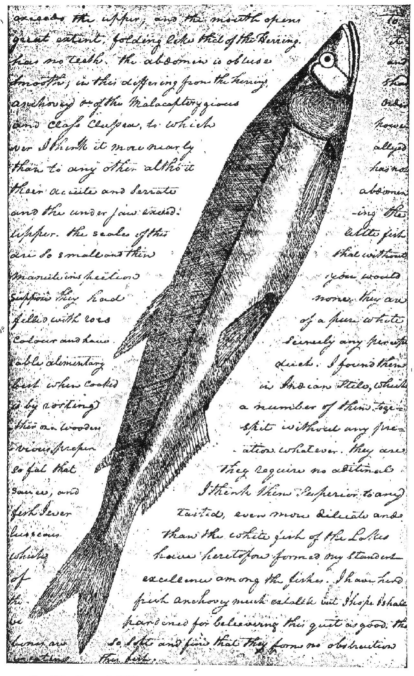

FIG. 253—Page of William Clark's handwriting with sketch of the Eulachon (*Thaleichthys pacificus*), the first notice of the species. Columbia River, 1805. (Expedition of Lewis & Clark.) (Reproduced from the original in the possession of his granddaughter Mrs. Julia Clark Voorhis, through the courtesy of Messrs. Dodd, Mead & Company, publishers of the "Original Journals of the Lewis and Clark Expedition.")

pan-fish in British Columbia The writer has had considerable experience with it, broiled and fried, in its native region, and has no hesitation in declaring it to be the best-flavored food-fish in American waters It is fat, tender, juicy, and richly flavored, with comparatively few troublesome bones It does not, however, bear transportation well The Indians in Alaska bury the eulachon in the ground in great masses After the fish are well decayed they are taken out and the oil pressed from them The odor of the fish and the oil is then very offensive, less so, however, than that of some forms of cheese eaten by civilized people

The capelin (*Mallotus villosus*) closely resembles the eulachon, differing mainly in its broader pectorals and in the peculiar scales of the males In the male fish a band of scales above

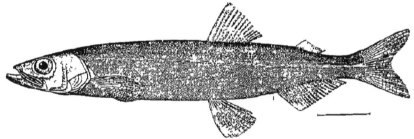

FIG 254 —Capelin, *Mallotus villosus* L Crosswater Bay

the lateral line and along each side of the belly become elongate, closely imbricated, with the free points projecting, giving the body a villous appearance It is very abundant on the coasts of Arctic America, both in the Atlantic and the Pacific, and is an important source of food for the natives of those regions

This species spawns in the surf, and the writer has seen them in August cast on the shores of the Alaskan islands (as at Metlakahtla in 1897), living and dead, in numbers which seem incredible The males are then distorted, and it seems likely that all of them perish after spawning The young are abundant in all the northern fiords Even more inordinate numbers are reported from the shores of Greenland

The capelin seems to be inferior to the eulachon as a food-fish, but to the natives of arctic regions in both hemispheres it is a very important article of food Fossil capelin are found

in abundance in recent shales in Greenland enveloped in nodules
of clay   In the open waters about the Aleutian Islands a small
smelt, *Therobromus callorhini*, occurs in very great abundance
and forms the chief part of the summer food of the fur-seal
Strangely enough, no complete specimen of this fish has yet
been seen by man, although thousands of fragments have been
taken from seals' stomachs   From these fragments Mr Frederick
A Lucas has reconstructed the fish, which must be an ally of
the surf-smelt, probably spawning in the open ocean of the north

The silvery species called *Argentina* live in deeper water
and have no commercial importance   *Argentina silus*, with
prickly scales, occurs in the North Sea   Several fossils have
been doubtfully referred to *Osmerus*

The Microstomidæ.—The small family of *Microstomidæ* consists of a few degraded smelt, slender in form, with feeble mouth
and but three or four branchiostegals, rarely taken in the deep
seas   *Nansenia grœnlandica* was found by Reinhardt off the
coast of Greenland, and six or eight other species of *Microstoma*
and *Bathylagus* have been brought in by the deep-sea explorations

The Salangidæ, or Icefishes.—Still more feeble and insignificant are the species of *Salangidæ*, icefishes, or Chinese whitebait,
which may be described as *Salmonidæ* reduced to the lowest
terms   The body is long and slender, perfectly translucent,
almost naked, and with the skeleton scarcely ossified   The
fins are like those of the salmon, the head is depressed, the jaws
long and broad, somewhat like the bill of a duck, and within
there are a few disproportionately strong canine teeth, those
of the lower jaw somewhat piercing the upper   The alimentary
canal is straight for its whole length, without pyloric cæca
These little fishes, two to five inches long, live in the sea in
enormous numbers and ascend the rivers of eastern Asia for
the purpose of spawning   It is thought by some that they are
annual fishes, all dying in the fall after reproduction, the species
living through the winter only within its eggs   But this is
only suspected, not proved, and the species will repay the careful study which some of the excellent naturalists of Japan are
sure before long to give to it   The species of *Salanx* are known
as whitebait, in Japan as *Shiro-uwo*, which means exactly the

same thing   They are also sometimes called icefish (*Hingio*), which, being used for no other fish, may be adopted as a group name for *Salanx*

The species are *Salanx chinensis* from Canton, *Salanx hyalo cranius* from Korea and northern China, *Salanx microdon* from northern Japan, and *Salanx ariakensis* from the southern island of Kiusiu   The Japanese fishes are species still smaller and feebler than their relatives from the mainland

The Haplochitonidæ. — The *Haplochitonidæ* are trout-like fishes of the south temperate zone, differing from the *Salmonidæ* mainly in the extension of the premaxillary until, as in the perch-like fishes, it forms the outer border of the upper jaw   The adipose fin is present as in all the salmon and smelt   *Haplochiton* of Tierra del Fuego and the Falkland Islands is naked, while in *Prototroctes* of Australia and New Zealand the body, as in all salmon, trout, and smelt, is covered with scales   *Prototroctes marœna* is the yarra herring of Australia   The closely related family of *Galaxiidæ*, also Australian, but lacking the adipose fin, is mentioned in a later chapter.

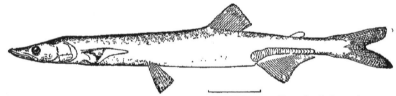

Fig 255 —Icefish, *Salanx hyalocranius* Abbott   Family *Salangidæ.*
Tientsin, China

Stomiatidæ. — The *Stomiatidæ*, with elongate bodies, have the mouth enormous, with fang-like teeth, usually barbed   Of

Fig 256 —*Stomias ferox* Reinhardt   Banquereau

the several species *Stomias ferox* is best known   According to Dr Boulenger, these fishes are true *Isospondyli.*

Astronesthidæ is another small group of small fishes naked and black, with long canines, found in the deep sea

The *Malacosteidæ* is a related group with extremely distensible mouth, the species capable of swallowing fishes much larger than themselves

The viper-fishes (*Chauliodontidæ*) are very feeble and very voracious little fishes occasionally brought up from the depths *Chauliodus sloanei* is notable for the length of the fangs

Much smaller and feebler are the species of the closely related family of *Gonostomidæ*   *Gonostoma* and *Cyclothone* dwell in oceanic abysses   One species, *Cyclothone elongata*, occurs at the depth of from half a mile to nearly four miles

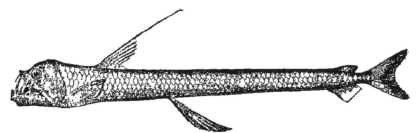

Fig 257 —*Chauliodus sloanei* Schneider   Grand Banks

almost everywhere throughout the oceans   It is probably the most widely distributed, as well as one of the feeblest and most fragile, of all bassalian or deep-sea fishes

Suborder Iniomi, the Lantern-fishes. — The suborder *Iniomi* (ἰνίον, nape, ὦμος, shoulder) comprises soft-rayed fishes, in which the shoulder-girdle has more or less lost its completeness of structure as part of the degradation consequent on life in the abysses of the sea   These features distinguish these forms from the true *Isospondyli*, but only in a very few of the species have these characters been verified by actual examination of the skeleton   The mesocoracoid arch is wanting or atrophied in all of the species examined, and the orbito-sphenoid is lacking, so far as known   The group thus agrees in most technical characters with the *Haplomi*, in which group they are placed by Dr Boulenger   On the other hand the relationships to the *Isospondyli* are very close, and the *Iniomi* have many traits suggesting degenerate *Isospondyli*   The post-temporal has lost its usual hold on the skull and may touch the occiput on the sides of the cranium   Nearly all the species are soft in body, black or silvery over black in color, and all that live in the deep sea are provided with luminous spots or glands giving light in the abysmal depths These spots are wanting in the few shore species, as also in those which approach most nearly to the *Salmonidæ*, these being presumably the most primitive of the group In these also the post-temporal touches the back of the cranium near the side In the majority of the *Iniomi* the adipose fin of the *Salmonidæ* is retained From the phosphorescent spots is derived the general name of lantern-fishes applied of late years to many of the species Most of these are of recent discovery, results of the remarkable work in deepsea dredging begun by the *Albatross* and the *Challenger* All of the species are carnivorous, and some, in spite of their feeble muscles, are exceedingly voracious, the mouth being armed with veritable daggers and spears

Aulopidæ.—Most primitive of the *Iniomi* is the family of *Aulopidæ*, having an adipose fin, a normal maxillary, and no luminous spots The rough firm scales suggest those of the berycoid fishes The few species of *Aulopus* and *Chlorophthalmus* are found in moderate depths *Aulopus purpurissatus* is the "Sergeant Baker" of the Australian fishermen

The Lizard-fishes.—The *Synodontidæ*, or lizard-fishes, have lizard-like heads with very large mouth The head is scaly, a character rare among the soft-rayed fishes The slender maxil-

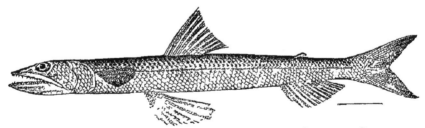

FIG 258 —Lizard-fish, *Synodus fœtens* I Charleston, S C

lary is grown fast to the premaxillary, and the color is not black Most of the species are shore-fishes and some are brightly colored *Synodus fœtens* is the common lizard-fish, or galliwasp, of our Atlantic coast *Synodus varius* of the Pacific is brightly colored, olive-green and orange-red types of coloration existing at different depths Most of the species lie close to the bottom and are mottled gray like coral sand A few occur in oceanic depths   The "Bombay duck" of the fishermen of India is a species of *Harpodon, H nehereus*, with large mouth and arrow-shaped teeth   The dried fish is used as a relish

The *Benthosauridæ* are deep-sea fishes of similar type, but with distinct maxillaries   The *Bathypteroidæ*, of the deep seas, resemble *Aulopus*, but have the upper and lower pectoral rays filiform, developed as organs of touch in the depths in which the small eyes become practically useless

Ipnopidæ.—In the *Ipnopidæ* the head is depressed above and the two eyes are flattened and widened so as to occupy most of its upper surface   These structures were at first supposed to be luminous organs, but Professor Moseley has thought them to be eyes   "They show a flattened cornea extending along the median line of the snout, with a large retina composed of peculiar rods which form a complicated apparatus

Fig 259 —*Ipnops murrayi* Gunther

destined undoubtedly to produce an image and to receive especial luminous rays"   The single species, *Ipnops murrayi*, is black in color and found at the depth of 2½ miles in various seas

The existence of well-developed eyes among fishes destined to live in the dark abysses of the ocean seems at first contradictory, but we must remember that these singular forms are descendants of immigrants from the shore and from the surface   "In some cases the eyes have not been specially modified, but in others there have been modifications of a luminous mucous membrane leading on the one hand to phosphorescent organs more or less specialized, or on the other to such remarkable structures as the eyes of *Ipnops*, intermediate between true eyes and phosphorescent plates   In fishes which cannot see, and which retain for their guidance only the general sensibility of the integuments and the lateral line, these parts soon acquire a very great delicacy   The same is the case with tactile organs (as in *Bathypterois* and *Benthosaurus*), and experiments show that barbels may become organs of touch adapted to aquatic life, sensitive to the faintest movements or the slightest displacement, with power to give the blinded fishes full cognizance of the medium in which they live"

Rondeletiidæ.—The *Rondeletiidæ* are naked black fishes with small eyes, without adipose fin and without luminous spots,

Fig 260 —*Cetomimus gilli* Goode & Bean   Gulf Stream.

taken at great depths in the Atlantic   The relationship of these fishes is wholly uncertain

The *Cetomimidæ* are near allies of the *Rondeletiidæ*, having the mouth excessively large, with the peculiar form seen in the right whales, which these little fishes curiously resemble

Myctophidæ.—The large family of *Myctophidæ*, or lanternfishes, is made up of small fishes allied to the *Aulopidæ*, but

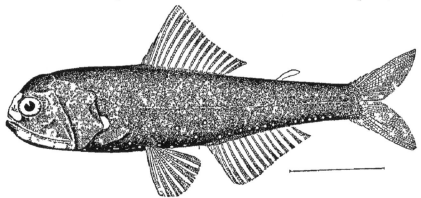

Fig 261 —Headlight Fish, *Diaphus lucidus* Goode and Bean   Gulf Stream

with the body covered with luminous dots, highly specialized and symmetrically arranged   Most of them belong to the deep sea, but others come to the surface in the night or during storms when the sunlight is absent   Through this habit they are often thrown by the waves on the decks of small vessels

Largely from Danish merchant-vessels, Dr Lütken has obtained the unrivaled collection of these sea-waifs preserved in the Museum of the University of Copenhagen   The species are all small in size and feeble in structure, the prey of the larger

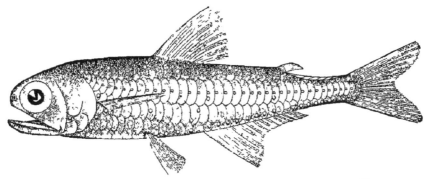

FIG 262 —Lantern-fish, *Myctophum opalinum* Goode & Bean   Gulf Stream

fishes of the depths, from which their lantern-like spots and large eyes help them to escape   The numerous species are now ranged in about fifteen genera, although earlier writers placed them all in a single genus *Myctophum (Scopelus)*.

In the genus *Diaphus (Æthoprora)* there is a large luminous gland on the end of the short snout, like the headlight of an

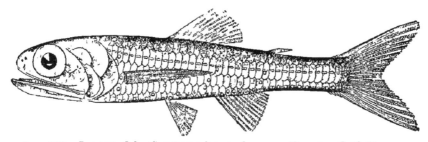

FIG 263 —Lantern-fish, *Ceratoscopelus madeirensis* (Lowe)   Gulf Stream

engine   In *Dasyscopelus* the scales are spinescent, but in most of the genera, as in *Myctophum*, the scales are cycloid and caducous, falling at the touch   In *Diaphus* the luminous spots are crossed by a septum giving them the form of the Greek letter θ (theta). One of the commonest species is *Myctophum humboldti*

Chirothricidæ.—The remarkable extinct family of *Chirothricidæ* may be related to the *Synodontidæ*, or *Myctophidæ* In this group the teeth are feeble, the paired fins much enlarged, and the ventrals are well forward The dorsal fin, inserted well forward, has stout basal bones *Chirothrix libanicus* of the Cretaceous of Mt Lebanon is remarkable for its excessively large ventral fins. *Telepholis* is a related genus *Exocœtoides* with rounded caudal fin is probably the type of a distinct family, *Exocœtoididæ*, the caudal fin being strongly forked in *Chirothrix* The small extinct group of *Rhinellidæ* is usually placed near the *Myctophidæ* They are distinguished by the very long gar-like jaws, whether they possessed adipose fins or luminous spots cannot be determined *Rhinellus furcatus* and other species occur in the Cretaceous of Europe and Asia Fossil forms more or less distinctly related to the *Mycto-*

Fig 204 —*Rhinellus furcatus* Agassiz Upper Cretaceous of Mt Lebanon (After Woodward)

phidæ are numerous *Osmeroides monasterii* (wrongly called *Sardinioides*), from the German Cretaceous, seems allied to *Myctophum*, although, of course, luminous spots leave no trace among fossils *Acrognathus boops* is remarkable for the large size of the eyes

Maurolicidæ. — The *Maurolicidæ* are similar in form and habit, but scaleless, and with luminous spots more highly specialized. *Maurolicus pennanti*, the "Sleppy Argentine," is occasionally taken on either side of the Atlantic Other genera are *Zalarges, Vinciguerria,* and *Valenciennellus*

The Lancet-fishes.—The *Plagyodontidæ (Alepisauridæ)* contains the lancet-fishes, large, swift, scaleless fishes of the ocean depths with very high dorsal fin, and the mouth filled with knife-like teeth. These large fish are occasionally cast up by storms or are driven to the shores by the torments of a parasite, *Tetrarhynchus*, found imbedded in the flesh

It is probable that they are sometimes killed by being forced above their level by fishes which they have swallowed In such cases they are destroyed through the reduction of pressure

Every part of the body is so fragile that perfect specimens are rare The dorsal fin is readily torn, the bones are very feebly ossified, and the ligaments connecting the vertebræ are very loose and extensible, so that the body can be considerably stretched "This loose connection of the parts of the body is found in numerous deep-sea fishes, and is merely the consequence of their withdrawal from the pressure of the water to which they are exposed in the depths inhabited by them When within the limits of their natural haunts, the osseous, muscular, and fibrous parts of the body will have that solidity which is required for the rapid and powerful movements of a predatory fish That the fishes of this genus (*Plagyodus*) belong to the most ferocious of the class is proved by their dentition and the contents of their stomach" (Gunther) Dr Gunther else-

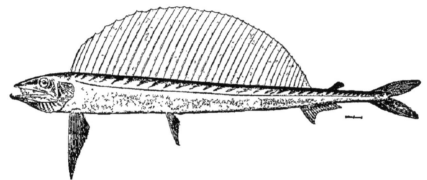

Fig 265 —Lancet-fish, *Plagyodus ferox* (Lowe)   New York

where observes "From the stomach of one example have been taken several octopods, crustaceans, ascidians, a young *Brama*, twelve young boarfishes (*Capros*), a horse-mackerel, and one young of its own species"

The lancet-fish, *Plagyodus ferox*, is occasionally taken on either side of the Atlantic and in Japan   The handsaw-fish, called *Plagyodus æsculapius*, has been taken at Unalaska, off San Luis Obispo, and in Humboldt Bay   It does not seem to differ at all from *Plagyodus ferox*   The original type from Unalaska had in its stomach twenty-one lumpfishes (*Eumicrotremus spinosus*)   This is the species described from Steller's manuscripts by Pallas under the name of *Plagyodus*   Another species, *Plagyodus borcalis*, is occasionally taken in the North Pacific

The *Evermannellidæ* is a small family of small deep-sea fishes with large teeth, distensible muscles, and an extraordinary power of swallowing other fishes, scarcely surpassed by *Chiasmodon* or *Saccopharynx* *Evermannella* (*Odontostomus*, the latter name preoccupied) and *Omosudis* are the principal genera

The *Paralepidæ* are reduced allies of *Plagyodus*, slender, silvery, with small fins and fang-like jaws As in *Plagyodus*, the adipose fin is developed and there are small luminous dots The species are few and mostly northern; one of them, *Sudis ringens*, is known only from a single specimen taken by the present writer from the stomach of a hake (*Merluccius productus*), the hake in turn swallowed whole by an albacore in the Santa Barbara Channel   The *Sudis* had been devoured by the hake, the hake by the albacore, and the albacore taken on the hook before the feeble *Sudis* had been digested

Perhaps allied to the *Plagyodontidæ* is also the large family of *Enchodontidæ*, widely represented in the Cretaceous rocks of

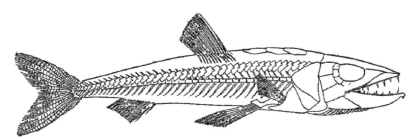

Fig 266 —*Eurypholis sulcidens* Pictet, restored   Family *Enchodontidæ*   Upper Cretaceous of Mt Lebanon   (After Woodward, as *E. boissieri*)

Syria, Europe, and Kansas   The body in this group is elongate, the teeth very strong, and the dorsal fin short   *Enchodus lewesiensis* is found in Mount Lebanon, *Halec sternbergi* in the German Cretaceous, and many species of *Enchodus* in Kansas, *Cimolichthys dirus* in North Dakota

Remotely allied to these groups is the extinct family of *Dercetidæ* from the Cretaceous of Germany and Syria   These are elongate fishes, the scales small or wanting, but with two or more series of bony scutes along the flanks   In *Dercetis scutatus* the scutes are large and the dorsal fin is very long   Other genera are *Leptotrachelus* and *Pelargorhynchus*   Dr Boulenger places the *Dercetidæ* in the order *Heteromi*   This is an expression of the fact that their relations are still unknown   Probably

related to the *Dercetidæ* is the American family of *Stratodontidæ*
with its two genera, *Stradodus* and *Empo* from the Cretaceous

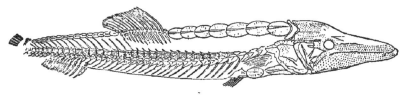

F:g. 267 —*Eurypholis freyeri* Heckel. Family *Enchodontidæ*. Cretaceous.
(After Heckel; the restoration of the jaws incorrect.)

(Niobrara) deposits of Kansas. *Empo nepaholica* is one of the
best-known species.

The Sternoptychidæ. — The *Sternoptychidæ* differ materi-
ally from all these forms in the short, compressed, deep body
and distorted form. The teeth are small, the body bright
silvery, with luminous spots. The species live in the deep
seas, rising in dark or stormy weather. *Sternoptyx diaphana* is
found in almost all seas, and species of *Argyropelecus* are almost

Fig. 268. —Monstrous Goldfish (bred in Japan), *Carassius auratus* (Linnæus).
(After Günther.)

as widely distributed. After the earthquakes in 1896, which
engulfed the fishing villages of Rikuzen, in northern Japan,

numerous specimens of this species were found dead, floating on the water, by the steamer *Albatross*

The *Idiacanthidæ* are small deep-sea fishes, eel-shaped and without pectorals, related to the *Iniomi*

Order Lyopomi.—Other deep-sea fishes constitute the order or suborder *Lyopomi* (λυός, loose, πῶμα, opercle)   These are elongate fishes having no mesocoracoid, and the preopercle rudimentary and connected only with the lower jaw, the large

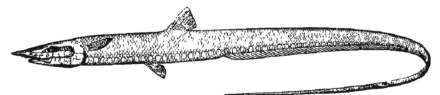

Fıg 269 —*Aldrovandıa gracılıs* (Goode & Bean)   Guadaloupe Island, West Indıes   Family *Halosaurıdæ*

subopercle usurping its place.   The group, which is perhaps to be regarded as a degenerate type of *Isospondyli*, contains the single family of *Halosauridæ*, with several species, black in color, soft in substance, with small teeth and long tapering tail, found in all seas   The principal genera are *Halosaurus* and *Aldrovandıa* (*Halosauropsis*).   *Aldrovandıa macrochıra* is the commonest species on our Atlantic coast

Several fossil *Halosaurıdæ* are described from the Cretaceous of Europe and Syria, referred to the genera *Echıdnocephalus* and *Enchelurus*.   Boulenger refers the *Lyopomi* to the suborder *Heteromi.*

CHAPTER XXII

THE APODES, OR EEL-LIKE FISHES

HE Eels—We may here break the sequence from the *Isospondyli* to the other soft-rayed fishes, to interpolate a large group of uncertain origin, the series or subclass of eels

The mass of apodal or eel-like fishes has been usually regarded as constituting a single order, the Apodes ($\check{a}$, without, $\pi o\hat{v}\varsigma$, foot) The group as a whole is characterized by the almost universal separation of the shoulder-girdle from the skull, by the absence of the mesocoracoid arch on the shoulder-girdle, by the presence of more than five pectoral actinosts, as in the Ganoid fishes, by the presence of great numbers of undifferentiated vertebræ, giving the body a snake-like form, by the absence in all living forms of the ventral fins, and, in all living forms, by the absence of a separate caudal fin. These structures indicate a low organization Some of them are certainly results of degeneration, and others are perhaps indications of primitive simplicity Within the limits of the group are seen other features of degeneration, notably shown in the progressive loss of the bones of the upper jaw and the membrane-bones of the head and the degradation of the various fins The symplectic bone is wanting, the notochord is more or less persistent, the vertebral centra always complete constricted cylinders, none coalesced But, notwithstanding great differences in these regards, the forms have been usually left in a single order, the more degraded forms being regarded as descended from the types which approach nearest to the ordinary fishes From this view Professor Cope dissents He recognizes several orders of eels, claiming that we should not unite all these various fishes into a single order on account of the eel-like form If we do so, we should place in another order those with the fish-like form

It is probable, though not absolutely certain, that the *Apodes* are related to each other   The loss among them, first, of the connection of the post-temporal with the skull, second, of the separate caudal fin and its hypural support, third, of the distinct maxillary and premaxillary, and fourth, of the pectoral fins, must be regarded as successive phases of a general line of degradation. The large number of actinosts, the persistence of the notochord, the absence of spines, and the large numbers of vertebræ seem to be traits of primitive simplicity   Special lines of degeneration are further shown by deep-sea forms   What the origin of the *Apodes* may have been is not known with any certainty They are soft-rayed fishes, with the air-bladder connected by a tube with the œsophagus, and with the anterior vertebræ not modified   In so far they agree with the *Isospondyli*   In some other respects they resemble the lower *Ostariophysi*, especially the electric eel and the eel-like catfishes   But these resemblances, mainly superficial, may be wholly deceptive, we have no links which certainly connect the most fish-like Apodes with any of the other orders   Probably Woodward's suggestion that they may form a series parallel with the *Isopondyli* and independently descended from Tertiary Ganoids deserves serious consideration   Perhaps the most satisfactory arrangement of these fishes will be to regard them as constituting four distinct orders for which we may use the names *Symbranchia* (including *Ichthyocephali* and *Holostomi*), *Apodes* (including *Enchelycephali* and *Colocephali*), *Carencheli*, and *Lyomeri*

Order Symbranchia.—The *Symbranchia* are distinguished by the development of the ordinary fish mouth, the maxillary and premaxillary being well developed.   The gill-openings are very small, and usually confluent below.   These fresh-water forms of the tropics, however eel-like in form, may have no real affinity with the true eels   In any event, they should not be placed in the same order with the latter

The eels of the suborder *Ichthyocephali* (ἰχθύς, fish, κεφαλή, head) have the head distinctly fish-like   The maxillary, premaxillary, and palatines are well developed, and the shoulder-girdle is joined by a post-temporal to the skull   The body is distinctly eel-like, the tail being very short and the fins inconspicuous The number of vertebræ is unusually large The order contains the single family *Monopteridæ*, the rice-field eels, one species, *Monopterus albus*, being excessively common in pools and ditches from China and southern Japan to India

The eels of the suborder *Holostomi* (ὁλός, complete, στόμα, mouth) differ from these mainly in the separation of the shoulder-girdle from the skull, a step in the direction of the true eels The *Symbranchidæ* are very close to the *Monopteridæ* in external appearance, small, dusky, eel-like inhabitants of sluggish ponds and rivers of tropical America and the East Indies The gill-openings are confluent under the throat *Symbranchus marmoratus* ranges northward as far as Vera Cruz, having much the habit of the rice-field eel of Japan and China The *Amphipnoidæ*, with peculiar respiratory structures, abound in India *Amphipnous cuchia*, according to Gunther, has but three gill-arches, with rudimentary lamina and very narrow slits To supplement this insufficient branchial apparatus, a lung-like sac is developed on each side of the body behind the head, opening between the hyoid and the first branchial arch The interior of the sac is abundantly provided with blood-vessels, the arterial coming from the branchial arch, whilst those issuing from it unite to form the aorta *Amphipnous* has rudimentary scales The other *Holostomi* and *Ichthyocephali* are naked and all lack the pectoral fin

The *Chilobranchidæ* are small sea-fishes from Australia, with the tail longer than the rest of the body, instead of much shorter as in the others

No forms allied to *Symbranchus* or *Monopterus* are recorded as fossils.

Order Apodes, or True Eels. — In this group the shoulder-girdle is free from the skull, and the bones of the jaws are reduced in number, through coalescence of the parts

Three well-marked suborders may be recognized, groups perhaps worthy of still higher rank *Archenceli, Enchelycephali,* and *Colocephali*

Suborder Archencheli —The *Archencheli*, now entirely extinct, are apparently the parents of the eels, having, however, certain traits characteristic of the *Isospondyli* They retain the separate caudal fin, with the ordinary hypural plate, and Professor

Hay has recently found, in an example from the Cretaceous of Mount Lebanon, remains of distinct ventral fins These traits seem to indicate an almost perfect transition from the *Isospondyli* to the *Archencheli*

One family may be recognized at present, *Urenchelyidæ*

The earliest known eel, *Urenchelys avus*, occurs in the upper Cretaceous at Mount Lebanon It represents the family *Urenchelyidæ*, apparently allied to the *Anguillidæ;* but having a separate caudal fin Its teeth are small, conical, blunt, in many series There are more than 100 vertebræ, the last expanded in a hypural Pectorals present Scales rudimentary, dorsal arising at the occiput Branchiostegals slender, not curved around the opercle *Urenchelys anglicus* is another species, found in the chalk of England

Suborder Enchelycephali. — The suborder *Enchelycephali* (ἔγχελυς, eel, κεφαλή, head) contains the typical eels, in which the shoulder-girdle is free from the skull, the palatopterygoid arch relatively complete, the premaxillaries wanting or rudimentary, the ethmoid and vomer coalesced, forming the front of the upper jaw, the maxillaries lateral, and the cranium with a single condyle In most of the species pectoral fins are present, and the cranium lacks the combined degradation and specialization shown by the morays (*Colocephali*).

Family Anguillidæ —The most primitive existing family is that of the typical eels, *Anguillidæ*, which have rudimentary scales oblong in form, and set separately in groups at right angles with one another These fishes are found in the fresh and brackish waters of all parts of the world, excepting the Pacific coast of North America and the islands of the Pacific In the upper Great Lakes and the upper Mississippi they are also absent unless introduced The species usually spawn in the sea and ascend the rivers to feed. But some individuals certainly spawn in fresh water, and none go far into the sea, or where the water is entirely salt The young eels sometimes ascend the brooks near the sea in incredible numbers, constituting what is known in England as "eel-fairs" They will pass through wet grass to surmount ordinary obstacles Niagara Falls they cannot pass, and according to Professor Baird "in the spring and summer the visitor who enters under the sheet of water at the foot of the falls will be astonished at the enormous numbers of young eels crawling over the slippery rocks and squirming in the seething whirlpools   An estimate of hundreds of wagon-loads, as seen in the course of the perilous journey referred to, would hardly be considered excessive by those who have visited the spot at a suitable season of the year"   "At other times large eels may be seen on their way down-stream, although naturally they are not as conspicuous then as are the hosts of the young on their way up-stream   Nevertheless it is now a well-assured fact that the eels are catadromous, that is, that the

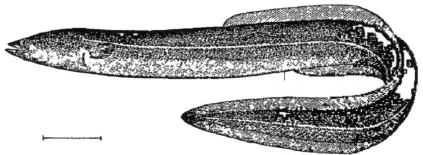

Fig 270 —Common Eel, *Anguilla chrisypa* Rafinesque   Holyoke, Mass

old descend the watercourses to the salt water to spawn, and the young, at least of the female sex, ascend them to enjoy life in the fresh water"

The Food of the Eel.—Eels are among the most voracious of all fishes   They devour dead flesh and they will attack any fish small enough for them to bite   They are among the swiftest of fishes   They work largely at night, and devour spawn as well as grown fishes

"On their hunting excursions they overturn huge and small stones alike, working for hours if necessary, beneath which they find species of shrimp and crayfish, of which they are exceedingly fond   Of shrimps they devour vast numbers   Their noses are poked into every imaginable hole in their search for food, to the terror of innumerable small fishes

Larva of the Eel.—The translucent band-shaped larva of the common eel has been very recently identified and described by Dr Eigenmann   It is probable that all true eels, *Enchely-*

cephali, pass through a band-shaped or leptocephalous stage, as is the case with *Albula* and other *Isospondyli* In the continued growth the body becomes firmer, and at the same time

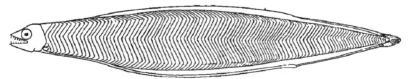

Fig 271 —Larva of Common Eel, *Anguilla chrisypa* (Rafinesque), called *Leptocephalus grassii* (After Eigenmann)

much shorter and thicker, gradually assuming the normal form of the species in question

In a recent paper Dr Carl H Eigenmann has very fully reviewed the life-history of the eel The common species live in fresh waters, migrating to the sea in the winter They deposit in deep water minute eggs that float at the surface The next year they develop into the band-shaped larva The young eels enter the streams two years after their parents drop down to the sea It is doubtful whether eels breed in fresh water The male eel is much smaller than the female

The eel is an excellent food-fish, the flesh being tender and oily, of agreeable flavor, better than that of any of its relatives Eels often reach a large size, old individuals of five or six feet in length being sometimes taken

Species of Eels —The different species are very closely related Not more than four or five of them are sharply defined, and these mostly in the South Seas and in the East Indies The three abundant species of the north temperate zone, *Anguilla anguilla* of Europe, *Anguilla chrisypa* of the eastern United States, and *Anguilla japonica* of Japan, are scarcely distinguishable In color, size, form, and value as food they are all alike

Fossil species referred to the *Anguillidæ* are known from the early Tertiary *Anguilla leptoptera* occurs in the Eocene of Monte Bolea, and *Anguilla elegans* in the Miocene of Œningen in Baden Other fossil eels seem to belong to the *Nettastomidæ* and *Myridæ*

Pug-nosed Eels.—Allied to the true eel is the pug-nosed eel, *Simenchelys parasiticus*, constituting the family of *Simenchelyidæ* This species is scaled like a true eel, has a short, blunt nose, and burrows its way into the bodies of halibut and other large fishes   It has been found in Newfoundland and

Fig 272 —Pug-nosed Eel, *Simenchelys parasiticus* Gill   Sable Island Bank

Madeira   Another family possessing rudimentary scales is that of the *Synaphobranchidæ*, slender eels of the ocean depths, widely distributed   In these forms the gill-openings are confluent *Synaphobranchus pinnatus* is the best-known species

Fig 273 —*Synaphobranchus pinnatus* (Gronow)   Le Have Bank

Conger-eels. — The *Leptocephalidæ*, or conger-eels, are very similar to the fresh-water eels, but are without scales and with a somewhat different mouth, the dorsal beginning nearer to the head

The principal genus is *Leptocephalus*, including the common conger-eel (*Leptocephalus conger*) of eastern America and Europe and numerous very similar species in the tropics of both continents   These fishes are strictly marine and, reaching the length of five or six feet, are much valued as food   The eggs are much larger than those of the eel and are produced in great numbers, so that the female almost bursts with their numbers Dr Hermes calculated that 3,300,000 were laid by one female in an aquarium

These eggs hatch out into transparent band-like larva, with very small heads formerly known as *Leptocephalus*, an ancient name which is now taken for the genus of congers, having been first used for the larva of the common conger-eel. The loose watery tissues of these "ghost-fishes" grow more and more compact and they are finally transformed into young congers

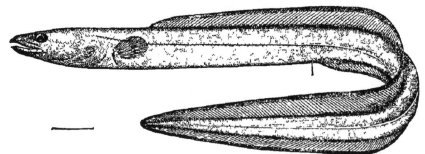

FIG 274 —Conger-eel, *Leptocephalus conger* (L.). Noank, Conn

The *Murænesocidæ* are large eels remarkable for their strong knife-like teeth. *Murænesox savanna* occurs in the West Indies and in the Mediterranean, *Murænesox cinereus* in Japan, and *Murænesox coniceps* on the west coast of Mexico, all large

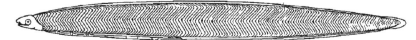

FIG 275 —Larva of Conger-eel (*Leptocephalus conger*), called *Leptocephalus morrissi*
(After Eigenmann)

and fierce, with teeth like shears   The *Myridæ* are small and worm-like eels closely allied to the congers, having the tail surrounded by a fin, but the nostrils labial   *Myrus myrus* is found in the Mediterranean   Species of *Eomyrus*, *Rhyncho-rhinus*, and *Paranguilla* apparently allied to *Myrus* occur in the Eocene   Other related families, mostly rare or living in the deep seas, are the *Ilyophidæ*, *Heterocongridæ*, and *Dysommidæ*

The Snake-eels.—Most varied of the families of eels is the *Ophichthyidæ*, snake-like eels recognizable by the form of the tail, which protrudes beyond the fins   Of the many genera found in tropical waters several are remarkable for the sharply defined coloration, suggesting that of the snake   Characteristic species are *Chlevastes colubrinus* and *Leiuranus semicinctus*, two beauti-fully banded species of Polynesia, living in the same holes in the reefs and colored in the same fashion.   Another is *Calle-*

chelys melanotænia   The commonest species on the Atlantic coast is the plainly colored *Ophichthus gomesi.*

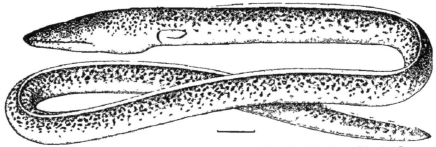

Fig 276 —*Xyrias revulsus* Jordan & Snyder   Family *Ophichthyidæ*   Misaki, Japan

In the genus *Sphagebranchus,* very slender eels of the reefs, the fins are almost wanting

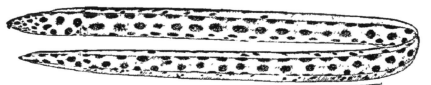

Fig 277.—*Myrichthys pantostigmius* Jordan & McGregor   Clarion Island

Allied to the Congers is the small family of duck-billed eels (*Nettastomidæ*) inhabiting moderate depths of the sea   *Nettastoma bolcense* occurs in the Eocene of Monte Bolca   The produced snout forms a transition to the really extraordinary type of thread-eels or snipe-eels (*Nemichthyidæ*), of which numerous genera and species live in the oceanic depths.   In *Nemichthys*

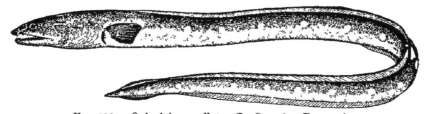

Fig 278 —*Ophichthus ocellatus* (Le Sueur)   Pensacola

the long, very slender, needle-like jaws are each curved backward so that the mouth cannot by any possibility be shut The body is excessively slender and the fish swims with swift undulations, often near the surface, and when seen is usually taken for a snake   The best-known species is *Nemichthys scolopaceus* of the Atlantic and Pacific   *Nemichthys avocetta*, very much like it, has been twice taken in Puget Sound

Suborder Colocephali, or Morays. — In the suborder *Colocephali* (κολός, deficient, κεφαλή, head) the palatopterygoid arch and the membrane-bones generally are very rudimentary   The skull is thus very narrow, the gill-structures are not well developed, and in the chief family there are no pectoral fins   This group is very closely related to the *Enchelycephali*, from which it is probably derived

In the great family of morays (*Murænidæ*) the teeth are often very highly developed   The muscles are always very strong and the spines bite savagely, a live moray, four to six feet long, being often able to drive men out of a boat   The skin is thick and leathery, and the coloration is highly specialized, the pattern of color

Fɪɢ 279   Fɪɢ 280

Fɪɢ 279 —Thread-eel, *Nemichthys avocetta* Jordan & Gilbert   Vancouver Island
Fɪɢ 280 —Jaws of *Nemichthys avocetta* Jordan & Gilbert

being often elaborate and brilliant   In *Echidna zebra* for example the body is wine-brown, with cross-stripes of golden yellow   In *Muræna* each nostril has a barbel   *Muræna helena*, the oldest moray known, is found in Europe   In *Gymnothorax*, the largest genus, only the anterior nostrils are thus provided   *Gymnothorax mordax* of California is a large food-fish, as are also the brown *Gymnothorax funebris* and the spotted *Gymnothorax moringa* in the West Indies   These and many other species may coil themselves in crevices in the reefs, whence they strike out at their prey like snakes, taking perhaps the head of a duck or the finger of a man

In many of the morays the jaws are so curved and the mouth so filled with knife-like teeth that the jaws cannot be closed   This fact, however, renders no assistance to their prey, as the teeth are adapted for holding as well as for cutting

In *Enchelynassa bleekeri*, a huge wine-colored eel of the South Seas, the teeth are larger than in any other species   *Evenchelys*

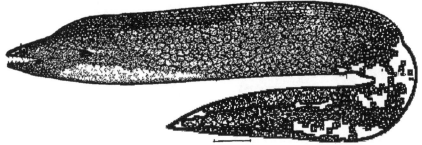

FIG 281 —*Muræna retifera* Garman   Charleston, S C

(*macrurus*) is remarkable for its extraordinary length of tail, *Echidna* for its blunt teeth, and *Scuticaria, Uropterygius*, and *Channomuræna* for the almost complete absence of fins.   In *Anarchias (allardicei, knighti)*, the anal fin is absent.   The flesh of the morays is rather agreeable in taste, but usually oily and not readily digestible, less wholesome than that of the true eels

The *Myrocongridæ* are small morays with developed pectoral fins   The species are few and little known

Family Moringuidæ.—Structurally one of the most peculiar of the groups of eels is the small family of *Moringuidæ* of the East and West Indies   In these very slender, almost worm-like fishes the heart is placed very far behind the gills and the tail is very short   The fins are very little developed, and some forms, as *Gordiichthys irretitus* of the Gulf of Mexico, the body as slender as a whiplash, possess a very great number of vertebræ   *Moringua hawaiensis* occurs in Hawaii, *M edwardsi* in the Bahamas   This family probably belongs with the morays to the group of *Colocephali*, although its real relationships are not wholly certain

Order Carencheli, the Long-necked Eels.—Certain offshoots from the Apodes so widely diverging in structure that they must apparently be considered as distinct orders occur sparingly in the deep seas. One of these, *Derichthys serpentinus*, the

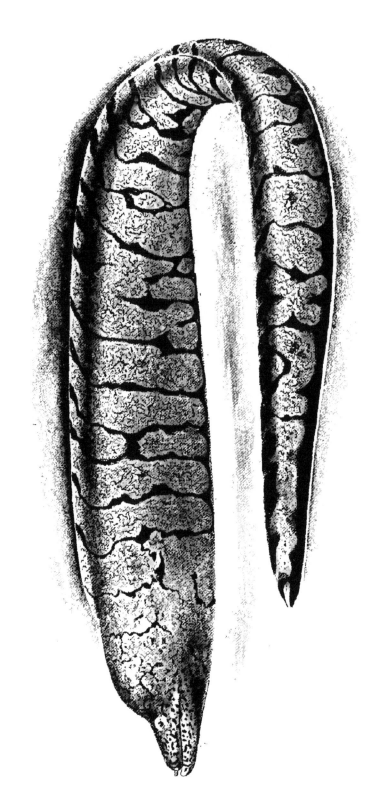

FIG. 282—*Gymnothorax berndti* Snyder. Hawaii. Family *Murænidæ*.

long-necked eel, constitutes the sole known species of the suborder *Carenchely* (*καρά*, head, *"ἔγχελυς*, eel). In this group
the premaxillaries and maxillaries are present as in ordinary

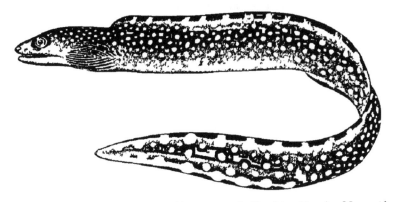

Fig 283 —*Gymnothorax jordani* (Evermann & Marsh) Family *Murænidæ*
Puerto Rico

fishes, but united by suture and soldered to the cranium As
in true eels, the shoulder-girdle is remote from the skull. The

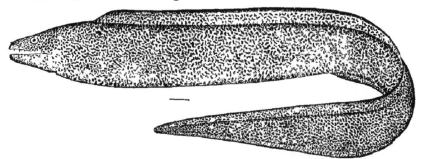

Fig 284 —Moray, *Gymnothorax moringa* Bloch Family *Murænidæ* Tortugas

head is set on a snake-like neck The single species representing
the family *Derichthyidæ* was found in the abysmal depths of
the Gulf Stream

Order Lyomeri, or Gulpers —Still more aberrant and in many
respects extraordinary are the eels of the order or suborder
Lyomeri (*λυός*, loose, *μέρος*, part), known as "Gulpers"
These are degenerate forms, possibly degraded from some con-
ger-like type, but characterized by an extreme looseness of
structure unique among fishes The gill-arches are reduced
to five small bars of bone, not attached to the skull, the palatopterygoid arch is wholly wanting, the premaxillaries are

wanting, as in all true eels, and the maxillaries loosely joined
to the skull The symplectic bone is wanting, and the lower jaw
is so hinged to the skull that it swings freely in various directions In place of the ·lateral line are singular appendages.

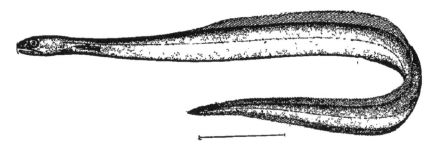

FIG 285 —*Derichthys serpentinus* Gill   Gulf Stream

Dr. Gill says of these fishes "The entire organization is peculiar
to the extent of anomaly, and our old conceptions of the characteristics of a fish require to be modified in the light of our
knowledge of such strange beings " Special features are the
extraordinary size of the mouth, which has a cavity larger than
that of the rest of the body, the insertion of the very small
eye at the tip of the snout, and the relative length of the tail
The whole substance is excessively fragile as usual with animals
living in great depths and the color is jet black   Three species

FIG 286 —Gulper-eel, *Gastrostomus bairdi* Gill & Ryder   Gulf Stream

have been described, and these have been placed in two families,
Saccopharyngidæ, with the trunk (gill-opening to the vent) much
longer than the head, and *Eurypharyngidæ*, with the trunk very
short, much shorter than the head   The best-known species
is the pelican eel (*Eurypharynx pelacanoides*), of the coast of
Morocco, described by Vaillant in 1882 *Gastrostomus bairdi*,
very much like it, occurs in the great depths under the Gulf
Stream   So fragile and so easily distorted are these fishes that

it is possible that all three are really the same species, for which the oldest name would be *Saccopharynx ampullaceus* Of this form four specimens have been taken in the Atlantic, one of them six feet long, carried to the surface through having swallowed fishes too large to be controlled To be carried above its depth in a struggle with its prey is one of the greatest dangers to which the abysmal fishes are subject

Order Heteromi —The order of *Heteromi* (ἕτερός, different, ὦμος, shoulder), or spiny eels, may be here noticed for want of a better place, as its affinities are very uncertain Some writers have regarded it as allied to the eels, some have placed it among the Ganoids Others have found affinities with the stickle-backs, and still others with the singular fresh-water fishes called *Mastacembelus* The *Heteromi* agree with the eels, as well as with *Mastacembelus*, in having the scapular arch separate from the cranium Unlike all the true eels, most of the species have true dorsal and anal spines, as in the *Percesoces* and *Hemi-branchii* The ventral fins, when present, are abdominal and each with several spines in front, a character not found among the *Acanthopteri* There is no mesocoracoid

The air-bladder has a duct, and the coracoids, much as in the *Xenomi*, are reduced to a single lamellar imperforate plate. The two groups have little else in common, however, and this trait is possibly primitive in both cases, more likely to have arisen through independent degeneration The separation of the shoulder-girdle doubtless indicates no affinity with the eels, as the bones of the jaws are quite normal Two families are known, both from the deep sea, besides an extinct family in which spines are not developed

The *Notacanthidæ* are elongate, compressed, ending in a band-shaped, tapering tail, the back has numerous free spines and few or no soft rays, and the mouth is normal, provided with teeth The species of *Notacanthus* are few and scantily pre-served Those of *Macdonaldia* are more abundant. *Mac-donaldia challengeri* is from the North Pacific, being once taken off Tokio The extinct family of *Protonotacanthidæ* differs in the total absence of dorsal spines and fin-rays, the single species, *Pronotocanthus sahel-almæ*, originally described as a primitive eel, occurs in the Cretaceous of Mount Lebanon

The *Lipogenyidæ* have a round, sucker-like mouth, with imperfect lower jaw, but are otherwise similar *Lipogenys gilli* was dredged in the Gulf Stream

Fig 287 —*Notacanthus phasganorus* Goode & Bean   Grand Banks

Dr Boulenger has recently extended the group of *Heteromi* by the addition of the *Dercetidæ*, *Halosauridæ* (*Lyopomi*), and the *Fierasferidæ* We can hardly suppose that all these forms are really allied to *Notacanthus*.

CHAPTER XXIII

SERIES OSTARIOPHYSI

STARIOPHYSI.—A large group of orders, certainly of common descent, may be brought together under the general name of *Ostariophysi* (ὀστάριον, a small bone; θυσός, inflated) These are in many ways allied to the *Isospondyli*, but they have undergone great changes of structure, some of the species being highly specialized, others variously degenerate A chief character is shared by all the species The anterior vertebræ are enlarged, interlocked, considerably modified, and through them a series of small bones connect the air-bladder with the ear. The air-bladder thus becomes apparently an organ of hearing through a form of connection which is lost in all the higher fishes

In all the members of this group excepting perhaps the degraded eel-like forms called *Gymnonoti*, the mesocoracoid arch persists, a trait found in all the living types of Ganoids, as well as in the *Teleost* order of *Isospondyli* Other traits of the Ostariophysan fishes are shared by the *Isospondyli* (herring, salmon) and other soft-rayed fishes The air-bladder is large, but not cellular It leads through life by an open duct to the œsophagus The ventral fins are abdominal in position The pectorals are inserted low A mesocoracoid arch is developed on the inner side of the shoulder-girdle. (See Fig 288) There are no spines on the fins, except in many cases a single one, a modified soft ray at front of dorsal or pectoral The scales, if present, are cycloid or replaced by bony plates

Many of the species have an armature much like that of the sturgeon, but here the resemblance ends, the bony plates in the two cases being without doubt independently evolved According to Cope, the affinities of the catfishes to the sturgeon are "seen in the absence of symplectic, the rudimentary maxillary bone, and, as observed by Parker, in the interclavicles. There is also a superficial resemblance in the dermal bones " But it is not likely that any real affinity exists

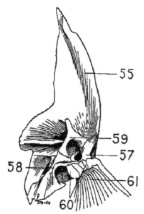

FIG 288 —Inner view of shoulder-girdle of the Buffalo-fish *Ictiobus bubalus* Rafinesque, showing the mesocoracoid (59) (After Starks)

The sturgeons lack the characteristic auditory ossicles, or "Weberian apparatus," which the catfishes possess in common with the carp family, the *Characins*, and the *Gymnonoti*. These orders must at least have a common origin, although this origin is obscure, and fossil remains give little help to the solution of the problem Probably the ancestors of the *Ostariophysi* are to be found among the allies of the *Osteoglossidæ*. Gill has called attention to the resemblance of *Erythrinus* to *Amia* In any event, all the *Ostariophysi* must be considered together, as it is not conceivable that so complex a structure as the Weberian apparatus should have been more than once independently evolved The branchiostegals, numerous among the *Isospondyli*, are mostly few among the *Ostariophysi*

To the *Ostariophysi* belong the vast majority of the freshwater fishes of the world. Their primitive structure is shown in

FIG 289 —Weberian apparatus and air-bladder of Carp (From Gunther, after Weber)

many ways, among others by the large number of vertebræ instead of the usual twenty-four among the more highly specialized families of fishes We may group the *Ostariophysi* under four orders *Heterognathi, Eventognathi (Plectospondyli), Nema-tognathi,* and *Gymnonoti*

The Heterognathi.—Of these the order of *Heterognathi* seems to be the most primitive, but in some ways the most highly developed, showing fewer traits of degeneration than any of the others   The presence of the adipose fin in this group and in the catfishes seems to indicate some sort of real affinity with the salmon-like forms, although there has been great change in other regards

The order *Heterognathi,* or *Characini* (ἕτερος, different; γνάθος, jaw), contains those *Ostariophysi* which retain the mesocoracoid and are not eel-like, and which have the lower pharyngeals developed as in ordinary fishes   In most cases an adipose fin is present and there are strong teeth in the jaws   There are no pseudobranchiæ, and, as in the *Cyprinidæ* usually but three branchiostegals   The *Characidæ* constitute the majority of the fresh-water fishes in those regions which have neither *Cyprinidæ* nor *Salmonidæ*   Nearly four hundred species are known from the rivers of South America and Africa   A single species, *Tetragonopterus argentatus,* extends its range northward to the Rio Grande in Texas   None are found in Asia, Europe, or, with this single exception, in the United States   Most of them are small fishes with deep bodies and very sharp, serrated, incisor-like teeth   Some are as innocuous as minnows, which they very much resemble, but others are extremely voracious and destructive in the highest degree   Of the caribe, belonging to the genus *Serrasalmo,* known by its serrated belly, Dr Günther observes

"Their voracity, fearlessness and number render them a perfect pest in many rivers of tropical America   In all the teeth are strong, short, sharp, sometimes lobed incisors, arranged in one or more series, by means of them they cut off a mouthful of flesh as with a pair of scissors, and any animal falling into the water where these fish abound is immediately attacked and cut to pieces in an incredibly short time   They assail persons entering the water, inflicting dangerous wounds before the victims are able to make their escape. In some localities it is scarcely possible to catch fishes with the hook and line, as the fish hooked is immediately attacked by the 'caribe' (as

these fish are called), and torn to pieces before it can be with-
drawn from the water   The caribes themselves are rarely
hooked, as they snap the hook or cut the line   The smell of
blood is said to attract at once thousands of these fishes to the
spot ''

Two families of *Heterognathi* are recognized· the *Erythrinidæ*, which lack the adipose fin, and the *Characidæ*, in which
this fin is developed   The *Erythrinidæ* are large pike-like
fishes of the South American rivers, robust and tenacious of
life, with large mouths armed with strong unequal teeth   The
best-known species is the *Trahira* (*Hoplias malabaricus*)

Among the *Characidæ, Serrasalmo* has been already noticed
Citharinus in Africa has very few teeth, and *Curimatus* in South
America none at all   *Nannocharax* in Africa is composed of

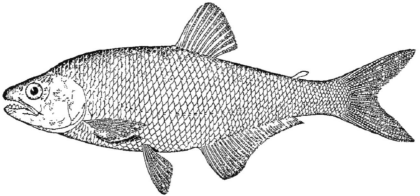

FIG 290 —*Brycon dentex* Gunther   Family *Characidæ*   Nicaragua

very diminutive fishes, *Hydrocyon* exceedingly voracious ones,
reaching a length of four feet, with savage teeth   Many of the
species are allies of *Tetragonopterus*, small, silvery, bream-like
fishes with flat bodies and serrated incisor teeth   Most of these
are American   A related genus is *Brycon*, found in the streams
about the Isthmus of Panama

Extinct *Characins* are very rare   Two species from the Tertiary lignite of São Paulo, Brazil, have been referred to *Tetragonopterus—T avus* and *T. ligniticus*

The Eventognathi.—The *Eventognathi* (εὖ, well, ἔν, within,
γνάθος, jaw) are characterized by the absence of teeth in the
jaws and by the high degree of specialization of the lower phar-

yngeals, which are scythe-shaped and in typical forms are armed
with a relatively small number of highly specialized teeth of
peculiar shape and arranged in one, two, or three rows. In
all the species the gill-openings are restricted to the sides, there is
no adipose fin, and the broad, flat branchiostegals are but three
in number. In all the species the scales, if present, are cycloid,
and the ventral fins, of course, abdominal. The modification
of the four anterior vertebræ and their connection with the
air bladder are essentially as seen in the catfishes.

The name *Plectospondyli* is often used for this group ($\pi\lambda\epsilon\kappa\tau\delta s$,
interwoven, $\sigma\pi\delta\nu\delta\nu\lambda os$, vertebra), but that term originally included the *Characins* as well.

The Cyprinidæ.—The chief family of the *Eventognathi* and the
largest of all the families of fishes is that of *Cyprinidæ*, comprising

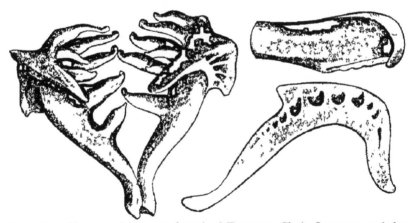

FIG 291 —Pharyngeal bones and teeth of European Chub, *Leuciscus cephalus*
(Linnæus)   (After Seelye)

200 genera and over 2000 species, found throughout the north temperate zone but not extending to the Arctic Circle on the north,
nor much beyond the Tropic of Cancer on the south. In this
family belong all the fishes known as carp, dace, chub, roach,
bleak, minnow, bream, and shiner. The essential character of the
family lies in the presence of one, two, or three rows of highly
specialized teeth on the lower pharyngeals, the main row containing 4, 5, 6, or 7 teeth, the others 1 to 3. The teeth of the
main row differ in form according to the food of the fish. They
may be coarse and blunt, molar-like in those which feed on shells,

they may be hooked at tip in those which eat smaller fishes; they may be serrated or not, they may have an excavated "grinding surface," which is most developed in the species which feed on mud and have long intestines. In the *Cyprinidæ*, or carp family, the barbels are small or wanting, the head is naked, the caudal fin forked, the mouth is toothless and without sucking lips, and the premaxillaries form its entire margin. With a few exceptions the *Cyprinidæ* are small and feeble fishes. They form most of the food of the predatory river fishes, and their great abundance in competition with these is due to their fecundity and their insignificance. They spawn profusely and find everywhere an abundance of food. Often they check the increase of predatory fish by the destruction of their eggs.

In many of the genera the breeding color of the males is very brilliant, rendering these little creatures for a time the most beautifully colored of fishes. In spring and early summer the fins, sides, and head in the males are often charged with pigment, the prevailing color of which is rosy, though often satin-white, orange, crimson, yellow, greenish, or jet black. Among American genera *Chrosomus*, *Notropis*, and *Rhinichthys* are most highly colored. *Rhodeus*, *Rutilus*, and *Zacco* in the Old World are also often very brilliant.

In very many species, especially in America, the male in the breeding season is often more or less covered with small,

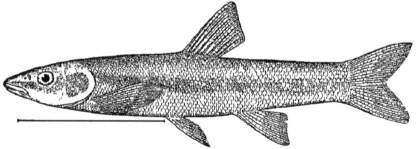

Fig 292 —Black-nosed Dace, *Rhinichthys dulcis* Girard. Yellowstone River

grayish tubercles or pearly bodies, outgrowths of the epidermis. These are most numerous on the head and fall off after the breeding season. They are most developed in *Campostoma*.

The *Cyprinidæ* are little valued as food-fishes. The carp, largely domesticated in small ponds for food, is coarse and

tasteless   Most of the others are flavorless and full of small
bones   One species, *Opsaruchthys uncirostris*, of Japan is an
exception in this regard, being a fish of very delicate flavor

In America 225 species of *Cyprinidæ* are known   One hundred of these are now usually held to form the single genus

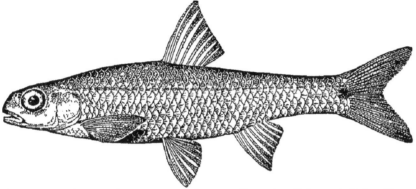

Fig 293 —White Chub, *Notropis hudsonius* (Clinton)   Kilpatrick Lake, Minn

Notropis   This includes the smaller and weaker species, from
two to seven inches in length, characterized by the loss, mostly
through degeneration, of special peculiarities of mouth, fins, and
teeth   These have no barbels and never more than four teeth

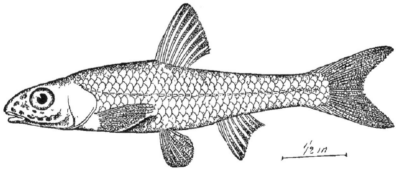

Fig 294 —Silver-jaw Minnow, *Ericymba buccata* Cope   Defiance, Ohio

in the main row   Few, if any, Asiatic species have so small
a number, and in most of these the maxillary still retains its
rudimentary barbel   But one American genus (*Orthodon*) has
more than five teeth in the main row and none have more than
two rows or more than two teeth in the lower row   By these
and other peculiarities it would seem that the American species
are at once less primitive and less complex than the Old World

forms   There is some evidence that the group is derived from Asia through western America, the Pacific Coast forms being much nearer the Old World types than the forms inhabiting the Mississippi Valley.   Not many *Cyprinidæ* are found in Mexico, none in Cuba, South America, Australia, Africa, or the islands to the eastward of Borneo   Many species are very widely distributed, many others extremely local   In the genus *Notropis*, each river basin in the Southern States has its series of different and mostly highly colored species   The presence of *Notropis niveus* in the Neuse, *Notropis pyrrhomelas* in the Santee, *Notropis zonistius* in the Chattahoochee, *Notropis callistius*, *trichroistius*, and *stigmaturus* in the Alabama, *Notropis whipplei* in

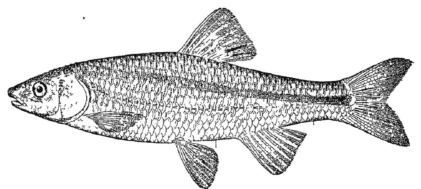

Fig 295 —Silverfin, *Notropis whipplei* (Girard)   White River, Indiana
Family *Cyprinidæ*

the Mississippi, *Notropis galacturus* in the Tennessee, and *Notropis cercostigma* in the Sabine forms an instructive series in this regard   These fishes and the darters (*Etheostominæ*) are, among American fishes, the groups best suited for the study of local problems in distribution.

Species of Dace and Shiner.—Noteworthy species in other genera are the following

Largest and best known of the species of *Notropis* is the familiar shiner or redfin, *Notropis cornutus*, found in almost every brook throughout the region east of the Missouri River

Campostoma anomalum, the stone-roller, has the very long intestines six times the length of its body, arranged in fifteen coils around the air-bladder.   This species feeds on mud and spawns in little brooks, swarming in early spring throughout the Mississippi Valley, and is notable for its nuptial tubercles and the black and orange fins

In the negro-chub, *Exoglossum maxillingua* of the Pennsyl-

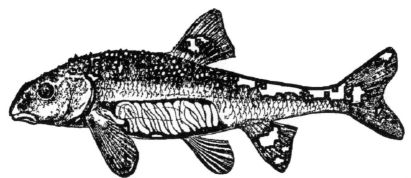

Fig 296 —Stone-roller, *Campostoma anomalum* (Rafinesque)   Family *Cyprinidæ*
Showing nuptial tubercles and intestines coiled about the air-bladder

vanian district, the rami of the lower jaw are united for their whole length, looking like a projecting tongue

The fallfish, *Semotilus corporalis*, is the largest chub of the Eastern rivers, 18 inches long, living in swift, clear rivers.   It is a soft fish, and according to Thoreau "it tastes like brown paper salted" when it is cooked Close to this is the horned dace, *Semotilus atromaculatus*, and the horny head, *Hybopsis kentuckiensis*, both among the most widely distributed of our river fishes These are all allied to the gudgeon (*Gobio gobio*), a common boys' fish of the rivers of Europe, and much sought by anglers who can get nothing better   The bream,

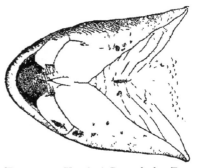

Fig 297 —Head of Day-chub, *Exoglossum maxillingua* (Le Sueur) Shenandoah River

Abramis, represented by numerous species in Europe, has a deep compressed body and a very long anal fin   It is also well represented in America, the golden shiner, common in Eastern and Southern streams, being *Abramis chrysoleucus*. The bleak of Europe (*Alburnus alburnus*) is a "shiner" close to some of our species of *Notropis*, while the minnow of Europe, *Phoxinus phoxinus*, resembles our gorgeously colored *Chrosomus erythro-*

gaster. Other European forms are the roach (*Rutilus rutilus*), the chub (*Leuciscus cephalus*), the dace (*Leuciscus leuciscus*),

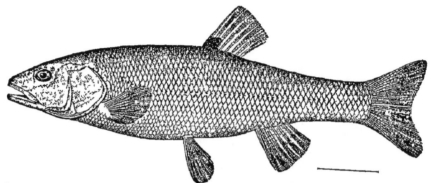

FIG 298 —Horned Dace, *Semotilus atromaculatus* (Mitchill) Aux Plaines River, Ills Family *Cyprinidæ*

the ide (*Idus idus*), the red-eye (*Scardinius erythropthalmus*), and the tench (*Tinca tinca*) The tench is the largest of the European species, and its virtues with those of its more or less

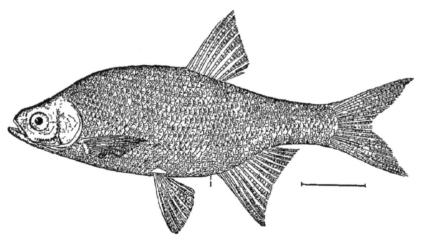

FIG 299 —Shiner, *Abramis chrysoleucus* (Mitchill) Hackensack River, N J

insignificant allies are set forth in the pages of Izaak Walton All of these receive more attention from anglers in England than their relatives receive in America All the American *Cyprinidæ* are ranked as "boys' fish," and those who seek the trout or black bass or even the perch or crappie will not notice them. Thoreau speaks of the boy who treasures the yellow perch as a real fish "So many unquestionable fish he counts, then so many chubs which he counts, then throws away "

Chubs of the Pacific Slope.—In the Western waters are numerous genera, some of the species reaching a large size The species

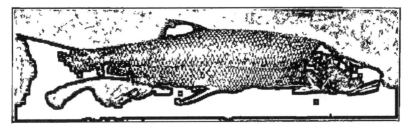

FIG 300 —The Squawfish, *Ptychocheilus grandis* Agassiz   (Photograph by Cloudsley Rutter)

of squawfish (*Ptychocheilus lucius* in the Colorado, *Ptychocheilus grandis* in the Sacramento, and *Ptychocheilus oregonensis* in the Columbia) reach a length of 4 or 5 feet or even more   These fishes are long and slender, with large toothless mouths and the aspect of a pike

Allied to these are the "hard tails" (*Gila elegans* and *Gila robusta*) of the Colorado Basin, strange-looking fishes scarcely eatable, with lean bodies, flat heads, and expanded tails   The split-tail, *Pogonichthys macrolepidotus*, is found in the Sacramento

In the chisel-mouth, *Acrocheilus alutaceus*, of the Columbia the lips have a hard cutting edge   In *Meda*, very small fishes

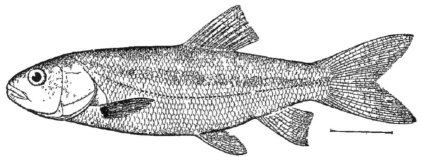

FIG 301 —Chub of the Great Basin, *Leuciscus lineatus* (Girard)   Heart Lake, Yellowstone Park   Family *Cyprinidæ*

of the Colorado Basin, the dorsal has a compound spine of peculiar structure   Many of the species of Western waters belong to the genus *Leuciscus*, which includes also many species of Asia and Europe The common Japanese dace (*Leuciscus hakuensis*) is often found out in the sea, but, in general, *Cyprinidæ* are only found in fresh waters The genus of barbels (*Barbus*) contains many large species in Europe and Asia In these the barbel is better developed than in most other genera, a character which seems to indicate a primitive organization *Barbus mosal* of the mountains of India is said to reach a length of more than six feet and to have "scales as large as the palm of the hand"

The Carp and Goldfish.—In the American and European *Cyprinidæ* the dorsal fin is few-rayed, but in many Asiatic species it is longer, having 15 to 20 rays and is often preceded by a serrated spine like that of a catfish Of the species with long dorsal the one most celebrated is the carp (*Cyprinus carpio*). This fish is a native of the rivers of China, where it has been domesticated for centuries Nearly three hundred years ago it was brought to northern Europe, where it has multiplied in domestication and become naturalized in many streams and ponds Of late years the cultivation of the carp has attracted much attention in America It has been generally satisfactory where the nature of the fish is understood and where expectations have not been too high

The carp is a dull and sluggish fish, preferring shaded, tranquil, and weedy waters with muddy bottoms Its food consists of water insects and other small animals, and vegetable matter, such as the leaves of aquatic plants They can be fed on much the same things as pigs and chickens, and they bear much the same relation to trout and bass that pigs and chickens do to wild game and game-birds The carp is a very hardy fish, grows rapidly, and has immense fecundity, 700,000 eggs having been found in the ovaries of a single individual It reaches sometimes a weight of 30 to 40 pounds As a food-fish the carp cannot be said to hold a high place It is tolerated in the absence of better fish

The carp, either native or in domestication, has many enemies. In America, catfish, sunfish, and pike prey upon its eggs or its young, as well as water-snakes, turtles, kingfishes, crayfishes, and many other creatures which live about our ponds and in sluggish streams In domestication numerous varieties of carp have been formed, the "leather-carp" (Lederkarpfen) being scaleless, others, "mirror-carp" (Spiegelkarpfen), having rows of large scales only along the lateral line or the bases of the fins

Closely allied to the carp is the goldfish (*Carassius auratus*) This is also a common Chinese fish introduced in domestication into Europe and America   The golden-yellow color is found only in domesticated specimens, and is retained by artificial selection   The native goldfish is olivaceous in color, and where the species has become naturalized (as in the Potomac River, where it has escaped from fountains in Washington) it reverts to its natural greenish hue.   The same change occurs in the rivers of Japan   The goldfish is valued solely for its bright colors as an ornamental fish   It has no beauty of form nor any interesting habits, and many of our native fishes (*Percidæ*, *Cyprinidæ*) far excel it in attractiveness as aquarium fishes Unfortunately they are less hardy   Many varieties and monstrosities of the goldfish have been produced by domestication.

The Catostomidæ.—The suckers, or *Catostomidæ*, are an offshoot from the *Cyprinidæ*, differing chiefly in the structure of the mouth and of the lower pharyngeal bones The border of the mouth above is formed mesially by the small premaxillaries and laterally by the maxillaries   The teeth of the lower pharyngeals are small and very numerous, arranged in one series like the teeth of a comb   The lips are usually thick and fleshy, and the dorsal fin is more or less elongate (its rays eleven to fifty in number), characters which distinguish the suckers from the American *Cyprinidæ* generally, but not from those of the Old World

About sixty species of suckers are known, all of them found in the rivers of North America except two, which have been recorded on rather uncertain authority from Siberia and China   Only two or three of the species extend their range south of the

Fig 302—Lower pharyngeal of *Placopharynx duquesnii* (Le Sueur)

Tropic of Cancer into Mexico or Central America, and none

occurs in Cuba nor in any of the neighboring islands. The majority of the genera are restricted to the region east of the Rocky Mountains, although species of *Catostomus*, *Chasmistes*, *Deltistes*, *Xyrauchen*, and *Pantosteus* are found in abundance in the Great Basin and the Pacific slope.

In size the suckers range from six inches in length to about three feet As food-fishes they are held in low esteem, the flesh of all being flavorless and excessively full of small bones Most of them are sluggish fishes, they inhabit all sorts of streams, lakes, and ponds, but even when in mountain brooks they gather in the eddies and places of greatest depth and least current They feed on insects and small aquatic animals, and also on mud, taking in their food by suction They are not very tenacious of life Most of the species swarm in the spring in shallow waters In the spawning season they migrate up smaller streams than those otherwise inhabited by them The

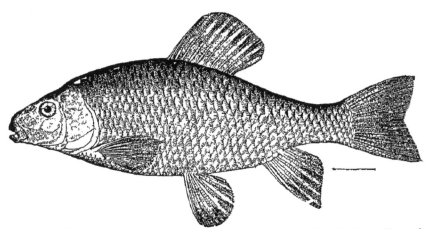

FIG 303 —Creekfish or Chub-sucker, *Erimyzon sucetta* (Lacépàde) Nipisink Lake, Illinois Family *Catostomidæ*

large species move from the large rivers into smaller ones, the small brook species go into smaller brooks In some cases the males in spring develop black or red pigment on the body or fins, and in many cases tubercles similar to those found in the *Cyprinidæ* appear on the head, body, and anal and caudal fins

The buffalo-fishes and carp-suckers, constituting the genera *Ictiobus* and *Carpiodes*, are the largest of the *Catostomidæ*, and

bear a considerable resemblance to the carp   They have the
dorsal fin many-rayed and the scales large and coarse   They

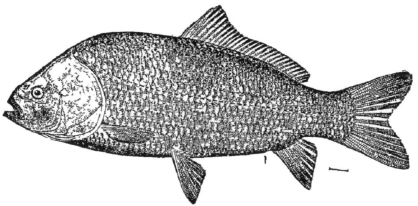

Fig 304 —Buffalo-fish, *Ictiobus cyprinella* (Cuv & Val)   Normal, Ill

abound in the large rivers and lakes between the Rocky Mountains
and the Alleghanies, one species being found in Central America
and a species of a closely related genus (*Myxocyprinus asiaticus*)

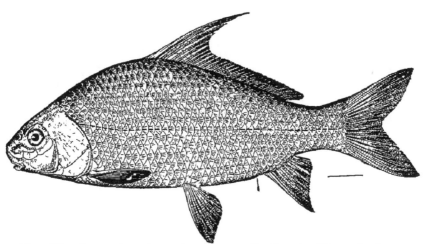

Fig 305 —Carp-sucker, *Carpiodes cyprinus* (Le Sueur)   Havre de Grace

being reported from eastern Asia   They rarely ascend the
smaller rivers except for the purpose of spawning   Although
so abundant in the Mississippi Valley as to be of importance
commercially, they are very inferior as food-fishes, being coarse
and bony   The genus *Cycleptus* contains the black-horse, or
Missouri sucker, a peculiar species with a small head, elongate

body, and jet-black coloration, which comes up the smaller rivers tributary to the Mississippi and Ohio in large numbers

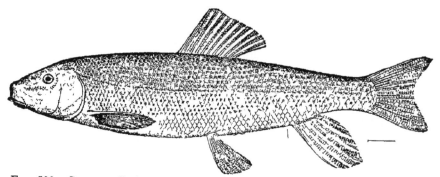

FIG 306 —Common Sucker, *Catostomus commersoni* (Le Sueur)   Ecorse, Mich

in the spring   Most of the other suckers belong to the genera *Catostomus* and *Moxostoma*, the latter with the large-toothed *Placopharynx* being known, from the red color of the fins, as

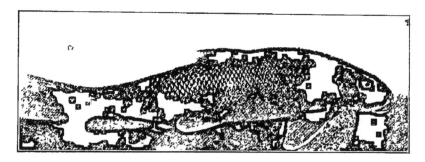

FIG 307 —California Sucker, *Catostomus occidentalis* Agassiz   (Photograph by Cloudsley Rutter)

red-horse, the former as sucker   Some of the species are very widely distributed, two of them (*Catostomus commersoni, Erimyzon sucetta*) being found in almost every stream east of the Rocky Mountains and *Catostomus catostomus* throughout Canada to the Arctic Sea   The most peculiar of the suckers in appearance is the harelip sucker (*Quassilabia lacera*) of the Western rivers   Very singular in form is the hump-back or razor-back sucker of the Colorado, *Xyrauchen cypho*

Fossil Cyprinidæ.—Fossil *Cyprinidæ*, closely related to existing forms, are found in abundance in fresh-water deposits of the Tertiary, but rarely if ever earlier than the Miocene   *Cyprinus* *priscus* occurs in the Miocene of Germany, perhaps showing that Germany was the original home of the so-called "German carp," afterwards actually imported to Germany from China.   Some specimens referred to *Barbus, Tinca, Rhodeus, Aspius,* and *Gobio* are found in regions now inhabited by these genera, and many species are referred to the great genus *Leuciscus, Leuciscus œningensis* from the Miocene of Germany being perhaps the best known Several species of *Leuciscus* or related genera are found in the Rocky Mountain region   Among these is the recently described *Leuciscus turneri.*

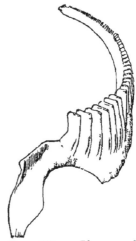

Fig 308 — Pharyngeal teeth of Oregon Sucker, *Catostomus macrocheilus*

Fossil *Catostomidæ* are very few and chiefly referred to the genus *Amyzon,* supposed to be allied to *Erimyzon,* but with a longer dorsal   *Amyzon commune* and other species are found in the Rocky Mountains, especially in the Miocene of the South Park in Colorado and the Eocene of Wyoming   Two or three species of

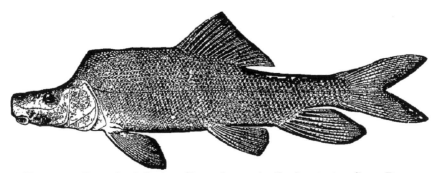

Fig 309 —Razor-back Sucker, *Xyrauchen cypho* (Lockington)   Green River, Utah

Catostomus, known by their skulls, are found in the Pliocene of Idaho

The Loaches.—The *Cobitidæ,* or loaches, are small fishes, all less than a foot in length, inhabiting streams and ponds of Europe and Asia.   In structure they are not very different from minnows, but they are rather eel-like in form, and the numerous long barbels about the mouth strongly suggest affinity with the catfishes   The scales are small, the pharyngeal teeth few, and the air-bladder, as in most small catfishes, enclosed in a capsule   The loaches are all bottom fishes of dark colors, tenacious of life, feeding on insects and worms   The species often bury themselves in mud and sand   They lie quiet on the bottom and move very quickly when disturbed much after the manner of darters and gobies   Species of *Cobitis* and *Misgurnus* are widely distributed from England to Japan   *Nemachilus barbatulus* is the commonest European species.   *Cobitis tænia* is found, almost unchanged, from England to the streams of Japan.

Remains of fossil loaches, mostly indistinguishable from *Cobitis*, occur in the Miocene and more recent rocks

From ancestors of loaches or other degraded *Cyprinidæ* we may trace the descent of the catfishes

The *Homalopteridæ* are small loaches in the mountain streams of the East Indies.   They have no air-bladder and the number of pharyngeal teeth (10 to 16) is greater than in the loaches, carp, or minnows.

CHAPTER XXIV

THE NEMATOGNATHI, OR CATFISHES

THE Nematognathi.—The *Nematognathi* (νῆμα, thread, γνάθος, jaw), known collectively as catfishes, are recognized at once by the fact that the rudimentary and usually toothless maxillary is developed as the bony base of a long barbel or feeler   Usually other feelers are found around the head, suggesting the "smellers" of a cat   The body is never scaly, being either naked and smooth or else more or less completely mailed with bony plates which often resemble superficially those of a sturgeon   Other distinctive characters are found in the skeleton, notably the absence of the subopercle, but the peculiar development of the maxillary and its barbel with the absence of scales is always distinctive   The symplectic is usually absent, and in some the air-bladder is reduced to a rudiment inclosed in a bony capsule   In almost all cases a stout spine exists in the front of the dorsal fin and in the front of each pectoral fin   This spine, made of modified or coalescent soft rays, is often a strong weapon with serrated edges and capable of inflicting a severe wound   When the fish is alarmed, it sets this spine by a rotary motion in its socket joint   It can then be depressed only by breaking it   By a rotary motion upward and toward the body the spine is again lowered   The wounds made by this spine are often painful, but this fact is due not to a specific poison but to the irregular cut and to the slime of the spine

In two genera, *Noturus* and *Schilbeodes*, a poison-gland exists at the base of the pectoral spine, and the wound gives a sharp pain like the sting of a hornet and almost exactly like the sting of a scorpion-fish   Most of the *Nematognathi* possess a fleshy or adipose fin behind the dorsal, exactly as in the salmon   In a few cases the adipose fin develops an anterior spine and occasionally supporting rays

All the *Nematognathi* are carnivorous bottom feeders, devouring any prey they can swallow Only a few enter the sea, and they occur in the greatest abundance in the Amazon region Upward of 1200 species, arranged in 150 genera, are recorded They vary greatly in size, from two inches to six feet in length All are regarded as food-fishes, but the species in the sea have very tough and flavorless flesh Some of the others are extremely delicate, with finely flavored flesh and a grateful absence of small bones

Families of Nematognathi.—According to Dr. Eigenmann's scheme of classification,* the most primitive family of Nematognathi is that of *Diplomystidæ*, characterized by the presence of a well-developed maxillary, as in other soft-rayed fishes The single species, *Diplomystes papillosus*, is found in the waters of Chile

Similar to the *Diplomystidæ* in all other respects is the great central family of *Siluridæ*, by far the most numerous and important of all the divisions of *Nematognathi*

The Siluridæ.—This group has the skin naked or imperfectly mailed, the barbels on the head well developed, the dorsal short, inserted forward, the adipose fin without spine, and the lower pharyngeals separate All the marine catfishes and most of the fresh-water species belong to this group, and its members, some 700 species, abound in all parts of the world where catfishes are known—"a bloodthirsty and bullying race of rangers inhabiting the river bottoms with ever a lance at rest and ready to do battle with their nearest neighbor"

The Sea Catfish.—In the tropical seas are numerous species of catfishes belonging to *Tachysurus, Arius, Galeichthys, Felichthys*, and other related genera These are sleek, silvery fishes covered with smooth skin, the head usually with a coat of mail, pierced by a central fontanelle Some of them reach a considerable size, swarming in sandy bays None are valued as food, being always tough and coarsely flavored Sea birds, as the pelican, which devour these catfishes are often destroyed by

* A Revision of the South American Nematognathi, 1890, p 7

the sudden erection of the pectoral spines   None of these are found in Europe or in Japan   Of the very many American species the gaff-topsail catfish (*Felichthys felis*), noted for its

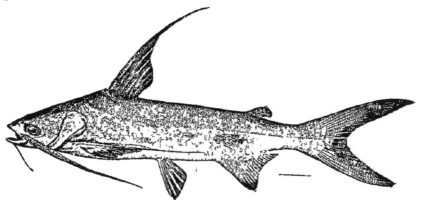

FIG 310 —Gaff-topsail Cat, *Felichthys felis* (L)   Woods Hole

very high spines, extends farthest north and is one of the very largest species   This genus has two barbels at the chin   Most others have four   The commonest sea catfish of the Carolina coast is *Galeichthys milberti*   In *Tachysurus* the teeth

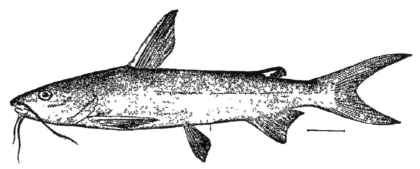

FIG. 311 —Sea Catfish, *Galeichthys milberti* (Cuv & Val)   Pensacola

on the palate are rounded, in most of the others they are in villiform bands

In most or all of the sea catfish the eggs, as large as small peas, are taken into the mouth of the male and there cared for until hatched

The Channel Cats—In all the rivers of North America east of the Rocky Mountains are found catfishes in great variety The channel cats, *Ictalurus*, known most readily by the forked tails, are the largest in size and most valued as food.   The tech·

nical character of the genus is the backward continuation of the supraoccipital, forming a bony bridge to the base of the dorsal The great blue cat, *Ictalurus furcatus*, abounds throughout the large rivers of the Southern States and reaches a weight of 150 pounds or more   It is an excellent food and its firm flesh is readily cut into steaks   In the Great Lakes and northward is a very similar species, also of large size, which has been called *Ictalurus*

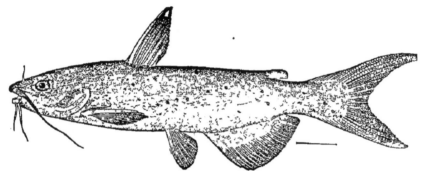

Fig 312 —Channel Catfish, *Ictalurus punctatus* (Rafinesque)   Illinois River
Family *Siluridæ*

lacustris   Another similar species is the willow cat, *Ictalurus anguilla*   The white channel-cat, *Ictalurus punctatus*, reaches a much smaller size and abounds on the ripples in clear swift streams of the Southwest, such as the Cumberland, the Alabama, and the Gasconade   It is a very delicate food-fish, with tender white flesh of excellent flavor

Horned Pout.—The genus *Ameiurus* includes the smaller brown catfish, horned pout, or bullhead   The body is more plump and the caudal fin is usually but not always rounded   The many species are widely diffused, abounding in brooks, lakes, and ponds   *Ameiurus nebulosus* is the best-known species, ranging from New England to Texas, known in the East as horned pout It has been successfully introduced into the Sacramento, where it abounds, as well as its congener, *Ameiurus catus*, the white bullhead, brought with it from the Potomac   The latter species has a broader head and concave or notched tail   All the species are good food-fishes   All are extremely tenacious of life, and all are alike valued by the urchin, for they will bite vigorously at any sort of bait   All must be handled with care, for the sharp pectoral spines make an ugly cut, a species of wound from which few boys' hands ın the catfish regıon are often free

In the caves about Conestoga Rıver ın Lancaster County, Pennsylvanıa, ıs a partly blınd catfish, evıdently derıved from

Fıg 313 —Horned Pout, *Ameıurus nebulosus* (Le Sueur)　(From lıfe by Dr R W Shufeldt)

local species outsıde the cave　It has been named *Gronıas nıgrılabrıs*

A few specıes are found ın Mexıco, one of them, *Ictalurus*

meridionalis, as far south as Rio Usamacinta on the boundary of Guatemala

Besides these, a large channel-cat of peculiar dentition, known as *Istlarius balsanus,* abounds in the basin of Rio Balsas In Mexico all catfishes are known as Bagre, this species as Bagre de Rio

The genus *Leptops* includes the great yellow catfish, or goujon, known at once by the projecting lower jaw It is a mottled olive and yellow fish of repulsive exterior, and it reaches a very great size It is, however, a good food-fish

The Mad-toms. — The genera *Noturus* and *Schilbeodes* are composed of diminutive catfishes, having the pectoral spine armed at base, with a poison sac which renders its sting ex

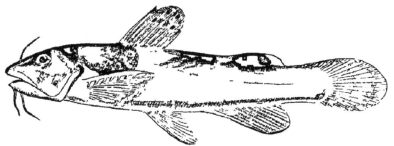

Fig. 314 —Mad-tom, *Schilbeodes furiosus* Jordan & Meek Showing the poisoned pectoral spine Family *Siluridæ* Neuse River

tremely painful though not dangerous The numerous species of this genus, known as "mad-toms" and "stone cats" live among weeds in brooks and sluggish streams Most of them rarely exceed three inches in length, and their varied colors make them attractive in the aquarium

The Old World Catfishes —In the catfishes of the Old World and their relatives, the adipose fin is rudimentary or wanting The chief species found in Europe is the huge sheatfish, or wels *Silurus glanis* This, next to the sturgeon, is the largest river fish in Europe, weighing 300 to 400 pounds It is not found in England, France, or Italy, but abounds in the Danube It is a lazy fish, hiding in the mud and thus escaping from nets It is very voracious, and many stories are told of the contents of its stomach A small child swallowed whole is recorded from Thorn, and there are still more remarkable stories, but not properly vouched for   The sheatfish is brown in color, naked, sleek, and much like an American *Ameiurus* save that its tail is much longer and more eel-like   Another large catfish, known to the ancients, but only recently rediscovered by Agassiz and Garman, is *Parasilurus aristotelis* of the rivers of Greece   In China and Japan is the very similar Namazu, or Japanese catfish, *Parasilurus asotus*, often found in ponds and used as food Numerous smaller related catfishes, *Porcus (Bagrus)*, *Pseudobagrus*, and related genera swarm in the brooks and ponds of the Orient

In the genus *Torpedo (Malapterurus)* the dorsal fin is wanting. *Torpedo electricus*, the electric catfish of the Nile, is a species of much interest to anatomists   The shock is like that of a Leyden jar   The structures concerned are noticed on p 58

FIG 315 —Electric Catfish., *Torpedo electricus* (Gmelin)   Congo River
(After Boulenger)

The generic name *Torpedo* was applied to the electric catfish before its use for the electric ray

In South America a multitude of genera and species cluster around the genus *Pimelodus*.   Some of them have the snout very long and spatulate   Most of them possess a very long adipose fin   The species are generally small in size and with smooth skin like the North American catfishes   Still other species in great numbers are grouped around the genus *Doras*. In this group the snout projects, bearing the small mouth at its end, and the lateral line is armed behind with spinous shields All but one of the genera belong to the Amazon district, *Synodontis* being found in Africa.

Concerning *Doras*, Dr Gunther observes· "These fishes have excited attention by their habit of traveling during the dry season from a piece of water about to dry up in quest of a pond of greater capacity   These journeys are occasionally of such a length that the fish spends whole nights on the way, and the bands of scaly travelers are sometimes so large that the Indians who happen to meet them fill many baskets of the prey thus placed in their hands The Indians suppose that the fish carry a supply of water with them, but they have no special organs and can only do so by closing the gill-openings or by retaining a little water between the plates of their bodies, as Hancock supposes The same naturalist adds that they make regular nests, in which they cover up their eggs with care and defend them, male and female uniting in this parental duty until the eggs are hatched The nest is constructed, at the beginning of the rainy season, of leaves and is sometimes placed in a hole scooped out of the beach ''

The Sisoridæ —The *Sisoridæ* are small catfishes found in swift mountain streams of northern India. In some of the genera (*Pseudecheneis*) in swift streams a sucking-disk formed of longitudinal plates of skin is formed on the breast This enables these fishes to resist the force of the water In one genus, *Exostoma*, plates of skin about the mouth serve the same purpose

The *Bunocephalidæ* are South American catfishes with the dorsal fin undeveloped and the top of the head rough In *Platystacus* (*Aspredo*), the eggs are carried on the belly of the female, which is provided with spongy tentacles to which the eggs are attached After the breeding season the ventral surface becomes again smooth

The Plotosidæ. — The *Plotosidæ* are naked catfishes, largely marine, found along the coasts of Asia In these fishes the second dorsal is very long *Plotosus anguillaris*, the sea catfish of Japan, is a small species striped with yellow and armed with sharp pectoral spines which render it a very disagreeable object to the fishermen In sandy bays like that of Nagasaki it is very abundant Allied to this is the small Asiatic family of *Chacidæ*

The Chlariidæ —The *Chlariidæ* are eel-like, with a soft skeleton and a peculiar accessory gill These abound in the swamps and muddy streams of India, where some species reach a length of six feet One species, *Chlarias magur*, has been brought by the Chinese to Hawaii, where it flourishes in the same waters as *Amerurus nebulosus*, brought from the Potomac and by Chinese carried from San Francisco

The Hypophthalmidæ and Pygidiidæ. — The *Hypophthalmidæ* have the minute air-bladder inclosed in a long bony capsule The eyes are placed very low and the skin is smooth The statement that this family lacks the auditory apparatus is not correct The few species belong to northern South America

Allied to this group is the family *Pygidiidæ* with a differently formed bony capsule and no adipose fin The numerous species are all South American, mostly of mountain streams of high altitude Some are very small Certain species are said to flee for protection into the gill-cavity of larger cat-

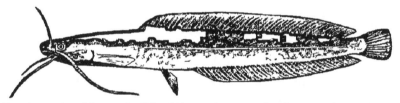

FIG 316 —An African Catfish, *Chlarias breviceps* Boulenger Congo River Family *Chlariidæ* (After Boulenger)

fishes Some are reported to enter the urethra of bathers, causing severe injuries The resemblance of certain species to the loaches, or *Cobitidæ*, is very striking This similarity is due to the results of similar environment and necessarily parallel habits The *Argidæ* have the capsule of the air-bladder formed in a still different fashion The few species are very small, inhabitants of the streams of the high Andes

The Loricariidæ.—In the family of *Loricariidæ* the sides and back are armed with rough bony plates The small air-bladder is still in a bony capsule, and the mouth is small with thick fringed lips The numerous species are all small fishes of the South American waters, bearing a strong external resemblance to *Agonidæ*, but wholly different in anatomy

The Callichthyidæ. — The *Callichthyidæ* are also small fishes armed with a bony interlocking coat of mail They are closely allied to the *Pygidiidæ* The body is more robust than in the *Callichthyidæ* and the coat of mail is differently formed The species swarm in the rivers of northern South America, where with the mailed *Loricariidæ* they form a conspicuous part of the fish fauna

Fossil Catfishes —Fossil catfishes are very few in number *Siluridæ*, allied to *Chlarias*, *Bagarius*, *Hetero-branchus*, and other fresh-water forms of India, are found in the late Tertiary rocks of Sumatra, and catfish spines exist in the Tertiary rocks of the United States Vertebræ in the Canadian Oligocene have been referred by Cope to species of *Ameiurus* (*A cancellatus* and *A maconnelli*) *Rhineastes peltatus* and six other species, perhaps allied to *Pimelodus*, have been described by Cope from Eocene of Wyoming and Colorado *Bucklandium diluvii* is found in the Eocene London clays, and several species apparently marine, referred to the neighborhood of *Tachysurus* or *Arius*, are found in Eocene rocks of England

There is no evidence that the group of catfishes has any great antiquity, or that its members were ever so numerous and varied as at the present time The group is evidently derived from scaly ancestors, and its peculiarities are due to specialization of certain parts and degeneration of others

There is not the slightest reason for regarding the catfishes as direct descendants of the sturgeon or other Ganoid type They should rather be looked upon as a degenerate and highly modified offshoot from the primitive Characins

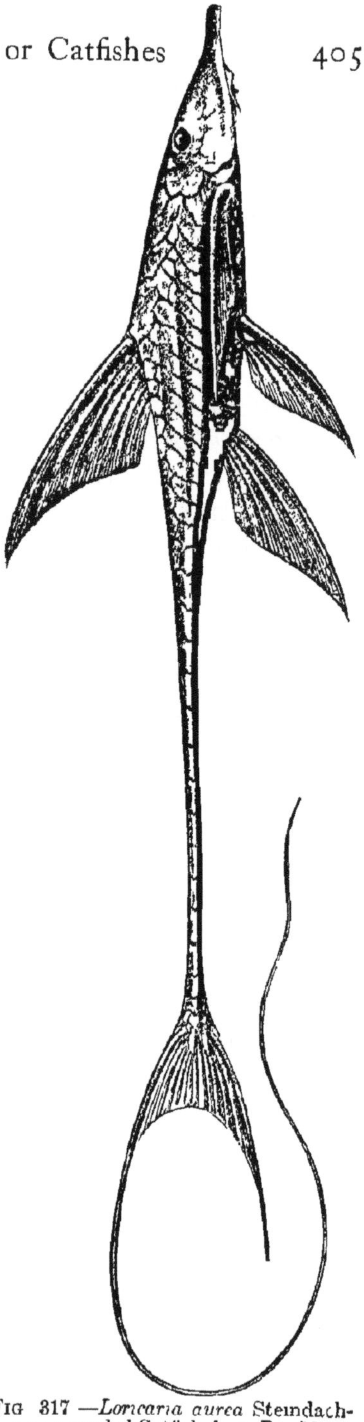

Fig 317 —*Loricaria aurea* Steindachner, a mailed Catfish from Rio Meta, Venezuela Family *Loricariidæ* (After Steindachner)

Order Gymnonoti.—At the end of the series of *Ostariophysans* we may place the *Gymnonoti* (γυμνός, bare, νῶτος, back)　This group contains about thirty species of fishes from the rivers of South America and Central America　All are eel-like in form, though the skeleton with the shoulder-girdle suspended from the cranium is quite unlike that of a true eel　There is no dorsal fin　The vent is at the throat and the anal is excessively long　The gill-opening is small as in the eel, and as in most elongate fishes, the ventral fins are undeveloped.　The body is naked or covered with small scales

Two families are recognized, differing widely in appearance　The *Electrophoridæ* constitutes by itself Cope's order of *Glanencheli* (γλανίς, catfish, ἔγχελυς, eel)　This group he regards as intermediate between the eel-like catfishes (*Chlarias*) and the true eels　It is naked and eel-shaped, with a short head and projecting lower jaw like that of the true eel　The single species, *Electrophorus electricus*, inhabits the rivers of Brazil, reaching a length of six feet, and is the most powerful of all electric fishes　Its electric organs on the tail are derived from modified muscular tissue

The *Gymnotidæ* are much smaller in size, with compressed scaly bodies and the mouth at the end of a long snout　The numerous species are all fishes without electric organs. *Eigenmannia humboldti* of the Panama region is a characteristic species　No fossil *Gymnonoti* are recorded

CHAPTER XXV

THE SCYPHOPHORI, HAPLOMI, AND XENOMI

ORDER Scyphophori. — The *Scyphophori* (σκύφος, cup, φορέω, to bear) constitutes a small order which lies apparently between the *Gymnonoti* and the *Isospondyli* Boulenger unites it with the *Isospondyli* The species, about seventy-five in number, inhabit the rivers of Africa, where they are important as food-fishes In all there is a deep cavity on each side of the cranium covered by a thin bony plate, the supertemporal bone There is no symplectic bone, and the subopercle is very small or concealed The gill-openings are narrow and there are no pharyngeal teeth. The air-bladder connects with the ear, but not apparently in the same way as with the *Ostariophysan* fishes, to which, however, the *Scyphophori* are most nearly related In all the *Scyphophori* the body is oblong, covered with cycloid scales, the head is naked, there are no barbels, and the small mouth is at the end of a long snout All the species possess a peculiar organ on the tail, which with reference to a similar structure in *Torpedo* and *Electrophorus* is held to be a degenerate electric organ According to Gunther, "it is without electric functions, but evidently representing a transitional condition from muscular substance to an electric organ It is an oblong capsule divided into numerous compartments by vertical transverse septa and containing a gelatinous substance"

The Mormyridæ. — There are two families of *Scyphophori* The *Mormyridæ* have the ordinary fins and tail of fishes and the *Gymnarchidæ* are eel-like, with ventrals, anal and caudal wanting *Gymnarchus niloticus* of the Nile reaches a length of six feet, and it is remarkable as retaining the cellular structure of the air-bladder as seen in the garpike and bowfin It doubtless serves as an imperfect lung

407

The best-known genus of *Scyphophori* is *Mormyrus*   Species
of this genus found in the Nile were worshiped as sacred by
the ancient Egyptians and pictures of *Mormyrus* are often
seen among the emblematic inscriptions   The Egyptians did not
eat the *Mormyrus* because with two other fishes it was accused
of having devoured a limb from the body of Osiris, so that Isis
was unable to recover it when she gathered the scattered remains of her husband

In *Mormyrus* the bones of the head are covered by skin,
the snout is more or less elongated, and the tail is generally
short and insignificant   One of the most characteristically
eccentric species is *Gnathonemus curvirostris*, lately discovered
by Dr Boulenger from the Congo   Fossil *Mormyridæ* are unknown

The Haplomi. — In the groups called *Iniomi* and *Lyopomi*,
the mesocoracoid arch is imperfect or wanting, a condition

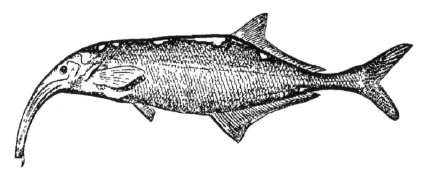

Fig 318 —*Gnathonemus curvirostris* Boulenger   Family *Mormyridæ*   Congo
River   (After Boulenger)

which in some cases may be due to the degeneration produced by
deep-sea life   In the eels a similar condition obtains   In the group
called *Haplomi* (ἁπλοός, simple, ὦμος, shoulder), as in all the
groups of fishes yet to be discussed, this arch is wholly wanting at
all stages of development   In common with the *Isospondyli* and
with soft-rayed fishes in general the air-bladder has a persistent
air-duct, all the fins are without true spines, the ventral fins
are abdominal, and the scales are cycloid   The group is a
transitional one, lying almost equidistant between the *Isospondyli*
and the *Acanthopterygii*   Gill unites it with the latter and
Woodward with the former   We may regard it for the present

as a distinct order, although no character of high importance separates it from either   Hay unites the *Haplomi* with the *Synentognathi* to form the order of *Mesichthyes*, or transitional fishes, but the affinities of either with other groups are quite as well marked as their relation to each other   Boulenger unites the *Iniomi* with the *Haplomi*, an arrangement which apparently has merit, for the most primitive and non-degenerate *Iniomi*, as *Aulopus* and *Synodus*, lack both mesocoracoid and orbitosphenoid   These bones are characteristic of the *Isospondyli*, but are wanting in *Haplomi*

There is no adipose dorsal in the typical *Haplomi*, the dorsal is inserted far back, and the head is generally scaly   Most but not all of the species are of small size, living in fresh or brackish water, and they are found in almost all warm regions, though scantily represented in California, Japan, and Polynesia   The four families of typical *Haplomi* differ considerably from one another and are easily distinguished, although obviously related   Several other families are provisionally added to this group on account of agreement in technical characters, but their actual relationships are uncertain

The Pikes—The *Esocidæ* have the body long and slender and the mouth large, its bones armed with very strong, sharp teeth of different sizes, some of them being movable   The upper jaw is not projectile, and its margin, as in the *Salmonidæ*, is formed by the maxillary   The scales are small, and the dorsal fin far back and opposite the anal, and the stomach is without pyloric cæca   There is but a single genus, *Esox* (*Lucius* of Rafinesque), with about five or six living species   Four of these are North American, the other one being found in Europe, Asia, and North America

All the pikes are greedy and voracious fishes, very destructive to other species which may happen to be their neighbors, "mere machines for the assimilation of other organisms"   Thoreau describes the pike as "the swiftest, wariest, and most ravenous of fishes, which Josselyn calls the river-wolf   It is a solemn, stately, ruminant fish, lurking under the shadow of a lily-pad at noon, with still, circumspect, voracious eye, motionless as a jewel set in water, or moving slowly along to take up its position; darting from time to time at such unlucky fish

FIG 319 —The Pike, *Esox-lucius* L (From life by R W Shufeldt)

or frog or insect as comes within its range, and swallowing it at one gulp Sometimes a striped snake, bound for greener meadows across the stream, ends its undulatory progress in the same receptacle "

As food-fishes, all the *Esocidæ* rank high. Their flesh is white, fine-grained, disposed in flakes, and of excellent flavor

The finest of the *Esocidæ*, a species to be compared, as a grand game fish, with the salmon, is the muskallunge (*Esox masquinongy*) Technically this species may be known by the fact that its cheeks and opercles are both naked on the lower half It may be known also by its great size and by its

Fig 320 —Muskallunge, *Esox masquinongy* Mitchill   Ecorse, Mich

color, young and old being spotted with black on a golden-olive ground

The muskallunge is found only in the Great Lake region, where it inhabits the deeper waters, except for a short time in the spring, when it enters the streams to spawn It often reaches a length of six feet and a weight of sixty to eighty pounds It is necessarily somewhat rare, for no small locality would furnish food for more than one such giant It is, says Hallock, "a long, slim, strong, and swift fish, in every way formed for the life it leads, that of a dauntless marauder."

A second species of muskallunge, *Esox ohiensis*, unspotted but vaguely cross-barred, occurs sparingly in the Ohio River and the upper Mississippi Valley It is especially abundant in Chautauqua Lake

The pike (*Esox lucius*) is smaller than the muskallunge, and is technically best distinguished by the fact that the opercles are naked below, while the cheeks are entirely scaly. The spots and cross-bars in the pike are whitish or yellowish, and always paler than the olive-gray ground color. It is the most

widely distributed of all fresh-water fishes, being found from
the upper Mississippi Valley, the Great Lakes, and New England
to Alaska and throughout northern Asia and Europe   It
reaches a weight of ten to twenty pounds or more, being a
large strong fish in its way, inferior only to the muskallunge.
In England *Esox lucius* is known as the pike, while its young
are called by the diminutive term pickerel   In America the name
pickerel is usually given to the smaller species, and sometimes
even to *Esox lucius* itself, the word being with us a synonym
for pike, not a diminutive

Of the small pike or pickerel we have three species in the
eastern United States.   They are greenish in color and banded
or reticulated, rather than spotted, and, in all, the opercles
as well as the cheeks are fully covered with scales   One of
these (*Esox reticulatus*) is the common pickerel of the Eastern
States, which reaches a respectable size and is excellent as
food   The others, *Esox americanus* along the Atlantic seaboard
and *Esox vermiculatus* in the middle West, seldom exceed a foot
in length and are of no economic importance

Numerous fossil species are found in the Tertiary of Europe,
Esox lepidotus from the Miocene of Baden being one of the

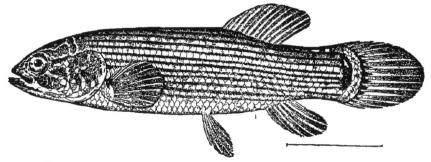

Fig 321 —Mud-minnow, *Umbra pygmua* (De Kay)   New Jersey

earliest and the best known, in this species the scales are much
larger than in the recent species   The fossil remains would seem
to indicate that the origin of the family was in southern Europe,
although most of the living species are American

The Mud-minnows.—Close to the pike is the family of *Umbridæ*, or mud-minnows, which technically differ from the pikes
only in the short snout, small mouth, and weak dentition   The

mud-minnows are small, sluggish, carnivorous fishes living in
the mud at the bottom of cold, clear streams and ponds   They
are extremely tenacious of life, though soon suffocated in warm
waters   The barred mud-minnow of the prairies of the middle
West (*Umbra limi*) often remains in dried sloughs and bog-
holes, and has been sometimes plowed up alive   *Umbra pygmæa*,
a striped species, is found in the Eastern States and *Umbra
crameri* in bogs and brooks along the Danube   This wide break
in distribution seems to indicate a former wide extension of
the range of *Umbridæ*, perhaps coextensive with *Esox*   Fossil
Umbridæ are, however, not yet recognized

The Killifishes.—Most of the recent *Haplomi* belong to the
family of *Pœciliidæ* (killifishes, or Cyprinodonts)   In this
group the small mouth is extremely protractile, its margin
formed by the premaxillaries alone much as in the spiny-
rayed fishes   The teeth are small and of various forms according to the food   In most of the herbivorous forms they are
incisor-like, serrate, and loosely inserted in the lips   In the
species that eat insects or worms they are more firmly fixed
The head is scaly, the stomach without cæca, and the intestines are long in the plant-eating species and short in the
others   There are nearly 200 species, very abundant from
New England and California southward to Argentina, and
in Asia and Africa also   In regions where rice is produced,
they swarm in the rice swamps and ditches   Some of them
enter the sea, but none of them go far from shore   Some
are brilliantly colored, and in many species the males are quite
unlike the females, being smaller and more showy   The largest
species (*Fundulus, Anableps*) rarely reach the length of a foot,
while *Heterandria formosa*, a diminutive inhabitant of the
Florida rivers, scarcely reaches an inch   Some species are
oviparous, but in most of the herbivorous forms, and some of
the others, the eggs are hatched within the body, and the anal
in the male is modified into a long sword-shaped intromittent
organ, placed farther forward than the anal in the female
The young when born closely resemble the parent   Most of
the insectivorous species swim at the surface, moving slowly
with the eyes partly out of water   This habit in the genus
Anableps (four-eyed fish, or *Cuatro ojos*) is associated with an

extraordinary structure of the eye   This organ is prominent and is divided by a horizontal partition into two parts, the upper, less convex, adopted for sight in the air, the lower in the water   The few species of *Anableps* are found in tropical America   The species of some genera swim near the bottom, but always in very shallow waters   All are very tenacious of life, and none have any commercial value although the flesh is good.

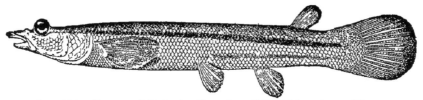

Fig 322 —Four-eyed Fish, *Anableps dovii* Gill   Tehuantepec, Mexico

The unique structure of the eye of this curious fish has been carefully studied by Mr M C Marsh, pathologist of the U S Fish Commission, who furnishes the following notes published by Evermann & Goldsborough

"The eye is crossed by a bar, like the diameter of a circle, and parallel with the length of the body   This bar is darker than the other external portions of the eyeball and has its edges darker still   Dividing the external aspect of the eye equally, it has its lower edge on the same level as the back of the fish, which is flat and straight from snout to dorsal, or nearly the whole length of the fish, so that when the body of the fish is just submerged the level of the water reaches to this bar, and the lower half of the eye is in water, the upper half in the air   Upon dissecting the eyeball from the orbit, it appears nearly round. A membranous sheath covers the external part and invests most of the ball   It may be peeled off, when the dark bar on the external portion of the eye is seen to be upon this membrane, which may correspond to the conjunctiva.   The back portion of the eyeball being cut off, one lens is found   The lining of the ball consists, in front, of one black layer, evidently choroid   Behind there is a retinal layer   The choroid layer turns up anteriorly, making a free edge comparable to an iris   The free edge is chiefly evident in the lower part of the eye   A large pupil is left, but is divided by two flaps, continuations of the choroid coat, projecting from either side and overlapping

There are properly then two pupils, an upper and lower, separated by a band consisting of the two flaps, which may probably, by moving upward and downward, increase or diminish the size of either pupil; an upward motion of the flaps increasing the lower pupil at the expense of the other, and vice versa."

This division of the pupil into two parts permits the fish, when swimming at the surface of the water, as is its usual custom, to see in the air with the upper portion and in the water with the lower   It is thus able to see not only such insects as are upon the surface of the water or flying in the air above, but also any that may be swimming beneath the surface

According to Mr E W Nelson, "the individuals of this species swim always at the surface and in little schools arranged in platoons or abreast. They always swim headed upstream against the current, and feed upon floating matter which the current brings them   A platoon may be seen in regular for-

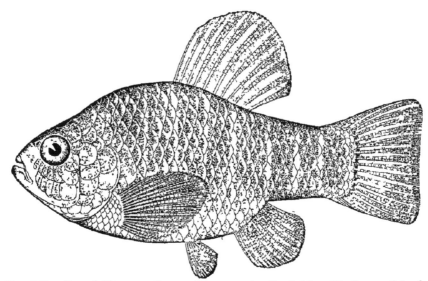

Fig 323 —Round Minnow, *Cyprinodon variegatus* Lacépède. St George Island, Maryland

mation breasting the current, either making slight headway upstream or merely maintaining their station, and on the qui vive for any suitable food the current may bring   Now and then one may be seen to dart forward, seize a floating food particle, and then resume its place in the platoon. And thus they may be observed feeding for long periods   They are almost invariably found in running water well out in the stream, or at least where the current is strongest and where floating matter is most abundant, for it is upon floating matter that they seem chiefly to depend   They are not known to jump out of the water to catch insects flying in the air or resting upon vegetation above the water surface, nor do they seem to feed to any extent upon all small crustaceans or other portions of the plankton beneath the surface

"When alarmed—and they are wary and very easily frightened—they escape by skipping or jumping over the water,

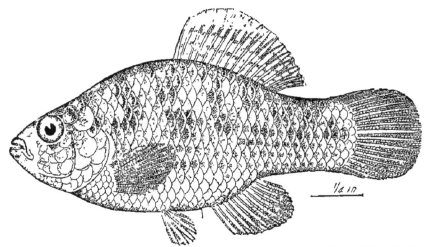

Fig 324 —Everglade Minnow, *Jordanella floridæ* Goode & Bean   Everglades of Florida

2 or 3 feet at a skip   They rise entirely out of the water, and at a considerable angle, the head pointing upward   In descending the tail strikes the water first and apparently by a sculling motion new impetus is acquired for another leap   This skipping may continue until the school is widely scattered   When a school has become scattered, and after the cause of their fright has disappeared, the individuals soon rejoin each other   First two will join each other and one by one the others will join them until the whole school is together again   Rarely do they attempt to dive or get beneath the surface, when they do they have great difficulty in keeping under and soon come to the surface again "

Of the many genera of *Pœciliidæ*, top-minnows, and killi-fishes we may mention the following. *Cyprinodon* is made

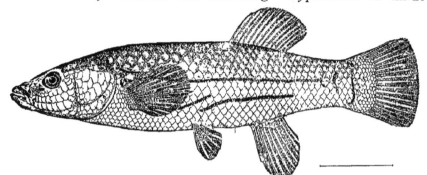

FIG 325 —Mayfish, *Fundulus majalis* (L) (male)   Woods Hole

up of chubby little fishes of eastern America with tricuspid, incisor teeth, oviparous and omnivorous   Very similar to

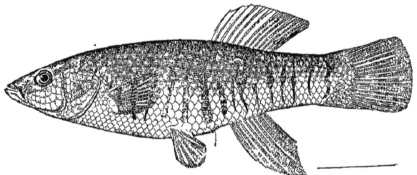

FIG 326 —Mayfish, *Fundulus majalis* (female)   Woods Hole

these but smaller are the species of *Lebias* in southern Europe *Jordanella floridæ* of the Florida everglades is similar, but with

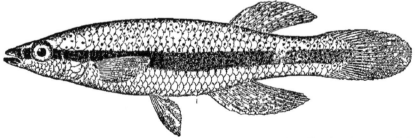

FIG 327 —Top-minnow, *Zygonectes notatus* (Rafinesque)   Eureka Springs, Ark

the dorsal fin long and its first ray enlarged and spine-like. It strongly resembles a young sunfish   Most of the larger forms belong to *Fundulus*, a genus widely distributed from Maine to Guatemala and north to Kansas and southern California *Fundulus majalis*, the Mayfish of the Atlantic Coast, is the largest of the genus   *Fundulus heteroclitus*, the killifish, the most abundant   *Fundulus diaphanus* inhabits sea and lake

FIG 328 —Death Valley Fish, *Empetrichthys merriami* Gilbert   Amargosa Desert, Cal   Family *Pœciladæ*   (After Gilbert)

indiscriminately   *Fundulus stellifer* of the Alabama is beautifully colored, as is *Fundulus zebrinus* of the Rio Grande   The genus *Zygonectes* includes dwarf species similar to *Fundulus*, and *Adinia* includes those with short, deep body. *Goodea atripinnis* with tricuspid teeth lives in warm springs in Mexico,

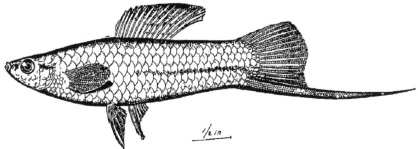

FIG 329 —Sword-tail Minnow, male, *Xiphophorus helleri* Heckel   The anal fin modified as an intromittent organ   Vera Cruz.

and several species of *Goodea*, *Gambusia*, *Pœcilia*, and other genera inhabit hot springs of Mexico, Central America, and Africa   The genus *Gambusia*, the top-minnows, includes numerous species with dwarf males having the anal modified *Gambusia affinis* abounds in all kinds of sluggish water in

the southern lowlands, gutters and even sewers included   It
brings forth its brood in early spring   Viviparous and herbivorous with modified anal are the species of *Pœcilia*, abundant
throughout·Mexico and southward to Brazil, *Mollienesia* very
similar, with a banner-like dorsal fin, showily marked, occurs
from Louisiana southward, and *Xiphophorus*, with a sword-
shaped lobe on the caudal, abounds in Mexico, *Characodon* and
Goodea in Mexico have notched teeth, and finally, *Heterandria*
contains some of the least of fishes, the handsomely colored
males barely half an inch long

In Lake Titicaca in the high Andes is a peculiar genus (*Orestias*) without ventral fins   Still more peculiar is *Empetrichthys
merriami* of the desert springs of the hot and rainless Death
Valley in California, similar to *Orestias*, but with enormously
enlarged pharyngeals and pharyngeal teeth, an adaptation to some
unknown purpose   Fossil Cyprinodonts are not rare from the
Miocene in southern Europe   The numerous species are allied
to *Lebias* and *Cyprinodon*, and are referred to *Prolebias* and
Pachylebias   None are American, although two American extinct
genera, *Gephyrura* and *Proballostomus*, are probably allied to this
group

Amblyopsidæ.—The cave-fishes, *Amblyopsidæ*, are the most
remarkable of the haplomous fishes   In this family the vent is

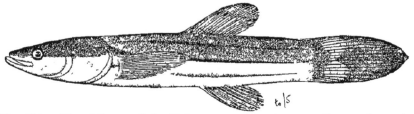

Fig 330 —Dismal Swamp Fish, *Chologaster cornutus* Agassiz   Supposed ancestor
of *Typhlichthys*   Virginia

placed at the throat   The form is that of the *Pœcilidæ*, but
the mouth is larger and not protractile   The species are viviparous, the young being born at about the length of a quarter of
an inch

In the primitive genus *Chologaster*, the fish of the Dismal
Swamp, the eyes are small but normally developed   *Chologaster cornutus* abounds in the black waters of the Dismal Swamp

of Virginia, thence southward through swamps and rice-fields
to Okefinokee Swamp in northern Florida   It is a small fish,
less than two inches long, striped with black, and with the habit
of a top-minnow   Other species of *Chologaster,* possessing
eyes and color, but provided also with tactile papillæ, are found
in cave springs in Tennessee and southern Illinois

From *Chologaster* is directly descended the small blindfish
Typhlichthys subterraneus of the caves of the Subcarboniferous
limestone rocks of southern Indiana and southward to northern
Alabama   As in *Chologaster*, the ventral fins are wanting
The eyes, present in the young, become defective and useless
in the adult, when they are almost hidden by other tissues
The different parts of the eye are all more or less incomplete,
being without function   The structure of the eye has been
described in much detail in several papers by Dr. Carl H Eigen-

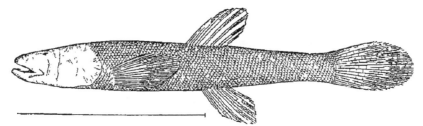

Fig. 331 —Blind Cave-fish, *Typhlichthys subterraneus* Girard   Mammoth Cave,
Kentucky

mann   As to the cause of the loss of eyesight two chief
theories exist—the Lamarckian theory of the inheritance in the
species of the results of disuse in the individual and the
Weissmannian doctrine that the loss of sight is a result of
panmixia or cessation of selection   This may be extended
to cover reversal of selection, as in the depths of the great
caves the fish without eyes would be at some slight advantage.
Dr Eigenmann inclines to the Lamarckian doctrine, but the
evidence brought forward fails to convince the present writer
that results of individual use or disuse ever become hereditary or that they are ever incorporated in the characters
of a species   In the caves of southern Missouri is an independent case of similar degradation   *Troglichthys rosæ*, the
blindfish of this region, has the eye in a different phase of
degeneration.   It is thought to be separately descended from

some other species of *Chologaster* Of this species Mr Garman
and Mr Eigenmann have given detailed accounts from somewhat different points of view

Concerning the habits of the blindfish (*Troglichthys rosæ*),
Mr Garman quotes the following from notes of Miss Ruth
Hoppin, of Jasper County, Missouri "For about two weeks
I have been watching a fish taken from a well I gave him
considerable water, changed once a day, and kept him in an
uninhabitated place subject to as few changes of temperature
as possible He seems perfectly healthy and as lively as when
first taken from the well If not capable of long fasts, he must
live on small organisms my eye cannot discern He is hardly
ever still, but moves about the sides of the vessel constantly,
down and up, as if needing the air He never swims through

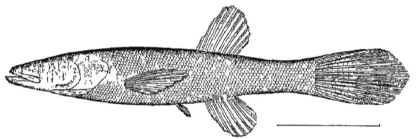

FIG 332 —Blindfish of the Mammoth Cave, *Amblyopsis spelæus* (De Kay)
Mammoth Cave, Kentucky

the body of the water away from the sides unless disturbed
Passing the finger over the sides of the vessel under water I
find it slippery I am careful not to disturb this slimy coating
when the water is changed   Numerous tests convince
me that it is through the sense of touch, and not through hearing, that the fish is disturbed, I may scream or strike metal
bodies together over him as near as possible, yet he seems to
take no notice whatever. If I strike the vessel so that the
water is set in motion, he darts away from that side through
the mass of water, instead of around in his usual way. If I
stir the water or touch the fish, no matter how lightly, his
actions are the same"

The more famous blindfish of the Mammoth Cave, *Amblyopsis spelæus*, reaches a length of five inches It possesses
ventral fins. From this fact we may infer its descent from

some extinct genus which, unlike *Chologaster*, retains these fins   The translucent body, as in the other blindfishes, is covered with very delicate tactile papillæ, which form a very delicate organ of touch

The anomalous position of the vent in *Amblyopsidæ* occurs again in an equally singular fish, *Aphredoderus sayanus*, which is found in the same waters throughout the same region in which *Chologaster* occurs   It would seem as if these lowland fishes of the southern swamps were remains of a once much more extensive fauna

No fossil allies of *Chologaster* are known

Kneriidæ, etc.—The members of the order of *Haplomi*, recorded above, differ widely among themselves in various details of osteology   There are other families, probably belonging here, which are still more aberrant   Among these are the *Kneriidæ*, and perhaps the entire series of forms called *Iniomi*, most of which possess the osteological traits of the *Haplomi*

The family of *Kneriidæ* includes a few very small fishes of the rivers of Africa.

The Galaxiidæ.—The *Galaxiidæ* are trout-like fishes of the southern rivers, where they take the place of the trout of the northern zones   The species lack the adipose fins and have the dorsal inserted well backward.   According to Boulenger these fishes, having no mesocoraoid, should be placed among the *Haplomi*   Yet their relation to the *Haplochitonidæ* is very close and both families may really belong to the *Isospondyli*. *Galaxias truttaceus* is the kokopu, or "trout," of New Zealand. *Galaxias ocellatus* is the yarra trout of Australia   Several other species are found in southern Australia, Tasmania, Patagonia, and the Falkland Islands, and even in South Africa   This very wide distribution in the rivers remote from each other has given rise to the suggestion of a former land connection between Australia and Patagonia.   Other similar facts have led some geologists to believe in the existence of a former great continent called Antarctica, now submerged except that part which constitutes the present unknown land of the Antarctic

Order Xenomi.—We must place near the *Haplomi* the singular group of *Xenomi* (ξενός, strange, ὦμος, shoulder), regarded by Dr Gill as a distinct order   Externally these fish much resemble the mud-minnows, differing mainly in the very broad pectorals   But the skeleton is thin and papery, the two coracoids forming a single cartilaginous plate imperfectly divided. The pectorals are attached directly to this without the intervention of actinosts, but in the distal third, according to Dr Charles H Gilbert, the coracoid plate begins to break up

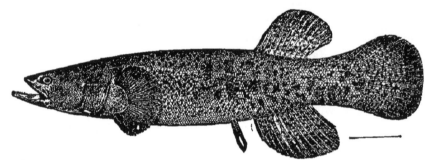

Fig 383 —Alaska Blackfish, *Dallia pectoralis* (Bean) St Michaels, Alaska

into a fringe of narrow cartilaginous strips

"In the deep-sea eels of the order *Heteromi* there is a somewhat similar condition of the coracoid elements inasmuch as the hypercoracoid and hypocoracoid though present are merely membranous elements surrounded by cartilage. and the actinosts are greatly reduced   It seems probable that we are dealing in the two cases with independent degeneration of the shoulder-girdle and that the two groups (*Xenomi* and *Heteromi*) are not really related " (Gilbert)

Of the single family *Dalliidæ*, one species is known, the Alaska blackfish, *Dallia pectoralis*

This animal, formed like a mud-minnow, reaches a length of eight inches and swarms in the bogs and sphagnum swamps of northwestern Alaska and westward through Siberia   It is found in countless numbers according to its discoverer, Mr L M. Turner, "wherever there is water enough to wet the skin of a fish," and wherever it occurs it forms the chief food of the natives. Its vitality is most extraordinary. Blackfishes will remain frozen in baskets for weeks and when thawed out are as lively as ever. Turner gives an account of a frozen individual swallowed by a dog which escaped in safety after being thawed out by the heat of the dog's stomach.

CHAPTER XXVI

ACANTHOPTERYGII; SYNENTOGNATHI

RDER Acanthopterygii, the Spiny-rayed Fishes. — The most of the remaining bony fishes constitute a natural group for which the name *Acanthopterygii* (ἄκανθα, spine, πτέρυξ, πτερόν, fin or wing) may be used   This name is often written *Actinopteri*, a form equally correct and more euphonious and convenient. These fishes are characterized, with numerous exceptions, by the presence of fin spines, by the connection of the ventral fins with the shoulder-girdle, by the presence in general of more than one spine in the anterior part of dorsal and anal fins, and as a rule of one spine and five rays in the ventral fins, and by the absence in the adult of a duct to the air-bladder   Minor characters are these the pectoral fins are inserted high on the shoulder-girdle, the scales are often ctenoid, and the edge of the upper jaw is formed by the premaxillary alone, the maxillary being always toothless

But it is impossible to define or limit the group by any single character or group of characters   It is connected with the *Malacopterygii* through the *Haplomi* on the one hand by transitional groups of genera which may lack any one of these characters   On the other hand, in the extreme forms, each of these distinctive characters may be lost through degeneration   Thus fin spines, ctenoid scales, and the homocercal tail are lost in the codfishes, the connection of ventrals with shoulder-girdle fails in the *Percesoces*, etc , and the development of the air-duct is subject to all sorts of variations   In one family even the adipose fin remains through all the changes and modifications the species have undergone

The various transitional forms between the *Haplomi* and the perch-like fishes have been from time to time regarded as

424

separate orders   Some of them are more related to the perch, others rather to ancestors of salmon or pike, while still others are degenerate offshoots, far enough from either

On the whole, all these forms, medium, extreme and transitional, may well be placed in one order, which would include the primitive flying-fishes and mullets, the degraded globefishes, and the specialized flounders   As for the most part these are spiny-rayed fishes, Cuvier's name *Acanthopterygii*, or *Acanthopteri*, will serve us as well as any. The *Physoclysti* of Muller, the *Thoracices* of older authors, and the *Ctenoidei* of Agassiz include substantially the same series of forms   The order *Teleocephali* of Gill (τελεός, perfect, κεφαλή, head) has been lately so restricted as to cover nearly the same ground   In Gill's most recent catalogue of families, the order *Teleocephali* includes the *Haplomi* and rejects the *Hemibranchii*, *Lophobranchii*, *Plectognathi*, and *Pediculati*, all of these being groups characterized by sharply defined but comparatively recent characters not of the highest importance   As originally arranged, the order *Teleocephali* included the soft-rayed fishes as well   From it the *Ostariophysi* were first detached, and still later the *Isospondyli* were regarded by Dr Gill as a separate order

We may first take up serially as suborders the principal groups which serve to effect the transition from soft-rayed to spiny-rayed fishes

Suborder Synentognathi. — Among the transitional forms between the soft-rayed and the spiny-rayed fishes, one of the most important groups is that known as *Synentognathi* (σύν, together; έν, within, γνάθος, jaw)   These have, in brief, the fins and shoulder-girdle of *Haplomi*, the ventral fins abdominal, the dorsal and anal without spines   At the same time, as in the spiny-rayed fishes, the air-bladder is without duct and the pectoral fins are inserted high on the side of the body   With these traits are two others which characterize the group as a suborder   The lower pharyngeal bones are solidly united into one bone and the lateral line forms a raised ridge along the lower side of the body   These forms are structurally allied to the pikes (*Haplomi*), on the one hand, and to the mullets (*Percesoces*), on the other, and this relationship accords with their general appearance   In this group as in all the remaining families of fishes, there is no mesocoracoid, and in very nearly all of these families the duct to the air-bladder disappears at an early stage of development

The Garfishes: Belonidæ. — There are two principal groups or families among the *Synentognathi*, the *Belonidæ*, with strong jaws and teeth, and the *Exocœtidæ*, in which these structures are feeble Much more important characters appear in the anatomy In the *Belonidæ* the third upper pharyngeal is small, with few teeth, and the maxillary is firmly soldered to the premaxillary The vertebræ are provided with zygapophyses. The species of *Belonidæ* are known as garfishes, or needle-fishes They resemble the garpike in form, but have nothing else in common The body is long and slender, covered with small scales Sharp, unequal teeth fill the long jaws and the

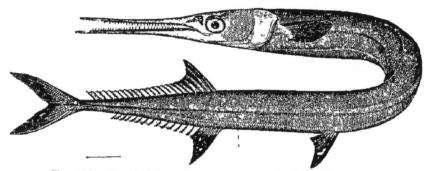

Fig 334 —Needle-fish, *Tylosurus acus* (Lacépède) New York

dorsal is opposite the anal, on the hinder part of the body These fishes are green in color, even the bones being often bright green, while the scales on the sides have a silvery luster The species are excellent as food, the green color being associated with nothing deleterious All are very voracious and some of the larger species, 5 or 6 feet long, may be dangerous even to man Fishermen have been wounded or killed by the thrust of the sharp snout of a fish springing into the air. The garfishes swim near the surface of the water and often move with great swiftness, frequently leaping from the water. The genus *Belone* is characterized by the presence of gill-rakers *Belone belone* is a small garfish common in southern Europe *Belone platura* occurs in Polynesia The American species (*Tylosurus*) lack gill-rakers *Tylosurus marinus*, the common garfish of the eastern United States, often ascends the rivers   *Tylosurus raphidoma*, *Tylosurus fodiator*, *Tylosurus acus*, and other species are very robust, with short strong jaws   *Athlennes hians* is a very large fish with the body strongly compressed, almost ribbon-like   It is found in the West Indies and across the Isthmus as far as Hawaii   Many other species, mostly belonging to *Tylosurus*, abound in the warm seas of all regions   *Tylosurus ferox* is the long tom of the Australian markets   *Potamorrhaphis* with the dorsal fin low is found in Brazilian rivers   A few fossil species are referred to *Belone*, *Belone flava* from the lower Eocene being the earliest

The Flying-fishes: Exocœtidæ.—The family of *Exocœtidæ* includes the flying-fishes and several related forms more or less intermediate between these and the garfishes   In these fishes the teeth are small and nearly equal and the maxillary is separate from the premaxillary   The third upper pharyngeal is much enlarged and there are no zygapophyses to the vertebræ

The skippers (*Scombresox*) have slender bodies, pointed jaws, and, like the mackerel, a number of detached finlets behind dorsal and anal, although in other respects they show no affinity to the mackerel   The common skipper, or saury (*Scombresox saurus*), is found on both shores of the North Atlantic swimming in large schools at the surface of the water, frequently leaping for a little distance like the flying-fish   They are pursued by the mackerel-like fishes, as the tunny or bonito, and sometimes by porpoises   According to Mr Couch, the skippers, when pursued, "mount to the surface in multitudes and crowd on each other as they press forward   When still more closely pursued, they spring to the height of several feet, leap over each other in singular confusion, and again sink beneath   Still further urged, they mount again and rush along the surface, by repeated starts, for more than one hundred feet, without once dipping beneath or scarcely seeming to touch the water. At last the pursuer springs after them, usually across their course, and again they all disappear together   Amidst such multitudes—for more than twenty thousand have been judged to be out of the water together—some must fall a prey to the enemy; but so many hunting in company, it must be long before the pursuers abandon.   From inspection we could scarcely judge the fish to be capable of such flights, for the fins, though numerous, are small, and the pectoral far from large, though the angle of their articulation is well adapted to raise the fish by the direction of their motions to the surface "

A similar species, *Cololabis saira*, with the snout very much shorter than in the Atlantic skipper, is the *Samma* of the fishermen of Japan

The hard-head (*Chriodorus atherinoides*) has no beak at all and its tricuspid incisor teeth are fitted to feed on plants. In this genus, as in the flying-fishes, there are no finlets. The hard-head is an excellent food-fish abundant about the Florida Keys but not yet seen elsewhere

Another group between the gars and the flying-fishes is that of the halfbeaks, or balaos, *Hemirhamphus*, etc. These are also

Fig 335 —Saury, *Scombresox saurus* (L)   Woods Hole

vegetable feeders, but with much smaller teeth, and the lower jaw with a spear-like prolongation to which a bright-red membrane is usually attached. Of the halfbeaks there are several genera, all of the species swimming near the surface in schools and sometimes very swiftly. Some of them leap into the air and sail for a short distance like flying-fishes, with which group the halfbeaks are connected by easy gradations. The com-

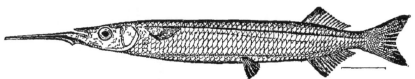

Fig 336 —Halfbeak, *Hyporhamphus unifasciatus* (Ranzani)   Chesapeake Bay

monest species along our Atlantic coast is *Hyporhamphus unifasciatus,* a larger species, *Hemirhamphus brasiliensis,* abounds about the Florida Keys. *Euleptorhamphus longirostris,* a ribbon-shaped elongate fish, with long jaw and long pectorals, is taken in the open sea, both in the Altantic and Pacific, being common in Hawaii. The Asiatic genus *Zenarchopterus* is viviparous,

Fig. 337.—Australian Flying-fish, *Exonautes unicolor* (Valenciennes). Specimen from Tasman Sea, having parasitic lernæan crustaceans, to which parasitic barnacles are attached. (After Kellogg.)

429

having the anal fin much modified in the male, forming an intromittent organ, as in the *Pœciliidæ*. One species occurs in the river mouths in Samoa

The flying-fishes have both jaws short, and at least the

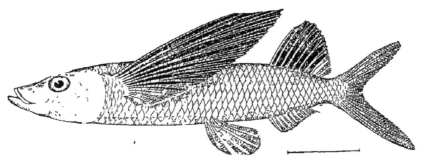

FIG 338 —Sharp-nosed Flying-fish, *Fodiator acutus* (Val)   Panama

pectoral fins much enlarged, so that the fish may sail in the air for a longer or shorter distance

The smaller species have usually shorter fins and approach more nearly to the halfbeaks   *Fodiator acutus*, with sharp jaws, and *Hemirevocatus*, with a short beak on the lower jaw, are especially intermediate   The flight of the flying-fishes is described in detail on p 44

The Catalina flying-fish, *Cypselurus californicus*, of the shore of southern California is perhaps the largest of the known species, reaching a length of 18 inches   To this genus, *Cypselurus*, having a long dorsal and short anal, and with ventrals enlarged as well as pectorals, belong all the species strongest in flight, *Cypselurus heterurus* and *furcatus* of the Atlantic, *Cypselurus simus* of Hawaii and *Cypselurus agoo* in Japan   The very young of most of these species have a long barbel at the chin which is lost with age

In the genus *Exonautes* the base of anal fin is long, as long as that of the dorsal   The species of this group, also strong in flight, are widely distributed   Most of the European flying-fishes, as *Exonautes rondeleti*, *Exonautes rubescens*, and *Exonautes vinciguerræ*, belong to this group, while those of *Cypselurus* mostly inhabit the Pacific   The large Australian species *Exonautes unicolor* belongs to this group   In the restricted genus *Exocætus* the ventral fins are short and not used in flight *Exocætus volitans* (*evolans*) is a small flying-fish, with short ventral fins not used for flight.   It is perhaps the most widely distributed of all, ranging through almost all warm seas. *Parexocœtus brachypterus*, still smaller, and with shorter, grasshopper-like wings, is also very widely distributed.   An excellent account of the flying-fishes of the world has been given by Dr. C. F. Lütken (1876), the University of Copenhagen,

Fig. 339.—Catalina Flying-fish, *Cypselurus californicus* (Cooper).   Santa Barbara.

which institution has received a remarkably fine series from trading-ships returning to that port.   Later accounts have been given by Jordan and Meek, and by Jordan and Evermann.

Very few fossil *Exocœtidæ* are found.   Species of *Scombresox* and *Hemirhamphus* are found in the Tertiary, the earliest being *Hemirhamphus edwardsi* from the Eocene of Monte Bolca.   No fossil flying-fishes are known, and the genera, *Exocœtus*, *Exonautes*, and *Cypselurus* are doubtless all of very recent origin.

CHAPTER XXVII

PERCESOCES AND RHEGNOPTERI

SUBORDER Percesoces.—In the line of direct ascending transition from the *Haplomi* and *Synentognathi*, the pike and flying-fish, towards the typical perch-like forms, we find a number of families, perch-like in essential regards but having the ventral fins abdominal

These types, represented by the mullet, the silverside, and the barracuda, have been segregated by Cope as an order called *Percesoces* (Perca, perch, Esox, pike), a name which correctly describes their real affinities In these typical forms, mullet, silverside, and barracuda, the affinities are plain, but in other transitional forms, as the threadfin and the stickleback, the relationships are less clear   Cope adds to the series of *Percesoces* the *Ophiocephalidæ*, which Gill leaves with the *Anabantidæ* among the spiny-rayed forms Boulenger adds also the sand-lances (*Ammodytidæ*) and the threadfins (*Polynemidæ*), while Woodward places here the *Crossognathidæ*   In the present work we define the *Percesoces* so as to include all spiny-rayed fishes in which the ventral fins are naturally abdominal, except-ing those having a reduced number of gill-bones, or of actinosts, or other peculiarities of the shoulder-girdle   The *Ammodytidæ* have no real affinities with the *Percesoces*   The *Crossognathidæ* and other families with abdominal ventrals and the dorsal spines wholly obsolete may belong with the *Haplomi*   Boulenger places the *Chiasmodontidæ*, the *Stromateidæ*, and the *Tetragonuridæ* among the *Percesoces*, an arrangement of very doubtful validity In most of the *Percesoces* the scales are cycloid, the spinous dorsal forms a short separate fin, and in all the air-duct is wanting

The Silversides· Atherinidæ.—The most primitive of living *Percesoces* constitute the large family of silversides (*Atherinidæ*),

432

known as "fishes of the King," Pescados del Rey, Pesce Rey, or
Peixe Re, wherever the Spanish or Portuguese languages are
spoken   The species are, in general, small and slender fishes
of dry and delicate flesh, feeding on small animals   The mouth
is small, with feeble teeth   There is no lateral line, the color
is translucent green, with usually a broad lateral band of silver
Sometimes this is wanting, and sometimes it is replaced by
burnished black   Some of the species live in lakes or rivers,
others in bays or arms of the sea, but never at a distance from
the shore or in water of more than a few feet in depth   The
larger species are much valued as food, the smaller ones, equally
delicate, are fried in numbers as "whitebait," but the bones are
firmer and more troublesome than in the smelts and young
herring   The species of the genus *Atherina*, known as "friars,"
or "brit," are chiefly European, although some occur in almost
all warm or temperate seas   These are small fishes, with the
mouth relatively large and oblique and the scales rather large
and firm   *Atherina hepsetus* and *A presbyter* are common in
Europe, *Atherina stipes* in the West Indies, *Atherina bleekeri*
in Japan, and *Atherina insularum* and *A lacunosa* in Polynesia.
The genus *Chirostoma* contains larger species, with projecting lower jaw, abounding in the lakes of Mexico   *Chirostoma humboldtianum* is very abundant about Mexico City
Like all the other species of this genus it is remarkably excellent
as food, the different species constituting the famous "Pescados
Blancos" of the great lakes of Chapala and Patzcuaro of the
western slope of Mexico   A very unusual circumstance is this:
that numerous very closely related species occupy the same
waters and are taken in the same nets   In zoology, generally,
it is an almost universal rule that very closely related species
occupy different geographical areas, their separation being
due to barriers which prevent interbreeding   But in the lake
of Chapala, near Guadalajara, Prof John O Snyder and the
present writer, and subsequently Dr S. E Meek, found ten
distinct species of *Chirostoma*, all living together, taken in the
same nets and scarcely distinguishable except on careful
examination   Most of these species are very abundant throughout the lake, and all reach a length of twelve to fifteen inches
These species are *Chirostoma estor, Ch. lucius, Ch sphyræna,*

Ch ocotlane, Ch lermæ, Ch chapalæ, Ch grandocule, Ch labarcæ, Ch promelas, and *Ch bartoni* A similar assemblage of species

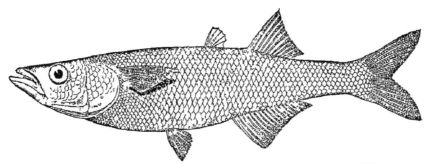

Fig 340 —Pescado blanco, *Chirostoma humboldtianum* (Val) Lake Chalco, City of Mexico

nearly all different from these was obtained by Dr Seth E Meek in the lake of Patzcuaro, farther south In this lake were found *Ch attenuatum, Ch patzcuaro, Ch humboldtianum, Ch grandocule,* and *Ch estor* The lake of Zirahuen, near Chapala, contains *Ch estor* and *Ch zirahuen*

Still another species, *Ch. jordani,* is found about the city of Mexico, where it is sold baked in corn-husks Along the coasts of Peru, Chile, and Argentina is found still another assemblage of fishes of the king, with very small scales, constituting the genera *Basilichthys* and *Gastropterus (Piscircgia). Basilichthys microlepidotus* is the common Pesca del Rey of Chile The small silversides, or "brit," of our Atlantic coast belong to numerous species of *Menidia, Menidia notata* to the northward and *Menidia menidia* to the southward being most abundant

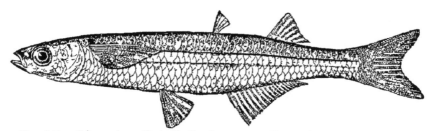

Fig 341 —Silverside or Brit, *Kirtlandia vagrans* (Goode & Bean) Pensacola

Kirtlandia laciniata, with ragged scales, is common along the Virginia coast, and *K vagrans* farther south Another small species, very slender and very graceful, is the brook silver-

side *Labidesthes sicculus*, which swarms in clear streams from
Lake Ontario to Texas   This species, three to four inches
long, has the snout produced and a very bright silvery stripe
along the side   Large and small species of silversides occur

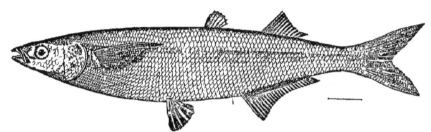

Fɪɢ 342 —Blue Smelt or Pez del Rey, *Atherinopsis californiensis* Girard
San Diego

in the sea along the California coast, where they are known
familiarly as "blue smelt" or "Peixe Re"   The most important of these and the largest member of the family, reaching
a length of eighteen inches, is *Atherinopsis californiensis*, an
important food-fish throughout California, everywhere wrongly
known as smelt   *Atherinops affinis* is much like it, but has

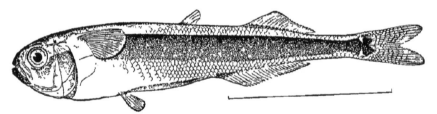

Fɪɢ 343—Flower of the surf *Iso flos-maris*, Jordan & Starks   Enoshima,

Y-shaped teeth   *Iso flos-maris*, called Nami-no-hana, or
flower of the surf, is a shining little fish with belly sharp like
that of a herring   It lives in the surf on the coast of Japan
Melanotænia nigrans of Australia (family *Melanotæniidæ*) has
the lateral band jet-black, as has also *Melaniris balsanus* of the
rivers of southern Mexico   *Atherinosoma vorax* of Australia has
strong teeth like those of a barracuda

Fossil species of *Atherina* occur in the Italian Eocene, the
best known being *Atherina macrocephala*.   Another species,
Rhamphognathus paralepoides, allied to *Menidia*, occurs in the
Eocene of Monte Bolca

The Mullets: Mugilidæ.—The mullets (*Mugilidæ*) are more
clumsy in form than the silversides, robust, with broad heads
and stouter fin-spines   The ventral fins are abdominal but
well forward, the pelvis barely touching the clavicle, a condition to be defined as "subabdominal"   The small mouth
is armed with very feeble teeth, often reduced to mere fringes
The stomach is muscular like the gizzard of a fowl and
the species feed largely on the vegetation contained in mud
There are numerous species, mostly living in shallow bays
and estuaries, but some of them are confined to fresh waters
All are valued as food and some of them under favorable conditions are especially excellent

Most of the species belong to the genera *Mugil*, the mullet of
all English-speaking people, although not at all related to the
red mullet or surmullet of the ancient Romans, *Mullus barbatus*

The mullets are stoutish fish from one to two feet long,
with blunt heads, small mouths almost toothless, large scales,
and a general bluish-silvery color often varied by faint blue
stripes   The most important species is *Mugil cephalus*, the
common striped mullet   This is found throughout southern
Europe and from Cape Cod to Brazil, from Monterey, California,
to Chile, and across the Pacific to Hawaii, Japan, and the Red
Sea

Mr Silas Stearns compares a school of mullets to barnyard
fowls feeding together   When a fish finds a rich spot the others
flock about it as chickens do   The pharyngeals form a sort of
filter, stopping the sand and mud, the coarse parts being ejected
through the mouth

The young mullet feed in schools and often swim with the
head at the surface of the water

The white or unstriped mullets are generally smaller, but
otherwise differ little   *Mugil curema* is the white mullet of
tropical America, ranging occasionally northward, and several
other species occur in the West Indies and the Mediterranean
The genus *Mugil* has the eye covered by thick transparent
tissue called the adipose eyelid   In *Liza* the adipose eyelid is
wanting   *Liza capito*, the big-headed mullet of the Mediterranean, is a well-known species.   Most of the mullets of the south
seas belong to the genus *Liza*   *Liza melinoptera* and *Liza*

cæruleomaculata are common in Samoa The genus *Querimana* includes dwarf-mullets, two or three inches long, known as whirligig-mullets. These little fishes gather in small schools and swim round and round on the surface like the whirligig-beetles, or *Gyrinidæ*, their habits being like those of the young mullets, some young mullets having been, in fact, described as species of *Querimana*. The genus *Agonostomus* includes fresh-water mullets of the mountain rivers of the East and West Indies and Mexico, locally known as trucha, or trout *Agonostomus nasutus* of Mexico is the best-known species

The Joturo, or Bobo, *Joturus pichardi*, is a very large robust and vigorous mullet which abounds at the foot of waterfalls

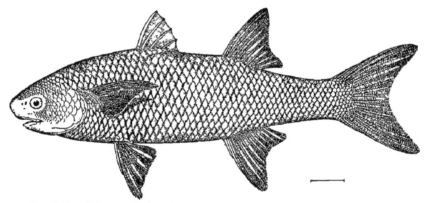

Fig 344 —Joturo or Bobo, *Joturus pichardi* Poey Rio Bayano, Panama

in the mountain torrents of Cuba, eastern Mexico, and Central America It is a good food-fish, frequently taken about Jalapa, Havana, and on the Isthmus of Panama Its lips are very thick and its teeth are broad, serrated, loosely inserted incisors

Fossil mullets are few *Mugil radobojanus* is the earliest from the Miocene of Croatia

The Barracudas: Sphyrænidæ.—The *Sphyrænidæ*, or barracudas, differ from the mullets in the presence of very strong teeth in the bones of the large mouth The lateral line is also developed, there is no gizzard, and there are numerous minor modifications connected with the food and habits The species are long, slender swift fishes, powerful in swimming and voracious to the last degree Some of the species reach a length of six feet or more, and these are almost as dangerous to bathers as sharks would be. The long, knife-like teeth render them very destructive to nets. The numerous species are placed in the single genus *Sphyræna*, and some of them are found in all warm seas, where they feed freely on all smaller fishes, their habits in the sea being much like those of the pike in the lakes The flesh is firm, delicate, and excellent in flavor   In the larger species, especially in the West Indies, it may be difficult of digestion and sometimes causes serious illness, or "ichthyosism "

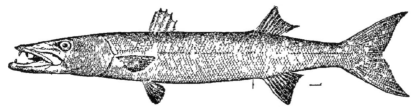

FIG 345 —Barracuda, *Sphyræna barracuda* Walbaum   Florida

Sphyræna sphyræna is the spet, or sennet, a rather small barracuda common in southern Europe   *Sphyræna borealis* of our eastern coast is a similar but still feebler species rarely exceeding a foot in length   These and other small species are feeble folk as compared with the great barracuda (*Sphyræna barracuda*) of the West Indies, a robust savage fish, also known as picuda or becuna   *Sphyræna commersoni* of Polynesia is a similar large species, while numerous lesser ones occur through the tropical seas   On the California coast *Sphyræna argentea* is an excellent food-fish, slenderer than the great barracuda but reaching a length of five feet

Several species of fossil barracuda occur in the Italian Eocene, *Sphyræna bolcensis* being the earliest

Stephanoberycidæ—We may append to the *Percesoces*, for want of a better place, a small family of the deep sea, its affinities at present unknown   The *Stephanoberycidæ* have the ventrals 1, 5, subabdominal, a single dorsal without spine, and the scales cycloid, scarcely imbricated, each with one or two central spines   The mouth is large, with small teeth, the skull cavernous, as in the berycoids, from which group the normally formed ventrals abdominal in position would seem to exclude it *Stephanoberyx monæ* and *S gilli* are found at the depth of a mile and a half below the Gulf Stream   Boulenger first placed them with the *Percesoces*, but more recently suggests their relationship with the *Haplomi* Perhaps, as supposed by Gill, they may prove to be degenerate berycoids in which the ventral fins have lost their normal connection

Crossognathidæ. — A peculiar primitive group referred by Woodward to the *Percesoces* is the family of *Crossognathidæ* of the Cretaceous period As in these fishes there are no fin-spines, they may be perhaps better placed with the *Haplomi* The dorsal fin is long, without distinct spines, and the abdominal ventrals have six to eight rays The mouth is small, with feeble teeth, and the body is elongate and compressed. *Crossognathus sabandianum* occurs in the Cretaceous of Switzerland and Germany, *Syllæmus latifrons* and other species in the Colorado Cretaceous, and *Syllæmus anglicus* in England The *Crossognathidæ* have probably the lower pharyngeals separate, else they would be placed among the *Synentognathi*, a group attached by Woodward, not without reason, to the *Percesoces*

Cobitopsidæ. — Near the *Crossognathidæ* may be placed the extinct *Cobitopsidæ*, *Cobitopsis acuta* being recorded from the

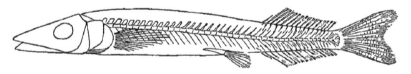

FIG 346 —*Cobitopsis acuta* Gervais, restored Oligocene of Puy-de-Dôme
(After Woodward)

Oligocene of Puy-de-Dôme in France In this species there is a short dorsal fin of about seventeen rays, no teeth, and the well-developed ventral fins are not far in front of the anal This little fish bears a strong resemblance to *Ammodytes*, but the affinities of the latter genus are certainly with the ophidioid fishes, while the real relationship of *Cobitopsis* is uncertain.

Suborder Rhegnopteri —The threadfins (*Polynemidæ*) are allied to the mullets, but differ from them and from all other fishes in the structure of the pectoral fin and its basal bones, or actinosts

The pectoral fin is divided into two parts, the lower composed of free or separate rays very slender and thread-like,

sometimes longer than the body   Two of the actinosts of the
pectoral support the fin, one is slender and has no rays, while
the fourth is plate-like and attached to the coracoids, supporting the pectoral filaments   The body is rather robust, covered
with large scales, formed much as in the mullet   The lateral

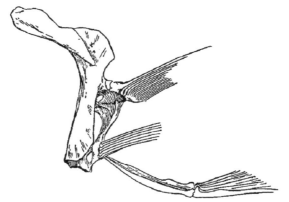

FIG 347 —Shoulder-girdle of a Threadfin, *Polydactylus approximans*
(Lay & Bennett).

line extends on the caudal fin as in the *Sciænidæ*, which group
these fishes resemble in many ways   The mouth is large,
inferior, with small teeth   The species are carnivorous fishes
of excellent flesh, abounding on sandy shores in the warm
seas   They are not very active and not at all voracious   The

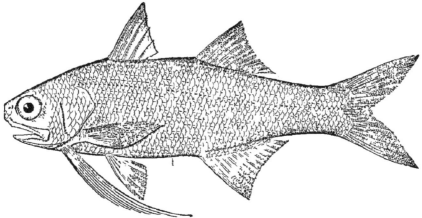

FIG 348 —Threadfin, *Polydactylus octonemus* (Girard).   Pensacola.

coloration is bluish and silvery, sometimes striped with black.
Most of the species belong to the genus *Polydactylus   Poly-*

dactylus virginicus, the barbudo, with seven filaments, is common
in the West Indies and Florida. *Polydactylus octonemus* with
eight filaments is more rare, but ranges further north *Polydactylus approximans*, the raton of western Mexico, with six
filaments, reaches San Diego *Polydactylus plebejus* is common
in Japan and other species range through Polynesia In India
isinglass is made from the large air-bladder of species of *Polydactylus* The rare *Polynemus quinquarius* of the West Indies
have five pectoral filaments, these being greatly elongate, much
longer than the body.

No extinct *Polynemidæ* are recorded.

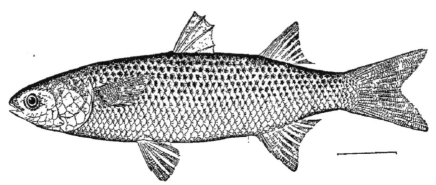

FIG 348a —Striped Mullet, *Mugil cephalus* (L) Woods Hole, Mass

CHAPTER XXVIII

PHTHINOBRANCHII: HEMIBRANCHII, LOPHO-
BRANCHII, AND HYPOSTOMIDES

SUBORDER **Hemibranchii.** — Still another transitional group, the *Hemibranchii*, is composed of spiny-rayed fishes with abdominal ventrals In this sub-order there are other points of divergence, though none of high importance In these fishes the bones of the shoulder-girdle are somewhat distorted, the supraclavicle reduced or wanting, and the gill structures somewhat degenerate The presence of bones called interclavicles or infraclavicles, below and behind the clavicle, has been supposed to characterize the order of *Hemibranchii*. But this character has very slight importance. In two families, *Macrorhamphosidæ* and *Centriscidæ*, the inter-clavicles are absent altogether In the *Fistularidæ* they are very large According to the studies of Mr Edwin C Starks,

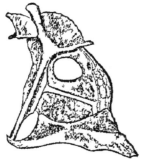

Fɪɢ 349   Fɪɢ 350

Fɪɢ 349 —Shoulder-girdle of a Stickleback, *Gasterosteus aculeatus* Linnæus. (After Parker)
Fɪɢ 350 —Shoulder-girdle of *Fistularia petimba* Lacépède, showing greatly extended interclavicle, the surface ossified

the bone in question is not a true infraclavicle It is not identical with the infraclavicle of the Ganoids, but it is only a backward extension of the hypocoracoid, there being no suture between

442

the two bones. In those species which have bony plates instead of scales, this bone has a deposit of bony substance or ganoid enamel at the surface. This gives it an apparent prominence as compared with other bones of the skeleton, but it has no great taxonomic importance. Dr Hay unites the suborders *Hemibranchii, Lophobranchii,* and *Hypostomides* to form the order *Phthinobranchii* (φθινάς, waning, βράγχος, gill), characterized by the reduction of the gill-arches. These forms are really nearly related, but their affinities with the *Percesoces* are so close that it may not be necessary to form a distinct order of the combined group. Boulenger unites the *Hemibranchii* with *Lampris* to form a group, *Catosteomi,* characterized by the development of infraclavicles, but we cannot see that *Lampris* bears any affinity to the sticklebacks, or that the presence of infraclavicle has any high significance, nor is it the supposed infraclavicle of *Lampris* homologous with that of the *Hemibranchii*. The dorsal fin in the *Hemibranchii* has more or less developed spines, spines are also present in the ventral fins. The lower pharyngeals are separated, there is no air-duct. The mouth is small and the bones of the snout are often much produced. The preopercle and symplectic are distinct. The group is doubtless derived from some transitional spiny-rayed type allied to the *Percesoces*. The Lophobranchs, another supposed order, represent simply a still further phase of degradation of gills and ventral fins. Dr Gill separates these two groups as distinct orders and places them, as aberrant offshoots, near the end of his series of bony fishes. We prefer to leave them with the other transitional forms, not regarding their traits of divergence as of any great importance in the systematic arrangement of families.

The Sticklebacks: Gasterosteidæ. — The sticklebacks (*Gasterosteidæ*) are small, scaleless fishes, closely related to the *Fistulariidæ* so far as anatomy is concerned, but with very different appearance and habits. The body often mailed, the dorsal is preceded by free spines and the ventrals are each reduced to a sharp spine with a rudimentary ray. The jaws are short, bristling with sharp teeth, and these little creatures are among the most active, voracious, and persistent of all fishes. They attack the fins of larger fishes, biting off pieces, and at the same time they devour the eggs of all species accessible to them   In almost all fresh and brackish waters of the north temperate zone these little fishes abound.   "It is scarcely to be conceived," Dr Gunther observes, "what damage these little fishes do, and how greatly detrimental they are to the increase of all the fishes among which they live, for it is with the utmost industry, sagacity, and greediness that they seek out and destroy all the young fry that come their way"

The sticklebacks inhabit brackish and fresh waters of the northern hemisphere, species essentially alike being found throughout northern Europe, Asia, and America   The same species is subject to great variation   The degree of development of spines and bony plates is greatest in individuals living in the sea and least in clear streams of the interior.   Each of the mailed species has its series of half-mailed or even naked varieties found in the fresh waters   This is true in Europe, New England, California, and Japan   The farther the individuals are from the sea, the less perfect is their armature   Thus, *Gasterosteus cataphractus*, which in the sea has a full armature of bony plates on the side, about 30 in number, will have in river mouths from 6 to 20 plates and in strictly fresh water only 2 or 3 or even none at all

The sticklebacks have been noted for their nest-building habits   The male performs this operation, and he is provided with a special gland for secretion of the necessary cement.   Dr Gill quotes from Dr John A Ryder an account of this process   The secretory gland is a "large vesicle filled with a clear secretion which coagulates into threads upon contact with water   It appears to open directly in front of the vent   As soon as it is ruptured, it loses its transparency, and whatever secretion escapes becomes whitish after being in contact with water for a short time   This has the same tough, elastic qualities as when spun by the animal itself, and is also composed of numerous fibers, as when a portion is taken that has been recently spun upon the nest   Thus provided, when the nuptial season has arrived the male stickleback prepares to build his nest, wherein his mate may deposit her eggs   How this nest is built, and the subsequent proceedings of the sticklebacks, have been told us in a graphic manner by Mr. John K.

Lord, from observations on *Gasterosteus cataphractus* on Vancouver Island, although the source of his secretion was misunderstood

"The site is generally amongst the stems of aquatic plants, where the water always flows but not too swiftly He first begins by carrying small bits of green material which he nips off the stalks and tugs from out the bottom and sides of the bank, these he attaches by some glutinous material, that he clearly has the power of secreting, to the different stems destined as pillars for his building During this operation he swims against the work already done, splashes about, and seems to test its durability and strength, rubs himself against the tiny kind of platform, scrapes the slimy mucus from his sides to mix with and act as mortar for his vegetable bricks Then he thrusts his nose into the sand at the bottom, and, bringing a mouthful, scatters it over the foundation, this is repeated until enough has been thrown on to weight the slender fabric down and give it substance and stability Then more twists, turns, and splashings to test the firm adherence of all the materials that are intended to constitute the foundation of the house that has yet to be erected on it The nest, or nursery, when completed is a hollow, somewhat rounded, barrel-shaped structure worked together much in the same way as the platform fastened to the water-plants, the whole firmly glued together by the viscous secretion scraped from off the body The inside is made as smooth as possible by a kind of plastering system, the little architect continually goes in, then, turning round and round, works the mucus from his body on to the inner sides of the nest, where it hardens like tough varnish There are two apertures, smooth and symmetrical as the hole leading into a wren's nest, and not unlike it.

"All this laborious work is done entirely by the male fish, and when completed he goes a-wooing Watch him as he swims towards a group of the fair sex enjoying themselves amidst the water-plants arrayed in his best and brightest livery, all smiles and amiability, steadily and in the most approved style of stickleback love-making this young and wealthy bachelor approaches the object of his affections, most likely tells her all about his house and its comforts, hints delicately at his readiness and ability to defend her children against every enemy, vows unfailing fidelity, and in lover fashion promises as much in a few minutes as would take a lifetime to fulfill Of course she listens to his suit, personal beauty, indomitable courage, backed by the substantial recommendations of a house ready built and fitted for immediate occupation, are gifts not to be lightly regarded

"Throwing herself on her side the captive lady shows her appreciation, and by sundry queer contortions declares herself his true and devoted spouse Then the twain return to the nest, into which the female at once betakes herself and therein deposits her eggs, emerging, when the operation is completed, by the opposite hole During the time she is in the nest (about six minutes) the male swims round and round, butts and rubs his nose against it, and altogether appears to be in a state of defiant excitement On the female leaving, he immediately enters, deposits the milt on the eggs, taking his departure through the back door So far his conduct is strictly pure, but I am afraid morality in stickleback society is of rather a lax order No sooner has this lady, his first love, taken her departure, than he at once seeks another, introduces her as he did the first, and so on, wife after wife, until the nest is filled with eggs, layer upon layer, milt being carefully deposited betwixt each stratum of ova As it is necessary there should be two holes, by which ingress and egress can be readily accomplished, so it is equally essential in another point of view To fertilize fish-eggs, running water is the first necessity, and, as the holes are invariably placed in the direction of the current, a steady stream of water is thus directed over them "

To the genus *Gasterosteus* the largest species belong, those having three dorsal spines, and the body typically fully covered with bony plates *Gasterosteus aculeatus* inhabits both shores of the Atlantic and the scarcely different *Gasterosteus cataphractus* swarms in the inlets from southern California to Alaska, Siberia, and northern Japan Half-naked forms have been called by various names and one entirely naked in streams of southern California is named *Gasterosteus williamsoni* Its traits are, however, clearly related to its life in fresh waters

In *Pygosteus pungitius*, a type of almost equally wide range, there are nine or ten dorsal spines and the body is more slender. All kinds of waters of the north on both continents may yield

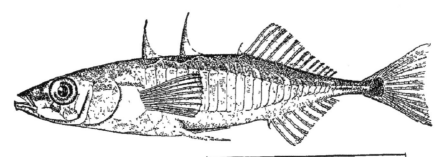

Fig 351.—Three-spined Stickleback, *Gasterosteus aculeatus* L   Woods Hole, Mass.

this species or its allies and variations, mailed or naked   The naked, *Apeltes quadracus*, is found in the sea only, along the New England coast.

Eucalia inconstans is the stickleback of the clear brook from New York to Indiana and Minnesota   The male is jet

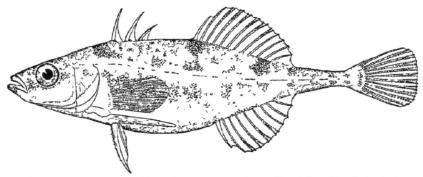

Fig 352 —Four-spined Stickleback, *Apeltes quadracus* Mitchill   Woods Hole, Mass

black in spring with the sheen of burnished copper and he is intensely active in his work of protecting the eggs of his own species and destroying the eggs and fry of others   *Spinachia spinachia* is a large sea stickleback of Europe with many dorsal spines

No fossil *Gasterosteidæ* are recorded, and the family, while the least specialized in most regards, is certainly not the most primitive of the suborder

The Aulorhynchidæ.—Closely related to the sticklebacks is the small family of *Aulorhynchidæ*, with four soft rays in the

ventral fins   Aulorhynchus, like *Spinachia*, has many dorsal
spines and an elongate snout approaching that of a trumpet-
fish   *Aulorhynchus flavidus* lives on the coast of California
and *Aulichthys japonicus* in Japan   The extinct family of *Pro-
tosyngnathidæ* is near *Aulorhynchus*, with the snout tubular, the
ribs free, not anchylosed as in *Aulorhynchus*, and with the first
vertebræ fused, forming one large one as in *Aulostomus*   *Proto-
syngnathus sumatrensis* occurs in Sumatra   *Protaulopsis bolcensis*
of the Eocene of Italy has the ventral fins farther back, and is
probably more primitive than the sticklebacks

Cornet-fishes: Fistularidæ. — Closely related to the sticklebacks so far as structure is concerned is a family of very different habit, the cornet-fishes, or cornetas (*Fistularidæ*)   In
these fishes the body is very long and slender, like that of a
garfish   The snout is produced into a very long tube, which
bears the short jaws at the end   The teeth are very small
There are no scales, but bony plates are sunk in the skin   The
ventrals are abdominal, each with a spine and four rays   The
four anterior vertebræ are very much elongate   There are
no spines in the dorsal and the backbone extends through the
forked caudal, ending in a long filament   The cornet-fishes
are dull red or dull green in color   They reach a length of
two or three feet, and the four or five known species are widely
distributed through the warm seas, where they swim in shallow
water near the surface   *Fistularia tabaccaria*, the tobacco-
pipe fish, is common in the West Indies, *Fistularia petimba*,
F serrata, and others in the Pacific   A fossil cornet-fish of very
small size, *Fistularia longirostris*, is known from the Eocene
of Monte Bolca, near Verona   *Fistularia kœnigi* is recorded
from the Oligocene of Glarus

The Trumpet-fishes: Aulostomidæ. — The *Aulostomidæ*, or trumpet-fishes are in structure entirely similar to the *Fistularidæ*, but the body is band-shaped, compressed, and scaly,
the long snout bearing the feeble jaws at the end   There
are numerous dorsal spines and no filament on the tail.
Aulostomus chinensis (*maculatus*) is common in the West Indies,
Aulostomus valentini abounds in Polynesia and Asia, where
it is a food-fish of moderate importance   A species of *Aulostomus* (*bolcensis*) is found in the Italian Eocene   Allied to it is

the extinct family *Urosphenidæ*, scaleless, but otherwise similar *Urosphen dubia* occurs in the Eocene at Monte Bolca *Urosphen*

FIG 353 —Trumpet-fish, *Aulostomus chinensis* (L) Virginia

is perhaps the most primitive genus of the whole suborder of *Hemibranchii*

The Snipefishes: Macrorhamphosidæ —Very remarkable fishes are the snipefishes, or *Macrorhamphosidæ* In these forms

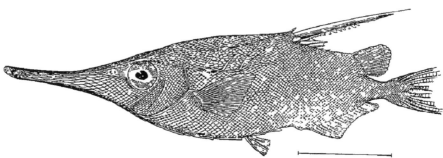

FIG 354 —Japanese Snipefish, *Macrorhamphosus sagifue* Jordan & Starks Misaki, Japan

the snout is still tubular, with the short jaws at the end The body is short and deep, partly covered with bony plates The dorsal has a very long serrated spine, besides several shorter ones, and the ventral fins have one spine and five rays

The snipefish, or woodcock-fish, *Macrorhamphosus scolopax*, is rather common on the coasts of Europe, and a very similar species (*M sagifue*) occurs in Japan The *Rhamphosidæ*, represented by *Rhamphosus*, an extinct genus with the ventrals further forward, are found in the Eocene rocks of Monte Bolca *Rhamphosus vastrum* has minute scales, short dorsal, and the snout greatly attenuate

The Shrimp-fishes: Centriscidæ.—One of the most extraordinary types of fishes is the small family of *Centriscidæ*, found in the East Indies The back is covered by a transparent bony cuirass which extends far beyond the short tail, on which the two dorsal fins are crowded. Anteriorly this cuirass is composed of plates which are soldered to the ribs.　The small toothless mouth is at the end of a long snout

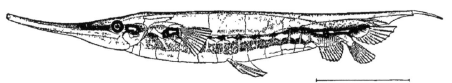

FIG 355 —Shrimp-fish, *Æoliscus strigatus* (Gunther)　Riu Kiu Islands, Japan

These little fishes with the transparent carapace look very much like shrimps　*Centriscus scutatus* (*Amphisile*) with the terminal spine fixed is found in the East Indies, and *Æoliscus strigatus* with the terminal spine movable is found in southern Japan and southwards

A fossil species, *Æoliscus heinrichi*, is found in the Oligocene

FIG 356 —*Æoliscus heinrichi* Heckel　Eocene of Carpathia　Family *Centriscidæ*
(After Heckel)

of various parts of Europe, and *Centriscus longirostris* occurs in the Eocene of Monte Bolca

In the *Centriscidæ* and *Macrorhamphosidæ* the expansions of the hypocoracoid called infraclavicles are not developed.

The Lophobranchs. — The suborder *Lophobranchii* (λοφός, tuft, βραγχός, gill) is certainly an offshoot from the *Hemibranchii* and belongs likewise among the forms transitional from soft to spiny-rayed fishes　At the same time it is a degenerate group, and in its modifications it turns directly away from the general line of specialization.

The chief characters are found in the reduction of the gills to small lobate tufts attached to rudimentary gill-arches　The so-called infraclavicles are present, as in most of the *Hemibranchii*　Bony plates united to form rings take the place of scales　The long tubular snout bears the short toothless jaws at the end　The preopercle is absent, and the ventrals are seven-rayed or wanting　The species known as pipefishes and sea-horses are all very small and none have any economic value.　They are numerous in all warm seas, mostly living in shallow bays among seaweed and eel-grass. The muscular system is little developed and all the species have the curious habit of carrying the eggs until hatched in a pouch of skin under the belly or tail, this structure is usually found in the male

The Solenostomidæ. — The *Solenostomidæ* of the East Indies are the most primitive of these fishes They have the body rather short and provided with spinous dorsal, and ventral fins The pretty species are occasionally swept northward to Japan in the Black Current *Solenostomus cyanopterus* is a characteristic species *Solenorhynchus elegans*, now extinct (with the trunk more elongate), preceded *Solenostomus* in the Eocene of Monte Bolca

The Pipefishes: Syngnathidæ.—The *Syngnathidæ* are very long and slender fishes, with neither spinous dorsal, nor ventral fins, the body covered by bony rings Of the pipefish, *Syngnathus*, there are very many species on all northern coasts. *Syngnathus acus* is common in Europe, *Syngnathus fuscum* along the New England coast, *Syngnathus californiense* in California, and *Syngnathus schlegeli* in Japan Numerous other species of *Syngnathus* and other genera are found further south in the same regions *Corythroichthys* is characteristic of coral reefs and *Microphis* of the streams of the islands of Polynesia. In general, the more northerly species have the greater number of vertebræ and of bony rings *Tiphle tiphle* is a large pipefish of the Mediterranean This species was preceded by *Tiphle albyi* (*Siphonostoma*) in the Miocene of Sicily. Other pipefishes, referred to as *Syngnathus* and *Calamostoma*, are found as fossils in Tertiary rocks

The Sea-horses: Hippocampus.—Both fossil and recent forms constitute a direct line of connection from the pipe-fishes to the sea-horses. In the latter the head has the form of the head of a horse. It is bent at right angles to the body like the head of a knight at chess There is no caudal fin, and the tail in typical species is coiled and can hardly be straightened out *Calamostoma* of the Eocene, *Gasterotokeus* of Polynesia, and *Acentronura* of Japan are forms which connect the true sea-horses with the pipefish. *Gasterotokeus* has the long head and slender body of the pipefish, with the prehensile finless

Phthinobranchii

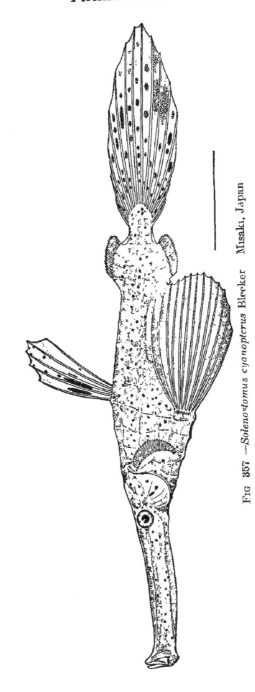

FIG. 357 —*Solenostomus cyanopterus* Bleeker Misaki, Japan

tail of a sea-horse   Most of the living species of the sea-horse belong to the genus *Hippocampus*   These little creatures have the egg-sac of the male under the abdomen   They range from two inches to a foot in length and some of the many species may be found in abundance in every warm sea   Some cling by the tails to floating seaweed and are swept to great distances, others cling to eel-grass and live very near the shore. The commonest European species is *Hippocampus hippocampus*   Most abundant on our Atlantic coast is *Hippocampus hudsonius*   *Hippocampus coronatus* is most common in Japan   The largest species, ten inches long, are *Hippocampus ingens* of Lower California and *kelloggi* in Japan   Many species, especially of the smaller ones, have the spines of the bony plates of the body ending in fleshy flaps   These are sometimes so enlarged as to simulate leaves of seaweed, thus serving for the efficient protection of the species   These flaps are developed to an extreme degree in

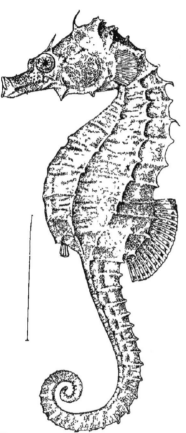

FIG 358 —Sea-horse, *Hippocampus hudsonius* Dekay. Virginia

Phyllopteryx eques, a pipefish of the East Indies.

No fossil sea-horses are known

The following account of the breeding-habits of our smallest sea-horse (*Hippocampus zosteræ*) was prepared by the writer for a book of children's stories

"He was a little bit of a sea-horse and his name was Hippocampus   He was not more than an inch long, and he had a red stripe on the fin on his back, and his head was made of bone and it had a shape just like a horse's head, but he ran out to a point at his tail, and his head and his tail were all covered with bone. He lived in the Grand Lagoon at Pensacola in Florida, where the water is shallow and warm and there are lots of seaweeds So he wound his tail around a stem of seaweed and hung with his head down, waiting to see what would happen next, and then he saw another little sea-horse hanging on another seaweed And the other sea-horse put out a lot of little eggs, and the little eggs all lay on the bottom of the sea at the foot of the seaweed So Hippocampus crawled down from the seaweed where he was and gathered up all those little eggs, and down on the under side of his tail where the skin is soft he made a long slit for a pocket, and then he stuffed all the eggs into this pocket and fastened it together and stuck it with some slime So he had all the other sea-horse's eggs in his own pocket

"Then he went up on the seawrack again and twisted his tail around it, and hung there with his head down to see what would happen next The sun shone down on him, and by and by all the little eggs began to hatch out, and each one of the eggs was a little sea-pony, shaped just like a sea-horse And when he hung there with his head down he could feel all the little sea-ponies squirming inside his pocket, and by and by they squirmed so much that they pushed the pocket open, and then every one crawled away from him, and he couldn't get them back, and so he went along with them and watched to see that nothing should hurt them And by and by they hung themselves all up on the seaweeds, and they are hanging there yet And so he crawled back to his own piece of seaweed and twisted his tail around it, and waited to see what would happen next And what happened next was just the same thing over again "

Suborder Hypostomides, the Sea-moths: Pegasidæ.—The small suborder of *Hypostomides* (ύπό, below, στόμα, mouth) consists of the family of *Pegasidæ* These "sea-moths" are fantastic little fishes, probably allied to the sticklebacks, but wholly unique in form The slender body is covered with bony plates, the gill-covers are reduced to a single plate The small mouth underneath a long snout has no teeth The preopercle and the symplectic are both wanting The ventrals are abdominal, formed of two rays, and the very large pectoral fin is placed horizontally like a great wing

The species, few in number, known as sea-moths and sea-dragons, rarely exceed four inches in length. They are found

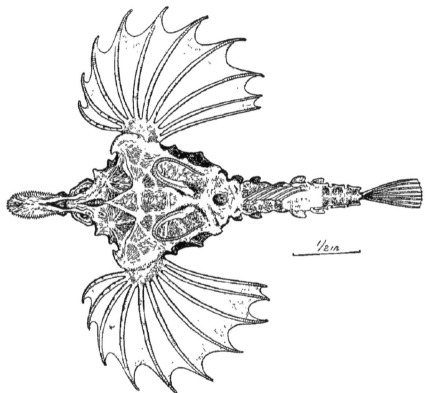

FIG 359 —Sea-moth, *Zalises umitengu* Jordan & Snyder   Misaki, Japan.
(View from below)

in the East Indies and drift with the currents northward to Japan   The genera are *Pegasus, Parapegasus,* and *Zalises.* The best-known species are *Zalises draconis* and *Pegasus volitans*

No fossil species of *Pegasidæ* are known.

CHAPTER XXIX

SALMOPERCÆ AND OTHER TRANSITIONAL GROUPS

SUBORDER Salmopercæ, the Trout-perches: Percopsidæ. —More ancient than the *Hemibranchii*, and still more distinctly in the line of transition from soft-rayed to spiny-rayed fishes, is the small suborder of *Salmopercæ* This is characterized by the presence of the adipose fin of the salmon,

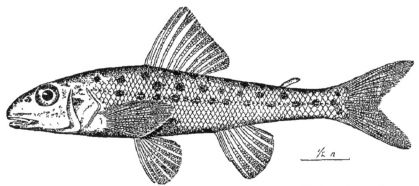

FIG 360 —Sand-roller, *Pecropsis guttatus* Agassiz Okoboji Lake, Ia

in connection with the mouth, scales, and fin-spines of a perch The premaxillary forms the entire edge of the upper jaw, the maxillary being without teeth The air-bladder retains a rudimentary duct. The bones of the head are full of mucous cavities, as in the European perch called *Gymnocephalus* and *Acerina* There are two spines in the dorsal and one or two in the anal, while the abdominal ventrals have each a spine and eight rays Two species only are known among living fishes, these emphasizing more perfectly than any other known forms the close relation really existing between spinous and soft-rayed forms The single family of *Percopsidæ* would seem to find its place in Cretaceous rocks rather than in the waters of to-day

456

Percopsis guttata, the trout-perch or sand-roller of the Great Lakes, is a pale translucent fish with dark spots, reaching a length of six inches   It abounds in the Great Lakes and their tributaries and is occasionally found in the Delaware, Ohio,

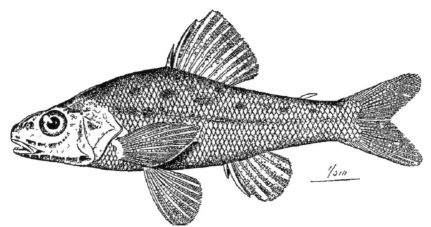

FIG 361 —Oregon Trout-perch, *Columbia transmontana* Eigenmann   Umatilla River, Oregon

Kansas, and other rivers and northwestward as far as Medicine Hat on the Saskatchewan   It is easily taken with a hook from the piers at Chicago

Columbia transmontana is another little fish of similar type, but rougher and more distinctly perch-like   It is found in sandy or weedy lagoons throughout the lower basin of the Columbia, where it was first noticed by Dr Eigenmann in 1892.

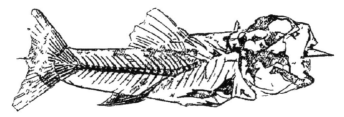

FIG 362 —*Erismatopterus endlicheri* Cope   Green River Eocene   (After Cope)

From the point of view of structure and classification, this left-over form is one of the most remarkable of American fishes.

Erismatopteridæ.—Here should perhaps be placed the family of *Erismatopteridæ*, represented by *Erismatopterus levatus* and other species of the Green River Eocene shales   In *Erismatopterus* the short dorsal has two or three spines, there are two or three spines in the anal, and the abdominal ventrals are opposite the dorsal   Allied to *Eris-matopterus* is *Amphiplaga* of the same deposits.

We cannot, however, feel sure that these extinct fragments, however well preserved, belonged to fishes having an adipose fin   Among spiny-rayed fishes the *Percopsidæ* alone retain this character, and the real affinities of *Erismatopterus* may be with *Aphredoderidæ* and other percoid forms

The relations of the extinct family of *Asineopidæ* are also still uncertain   This group comprises fresh-water fishes said to be allied to the *Aphre-doderidæ*, but with the pelvic bones not forked   *Asineops pauciradiata, squamifrons* and *viridensis* are described from the Green River shales   With *Erismatopterus* all these fishes may belong to the suborder of *Salmopercæ*, but, as above

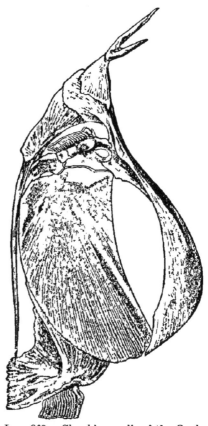

F IG 363 —Shoulder-girdle of the Opah, *Lampris guttatus* (Brunnich), showing the enlarged infraclavicle   (After Boulenger)

stated, the possession of the adipose fin, the most characteristic trait of the *Salmopercæ*, cannot be verified in the fossil remains

Suborder Selenichthyes, the Opahs: Lamprididæ.—We may bring together as constituting another suborder certain forms of uncertain relationship, but which seem to be transitional between deep-bodied extinct Ganoids and the forms allied to *Platax, Zeus*, and *Antigonia*   The name of *Selenichthyes* (σηλήνη, moon, ιχθύς, fish) is suggested by Boulenger for the group of opahs, or moonfishes   These are characterized by the highly compressed body, the great development of a large hypocoracoid, and especially by the structure of the ventral fins, which are composed of about fifteen rays instead of the one spine and five rays characteristic of the specialized perch-like fishes The living forms of this type are further characterized by the partial or total absence of the spinous dorsal, by the small oblique mouth, and the prominence of the ventral curve of the body A thorough study of the osteology of these forms living and fossil will be necessary before the group can be properly defined The large bone above mentioned was at first considered by Boulenger as the interclavicle or infraclavicle, the hypocoracoid being regarded by him as displaced, lying with the actinosts But it is certain, from the studies of Mr Starks, that this bone is the real hypocoracoid, which in this case is simply exaggerated in size, but placed as in ordinary fishes.

The single living family, *Lamprididæ*, contains but one species, *Lampris guttatus*, known as opah, moonfish, mariposa, cravo, Jerusalem haddock, or San Pedro fish This species reaches a length of six feet and a weight of 500 to 600 pounds Fig 84 is taken from a photograph of an example weighing 317½ pounds taken near Honolulu by Mr E L Berndt The body is almost as deep as long, plump and smooth, without scales or bony plates The vertebræ are forty-five in number, and the large ventrals contain about fifteen rays The dorsal is without spines, the small mouth without teeth The color is a "rich brocade of silver and lilac, rosy on the belly, everywhere with round silvery spots" The head and back have ultramarine tints, the jaws and fins are vermilion On a drawing of this fish made at Sable Island in 1856, Mr James Farquhar wrote (to Dr J Bernard Gilpin) "Just imagine the body, a beautiful silver interspersed with spots of a lighter color about the size of sixpence, the eyes very large and brilliant, with a golden ring around them You will then have some idea of the splendid appearance of the fish when fresh If Caligula had seen them I might have realized a fortune."

The skeleton of the opah is very firm and heavy The flesh is of varying shades of salmon-red, tender, oily, and of a rich, exquisite flavor scarcely surpassed by any other fish whatsoever

The opah is a rare fish, swimming slowly near the surface and ranging very widely in all the warm seas   It was first noticed in Norway by Gunner, the good bishop of Throndhjem, about 1780   It was soon after recorded from Elsinore, Torbay, and Madeira, and is occasionally taken in various places in Europe It is also recorded from Newfoundland, Sable Island, Cuba, Monterey, San Pedro Point (near San Francisco), Santa Catalina, Honolulu, and Japan

The specimen studied by the writer came ashore at Monterey in an injured condition, having been worsted in a struggle with some better-armed fish

Allied to *Lampris* is the imposing extinct species known as *Semiophorus velifer* from the Eocene of Monte Bolca near Verona, the type of the extinct family of *Semiophoridæ*   This is a deep compressed fish, with very high spinous dorsal and very long, many-rayed ventrals   Other related species are known also from the Eocene   There is no evidence of any close relation between these fishes with *Caranx* or *Platax*, with which Woodward associates *Semiophorus*

The *Semiophoridæ* differ from the *Lampridæ* chiefly in the development of the spinous dorsal fin, which is composed of many slender rays

Suborder Zeoidea. — Not far from the *Selenichthyes* and the *Berycoidei* we may place the singular group of John Dories, or zeoid fishes   These have the ventral fins thoracic and many-rayed, the dorsal fin provided with spines, and the post-temporal, as in the *Chætodontidæ*, fused with the skull Dr Boulenger calls attention to the close relation of these fishes to the flounders, and suggests the possible derivation of both from a synthetic type, the *Amphistiidæ*, found in the European Eocene   The *Amphistiidæ*, *Zeidæ*, and flounders are united by him to form the group or suborder *Zeorhombi*, characterized by the thoracic ventrals, which have the rays not I, 5 in number, by the progressive degeneration of the fin-spines and the progressive twisting of the cranium, bringing the two eyes to the same side of the head   It is not certain that the flounders are really derived from Zeus-like fishes, but no other guess as to their origin has more elements of probability

FIG. 364.—*Semiophorus velifer* Volta. Eocene. (After Agassiz, per Zittel.)

We may, however, regard the *Zeoidea* on the one hand and the *Heterosomata* on the other as distinct suborders.   This is

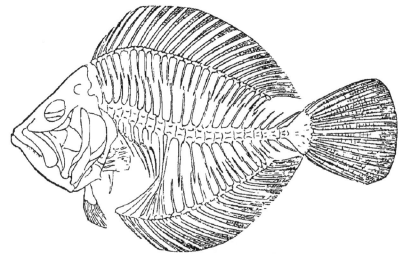

FIG 365 —*Amphistium paradoxum* Agassiz   Upper Eocene, (Supposed ancestor of the flounders)   (After Boulengei)

certain, that the flounders are descended from spiny-rayed forms and that they have no affinities with the codfishes

Amphistiidæ —The *Amphistiidæ*, now extinct, are deep-bodied, compressed fishes, with long, continuous dorsal and anal in which a few of the anterior rays are simple, slender spines scarcely differentiated from the soft rays   The form of body and the structure of the fins are essentially as in the flounders, from which they differ chiefly by the symmetry of the head, the eyes being normally placed   *Amphistium paradoxum* is described by Agassiz from the upper Eocene   It occurs in Italy and France. In its dorsal and anal fins there are about twenty-two rays, the first three or four undivided   The teeth are minute or absent and there is a high supraoccipital crest

The John Dories: Zeidæ. — The singular family of *Zeidæ*, or John Dories, agrees with Chætodonts in the single character of the fusion of the post-temporal with the skull   The species, however, diverge widely in other regards, and their ventral fins are essentially those of the Berycoids   In all the species there are seven to nine soft rays in the ventral fins, as in the Berycoid fishes   Probably the character of the fused

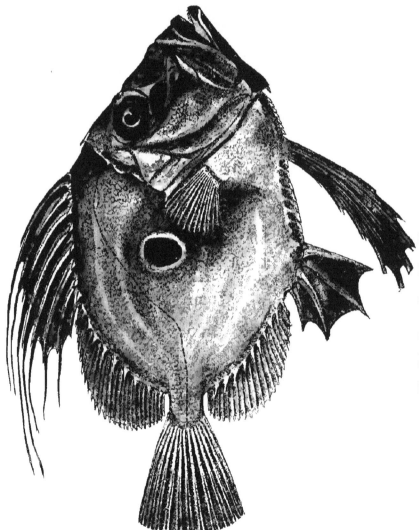

FIG. 366.—The John Dory, *Zeus faber*, Linnæus.   Devon, England.

post temporal has been independently derived The anterior vertebræ in *Zeus*, as in *Chætodon*, are closely crowded together In the *Zeidæ* the spinous dorsal is well developed, the body naked or with very thin scales, and provided with bony warts at least around the bases of dorsal and anal fins The species are mostly of small size, silvery in color, living in moderate depths in warm seas The best-known genus is *Zeus*, which is a group of shore-fishes of the waters of Asia and Europe The common John Dory (called in Germany Harings-Konig, or king of the herrings), *Zeus faber*, abounds in shallow bays on the coasts of Europe It reaches a length of nearly a foot, and is a striking feature of the markets of southern Europe The dorsal spines are high, the mouth large, and on the sides is a black ring, said by some to be the mark of the thumb of St Peter, who is reported to have taken a coin from the mouth of this species A black spot on several other species is associated with the same legend

On the coasts of Japan abounds the Matao, or target-fish (*Zeus japonicus*), very similar to the European species and like it in form and color *Zenopsis nebulosa* and *Zen itea* also occur on the coasts of Japan The remaining *Zeidæ* (*Cyttus*, *Zenopsis*, *Zenion*, etc) are all rare species occasionally dredged especially in the Australian region *Zeus priscus* is recorded from the Tertiary, and *Cyttoides glaronensis* from the upper Eocene of Glavus

Grammicolepidæ.—The *Grammicolepidæ*, represented by a single species, *Grammicolepis brachiusculus*, rarely taken off the coast of Cuba, is related to the *Zeidæ* It has rough, ridged, parchment-like scales deeper than long The ventrals are thoracic, with the rays in increased number, as in *Zeus* and *Beryx*, with each of which it suggests affinity.

CHAPTER XXX

BERYCOIDEI

THE **Berycoid Fishes.** — We may place in a separate order a group of fishes, mostly spiny-rayed, which appeared earlier in geological time than any other of the spinous forms, and which in several ways represent the transition from the isospondylous fishes to those of the type of the mackerel and perch In the berycoid fishes the ventral fins are always thoracic, the number of rays almost always greater than I, 5, and in all cases an orbitosphenoid bone is developed in connection with the septum between the orbits above This bone is found in the *Isospondyli* and other primitive fishes, but according to the investigations

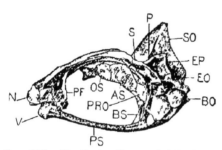

FIG 367 —Skull of a Berycoid fish, *Beryx splendens* Cuv & Val, showing the orbitosphenoid (OS), characteristic of all Berycoid fishes

of Mr E C Starks it is wanting in all percoid and scombroid forms, as well as in the *Haplomi* and in all the higher fishes. This trait may therefore, among thoracic fishes, be held to define the section or suborder of *Berycoidei*

These fishes, most primitive of the thoracic types, were more abundant in Cretaceous and Eocene times than now The possession of an increased number of soft rays in the ventral fins is archaic, although in one family, the *Monocentridæ*, the number is reduced to three Most of the living *Berycoidei* retain through life the archaic duct to the air-bladder characteristic of most abdominal or soft-rayed fishes. In some however, the duct is lost For the first time in the fish series the number of twenty-four vertebræ appears In most spiny-rayed fishes of the tropics, of whatever family, this number is retained

In every case spines are present in the dorsal fin, and in certain cases the development of the spinous dorsal surpasses that of the most extreme perch-like forms   In geological times the Berycoids preceded all other perch-like fishes   They are probably ancestral to all the latter   All the recent species, in spite of high specialization, retain some archaic characters

The Alfonsinos· Berycidæ.—The typical family, *Berycidæ*, is composed of fishes of rather deep water, bright scarlet or black in color, with the body short and compressed, the scales varying in the different genera   The single dorsal fin has a few spines in front, and there are no barbels   The suborbitals are not greatly developed

The species of *Beryx*, called in Spanish *Alfonsino*, *Beryx elegans* and *Beryx decadactylus*, are widely distributed at mod-

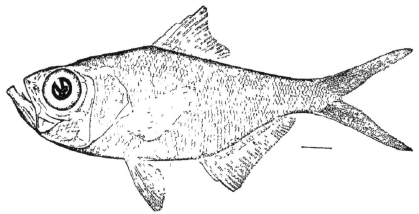

FIG 368.—*Beryx splendens* Lowe   Gulf Stream

erate depths, the same species being recorded from Portugal, Madeira, Cuba, the Gulf Stream, and Japan   The colors are very handsome, being scarlet with streaks of white or golden. These fishes reach the length of a foot or more and are valued as food where sufficiently common.

Numerous species of *Beryx* and closely allied genera are found in all rocks since Cretaceous times; *Beryx dalmaticus*, from the Cretaceous of Dalmatia, is perhaps the earliest   *Beryx insculptus* is found in New Jersey, but no other Berycoids are yet known as fossils from North America. *Sphenocephalus*, with four anal spines, is found in the chalk, as are also species of *Acrogaster* and *Pycnosterinx*, these being the earliest of fishes with distinctly spiny fins.

The *Trachichthyidæ* are deep-sea fishes with short bodies, cavernous skulls, and rough scales. The dorsal is short, with a few spines in front. The suborbitals are very broad, often covering the cheeks, and the anal fin is shorter than the dorsal, a character which separates these fishes from the *Berycidæ*, in

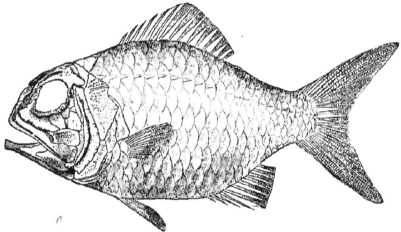

FIG. 369.—*Hoplopteryx lewesiensis* (Mantell), restored. English Cretaceous Family *Berycidæ*. (After Woodward.)

which group the anal fin is very long. The belly has often a serrated edge, and the coloration is red or black, the black species being softer in body and living in deeper water. Species of *Hoplostethus*, notably *Hoplostethus mcditerraneus*, are found in most seas at a considerable depth. *Trachichthys*, a genus scarcely distinguishable from *Hoplostethus*, is found in various seas. The genus *Paratrachichthys* is remarkable for the anterior position of the vent, much as in *Aphrcdoderus*. Species occur in Japan and Australia. *Gephyroberyx*, with the dorsal fin notched, is known from Japan (*G. japonicus*) and Madeira (*G. darwini*).

We may also refer to the *Trachichthyidæ* certain species of still deeper waters, black in color and still softer in texture, with smaller scales which are often peculiar in form. These constitute the genera *Caulolepis*, *Anoplogaster*, *Melamphaës*, and *Plectromus*.   In *Caulolepis* the jaws are armed with very strong canines.

Allied to the *Trachichthyidæ* are also the fossil genera *Hoplopteryx* and *Homonotus*.   *Hoplopteryx lewesiensis*, from the English chalk, is one of the earliest of the spiny-rayed fishes.

The Soldier-fishes: Holocentridæ. — The soldier-fishes (*Holocentridæ*), also known as squirrel-fishes, Welshmen, soldados, matajuelos, malau, alehi, etc., are shore fishes very characteristic

FIG. 370.—*Paratrachichthys prosthemius* Jordan & Fowler, Misaki, Japan.   Family *Trachichthyidæ*.

of rocky banks in the tropical seas.   In this family the flesh is firm and the large scales very hard and with very rough edges.   There are eleven spines in the dorsal and four in the anal, the third being usually very long.   The ventral fins have one spine and seven soft rays.   The whole head and body are rough with prickles.   The coloration is always brilliant, the ground hue being scarlet or crimson, often with lines or stripes of white, black, or golden.   The fishes are valued as food, and they furnish a large part of the beauty of coloration so characteristic of the fishes of the coral reefs.   The species are active, pugnacious, carnivorous, but not especially voracious, the mouth being usually small.

The genus *Holocentrus* is characterized by the presence of a large spine on the angle of the preopercle.   Its species are especially numerous, *Holocentrus ascenscionis*, abundant in Cuba, ranges northward in the Gulf Stream. *Holocentrus*

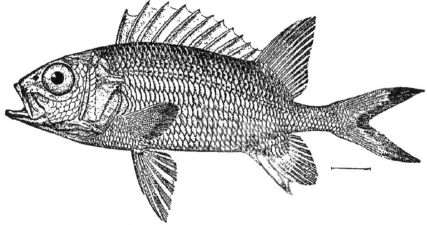

Fig. 371.—Soldier-fish, *Holocentrus ascenscionis* (Osbeck).

suborbitalis, the mojarra cardenal, is a small, relatively dull species swarming about the rocks of western Mexico. *Holo-*

Fig. 372.—Soldier-fish, *Holocentrus ittodai* Jordan & Fowler. Riu Kiu Islands, Japan.

centrus spinosissimus is a characteristic fish of Japan. Many other species abound throughout Polynesia and the East Indies, as well as in tropical America. *Holocentrus ruber* and *Holo-*

centrus diadema are common species of Polynesia and the East
Indies. Other abundant species are *H spinifer, H microstomus,*
and *H violascens*

Holocentrus marianus is the marian of the French West
Indies, *Holocentrus sammara,* and related large-mouthed species
occur in Polynesia

In *Myripristis* the preopercular spine is wanting and the
air-bladder is divided into two parts, the anterior extending
to the ear *Myripristis jacobus* is the brilliantly colored candil,

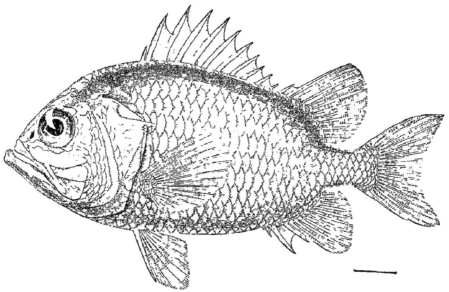

Fig 373 —*Ostichthys japonicus* (Cuv & Val) Giran, Formosa

or "Frère Jacques," of the West Indies. Species of *Myripristis* are known in Hawaii as *u-u* A curious method of catching
Myripristis murdjan is pursued on the Island of Hawaii
A living fish is suspended by a cord in front of a reef inhabited
by this species It remains with scarlet fins spread and glistening red scales Its presence is a challenge to other individuals,
who rush out to attack it These are then drawn out by a
concealed scoop-net, and a fresh specimen is taken as a decoy
Myripristis pralinius, M. multiradiatus, and other species
occur in Polynesia *Ostichthys* is allied to *Myripristis* but
with very large rough scales *Ostichthys japonicus* is a large
and showy fish of the waters of Japan *Ostichthys pillwaxi*

occurs at Honolulu. *Holotrachys lima* is a small, brick-red fish with small very rough scales found throughout Polynesia.

Fossil species of *Holocentrus, Myripristis,* and related extinct genera occur in the Eocene and Miocene. *Holocentrus macro-cephalus,* from Monte Bolca Eocene, is one of the best known. *Myricanthus leptacanthus* from the same region, has very slender spines in the fins.

The Polymixiidæ.—The family of *Polymixiidæ,* or barbudos, is one of the most interesting in Ichthyology from its bewildering combination of characters belonging to different groups. With the general aspect of a Berycoid, the ventral rays I, 7,

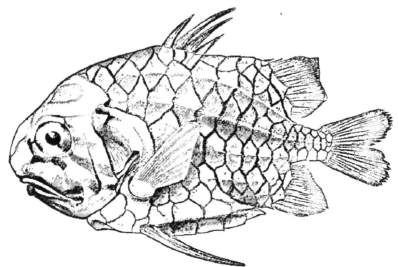

FIG. 374.—Pine-cone Fish, *Monocentris japonicus* (Houttuyn). Waka, Japan.

and the single dorsal fin with a few spines, *Polymixia* has the scales rather smooth and at the chin are two long barbels which look remarkably like those of the family of *Mullidæ* or *Surmullets.* As in the *Mullidæ,* there are but four branchiostegals. In other regards the two groups seem to have little in common. According to Starks, the specialized feelers at the chin are different in structure and must have been independently developed in the two groups. In *Polymixia,* each barbel is suspended from the hypohyal; three rudimentary branchiostegals forming its thickened base. In *Mullus,* each barbel is suspended from the trip of a slender projection of the ceratohyal, having no connection with the branchiostegals. *Polymixia* possesses the orbitosphenoid bone and is a true berycoid, while the *Mullidæ* are genuine percoid fishes

Four species of *Polymixia* are recorded from rather deep water· *Polymixia nobilis* from Madeira, *Polymixia lowei* from the West Indies, *Polymixia berndti* from Hawaii, and *Polymixia japonica* from Japan. All are plainly colored, without red

The Pine-cone Fishes: Monocentridæ.—Among the most extraordinary of all fishes is the little family of *Monocentridæ*, or pine-cone fishes *Monocentris japonicus*, the best-known species, is common on the coasts of Japan It reaches the length of five inches The body is covered with a coat of mail, made of rough plates which look as though carelessly put together. The dorsal spines are very strong, and each ventral fin is replaced by a very strong rough spine. The animal fully justifies the remark of its discoverer, Houttuyn (1782), that it is "the most remarkable fish which exists" It is dull golden brown in color, and in movement as sluggish as a trunkfish A similar species, called knightfish, *Monocentris gloriæ-maris*, is found in Australia. No fossils allied to *Monocentris* are known

CHAPTER XXXI

PERCOMORPHI

SUBORDER Percomorphi, the Mackerels and Perches. — We may place in a single suborder the various groups of fishes which cluster about the perches, and the mackerels The group is not easily definable and may contain heterogeneous elements. We may, however, arrange in it, for our present purposes, those spiny-rayed fishes having the ventral fins thoracic, of one spine and five rays (the ventral fin occasionally wanting or defective, having a reduced number of rays), the lower pharyngeal bones separate, the suborbital chain without backward extension or bony stay, the post-temporal normally developed and separate from the cranium, the premaxillary and maxillary distinct, the cranium itself without orbitosphenoid bone, having a structure not greatly unlike that of perch or mackerel, and the backbone primitively of twenty-four vertebræ, the number increased in arctic, pelagic, or fresh-water offshoots

The species, comprising the great body of the spiny-rayed forms, group themselves chiefly about two central families, the *Scombridæ*, or mackerels, and the *Serranidæ*, the sea-bass, with their fresh-water allies, the *Percidæ*, or perch

The Mackerel Tribe: Scombroidea.—The two groups of *Percomorphi*, the mackerel-like and the perch-like, admit of no exact definition, as the one fully grades into the other The mackerel-like forms, or *Scombroidea*, as a whole are defined by their adaptation for swift movement. The profile is sharp anteriorly, the tail slender, with widely forked caudal, the scales are usually small, thin, and smooth, of such a character as not to produce friction in the water

In general the external surface is smooth, the skeleton light and strong, the muscles firm, and the species are carniv-

473

orous and predaceous. But among the multitude of forms are many variations, and some of these will seem to be exceptions to any definition of mackerel-like fishes which could possibly be framed

The mackerels, or *Scombroidea*, have usually the tail very slender, composed of very strong bones, with widely forked fin In the perch and bass the tail is stout, composed largely of flesh, the supporting vertebræ relatively small and spread out fan-fashion behind Neither mackerels nor perch nor any of their near allies ever have more than five soft rays in the ventral fins, and the persistence of this number throughout the *Percomorphi*, *Squamipinnes*, *Pharyngognathi*, and spiny fishes generally must be attributed to inheritance from the primitive perch-like or mackerel-like forms In almost all the groups to be considered in this work, after the *Berycoidea* the ventral rays are I, 5, or else fewer through degeneration, never more In the central or primitive members of most of these groups there are twenty-four vertebræ, the number increased in certain forms, probably through repetitive degeneration

The True Mackerels· Scombridæ —We may first consider the great central family of *Scombridæ*, or true mackerels, distinguished among related families by their swift forms, smooth scales, metallic coloration, and technically by the presence of a number of detached finlets behind the dorsal and anal fins The cut of the mouth is peculiar, the spines in the fins are feeble, the muscular system is extremely strong, the flesh oily, and the air-bladder reduced in size or altogether wanting As in most swift-swimming fishes and fishes of pelagic habit, the vertebræ are numerous and relatively small, an arrangement which promotes flexibility of body. It is not likely that this group is the most primitive of the scombroid fishes In some respects the *Stromateidæ* stand nearer the primitive stock The true mackerels, however, furnish the most convenient point of departure in reviewing the great group

In the genus of true mackerels, *Scomber*, the dorsal fins are well separated, the first being rather short, and the scales of the shoulders are not modified to form a corselet There are numerous species, two of them of general interest. The common mackerel, *Scomber scombrus*, is one of the best known of food-fishes It is probably confined to the Atlantic, where on both shores it runs in vast schools, the movements varying greatly from season to season, the preference being for cool waters The female mackerel produces about 500,000 eggs each year, according to Professor Goode These are very minute and each is provided with an oil-globule, which causes it to float on the surface About 400,000 barrels of mackerel are salted yearly by the mackerel fleet of Massachusetts Single schools of mackerel, estimated to contain a million barrels, have been recorded Captain Harding describes such a school

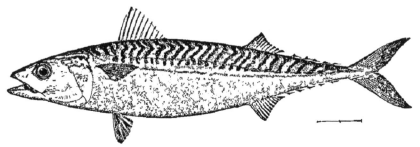

FIG 375 —Mackerel, *Scomber scombrus* L New York

as "a windrow of fish half a mile wide and twenty miles long"

Professor Goode writes

"Upon the abundance of mackerel depends the welfare of many thousands of the citizens of Massachusetts and Maine The success of the mackerel-fishery is much more uncertain than that of the cod-fishery, for instance, for the supply of cod is quite uniform from year to year The prospects of each season are eagerly discussed from week to week in thousands of little circles along the coast, and are chronicled by the local press The story of each successful trip is passed from mouth to mouth, and is a matter of general congratulation in each fishing community A review of the results of the American mackerel-fishery, and of the movements of the fish in each part of the season, would be an important contribution to the literature of the American fisheries

"The mackerel-fishery is peculiarly American, and its history is full of romance. There are no finer vessels afloat than the

American mackerel-schooners—yachts of great speed and unsurpassed for seaworthiness The modern instruments of capture are marvels of inventive skill, and require the highest degree of energy and intelligence on the part of the fishermen The crews of the mackerel-schooners are still for the most part Americans of the old colonial stock, although the cod and halibut fisheries are to a great extent given up to foreigners.

"When the mackerel is caught, trout, bass, and sheepshead cannot vanquish him in a gastronomic tournament. In Holland, to be sure, the mackerel is not prized, and is accused of tasting like rancid fish-oil, and in England, even, they are usually lean and dry, like the wretched skeletons which are brought to market in April and May by the southern fleet, which goes forth in the early spring from Massachusetts to intercept the schools as they approach the coasts of Carolina and Virginia They are not worthy of the name of mackerel *Scomber Scombrus* is not properly in season until the spawning time is over, when the schools begin to feed at the surface in the Gulf of Maine and the 'North Bay'

"Just from the water, fat enough to broil in its own drippings, or slightly corned in strong brine, caught at night and eaten in the morning, a mackerel or a bluefish is unsurpassable A well-cured autumn mackerel is perhaps the finest of all salted fish, but in these days of wholesale capture by the purse-seine, hasty dressing and careless handling, it is very difficult to obtain a sweet and sound salt mackerel Salt mackerel may be boiled as well as broiled, and a fresh mackerel may be cooked in the same manner Americans will usually prefer to do without the sauce of fennel and gooseberry which transatlantic cooks recommend Fresh and salt, fat and lean, new or stale, mackerel are consumed by Americans in immense quantities, as the statistics show, and whatever their state, always find ready sale "

Smaller, less important, less useful, but far more widely distributed is the chub-mackerel, or thimble-eyed mackerel, *Scomber japonicus* (Houttuyn, 178ᴣ), usually known by the later name of *Scomber colias* (Gmelin, 1788) In this species the air-bladder (absent in the common mackerel) is moderately developed. It very much resembles the true mackerel, but is of smaller size, less excellence as a food-fish, and keeps nearer to the shore. It may be usually distinguished by the presence of vague, dull-gray spots on the sides, where the true mackerel is lustrous silvery

This fish is common in the Mediterranean, along our Atlantic coast, on the coast of California, and everywhere in Japan

Scomber antarcticus is the familiar mackerel of Australia. *Scomber loo*, silvery, with round black spots, is the common mackerel of the South Seas, locally known as *Ga*

Scomber priscus is a fossil mackerel from the Eocene

Auxis thazard, the frigate mackerel, has the scales of the shoulders enlarged and somewhat coalescent, forming what is called a corselet. The species ranges widely through the seas of the world in great numbers, but very erratic, sometimes myriads reaching our Eastern coast, then none seen for years It is more constant in its visits to Japan and Hawaii Fossil species of *Auxis* are found in the Miocene

The genus *Gymnosarda* has the corselet as in *Auxis*, but the first dorsal fin is long, extending backward to the base of the second Its two species, *Gymnosarda pelamis*, the Oceanic bonito, and *Gymnosarda alleterata*, the little tunny, are found in all warm seas, being especially abundant in the Mediterranean, about Hawaii and Japan These are plump fish of moderate size, with very red and very oily flesh

Closely related to these is the great tunny, or Tuna (*Thunnus thynnus*) found in all warm seas and reaching at times a weight of 1500 pounds These enormous fishes are much valued by anglers, a popular "Tuna Club' devoted to the sport of catching them with a hook having its headquarters at Avalon, on Santa Catalina Island in California They are good food, although the flesh of the large ones is very oily. The name horse-mackerel is often given to these monsters on the New England coast In California, the Spanish name of tuna has become current among fisherman

Very similar to the tuna, but much smaller, is the Albacore (*Germo alalonga*) This reaches a weight of fifteen to thirty pounds, and is known by its very long, almost ribbon-like pectoral fins This species is common in the Mediterranean, and

about the Santa Barbara Islands, where it runs in great schools
in March   The flesh of the albacore is of little value, unless,
as in Japan, it is eaten raw   The Japanese (*Germo macropterus*)
is another large albacore, having the finlets bright yellow   It is
found also at Hawaii and in Southern California.

The bonito (*Sarda sarda*) wanders far throughout the Atlantic, abounding on our Atlantic coast as in the Mediterranean,
coming inshore in summer to spawn or feed   Its flesh is red
and not very delicate, though it may be reckoned as a fair food-

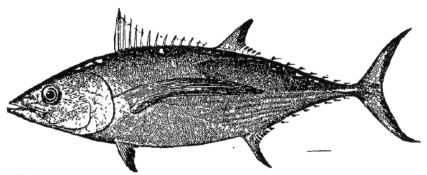

Fig 376 —The Long-fin Albacore, *Germo alalunga* (Gmelin).   Gulf Stream

fish   It is often served under the name of "Spanish mackerel"
to the injury of the reputation of the better fish

Professor Goode writes

"One of these fishes is a marvel of beauty and strength
Every line in its contour is suggestive of swift motion   The
head is shaped like a minie bullet, the jaws fit together so
tightly that a knife-edge could scarcely pass between, the eyes
are hard, smooth, their surfaces on a perfect level with the
adjoining surfaces   The shoulders are heavy and strong, the
contours of the powerful masses of muscle gently and evenly
merging into the straighter lines in which the contour of the
body slopes back to the tail   The dorsal fin is placed in a
groove into which it is received, like the blade of a clasp-knife
in its handle   The pectoral and ventral fins also fit into depres-
sions in the sides of the fish   Above and below, on the posterior third of the body, are placed the little finlets, each a little
rudder with independent motions of its own, by which the
course of the fish may be readily steered   The tail itself is a

crescent-shaped oar, without flesh, almost without scales, composed of bundles of rays flexible, yet almost as hard as ivory. A single sweep of this powerful oar doubtless suffices to propel the bonito a hundred yards, for the polished surfaces of its body can offer little resistance to the water I have seen a common dolphin swimming round and round a steamship, advancing at the rate of twelve knots an hour, the effort being hardly perceptible The wild duck is said to fly seventy miles in an hour Who can calculate the speed of the bonito? It might be done by the aid of the electrical contrivances by which is calculated the initial velocity of a projectile The bonitoes in our sounds to-day may have been passing Cape Colony or the Land of Fire day before yesterday "

Another bonito, *Sarda chilensis*, is common in California, in Chile, and in Japan This species has fewer dorsal spines than the bonito of the Atlantic, but the same size, coloration, and flesh Both are blue, with undulating black stripes along the side of the back

The genus *Scomberomorus* includes mackerels slenderer in form, with larger teeth, no corselet, and the flesh comparatively pale and free from oil

Scomberomorus maculatus, the Spanish mackerel of the West Indies, is one of the noblest of food-fishes Its biography

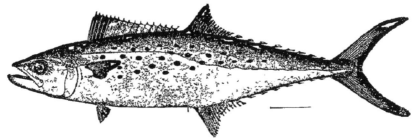

Fig 877 —The Spanish Mackerel, *Scombcromorus maculatus* (Mitchill) New York

was written by Mitchill almost a century ago in these words:

"A fine and beautiful fish, comes in July "

Goode thus writes of it

"The Spanish mackerel is surely one of the most graceful

of fishes It appeals as scarcely any other can to our love of beauty, when we look upon it, as shown in Kilbourn's well-known painting, darting like an arrow just shot from the bow, its burnished sides, silver flecked with gold, thrown into bold relief by the cool green background of the rippled sea, the transparent grays, opalescent whites, and glossy blacks of its trembling fins enhance the metallic splendor of its body, until it seems to rival the most brilliant of tropical birds Kilbourn made copies of his large painting on the pearly linings of sea-shells and produced some wonderful effects by allowing the natural luster of the mother-of-pearl to show through his transparent pigments and simulate the brilliancy of the life-inspired hues of the quivering, darting sea-sprite, whose charms even his potent brush could not properly depict

"It is a lover of the sun, a fish of tropical nature, which comes to us only in midsummer, and which disappears with the approach of cold, to some region not yet explored by ichthyologists It is doubtless very familiar in winter to the inhabitants of some region adjacent to the waters of the Caribbean or the tropical Atlantic, but until this place shall have been discovered it is more satisfactory to suppose that with the bluefish and the mackerel it inhabits that hypothetical winter resort to which we send the migratory fishes whose habits we do not understand—the middle strata of the ocean, the floating beds of Sargassum, which drift hither and thither under the alternate promptings of the Gulf-stream currents and the winter winds "

The Spanish mackerel swims at the surface in moderate schools and is caught in abundance from Cape May southward Its white flesh is most delicious, when properly grilled, and Spanish mackerel, like pampano, should be cooked in no other way

A very similar species, *Scomberomorus sierra*, occurs on the west coast of Mexico For some reason it is little valued as food by the Mexicans In California, the Monterey Spanish mackerel (*Scomberomorus concolor*) is equally excellent as a food-fish This fish lacks the spots characteristic of most of its relatives It was first found in the Bay of Monterey, especially at Santa Cruz and Soquel, in abundance in the autumn of 1879 and 1880 It has not, so far as is known, been seen since, nor is the species recorded from any other coast

The true Spanish mackerel has round, bronze-black spots upon its sides Almost exactly like it in appearance is the pintado, or sierra (*Scomberomorus regalis*), but in this species the spots are oblong in form The pintado abounds in the West Indies Its flesh is less delicate than that of the more true Spanish mackerel The name *sierra*, saw, commonly applied to these fishes by Spanish-speaking people, has been corrupted into *cero* in some books on angling

Still other Spanish mackerel of several species occur on the coasts of India, Chile, and Japan

The great kingfish, or cavalla (*Scomberomorus cavalla*), is a huge Spanish mackerel of Cuba and the West Indies, reaching a weight of 100 pounds It is dark iron-gray in color, one of the best of food-fishes, and is unspotted, and its firm, rich flesh resembles that of the barracuda

Still larger is the great guahu, or peto, an immense sharp-nosed, swift-swimming mackerel found in the East and West Indies, as well as in Polynesia, reaching a length of six feet and a weight of more than a hundred pounds Its large knife-like teeth are serrated on the edge and the color is almost black *Acanthocybium solandri* is the species found in Hawaii and Japan The American *Acanthocybium petus*, occasionally also taken in the Mediterranean, may be the same species

Fossil Spanish mackerels, tunnies, and albacores, as well as representatives of related genera now extinct, abound in the Eocene and Miocene, especially in northern Italy Among them are *Scomber antiquus* from the Miocene, *Scombrinus macropomus* from the Eocene London clays, much like *Scomber*, but with stronger teeth, *Sphyrænodus priscus* from the same deposits, the teeth still larger, *Scombramphodon crossidens*, from the same deposits, also with strong teeth, like those of *Scomberomorus*. *Scomberomorus* is the best represented of all the genera as fossil, *Scomberomorus speciosus* and numerous other species occurring in the Eocene A fossil species of *Germo*, *G lanceolatus*, occurs at Monte Bolca in Eocene rocks. Another tunny, with very small teeth is *Eothynnus salmonens,* from the lower Eocene near London Several other tunny-like fishes occur in the lower Tertiary

The Escolars: Gempylidæ.—More predaceous than the mackerels and tunnies are the pelagic mackerels, *Gempylidæ*, known as *escolars* ("scholars"), with the body almost band-shaped and the teeth very large and sharp Some of these, from the ocean depths, are violet-black in color, those near the surface being silvery *Escolar violaceus* lives in the abysses of the Gulf Stream *Ruvettus pretiosus*, the black escolar, lives in more moderate depths and is often taken in Cuba, Madeira, Hawaii, and Japan It is a very large fish, black, with very rough scales The flesh is white, soft, and full of oil, sometimes rated very high, and at other times too rank to be edible The name *escolar* means *scholar* in Spanish, but its root meaning, as applied to this fish, comes from a word meaning *to scour*, in allusion to the very rough scales

Promethichthys prometheus, the rabbit-fish, or conejo, so-called from its wariness, is caught in the same regions, being especially common about Madeira and Hawaii *Gempylus serpens*, the snake-mackerel, is a still slenderer and more voracious fish of the open seas *Thyrsites atun* is the Australian "barracuda," a valued food-fish, voracious and predaceous

Scabbard- and Cutlass-fishes. Lepidopidæ and Trichiuridæ. — The family of *Lepidopidæ*, or scabbard-fishes, includes degenerate mackerels, band-shaped, with continuous dorsal fin, and the long jaws armed with very small teeth These are found in the open sea, *Lepidopus caudatus* being the most common. This species reaches a length of five or six feet and comes to different coasts occasionally to deposit its spawn. It lives in warm water and is at once chilled by the least cold , hence the name of frostfish occasionally applied to it Several species of *Lepidopus* are fossil in the later Tertiary *Lepidopus glarisianus* occurs in the Swiss Oligocene, and with it *Thyrsitocephalus alpinus*, which approaches more nearly to the *Gempylidæ*

Still more degenerate are the *Trichiuridæ*, or cutlass-fishes, in which the caudal fin is wanting, the tail ending in a hair-like filament The species are bright silvery in color, very slender, and very voracious, reaching a length of three to five feet.

Trichiurus lepturus is rather common on our Atlantic coast. The names hairfish and silver-eel, among others, are often given to it *Trichiurus japonicus*, a very similar species, is common

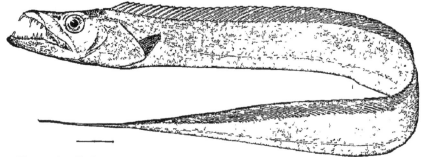

FIG 378.—Cutlass-fish, *Trichiurus lepturus* Linnæus St Augustine, Fla

in Japan, and other species inhabit the tropical seas *Trichiurichthys*, a fossil genus with well-developed scales, precedes *Trichiurus* in the Miocene

The Palæorhynchidæ.—The extinct family of *Palæorhynchidæ* is found from the Eocene to the Oligocene It contains very

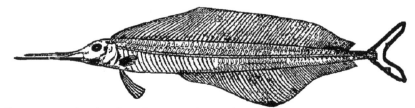

FIG 379 —*Palæorhynchus glarisianus* Blainville Oligocene (After Woodward)

long and slender fishes, with long jaws and small teeth, the dorsal fin long and continuous The species resembles the *Escolar* on the one hand and the sailfishes on the other, and they may prove to be ancestral to the *Istiophoridæ Hemirhynchus deshayesi* with the upper jaw twice as long as the lower, sword-like, occurs in the Eocene at Paris, *Palæorhynchum glarisianum*, with the jaws both elongate, the lower longest, is in the Oligocene of Glarus. Several other species of both genera are recorded

The Sailfishes: Istiophoridæ.—Remotely allied to the cutlass-fishes and still nearer to the *Palæorhynchidæ* is the family of sailfishes, *Istiophoridæ*, having the upper jaw prolonged into

a sword made of consolidated bones. The teeth are very feeble
and the ventral fins reduced to two or three rays. The species
are few in number, of large size, and very brilliant metallic
coloration, inhabiting the warm seas, moving northward in
summer They are excellent as food, similar to the swordfish
in this as in many other respects The species are not well
known, being too large for museum purposes, and no one having
critically studied them in the field *Istiophorus* has the dorsal
fin very high, like a great sail, and undivided, *Istiophorus nigricans* is rather common about the Florida Keys, where it
reaches a length of six feet Its great sail, blue with black
spots, is a very striking object Closely related to this is
Istiophorus orientalis of Japan and other less known species
of the East Indies

Tetrapturus, the spearfish, has the dorsal fin low and divided
into two parts Its species are taken in most warm seas,
Tetrapturus imperator throughout the Atlantic, *Tetrapturus am-
plus* in Cuba, *Tetrapturus mitsukurii* in Japan and in Southern
California These much resemble swordfish in form and habits,
and they have been known to strike boats in the same way

Fossil *Istiophoridæ* are known only from fragments of the
snout, in Europe and America, referred provisionally to *Istiophorus* The genus *Xiphiorhynchus*, fossil swordfishes from the
Eocene, known from the skull only, may be referred to this
family, as minute teeth are present in the jaws *Xiphiorhynchus priscus* is found in the London Eocene

The Swordfishes: Xiphiidæ. — The family of swordfishes,
Xiphiidæ, consists of a single species, *Xiphias gladius*, of world-

Fig 380 —Young Swordfish, *Xiphias gladius* (Linnæus)   (After Lutken)

wide distribution in the warm seas The snout in the swordfish is still longer, more perfectly consolidated, and a still more
effective weapon of attack The teeth are wholly wanting,
and there are no ventral fins, while the second of the two fins
on the back is reduced to a slight finlet

The swordfish follows the schools of mackerel to the New England coasts "Where you see swordfish, you may know that mackerel are about," Goode quotes from an old fisherman The swordfish swims near the surface, allowing its dorsal fin to appear, as also the upper lobe of the caudal It often leaps out of the water, and none of all the fishes of the sea can swim more swiftly

"The pointed head," says Goode, "the fins of the back and abdomen snugly fitting into grooves, the absence of ventrals, the long, lithe, muscular body, sloping slowly to the tail, fit

Fig 381 —Swordfish, *Xiphias gladius* (Linnæus)   (After Day)

it for the most rapid and forcible movement through the water Prof Richard Owen, testifying in an England court in regard to its power, said:

"'It strikes with the accumulated force of fifteen double-handed hammers. Its velocity is equal to that of a swivel-shot, and is as dangerous in its effects as a heavy artillery projectile '

"Many very curious instances are on record of the encounters of this fish with other fishes, or of their attacks upon ships What can be the inducement for it to attack objects so much larger than itself it is hard to surmise

"It surely seems as if a temporary insanity sometimes takes possession of the fish It is not strange that, when harpooned, it should retaliate by attacking its assailant An old swordfish fisherman told Mr. Blackford that his vessel had been struck twenty times There are, however, many instances of entirely unprovoked assault on vessels at sea Many of these are recounted in a later portion of this memoir Their movements when feeding are discussed below, as well as their alleged peculiarities of movement during the breeding season

"It ıs the universal testımony of our fishermen that two are never seen swımmıng close together. Capt Ashby says that they are always dıstant from each other at least thırty or forty feet

"The pugnacıty of the swordfish has become a byword Wıthout any specıal effort on my part numerous ınstances of theır attacks upon vessels have ın the last ten years found theır way ınto the pıgeon-hole labeled 'Swordfish '''

Swordfishes are common on both shores of the Atlantıc wherever mackerel run They do not breed on our shores, but probably do so ın the Medıterranean and other warm seas. They are rare off the Calıfornıa coast, but five records exıstıng (Anacapa, Santa Barbara, Santa Catalına, San Dıego, off Cerros Island) The wrıter has seen two large ındıvıduals ın the market of Yokohama, but ıt ıs scarcely known ın Japan   As a food-fish, the swordfish ıs one of the best, ıts dark-colored oıly flesh, though a lıttle coarse, makıng most excellent steaks. Its average weıght on our coast ıs about 300 pounds, the maxımum 625

The swordfish undergoes great change ın the process of development, the very young havıng the head armed wıth rough spınes and ın nowıse resemblıng the adult

Fossıl swordfishes are unknown, or perhaps cannot be dıstınguıshed from remaıns of *Istıophorıdæ*.

CHAPTER XXXII

CAVALLAS AND PAMPANOS

THE **Pampanos: Carangidæ** —We next take up the great family of Pampanos, *Carangidæ*, distinguished from the *Scombridæ* as a whole by the shorter, deeper body, the fewer and larger vertebræ, and by the loss of the provision for swift movement in the open sea characteristic of the mackerels and their immediate allies. A simple mark of the *Carangidæ* is the presence of two separate spines in front of the anal fin. These spines are joined to the fin in the young. All of the species undergo considerable changes with age, and almost all are silvery in color with metallic blue on the back.

Most like the true mackerel are the "leather-jackets," or "runners," forming the genera *Scomberoides* and *Oligoplites*. *Scomberoides* of the Old World has the body scaly, long, slender, and fitted for swift motion, *Scomberoides sancti-petri* is a widely diffused species, and others are found in Polynesia. In the New World genus *Oligoplites* the scales are reduced to linear ridges imbedded in the skin at different angles. *Oligoplites saurus* is a common dry and bony fish abounding in the West Indies and ranging north in summer to Cape Cod.

Naucrates ductor, the pilotfish, or romero, inhabits the open sea, being taken—everywhere rarely—in Europe, the West Indies, Hawaii, and Japan. It is marked by six black cross-bands. Its tail has a keel, and it reaches a length of about two feet. In its development it undergoes considerable change, its first dorsal fin being finally reduced to disconnected spines.

The amber-fishes, forming the genus *Seriola*, are rather robust fishes, with the anal fin much shorter than the soft dorsal. The sides of the tail have a low, smooth keel. From a yellow streak obliquely across the head in some species they receive their Spanish name of coronado. The species are

numerous, found in all warm seas, of fair quality as food, and
range in length from two to six feet

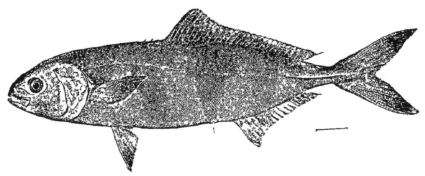

Fig 382 —Pilot-fish, *Naucrates ductor* (Linnæus)   New Bedford, Mass

Seriola dorsalis is the noted yellow-tail of California, valued
by anglers for its game qualities   It comes to the Santa Bar-

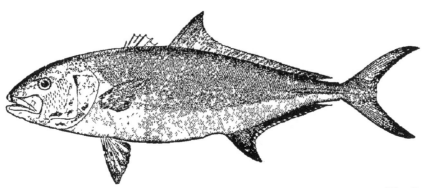

Fig 383 —Amber-fish, *Seriola lalandi* (Cuv & Val)   Family *Carangidæ*.   Wood's
Hole

bara Islands in early summer   *Seriola zonata* is the rudder-
fish, or shark's pilot, common on our New England coast   The
banded young, abundant off Cape Cod, lose their marks with
age. *Seriola hippos* is the "samson-fish" of Australia   *Seriola lalandi* is the great amber-fish of the West Indies, occasionally venturing farther northward, and *Seriola dumerili*
the amber-jack, or coronado, of the Mediterranean   The deep-
bodied medregal (*Seriola fasciata*) is also taken in the West
Indies, as is also the high-finned *Seriola rivoliana*   Species
very similar to these occur in Hawaii and Japan, where they

are known as *Ao*, or bluefishes   *Seriola lata* is fossil in the mountains of Tuscany

The runner, *Elegatis bipinnulatus*, differs from *Seriola* in having a finlet behind dorsal and anal   It is found in almost all warm seas, ranging north once in a while to Long Island

The mackerel scads (*Decapterus*) have also a finlet, and on the posterior part of the body the lateral line is shielded with bony plates   In size and form these little fishes much resemble small mackerel, and they are much valued as food wherever abundant   *Decapterus punclatus*, known also as cigar-fish and round-robin, frequently visits our Atlantic coasts from the West Indies, where it is abundant   *Decapterus russelli* is the *Maru-aji*, highly valued in Japan for its abundance, while *Decapterus muroadsi* is the Japanese muroaji

Megalaspis cordyla abounds in the East Indies and Poly-

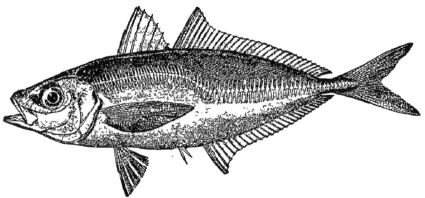

FIG 384 —The Saurel, *Trachurus trachurus* (Linnæus)   Newport, R I

nesia. It has many finlets, and the bony plates on the lateral line are developed to an extraordinary degree

In *Trachurus* the finlets are lost and the bony plates extend the whole length of the lateral line   The species known as saurel and wrongly called horse-mackerel are closely related and some of them very widely distributed

Trachurus trachurus common in Europe, extends to Japan where it is the abundant maaji   *Trachurus mediterraneus* is common in southern Europe and *Trachurus symmetricus* in California   *Trachurus picturatus* of Madeira is much the same as the last named, and there is much question as to the right names and proper limits of all these species.

In *Trachurops* the bony plates are lacking on the anterior half of the body, and there is a peculiar nick and projection on the lower part of the anterior edge of the shoulder-girdle *Trachurops crumenophthalma*, the goggler, or big-eyed scad, ranges widely in the open sea and at Hawaii, as the *Akule*, is the most highly valued because most abundant of the migratory fishes   At Samoa it is equally abundant, the name being here *Atule*   *Trachurops torva* is the meaji, or big-eyed scad, of the Japanese, always abundant

To *Caranx, Carangus,* and a number of related genera, characterized by the bony armature on the narrow caudal peduncle, a host of species may be referred   These fishes, known as cavallas,

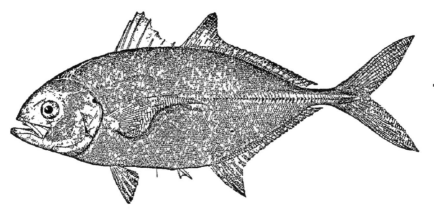

Fig   385 —Yellow Mackerel, *Carangus chrysos* (Mitchill)   Wood's Hole

hard-tails, jacks, etc , are broad-bodied, silvery or metallic black in color, and are found in all warm seas   They usually move from the tropics northward in the fall in search of food and are especially abundant on our Atlantic coast, in Polynesia, and in Japan   About the Oceanic Islands they are resident, these being their chosen spawning-grounds   In Hawaii and Samoa they form a large part of the food-supply, the ulua (*Carangus forsteri*) and the malauli (*Carangus melampygus*) being among the most valuable food-fishes, large in size and excellent in flesh, unsurpassed in fish chowders   Of the American species *Carangus chrysos*, called yellow mackerel, is the most abundant, ranging from Cape

Cod southward. This is an elongate species of moderate size The cavalla, or jiguagua, *Carangus hippos*, known by the black spot on the opercle, with another on the pectoral fin, is a widely distributed species and one of the largest of the tribe Another important food-fish is the horse-eye-jack, or jurel, *Carangus latus*, which is very similar to the species called ulua in the Pacific The black jack, or tiñosa, of Cuba, *Carangus funebris*, is said to be often poisonous This is a very large species, black in color, the sale of which has been long forbidden in the markets of Havana. The young of different species of *Carangus* are often found taking refuge under the disk of jelly-fishes protected by the stinging feelers The species of the genus *Carangus* have well-developed teeth. In the restricted genus of *Caranx* proper, the jaws are toothless. *Caranx speciosus*, golden with dark cross-bands, is a large food-fish of the Pacific. *Citula armata* is another widely distributed species, with some of the dorsal rays produced in long filaments

In *Alectis ciliaris*, the cobbler-fish, or threadfish, the armature of the tail is very slight and each fin has some of its rays drawn out into long threads. In the young these are very much longer than the body, but with age they wear off and grow shorter, while the body becomes more elongate In *Vomer*, *Selene*, and *Chloroscombrus* the bony armature of the tail, feeble in *Alectis*, by degrees entirely disappears

Vomer setipinnis, the so-called moonfish, or jorobado, has the body greatly elevated, compressed, and distorted, while the fins, growing shorter with age, become finally very low *Selene vomer*, the horse-head-fish, or look-down, is similarly but even more distorted The fins, filamentous in the young, grow shorter with age, as in *Vomer* and *Alectis* The skeleton in these fishes is essentially like that of *Carangus*, the only difference lying in the compression and distortion of the bones *Chloroscombrus* contains the casabes, or bumpers, thin, dry, compressed fish, of little value as food, the bony armature of the tail being wholly lost

To the genus *Trachinotus* belong the pampanos, broad-bodied, silvery fishes, toothless when adult, the bodies covered with small scales and with no bony plates

The true pampano, *Trachinotus carolinus*, is one of the

finest of all food-fishes, ranking with the Spanish mackerel and to be cooked in the same way, only by broiling. The flesh is white, firm, and flaky, with a moderate amount of delicate oil. It has no especial interest to the angler and it is not abundant enough to be of great commercial importance, yet few fish bring or deserve to bring higher prices in the markets of the

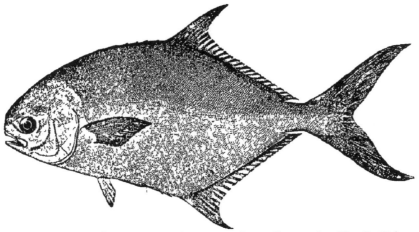

FIG 386 —The Pampano, *Trachinotus carolinus* (Linnæus). Wood's Hole

epicures   The species is most common along our Gulf coast, ranging northward along the Carolinas as far as Cape Cod

Pampano in Spanish means the leaf of the grape, from the broad body of the fish   The spelling "pompano" should therefore be discouraged

The other pampanos, of which there are several in tropical America and Asia, are little esteemed, the flesh being dry and relatively flavorless   *Trachinotus palometa*, the gafftopsail pampano, has very high fins and its sides have four black bands like the marks of a grill   The round pampano, *Trachinotus falcatus*, is common southward, as is also the great pampano, *Trachinotus goodei*, which reaches a length of three feet   *Trachinotus ovatus*, a large deep-bodied pampano, is common in Polynesia and the East Indies   No pampanos are found in Europe, but a related genus, *Lichia*, contains species which much resemble them, but in which the body is more elongate and the mouth larger

Numerous fossils are referred to the *Carangidæ* with more

or less certainty *Aipichthys pretiosus* and other species occur
in the Cretaceous These are deep-bodied fishes resembling
Seriola, having the falcate dorsal twice as long as the anal and
the ventral ridge with thickened scales *Vomeropsis* (*longispina
elongata*, etc), also from the Eocene, with rounded caudal,
the anterior dorsal rays greatly elongate, and the supraoccipital
crest highly developed, probably constitutes with it a distinct
family, *Vomeropsidæ* Several species referable to *Carangus*
are found in the Miocene *Archæus glarisianus*, resembling
Carangus, but without scales so far as known, is found in the
Oligocene of Glarus, *Seriola prisca* and other species of *Seriola*
occur in the Eocene, *Carangopsis brevis*, etc , allied to *Caranx*,
but with the lateral line unarmed, is recorded from the Eocene
of France and Italy

Ductor leptosomus from the Eocene of Monte Bolca
resembles *Naucrates; Trachinotus tenuiceps* is recorded from
Monte Bolca, and a species of uncertain relationship, called
Pseudovomer minutus, with sixteen caudal vertebræ is taken
from the Miocene of Licata

The Papagallos: Nematistiidæ.—Very close to the *Carangidæ*,
and especially to the genus *Seriola*, is the small family of
Nematistiidæ, containing the papagallo, *Nematistius pectoralis*
of the west coast of Mexico This large and beautiful fish has
the general appearance of an amber-fish, but the dorsal spines
are produced in long filaments The chief character of the
family is found in the excessive division of the rays of the
pectoral fins

The Bluefishes: Cheilodipteridæ.—Allied to the *Carangidæ* is
the family of bluefishes (*Cheilodipteridæ*, or *Pomatomidæ*) The
single species *Cheilodipterus saltatrix*, or *Pomatomus saltatrix*,
known as the bluefish, is a large, swift, extremely voracious fish,
common throughout most of the warmer parts of the Atlantic,
but very irregularly distributed on the various coasts Its
distribution is doubtless related to its food It is more abundant on our Eastern coast than anywhere else, and its chief
food here is the menhaden. The bluefish differs from the
Carangidæ mainly in its larger scales, and in a slight serration
of the bones of the head Its flesh is tender and easily torn
As a food-fish, rich, juicy, and delicate, it has few superiors

Its maximum weight is from twelve to twenty pounds, but most of those taken are much smaller. It is one of the most voracious of all fish Concerning this, Professor Baird observes:

"There is no parallel in point of destructiveness to the bluefish among the marine species on our coast, whatever may be the case among some of the carnivorous fish of the South American waters The bluefish has been well likened to an animated chopping-machine the business of which is to cut to pieces and otherwise destroy as many fish as possible in a

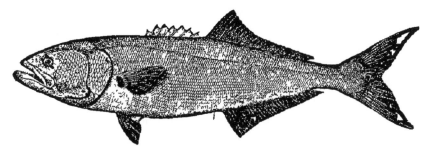

Fig. 387 —Bluefish, *Cheilodipterus saltatrix* (L) New York

given space of time All writers are unanimous in regard to the destructiveness of the bluefish Going in large schools in pursuit of fish not much inferior to themselves in size, they move along like a pack of hungry wolves, destroying everything before them Their trail is marked by fragments of fish and by the stain of blood in the sea, as, where the fish is too large to be swallowed entire, the hinder portion will be bitten off and the anterior part allowed to float away or sink It is even maintained with great earnestness that such is the gluttony of the fish, that when the stomach becomes full the contents are disgorged and then again filled It is certain that it kills many more fish than it requires for its own support.

"The youngest fish, equally with the older, perform this function of destruction, and although they occasionally devour crabs, worms, etc , the bulk of their sustenance throughout the greater part of the year is derived from other fish Nothing is more common than to find a small bluefish of six or eight inches in length under a school of minnows making continual dashes and captures among them The stomachs of the bluefish of all sizes, with rare exceptions, are found loaded with the other fish, sometimes to the number of thirty or forty, either entire or in fragments

"As already referred to, it must also be borne in mind that it is not merely the small fry that are thus devoured, and which it is expected will fall a prey to other animals, but that the food of the bluefish consists very largely of individuals which have already passed a large percentage of the chances against their reaching maturity, many of them, indeed, having arrived at the period of spawning To make the case more clear, let us realize for a moment the number of bluefish that exist on our coast in the summer season. As far as I can ascertain by the statistics obtained at the fishing-stations on the New England coast, as also from the records of the New York markets, kindly furnished by Middleton & Carman, of the Fulton Market, the capture of bluefish from New Jersey to Monomoy during the season amounts to no less than one million individuals, averaging five or six pounds each Those, however, who have seen the bluefish in his native waters and realized the immense numbers there existing will be quite willing to admit that probably not one fish in a thousand is ever taken by man If, therefore, we have an actual capture of one million, we may allow one thousand millions as occurring in the extent of our coasts referred to, even neglecting the smaller ones, which, perhaps, should also be taken into account

"An allowance of ten fish per day to each bluefish is not excessive, according to the testimony elicited from the fishermen and substantiated by the stomachs of those examined; this gives ten thousand millions of fish destroyed per day And as the period of the stay of the bluefish on the New England coast is at least one hundred and twenty days, we have in round numbers twelve hundred million millions of fish devoured in the course of a season Again, if each bluefish, averaging five pounds, devours or destroys even half its own weight of other fish per day (and I am not sure that the estimate of some witnesses of twice this weight is not more nearly correct), we will have, during the same period, a daily loss of twenty-five hundred million pounds, equal to three hundred thousand millions for the season.

"This estimate applies to three or four year old fish of at least three to five pounds in weight We must, however, allow for those of smaller size, and a hundred-fold or more in number, all engaged simultaneously in the butchery referred to.

"We can scarcely conceive of a number so vast; and however much we may diminish, within reason, the estimate of the number of bluefish and the average of their capture, there still remains an appalling aggregate of destruction While the smallest bluefish feed upon the diminutive fry, those of which we have taken account capture fish of large size, many of them, if not capable of reproduction, being within at least one or two years of that period

"It is estimated by very good authority that of the spawn deposited by any fish at a given time not more than 30 per cent are hatched, and that less than 10 per cent. attain an age when they are able to take care of themselves. As their age increases the chances of reaching maturity become greater and greater It is among the small residuum of this class that the agency of the bluefish is exercised and whatever reasonable reduction may be made in our estimate, we cannot doubt that they exert a material influence

"The rate of growth of the bluefish is also an evidence of the immense amount of food they must consume The young fish which first appear along the shores of Vineyard Sound, about the middle of August, are about five inches in length By the beginning of September, however, they have reached six or seven inches, and on their reappearance in the second year they measure about twelve or fifteen inches After this they increase in a still more rapid ratio A fish which passes eastward from Vineyard Sound in the spring weighing five pounds is represented, according to the general impression, by the ten- to fifteen-pound fish of the autumn If this be the fact, the fish of three or four pounds which pass along the coast of North Carolina in March return to it in October weighing ten to fifteen pounds

"As already explained, the relationship of these fish to the other inhabitants of the sea is that of an unmitigated butcher, and it is able to contend successfully with any other species not superior to itself in size It is not known whether an entire school ever unite in an attack upon a particular object of prey, as is said to be the case with the ferocious fishes of the South American rivers, should they do so, no animal, however large, could withstand their onslaught

"They appear to eat anything that swims of suitable size—fish of all kinds, but perhaps more especially the menhaden, which they seem to follow along the coast, and which they atack with such ferocity as to drive them on the shore, where

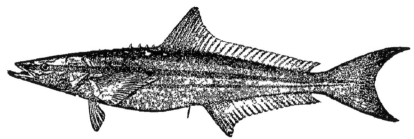

Fig 388 —Sergeant-fish, *Rachycentron canadum* (Linnæus)   Virginia

they are sometimes piled up in windrows to the depth of a foot or more "

The Sergeant-fishes: Rachycentridæ. — The *Rachycentridæ*, or sergeant-fishes, are large, strong, swift, voracious shore fishes, with large mouths and small teeth, ranging northward from the warm seas   The dorsal spines are short and stout, separate from the fin, and the body is almost cylindrical, somewhat like that of the pike

Rachycentron canadum, called cobia, crab-eater, snooks, or sergeant-fish, reaches a length of about five feet   The last name is supposed to allude to the black stripe along its side, like the stripe on a sergeant's trousers   It is rather common in summer along our Atlantic coast as far as Cape Cod, especially in Chesapeake Bay   *Rachycention pondicerrianum*, equally voracious, extends its summer depredations as far as Japan The more familiar name for these fishes, *Elacate*, is of later date than *Rachycentron*

Mr. Prime thus speaks of the crab-eater as a game-fish·

"In shape he may be roughly likened to the great northern pike, with a similar head, flattened on the forehead   He is dark green on the back, growing lighter on the sides, but the distinguishing characteristic is a broad, dark collar over the neck, from which two black stripes or straps, parting on the shoulders, extend, one on each side, to the tail He looks as if harnessed with a pair of traces, and his behavior on a fly-rod is that of a wild horse The first one that I struck, in the brackish water of Hillsborough River at Tampa, gave me a hitherto unknown sensation The tremendous rush was not unfamiliar, but when the fierce fellow took the top of the water and went along lashing it with his tail, swift as a bullet, then descended, and with a short, sharp, electric shock left the line to come home free, I was for an instant confounded It was all over in ten seconds Nearly every fish that I struck after this behaved in the same way, and after I had got 'the hang of them' I took a great many "

The Butter-fishes: Stromateidæ. — The butter-fishes (*Stromateidæ*) form a large group of small fishes with short, compressed bodies, smooth scales, feeble spines, the vertebræ in increased number and especially characterized by the presence of a series of tooth-like processes in the œsophagus behind the pharyngeals. The ventral fins present in the young are often lost in the process of development

According to Mr Regan, the pelvic bones are very loosely attached to the shoulder-girdle as in the extinct genera *Platycormus* and *Homosoma*. This is perhaps a primitive feature, indicating the line of descent of these fishes from berycoid forms

We unite with the *Stromateidæ* the groups or families of *Centrolophidæ* and *Nomeidæ*, knowing no characters by which to separate them

Stromateus fiatola, the fiatola of the Italian fishermen, is an excellent food-fish of the Mediterranean *Poronotus triacanthus*, the harvest-fish, or dollar-fish, of our Atlantic coast, is a common little silvery fish six to ten inches, as bright and almost as round as a dollar Its tender oily flesh has an excellent flavor Very similar to it is the poppy-fish (*Palometa simillima*) of the sandy shores of California, miscalled the "California pampano," valued by the San Francisco epicure, who pays large prices for it supposing it to be pampano, although admitting that the pampano in New Orleans has firmer flesh and better flavor. The harvest-fish, *Peprilus paru*, frequently taken on our Atlantic coast, is known by its very high fins

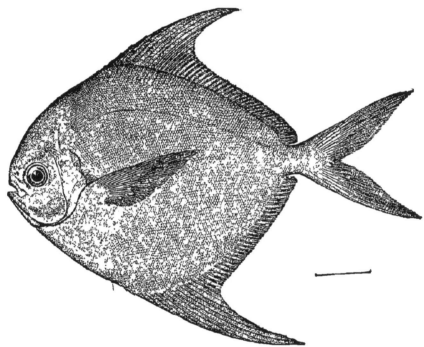

Fig 389 —Harvest-fish, *Peprilus paru* (Linnæus) Virginia

Stromateoides argenteus, a much larger fish than any of these, is a very important species on the coasts of China

Psenopsis anomala takes the place of our butter-fishes in Japan, and much resembles them in appearance as in flavor

To the *Stromateidæ* we also refer the black ruff of Europe, *Centrolophus niger*, an interesting deep-sea fish rarely straying to our coast   Allied to it is the black rudder-fish, *Palinurichthys perciformis*, common on the Massachusetts coast, where it is of some value as a food-fish   A specimen in a live-box once drifted to the coast of Cornwall, where it was taken uninjured, though doubtless hungry   Other species of ruff- and rudder-fish are recorded from various coasts

Allied to the *Stromateidæ* are numerous fossil forms. *Omosoma sachelalmæ* and other species occur in the Cretaceous at Mount Lebanon.   *Platycormus germanus*, with ctenoid scales resembling a berycoid, but with the ventral rays I, 5, occurs in the Upper Cretaceous. Closely related to this is *Berycopsis elegans*, with smoother scales, from the English Chalk.

Gobiomorus gronovii (usually called *Nomeus gronovii*), the Portuguese man-of-war-fish, is a neat little fish about three inches long, common in the Gulf of Mexico and the Gulf Stream, where it hides from its enemies among the poisoned tentacles of the Portuguese man-of-war. Under the Portuguese man-of-war and also in or under large jelly-fishes several other species are found, notably *Carangus medusicola* and *Peprilus paru*. Many small species of *Psenes*, a related genus, also abound in the warm currents from tropical seas.

FIG. 390.— Portuguese Man-of-war Fish, *Gobiomorus gronovii*. Family *Stromateidæ*.

The Rag-fishes: Icosteidæ. — Allied to the butter-fishes are the deep-water *Icosteidæ*, fishes of soft, limp bodies as unresistent as a wet rag, *Icosteus ænigmaticus* of the California coast being known as ragfish. *Schedophilus medusophagus* feeds on medusæ and salpa, living on the surface in the deep seas. Mr. Ogilby thus speaks of a specimen taken in Ireland:

"It was the most delicate adult fish I ever handled; within twenty-four hours after its capture the skin of the belly and the intestines fell off when it was lifted, and it felt in the hand quite soft and boneless." A related species (*S. heathi*) has been lately taken by Dr. Charles H. Gilbert at Monterey in California.

The family of *Acrotidæ* contains a single species of large size. *Acrotus willoughbyi*, allied to *Icosteus*, but without ventral fins and with the vertebræ very numerous. The type, five and one-quarter feet long, was thrown by a storm on the coast of Washington, near the Quinnault agency.

The family of *Zaproridæ* contains also a single large species, *Zaprora silenus*, without ventrals, but scaly and firm in substance   One specimen 2½ feet long was taken at Nanaimo on Vancouver Island and a smaller one at Victoria

The Pomfrets: Bramidæ. — The *Bramidæ* are broad-bodied fishes of the open seas, covered with firm adherent scales   The flesh is firm and the skeleton heavy, the hypercoracoid especially much dilated   Of the various species the pomfret, or black bream (*Brama rau*), is the best known and most widely diffused   It reaches a length of two to four feet and is sooty black in color   It is not rare in Europe and has been occasionally taken at Grand Bank off Newfoundland, at the Bermudas, off the coast of Washington, on Santa Catalina Island, and in Japan It is an excellent food-fish, but is seldom seen unless driven ashore by storms

Steinegeria rubescens of the Gulf of Mexico is a little-known deep-sea fish allied to *Brama*, but placed by Jordan and Evermann in a distinct family, *Steinegeriidæ*

Closely related to the *Bramidæ* is the small family of *Pteraclidæ*, silvery fishes with large firm scales, living near the surface in the ocean currents   In these fishes the ventral fins are placed well forward, fairly to be called jugular, and the rays of the dorsal and anal, all inarticulate or spine-like, are excessively prolonged   The species, none of them well known, are referred to four genera—*Pteraclis, Bentenia, Centropholis,* and *Velifer*.   They are occasionally taken in ocean currents, chiefly about Japan and Madeira.

Fossil forms more or less remotely allied to the *Bramidæ* are recorded from the Eocene and Miocene   Among these are *Acanthonemus*, and perhaps *Pseudovomer*

The Dolphins: Coryphænidæ. — The dolphins, or dorados (*Coryphænidæ*), are large, swift sea-fishes, with elongate, compressed bodies, elevated heads, sharp like the cut-water of a boat, and with the caudal fin very strong   The long dorsal fin, elevated like a crest on the head, is without spines   The high forehead characteristic of the dolphin is developed only in the adult male.   The flesh of the dolphin is valued as food

Its colors, golden-blue with deep-blue spots, fade rapidly at death, though the extent of this change has been much exaggerated   Similar changes of color occur at death in most bright-colored fishes, especially in those with thin scales   The common dolphin, or dorado (*Coryphæna hippurus*), is found in all warm

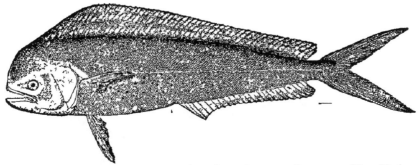

Fig 391 —Dolphin or Dorado, *Coryphæna hippurus* Linnæus   New York

seas swimming near the surface, as usual in predatory fishes, and reaches a length of about six feet   The small dolphin, *Coryphæna equiselis*, rarely exceeds 2½ feet, and is much more rare than the preceding, from which the smaller number of dorsal rays (53 instead of 60) best distinguishes it   Young dolphins of both species are elongate in form, the crest of the head not elevated, the physiognomy thus appearing very different from that of the adult   *Goniognathus coryphænoides* is an extinct dolphin of the Eocene

The name dolphin, belonging properly to a group of small whales or porpoises, the genus *Delphinus*, has been unfortunately used in connection with this very different animal, which bears no resemblance to the mammal of the same name

Other mackerel-like families not closely related to these occur in the warm seas   The *Leiognathidæ* are small, silvery fishes of the East Indies   *Leiognathus argentatus* (*Equula*) is very common in the bays of Japan, a small silvery fish of moderate value as food   *Gazza minuta*, similar, with strong teeth, abounds farther south   *Leiognathus fasciatum* is common in Polynesia.   A fossil species called *Parequula albyi* occurs in the Miocene of Licata

The *Kurtidæ* are small, short-bodied fishes of the Indian seas, with some of the ribs immovably fixed between rings formed by the ossified cover of the air-bladder and with the hypocoracoid obsolete. *Kurtus indicus* is the principal species.

The Menidæ.—Near the *Kurtidæ* we may perhaps place the family of *Menidæ*, of one species, *Mene maculata*, the moon-fish of the open seas of the East Indies and Japan. This is a small fish, about a foot long, with the body very closely compressed, the fins low and the belly, through the extension of the pelvic bone, a good deal more prominent than the back. The ventral

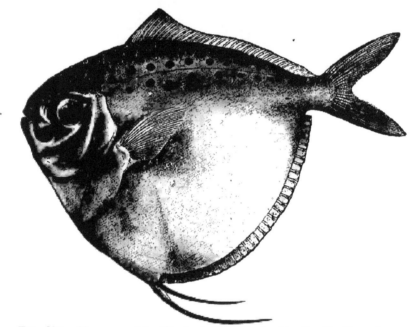

Fig. 392.—*Mene maculata* (Bloch & Schneider). Family Menidæ. Japan.

fins have the usual number of one spine and five soft rays, a character which separates *Mene* widely from *Lampris*, which in some ways seems allied to it.

Another species of *Menidæ* is the extinct *Gasteronemus rhombeus* of the Eocene of Monte Bolca. It has much the same form, with long pubic bones. The very long ventral fins are, however, made of one spine and one or two rays. A second species, *Gasteronemus oblongus*, is recorded from the same rocks.

The Pempheridæ.—The *Pempheridæ*, "deep-water catalufas," or "magifi," are rather small deep-bodied fishes, reddish in color, with very short dorsal, containing a few graduated spines.

and with a very long anal fin. These inhabit tropical seas at moderate depths. *Pempheris* bears a superficial resemblance to

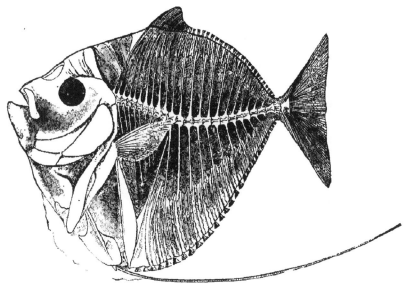

FIG. 393 —*Gasteronemus rhombeus* Agassiz. (After Woodward.) Menidæ.

Bcryx, but, according to Starks, this resemblance is not borne out by the anatomy. *Pempheris mulleri* and *P. poeyi* are found

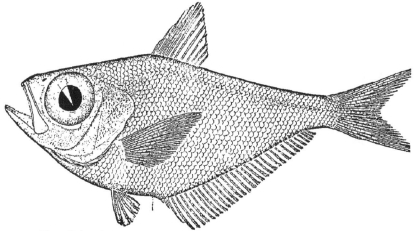

FIG. 394.—Catalufa de lo Alto, *Pempheris mulleri* Poey. Havana.

in the West Indies. *Pempheris otaitensis* and *P. mangula* range through Polynesia.

Very close to the *Pempheridæ* is the small family of *Bathy-clupeidæ*. These are herring-like fishes, much compressed and

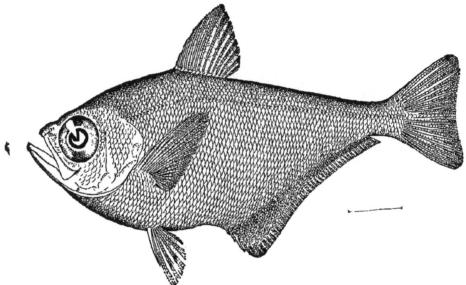

FIG 395 —*Pempheris nyctereutes.* Jordan & Evermann. Giran, Formosa

with a duct to the air-bladder There are but one or two dorsal spines The ventrals are of one spine and five rays as in perch, like fishes, but placed behind the pectoral fins This feature-due to the shortening of the belly, is regarded by Alcock, the discoverer, as a result of degeneration, and the family was

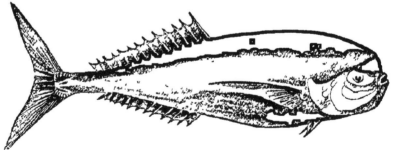

FIG. 396 —The Louvar, *Luvarus imperialis* Rafinesque Family Luvaridæ. (After Day)

placed by him among the herrings The persistent air-duct excludes it from the *Percesoces*, the normally formed ventrals from the *Berycoidei*. If we trust the indications of the skeleton, we must place the family with *Pempheris*, near the scombroid fishes

Luvaridæ.—Another singular family is the group of *Louvars*, *Luvaridæ Luvaris imperialis* The single known species is a large, plump, voracious fish, with the dorsal and anal rays all unbranched, and the scales scurf-life over the smooth skin It is frequently taken in the Mediterranean, and was found on the island of Santa Catalina, California, by Mr C. F. Holden.

The Square-tails: Tetragonuridæ.—The *Tetragonuridæ* are long-bodied fishes of a plump or almost squarish form, covered with hard, firm, very adherent scales *Tetragonurus cuvieri*, the single species, called square-tail, or escolar de natura, is a curious fish, looking as if whittled out of wood, covered with a compact armor of bony scales, and swimming very slowly in deep water It is known from the open Atlantic and Mediterranean and has been once taken at Woods Hole in Massachusetts. According to Mr C T Regan the relations of this eccentric fish are with the *Stromateidæ* and *Bramidæ*, the skeleton being essentially that of *Stromateus*, and Boulenger places both *Tetragonurus* and *Stromateus* among the *Percesoces*

The Crested Band-fishes· Lophotidæ.—The family of *Lophotidæ* consists of a few species of deep-sea fishes, band-shaped, naked, with the dorsal of flexible spines beginning as a high crest on the elevated occiput The first spine is very strong The ventrals are thoracic with the normal number, I, 5, of fin-rays *Lophotes cepedianus*, the crested bandfish, is occasionally taken in the Mediterranean in rather deep water. *Lophotes capellei* is rarely taken in the deep waters of Japan.

It is thought that the *Lophotidæ* may be related to the ribbon-fishes, *Tæniosomi*, but on the whole they seem nearer to the highly modified *Scombroidei*, the *Pteraclidæ* for example.

In a natural arrangement, we should turn from the *Bramidæ* to the *Antigoniidæ* and the *Ilarchidæ*, then passing over the series which leads through *Chætodontidæ* and *Teuthidæ* to the *Plectognaths* It is, however, necessary to include here, alongside the mackerels, though not closely related to them, the parallel series of perch-like fishes, which at the end become also hopelessly entangled, through aberrant forms, with other

series of which the origin and relations are imperfectly understood As the relations of forms cannot be expressed in a linear
series, many pages must intervene before we can take up the
supposed line of development from the Scombroid fishes to
those called *Squamipinnes.*

CHAPTER XXXIII

PERCOIDEA, OR PERCH-LIKE FISHES

PERCOID Fishes.—We may now take up the long series of the *Percoidea*, the fishes built on the type of the perch or bass This is a group of fishes of diverse habits and forms, but on the whole representing better than any other the typical *Acanthopterygian* fish The group is incapable of concise definition, or, in general, of any definition at all, still, most of its members are definitely related to each other and bear in one way or another a resemblance to the typical form, the perch, or more strictly to its marine relatives, the sea-bass, or *Serranidæ* The following analysis gives most of the common characters of the group

Body usually oblong, covered with scales, which are typically ctenoid, not smooth nor spinous, and of moderate size Lateral line typically present and concurrent with the back Head usually compressed laterally and with the cheeks and opercles scaly Mouth various, usually terminal and with lateral cleft, the teeth various, but typically pointed, arranged in bands on the jaws, and in several families on the vomer and palatine bones also, as well as on the pharyngeals, gill-rakers usually sharp, stoutish, armed with teeth, but sometimes short or feeble, lower pharyngeals almost always separate, usually armed with cardiform teeth, third upper pharyngeal moderately enlarged, elongate, not articulated to the cranium, the fourth typically present, gills four, a slit behind the fourth, gill membranes free from the isthmus, and usually not connected with each other, pseudobranchiæ typically well developed Branchiostegals few, usually six or seven No bony stay connecting the suborbital chain to the preopercle Opercular bones all well developed, normal in position, the preopercle typically serrate No cranial spines Dorsal fin

508

variously developed, but always with some spines in front, these typically stiff and pungent, anal fin typically short, usually with three spines, sometimes with a larger number, rarely with none, caudal fin various, usually lunate, pectoral fins well developed, inserted high, ventral fins always present, thoracic, separate, almost always with one spine and five rays, the *Aphredoderidæ* having more, a few *Serranidæ* having fewer. Air-bladder usually present, without air-duct in adult, simple and generally adherent to the walls of the abdomen Stomach cæcal, with pyloric appendages, the intestines short in most species, long in the herbivorous forms Vertebral column well developed, none of the vertebræ especially modified, the number $10 + 14 = 24$, except in certain extratropical and fresh-water forms, which retain primitive higher numbers Shoulder-girdle normally developed, the post-temporal bifurcate attached to the skull, but not coossified with it, none of the epipleural bones attached to the center of the vertebræ, coracoids normal, the hypercoracoid always with a median foramen, the basal bones of the pectoral (actinosts or pterygials) normally developed, three or four in number, hour-glass-shaped, longer than broad, premaxillary forming the border of the mouth usually protractile, bones of the mandible distinct Orbitosphenoid wanting

The most archaic of the perch-like types are apparently some of those of the fresh waters Among these the process of evolution has been less rapid In some groups, as the *Percidæ*, the great variability of species is doubtless due to the recent origin, the characters not being well fixed

The Pirate-perches: Aphredoderidæ. — Among the most remarkable of the living percoid fishes and probably the most primitive of all, showing affinities with the *Salmopercæ*, is the pirate-perch, *Aphredoderus sayanus*, a little fish of the lowland streams of the Mississippi Valley The family of *Aphredoderidæ* agrees with the berycoid fishes in scales and structure of the fins, and Boulenger places it with the Berycidæ Starks has shown, however, that it lacks the orbitosphenoid, and the general osteology is that of the perch-like fishes The dorsal and anal have a few spines The thoracic ventrals have one spine and eight rays There is no adipose fin and probably no duct to the air-bladder. A singular trait is found in the posi-

tion of the vent   In the adult this is in front of the ventral
fins, at the throat   In the young it is behind the ventral fins

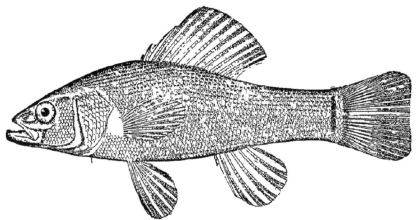

Fig 397 —Pirate Perch, *Aphredoderus sayanus* (Gilliams)   Illinois River

as in ordinary fishes   With age it moves forward by the prolongation of the horizontal part of the intestine or rectum·
The same peculiar position of the vent is found in the berycoid
genus *Paratrachichthys*

In the family *Aphredoderidæ* but one species is known,
Aphredoderus sayanus, the pirate-perch   It reaches a length

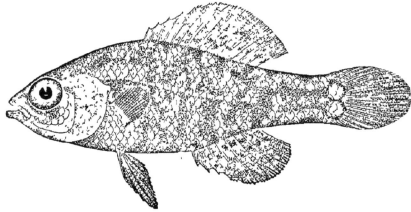

Fig 398.—Everglade Pigmy Perch, *Elassoma everglader* Jordan   Everglades of
Florida

of five inches and lives in sluggish lowland streams with muddy
bottom from New Jersey and Minnesota to Louisiana.   It is

dull green in color and feeds on insects and worms. It has no
economic value, although extremely interesting in its anatomy
and relationship

Whether the *Asineopidæ*, fresh-water fishes of the American
Eocene, and the *Erismatopteridæ*, of the same deposits (see page
450) are related to *Aphredoderus* or to *Percopsis* is still uncertain

The Pigmy Sunfishes: Elassomidæ.—One of the most primitive
groups is that of *Elassomidæ*, or pigmy sunfishes. These are

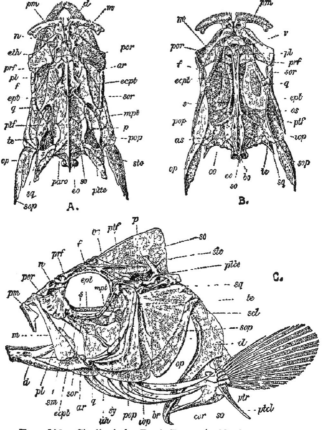

FIG 399 —Skull of the Rock Bass, *Ambloplites rupestris*,

very small fishes, less than two inches long, living in the swamps
of the South, resembling the sunfishes, but with the number of
dorsal spines reduced to from three to five. *Elassoma zonatum*
occurs from southern Illinois to Louisiana. *Elassoma ever-
gladei* abounds in the Everglades of Florida. In both the body

is oblong and compressed, the color is dull green crossed by black bars or blotches

The Sunfishes: Centrarchidæ.—The large family of *Centrarchidæ*, or sunfishes, is especially characteristic of the rivers of the eastern United States, where the various species are inordinately abundant The body is relatively short and deep, and the axis passes through the middle so that the back has much the same outline as the belly The pseudobranchiæ are imperfect, as in many fresh-water fishes, and the head is feebly armed, the bones being usually without spines or serratures The colors are often brilliant, the sexes alike, and all are carnivorous, voracious, and gamy, being excellent as food. The origin of the group is probably Asiatic, the fresh-water serranoid of Japan, *Bryttosus*, resembling in many ways an American sunfish, and the genus *Kuhlia* of the Pacific showing many homologies with the black bass, *Micropterus*

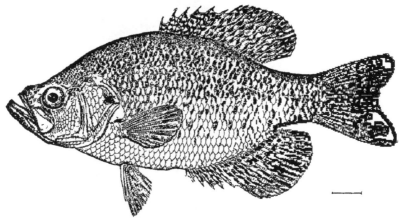

Fig 400 —Crappie, *Pomoxis annularis* Rafinesque   Ohio River

Crappies and Rock Bass. — *Pomoxis annularis*, the crappie, and *Pomoxis sparoides*, the calico-bass, are handsome fishes, valued by the angler These are perhaps the most primitive of the family, and in these species the anal fin is larger than the dorsal The flier, or round bass, *Centrarchus macropterus*, with eight anal spines, is abundant in swamps and lowland ponds of the Southern States It is a pretty fish, attractive in the aquarium *Acantharchus pomotis* is the mud-bass of the Delaware, and *Archoplites interruptus*, the

FIG. 401 —Crappie, *Pomoxis annularis* (Raf.). (From life by Dr. R. W. Shufeldt.)

513

"perch" of the Sacramento. The latter is a large and gamy fish, valued as food and interesting as being the only fresh-

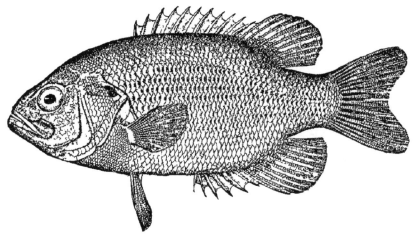

Fig 402 —Rock Bass, *Ambloplites rupestris* (Rafinesque) Ecorse, Mich

water fish of the nature of perch or bass native to the west of the Rocky Mountains   The numbers of this species, according

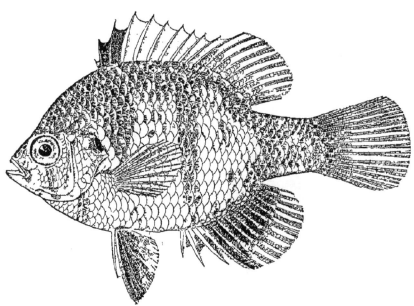

Fig 403 —Banded Sunfish, *Mesogonistius chatodon* (Baird)   Delaware River

to Mr Will S Green of Colusa, California, have been greatly reduced by the introduction of the catfish (*Amerurus nebulosus*) into the Sacramento The perch eats the young catfish, and its stomach is torn by their sharp pectoral spines Another

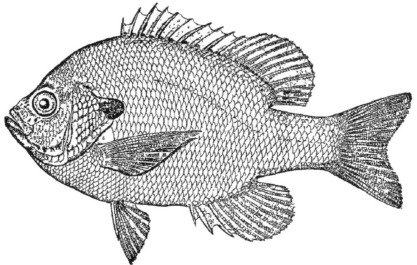

FIG 404 —Blue-Gill, *Lepomis pallidus* (Mitchill) Potomac River

species of this type is the warmouth (*Chænobryttus gulosus*) of the ponds of the South, and still more familiar rock-bass

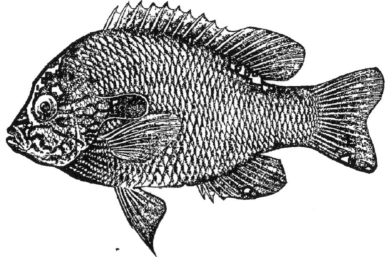

FIG 405 —Long-eared Sunfish, *Lepomis megalotis* (Rafinesque) From Clear Creek, Bloomington, Indiana Family *Centrarchidæ*

or redeye (*Ambloplites rupestris*) of the more northern lakes and rivers valued as a game- and food-fish A very pretty aquarium fish is the black-banded sunfish, *Mesogonistius chæto-don*, of the Delaware, as also the nine-spined sunfish, *Enneacanthus gloriosus*, of the coast streams southward *Apomotis cyanellus*, the blue-green sunfish or little redeye, is very widely distributed from Ohio westward, living in every brook. The dissection of this species is given on page 26 To *Lepomis* belong numerous species having the opercle prolonged in a long flap which is always black in color, often with a border of scarlet or blue The yellowbelly of the South (*Lepomis auritus*), ear-like the showily colored long-eared sunfish (*Lepomis megalotis*) of the

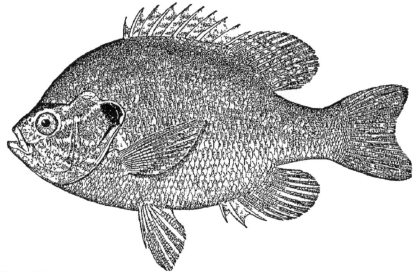

FIG 406 —Common Sunfish, *Eupomotis gibbosus* (Linnæus) Root River, Wis.

southwest, figured on page 2, the bluegill (*Lepomis pallidus*), abundant everywhere south and west of New York, are members of this genus The genus *Eupomotis* differs in its larger pharyngeals, which are armed with blunt teeth. The common sunfish, or pumpkinseed, *Eupomotis gibbosus*, is the most familiar representative of the family, abounding everywhere from Minnesota to New England, then south to Carolina on the east slope of the Alleghanies, breeding everywhere in ponds and in the eddies of the clear brooks.

The Black Bass.—The black bass (*Micropterus*) belong to the same family as the sunfish, differing in the larger size, more elongate form, and more voracious habit The two species are among the most important of American game-fishes, abounding in all clear waters east of the Alleghanies and resisting the evils of civilization far better than the trout

The small-mouthed black bass, *Micropterus dolomieu*, is the most valuable of the species Its mouth, although large, is relatively small, the cleft not extending beyond the eye The green coloration is broken in the young by bronze cross-bands The species frequents only running streams, preferring clear and cold waters, and it extends its range from Canada as far to the southward as such streams can be found Dr James A Henshall, an accomplished angler, author of the "Book of the Black Bass," says "The black bass is eminently an American fish, he has the faculty of asserting himself and of making himself completely at home wherever placed He is plucky, game, brave, unyielding to the last when hooked He has the arrowy rush and vigor of a trout, the untiring strength and bold leap of a salmon, while he has a system of fighting tactics peculiarly his own. I consider him inch for inch and pound for pound the gamest fish that swims "

In the same vein Charles Hallock writes "No doubt the bass is the appointed successor of the trout, not through heritage, nor selection, nor by interloping, but by forcordination Truly, it is sad to contemplate, in the not distant future, the extinction of a beautiful race of creatures, whose attributes have been sung by all the poets, but we regard the inevitable with the same calm philosophy with which the astronomer watches the burning out of a world, knowing that it will be succeeded by a new creation As we mark the soft varitinted flush of the trout disappear in the eventide, behold the sparkle of the coming bass, as he leaps in the morning of his glory! We hardly know which to admire the most—the velvet livery and the charming graces of the departing courtier, or the flash of the armor-plates of the advancing warrior The bass will unquestionably prove himself a worthy substitute for his predecessor and a candidate for a full legacy of honors

"No doubt, when every one of the older states shall become as densely settled as Great Britain itself, and all the rural aspects of the crowded domain resemble the suburban surroundings of our Boston, when every feature of the pastoral landscape

shall wear the finished appearance of European lands, and every
verdant field be closely cropped by lawn-mowers and guarded
by hedges, and every purling stream which meanders through
it has its water-bailiff, we shall still have speckled trout from
which the radiant spots have faded, and tasteless fish, to catch
at a dollar a pound (as we already have on Long Island), and
all the appurtenances and appointments of a genuine English
trouting privilege and a genuine English 'outing'

"In those future days, not long hence to come, some ven-
erable piscator, in whose memory still lingers the joy of fishing,
the brawling stream which tumbled over the rocks in the tangled
wildwood, and moistened the arbutus and the bunchberries

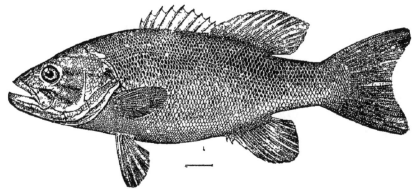

Fig 407 —Small Mouth Black Bass *Micropterus dolomieu* Lacèpède.

which garnished its banks, will totter forth to the velvet edge
of some peacefully flowing stream, and having seated himself
on a convenient point in a revolving easy-chair, placed there
by his careful attendant, cast right and left for the semblance
of sport long dead

"Hosts of liver-fed fish rush to the signal for their early
morning meal, and from the center of the boil which follows
the fall of the handfuls thrown in my piscator of the ancient
days will hook a two-pound trout, and play him hither and yon,
from surface to bottom, without disturbing the pampered gour-
mands which are gorging themselves upon the disgusting viands,
and when he has leisurely brought him to land at last, and the
gillie has scooped him with his landing-net, he will feel in his
capacious pocket for his last trade dollar, and giving his friend
the tip, shuffle back to his house, and lay aside his rod forever "

The black bass is now introduced into the streams of Europe and California. There is little danger that it will work injury to the trout, for the black bass prefers limestone streams, and the trout rarely does well in waters which do not flow over granite rock or else glacial gravel.

The large-mouth black bass (*Micropterus salmoides*) is very much like the other in appearance. The mouth is larger, in the adult cleft beyond the eye, the scales are larger, and in the young there is always a broad black stripe along the sides and no cross-bands. The two are found in the same region, but almost never in the same waters, for the large-mouth bass is a fish of the lakes, ponds, and bayous, always avoiding the swift currents. The young like to hide among weeds or beneath lily-pads. From its preference for sluggish waters, its range extends farther to the southward, as far as the Mexican State of Tamaulipas.

Plioplarchus is a genus of fossil sunfishes from the Eocene of South Dakota and Oregon. *Plioplarchus sevspinosus, septemspinosus*, and *whitei* are imperfectly known species.

The Saleles: Kuhliidæ.—Much like the sunfishes in anatomy, though more like the white perch in appearance and habit, are the members of the little family of *Kuhliidæ*. These are active silvery perches of the tropical seas, ponds, and river-mouths, especially abundant in Polynesia. *Kuhlia malo* is the aholehole of the Hawaiians, a silvery fish living in great numbers in brackish waters. *Kuhlia rupestris*, the salele of the Samoan rivers, is a large swift fish of the rock pools, in form, color, and habits remarkably like the black bass. It is silvery bronze in hue, everywhere mottled with olive-green. The sesele, *Kuhlia marginata*, lives with it in the rivers, but is less abundant. The saboti, *Kuhlia tæniura*, a large silvery fish with cross-bands on the caudal fin, lives about lava-rocks in Polynesia from the Galapagos to Samoa and the East Indies, never entering rivers. Still other species are found in the rock pools and streams of Japan and southward.

The skeleton in *Kuhlia* is essentially like that of the black bass, and Dr. Boulenger places the genus with the *Centrarchidæ*.

The True Perches: Percidæ.—The great family of *Percidæ* includes fresh-water fishes of the northern hemisphere, elon-

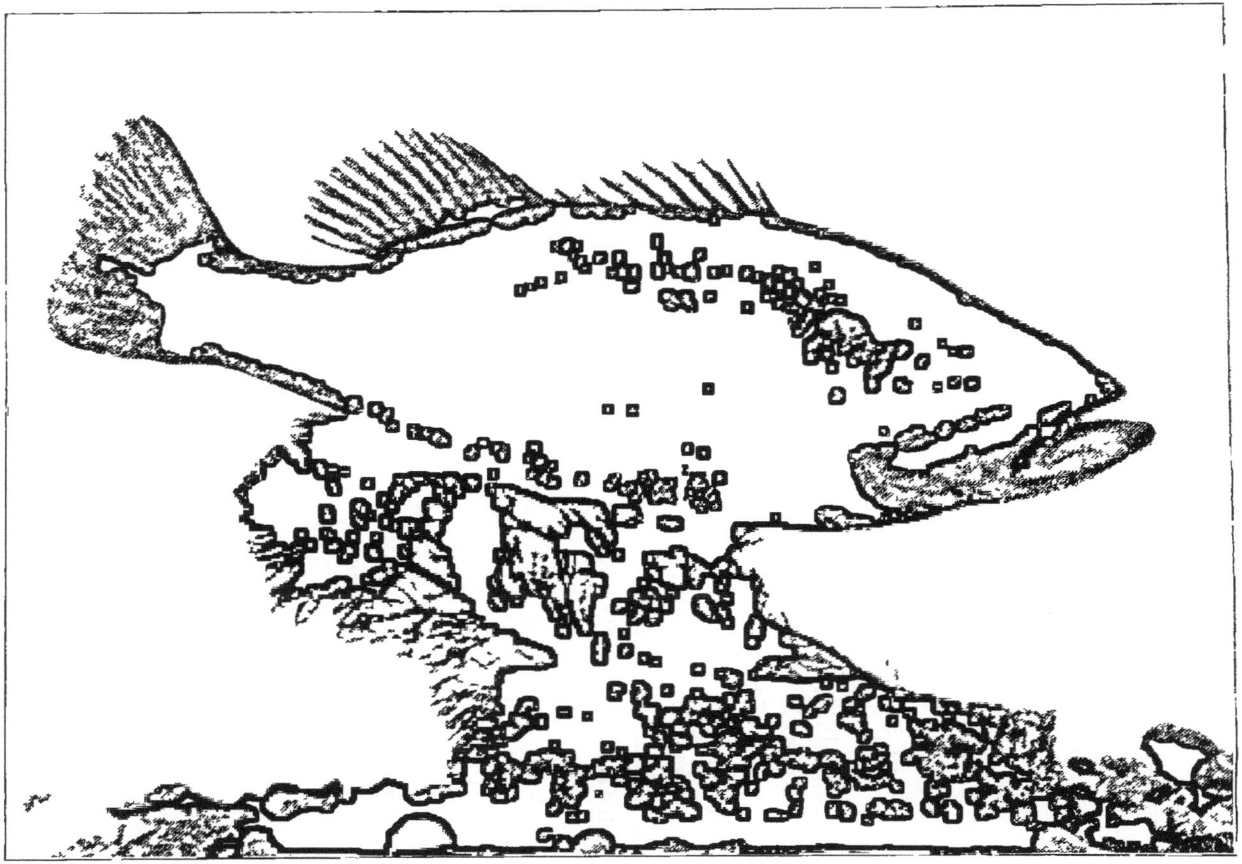

Fig 408 —Large-mouthed Black Bass, *Micropterus salmoides* (Lac) (From life by Dr R W Shufeldt)

529

gate in body, with the vertebræ in increased number and with only two spines in the anal fin About ninety species are recorded, the vast majority being American. The dwarf perches, called darters (*Etheostominæ*), are especially characteristic of the clear streams to the eastward of the plains of the Missouri These constitute one of the greatest attractions of our American river fauna They differ from the perch and its European allies in their small size, bright colors, and large fins, and more technically in the rudimentary condition of the pseudobranchiæ and the air-bladder, both of which organs are almost inappreciable The preopercle is unarmed, and the number of the branchiostegals is six The anal papilla is likewise developed, as in the *Gobiidæ*, to which group the darters bear a considerable superficial resemblance, which, however, indicates no real affinity.

Relations of Darters to Perches. — The colors of the *Etheostominæ*, or darters, are usually very brilliant, species of *Etheostoma* especially being among the most brilliantly colored fishes known, the sexual differences are often great, the females being, as a rule, dull in color and more speckled or barred than the males Most of them prefer clear running water, where they lie on the bottom concealed under stones, darting, when frightened or hungry, with great velocity for a short distance, by a powerful movement of the fan-shaped pectorals, then stopping as suddenly They rarely use the caudal fin in swimming, and they are seldom seen floating or moving freely in the water like most fishes When at rest they support themselves on their expanded ventrals and anal fin All of them can turn the head from side to side, and they frequently lie with the head in a curved position or partly on one side of the body The species of *Ammocrypta*, and perhaps some of the others, prefer a sandy bottom, where, by a sudden plunge, the fish buries itself in the sand, and remains quiescent for hours at a time with only its eyes and snout visible. The others lurk in stony places, under rocks and weeds Although more than usually tenacious of vitality, the darters, from their bottom life, are the first to be disturbed by impurities in the water. All the darters are carnivorous, feeding chiefly on the larvæ of *Diptera*, and in their way voracious. All are of small size; the largest (*Percina rex*) reaches a length of six inches, while the smallest (*Microperca punctulata*) is one of the smallest spiny-rayed fishes known, barely attaining the length of an inch and a half   In Europe no *Etheostominæ* are found, their place being filled by the genera *Zingel* and *Aspro*, which bear a strong resemblance to the American forms, a resemblance which may be a clew to the origin of the latter

The Perches. — The European perch, *Perca fluviatilis*, is placed by Cuvier at the head of the fish series, as representing in a high degree the traits of a fish without sign of incomplete development on the one hand or of degradation on the other   Doubtless the increased number of the vertebræ is the chief character which would lead us to call in question this time-honored arrangement   Because, however, the perch has a relatively degenerate vertebral column, we have used an allied form, the striped bass, as a fairer type of the perfected spiny-rayed fish.   Certainly the bass represents this type better than the perch

But though we may regard the perch as nearest the typically perfect fish, it is far from being one of the most highly specialized, for, as we have seen in several cases, a high degree of specialization of a particular structure is a first step toward its degradation.

The perch of Europe is a common game-fish of the rivers. The yellow perch of America (*Perca flavescens*) is very much like it, a little brighter in color, olive and golden with dusky cross-bands   It frequents quiet streams and ponds from Minnesota eastward, then southward east of the Alleghanies   "As a still-pond fish," says Dr Charles Conrad Abbott, "if there is a fair supply of spring-water, they thrive excellently, but the largest specimens come either from the river or from the inflowing creeks   Deep water of the temperature of ordinary spring-water, with some current and the bed of the stream at least partly covered with vegetation, best suits this fish "   The perch is a food-fish of moderate quality.   In spite of its beauty and gaminess, it is little sought for by our anglers, and is much less valued with us than is the European perch in England   But Dr. Goode ventures to prophesy that "before many years the perch will have as many followers as the black bass among those who fish for pleasure" in the region it inhabits.   "A fish for the people it is, we will grant, and it is the anglers from among the people who have neither time nor patience for long trips nor complicated tackle who will prove its steadfast friends" The boy values it, according to Thoreau When he returns from the mill-pond, he numbers his perch as "real fishes" "So many unquestionable fish he counts, and so many chubs, which he counts, then throws away."

In the perch, the oral valves, characteristic of all bony fishes, are well developed. These structures recently investigated by

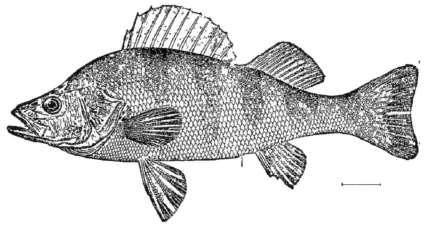

FIG. 409 —Yellow Perch, *Perca flavescens* Mitchill   Potomac River.

Evelyn G Mitchill, form a fold of connective tissue just behind the premaxillary and before the vomer   They are used in respiration, preventing the forward flow of water as the mouth closes

Several perch-like fishes are recorded as fossils from the Miocene

Allied to the perch, but long, slender, big-mouthed, and voracious, is the group of pike perches, found in eastern America and Europe   The wall-eye or glass-eye (*Stizostedion vitreum*), is the largest of this tribe, reaching a weight of ten to twenty pounds   It is found throughout the region east of the Missouri in the large streams and ponds, an excellent food-fish, with white, flaky flesh and in the north a game fish of high rank.   The common names refer to the large glassy eye, concerning which Dr Goode quotes from some "ardent admirer" these words   "Look at this beautiful fish, as symmetrical in form as the salmon. Not a fault in his make-up, not a scale

disturbed, every fin perfect, tail clean-cut, and his great, big
wall-eyes stand out with that life-like glare so characteristic of
the fish "

Similar to the wall-eye, but much smaller and more translucent in color, is the sauger, or sand-pike, of the Great Lakes and

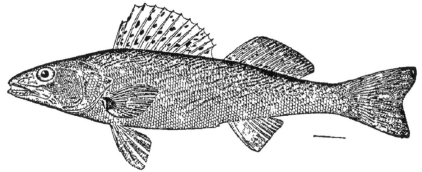

FIG 410 —Sauger, *Stizostedion canadense* (Smith)   Ecorse, Mich

Northern rivers, *Stizostedion canadense*   This fish rarely exceeds
fifteen inches in length, and as a food-fish it is of correspondingly less importance

The pike-perch, or zander, of central Europe, *Centropomus*
(or *Sandrus*) *lucioperca*, is an excellent game-fish, similar to

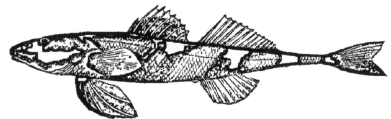

FIG 411 —The Aspron, *Aspro asper* (Linnæus)   Rhone River   Family *Percidæ*
(After Seelye)

the sauger, but larger, characterized technically by having the
ventral fins closer together   Another species, *Centropomus vol-
gensis*, in Russia, looks more like a perch than the other species
do. *Sandroserrus*, a fossil pike-perch, occurs in the Pliocene
Another European fish related to the perch is the river ruff,
or pope, *Acerina cernua*, which is a small fish with the
form of a perch and with conspicuous mucous cavities in
the skull   It is common throughout the north of Europe

and especially abundant at the confluence of rivers *Gymno-cephalus schrœtzer* of the Danube has the head still more cavernous. *Percarina demidoffi* of southern Russia is another dainty little fish of the general type of the perch A fossil genus of this type called *Smerdis* is numerously represented in the Miocene and later rocks. The aspron, *Aspro asper*, is a species like a darter found lying on the bottoms of swift rivers, especially the Rhone The body is elongate, with the paired fins highly developed *Zingel zingel* is found in the Danube, as is also a third species called *Aspro streber* In form and coloration these species greatly resemble the American darters, and the genus *Zingel* is, perhaps, the ancestor of the entire group *Zingel* differs from *Percina* mainly in having seven instead of six branchiostegals and the pseudobranchiæ better

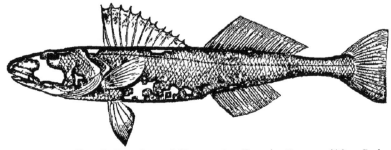

Fig 412.—The Zingel, *Zingel zingel* (Linnæus). Danube River   (After Seelye)

developed The differences in these and other regards which distinguish the darters are features of degradation, and they are also no doubt of relatively recent acquisition To this fact we may ascribe the difficulty in finding good generic characters within the group. Sharply defined genera occur where the intervening types are lost The darter is one of the very latest products in the evolution of fishes

The Darters: Etheostominæ. — Of the darters, or etheostomine perches, over fifty species are known, all confined to the streams of the region bounded by Quebec, Assiniboia, Colorado, and Nuevo Leon All are small fishes and some of them minute, and some are the most brilliantly colored of all freshwater fishes of any region, the most ornate belonging to the large genus called *Etheostoma* The largest species, the most primitive because most like the perch, belong to the genus *Percina*.

First among the darters because largest in size, most perch-like in structure, and least degenerate, we place the king darter, *Percina rex* of the Roanoke River in Virginia. This species reaches a length of six inches, is handsomely colored, and looks like a young wall-eye

The log-perch, *Percina caprodes*, is near to this, but a little smaller, with the body surrounded by black rings alternately

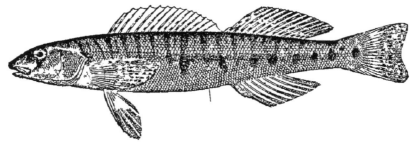

Fig 413 —Log-perch, *Percina caprodes* (Rafinesque)   Licking Co , Ohio

large and small. In this widely distributed species, large enough to take the hook, the air-bladder is present although small   In the smaller species it vanishes by degrees, and in proportion as in their habits they cling to the bottom of the stream

The genus *Hadropterus* includes many handsome species, most of them with a black lateral band widened at intervals.

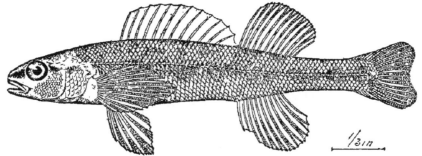

Fig 414 —Black-sided Darter, *Hadropterus aspro* (Cope & Jordan). Chickamauga River

The black-sided darter, *Hadropterus aspro*, is the best-known species and one of the most elegant of all fishes, abounding in the clear gravelly streams of the Ohio basin and northwestward

Hadropterus evides of the Ohio region is still more brilliant, with alternate bands of dark blue-green and orange-red, most exquisite in their arrangement In the South, *Hadropterus nigrofasciatus*, the crawl-a-bottom of the Georgia rivers, is a heavily built darter, which Vaillant has considered the ancestral species of the group Still more swift in movement and bright in color are the species of *Hypohomus*, which flash their showy hues in the sparkling brooks of the Ozark and the Great Smoky Mountains. *Hypohomus aurantiacus* is the best-known species

Diplesion blennioides, the green-sided darter, is the type of numerous species with short heads, large fins, and coloration

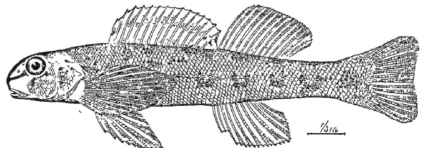

FIG 415 —Green-sided Darter *Diplesion blennioides* Rafinesque   Clinch River
Family *Percidæ*

of speckled green and golden It abounds in the streams of the Ohio Valley.

The tessellated darters, *Boleosoma*, are the most plainly colored of the group and among the smallest, yet in the

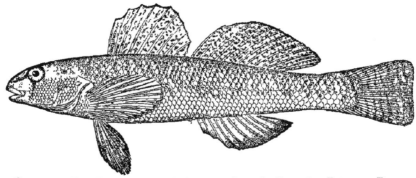

FIG. 416 —Tessellated Darter, *Boleosoma olmstedi* (Storer)   Potomac River.

delicacy, wariness, and quaintness of motion they are among the most interesting, especially in the aquarium. *Boleosoma*

nigrum, the Johnny darter in the West, and *Boleosoma olmstedi*
in the East are among the commonest species, found half hidden in the weeds of small brooks, and showing no bright colors,
although the male in the spring has the head, and often the
whole body, jet black.

Crystallaria asprella, a large species almost transparent,
is occasionally taken in swift currents along the limestone

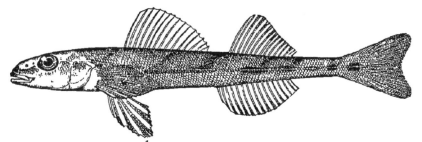

Fig. 417 —Crystal Darter, *Crystallaria asprella* (Jordan)   Wabash River.

banks of the Mississippi   Still more transparent is the small
sand-darter, *Ammocrypta pellucida*, which lives in the clearest
of waters, concealing itself by plunging into the sand. Its
scales are scantily developed, as befits a fish that chooses this

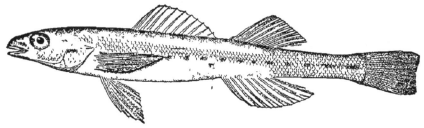

Fig. 418 —Sand-darter, *Ammocrypta clara* (Jordan & Meek)   Des Moines River

method of protection, and in the related *Ammocrypta beani* of
the streams of the Louisiana pine-woods. the body is almost
naked, as also in *Ioa vitrea*, the glassy darter of the pine-woods
of North Carolina

In the other darters the body is more compressed, the movements less active, the coloration even more brilliant in the
males, which are far more showy than their dull olivaceous
mates

To *Etheostoma* nearly half of the species belong, and they

form indeed a royal series of little fishes. Only a few can be noticed here, but all of them are described in detail and many

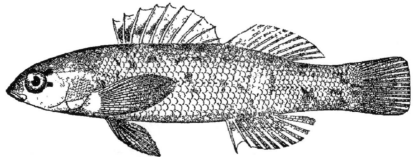

FIG 419 —*Etheostoma jordani* Gilbert. Chestnut Creek, Verbena, Ala.

are figured by Jordan and Evermann ("Fishes of North and Middle America," Vol. I).

Most beautiful of all fresh-water fishes is the blue-breasted darter, *Etheostoma camurum*, red-blue and olive, with red spots,

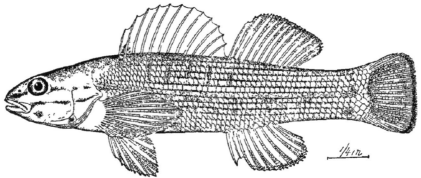

FIG 420 —Blue-breasted Darter, *Etheostoma camurum* (Cope) the most brilliantly colored of American river fishes   Cumberland Gap, Tenn

like a trout   This species lives in clear streams of the Ohio valley, a region perhaps to be regarded as the center of abundance of these fishes

Very similar is the trout-spotted darter, *Etheostoma maculatum*, dusky and red, with round crimson spots   *Etheostoma rufilineatum* of the French Broad is one of the most gaudy of fishes. *Etheostoma australe* of Chihuahua ranges farthest south of all the darters, and *Etheostoma boreale* of Quebec perhaps farthest north, though *Etheostoma iowæ*, found from Iowa to the Saskatchewan, may dispute this honor. *Etheostoma cæruleum*, the rainbow darter or soldier-fish, with alternate oblique bands of blue and scarlet, is doubtless the most familiar of the brilliantly colored species, as it is the most abundant throughout the Ohio valley.

Etheostoma flabellare, the fan-tailed darter, discovered by Rafinesque in Kentucky in 1817, was the first species of the series made known to science It has no bright colors, but its movements in water are more active than any of the others, and it is the most hardy in the aquarium

Psychromaster tuscumbia abounds in the great limestone springs of northern Alabama, while *Copelandellus quiescens* swarms in the black-water brooks which flow into the Dismal Swamp and thence southward to the Suwanee. It is a little fish not very active, its range going farther into the southern lowlands than any other Finally, *Microperca punctulata*, the least darter, is the smallest of all, with fewest spines and dullest colors, must specialized in the sense of being least primitive, but at the same time the most degraded of all the darters.

No fossil forms nearly allied to the darters are on record The nearest is perhaps *Mioplosus labracoides* from the Eocene at Green River, Wyoming This elongate fish, a foot long, has the dorsal rays IX-1, 13, and the anal rays II, 13, its scales finely serrated, and the preopercle coarsely serrated on the lower limb only This species, with its numerous congeners from the Rocky Mountain Eocene, is nearer the true perch than the darters. Several species related to Perca are also recorded from the Eocene of England and Germany A species called *Lucioperca skorpili*, allied to *Centropomus*, is described from the Oligocene of Bulgaria, besides several other forms imperfectly preserved, of still more doubtful affinities.

CHAPTER XXXIV

THE BASS AND THEIR RELATIVES

THE Cardinal-fishes. Apogonidæ.—The *Apogonidæ* or cardinal-fishes are perch-like fishes, mostly of small size, with two distinct short dorsal fins. They are found in the warm seas, and many of them enter rivers, some even inhabiting hot springs Many of the shore species are bright red in color, usually with black stripes, bands, or spots Still others, however, are olive or silvery, and a few in deeper water are violet-black

The species of *Apogon* are especially numerous, and in regions where they are abundant, as in Japan, they are much

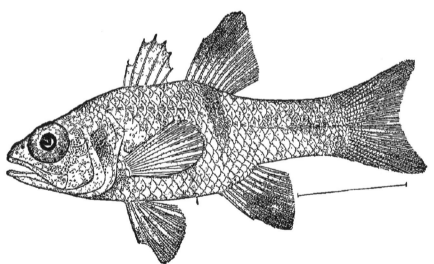

Fig 421 —Cardinal-fish, *Apogon retrosella* Gill Mazatlan

valued as food. *Apogon imberbis*, the "king of the mullet," is a common red species of southern Europe. *Apogon maculatus* is found in the West Indies. *Apogon retrosella* is the pretty "cardenal" of the west coast of Mexico. *Apogon lineatus, semilineatus* and other species abound in Japan, and many species occur about the islands of Polynesia *Epigonus telescopium* is a deep-sea fish of the Mediterranean and *Telescopias* and *Synagrops* are genera of the depths of the Pacific   *Paramia* with strong canines is allied to *Apogon*, and similar in color and habit

Allied to *Apogon* are several small groups often taken as distinct families   The species of *Ambassis* (*Ambassidæ*) are little fishes of the rivers and bays of India and Polynesia, resembling small silvery perch or bass   All these have three anal spines instead of two as in *Apogon*   Some of these enter rivers and several are recorded from hot springs   *Scombrops boops*, the mutsu of Japan, is a valued food-fish found in rather deep water   It is remarkable for its very strong teeth, although its flesh is feeble and easily torn   A still larger species in Cuba, *Scombrops oculata*, known as *Escolar chino*, resembles a barracuda   These fishes with fragile bodies and very strong teeth are placed by Gill in a separate family (*Scombropidæ*)   *Acropoma japonicum* is a neat little fish of the Japanese coast, with the vent placed farther forward than in *Apogon*   It is the type of the *Acropomidæ*, a small family of the Pacific   *Enoplosus armatus* is an Australian fish with high back and fins, with a rather stately appearance, type of the *Enoplosidæ*   In his last catalogue of families of fishes Dr Gill recognizes *Scombropidæ* and *Acropomidæ* as distinct families, but their relationships with *Apogon* are certainly very close   Many genera allied to *Apogon* and *Ambassis* occur in Australian rivers Several fossils referred to *Apogon* (*Apogon spinosus*, etc) occur in the Eocene of Italy and Germany

The Anomalopidæ.—The family of *Anomalopidæ* is a small group of deep-sea fishes of uncertain relationship, but perhaps remotely related to *Apogon*   *Anomalops palpebrata* is found in Polynesia and has beneath the eye a large luminous organ unlike anything seen elsewhere among fishes

The Asineopidæ. — Another family of doubtful relationship is that of *Asineopidæ*, elsewhere noticed   It is composed of extinct fresh-water fishes found in the Green River shales   In *Asineops squamifrons* the opercles are unarmed, the teeth villiform, and the dorsal fin undivided, composed of eight or nine spines and twelve to fourteen soft rays   The anal spines, as in *Apogon*, are two only, and the scales are cycloid.

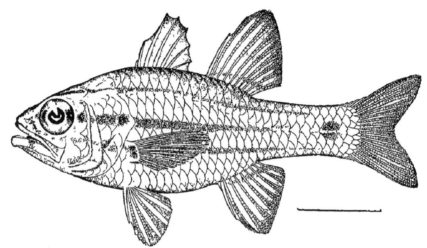

FIG 422 —*Apogon semilineatus* Schlegel   Misaki, Japan

The Robalos:* Oxylabracidæ. — The family of Robalos (*Oxylabracidæ* or *Centropomidæ*) is closely related to the *Serranidæ*, differing among other things in having the conspicuous lateral line extended on the caudal fin   These are silvery fishes with

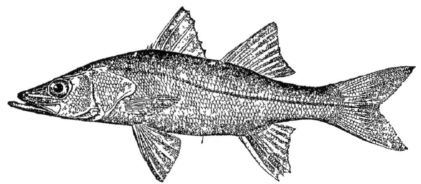

FIG. 423 —Robalo, *Oxylabrax undecimalis* (Bloch)   Florida

elongate bodies, large scales, a pike-like appearance, the first dorsal composed of strong spines and the second spine of the

* The European zander is the type of Lacépède's genus *Centropomus*. The name *Centropomus* has been wrongly transferred to the robalo by most authors

anal especially large   They are found in tropical America
only, where they are highly valued as food, the flesh being
like that of the striped bass, white, flaky, and of fine flavor
The common robalo, or snook, *Oxylabrax* (or *Centropomus*) *undecimalis*, reaches a weight of fifteen to twenty pounds   It
ranges north as far as Texas   In this species the lateral line
is black.   The smaller species, of which several are described,
are known as *Robalito* or *Constantino*.

The Sea-bass: Serranidæ.—The central family of the percoid
fishes is that of the *Serranidæ*, or sea-bass   Of these about
400 species are recorded, carnivorous fishes found in all warm
seas, a few ascending the fresh waters   In general, the species
are characterized by the presence of twenty-four vertebræ and
three anal spines, never more than three   The fresh-water
species are all more or less archaic and show traits suggesting
the *Oxylabracidæ*, *Percidæ*, or *Centrarchidæ*, all of which are
doubtless derived from ancestors of *Serranidæ*.   Among the
connecting forms are the perch-like genera *Percichthys* and
Percilia of the rivers of Chile   These species look much like
perch, but have three anal spines, the number of vertebræ
being thirty-five   *Percichthys trucha* is the common trucha, or
trout, of Chilean waters

Lateolabrax japonicus, the susuki, or bass, of Japan, is one
of the most valued food-fishes of the Orient, similar in quality to
the robalo, which it much resembles   This genus and the
East Indian *Centrogenys waigiensis* approach *Oxylabrax* in
appearance and structure   *Niphon spinosus*, the ara of Japan,
is a very large sea-bass, also of this type   Close to these bass,
marine and fresh water, are the Chinese genus *Siniperca* and
the Korean genus *Coreoperca*, several species of which abound
in Oriental rivers   In southern Japan is the rare *Bryttosus
kawamebari*, a bass in structure, but very closely resembling
the American sunfish, even to the presence of the bright-edged
black ear-spot   There is reason to believe that from some
such form the *Centrarchidæ* were derived

Other bass-like fishes occur in Egypt (*Lates*), Australia
(*Percalates*, etc), and southern Africa   *Oligorus macquariensis*
is the great cod of the Australian rivers and *Ctenolates ambiguus*
is the yellow belly, while *Percalates colonorum* is everywhere

the "perch" in Australian rivers The most important member of these transitional types between perch and sea-bass is the striped bass, or rockfish (*Roccus lineatus*), of the Atlantic coast of the United States. This large fish, reaching in extreme cases a weight of 112 pounds, lives in shallow waters in the sea and ascends the rivers in spring to spawn It is olivaceous in color, the sides golden silvery, with narrow black stripes About 1880 it was introduced by the United States Fish Commission into the Sacramento, where it is now very abundant and a fish of large commercial importance To the angler the striped bass is always "a gallant fish and a bold biter," and Genio Scott places it first among the game-fishes of America

The white bass (*Roccus chrysops*) is very similar to it, but shorter and more compressed, reaching a smaller size This fish is abundant in the Great Lakes and the upper Mississippi as far south as Arkansas

The yellow bass (*Morone interrupta*), a coarser and more brassy fish, replaces it farther south It is seldom seen above Cincinnati and St Louis The white perch (*Morone americana*) is a little fish of the Atlantic seaboard, entering the sea, but running up all the rivers, remaining contentedly landlocked in ponds It is one of the most characteristic fishes of the coast from Nova Scotia to Virginia It is a good pan fish, takes the hook vigorously, and in a modest way deserves the good-will of the angler who cannot stray far into the mountains. Very close to these American bass is the bass, bars, or robalo, of southern Europe, *Dicentrarchus labrax*, a large olive-colored fish, excellent as food, living in the sea about the mouths of rivers.

The Jewfishes.—In the warm seas are certain bass of immense size, reaching a length of six feet or more, and being robust in form, a weight of 500 or 600 pounds These are dusky green in color, thick-headed, rough-scaled, with low fins, voracious disposition, and sluggish movements In almost all parts of the world these great bass are called jewfish, but no reason for this name has ever been suggested In habit and value the species are much alike, and the jewfish of California, *Stereolepis gigas*, the prize of the Santa Catalina anglers, may be taken as the type of them all Closely related

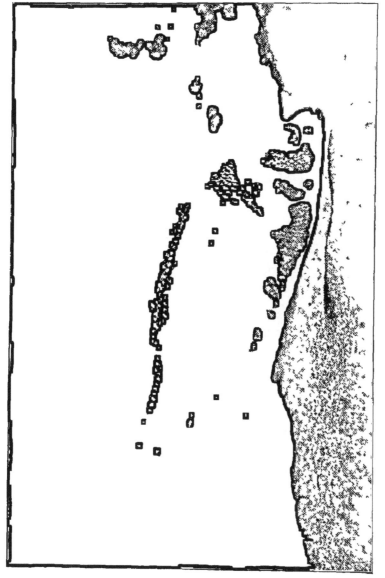

Fig 434—White Perch, *Morone americana* Gmelin (From life by Dr R W Shufeldt, one half natural size)

to this is the Japanese ishinagi, *Megaperca ischinagi*, the jew-fish, or stone-bass, of Japan Another Japanese jewfish is the Abura bodzu, or "fat priest," *Ebisus sagamius* In the West Indies, as also on the west coast of Mexico, the jewfish, or guasa, is *Promicrops itaiara*. The black grouper, *Garrupa nigrita*, is the jewfish of Florida The European jewfish, more often called wreckfish, or stone-bass, is *Polyprion americanus*, and the equally large *Polyprion oxygeneios* is found in Australia, as is also another jewfish, *Glaucosoma hebraicum*, the last belonging to the *Lutianidæ*. Largest of all these jewfishes is *Promicrops lanceolata* of the South Pacific This huge bass,

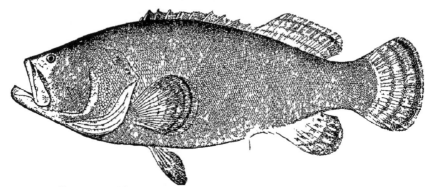

Fig 425 —Florida Jewfish, *Promicrops itaiara* (Lichtenstein)
St John's River, Fla

according to Dr Boulenger, sometimes reaches a length of twelve feet.

Related to the jewfishes are numerous smaller fishes One of these, the Spanish-flag of Cuba, *Gonioplectrus hispanus*, is rose-colored, with golden bands like the flag of Spain itself Other species referred to *Acanthistius* and *Plectropoma* have, like this, hooked spines on the lower border of the preopercle

The Groupers.—In all warm seas abound species of *Epinephelus* and related genera, known as sea-bass, groupers, or merous They are mostly large voracious fishes with small scales, pale flesh of fair quality, and from their abundance they are of large commercial importance To English-speaking people these fishes are usually known as grouper, a corruption of the Portuguese name garrupa In the West Indies and about Panama there are very many species, and still others abound in the Mediter-

ranean, in southern Japan, and throughout Polynesia and
the West Indies   They have very much in common, but differ
in size and color, some being bright red, some gaudily spotted
with red or blue, but most of them are merely mottled green
or brown   In many cases individuals living near shore are
olivaceous, and those of the same species in the depths are
bright crimson or scarlet   We name below a few of the most
prominent species   Even a bare list of all of them would take

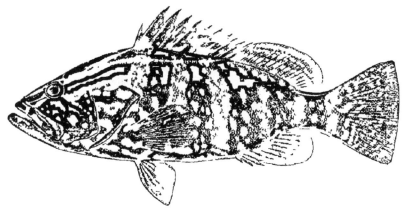

FIG 426 —*Epinephelus striatus* (Bloch), Nassau Grouper   *Cherna criolla*
Family *Serranidæ*

many pages *Cephalopholis cruentatus*, the red hind of the
Florida Keys, is one of the smallest and brightest of all of them
Cephalopholis fulvus, the blue-spotted guativere of the Cubans,
is called negro-fish, butter-fish, yellow-fish, or redfish, according to its color, which varies with the depth   It is red, yellow,
or olive, with many round blue spots   *Epinephelus adscen-
scionis*, the rock-hind, is spotted everywhere with orange
Epinephelus guaza is the merou, or giant-bass, of Europe, a
large food-fish of value, rather dull in color   *Epinephelus striatus*
is the Nassau grouper, or *Cherna criolla*, common in the West
Indies *Epinephelus maculosus* is the cabrilla of Cuba   *Epinephelus drummond-hayi*, the speckled hind, umber brown, spotted
with lavender, is one of the handsomest of all the groupers
Epinephelus morio, the red grouper, is the commonest of all
these fishes in the American markets   In Asia the species
are equally numerous, *Epinephelus quernus* of Hawaii and the
red *Epinephelus fasciatus* of Japan and southward being food-

fishes of importance. *Epinephelus merra, Epinephelus gilberti,* and *Epinephelus tauvina* are among the more common species of Polynesia. *Epinephelus corallicola,* a species profusely

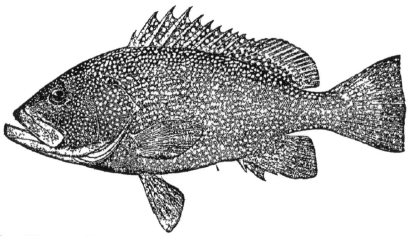

Fig 427 —John Paw or Speckled Hind, *Epinephelus drummond-hayi* Goode Pensacola

spotted, abounds in the crevices of coral reefs, while *Cepholopholis argus* and *C leopardus* are showy fishes of the deeper channels *Mycteroperca venenosa,* the yellow-finned grouper, is a large and handsome fish of the coast of Cuba, the flesh sometimes poisonous; when red in deep water it is known as

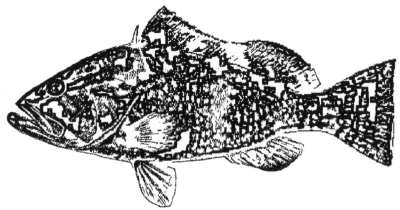

Fig 428 —*Epinephelus morio* (Cuvier & Valenciennes), Red Grouper, or Mero. Family *Serranidæ*

the bonaci cardenal. *Mycteroperca bonaci,* the bonaci arara sells in our markets as black grouper *Mycteroperca microlepis*

Fig. 429.—Red Hind, *Epinephelus adscensionis* (Osbeck). Puerto Rico. (After Evermann.)

540

is commonest along our South Atlantic coast, not reaching the West Indies, and *Mycteroperca rubra*, which is never red, enters the Mediterranean. *Mycteroperca falcata* is known in the markets as scamp, and *Mycteroperca venadorum* is a giant species from the Venados Islands, near Mazatlan *Diploprion bifasciatus* is a handsome grouper-like fish with two black cross-bands, found in Japan and India *Variola louti*, red, with crimson spots and a forked caudal fin, is one of the most showy fishes of the equatorial Pacific

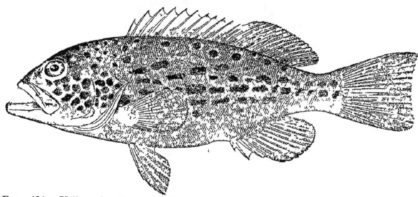

Fig 430 —Yellow-fin Grouper, *Mycteroperca venenosa* (Linnæus) Havana

The small fishes called Vaca in Cuba belong to the genus *Hypoplectrus* Their extraordinary and unexplained variations in color have been noticed on page 88 The common species— blue, orange, green, plain, striated, checkered, or striped— bears the name of *Hypoplectrus unicolor* (Fig 431)

The Serranos. — In all the species known as jewfish and grouper, as also in the *Oxylabracidæ* and most *Centrarchidæ*, the maxillary bone is divided by a lengthwise suture which sets off a distinct supplemental maxillary This bone is wanting in the remaining species of *Serranidæ*, as it is also in those forms already noticed which are familiarly known as bass The species without the supplemental maxillary are in general smaller in size, the canines are on the sides of the jaws instead of in front, and there is none of the hinged depressible teeth which are conspicuous in the groupers The species are abundant in the Atlantic, but scarcely any are found in Polynesia, and few in Japan or India

Serranus cabrilla is the Cabrilla of the Mediterranean, a well-known and excellent food-fish, the original type of the family of *Serranidæ*. *Serranellus scriba* is the serran, a very pretty shore-fish of southern Europe, longer known than any other of the tribe.   On the coast of southern California are also species called Cabrillas, fine, large, food-fish, bass-like in form, *Paralabrax clathratus*, and other less common species The *Cabrillas* and their relatives are almost all American, a few straying across to Europe.   One of the most important in the number is the black sea-bass, or black will, of our Atlantic

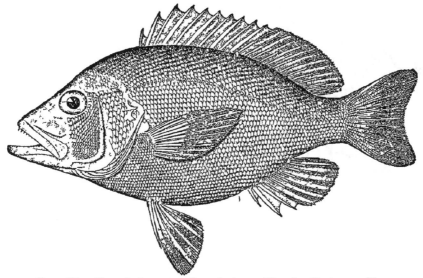

FIG. 431 —*Hypoplectrus unicolor nigricans* (Poey)   Tortugas, Fla.

coast, *Centropristes striatus*   This is a common food- and game-fish, dusky in color, gamy, and of fine flesh.   The squirrel-fishes (*Diplectrum*) and the many serranos (*Prionodes*) of the tropics, small bright-colored fishes of the rocks and reefs, must be passed with a word, as also the small *Paracentropristis* of the Mediterranean and the fine red creole-fish of the West Indies, *Paranthias furcifer*   In one species, *Anyperodon leucogrammicus* of Polynesia, there are no teeth on the palatines

The barber-fish (*Anthias anthias*) of southern Europe, bright red and with the lateral line running very high, is the type of a numerous group found at the lowest fishing level in all warm seas   All the species of this group are bright red, very hand-

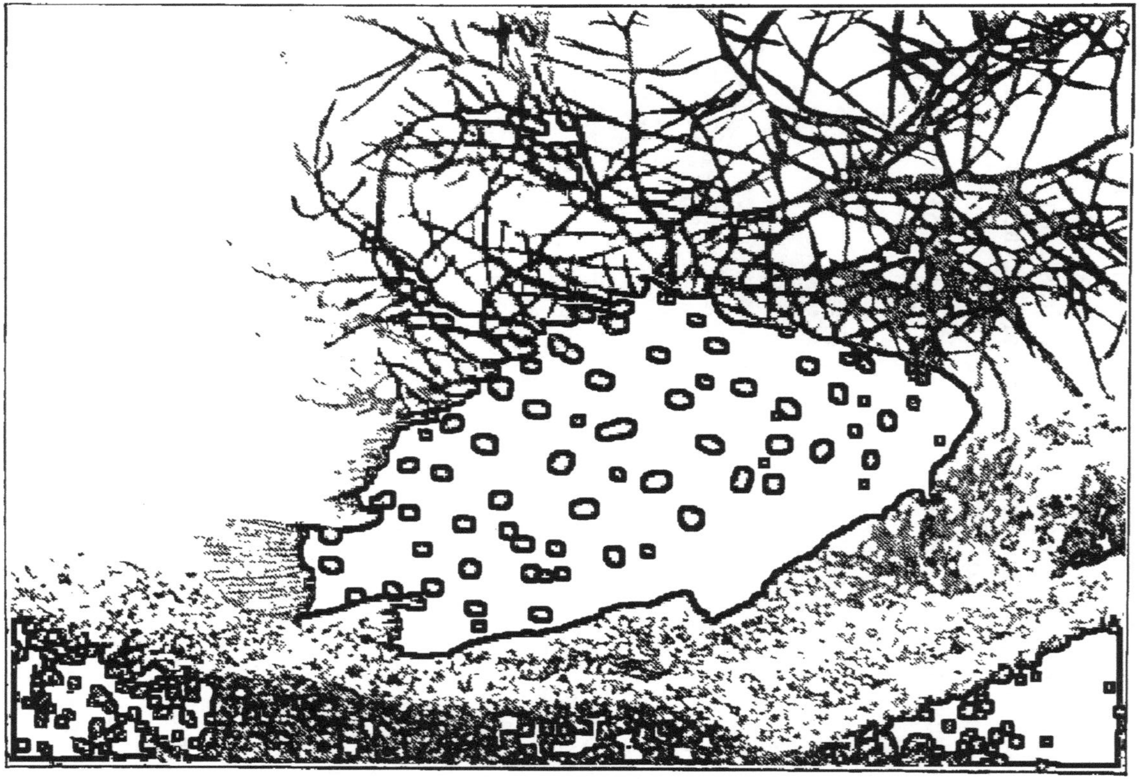

FIG 432—Snowy Grouper, *Epinephelus niveatus* (Cuv. & Val.) Natural size young.
(Photograph by Dr R W Shufeldt)

543

some, and excellent as food Hemianthias vivanus, known only from the spewings of the red snapper (Lutianus aya) at Pensacola, is one of the most brilliant species, red, with golden streaks The genus Plesiops consists of small fishes almost black in color, with blue spots and other markings, abounding about the coral reefs In this genus the lateral line is interrupted and there is some indication of affinity with the Opisthognathidæ.

In the soapfishes (Rypticus) the supplemental maxillary appears again, but in these forms the dorsal fin is reduced to two or three spines and there is none in the anal Rypticus saponaceus, so called from the smooth or soapy scales, is the

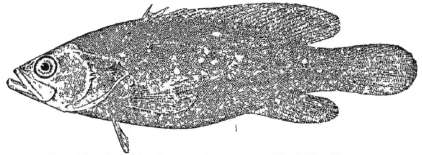

Fig 433 —Soapfish, Rypticus bistrispinus (Mitchill) Virginia

best known of the numerous species, which all belong to tropical America Grammistes, with eight dorsal spines, is a related form in Polynesia, bright yellow, with numerous black stripes Numerous species referred to the Serranidæ occur in the Eocene and Miocene rocks Some are related to Epinephelus, others to Roccus and Lates In the Tertiary lignite of Brazil is a species of Percichthys, Percichthys antiquus, with Properca beaumonti, which seem to be a primitive form of the bass, allied to Dicentrarchus Prolates heberti of the Cretaceous, one of the earliest of the series, has the caudal rounded and is apparently allied to Lates, as is also the heavily armed Acanus regleysianus of the Oligocene Smerdis minutus, a small fish from the Oligocene, is also related to Lates, which genus with Roccus and Dicentrarchus must represent the most primitive of existing members of this family Of both Smerdis and Dicentrarchus (Labrax) numerous species are recorded, mostly from the Miocene of Europe

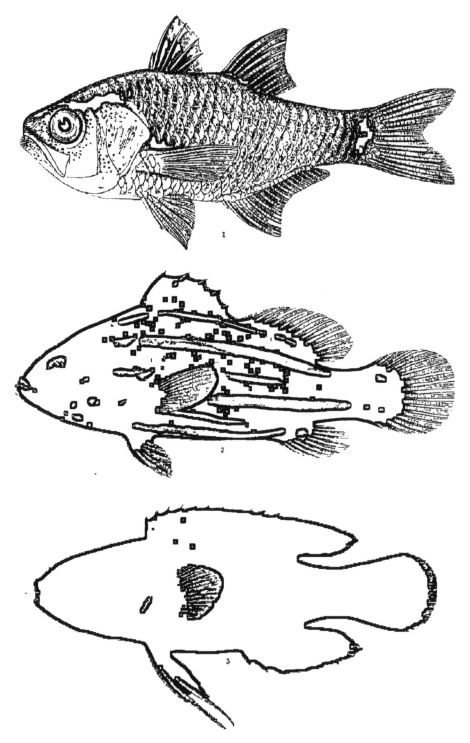

1 ARCHAMIA LINEOLATA (EHRENBERG)

The Flashers. Lobotidæ.—The small family of *Lobotidæ*, flashers, or triple-tails, closely resembles the *Serranidæ*, but there

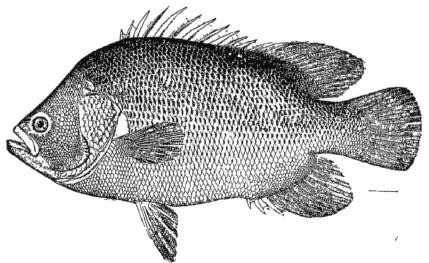

Fig 434 —Flasher, *Lobotes surinamensis* (Bloch)   Virginia.

are no teeth on vomer or palatines. The three species are robust fishes, of a large size, of a dark-green color, the front part of the head very short   They reach a length of about

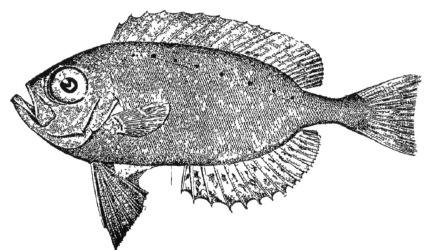

Fig 435 —Catalufa, *Priacanthus arenatus* Cuv. & Val   Woods Hole, Mass

three feet and are good food-fishes   *Lobotes surinamensis* comes northward from the West Indies as far as Cape Cod

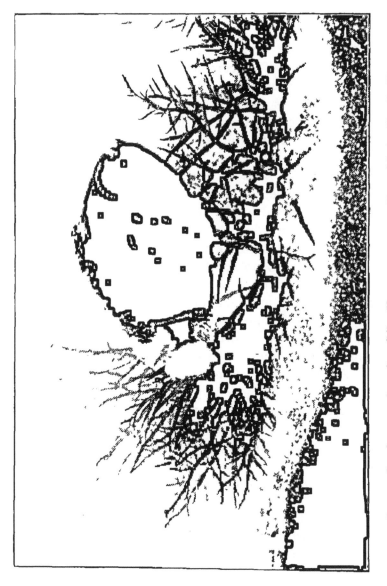

FIG 436 —Bigeye, *Pseudopriacanthus altus* Gill Young specimen (From life by Dr R W Shufeldt.)

545

Lobotes pacificus is found about Panama   *Lobotes erate*, common in India, was taken by the writer at Misaki, Japan.

The Bigeyes: Priacanthidæ.—The *Catalufas* or bigeyes (*Priacanthidæ*) are handsome fishes of the tropics, with short, flattened bodies, rough scales, large eyes, and bright-red coloration. The mouth is very oblique, and the anal fin about as large as the dorsal   The commonest species is *Priacanthus cruentatus*, widely diffused through the Pacific and also in the West Indies. This is the noted Aweoweo of the Hawaiians, which used to come into the bays in myriads at the period of death of royalty. It is still abundant, even after Hawaiian royalty has passed away.

Pseudopriacanthus altus is a short, very deep-bodied, and very rough fish, scarlet in color, occasionally taken along our coast, driven northward by the Gulf Stream   The young fishes are quite unlike the adult in appearance   Numerous other species of *Priacanthus* occur in the Indies and Polynesia

The Histopteridæ.—Another family with strong spines and rough scales is the group of *Histopteridæ*   *Histiopterus typus*, the Matodai, is found in Japan, and is remarkable for its very deep body and very high spines   Equally remarkable is the Tengudai, *Histiopterus acutirostris*, also Japanese, remarkable for the long snout and high fins   Both are rare in Japanese markets   All these are eccentric variations from the perchlike type

The Snappers: Lutianidæ.—Scarcely less numerous and varied than the sea-bass is the great family of *Lutianidæ*, known in America as snappers or pargos.   In these fishes the maxillary slips along its edge into a sheath formed by the broad preorbital   In the *Serranidæ* there is no such sheath   In the *Lutianidæ* there is no supplemental maxillary, teeth are present on the vomer and palatines, and in the jaws there are distinct canines   These fishes of the warm seas are all carnivorous, voracious, gamy, excellent as food though seldom of fine grain, the flesh being white and not flaky. About 250 species are known, and in all warm seas they are abundant

To the great genus *Lutianus* most of the species belong   These are the snappers of our markets and the pargos of the Spanish-speaking fishermen.   The shore species are green in color, mostly

FIG. 437.—Gray Snapper, *Lutianus griseus* L. Puerto Rico. (After Evermann.)

548

banded, spotted, or streaked. In deeper water bright-red species are found. One of these, *Lutianus aya*, the red snapper or pargo guachinango of the Gulf of Mexico, is, economically speaking, the most important of all these fishes in the United States. It is a large, rather coarse fish, bright red in color, and it is taken on long lines on rocky reefs chiefly about Pensacola and Tampa in Florida, although similar fisheries exist on the shores of Yucatan and Brazil.

A related species is the *Lutianus analis*, the mutton snapper or pargo criollo of the West Indies. This is one of the staple

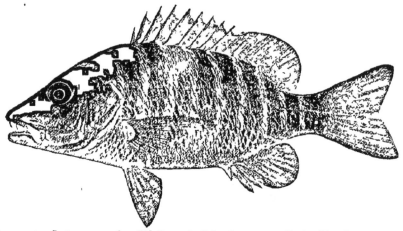

Fig 438 —*Lutianus apodus* (Walbaum), Schoolmaster or Cají   Family *Lutianidæ*

fishes of the Havana market, always in demand for banquets and festivals, because its flesh is never unwholesome. The mangrove snapper, or gray-snapper, *Lutianus griseus*, called in Cuba, Caballerote, is the commonest species on our coasts. The common name arises from the fact that the young hide in the mangrove bushes of Florida and Cuba, whence they sally out in pursuit of sardines and other small fishes. It is a very wary fish, to be sought with care, hence the name "lawyer," sometimes heard in Florida. The cubero (*Lutianus cyanopterus*) is a very large snapper, often rejected as unwholesome, being said to cause the disease known as ciguatera. Certain snappers in Polynesia have a similar reputation. The large red mumea, *Lutianus bohar*, is regarded as always poisonous in Samoa—the most dangerous fish of the islands. *L leioglossus* is also held under suspicion on Tutuila, though other fishes of this type are regarded as always safe. Other common snappers

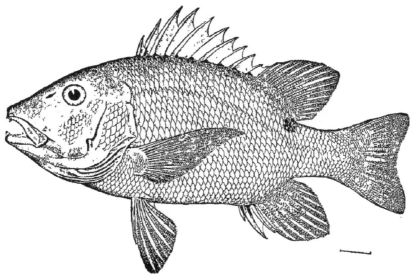

FIG 439.—*Hoplopagrus guntheri* Gill. Mazatlan.

of Florida and Cuba are the dog snapper or jocú (*Lutianus jocu*), the schoolmaster or cají (*Lutianus apodus*), the black-fin snapper or sese de lo alto (*Lutianus buccanella*), the silk snapper or

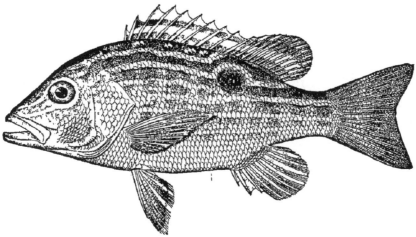

FIG 440 —Lane Snapper or Biajaiba, *Lutianus synagris* (Linnæus)   Key West

pargo de lo alto (*Lutianus vivanus*), the abundant lane snapper or biajaiba (*Lutianus synagris*), and the mahogany snapper

or ojanco (*Lutianus mahogani*) Numerous other species occur
on both coasts of tropical America, and a vastly larger assemblage is found in the East Indies, some of them ranging northward to Japan.

Hoplopagrus guntheri is a large snapper of the west coast
of Mexico, having very large molar teeth in its jaws besides slit-

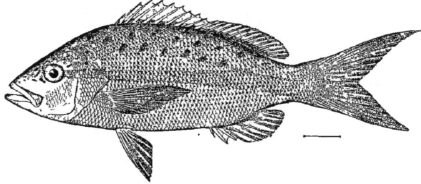

FIG 441 —Yellow-tail Snapper, *Ocyurus chrysurus* (Linnæus). Key West.

like nostrils and other notable peculiarities From the stand-
point of structure this species, with its eccentric characters—
is especially interesting The yellow-tail snapper or rabirubia
(*Ocyurus chrysurus*) is a handsome and common fish of the

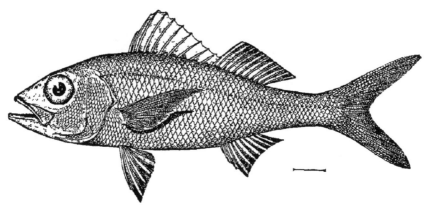

FIG. 442 —Cachucho, *Etelis oculatus* (Linnæus) Havana

West Indies, with long, deeply forked tail, which makes it a
swifter fish than the others Another red species is the dia-
mond snapper or cagon de lo alto, *Rhomboplites aurorubens*.
All these true snappers have the soft fins more or less scaly.

In certain species that swim more freely in deep waters, these fins are naked   Among them is the Arnillo, *Apsilus dentatus*, a pretty brown fish of the West Indies, and its analogue in Hawaii, *Apsilus brighami*, red, with golden cross-bands   *Aprion virescens*, the Uku of Hawaii, is a large fish of a greenish color and elongate body, widely diffused throughout Polynesia and one of the best of food-fishes   A related species is the red voraz (*Aprion macrophthalmus*) of the West Indies

Most beautiful of all the group are the species of *Etelis*, with the dorsal fin deeply divided and the head flattened above These live in rather deep water about rocky reefs and are fiery red in color   Best known is the Cuban species, *Etelis oculatus*, the cachucho of the markets   Equally abundant and equally

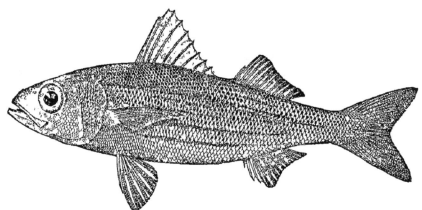

FIG   443 —*Xenocys jessiæ* Jordan & Bollman   Family *Lutianidæ*. Galapagos Islands

beautiful are *Etelis carbunculus* of Polynesia, *Etelis evurus* of Hawaii, and other species of the Pacific islands.

Verilus sordidus, the black escolar of Cuba, has the form of *Etelis*, but the flesh is very soft and the color violet-black, indicating its life in very deep water   Numerous small silvery snappers living near the shore along the coast of western Mexico belong to the genera called *Xenichthys*, *Xenistius*, and *Xenocys* *Xenistius californiensis* is the commonest of these species, *Xenocys jessiæ*, the largest in size, with black lines like a striped bass   To the genus *Dentex* belongs a large snapper-like fish of

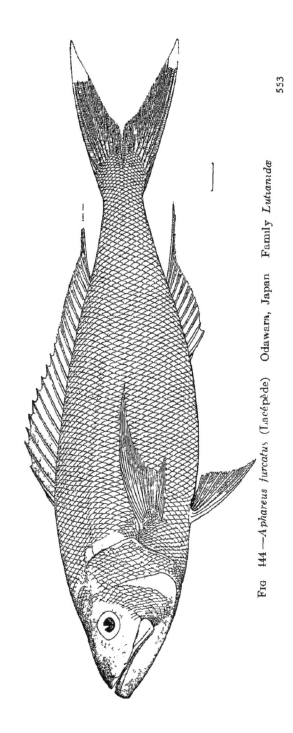

FIG. 144—*Aphareus furcatus* (Lacépède)   Odawara, Japan   Family *Lutianidæ*

the Mediterranean, *Dentex dentex*   Very many related species occur in the old world, the prettily colored *Nemipterus virgatus*, the *Itoyori* of Japan being one of the best known.   Another interesting fish is *Aphareus furcatus*, a handsome, swift fish of the open seas occasionally taken in Japan and the East Indies. *Glaucosoma burgeri* is a large snapper of Japan, and a related species, *Glaucosoma hebraicum*, is one of the "jewfishes" of Australia.   Numerous fossil forms referred to *Dentex* occur in the Eocene of Monte Bolca, as also a fish called *Ctenodentex lackeniensis* from the Eocene of Belgium.

The Grunts: Hæmulidæ. — The large family of *Hæmulidæ*, known in America as grunters or roncos, is represented with the

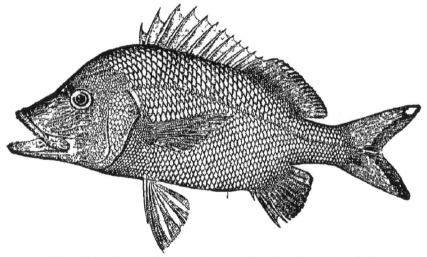

Fig   445 —Grunt, *Hæmulon plumieri* (Bloch)   Charleston, S C

snappers in all tropical seas   The common names (Spanish, *roncar*, to grunt or snore) refer to the noise made either with their large pharyngeal teeth or with the complex air-bladder. These fishes differ from the *Lutianinæ* mainly in the feebler detention, there being no canines and no teeth on the vomer Most of the American species belong to the genus *Hæmulon* or red-mouth grunts, so called from the dash of scarlet at the corner of the mouth   *Hæmulon plumieri*, the common grunt, or ronco arará, is the most abundant species, known by the narrow blue stripes across the head   In the yellow grunt, ronco amarillo (*Hæmulon sciurus*), these stripes cross the whole

body. In the margate-fish, or Jallao (*Hæmulon album*), the largest of the grunts, there are no stripes at all   Another common
grunt is the black spotted sailor's choice, *Ronco prieto* (*Hæmulon
parra*), very abundant from Florida southward   Numerous other
grunts and "Tom Tates" are found on both shores of Mexico,
all the species of *Hæmulon* being confined to America. *Anisotremus* includes numerous deep-bodied species with smaller
mouth, also all American *Anisotremus surinamensis*, the
pompon, abundant from Louisiana southward is the commonest
species. *Anisotremus virginicus*, the porkfish or Catalineta,

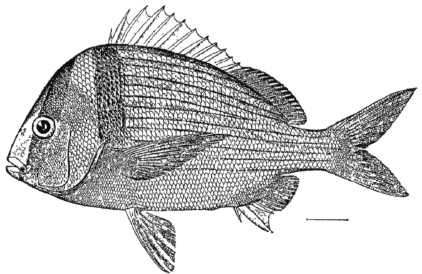

FIG. 446 —Porkfish, *Anisotremus virginicus* (Linnæus)   Key West

beautifully striped with black and golden, is very common
in the West Indies   *Plectorhynchus* of Polynesia and the coasts
of Asia contains numerous large species closely resembling
Anisotremus, but lacking the groove at the chin characteristic of *Anisotremus* and *Hæmulon*   Some of these are striped
or spotted with black in very gaudy fashion   *Pomadasis*, a
genus equally abundant in Asia and America, contains silvery
species of the sandy shores, with the body more elongate and
the spines generally stronger. *Pomadasis crocro* is the commonest West Indian species, *Pomadasis hasta* the best known
of the Asiatic forms   *Gnathodentex aurolineatus* with golden
stripes is common in Polynesia

The pigfishes, *Orthopristis*, have the spines feebler and the anal fin more elongate. Of the many species, American and Mediterranean, *Orthopristis chrysopterus* is most familiar, ranging northward to Long Island, and excellent as a pan fish. *Parapristipoma trilineatum*, the Isaki of Japan, is equally abundant and very similar to it. Many related species belong to the Asiatic genera, *Terapon*, *Scolopsis*, *Cæsio*, etc., sometimes placed in a distinct family as *Teraponidæ*. *Terapon servus* enters the streams of Polynesia, and is a very common fish of the river mouths, taken in Samoa by the boys. *Terapon theraps* is found throughout the East Indies. *Terapon richardsoni* is the Australian silver perch. *Cæsio* contains numerous small species, elongate and brightly colored, largely blue and golden. *Scolopsis*, having a spine on the preorbital, contains numerous species in the East Indies and Polynesia. These are often handsomely colored. Among them is the taiva, *Scolopsis trilineatus* of Samoa, gray with white streaks and markings of delicate pattern. A fossil species in the Italian Eocene related to *Pomadasis* is *Pomadasis furcatus*. Another, perhaps allied to *Terapon*, is called *Pelates quindecimalis*.

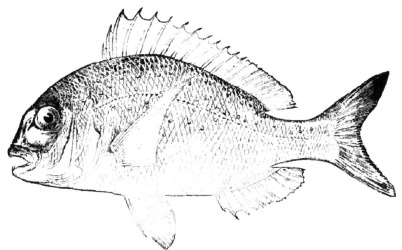

FIG. 447.—The Red Tai of Japan, *Pagrus major* Schlegel. Family *Sparidæ*. (After Kishinouye.)

The Porgies: Sparidæ. — The great family of *Sparidæ* or porgies is also closely related to the *Hæmulidæ*. The most tangible difference rests in the teeth, which are stronger, and

some of those along the side of the jaw are transformed into
large blunt molars, fitted for grinding small crabs and shells.
The name porgy, in Spanish pargo, comes from the Latin
Pagrus and Greek πάγρος, the name from time immemorial
of the red porgy of the Mediterranean, *Pagrus pagrus*. In this

FIG. 448.—Ebisu, the Fish-god of Japan, bearing a Red Tai
(Sketch by Kako Morita.)

species the front teeth are canine-like, the side teeth molar. It
is a fine food-fish, very handsome, being crimson with blue
spots, and in the Mediterranean it is much esteemed. It also
breeds sparingly on our south Atlantic and Gulf coasts.

Very similar to the porgy is the famous red tai or akadai of Japan (*Pagrus major*), a fish so highly esteemed as to be, with the rising sun and the chrysanthemum, a sort of national emblem   In all prints and images the fish-god Ebisu (Fig 448), beloved of the Japanese people, appears with a red tai under his arm   This species, everywhere abundant, is crimson in color, and the flesh is always tender and excellent   A similar species is

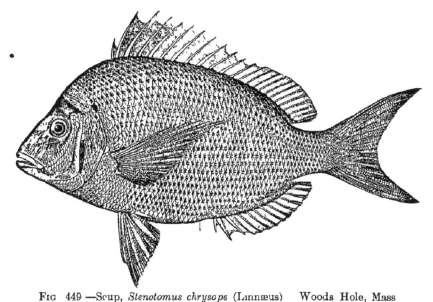

Fig 449 —Scup, *Stenotomus chrysops* (Linnæus)   Woods Hole, Mass

the well-known and abundant "schnapper" of Australia, *Pagrus unicolor*   Another but smaller tai or porgy, crimson, sprinkled with blue spots, *Pagrus cardinalis*, occurs in Japan in great abundance, as also two species similar in character but without red, known as *Kurodai* or black tai   These are *Sparus latus* and *Sparus berda*   The gilt-head of the Mediterranean, *Sparus aurata*, is very similar to these Japanese species   *Sparus sarba* in Australia is the tarwhine, and *Sparus australis* the black bream   The numerous species of *Pagellus* abound in the Mediterranean   These are smaller in size than the species of *Pagrus*, red in color and with feebler teeth   *Monotaxis grandoculis*, known as the "mu," is a widely diffused and valuable food-fish of the Pacific islands, greenish in color, with pale cross-bands   Very closely related is also the American scup or fair maid (*Stenotomus chrysops*), one of our commonest pan fishes.   In this genus and in *Calamus* the second interhæmal spine is very greatly enlarged, its concave end formed like a quill-pen and

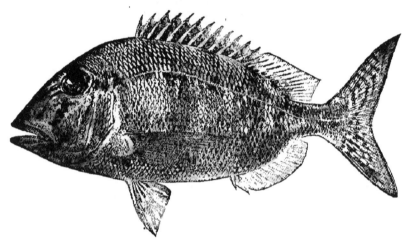

Fig. 450.—*Calamus bajonado* (Bloch & Schneider), Jolt-head Porgy. Pez de Pluma. Family *Sparidæ*.

including the posterior end of the large air-bladder. This arrangement presumably assists in hearing. Of the penfishes,

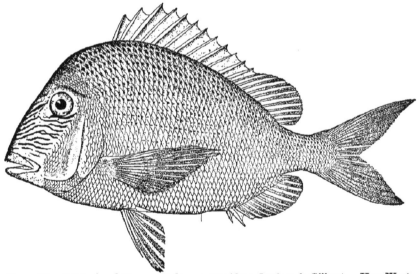

Fig. 451.—Little-head Porgy, *Calamus proridens* Jordan & Gilbert. Key West.

or pez de pluma, numerous species abound in tropical America, where they are valued as food. Of these the bajonado or jolt-head porgy (*Calamus bajonado*) is largest, most common and dullest in color   *Calamus calamus* is the saucer-eye porgy, and *Calamus providens*, the little-head porgy   *Calamus leucosteus* is called white-bone porgy, and the small *Calamus arctifrons* the grass-porgy

The Chopa spina, or pinfish, *Lagodon rhomboides*, is a little porgy with notched incisors, exceedingly common on our South Atlantic coast

In some of the porgies the front teeth instead of being canine-like are compressed and truncate, almost exactly like human incisors   These species are known as sheepshead, or sargos

Diplodus sargus and *Diplodus annularis* are common sargos of the Mediterranean, silvery, with a black blotch on the back of

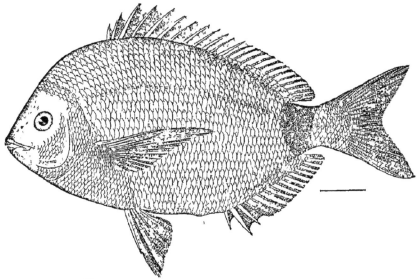

FIG 452 —*Diplodus holbrooki* Bean   Pensacola.

the tail   *Diplodus argenteus* of the West Indies and *Diplodus holbrooki* of the Carolina coast are very close to these

The sheepshead, *Archosargus probatocephalus*, is much the most valuable fish of this group   The broad body is crossed by about seven black cross-bands   It is common from Cape Cod to Texas in sandy bays, reaching rarely a weight of fifteen pounds.   Its flesh is most excellent, rich and tender   The sheepshead is a quiet bottom-fish, but takes the hook readily and with some spirit.   Close to the sheepshead is a smaller species known as Salema (*Archosargus unimaculatus*), with blue and golden stripes and a black spot at the shoulder. It abounds in the West Indies.

On the coast of Japan and throughout Polynesia are numerous species of *Lethrinus* and related genera, formed and

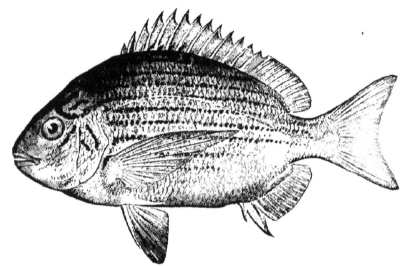

Fig. 453.—*Archosargus unimaculatus* (Bloch), Salema, Striped Sheepshead. Family *Sparidæ*.

colored like snappers, but with molar teeth and the cheek without scales. A common species in Japan is *Lethrinus richardsoni*.

Fossil species of *Diplodus*, *Sparus*, *Pagrus*, and *Pagellus* occur in the Italian Eocene, as also certain extinct genera, *Sparnodus* and *Trigonodon*, of similar type. *Sparnodus macrophthalmus* is abundant in the Eocene of Monte Bolca.

The Picarels: Mænidæ.—The *Mænidæ*, or *Picarels*, are elongate, gracefully formed fishes, remarkable for the extreme protractility of the upper jaw. *Spicara smaris* and several other small species are found in the Mediterranean. *Emmelichthys* contains species of larger size occurring in the West Indies and various parts of the Pacific, chiefly red and very graceful in form and color. *Emmelichthys villatus*, the boga, is occasionally taken in Cuba, *Erythrichthys schlegeli* is found in Japan and Hawaii.

The Mojarras: Gerridæ.—The *Gerridæ*, or *Mojarras*, have the mouth equally protractile, but the form of the body is different, being broad, compressed, and covered with large silvery scales   In some species the dorsal spines and the third anal spine are very strong, and in some the second interhæmal is quill-shaped, including the end of the air-bladder, as in *Calamus.* Most of the species, including all the peculiar ones, are American The smallest, *Eucinostomus*, have the quill-shaped interhæmal

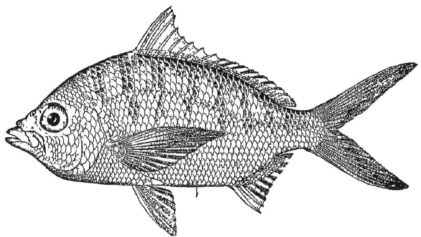

FIG 454 —Mojarra, *Xystæma cinereum* (Walbaum)   Key West.

and the dorsal and anal spines are very weak   The commonest species is the silver jenny, or mojarra de Ley, *Eucinostomus gula*, which ranges from Cape Cod to Rio Janeiro, in the surf along sandy shores   Equally common is *Eucinostomus californiensis* of the Pacific Coast of Mexico, while *Eucinostomus harengulus* of the West Indies is also very abundant. *Ulæma lefroyi* has but two anal spines and the interhæmal very small It is common through the West Indies   *Xystæma*, with the interhæmal spear-shaped and normally formed, is found in Asia and Polynesia more abundantly than in America, although one species, *Xystæma cinereum*, the broad shad, or Mojarra blanca, is common on both shores of tropical America *Xystæma gigas* is found in Polynesia, *X oyena* in Japan, and *X filamentosum* in Formosa and India   *Xystæma massalongoi* is also fossil in the Miocene of Austria   The species of *Gerres* have very strong dorsal and anal spines and the back much elevated   *Gerres plumieri*, the striped mojarra, *Gerres brasiliensis*, the patao, *Gerres olisthostomus*, the Irish pampano, and *Gerres rhombeus* are some of the numerous species found on the Florida coast and in the West Indies   The family of *Leiognathidæ*, already noticed (page 502), should stand next to the *Gerridæ*.

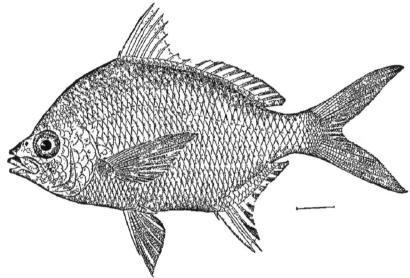

FIG 455 —Irish Pampano, *Gerres olisthostomus* Goode & Bean   Indian River, Fla

The Rudder-fishes: Kyphosidæ.—The *Kyphosidæ*, called rudder-fishes, have no molars, the front of the jaws being occupied by incisors, which are often serrated, loosely attached,

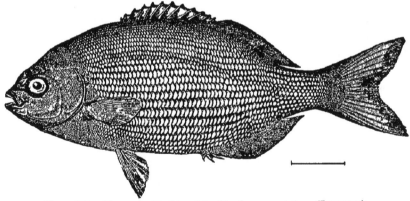

FIG. 456 —Chopa or Rudder-fish, *Kyphosus sectatrix* (Linnæus)
Woods Hole, Mass

and movable. The numerous species are found in the warm seas and are chiefly herbivorous   ·

Boops boops and *Boops salpa*, known as boga and salpa,

are elongate fishes common in the Mediterranean. Other Mediterranean forms are *Spondyliosoma cantharus*, *Oblata melanura*, etc. *Girella nigricans* is the greenfish of California, everywhere abundant about rocks to the south of San Francisco, and of considerable value as food. Almost exactly like it is the Mejinadai (*Girella punctata*) of Japan. The best-known members of this group belong to the genus *Kyphosus*. *Kyphosus sectatrix* is the rudder-fish, or Chopa blanca, common in the West Indies and following ships to the northward even as far as Cape Cod, once even taken at Palermo. It is supposed that it is enticed by the waste thrown overboard. *Kyphosus elegans* is found on the west coast of Mexico, *Kyphosus tahmel* in the East Indies and Polynesia, and numerous other species occur in tropical America and along the coasts of southern Asia. *Sectator ocyurus* is a more elongate form of rudder-fish, striped with bright blue and yellow, found in the Pacific. *Medialuna californiensis* is the half-moon fish, or medialuna, of southern California, an excellent food-fish frequently taken on rocky shores. Numerous related species occur in the Indian seas.

Fossil fragments in Europe have been referred to *Boops*, *Spondyliosoma*, and other genera.

Fig. 457.—Blue-green Sunfish, *Apomotis cyanellus* (Rafinesque). Kansas River. (After Kellogg.)

CHAPTER XXXV

THE SURMULLETS, THE CROAKERS AND THEIR RELATIVES

THE Surmullets, or Goatfishes: Mullidæ.—The *Mullidæ* (Surmullets) are shore-fishes of the warm seas, of moderate size, with small mouth, large scales, and possessing the notable character of two long, unbranched barbels of firm substance at the chin. The dorsal fins are short, well separated, the first of six to eight firm spines There are two anal spines and the ventral fins, thoracic, are formed of one spine and five rays The flesh is white and tender, often of very superior flavor The species are carnivorous,

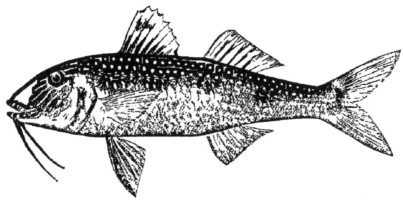

FIG 458 —Red Goatfish, or Salmonete, *Pseudupeneus maculatus* Bloch
Family *Mullidæ* (Surmullets)

feeding chiefly on small animals They are not voracious, and predaceous fishes feed freely on them The coloration is generally bright, largely red or golden, in nearly all cases with an under layer, below the scales, of red, which appears when the fish is scaled or placed in alcohol The barbels are often bright yellow, and when the fish swims along the bottom these are carried in advance, feeling the way Testing the bottom

565

with their feelers, these fishes creep over the floor of shallow waters, seeking their food

The numerous species are all very much alike in form, and the current genera are separated by details of the arrangement of the teeth   But few are found outside the tropics

The surmullet or red mullet of Europe, *Mullus barbatus*, is the most famous species, placed by the Romans above all other fishes unless it be the scarus, *Sparisoma cretense*   From the satirical poets we learn that "enormous prices were paid for a fine fish, and it was the fashion to bring the fish into the dining-room and exhibit it alive before the assembled guests, so that they might gloat over the brilliant and changing colors during the death-agonies"   It is red in life, and when the scales are removed, the color is much brighter.

It is an excellent fish, tender and rich, but nowhere so extravagantly valued to-day as was formerly the case in Rome.

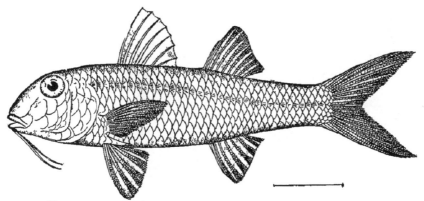

Fig   459 —Golden Surmullet, *Mullus auratus* Jordan & Gilbert
Wood's Hole, Mass

Mullus surmuletus is a second European species, scarcely different from *Mullus barbatus*

Equally excellent as food and larger in size are two Polynesian species known as kumu and munu (*Pseudupeneus porphyreus* and *Pseudupeneus bifasciatus*).   *Mullus auratus* is a small surmullet occasionally taken off our Atlantic coast, but in deeper water than that frequented by the European species   *Pseudupeneus maculatus* is the red goatfish or salmonete, common from Florida to Brazil, as is also the yellow goatfish, *Pseudu-*

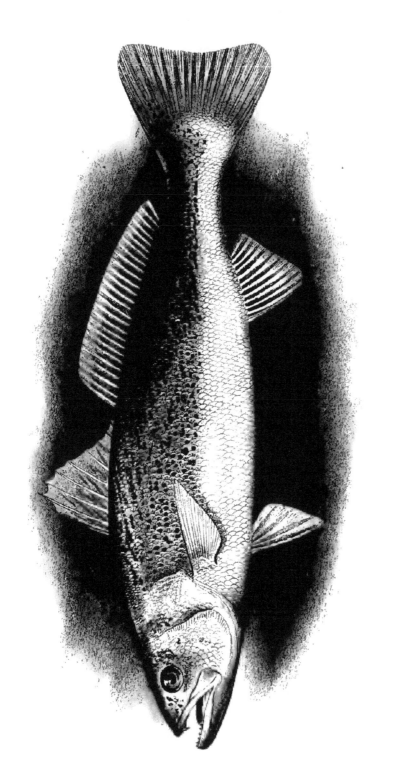

SQUETEAGUE; WEAKFISH (CYNOSCION REGALIS)

peneus martinicus, equally valued.   Many other species are
found in tropical America, Polynesia, and the Indies and Japan
Perhaps the most notable are *Upeneus vittatus*, striped with
yellow and with the caudal fin cross-barred and the belly sul-
phur-yellow, and *Upeneus arge*, similar, the belly white   The
common red and black-banded "moana" or goatfish of Hawaii
is *Pseudupeneus multifasciatus*

No fossil *Mullidæ* are recorded, so far as known to us

The Croakers: Sciænidæ. — The family of *Sciænidæ* (croakers, roncadors) is another of the great groups of food-fishes
The species are found on every sandy shore in warm regions
and all of them are large enough to have value as food, while
many have flesh of superior quality   None is brightly colored,
most of the species being nearly plain silvery

Special characters are the cavernous structure of the bones
of the head, which are full of mucous tracts, the specialization

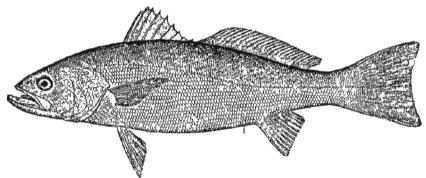

Fig 460 —Spotted Weakfish, *Cynoscion nebulosus* Virginia

(and occasional absence) of the air-bladder, and the presence
of never more than two anal spines, one of these being sometimes very large   Most of the species are marine, all are carnivorous, none inhabits rocky places and none descends to depths
in the sea   At the least specialized extreme of the family,
the mouth is large with strong canines and the species are
slender, swift, and predaceous

The weakfish or squeteague (*Cynoscion regalis*) is a type
of a multitude of species, large, swift, voracious, but with tender flesh, which is easily torn   The common weakfish, abundant on our Atlantic coast, suffers much at the hands of its

enemy and associate, the bluefish. It is one of the best of all our food-fishes Farther south the spotted weakfish (*Cynoscion nebulosus*), very incorrectly known as sea-trout, takes its place, and about New Orleans is especially and justly prized.

The California "bluefish," *Cynoscion parvipinnis*, is very similar to these Atlantic species, and there are many other species of *Cynoscion* on both coasts of tropical America, forming a large part of the best fish-supply of the various markets of the mainland On the rocky islands, as Cuba, and about coral reefs, *Sciænidæ* are practically unknown In the Gulf of California, the totuava, *Cynoscion macdonaldi*, reaches a weight of 172 pounds, and the stateliest of all, the great "white sea-bass" of California, *Cynoscion nobilis*, reaches 100 pounds In these large species the flesh is much more firm than in the weakfish and thus bears shipment better *Cynoscion* has canines in the upper jaw only and its species are all American In the East Indies the genus *Otolithes* has strong canines in both jaws Its numerous species are very similar in form, habits, and value to those of *Cynoscion* The queenfish, *Seriphus politus*, of the California coast, is much like the others of this series, but smaller and with no canines at all It is a very choice fish, as are also the species of *Macrodon* (*Ancylodon*) known as pescadillo del red, voracious fishes of both shores of South America

Plagioscion squamosissimus and numerous species of *Plagioscion* and other genera live in the rivers of South America A single species, the river-drum, gaspergou, river sheepshead, or thunder-pumper (*Aplodinotus grunniens*), is found in streams in North America This is a large fish reaching a length of nearly three feet It is very widely distributed, from the Great Lakes to Rio Usumacinta in Guatemala, whence it has been lately received by Dr Evermann This species abounds in lakes and sluggish rivers The flesh is coarse, and in the Great Lakes it is rarely eaten, having a rank odor In Louisiana and Texas it is, however, regarded as a good food-fish In this species the lower pharyngeals are very large and firmly united, while, as in all other *Sciænidæ*, except the genus *Pogonias*, these bones are separated In all members of the family the ear-bones or otoliths are largely developed, often finely sculptured.

The otoliths of the river-drum are known to Wisconsin boys as "lucky-stones," each having a rude impress of the letter L The names roncador, drum, thunder-pumper, croaker, and the like refer to the grunting noise made by most *Sciænidæ* in the water, a noise at least connected with the large and divided air-bladder.

Numerous silvery species belong to *Larimus, Corvula, Odontoscion*, and especially to *Bairdiella*, a genus in which the second anal spine is unusually strong   The mademoiselle, *Bairdiella*

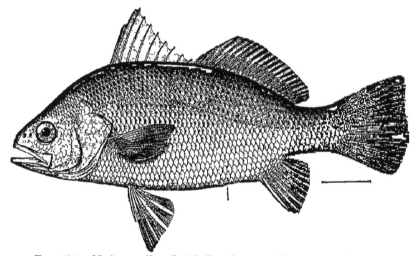

Fig 461 —Mademoiselle, *Bairdiella chrysura* (Linnæus) Virginia

chrysura is a pretty fish of our Atlantic coast, excellent as a pan fish   In *Bairdiella ensifera* of Panama the second anal spine is enormously large, much as in a robalo (*Oxylabrax*).

In *Stellifer* and *Nebris*, the head is soft and spongy   *Stellifer lanceolatus* is occasionally taken off South Carolina, and numerous other species of this and related genera are found farther South

Sciænops ocellata is the red-drum or channel bass of our South Atlantic coast, a most important food-fish reaching a weight of seventy-five pounds.   It is well marked by a black ocellus on the base of the tail.   On the coast of Texas, this species, locally called redfish, exceeds in economic value all other species found in that State

Pseudosciæna aquila, the maigre of southern Europe, is

another large fish, similar in value to the red drum.   *Pseudo-sciæna antarctica* is the kingfish of Australia   To *Sciæna* belong many species, largely Asiatic, with the mouth inferior, without barbels, the teeth small, and the convex snout marked with mucous pores   *Sciæna umbra*, the ombre, is the common European species, *Sciæna saturna*, the black roncador of California, is much like it   *Sciæna deliciosa* is one of the most valued

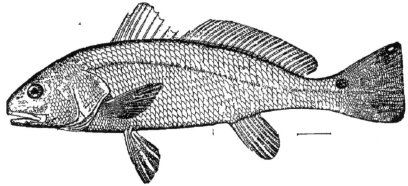

Fig   462 —Red Drum, *Sciænops ocellata* Linnæus.   Texas

food-fishes of Peru, and *Sciæna argentata* is valued in Japan. Species of *Sciæna* are especially numerous on the coasts of India

Ronaador stearnsi, the California roncador, is a large fish with a black ocellus at the base of the pectoral   It has some importance in the Los Angeles market   The goody, spot, or lafayette (*Leiostomus xanthurus*) is a small, finely flavored species abundant from Cape Cod to Texas   Similar to it but inferior is the little roncador (*Genyonemus lineatus*) of California. The common croaker, *Micropogon undulatus*, is very abundant on our Eastern coast, and other species known as verrugatos or white-mouthed drummers replace it farther South

In, *Umbrina* the chin has a short thick barbel   The species abound in the tropics, *Umbrina cirrosa* in the Mediterranean, *Umbrina coroides* in California, and the handsome *Umbrina roncador*, the yellow-tailed roncador, in southern California   The kingfish, *Menticirrhus*, differs in lacking the air-bladder, and lying on the bottom in shallow water the lower fins are enlarged much as in the darters or gobies   All the species are American.   All are dull-colored and all excellent as food   *Menticirrhus saxatilis* is the common kingfish or sea-mink, abundant from Cape Ann southward, *Menticirrhus americanus* is the equally common sand-whiting of Carolina, and *Menticirrhus*

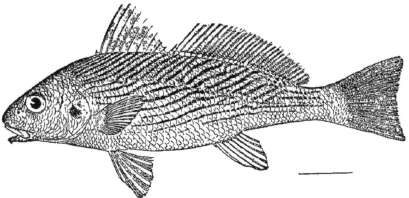

FIG 463 —Yellow-fin Roncador, *Umbrina sinaloæ* Scofield   Mazatlan

littoralis the surf-whiting   The California whiting or sand-sucker is *Menticirrhus undulatus*

Pogonias chromis, the sea-drum, has barbels on the chin and the lower pharyngeals are enlarged and united as in the river-

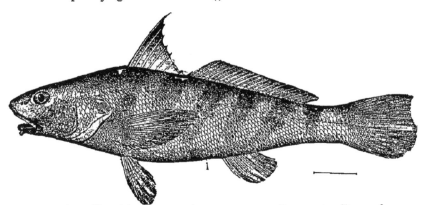

FIG 464 —Kingfish, *Menticirrhus americanus* (Linnæus)   Pensacola

drum, *Aplodinotus*. It is a coarse fish common on our Atlantic coasts, a large specimen taken at St Augustine weighing 146 pounds   Other species of this family, belonging to the genus *Eques*, are marked with ribbon-like stripes of black   *Eques lanceolatus*, known in Cuba as serrana, is the most ornate of these species, looking like a butterfly-fish or Chætodon.

Several fossil fragments have been doubtfully referred to *Sciæna, Umbrina, Pogonias,* and other genera   Otoliths or ear-bones not clearly identifiable are found from the Miocene on These structures are more highly specialized in this group than in any other

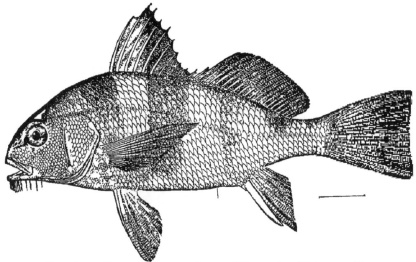

FIG 465 —Drum, *Pogonias chromis* (Linnæus) Matanzas, Fla

The Sillaginidæ, etc.—Allied to the *Sciænidæ* is the small family of Kisugos, *Sillaginidæ*, of the coasts of Asia These are slender, cylindrical fishes, silvery in color, with a general resemblance to small *Sciænas*

Sillago japonicus, the kisugo of Japan, is a very abundant species, valued as food *Sillago sihama* ranges from Japan to Abyssinia

A number of small families, mostly Asiatic, may be appended to the percoid series, with which they agree in general characters, especially in the normal structure of the shoulder-girdle and in the insertion of the pectoral and ventral fins

The *Lactariidæ* constitute a small family of the East Indies, allied to the *Sciænidæ*, but with three anal spines. The mouth is armed with strong teeth *Lactarius lactarius* is a food-fish of India

The *Nandidæ* are small spiny-rayed fishes of the East Indian streams, without pseudobranchiæ

The *Polycentridæ* are small fresh-water perch-like fishes of the streams of South America, without lateral line and with many anal spines

The Jawfishes: Opisthognathidæ, etc. — The *Pseudochromi-pidæ* are marine-fishes of the tropics with the lateral line inter-rupted, and with a single dorsal. They bear some resemblance to *Plesiops* and other aberrant *Serranidæ*

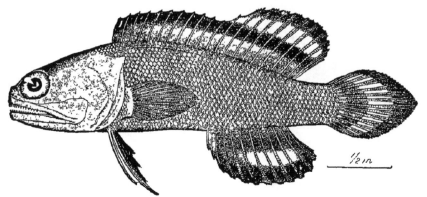

Fig **466** —*Gnathypops evermanni* Jordan & Snyder. Misaki, Japan

Very close to these are the *Opistognathidæ* or jawfishes with a single lateral line and the mouth very large In certain species of *Opisthognathus*, the maxillary, long and curved, extends far behind the head. The few species are found in warm

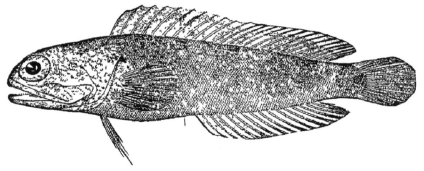

Fig **467** —Jawfish, *Opisthognathus macrognathus* Poey. Tortugas, Fla

seas, but always very sparingly   Some of them are handsomely colored.

The Stone-wall Perch: Oplegnathidæ.—A singular group evi-dently allied to the *Hæmulidæ* is the family of *Oplegnathidæ* In these fishes the teeth are grown together to form a bony beak like the jaw of a turtle   Except for this character, the species are very similar to ordinary grunts   While the mouth resembles that of the parrot-fish, it is structurally different and must have been independently developed *Oplegnathus punctatus*, the "stonewall perch" (ishigakidai), is common in Japan, as is also

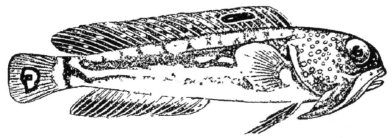

FIG 468 —*Opisthognathus nigromarginatus*   India   (After Day)

the banded *Oplegnathus fasciatus*   Other species are found in Australia and Chile.

The Swallowers: Chiasmodontidæ.—The family of swallowers *Chiasmodontidæ*, is made up of a few deep-sea fishes of soft flesh and feeble spines, the opercular apparatus much reduced.

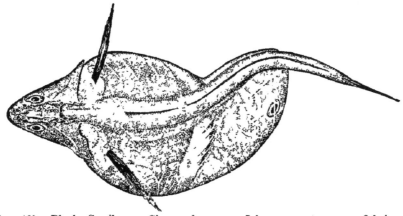

FIG 469 —Black Swallower, *Chiasmodon niger* Johnson, containing a fish larger than itself   Le Have Bank

The ventrals are post-thoracic, the rays 1, 5, facts which point to some affinity with the *Opisthognathidæ*, although Boulenger places these fishes among the *Percesoces*   *Chiasmodon niger*, the black swallower of the mid-Atlantic, has exceedingly long teeth and the whole body so distensible that it can swallow fishes of many times its own size   According to Gill

"It espies a fish many times larger than itself, but which, nevertheless, may be managed, it darts upon it, seizes it by

OCHANOPS LATOVITTATA (LACÉPÈDE)

the tail and gradually climbs over it with its jaws, first using one and then the other, as the captive is taken in the stomach and integuments stretch out, and at last the entire fish is passed through the mouth and into the stomach, and the distended belly appears as a great bag, projecting out far backwards and forwards, over which is the swallower with the ventrals dislocated and far away from their normal place   The walls of the stomach and belly have been so stretched that they are transparent, and the species of the fish can be discerned within   But such rapacity is more than the captor itself can stand.   At length decomposition sets in, the swallower is forced belly up. wards, and the imprisoned gas, as in a balloon, takes it upwards from the depths to the surface of the ocean, and there, perchance, it may be found and picked up, to be taken home for a wonder, as it is really   Thus have at least three specimens found their way into museums—one being in the United States National Museum—and in each the fish in the stomach has been about twice as long, and stouter in proportion, than the swallower— six to twelve times bulkier! Its true habitat seems to be at a depth of about 1,500 fathoms "

Allied to this family is the little group of *Champsodontidæ* of Japan and the East Indies   *Champsodon vorax* looks like a young *Uranoscopus*   The body is covered with numerous lateral lines and cross-lines.

The Malacanthidæ. — The *Malacanthidæ* are elongate fishes, rather handsomely colored, with a strong canine on the premaxillary behind   *Malacanthus plumieri*, the matajuelo blanco, a slender fish of a creamy-brown color, is common in the West Indies.   Other species are found in Polynesia, the most notable being *Malacanthus* (or *Oceanops*) *latovittatus*, a large fish of a brilliant sky-blue, with a jet-black lateral band   In Samoa this species is called gatasami, the "eye of the sea."

The Blanquillos: Latilidæ.—The *Latilidæ*, or blanquillos, have also an enlarged posterior canine, but the body is deeper and the flesh more firm   The species reach a considerable size and are valued as food   *Lopholatilus chamæleonticeps* is the famous tilefish dredged in the depths under the Gulf Stream   It is a fish of remarkable beauty, red and golden   This species, Professor Gill writes, "was unknown until 1879, when specimens were brought by fishermen to Boston from a previously unexplored bank about eighty miles southeast of No Man's Land, Mass In the fall of 1880 it was found to be extremely abundant everywhere off the coast of southern New England at a depth of from seventy-five to two hundred and fifty fathoms The form of the species is more compressed, and higher, than in most of the family, and what especially distinguishes it is the development of a compressed, 'fleshy, fin-like appendage over the back part of the head and nape, reminding one of the adipose fin of the salmonids and catfishes' It is especially notable, too, for the brilliancy of its colors, as well as for its size, being by far larger than any other member of its family A weight of fifty pounds or more is, or rather, one might say, was frequently attained by it, although such was very far above the average, that being little over ten pounds In the reach of water referred to, it could once be found abundantly at any time, and caught by hook and line After a severe gale in March, 1882, millions of tilefish could be seen, or calculated for, on the surface of the water for a distance of about three hundred miles from north to south, and fifty miles from east to west It has been calculated by Capt Collins that as many as one thousand four hundred and thirty-eight millions were scattered over the surface This would have allowed about two hundred and twenty-eight pounds to every man, woman and child of the fifty million inhabitants of the United States! On trying at their former habitat the next fall, as well as all successive years to the present time, not a single specimen could be found where formerly it was so numerous. We have thus a case of a catastrophe which, as far as has been observed, caused complete annihilation of an abundant animal in a very limited period. Whether the grounds it formerly held will be reoccupied subsequently by the progeny of a protected colony remains to be seen, but it is scarcely probable that the entire species has been exterminated " It is now certain that the species is not extinct

Caulolatilus princeps is the blanquillo or "whitefish" of southern California, a large handsome fish formed like a dolphin, of purplish, olivaceous color and excellent flesh. Other species of *Caulolatilus* are found in the West Indies *Latilus*

japonicus is the amadai or sweet perch of Japan, an excellent food-fish of a bright crimson color

The *Pinguipedidæ* of Chile resemble the *Latilidæ*, having also the enlarged premaxillary tooth The ventrals are, however, thickened and placed farther forward

The Bandfishes Cepolidæ.—The small family of *Cepolidæ*, or bandfishes, resemble the *Latilidæ* somewhat and are probably related to them. The head is normally formed, the ventral fins are thoracic, with a spine and five rays, but the body is drawn out into a long eel-like form, the many-rayed dorsal and anal fins meeting around the tail The few species are crimson in color with small scales They are used as food, but the flesh is dry and the bones are stiff and numerous *Cepola tænia* is common in the Mediterranean, and *Acanthocepola krusensterni* abounds in the bays of southern Japan

The Cirrhitidæ.—The species of the family *Cirrhitidæ* strongly resemble the smaller *Serranidæ* and even *Serranus* itself, but the lower rays of the pectoral fins are enlarged and are undivided, as in the sea-scorpions and some sculpins In these fishes, however, the bony stay, which characterizes *Scorpænidæ* and *Cottidæ*, is wholly absent It is, however, considered possible that this interesting family represents the point of separation at which the mail-cheeked fishes become differentiated from the typical perch-like forms *Goniistius zonatus*, the takanohadai, is a valuable food-fish of Japan, marked by black cross-bands *Paracirrhites forsteri* and other species of *Cirrhitus* and *Paracirrhites* are very pretty fishes of the coral reefs, abundant in the markets of Honolulu, the spotted *Cirrhitus marmoratus* being the most widely diffused of these. Only one species of this family, *Cirrhitus rivulatus*, a large fish, green, with blue markings, is found in American waters It frequents the rocky shores of the west coast of Mexico

Allied to the *Cirrhitidæ* is the small family of *Latriddidæ*, with a long dorsal fin deeply divided, and the lower rays of the pectoral similarly modified *Latris hecateia* is called the "trumpeter" in Australian waters It is one of the best food-fishes of Australia, reaching a weight of sixty to eighty pounds

Another small family showing the same peculiar structure of the pectoral fin is that of the *Aplodactylidæ* The species of *Aplodactylus* live on the coasts of Chile and Australia   They are herbivorous fishes, with flat, tricuspid teeth, and except for their pectoral fins are very similar to the *Kyphosidæ*.

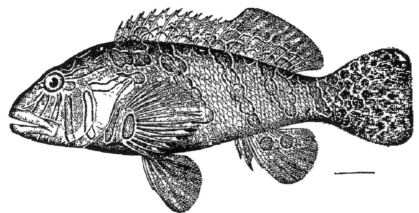

FIG 470 —*Cirrhitus rivulatus* Valenciennes   Mazatlan

The Sandfishes: Trichodontidæ.—In the neighborhood of the *Latrididæ*, Dr Boulenger places the *Trichodontidæ* or sandfishes, small, scaleless, silvery fishes of the northern Pacific. These

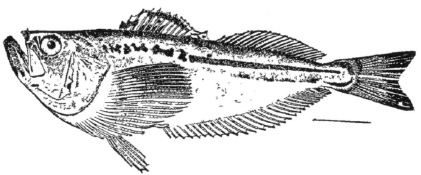

FIG 471—Sandfish, *Trichodon trichodon* (Tilesius). Shumagin Islands, Alaska

are much compressed in body, with very oblique mouths, with fringed lips and, as befits their northern habitat, with a much increased number of vertebræ   They bury themselves in sand under the surf, and the two species, *Trichodon trichodon* and *Arctoscopus japonicus*, range very widely in the regions washed by the Japan current   These species bear a strong resemblance to the star-gazers (*Uranoscopus*), but this likeness seems to be superficial only

CHAPTER XXXVI

LABYRINTHICI AND HOLCONOTI

THE Labyrinthine Fishes.—An oftshoot of the Percomorphi is the group of Labyrinthici, composed of perch-like fishes which have a very peculiar structure to the pharyngeal bones and respiratory apparatus This feature is thus described by Dr. Gill.

"The upper elements of one of the pairs of gill-bearing arches are peculiarly modified The elements in question (called branchihyal) of each side, instead of being straight and solid, as in most fishes, are excessively developed and provided with several thin plates or folds, erect from the surface of the bones and the roof of the skull, to which the bones are attached These plates, by their intersection, form chambers, and are lined with a vascular membrane, which is supplied with large blood-vessels It was formerly supposed that the chambers referred to had the office of receiving and retaining supplies of water which should trickle down and keep the gills moist, such was supposed to be an adaptation for the sustentation of life out of the water The experiments of Surgeon Day, however, throw doubt upon this alleged function, and tend to show (1) that these fishes died when deprived of access to atmospheric air, not from any deleterious properties either in the water or in the apparatus used, but from being unable to subsist on air obtained solely from the water, aerial respiration being indispensable, (2) that they can live in moisture out of the water for lengthened periods, and for a short, but variable period in water only, and (3) that the cavity or receptacle does not contain water, but has a moist secreting surface, in which air is retained for the purpose of respiration It seems probable that the air, after having been supplied for aerial respiration, is ejected by the mouth, and not swallowed to be

discharged per anum. In fine, the two respiratory factors
of the branchial apparatus have independent functions (1)
the labyrinthiform, or branchihyal portion, being a special modification for the respiration of atmospheric air, and (2) the gill
filaments discharging their normal function. If, however,
the fish is kept in water and prevented from coming to the
surface to swallow the atmospheric air, the labyrinthiform
apparatus becomes filled with water which cannot be discharged, owing to its almost non-contractile powers   There
is thus no means of emptying it, and the water probably
becomes carbonized and unfit for oxygenizing the blood, so
that the whole of the respiration is thus thrown on the branchiæ
This will account for the fact that when the fish is in a state
of quiescence, it lives much longer than when excited, whilst
the sluggishness sometimes evinced may be due to poisoned
or carbonized blood "

Four families of labyrinth-gilled fishes are recognized by
Professor Gill, and to these we may append a fifth, which, however, lacks the elaborate structures mentioned above and
which shows other evidences of degeneration.

The Climbing-perches: Anabantidæ.—The family of *Anabantidæ*, according to Gill, "includes those species which have the

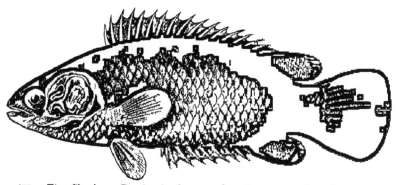

FIG 472 —The Climbing Perch, *Anabas scandens* Linnæus   Opercle cut away to
show the gill-labyrinth

mouth of moderate size and teeth on the palate (either on the
vomer alone, or on both the vomer and palatine bones).   To
the family belongs the celebrated climbing-fish

"The climbing-fish (*Anabas scandens*) is especially noteworthy for the movability of the sub-operculum.   The oper-

culum is serrated. The color is reddish olive, with a blackish spot at the base of the caudal fin, the head, below the level of the eye, grayish, but relieved by an olive band running from the angle of the mouth to the angle of the pre-operculum, and with a black spot on the membrane behind the hindermost spines of the operculum

"The climbing-fish was first made known in a memoir, printed in 1797, by Daldorf, a lieutenant in the service of the Danish East India Company at Tranquebar Daldorf called it *Perca scandens*, and affirmed that he himself had taken one of these fishes, clinging by the spine of its operculum in a slit in the bark of a palm (*Borassus flabelliformis*) which grew near a pond He also described its mode of progression, and his observations were substantially repeated by the Rev. Mr. John, a missionary resident in the same country. His positive evidence was, however, called into question by those who doubted on account of hypothetical considerations Even in popular works not generally prone to even a judicious skepticism, the accounts were stigmatized as unworthy of belief. We have, however, in answer to such doubts, too specific information to longer distrust the reliability of the previous reports

"Mr. Rungasawmy Moodeliar, a native assistant of Capt. Jesse Mitchell of the Madras Government Central Museum, communicated to his superior the statement that 'this fish inhabits tanks or pools of water, and is called *Panai jeri*, i e , the fish that climbs palmyra-trees. When there are palmyra-trees growing by the side of a tank or pool, when heavy rain falls and the water runs profusely down their trunks, this fish, by means of its opercula, which move unlike those of other fishes, crawls up the tree sideways (i e , inclining to the sides considerably from the vertical) to a height of from five to seven feet, and then drops down. Should this fish be thrown upon the ground, it runs or proceeds rapidly along in the same manner (sideways) as long as the mucus on it remains '

"These movements are effected by the opercula, which, it will be remembered, are unusually mobile in this species, they can, according to Captain Mitchell (and I have verified the statement), be raised or turned outwards to nearly a right angle with the body, and when in that position, the suboperculum distends a little, and it appears that it is chiefly by the spines of this latter piece that the fish takes a purchase on the tree or ground. 'I have,' says Captain Mitchell, 'ascertained by experiment that the mere closing of the operculum, when the spines are in contact with any surface, even common glass, pulls an ordinary-sized fish forwards about half an inch,' but it is probable that additional force is supplied by the caudal and anal fins, both of which, it is said, are put in use when climbing or advancing on the ground, the motion, in fact, is described as a wriggling one

"The climbing-fish seems to manifest an inclination to ascend streams against the current, and we can now understand how, during rain, the water will flow down the trunk of a tree, and the climbing-fish, taking advantage of this, will ascend against the down-flow by means of the mechanism already described, and by which it is enabled to reach a considerable distance up the trunk" (Gill)

The Gouramis Osphromenidæ —"The *Osphromenidæ* are fishes with a mouth of small size, and destitute of teeth on the palate. To this family belongs the gourami, whose praises have been so often sung, and which has been the subject of many efforts for acclimatization in France and elsewhere by the French

"The gourami (*Osphromenus goramy*) has an oblong, oval form, and, when mature, the color is nearly uniform, but in the young there are black bands across the body, and also a blackish spot at the base of the pectoral fin The gourami, if we can credit reports, occasionally reaches a gigantic size, for it is claimed that it sometimes attains a length of 6 feet, and weighs 150 pounds, but if this is true, the size is at least exceptional, and one of 20 pounds is a very large fish, indeed, they are considered very large if they weigh as much as 12 or 14 pounds, in which case they measure about 2 feet in length

"The countries in which the gourami is most at home lie in the intertropical belt The fish is assiduous in the care of its young, and prepares a nest for the reception of eggs The bottom selected is muddy, the depth variable within a narrow area, that is, in one place about a yard, and near by several yards deep

"They prefer to use, for the nests, tufts of a peculiar grass

(*Panicum jumentorum*) which grows on the surface of the water, and whose floating roots, rising and falling with the movements of the water, form natural galleries, under which the fish can conceal themselves In one of the corners of the pond, among the plants which grow there, the gouramis attach their nest, which is of a nearly spherical form, and composed of plants and mud, and considerably resembles in form those of some birds.

"The gourami is omnivorous, taking at times flesh, fish, frogs, insects, worms, and many kinds of vegetables, and on account of its omnivorous habit, it has been called by the French colonists of Mauritius *porc des rivières*, or 'river-pig' It is, however, essentially a vegetarian, and its adaptation for this diet is indicated by the extremely elongated intestinal canal, which is many times folded upon itself It is said to be especially fond of the leaves of several araceous plants Its flesh is, according to several authors, of a light-yellow straw-color, firm and easy of digestion They vary in quality with the nature of the waters inhabited, those taken from a rocky river being much superior to those from muddy ponds, but those dwelling at the mouth of rivers, where the water is to some extent brackish, are the best of all Again, they vary with age, and the large, overgrown fishes are much less esteemed than the small ones They are in their prime when three years old Dr Vinson says the flavor is somewhat like that of carp, and, if this is so, we may entertain some skepticism as to its superiority, but the unanimous testimony in favor of its excellence naturally leads to the belief that the comparison is unfair to the gourami

"Numerous attempts have been made by the French to introduce the gourami into their country, as well as into several of their provinces, and for a number of years consignments of the eggs, or the young, or adult fish, were made Although at least partially successful, the fish has never been domiciliated in the Republic, and, indeed, it could not be reasonably expected that it would be, knowing, as we do, its sensitiveness to cold and the climates under which it thrives

"The fish of paradise (*Macropodus viridi-auratus*) is a species remarkable for its beauty and the extension of its fins, and especially of the ventrals, which has obtained for it the generic name *Macropodus* To some extent this species has also been made the subject of fish-culture, but with reference to its beauty and exhibition in aquaria and ponds, like the goldfish, rather than for its food qualities

"The only other fish of the family that needs mention is the fighting-fish (*Betta pugnax*) It is cultivated by the natives of Siam, and a special race seems to have been the result of such cultivation The fishes are kept in glasses of water and fed, among other things, with the larvæ of mosquitoes or other aquatic insects 'The Siamese are as infatuated with the combats of these fishes as the Malays are with their cock-fights, and stake on the issue considerable sums, and sometimes their own persons and families The license to exhibit fish-fights is farmed, and brings a considerable annual revenue to the king of Siam The species abounds in the rivulets at the foot of the hills of Penang The inhabitants name it 'pla-kat,' or the 'fighting-fish ' ''

The *Helostomidæ* are herbivorous, with movable teeth on the lips and with long intestines *Helostoma teminincki* lives in the rivers of Java, Borneo, and Sumatra

The *Luciocephalidæ* of East Indian rivers have the supra-branchial organ small, formed of two gill-arches dilated by a membrane In these species there are no spines in the dorsal and anal, while in the *Anabantidæ* and *Osphromenidæ* numerous spines are developed both in the dorsal and anal *Luciocephalus pulcher* indicates a transition toward the *Ophicephalidæ*

The Snake-head Mullets: Ophicephalidæ —The family of *Ophicephalidæ*, snake-head mullets, or China-fishes, placed among the *Percesoces* by Cope and Boulenger, seems to us nearer the Labyrinthine fishes, of which it is perhaps a degenerate descendant The body is long, cylindrical, covered with firm scales which on the head are often larger and shield-like The mouth is large, the head pike-like, and the habit carnivorous and voracious There are no spines in any of the fins, but the thoracic position of the ventrals indicates affinity with perch-like forms and the absence of ventral spines seems rather a feature of degradation, the more so as in one genus (*Channa*) the ventrals are wanting altogether The numerous species are found in the rivers of southern China and India, crossing to Formosa and to Africa They are extremely tenacious of life, and are carried alive by the Chinese to San Francisco and to Hawaii, where they are now naturalized, being known as "China-fishes"

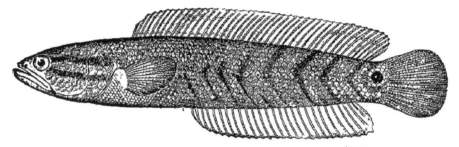

Fig 473 —*Channa formosana* Jordan & Evermann   Streams of Formosa

These fishes have no special organ for holding water on the gills, but the gill space may be partly closed by a membrane According to Dr Gunther, these fishes are "able to survive drought living in semi-fluid mud or lying in a torpid state below the hard-baked crusts of the bottom of a tank from which every drop of water has disappeared Respiration is

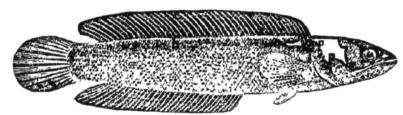

Fig 474 —Snake-headed China-fish, *Ophicephalus barca*   India   (After Day)

probably entirely suspended during the state of torpidity, but whilst the mud is still soft enough to allow them to come to the surface, they rise at intervals to take in a quantity of air, by means of which their blood is oxygenized This habit has been observed in some species to continue also to the period of the year in which the fish lives in normal water, and individuals which are kept in a basin and prevented from coming to the surface and renewing the air for respiratory purposes are suffocated The particular manner in which the accessory branchial cavity participates in respiratory functions is not known It is a simple cavity, without an accessory branchial organ, the opening of which is partly closed by a fold of the mucous membrane "

Ophicephalus striatus is the most widely diffused species in China, India, and the Philippines, living in grassy swamps and biting at any bait from a live frog to an artificial salmon-fly. It has been introduced into Hawaii   *Ophicephalus marulius* is another very common species, as is also *Channa orientalis*, known by the absence of ventral fins

Suborder Holconoti, the Surf-fishes —Another offshoot from the perch-like forms is the small suborder of *Holconoti* (ὄλκος, furrow, νῶτος, back)   It contains fishes percoid in appearance, with much in common with the *Gerridæ* and *Sparidæ*, but with certain

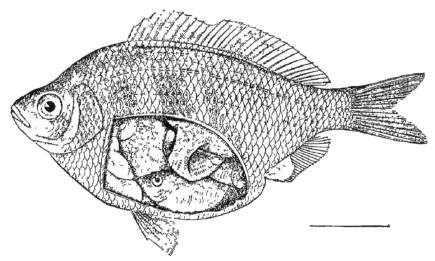

Fig 475 —White Surf-fish, viviparous, with young, *Cymatogaster aggregatus* Gibbons San Francisco

striking characteristics not possessed by any perch or bass   All the species are viviparous, bringing forth their young alive, these being in small number and born at an advanced stage of development The lower pharyngeals are solidly united, as in the *Labridæ*, a group which these fishes resemble in scarcely any other respects. The soft dorsal and anal are formed of many fine rays, the anal being peculiarly modified in the male sex.   The nostrils, ventral fins, and shoulder-girdle have the structure normal among perch-like fishes, and the dorsal furrow, which suggested to Agassiz the name of *Holconoti*, is also found among various perch-like forms

The Embiotocidæ.—The group contains a single family, the *Embiotocidæ*, or surf-fishes   All but two of the species are confined

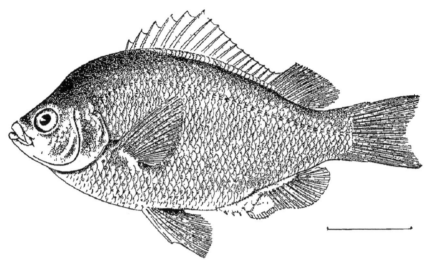

FIG. 476 —Fresh-water Viviparous Perch, *Hysterocarpus traski* Gibbons.
Sacramento River

to California, these two living in Japan   The species are relatively small fishes, from five inches to eighteen inches in length, with rather large, usually silvery scales, small mouths and small teeth.   They feed mainly on crustaceans, two or three species being herbivorous.   With two exceptions, they inhabit

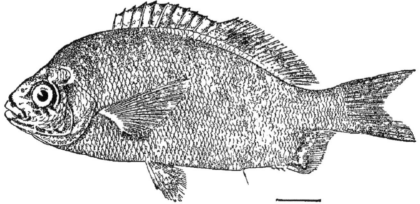

FIG 477 —*Hypsurus caryi* (Agassiz)   Monterey.

the shallow waters on sandy beaches, where they bring forth their young.   They can be readily taken in nets in the surf.

As food-fishes they are rather inferior, the flesh being somewhat watery and with little flavor   Many are dried by the

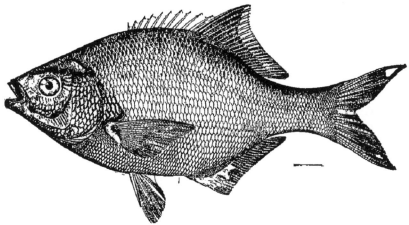

Fɪɢ 478 —White Surf-fish, *Damalichthys argyrosomus* (Girard).   British Columbia

Chinese   The two exceptions in distribution are *Hysterocarpus traski*, which lives exclusively in fresh waters, being confined to the lowlands of the Sacramento Basin, and *Zalembius
rosaceus*, which descends to considerable depths in the sea   In
Hysterocarpus the spinous dorsal is very greatly developed,

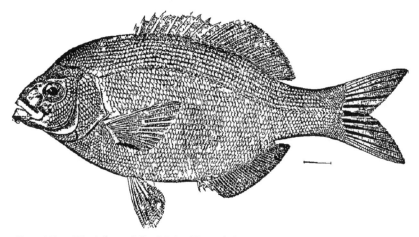

Fɪɢ 479 —Thick-lipped Surf-fish, *Rhacochilus toxotes* Agassiz   Monterey, Cal.

seventeen stout spines being present, the others having but
eight to eleven and these very slender.

The details of structure vary greatly among the different

species, for which reason almost every species has been properly made the type of a distinct genus   The two 'species found in Japan are *Ditrema temmincki* and *Neoditrema ransonneti*   In the latter species the female is always toothless   Close to *Ditrema* is the blue surf-fish of California, *Embiotoca jacksoni*, the first discovered and perhaps the commonest species   *Tæniotoca lateralis* is remarkable for its bright coloration, greenish, with orange stripes   *Hypsurus caryi*, still brighter in color, orange, green and black, has the abdominal region very long.   *Phanerodon furcatus* and *P atripes* are dull silvery in color, as in *Damalichthys argyrosomus*, the white surf-fish, which ranges northward to Alaska, and is remarkable for the extraordinary size of its lower pharyngeals   *Holconotus rhodoterus* is a large, rosy species, and *Amphistichus argenteus* a large

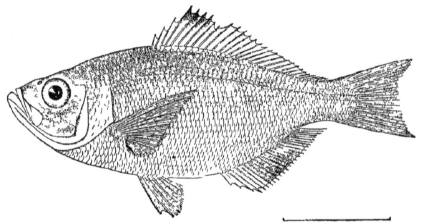

Fig. 480 —Silver Surf-fish (viviparous), *Hypocritichthys analis* (Agassiz).
Monterey

species with dull yellowish cross-bands   *Rhachochilus toxotes* is the largest species in the family and the one most valued as food   It is notable for its thick, drooping, ragged lips   *Hyperprosopon arcuatus*, the wall-eye surf-fish, is brilliantly silvery, with very large eyes   *H agassizi* closely resembles it, as does also the dwarf species, *Hypocritichthys analis*, to which the Japanese *Neoditrema ransonneti* is very nearly related   The other species are all small   *Abeona minima* and *A aurora* feed on seaweed   *Brachyistius frenatus* is the smallest of all, orange-red in color, while its relative, *Zalembius rosaceus*, is handsomest of all, rose-red with a black lateral spot *Cyma-togaster aggregatus*, the surf-shiner, is a little fish, excessively common along the California coast, and from its abundance it has been selected by Dr Eigenmann as the basis of his studies

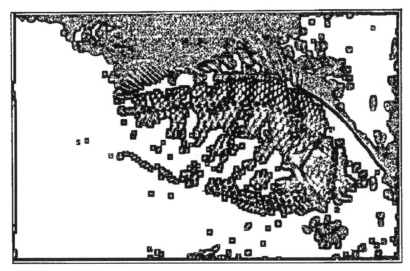

FIG 481 —Viviparous Perch (male), *Hysterocarpus traski* Gibbons   Battle Creek, Sacramento River.   (Photograph by Cloudsley Rutter)

of these fishes   In this species the male shows golden and black markings, which are wanting in the silvery female, and the anterior rays of the anal are thickened or otherwise modified

No fossil embiotocoids are recorded

CHAPTER XXXVII

CHROMIDES AND PHARYNGOGNATHI

SUBORDER Chromides.—The suborder *Chromides* contains spiny-rayed fishes similar to the perch-like forms in most regards, but strikingly distinguished by the complete union of the lower pharyngeal bones, as in the *Holconoti* and *Pharyngognathi*, and still more remarkably by the presence of but one nasal opening on each side In all the perch-like fishes and in nearly all others there are two nasal openings or nostrils on each side, these two entering into the same nasal sac In all the *Chromides* the lateral line is incomplete or interrupted, and the scales are usually large and ctenoid

The Cichlidæ.—The suborder *Chromides* includes two families, *Cichlidæ*, and *Pomacentridæ* The *Cichlidæ* are fresh-water fishes of the tropics, characterized by the presence of three to ten spines in the anal fin In size, color, appearance, habits, and food value they bear a striking resemblance to the fresh-water sunfishes, or *Centrarchidæ*, of the eastern United States This resemblance is one of analogy only, for in structure the *Cichlidæ* have no more in common with the *Centrarchidæ* than with other families of perch or bass The numerous species of *Cichlidæ* are confined to tropical America and to corresponding districts in Africa and western Asia *Tilapia nilotica* abounds in the Nile *Tilapia galilæa* is found in the river Jordan and the Lake of Galilee This species is supposed to form part of the great draught of fishes recorded in the Gospels, and a black spot on the side is held to commemorate the touch of Simon Peter Numerous other species of *Cichlidæ*, large and small, abound in central Africa, even in the salt ditches of the Sahara

The species of *Cichla*, especially *Cichla ocellaris*, of the rivers of South America, elongate and large-mouthed, bear a strong

591

analogy to the black bass of farther north A vast number
of species belonging to *Heros*, *Acara*, *Cichlasoma*, *Geophagus*,
Chætobranchus, and related genera swarm in the Amazon region
Each of the large rivers of Mexico has one or more species, one
of these, *Heros cyanoguttatus*, occurs in the Rio Grande and the
rivers of southern Texas, its range corresponding with that of
Tetragonopterus argentatus, just as the range of the whole family
of *Cichlidæ* corresponds with that of the *Characinidæ* No other
species of either family enters the United States A similar
species, *Heros tetracanthus*, abounds in the rivers of Cuba, and
another, *Heros beani*, called the mojarra verde, in the streams
of Sinaloa In the lakes and swamps of Central America *Cichlidæ* and *Characinidæ* are very abundant One fossil genus is
known, called *Priscacara* by Cope *Priscacara clivosa* and
other species occur in the Eocene of Green River and the Great
Basin of Utah In this genus vomerine teeth are said to be
present, and there are three anal spines. None of the living
Cichlidæ has vomerine teeth

The Damsel-fishes· Pomacentridæ. –The *Pomacentridæ*, called
rock-pilots or damsel-fishes, are exclusively marine and have in
all cases but two anal spines The species are often very brilliantly colored, lustrous metallic blue and orange or scarlet
being the prevailing shades among the bright-colored species.
Their habits in the reef pools correspond very closely with those
of the *Chætodontidæ* With the rock-pilots, as with the butterfly-
fishes, the exceeding alertness and quickness of movement make
up for lack of protective colors With both groups the choice
of rocky basins, crevices in the coral, and holes in coral reefs
preserves them from attacks of enemies large enough to destroy
them In Samoa the interstices in masses of living coral are
often filled with these gorgeous little fishes The *Pomacentridæ*
are chiefly confined to the coral reefs, few ranging to the northward of the Tropic of Cancer Sometimes the young are colored
differently from the adult, having sky-blue spots and often
ocelli on the fins, which disappear with age But one species
Chromis chromis is found in the Mediterranean *Chromis
punctipinnis*, the blacksmith, is found in southern California,
and *Chromis notatus* is the common dogoro of Japan One of
the largest species, reaching the length of a foot, is the Gari-

baldi, *Hypsypops rubicundus*, of the rocky shores of southern California. This fish, when full grown, is of a pure bright

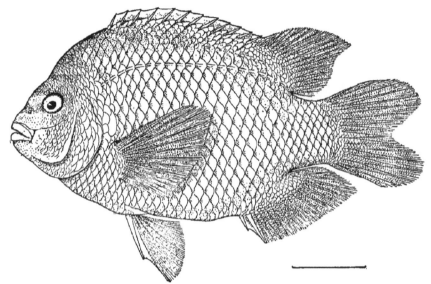

Fig. 482.—Garibaldi (scarlet in color), *Hypsypops rubicunda* (Girard). La Jolla, San Diego, Cal.

Fig. 483.—*Pomacentrus leucostictus* (Müller & Troschel), Damsel-fish. Family *Pomacentridæ*.

scarlet. The young are greenish, marked with blue spots. Species of *Pomacentrus*, locally known as pescado azul, abound in the West Indies and on the west coast of Mexico. *Pomacentrus fuscus* is the commonest West Indian species, and *Pomacentrus rectifrenum* the most abundant on the west coast of Mexico, the young, of an exquisite sky-blue, crowding the rock pools. *Pomacentrus* of many species, blue, scarlet, black, and golden, abound in Polynesia, and no rock pool in the East Indies is without several forms of this type. The type reaches its greatest development in the south seas About forty different species of *Pomacentrus* and *Glyphisodon* occur in the corals of the harbor of Apia in Samoa

Almost equally abundant are the species of *Glyphisodon* The "cockeye pilot," or jaqueta, *Glyphisodon marginatus*, green with

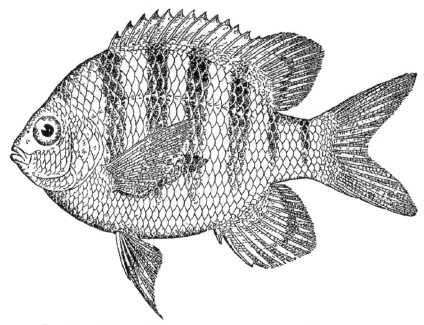

Fig 484 —Cockeye Pilot, *Glyphisodon marginatus* (Bloch) Cuba.

black bands, swarms in the West Indies, occasionally ranging northward, and is equally common on the west coast of Mexico *Glyphisodon abdominalis* replaces it in Hawaii, and the Asiatic *Glyphisodon saxatilis* is perhaps the parent of both *Glyphisodon sordidus* banded with pale and with a black ocellus below the soft dorsal is very common from Hawaii to the Red Sea, and is a food-fish of some importance *Glyphisodon cœlestinus* blue, with black bands, abounds in the south seas

The many species of *Amphiprion* are always brilliant, red or orange, usually marked by one or two cross-bands of creamy blue *Amphiprion melanopus* abounds in the south seas *Azurina hirundo* is a slender species of lower California of a brilliant metallic blue All these species are carnivorous, feeding on shrimps, worms, and the like

Microspathodon is herbivorous, the serrated incisors being loosely implanted in the jaws. *Microspathodon dorsalis*, of the west coast of Mexico, is of a deep indigo-blue color, with streamer-like fins. *Microspathodon chrysurus*, of the West Indian coral reefs, black with round blue spots and the tail yellow This

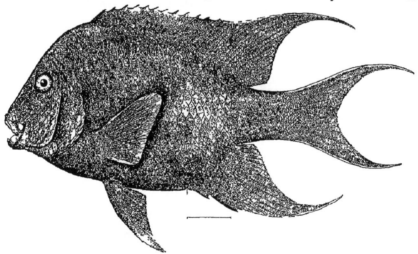

FIG 485 —Indigo Damsel fish, *Microspathodon dorsalis* (Gill) Mazatlan, Mex

family is probably of recent origin, as few fossils are referred to it. *Odonteus pygmæus* of the Eocene perhaps belongs to it

Suborder Pharyngognathi.—The wrasses and parrot-fishes, constituting the group called *Pharyngognathi* (φαρύγξ, gullet, γνάθος, jaw), by Johannes Muller, have the lower pharyngeal bones much enlarged and solidly united, their teeth being either rounded or else flat and paved The nostrils, ventral fins, pectoral fins and shoulder-girdle are of the ordinary perch-like type The teeth are, however, highly specialized, usually large and canine-like, developed in the jaws only, and the gills are reduced in number, 3½ instead of 4, with no slit behind the last half gill. The scales are always cycloid and are usually large In the tropical forms the vertebræ are always twenty-four in number (10 + 14), but in northern forms the number is largely increased with a proportionate increase in the number and strength of the dorsal spines All the species are strictly marine, and the coloration is often the most highly specialized and brilliant known among fishes, the predominant shade being blue

All are carnivorous, feeding mainly on crustaceans and snails, which they crush with their strong teeth, there being often a strong canine at the posterior end of the premaxillary, which holds the snail while the lower jaw acts upon it The species are very numerous and form the most conspicuous feature in the fish markets of every tropical port They abound

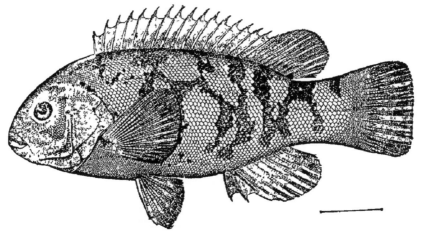

Fig 486 —Tautog, *Tautoga onitis* (L). Wood's Hole, Mass

especially in the pools and openings in the coral reefs All are good for food, though all are relatively flavorless, the flesh being rather soft and not oily

The Wrasse Fishes. Labridæ.—The principal family is that of the *Labridæ*, characterized by the presence of separate teeth in the front of the jaws. Numerous fossil species are known from the Eocene and Miocene Most of these are known only from the lower pharyngeal bones. *Labrodon* is the most widely diffused genus, probably allied to *Labrus*, but with a pile of successional teeth beneath each functional tooth. The species are mostly from the Miocene

The northern forms of *Labridæ* are known as wrasse on the

coasts of England   Among these are *Labrus bergylta*, the ballan wrasse, *Labrus viridis*, the green wrasse, *Labrus ossiphagus*, the red wrasse, and *Labrus merula*, the black wrasse   *Acantholabrus palloni* and *Centrolabrus exoletus* have more than three anal spines   The latter species, known as rock cook, is abundant in western Norway, as far north as Throndhjem, its range extending to the northward beyond that of any other Labroid   Allied to these, on the American coast, is the tautog or blackfish, *Tautoga onitis*, a common food-fish, dusky in color with excellent white flesh, especially abundant on the coast of New England   With this, and still more abundant, is the cunner or chogset, *Tautogolabrus adspersus*, greenish-blue

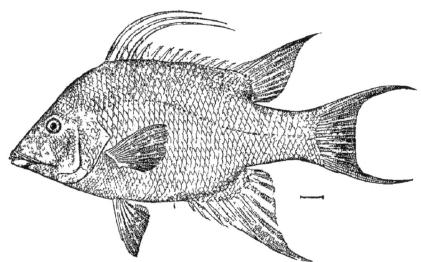

Fig 488 —Capitaine or Hogfish, *Lachnolaimus falcatus*   Florida

in color, the flesh being also more or less blue   This fish is too small to have much value as food, but it readily takes the hook set for better fishes

In the Mediterranean are found many species of *Crenilabrus*, gaily colored, each species having its own peculiar pattern and its own arrangement of inky spots   Among these are *Crenilabrus mediterraneus*, *Crenilabrus pavo*, and *Crenilabrus griseus*   With these are the small species called *Ctenolabrus rupestris*, the goldsinny, much like the American cunner, and the long-nosed *Symphodus scina*

Of the many West Indian species we may notice the Capitaine or hogfish, *Lachnolaimus maximus*, a great fish, crimson in color, with its fin spines ending in long streamers, *Bodianus rufus*, the Spanish lady-fish or pudiano, half crimson, half golden *Halichæres radiatus*, the pudding-wife (a mysterious word derived from "oldwife" and the Portuguese name, pudiano), a blue fish handsomely mottled and streaked Of the smaller species, *Clepticus parræ*, the janissary, with very small teeth, *Halichæres bivittatus*, the slippery-dick, ranging northward to Cape Hatteras, and *Doratonotus megalepis*, of an intense grass-green color, are among the most notable The razorfish, *Xyrichthys psittacus*, red, with the forehead compressed to a sharp edge, is found in the Mediterranean as well as throughout the West Indies, where several other species of razor-fish also occur

Scarcely less numerous are the species of the Pacific Coast of America *Pimelometopon pulcher*, the redfish or fathead of

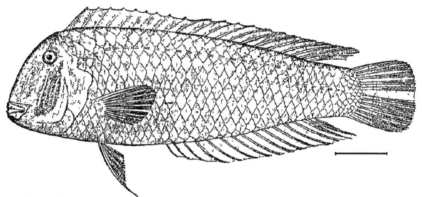

FIG 489 —Razor-fish, *Xyrichthys psittacus* (Linnæus) Tortugas, Fla

southern California, reaches a length of two feet or more It abounds in the broad band of giant kelp which lines the California coast and is a food-fish of much importance The female is dull crimson In the male the head and tail are black and on the top of the head is developed with age a great adipose hump A similar hump is found on the adult of several other large labroids Similar species on the coast of South America, differing in color and size of scales, are *Pimelometopon darwini*, *Trochocopus opercularis*, and *Bodianus diplotænia* The señorita, *Oxyjulis californica*, is a dainty cream-colored little fish of the California coast, *Halichæres semicinctus*, the kelpfish, light olive, the male with a blue shoulder bar, is found in southern California On the west coast of Mexico are numerous species of *Thalassoma, Halichæres, Pseudojulis, Xyrichthys* and *Iniistius*, all different from the corresponding species in the West Indies, and equally different from the much greater

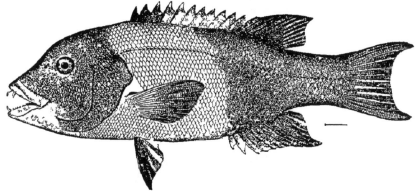

FIG 490 —Redfish (male), *Pimelometopon pulcher* (Ayres) San Diego

variety found in Hawaii and in Samoa About the Polynesian and West Indian islands abound a marvelous wealth of forms of

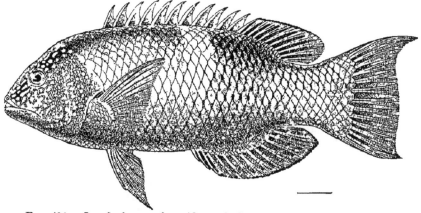

FIG 491 —*Lepidaplois perditio* (Quoy & Gaimard) Wakanoura, Japan

every shade and pattern of bright colors—blue, green, golden, scarlet, crimson, purple—as if painted on with lavish hand and often in the most gaudy pattern, although at times laid on with the greatest delicacy The most brilliant species belong to *Thalassoma* and *Julis*, the most delicately colored to *Stetho-*

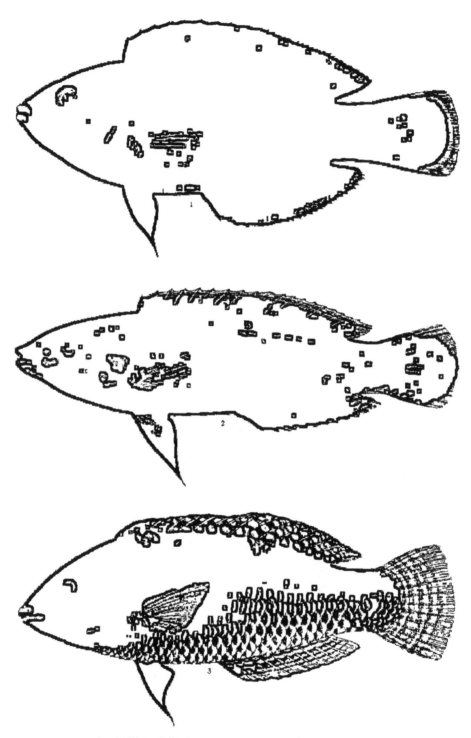

1 PLATYGLOSSUS MARGINATUS (RUPPELL)
2 PLATYGLOSSUS FLOS CORALLIS JORDAN & SEALE TYPE

julis and *Cirrhilabrus* In *Gomphosus* the snout is prolonged on a long slender tube. In *Cheilio* the whole body is elongate In *Iniistius* the first two dorsal spines form a separate fin, the forehead being sharp as in *Xyrichthys* Other widely distributed genera are *Anampses, Lepidaplois, Semicossyphus, Duymæria, Platyglossus, Pseudolabrus, Hologymnosus, Macropharyngodon, Coris, Julis, Hemipteronotus, Novaculichthys, Cheilinus, Hemigymnus,* and *Cymolutes* *Halichæres* is as abundant in the East Indies as in the West, one of its species *Halichæres pæcilopterus* being common as far north as Hakodate in Japan In this species as in a few others the sexes are very different in color, although in most species no external sexual differences of any sort appear In the East Indian genus, *Pseudocheilinus,* the eye is very greatly modified The cornea is thickened, forming two additional lens-like structures

The small family of *Odacidæ* differs from the *Labridæ* in having in each jaw a sharp cutting edge without distinct teeth anteriorly, the pharyngeal teeth being pavement-like The scales are small, very much smaller than in the *Scaridæ,* the body more elongate, and the structure of the teeth different The species are mostly Australian, *Odax balteatus* being the most abundant It is locally known as kelpfish

In the *Siphonognathidæ* the teeth are much as in the *Odacidæ,* but the body is very elongate, the snout produced as in the cornet-fishes (*Fistularia*), and the upper jaw ends in a long skinny appendage *Siphonognathus argyrophanes,* from Australia, reaches a length of sixteen inches

The Parrot-fishes: Scaridæ.—The parrot-fishes, or *Scaridæ,* are very similar to the *Labridæ* in form, color, and scales, but differ in the more or less complete fusion of the teeth, a character which varies in the different genera

Of these the most primitive is *Calotomus,* confined to the East Indies and Polynesia In this genus the teeth are united at base, their tips free and imbricated over the surface of the jaw

The species are dull in color, reddish or greenish *Calotomus japonicus* is the Budai or Igami of Japan *Calotomus sandwichensis* and *Calotomus irradians* are found in Hawaii, and *Calotomus xenodon* on the offshore islands of Mexico.

In *Calotomus* the dorsal spines are slender.   In *Scaridea* (*balia*) of the Hawaiian Islands the first dorsal is formed of pungent spines as in *Sparisoma*

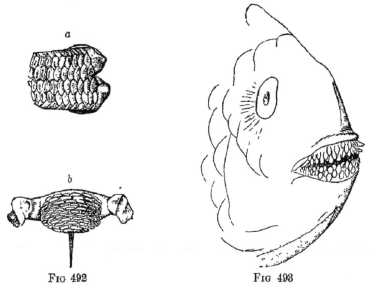

FIG 492   FIG 493

FIG 492 —Pharyngeals of Italian Parrot-fish, *Sparisoma cretense* (L).
 a, upper, *b*, lower
FIG 493 —Jaws of a Parrot-fish, *Calotomus xenodon* Gilbert

Cryptotomus of the Atlantic is also a transitional group having the general characters of *Sparisoma*, but the anterior

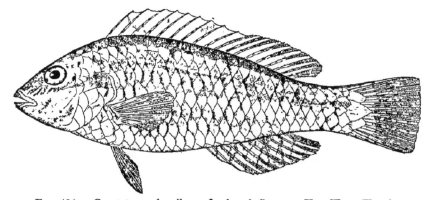

FIG 494 —*Cryptotomus beryllinus* Jordan & Swain.   Key West, Florida

teeth more separate   The several species are all small and characteristic of the West Indian fauna, one species, *Cryptotomus beryllinus*, ranging northward to Long Island

1 STETHOJULIS CASTURI GÜNTHER
2 STETHOJULIS BANDANENSIS (BLEEKER)
3 LEPTOJULIS PARDALIS KNER

In the large genus *Sparisoma* the teeth are more completely joined In this group, which is found only in the tropical Atlantic, the lower pharyngeals are broader than long and

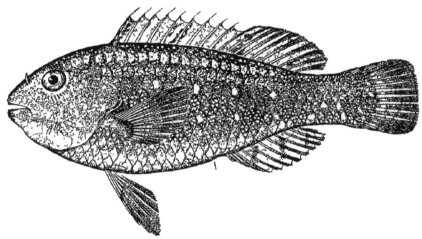

FIG. 495 —*Sparisoma hoplomystax* (Cope). Key West

hexagonal. The teeth of the jaws are not completely united, the dorsal spines are pungent, the lateral line not interrupted, and the gill membranes broadly united to the isthmus

Of the numerous species the dull-colored *Sparisoma flaves-*

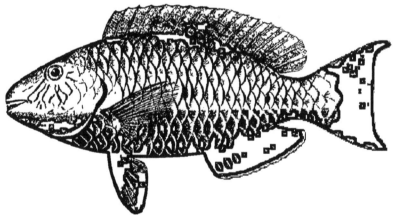

FIG 496 —*Sparisoma abildgaardi* (Bloch), Red Parrot-fish   Loro Colorado
Family *Scaridæ*

cens is most abundant in the West Indies and ranges farther north than any other. *Sparisoma cretense*, the *Scarus* of the

ancients, is found in the Mediterranean, being the only member
of the family known in Europe and the only *Sparisoma* known
from outside the West Indian fauna

Other West Indian species are the red parrot-fish, *Sparisoma
abildgaardi*, *Sparisoma xystrodon*, *Sparisoma hoplomystax*, the
last two being small species about the Florida Keys, and the
handsome *Sparisoma viride* from the West Indies.

Scarus is the great central genus of parrot-fishes   Its members are especially abundant in Polynesia and the East Indies,
the center of distribution of the group,
although some extend their range to
western Mexico, Japan, the Red Sea, and
Australia, and a large number are found
in the West Indies   Most of them are
fishes of large size, but a few, as the West
Indian *Scarus croicensis*, reach the length
of less than a foot, and other still smaller
species (*Scarus evermanni*, *Scarus boll-
mani*) are found only in water of considerable depth (200 fathoms)

The genus *Scarus* is characterized by
not only the almost complete fusion of its
teeth, but by numerous other characters

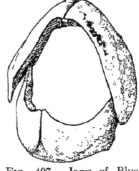

Fig   497 —Jaws of Blue
Parrot-fish, *Scarus cœruleus* (Bloch)

Its lower pharyngeals are oblong and spoon-shaped, the teeth
appearing as a mosaic on the concave surface   The gill-mem-

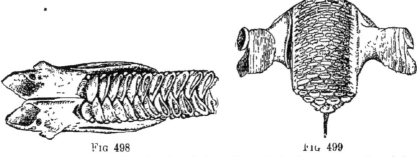

Fig 498   Fig 499

Fig 498 —Upper pharyngeals of an Indian Parrot-fish, *Scarus strongylocephalus*
Fig 499 —Lower pharyngeals of a Parrot-fish, *Scarus strongylocephalus* (Bleeker)

branes are scarcely united to the narrow isthmus, the lateral
line is interrupted, the dorsal spines are flexible, and there

are but few scales on the head. These, as well as the scales of the body, are always large. The most highly specialized

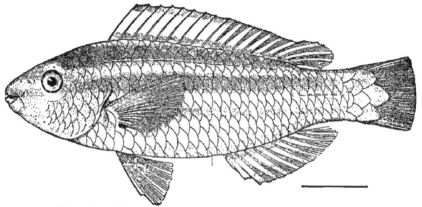

Fig. 500.—*Scarus emblematicus* Jordan & Rutter. Jamaica.

of its species have the teeth deep blue in color, a character which marks the genus or subgenus *Pseudoscarus*. Of the species of this type, the loro, *Pseudoscarus cœlestinus*, and the more abundant guacamaia, *Pseudoscarus guacamaia* (Fig. 100) of the West Indies, are characteristic forms. The perrico, *Pseudo-*

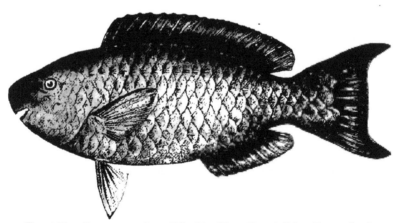

Fig. 501.—*Scarus cœruleus* (Bloch). Blue Parrot-fish. Loro, Azul.
Family *Scaridæ*.

scarus perrico of the west coast of Mexico, and the great blue parrot-fish, or galo, of Hawaii and Samoa, *Pseudoscarus jordani,* belong to this type. *Pseudoscarus jordani* was formerly tabu to the king in Hawaii, and its brilliant colors and toothsome

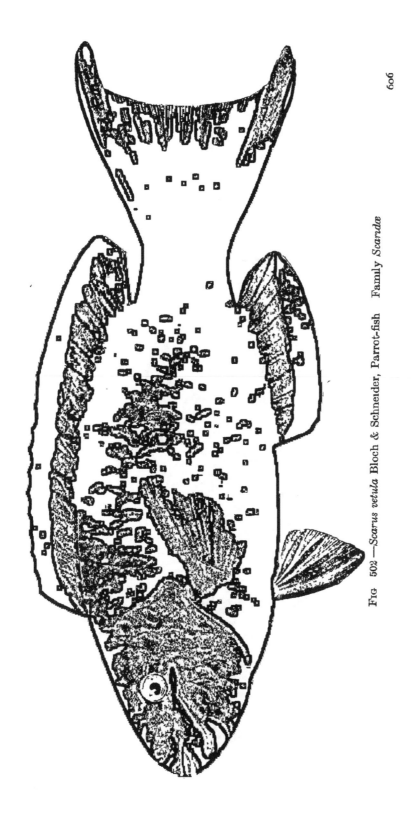

Fig. 502.—*Scarus vetula* Bloch & Schneider, Parrot-fish   Family *Scaridæ*

PSEUDOSCARUS OR CALLYODON LATAX JORDAN & SEALE TYPE

flesh (when eaten raw) made it the most highly valued fish at the royal banquets of old Hawaii. It still sells readily at a dollar or more per pound To this type belong also the blue parrot-fish, *Pseudoscarus ovifrons*, of Japan In the restricted genus *Scarus* proper the teeth are pale The great blue parrot-fish, of the West Indies, *Scarus cæruleus*, belongs to this group This species, deep blue in color, reaches a large size, and the adult has a large fleshy hump on the forehead. Lesser parrot-fish with pale teeth and with showy coloration are the West Indian species *Scarus tæniopterus, Scarus vetula, Scarus croicensis*, etc

Very many species of both *Scarus* and *Pseudoscarus*, green, blue, red-brown, or variegated, abound about the coral reefs of Polynesia. About twenty-five species occur in Samoa

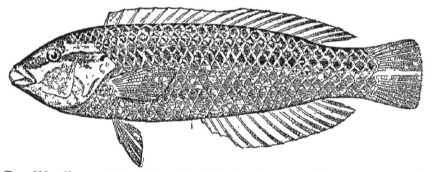

Fig. 503 —Slippery-dick or Doncella, *Halichæres bivittatus* (Bloch), a fish of the coral reefs, Key West Family *Labridæ*

Pseudoscarus latax and *P. ultramarinus* being large and showy species, chiefly blue *Pseudoscarus prasiognathus* is deep red with the jaws bright blue

Fossil species referred to *Scarus* but belonging rather to *Sparisoma* are found in the later Tertiary. The genera *Phyllodus, Egerionia*, and *Paraphyllodus* of the Eocene perhaps form a transition from *Labridæ* to *Scaridæ* In *Paraphyllodus medius* the three median teeth of the lower pharyngeals are greatly widened, extending across the surface of the bone.

CHAPTER XXXVIII

THE SQUAMIPINNES

THE Squamipinnes. — Very closely allied to the *Percomorphi* is the great group called *Squamipinnes* (*squama*, scale; *pinna*, fin) by Cuvier and *Epelasmia* by Cope. With a general agreement with the *Percomorphi*, it is distinguished by the more or less complete soldering of the post-temporal with the cranium. In the more specialized forms we find also a soldering of the elements of the upper

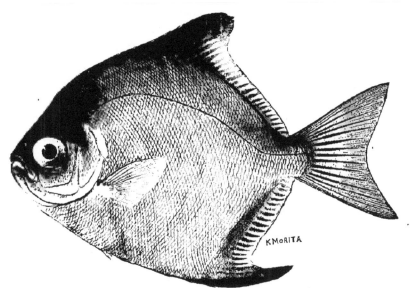

FIG. 504.—*Monodactylus argenteus* (Linnæus). From Apia, Samoa.
Family *Scorpididæ*.

jaw, and a progressive reduction in the size of the gill-opening. The ventral fin retains its thoracic insertion, and, as in the perch mackerel-like forms, it has one spine and five rays, never any more. The ventral fins are occasionally lost in the adult, as in the *Stromateidæ*, or they may lose part of their rays. The name *Squamipinnes* refers to the scaly fins, the typical species having the soft rays of dorsal, anal, and caudal, and sometimes of other fins densely covered with small scales. In various aberrant forms these scales are absent. The name *Epelasmia* (ἔπι, above, ἐλάσμος, plate) refers to the thin upper pharyngeals characteristic of certain forms. The transition from this group to the *Sclerodermi* is very clear and very gradual. The *Squamipinnes*, *Sclerodermi*, *Ostracodermi*, and *Gymnodontes* form a continuous degenerating series. On the other hand the less specialized *Squamipinnes* approach very closely to forms already considered. The *Antigoniidæ* are of uncertain affinities, possibly derived from such forms as *Histiopteridæ*, while *Platax* show considerable resemblance to scaly-finned fishes like the *Kyphosidæ* and *Stromateidæ*. The *Scorpididæ* seem intermediate between *Stromateidæ* and *Platacidæ*. In such offshoots from *Scombroidei* or *Percoidei* the group doubtless had its origin.

We may begin the series with some forms which are of doubtful affinity and more or less intermediate between the *Squamipinnes* and the more primitive *Percomorphi*.

The Scorpididæ—This family has the general appearance of *Platax* and *Ilarches*, but the teeth are not brush-like, and the post-temporal is free from the skull as in perch-like fishes. The species inhabit the Pacific. *Scorpis georgianus* is a food-fish of Australia, with the body oblong. *Monodactylus argenteus*, the toto of Samoa, is almost orbicular in form, while *Psettias sebæ* is twice as deep as long, the deepest-bodied of all fishes in proportion to its length.

The Boarfishes: Antigoniidæ.—The boarfishes (*Antigoniidæ*) are characterized by a very deep body covered with rough scales, the post-temporal, as in the *Chætodontidæ* and the *Zeidæ*, being adnate to the skull.

These fishes bear some resemblance to *Zeus*, but there is no evidence of close affinity nor is it clear that they are related to the *Chætodontidæ*. *Capros aper*, the boarfish, is common in southern Europe, reaching a length of less than a foot, the protractile mouth suggesting that of a pig. The diamond-fishes, *Antigonia*, are deeper than long and strongly compressed, the body being covered with roughish scales. The color is

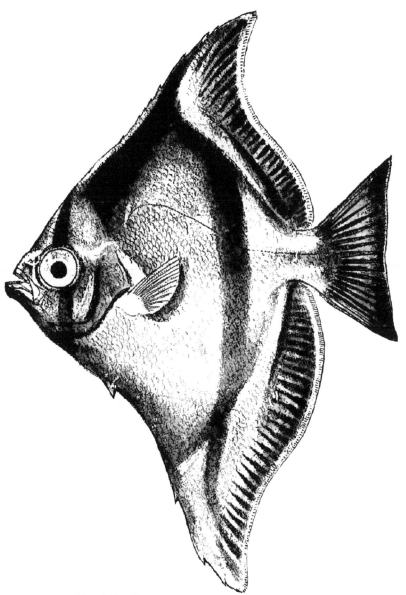

FIG. 505.—*Psettia sebæ* Cuv. & Val.   East Indies.

salmon-red and the species live just below the depths ordinarily
explored by fishermen. *Antigonia capros* is found at Madeira
and in the West Indies, *Antigonia steindachneri* about Hawaii
and in Japan, while the smaller *Antigonia rubescens* is abundant
in the Japanese bays at a depth reached by the dredge An
extinct genus, *Proantigonia* from the Miocene is said to connect
Antigonia with *Capros*

The Arches: Toxotidæ.—The archers, *Toxotidæ*, have the body
compressed, the snout produced, and the dorsal fin with but five
spines The skeleton differs widely from that of *Chætodon* and
the family should perhaps rather find its place among the per-
coids. *Toxotes jaculatrix* is found in the East Indies The
name alludes to its supposed habit of catching insects by shoot-
ing drops of water at them through its long mouth

The Ephippidæ.—With the typical *Squamipinnes*, the teeth
become very slender, crowded in brush-like bands The least
specialized family is that of *Ephippidæ*, characterized by the
presence of four anal spines and a recumbent spine before the
dorsal The principal genus, *Ephippus* (*Scatophagus*), is represented by *Ephippus argus*, a small, bass-like fish, spotted with
black, found in the Indian seas, and ranging northward to Formosa Species referred to *Ephippus* (*Scatophagus*) are recorded
from the Italian Eocene of Monte Bolca, where a species of
Toxotes has been also found

The Spadefishes: Ilarchidæ. — In the *Ilarchidæ* the dorsal is
divided into two fins, the spinous part being free from scales
In various regards the species are intermediate between ordinary
perch-like forms and the chætodonts In these fishes the body
is very deep and, with the soft fins, closely covered with roughish
scales In *Ilarches* (*Ephippus*), represented by *Ilarches orbis*
of the Indian seas, these scales are relatively large. This
species is a common food-fish from India to Formosa

In the American genus, *Chætodipterus*, the scales are quite
small The spadefish (*Chætodipterus faber*), sometimes called also
moonfish or angel-fish, is a large, deep-bodied fish, reaching a
length of two feet. It is rather common from Cape Cod to Cuba,
and is an excellent pan fish, with finely flavored white flesh.
The young are marked by black cross-bands which disappear
with age, and in the adult the supraoccipital crest is greatly

thickened and the skull otherwise modified   A very similar species, *Chætodipterus zonatus*, occurs on the west coast of Mexico   Species allied to *Chætodipterus* are fossil in the Italian Eocene   The *Drepanidæ* of the East Indies are close to the *Ilarchidæ*   *Drepane punctata* is a large, deep-bodied fish resembling the spadefish but with larger scales

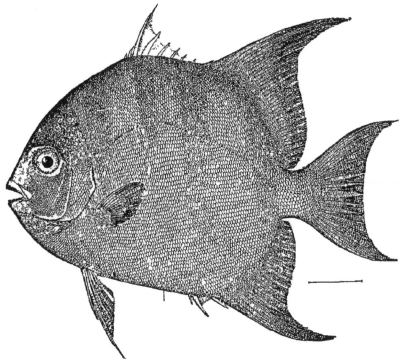

FIG   506 —Spadefish, *Chætodipterus faber* (L)   Virginia

The Platacidæ.—Closely related to the *Ilarchidæ* is also the East Indian family of *Platacidæ*, remarkable for the very great depth and compression of the body, which is much deeper than long, and the highly elevated dorsal and anal still further emphasize this peculiarity of form   In this group the few dorsal spines are closely attached to the soft rays and the general color is dusky   In the young the body is deeper than in the adult and the ventral fins much more produced   The best-known species is the tsuzume or batfish (*Platax orbicularis*), which ranges from India through the warm current to northern Japan. *Platax teira*, farther south, is very similar. *Platax* *altissimus,* with a very high dorsal, is fossil in the Eocene of Monte Bolca

The Butterfly-fishes: Chætodontidæ.—The central family of *Squamipinnes* is that of the butterfly-fishes or *Chætodontidæ*. In this group the teeth are distinctly brush-like, the mouth small, the dorsal fin continuous and closely scaly, and the ventral fins with one spine and five rays   The species are mostly of small size and brilliant and varied coloration, yellow and black being the leading colors   They vary considerably with age, the young having the posterior free edges of the bones of

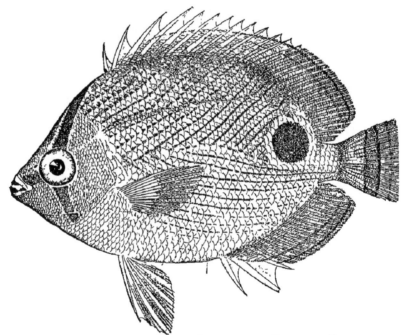

Fig 507 —Butterfly-fish, *Chætodon capistratus* Linnæus   Jamaica

the head produced, forming a sort of collar   These forms have received the name of *Tholichthys,* but that supposed genus is merely the young of *Chætodon*   The species of *Chætodontidæ* abound in rock pools and about coral reefs in clear water.   They are among the most characteristic forms of these waters and their excessive quickness of movement compensates for their conspicuous coloration   In these confined localities they have, however, few enemies   The broad bodies and spinous fins make them rather difficult for a large fish to swallow.   They feed

on small crustaceans, worms, and the like   The analogy to the
butterfly is a striking one, giving rise to the English name,
butterfly-fish, the Spanish mariposa, and the Japanese chocho-
uwo, all having the same meaning   Fossil chætodonts are
rather few, *Chætodon pseudorhombus* of the Pliocene of France,
Holocanthus microcephalus and *Pomacanthus subarcuatus* of the
Eocene, being the only species recorded by Zittel

   In the principal genus, *Chætodon*, the colors are especially

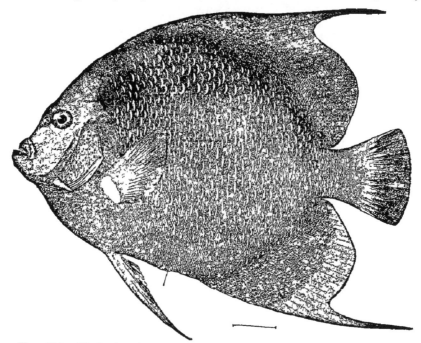

Fig 508 —Black Angel-fish, *Pomacanthus arcuatus* (Linnæus)   Barnegat,
New Jersey

bright   There is almost always a black bar across the eye,
and often black ocelli adorn the fins   This genus is wanting
in Europe   *Chætodon capistratus*, *striatus*, and numerous other
species are found in the West Indies, *Chætodon humeralis* and
nigrirostris are common on the coast of Mexico   The center
of their distribution is in Polynesia and the East Indian Archipelago   *Chætodon reticulatus*, *lineolatus*, *ulietensis*, *ornatis-
simus*, *ephippion*, *setifer*, and *auriga* are among the most showy
species   Numerous closely related genera are described   In
some of these the snout is prolonged into a long tube, bearing

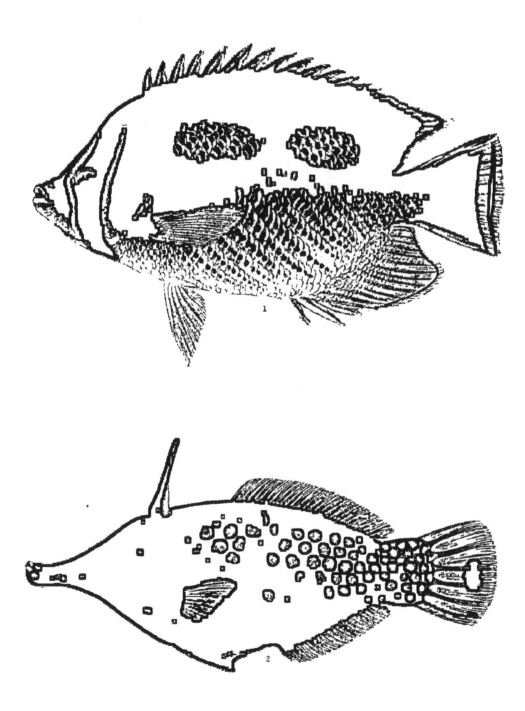

1 MEGAPROTODON TRIFASCIALIS (QUOY & GAIMARD) (FAMILY CHAETODONTIDÆ)
2 OXYMONACANTHUS LONGIROSTRIS (BLOCH & SCHNEIDER) (FAMILY MONACANTHIDÆ)

FISHES OF THE CORAL REEFS, SAMOA

the jaws at its end Of this type are *Chelmo* in India, *Forcipiger* in Polynesia, and *Prognathodes* in the West Indies. *Heniochus* (*macrolepidotus*) has one dorsal spine greatly elongated *Micro-canthus strigatus*, one of the most widely distributed species, is known by its small scales *Megaprotodon* (*trifascialis*) has four anal spines instead of three as in the others.

The species of *Holacanthus*, known as angel-fishes, are larger in size, and their colors are still more showy, being often scarlet or blue. In this genus the preopercle is armed with a strong

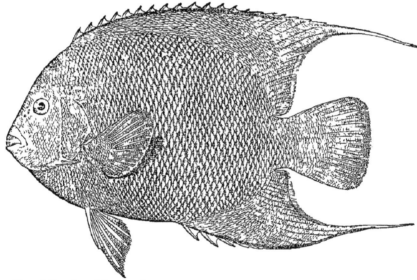

Fig 509 —Angel-fish or Isabelita, *Holacanthus ciliaris* (Linnæus) Jamaica Family *Chætodontidæ*

spine, and there are fourteen or more strong spines in the dorsal This genus has also its center of distribution in the East Indies, whence two species (*septentrionalis* and *ronin*) with concentric stripes of blue range northward to Japan *Holacanthus tibicen*, jet-black with one yellow cross-band, is found from the Riu Kiu Islands southward The angel-fish or isabelita (*Holacanthus ciliaris*), orange-red, sky-blue, and golden, as though gaudily painted, is the best-known species The vaqueta de dos colores or rock beauty (*Holacanthus bicolor*), half jet-black, half golden, is scarcely less remarkable Both are excellent food-fishes of the West Indies *Holacanthus passer* is a showy inhabitant of the west coast of Mexico *Holacanthus diacanthus*, orange, barred with blue, is one of the gaudiest inhabitants of the coral reefs of Polynesia. *Holacanthus flavissimus*, golden with some deep-blue markings, and *Holacanthus nicobariensis*, blackish with white circles, are found with other species in the same waters

The genus *Pomacanthus* (*Pomacanthodes*) includes American species only, still larger in size and differing from *Holacanthus* in having nine to eleven spines only in the dorsal fin   The young of *Pomacanthus* are blackish, crossed by many curved yellow cross-bands, which disappear entirely with age   Three species

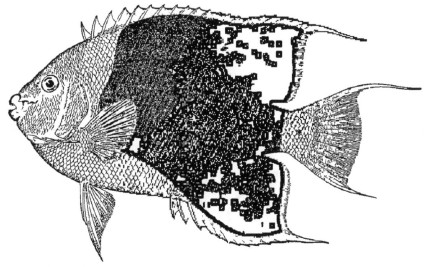

Fig   510—Rock Beauty, *Holacanthus tricolor* (L)   Puerto Rico.

are known, *Pomacanthus arcuatus*, the black angel, chirivita or portugais, *Pomacanthus paru*, the Indian-fish or paru of the West Indies, and *Pomacanthus zonipectus*, "Mojarra de las Piedras," of the west coast of Mexico   All are good food-fishes, but lacking the brilliant colors of *Holacanthus* and the fine pattern usual in *Chætodon*

The Pygæidæ —Between the *Chætodontidæ* and the *Acanthuridæ* we would place the extinct family of *Pygæidæ*, of the Eocene   In *Pygæus gigas* and other species the dorsal spines are strong and numerous, there are 5 to 8 species in the anal fin, the scales are shagreen-like, and the teeth seem coarser than in the *Chætodontidæ*   The tail is apparently unarmed, and the soft dorsal, as in *Chætodon*, is much shorter than the spinous.   To this family the Eocene genera, *Aulorhamphus* (*bolceusis*), with produced snout, and *Apostasis* (*croaticus*), with long spinous dorsal, probably belong.

The Moorish Idols: Zanclidæ. — The family of *Zanclidæ* includes a single species, the Moorish idol or kihi kihi, *Zanclus canescens*. In this family the scales are reduced to a fine sha-

FIG 511 —The Moorish Idol, *Zanclus canescens* (Linnæus) From Hawaii
Family *Zanclidæ* (Painting by Mrs E G Norris)

green, and in the adult two bony horns grow out over the eye The dorsal spines are prolonged in filaments and the color is yellow crossed by bars of black *Zanclus canescens* is a very handsome fish with the general appearance and habit of a *Chætodon*, but the form is more exaggerated It is found throughout Polynesia, from Japan to the off-shore islands of

Mexico, and is generally common, though rarely entering rock pools.

Zanclus eocœnus is recorded from the Italian Eocene

The Tangs: Acanthuridæ.—In the next family, *Acanthuridæ*, the surgeon-fishes or tangs, the scales remain small and shagreen-like, the body is more elongate, the gill-openings still more restricted, and the teeth are flattened and incisor-like The pubic bone is more elongate, and in all the species some sort of armature is developed on the side of the tail The spinous dorsal

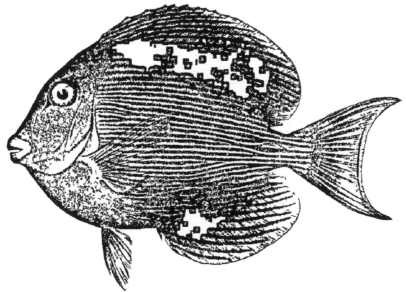

Fig 512 —*Teuthis cœruleus* (Bloch & Schneider), Blue Tang, Medico
Family *Teuthididæ*

in all is less developed than the soft dorsal The species abound in the warm seas, especially about the tide pools, and are used as food. They undergo considerable changes with age, the caudal armature being developed by degrees. Nearly all are dull brown in color, but in some a vivid ornamentation is added Fossil forms are found from the Eocene and later. Most of these are referable to *Teuthis* and *Acanthurus*

The principal genus is *Teuthis*, characterized by the presence on each side of the tail of a sharp, knife-like, movable spine with the point turned forwards and dropping into a sheath This spine gives these fishes their name of surgeon-fish, doctorfish, lancet-fish, tang, barbero, etc , and it forms a very effective weapon against fish or man who would seize one of these creatures by the tail   The species have the center of distribution in the East Indies and have not reached Europe   Three species are found in the West Indies   The blue tang (*Teuthis cœruleus*) is chiefly bright blue.   The common tang, *Teuthis chirurgus*, is brown with bluish streaks, while a third species, *Teuthis bahianus*, has a forked caudal fin   Very close to this species is *Teuthis crestonis*, of the west coast of Mexico, and both are closely related to *Teuthis matoides*, found from India to Hawaii

Teuthis triostegus, of Japan and Polynesia and the East Indies, is covered with cross-bands alternately black and pale

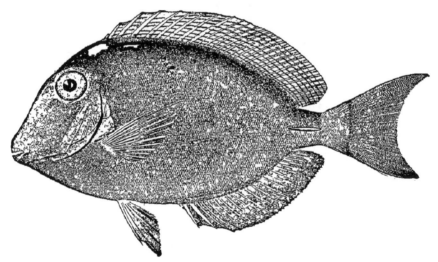

FIG. 513 —Brown Tang, *Teuthis bahianus* (Ranzani)   Tortugas, Fla

In Hawaii this is replaced by the very similar *Teuthis sandwichensis*.   Many species are found about Hawaii and the other Polynesian Islands   *Teuthis achilles* has a large blotch of brilliant scarlet on the tail, and *Teuthis olivaceus* a bright-colored mark on the shoulder   *Teuthis lineatus*, yellow with blue stripes, a showily colored fish of the coral reefs, is often poisonous, its flesh producing ciguatera

Zebrasoma differs from *Teuthis* in having but 4 or 5 dorsal spines instead of 10 or 11   In this genus the soft dorsal fin is very high.   *Zebrasoma flavescens*, sometimes brown, sometimes bright yellow, is common in Polynesia, *Zebrasoma veliferum*, cross-barred with black, is also common

Ctenochætus (strigosus), unlike the others, is herbivorous and has its teeth loosely implanted in the gums This species, black with dull orange streaks, was once tabu to the king of Hawaii, who ate it raw, and common people who appropriated it were put to death

In *Xesurus* the caudal lancelet is replaced by three or four bony tubercles which have no sharp edge *Xesurus scalprum* is common in Japan, and there are three species or more on the west coast of Mexico, *Xesurus punctatus* and *Xesurus laticlavius* being most abundant

In *Prionurus (microlepidotus)* of the tropical Pacific the armature is still more degraded, about six small plates being developed

In *Acanthurus (Monoceros, Naseus)*, the unicorn-fish and its relatives, the ventral fins are reduced, having but three soft rays, the caudal spines are very large, blunt, immovable, one placed in front of the other In most of the species of *Acanthurus* a long, bony horn grows forward from the cranium above the eye This is wanting in the young and has various degrees of development in the different species, in some of which it is wholly wanting The species of *Acanthurus* reach a large size, and in some the caudal spines are bright scarlet, in others blue *Acanthurus unicornis*, the unicorn-fish, is the commonest species and the one with the longest horn It is abundant in Japan, in Hawaii, and in the East Indies

Axinurus thynnoides of the East Indies has a long, slim body, with slender tail like a mackerel

Suborder Amphacanthi, the Siganidæ. — The *Amphacanthi* (ἄμφι, everywhere, ἄκανθα, spine) are spiny-rayed fishes certainly related to the *Teuthididæ*, but differing from all other fishes in having the last ray of the ventrals spinous as well as the first, the formula being I, 4, I The anal fin has also six or seven spines, and the maxillary is soldered to the premaxillary The skeleton is essentially like that of the *Acanthuridæ*

The single family, *Siganidæ*, contains fishes of moderate size, valued as food, and abounding about rocks in shallow

water from the Red Sea to Tahiti   The coloration is rather
plain olive or brown, sometimes with white spots, sometimes
with bluish lines   The species are very much alike and all
belong to the single genus *Siganus*   One species, *Siganus
fuscescens*, dusky with small, pale dots, is a common food-
fish of Japan   Others, as *Siganus oramin* and *Siganus vermiculatus*, occur in India, and *Siganus punctatus*, known as Io,
abounds about the coral reefs of Samoa. *Siganus vulpinus*
differs from the others in the elongate snout

A fossil genus, *Archoteuthis* (*glaronensis*), is found in the
Tertiary of Glarus   It differs from *Siganus* in the deeper body
and in the presence of six instead of seven spines in the anal
fin

CHAPTER XXXIX

SERIES PLECTOGNATHI

THE Plectognaths.—Derived directly from the *Acanthuridæ*, from which they differ by progressive steps of degeneration, are the three suborders of *Sclerodermi*, *Ostracodermi*, and *Gymnodontes*, forming together the series or suborder of *Plectognathi* As the members of this group differ from one another more widely than the highest or most generalized forms differ from the *Acanthuridæ*, we do not regard it as a distinct order The forms included in it differ from the *Acanthuridæ* much as the swordfishes differ from ordinary mackerel The *Plectognathi* (πλεκτός, woven together, γνάθος, jaw) agree in the union of the maxillary and premaxillary, in the union of the post-temporal with the skull, in the great reduction of the gill-opening, and in the elongation of the pelvic bones All these characters in less degree are shown in the *Squamipinnes* We have also the reduction and final entire loss of ventral fins, the reduction and loss of the spinous dorsal, the compression and final partial or total fusion of the teeth of the upper jaw, the specialization of the scales, which change from bony scutes into a solid coat of mail on the one hand, and on the other are reduced to thorns or prickles and are finally altogether lost The number of vertebræ is also progressively reduced until in the extreme forms the caudal fin seems attached to the head, the body being apparently wanting Throughout the group poisonous alkaloids are developed in the flesh These may produce the violent disease known as ciguatera, directly attacking the nervous system

The three suborders of plectognathous are easily recognized by external characters In the *Sclerodermi* (σκληρός, hard, δέρμα, skin) the spinous dorsal is present and the body is more or less distinctly scaly The teeth are separate and incisor-like and the form is compressed In the *Ostracodermi* (ὀστράκος, a box, δέρμα, skin) there is no spinous dorsal, the teeth are slender, and the body is inclosed in an immovable, bony box In the *Gymnodontes* (γυμνός, naked, ὀδούς, tooth) the teeth are fused into a beak like that of a turtle, either continuous or divided by a median suture in each jaw, the spinous dorsal is lost, and the body is covered with thorns or prickles or else is naked

The Scleroderms.—The *Sclerodermi* include three recent and one extinct families Of the recent forms, *Triacanthidæ* is the most primitive, having the ventral fins each represented by a stout spine and the skin covered with small, rough scales. The dorsal has from four to six stiff spines

Triacanthodes anomalus is found in Japan, *Hollardia hollardi* in Cuba *Triacanthus brevirostris*, with the first spine very large, is the common hornfish of the East Indies ranging northward to Japan

The Trigger-fishes· Balistidæ.—The *Balistidæ*, or trigger-fishes, have the body covered with large rough scales regularly arranged

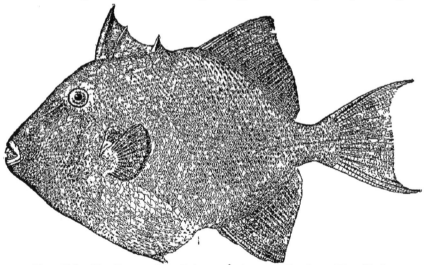

FIG 514 —The Trigger-fish, *Balistes carolinensis* Gmelin   New York

The first dorsal fin is composed of a short stout rough spine, with a smaller one behind it and usually a third so placed that by touching it the first spine may be set or released This

peculiarity gives the name of trigger-fish as well as the older
name of *Balistes*, or cross-bow shooter.   There are no ventral
fins, the long pelvis ending in a single blunt spine.   The numerous species of trigger-fishes are large coarse fishes of the tropical seas occasionally ranging northward   The center of distribution is in the East Indies, where many of the species are
most fantastically marked *Balistes carolinensis*, the leather-
jacket, or cucuyo, is found in the Mediterranean as also on the
American coast *Balistes vetula*, the oldwife, oldwench, or
cochino, marked with blue, is common in the West Indies,
as are several other species, as *Canthidermis sufflamen*, the
sobaco, and the jet-black *Melichthys piceus*, the black oldwife,
or galafata   Several species occur on the Pacific Coast of
Mexico, the Pez Puerco, *Balistes verres*, being commonest
Still others are abundant about the Hawaiian Islands and
Japan   The genus *Balistapus*, having spinous plates on the
tail, contains the largest number of species, these being at the
same time the smallest in size and the most oddly colored
Balistapus aculeatus and *Balistapus undulatus* are common
through Polynesia to Japan   Most of the tropical species
of *Balistidæ* are more or less poisonous, causing ciguatera, the
offensive alkaloids becoming weaker in the northern species
Melichthys radula abounds in Polynesia   In this species great
changes take place at death, the colors changing from blue and
mottled golden green to jet black   Other abundant Polynesian
species are *Xanthichthys lineopunctatus*, *Balistes vidua*, *Balistes
bursa*, and *Balistes flavomarginatus*

The File-fishes· Monacanthidæ.—Closely related to the *Balistidæ* are the *Monacanthidæ*, known as filefishes, or foolfishes   In
these the body is very lean and meager, the scales being
reduced to shagreen-like prickles   The ventral fins are
replaced by a single movable or immovable spine, which is
often absent, and the first dorsal fin is reduced to a single spine
with sometimes a rudiment behind it.   The species are in
general smaller than the *Balistidæ* and usually but not always
dull in color   They have no economic value and are rarely
used as food, the dry flesh being bitter and offensive   The
species are numerous in tropical and temperate seas, although
none is found in Europe   On our Atlantic coast, *Stephano-*

lepis hispidus and *Ceratacanthus schœpfi* are common species. In the West Indies are numerous others, *Osbeckia lœvis* and

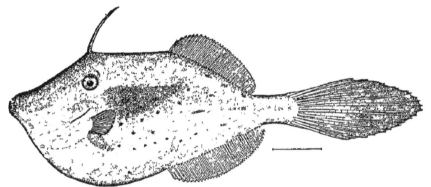

FIG 515 —File-fish, *Osbeckia lœvis* (*scripta*)   Woods Hole, Mass.

Alutera guntheriana, largest in size, among the commonest   Both of these are large fishes without ventral spine. *Monacanthus chinensis*, with a great, drooping dewlap of skin behind the

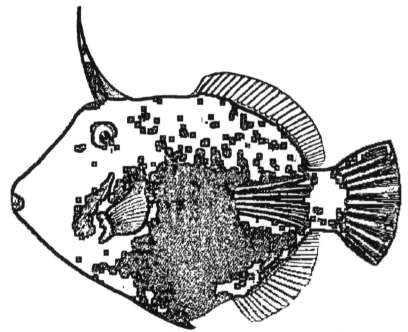

FIG 516 —The Needle-bearing File-fish, *Amanses scopas* of Samoa

ventral spine, is found on the coast of China.   Of the numerous Japanese species, the most abundant and largest is *Pseudomon-*

acanthus modestus, with deep-blue fins and the ventral spine immovable   Another is *Stephanolepis cirrhifer*, known as *Kawa-muki*, or skin-peeler   *Alutera monoceros*, and *Osbeckia scripta*, the unicorn fish, abound in the East Indies, with numerous others of less size and note   In the male of the Polynesian *Amanses scopas* (Fig 516) the tail is armed with a brush of extraordinarily long needle-like spines

In *Stephanolepis spilosomus* the caudal fin is of a brilliant scarlet color, contrasting with the usual dull colors of these fishes   In *Oxymonacanthus longirostris* the body is blue with orange checker-like spots and the snout is produced in a long tube   About the islands of Polynesia, filefishes are relatively few, but some of them are very curious in form or color

The Spinacanthidæ —In the extinct family *Spinacanthidæ* the body is elongate, high in front and tapering behind   The

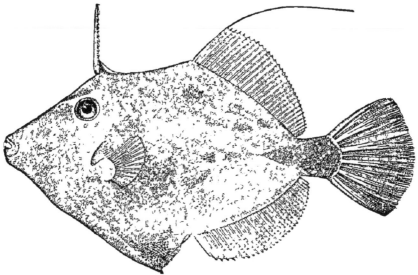

Fig 517 —Common File fish, *Stephanolepis hispidus* (Linnæus)   Virginia

first dorsal has six or seven spines, and there are rough spines in the pectoral   The teeth are bluntly conical   *Spinacanthus blennioides* and *S imperalis* are found in the Eocene of Monte Bolca.   These are probably the nearest to the original ancestor among known scleroderms

The Trunkfishes: Ostraciidæ.—The group *Ostracodermi* contains the single family of *Ostraciidæ*, the trunkfishes or cuck-

olds In this group, the body is enveloped in a bony box,
made of six-sided scutes connected by sutures, leaving only

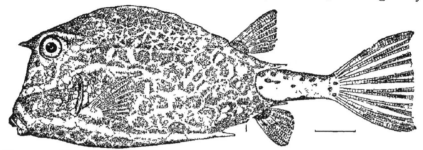

Fig 518—Horned Trunkfish, Cowfish, or Cuckold, *Lactophrys tricornis* (Linnæus)
Charleston, S C

the jaws, fins and tail free The spinous dorsal fin is wholly
wanting There are no ventral fins, and the outer fins are

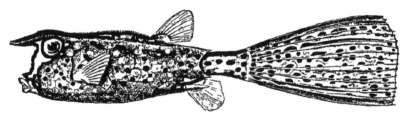

Fig 519 —Horned Trunkfish, *Ostracion cornutum* (Linnæus). East Indies.
(After Bleeker)

short and small. The trunkfishes live in shallow water in
the tropical seas They are slow of motion, though often
brightly colored.

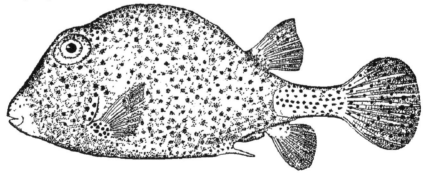

Fig 520 —Spotted Trunkfish, *Lactophrys bicaudalis* (Linnæus) Cozumel Island,
Yucatan

Against most of their enemies they are protected by the
bony case The species range from four inches to a foot in

length, so far as known. They are not poisonous, and are often baked in the shell Three genera are recognized. *Lactophrys* with the *carapace*, three-angled, *Ostracion* with four angles, and *Aracana*, resembling *Ostracion*, but with the carapace not closed behind the anal fin   In each of these genera there is considerable minor variation due to the presence or absence of spines on the bony shell In some species, called cuckolds, or cowfishes, long horns are developed over the eye Others have spines on some other part of the shield and some have no spines at all. No species are found in Europe, and none on the Pacific coast of America The three-angled species, called

Fig 521 —Spotted Trunkfish (face view), *Lactophrys bicaudalis* (Linnæus).

Lactophrys, are native chiefly to the West Indies, sometimes carried by currents to Guinea, and one is described from Australia. *Lactophrys tricornis* of the West Indies has long

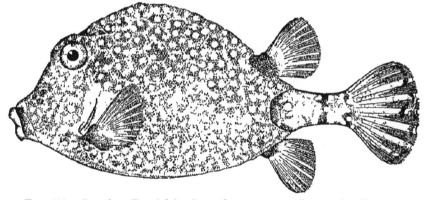

Fig 522 —Spineless Trunkfish, *Lactophrys triqueter* (Linnæus)   Tortugas

horns over the eye, *Lactophrys trigonus* has spines on the lower parts only *Lactophrys triqueter* is without spines, and the fourth American species, *Lactophrys bicaudalis*, is marked by large black spots. The species of *Ostracion* radiate from the East Indies One of them, *Ostracion gibbosum*, has a turret-like spine on the middle of the back, causing the carapace to appear five-angled, *Ostracion diaphanum* has short horns over the eye, and *Ostracion cornutum* very long ones, *Ostracion immaculatus*, the common species of Japan, is without spines, *Ostracion sebæ* of Hawaii and Samoa is deep, rich blue with spots of golden. *Aracana* is also of East Indian origin; *Aracana aculeata*, with numerous species, is common in Japan.

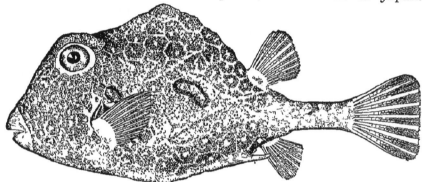

Fig 523—Hornless Trunkfish, *Lactophrys trigonus* (Linnæus)   Tortugas, Fla

A fossil species of *Ostracion* (*O micrurum*) is known from the Eocene of Monte Bolca.

The Gymnodontes. — The group of *Gymnodontes*, having the teeth united in a turtle-like beak, carry still further the degen-

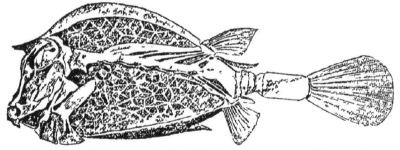

Fig 524 —Skeleton of the Cowfish, *Lactophrys tricornis* (Linnæus)

eration of scales and fins   There is no trace of spinous dorsal, or ventral   The scales are reduced to thorns or prickles, or are lost altogether   All the species have the habit of inflating themselves with air when disturbed, thus floating, belly upward, on the surface of the water   Very few, and these only northern species, are used as food, the flesh of the tropical forms being generally poisonous, and that often in a higher degree than any other fishes whatever

The Triodontidæ. — The most generalized family is that of the *Triodontidæ*. These fishes approach the *Balistidæ* in several regards, having the body compressed and covered with rough scales   The teeth form a single plate in the lower jaw, but are divided on the median line above   The compressed, fanlike, ventral flap is greatly distensible   *Triodon bursarius*, of the East Indies and northward to Japan, is the sole species of the family

The Globefishes. Tetraodontidæ.—In the *Tetraodontidæ* (globefishes, or puffers), each jaw is divided by a median suture The dorsal and anal are short, and the ventrals are reduced

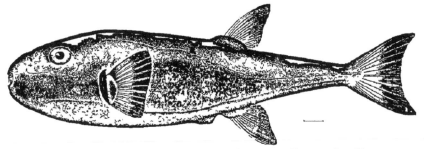

FIG 525 —Silvery Puffer, *Lagocephalus lævigatus* (Linnæus)   Virginia

in number, usually fifteen to twenty (7+13 to 7+9)   The walls of the belly are capable of extraordinary distension, so that when inflated, the fish appears like a globe with a beak and a short tail attached   The principal genus *Spheroides* contains a great variety of forms, forming a closely intergrading series   In some of these the body is smooth, in others more or less covered with prickles, usually three-rooted   In some the form is elongate, the color silvery, and the side of the belly with a conspicuous fold of skin   In these species, the caudal is lunate and the other fins falcate, and with numerous rays But these forms (called *Lagocephalus*) pass by degrees into the short-bodied forms with small rounded fins, and no clear line has yet been drawn of the genera of this group   In these species each nostril has a double opening   *Lagocephalus lagocephalus*, large and silvery, is found in Europe   *Lagocephalus lævigatus* replaces it on the Atlantic Coast of North America In Japan are numerous forms of this type, the venomous *Lagocephalus sceleratus* being one of the best known.   Numerous other Japanese species, *Spheroides xanthopterus, rubripes, pardalis, ocellatus, vermiculatus, chrysops*, etc , mark the transition to typical *Spheroides* *Spheroides maculatus* is common on our Atlantic coast, the puffer, or swell-toad of the

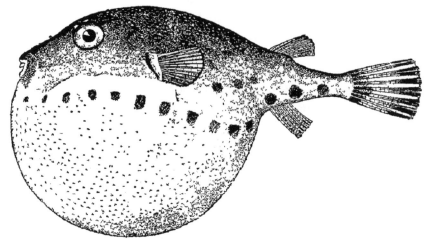

FIG 526 —Puffer, inflated, *Spheroides spengleri* (Bloch) Woods Hole, Mass

coastwise boys who tease it to cause it to swell *Spheroides spengleri* and *S testudineus* abound in the West Indies. *Spheroides politus* on the west coast of Mexico

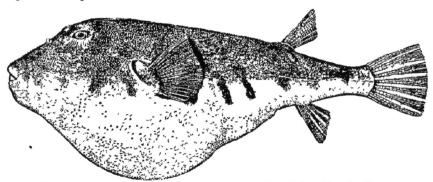

FIG 527 —Puffer, *Spheroides maculatus* (Schneider). Noank, Conn.

In *Tetraodon* the nasal tentacle is without distinct opening, its tip being merely spongy The species of this genus are even more inflatable and are often strikingly colored, the young sometimes having the belly marked by concentric stripes of black which disappear with age *Tetraodon hispidus* abounds in estuaries and shallow bays from Hawaii to India In Hawaii, it is regarded as the most poisonous of all fishes (muki-muki) and it is said that its gall was once used to

poison arrows   *Tetraodon fahaka* is a related species, the
first known of the family   It is found in the Nile   *Tetraodon
lacrymatus,* black with white spots, is common in Polynesia
Tetraodon aerostaticus, with black spots, is frequently taken in
Japan, and *Tetraodon setosus* is frequent on the west coast
of Mexico   This species is subject to peculiar changes of color
Normally dark brown, with paler spots, it is sometimes deep
blue, sometimes lemon-yellow and sometimes of mixed shades

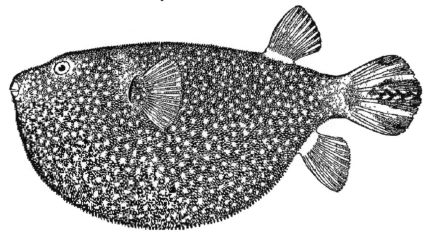

FIG 528 —*Tetraodon meleagris* (Lacépède)   Riu Kiu Islands

Specimens showing these traits were obtained about Clarion
Island of the Revillagigedos   No *Tetraodon* occurs in the West
Indies *Colomesus psittacus,* a river fish of the northern part
of South America, resembles *Spheroides,* but shows considerable difference in the skull

But few fossil *Tetraodontidæ* have been recognized   These
are referred to *Tetraodon*   The earliest is *Tetraodon pygmæus*
from Monte Bolca

The *Chonerhinidæ* of the East Indies are globefishes having the dorsal and anal fins very long, the vertebræ more
numerous (12 + 17), twenty-nine in number   *Chonerhinus
naritus* inhabits the rivers of Sumatra and Java

The little family of *Tropidichthyidæ* is composed of small
globefishes, with a sharply-keeled back, and the nostrils almost,
or quite, wanting   The teeth are as in the *Tetraodontidæ*.
The skeleton differs considerably from that of *Spheroides,*
apparently justifying their separation as a family   The species

are all very small, three to six inches in length, and prettily colored   In the West Indies *Tropidichthys rostratus* is found. *Tropidichthys solandri* abounds in the South Seas, dull orange with blue spots   *Tropidichthys rivulatus* is common in Japan and several other species are found in Hawaii.

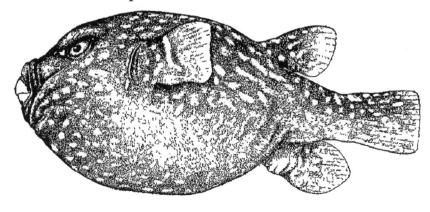

FIG 529 —Bristly Globefish, *Tetraodon setosus* Rosa Smith   Clarion Island, Mex

Other species occur on the west coast of Mexico, in Polynesia, and in the East Indies

The Porcupine-fishes: Diodontidæ. — In the remaining families of *Gymnodontes*, there is no suture in either jaw, the teeth

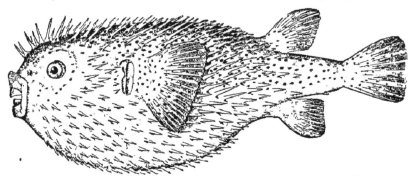

FIG 530 —Porcupine-fish, *Diodon hystrix* (Linnæus)   Tortugas Islands

forming an undivided beak   The *Diodontidæ*, or porcupine-fishes, have the body spherical or squarish, and armed with sharp thorns, the bases of which are so broad as to form a continuous coat of mail   In some of them, part of the spines are movable, these being usually two-rooted, in others, all are immovable and three-rooted   All are reputed poisonous, especially in the equatorial seas

In *Diodon* the spines are very long, the anterior ones, at least, movable   The common porcupine-fish, *Diodon hystrix*, is found in all seas, and often in abundance   It is a sluggish fish, olive and spotted with black   It reaches a length of two feet or more, and by its long spines it is thoroughly protected from all enemies   A second species, equally common, is the lesser porcupine-fish, *Diodon holacanthus*   In this species, the frontal spines are longer than those behind the pectoral, instead of the reverse, as in *Diodon hystrix*   Many species of *Diodon* are recorded from the Eocene, besides numerous species from later deposits   One of these, as *Heptadiodon heptadiodon* from the Eocene of Italy, with the teeth subdivided, possibly represents a distinct family   *Diodon erinaceus* is found in the Eocene of Monte Bolca and *Progymnodon hilgendorfi* in the Eocene of Egypt

In the rabbit-fishes (*Chilomycterus*) the body is box-shaped,

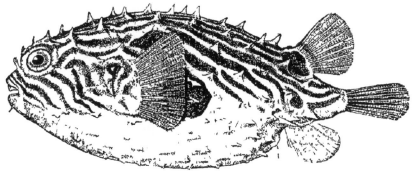

Fig 531 —Rabbit-fish, *Chilomycterus schœpfi* (Walbaum)   Noank, Conn.

covered with triangular spines, much shorter and broader at base than those of *Diodon*   Numerous species are known

Chilomycterus schœpfi is the common rabbit-fish, or swelltoad of our Atlantic coast, light green, prettily varied with black lines   The larger *Chilomycterus affinis*, with the pectoral fin spotted with black, is widely diffused through the Pacific   It is rather common in Japan, where it is the torabuku, or tiger puffer   It is found also in Hawaii, and it is once recorded by Dr Eigenmann from San Pedro, California, and once by Snodgrass and Heller, from the Galapagos

The Head-fishes: Molidæ.—The head-fishes, or *Molidæ*, also called sunfishes, have the body abbreviated behind so that the dorsal, anal, and caudal seem to be attached to the posterior outline of the head This feature, constituting the so-called gephyrocercal tail is a trait of specialized degradation.

Mola mola, the common head-fish or sunfish, is found occasionally in all tropical and temperate seas.   Its form is almost

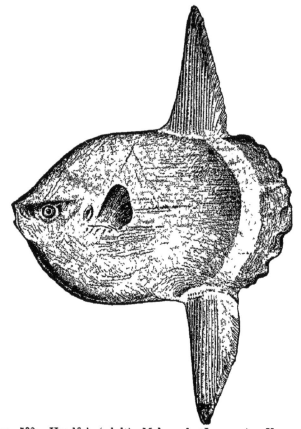

FIG 532 —Headfish (adult), *Mola mola* (Linnæus)   Virginia

circular, having been compared by Linnæus to a mill-wheel (mola), and its surface is covered with a rough, leathery skin It swims very lazily at the surface of the water, its high dorsal often rising above the surface   It is rarely used as food, though not known to be poisonous   The largest example known to the writer was taken at Redondo Beach, California, by Mr Thomas Shooter, of Los Angeles   This specimen was 8 feet 2 inches in length, and weighed 1200 pounds. Another, almost as large, was taken at San Diego, in April, 1904. No difference has been noticed among specimens from California, Cape Cod, Japan, and the Mediterranean. The young, however, differ considerably from the adult, as might be expected in a fish of such great size and extraordinary form.

Fragments named *Chelonopsis*, and doubtfully referred to *Mola*, are found in the Pliocene of Belgium. Certain jaws of cretaceous age, attributed to *Mola*, probably belong, according to Woodward, to a turtle.

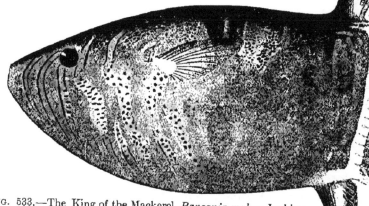

FIG. 533.—The King of the Mackerel, *Ranzania makua* Jenkins, from Honolulu. (After Jenkins.)

In the genus *Ranzania*, the body is more elongate, twice as long as deep, but as in *Mola*, the body appears as if bitten off and then provided with a fringe of tail. The species are rarely taken. *Ranzania truncata* is found in the Mediterranean and once at Madeira. *Ranzania makua*, known as the king of the mackerels about Hawaii, is beautifully colored brown and silvery. This species has been taken once in Japan.

In Hawaii it is believed that all the Scombroid fishes are subject to the rule of the makua and that they will disappear if this fish be killed. By a similar superstition, *Regalecus glesne* is "king of the herrings" in Norway and about Cape Flattery, *Trachypterus rex salmonorum* is "king of the salmon."

CHAPTER XL

PAREIOPLITÆ, OR MAILED-CHEEK FISHES

THE Mailed-cheek Fishes. — The vast group of *Pareioplitæ* (*Loricati*) or mailed-cheek fishes is characterized by the presence of a "bony stay" or backward-directed process from the third suborbital This extends backward across the cheek toward the preopercle In the most generalized forms this bony stay is small and hidden under the skin In more specialized forms it grows larger, articulates with the preopercle, and becomes rough or spinous at its surface Finally, it joins the other bones to form a coat of mail which covers the whole head In degenerate forms it is again reduced in size, finally becoming insignificant

The more primitive *Pareioplitæ* (παρεία, cheek, ὁπλιτής, armed) closely resemble the *Percomorphi*, having the same fins, the same type of shoulder-girdle, and the same insertion of the ventral fins In the more specialized forms the ventral fins remain thoracic, but almost all other parts of the anatomy are greatly distorted In all cases, so far as known to the writer, the hypercoracoid is perforate as in the *Percomorphi* There are numerous points of resemblance between the *Cirrhitidæ* and the *Scorpænidæ*, and it is probable that the *Scorpænidæ* with all the other *Pareioplitæ* sprang from some perciform stock allied to *Cirrhitidæ* and *Latrididæ*

Fossil mailed-cheek fishes are extremely few and throw little light on the origin of the group Those belong chiefly to the *Cottidæ Lepidocottus*, recorded from the Miocene and Oligocene, seems to be the earliest genus

The Scorpion-fishes: Scorpænidæ. — The vast family of *Scorpænidæ*, or scorpion-fishes, comprises such a variety of forms as almost to defy diagnosis The more primitive types are

637

percoid in almost all respects, save in the presence of the sub-ocular stay Their scales are ctenoid and well developed The dorsal spines are numerous and strong. The ventral fins are complete and normally attached; the anal has three strong

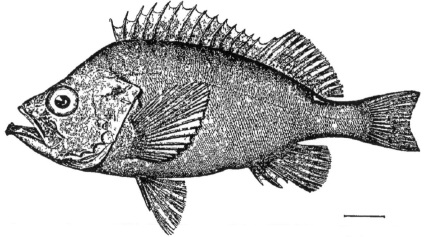

Fig 534 —Rosefish, *Sebastes marinus* Linnæus Cape Cod

spines The cranium shows only a trace of spiny ridges, and the five spines on the preoperculum are not very different from those seen in some species of bass The gill-arches are, however, different, there being but 3½ gills and no slit behind the last

Fig 535 —Skull of *Scorpænichthys marmoratus* Girard, showing the suborbital stay (a)

Otherwise the mouth and pharanx show no unusual characters In the extremes of the group, however, great changes take place, the head becomes greatly distorted with ridges and grooves, the anal spines are lost, and the dorsal spines variously modified The scales may be lost or replaced by warts or prickles and the ventral fins may be greatly reduced   Still the changes are very gradual, and it is not easy to divide the group into smaller families

The most primitive existing genus is doubtless *Sebastes*. The familiar rosefish, *Sebastes marinus*, is found on both shores of the north Atlantic   It is bright red in color and is valued as food   As befits a northern fish, it has an increased number of vertebræ (31) and the dorsal spines number 15   From its large haddock-like eye it has been called the Norway haddock It is an important food-fish in New England as well as in northern Europe

In the north Pacific *Sebastes* gives place to *Sebastolobus*, with three species (*macrochir, altivelis,* and *alascanus*), all bright-

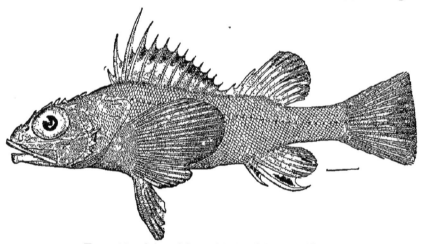

Fig 536 —*Sebastolobus altivelis* Gilbert   Alaska

red fishes of soft substance and living in rather deep water *Sebastolobus* is characterized by its two-lobed pectoral fin, the lower rays being enlarged

The genus *Sebastodes*, with its rougher-headed ally *Sebastichthys*, with 13 dorsal spines and the vertebræ 27, ranges farther south than *Sebastes* and forms one of the most characteristic features of the fauna of California and Japan, 50 species occurring about California and 25 being already known from Japan   One species (*Sebastichthys capensis*) is recorded from the Cape of Good Hope, and two, *Sebastichthys oculatus* and *S darwini*, from the coast of Chile

Within the limits of *Sebastodes* and *Sebastichthys* is a very large range of form and color, far more than should exist within the range of a natural genus. On the other hand, all attempts at generic subdivision have failed because the species form a number of almost perfectly continuous series. At one extreme are species with large mouths, small scales, relatively smooth cranium, and long gill-rakers. At the other extreme are robust species, with the head very rough, the mouth moderate, the scales larger, and the gill-rakers short and thick. Still other species have slender cranial spines and spots of bright pink in certain specialized localities. These approach the genus *Helicolenus* as other species approach *Scorpæna*.

The various species are known in California as rockfish, or rock-cod, in Japan as Soi and Mebaru. In both regions they form a large part of the bulk of food-fishes, the flesh being rather coarse and of moderate flavor. All the species so far as known are ovoviviparous, the young being brought forth in summer in very great number, born at the length of about $\frac{1}{4}$ of an inch. The species living close to shore are brown, black, or green. Those living in deeper waters are bright red, and in still deeper waters often creamy or gray, with the lining of the mouth and the peritoneum black. The largest species reach a length of two or three feet, the smallest eight or ten inches. None is found between Lower California and Peru and none south of Nagasaki in Japan. Of the California species the following are of most note. *Sebastodes paucispinis*, the Bocaccio of the fishermen, from its large mouth, is an elongate fish, dull red in color, and reaching a very large size. In deeper waters are *Sebastodes jordani* and *Sebastodes goodei*, the former elongate and red, the latter more robust and of a very bright crimson color. *Sebastodes ovalis*, the viuva, and *Sebastodes entomelas* are grayish in hue, and the related *Sebastodes proriger* is red. The green rockfish *Sebastodes flavidus* is common along the shore, as also the black rockfish, known as pêche prêtre or priestfish, *Sebastodes mystinus*. Less common is *Sebastodes melanops*. Similar to this but more orange in color is the large *Sebastodes miniatus*. Somewhat rougher-headed is the small grass rockfish, *Sebastodes atrovirens*. On the large red rockfish, *Sebastichthys ruberrimus*, the spinous ridges are all large and rough serrate On the equally large *Sebastichthys levis* these ridges are smooth Both these species are bright red in color *Sebastichthys rubrovinctus*, called the Spanish-flag, is covered with broad alternating bands of deep crimson and creamy pink It is the most handsomely colored of our marine fishes and is often taken in southern California *Sebastichthys elongatus* is a red species with very large mouth. Several other species small in size are red, with three or four spots of bright pink. The commonest of these is the corsair,

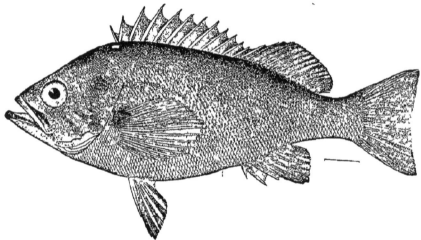

Fig 537 —Priest-fish, *Sebastodes mystinus* Jordan & Gilbert. Monterey, Cal

Sebastichthys rosaceus, plain red and golden Another species is the green and red flyfish, *Sebastichthys rhodochloris*. *Sebastichthys constellatus* is spotted with pink and *Sebastichthys chlorostictus* with green To this group with pink spots the South American and African species belong, but none of the Japanese *Sebastodes aleutianus* is a large red species common in Alaska and *Sebastodes ciliatus* a green one About the wharves in California and northward the brown species called *Sebastichthys auriculatus* is abundant In the remaining species the spinous ridges are progressively higher, though not so sharp as in some of those already named *Sebastichthys maliger* has very high dorsal spines and a golden blotch on the back In *Sebastichthys caurinus* and especially *Sebastichthys vexillaris* the spines are very high, but the coloration is different, being reddish brown. *Sebastichthys nebulosus* is blue-black with golden spots   *Sebastichthys chrysomelas* is mottled black and yellow *Sebastichthys carnatus* is flesh-color and green   *Sebastichthys rastrelliger* is a small, blackish-green species looking like *Sebastodes atrovirens*, but with short gill-rakers.   *Sebastichthys hopkinsi* and *Sebastichthys gilberti* are small species allied to it The treefish, *Sebastichthys serriceps*, has very high spines on the head, and the olive body is crowned by broad black bands Still more striking is the black-banded rockfish, *Sebastichthys*

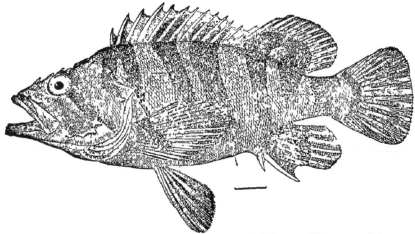

FIG 588 —*Sebastichthys serriceps* Jordan & Gilbert   Monterey, Cal.

nigrofasciatus, with very rough head and bright red body with broad cross-bands of black

Of the Japanese species the commonest, *Sebastodes inermis*, the Mebaru, much resembles *Sebastodes flavidus Sebastodes fuscescens* looks like *Sebastodes melanops*, as does also *Sebastodes taczanowskii Sebastodes matsubaræ* and *S. flammeus* and *S iracundus*, bright-red off-shore species, run close to *Sebastodes aleutianus. Sebastichthys pachycephalus* suggests *Sebastichthys chrysomelas. Sebastodes steindachneri* and *S itinus* are brighter-colored allies of *Sebastodes ovalis* and *Sebastodes scythropus* and *Sebastodes joyneri* represent *Sebastodes proriger. Sebastichthys trivittatus*, green, striped with bright golden, bears some resemblance to *Sebastichthys maliger Sebastichthys elegans, Sebastichthys oblongus*, and *Sebastichthys mitsukurii*, dwarf species, profusely spotted, have no analogues among the American forms. *Sebastodes glaucus* of the Kurile Islands has 14 dorsal spines and is not closely related to any other   Fourteen dorsal spines are occasionally present in *Sebastichthys elegans*.   All the other species show constantly 13

The genus *Sebastiscus* has the general appearance of *Sebastodes*, and like the latter possesses a large air-bladder   It however agrees with *Scorpæna* in the possession of but 12 dorsal spines and 24 vertebræ   The two known species are common in Japan   *Sebastiscus marmoratus*, mottled brown, is everywhere

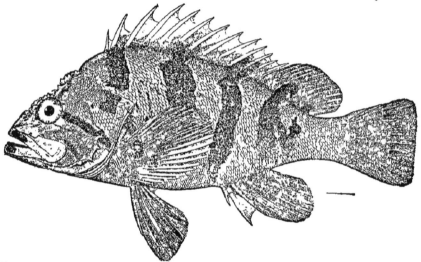

Fig 539 —Banded Rockfish, *Sebastichthys nigrocinctus* (Ayres)   Straits of Fuca

abundant along the coast, and the pretty *Sebastiscus albofasciatus*, pink, violet, and golden, represents it in equal abundance in deeper water

The genus *Sebastopsis* differs from *Sebastodes* only in having no teeth on the palatines   The species, all of small size and red or varied coloration, are confined to the Pacific   *Sebastopsis xyris* occurs in Lower California and *Sebastopsis guamensis* and *S scaber* in Polynesia   Species of this genus are often found dried in Chinese insect boxes.

Helicolenus differs from *Sebastiscus* only in the total absence of air-bladder   The species are all bright crimson in color, very handsome, and live in deep water   *Helicolenus dactylopterus* is rather common in the Mediterranean, and is sometimes taken in the Gulf Stream, and also in Japan, where two or three other species occur

Neosebastes is much like *Sebastodes*, but the suborbital stay bears strong spines and the dorsal is very high *Neosebastes panda* is found in Australia, and *N entaxis* in Japan *Setarches* is distinguished by the cavernous bones of its head. Species are found in both the Atlantic and Pacific in deep water. Several other peculiar or transitional genera are found in different parts of the Pacific

In *Scorpæna* the head is more uneven in outline than in *Sebastodes* and *Sebastichthys*, skinny flaps are often present on head and body, the air-bladder is wanting, there are 12 dorsal

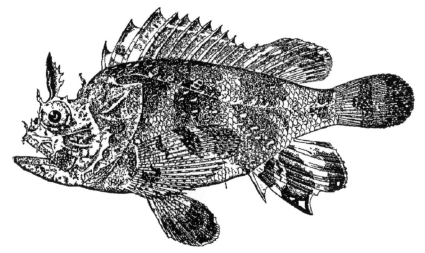

Fig 540 —Florida Lion fish, *Scorpæna grandicornis* Cuv & Val Key West.

spines and 24 vertebræ, and on each dorsal spine is a small venom-secreting gland   The species are very numerous, highly varied in color, and found in all warm seas, being known as scorpion-fishes or *Rascacios*   Two species, *Scorpæna scrofa* and *Scorpæna porcus*, are common in the Mediterranean, being regarded as good food-fishes, though disliked by the fishermen

Of the numerous West Indian species, *Scorpæna plumieri*, *Scorpæna grandicornis*, and *Scorpæna brasiliensis* are best known *Scorpæna guttata* is common in southern California and is an excellent food-fish   *Scorpæna mystes* is found on the west coast of Mexico   *Scorpæna onaria* and *S izensis* are found in Japan Fossil remains referred to *Scorpæna* are recorded from the Tertiary rocks.

VARIATIONS IN THE COLOR OF FISHES

The Oniokose or Demon Stinger, *Inimicus japonicus* (Cuv and Val), from
Wakanoura, Japan   From nature by Kako Morita

Surface coloration about lava rocks

Coloration of specimens living among red algæ

Coloration in deep water, *Inimicus aurantiacus* (Schlegel)

In the islands of the Pacific are numerous dwarf species less than three inches long, which have been set apart as a separate genus, *Sebastapistes* The longest known of these is *Sebastapistes strongensis*, named from Strong Island, abundant in crevices in the corals throughout Polynesia, and much disliked by fishermen

The genus *Scorpænopsis* differs from *Scorpæna* in the absence of palatine teeth It is still more fantastic in form and color

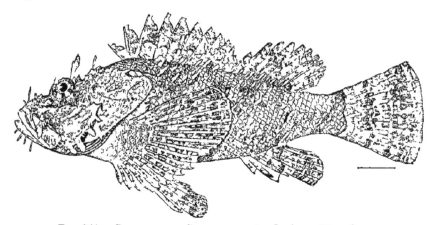

FIG 541 —Sea-scorpion, *Scorpæna mystes* Jordan Mazatlan

Scorpænopsis cirrhosa, *Scorpænopsis fimbriata*, and other species are widely distributed through the East Indies and Polynesia

The lion-fishes (*Pterois*) of the tropical Pacific are remarkable for their long pectoral fins, elongate dorsal spines, and zebra-like coloration The numerous species are fantastic and handsomely colored, but their poisoned, needle-like spines are dreaded by fishermen They lurk in crevices in the coral reefs, some of them reaching a foot in length

Inimicus japonicus, common in Japan, has a depressed and monstrous head and a generally bizarre appearance It is usually black in color but is largely bright red when found among red algæ A related species, *Inimicus aurantiacus*, is blackish when near shore, but lemon-yellow in deep water (see plate) A related species in the East Indies is *Pelor filamentosum*, called *Nohu* or *Gofu* in Polynesia

Still more monstrous are the species of *Synanceia*, short, thick-set, irregularly formed fishes, in which the poisoned spines

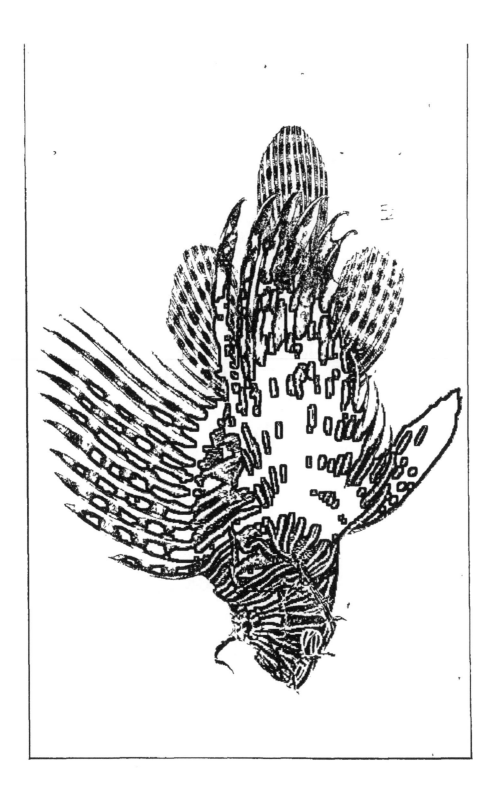

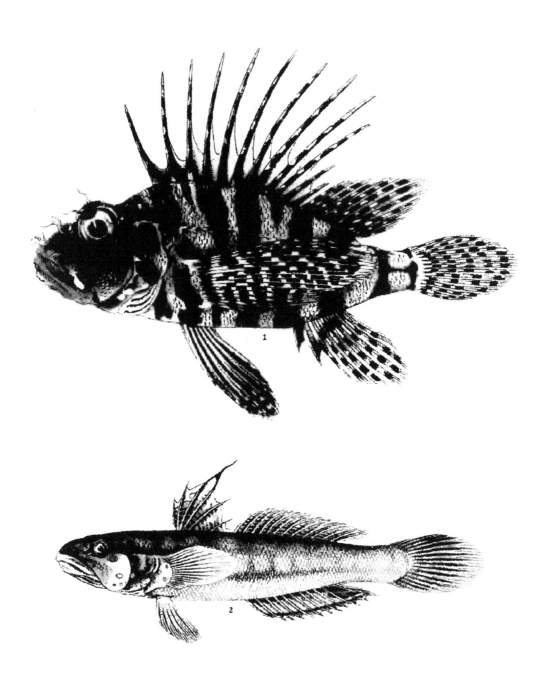

1 PTEROIS SAUSAULELE JORDAN & SEALE. (FAMILY SCORPÆNIDÆ)
2 VALENCIENNEA VIOLIFERA JORDAN & SEALE. TYPE. (FAMILY GOBIIDÆ)

FISHES OF THE CORAL POOLS, SAMOA

reach a high degree of venom. The flesh in all these species is wholesome, and when the dorsal spines are cut off the fishes sell readily in the markets. These fishes lie hidden in cavities of the reefs, being scarcely distinguishable from the rock itself. (See Fig. 64.)

The black *Emmydrichthys vulcanus* of Tahiti lies in crevices of lava, and could scarcely be distinguished from an irregular lump of lava-rock.

FIG. 543.—Black Nohu, or Poison-fish, *Emmydrichthys vulcanus* Jordan. A species with stinging spines, showing resemblance to lumps of lava among which it lives. Family *Scorpænidæ*. From Tahiti.

A related form, *Erosa erosa*, the daruma-okose of Japan, is monstrous in form but often beautifully colored with crimson and gray.

In *Congiopus* the very strong dorsal spines begin in the head, and the mouth is very small. Dr. Gill makes this genus the type of a distinct family, *Congiopodidæ*.

Besides these, very many genera and species of small poison-fishes, called okose in Japan, abound in the sandy bays from Tokio to Hindostan and the Red Sea. Some of these are handsomely colored, others are fantastically formed. *Paracentropogon rubripinnis* and *Minous adamsi* are the commonest species in Japan. *Trachicephalus uranoscopus* abounds in the bays of hina. *Snyderina yamanokami* occurs in Southern Japan.

But few fossil *Scorpænidæ* are recorded. *Scorpænopterus siluridens*, a mailed fish from the Vienna Miocene, with a warty head, seems to belong to this group, and *Ampherisius toliapicus*,

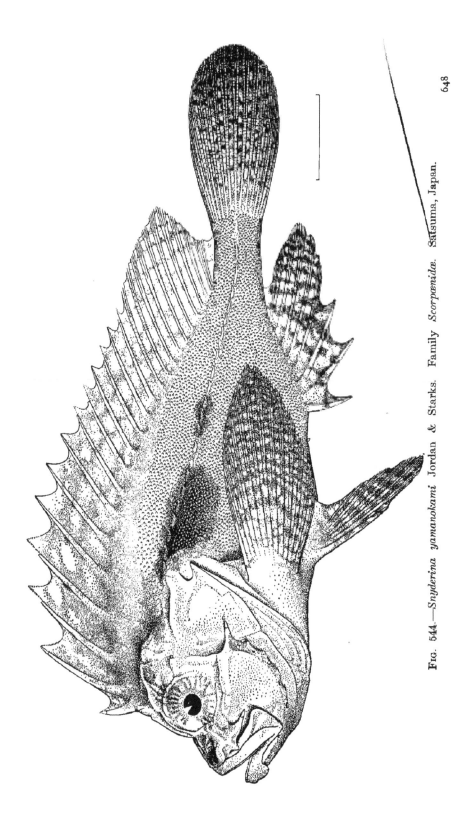

Fig. 544.—*Snyderina yamanokami* Jordan & Starks. Family *Scorpænidæ*. Satsuma, Japan.

648

with a broad, depressed head, is found in the London Eocene, and various Miocene species have been referred to *Scorpæna*. *Sebastodes rosæ* is based on a fragment, probably Pleistocene, from Port Harford, California

The small family of the *Caracanthidæ* consists of little fishes

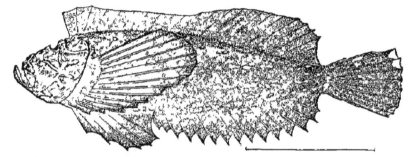

Fig 545 —*Trachicephalus uranoscopus* Family *Scorpænidæ* From Swatow, China

of the coral reefs of the Pacific   These are compressed in form, and the skin is rough with small prickles, the head being feebly armed   The species are rare and little known, brown in color with pale spots

The Skilfishes: Anoplopomidæ. — The small family of skilfishes or *Anoplopomidæ* consists of two species found on the

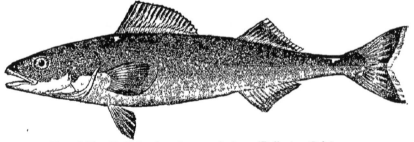

Fig 546 —Skilfish, *Anoplopoma fimbria* (Pallas) California

coast of California and northward   These resemble the *Scorpænidæ*, having the usual form of nostrils, and the suborbital stay well developed   The skull is, however, free from spines, the scales are small and close-set, and the sleek, dark-colored body has suggested resemblance to the mackerel or hake. *Anoplopoma fimbria*, known as skilfish, beshow, or coalfish, is rather common from Unalaska to Monterey, reaching a length of two feet or more.   In the north it becomes very

fat and is much valued as food   About San Francisco it is
dry and tasteless

The Greenlings: Hexagrammidæ. — The curious family of
greenlings, *Hexagrammidæ*, is confined to the two shores of the
North Pacific.   The species vary much in form, but agree in
the unarmed cranium and in the presence of but a single nostril
on each side, the posterior opening being reduced to a minute
pore   The vertebræ are numerous, the scales small, and the
coloration often brilliant   The species are carnivorous and
usually valued as food   They live in the kelp and about rocks
in California and Japan and along the shores of Siberia and

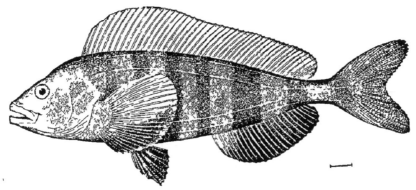

FIG 547 —Atka-fish, *Pleurogrammus monopterygius* (Pallas)   Atka Island

Alaska.   The atka-fish (*Pleurogrammus monopterygius*) is one
of the finest of food-fishes   This species reaches a length of
eighteen inches   It is yellow in color, banded with black, and
the flesh is white and tender, somewhat like that of the Lake
whitefish (*Coregonus clupeiformis*), and is especially fine when
salted   This fish is found about the Aleutian Islands, especially the island of Atka, from which it takes its name   It is
commercially known as Atka mackerel

In this genus there are numerous lateral lines, and the dorsal
fin is continuous   In *Hexagrammos*, the principal genus of the
family, the dorsal is divided into two fins, and there are about
five lateral lines on each side

Hexagrammos decagrammus is common on the coast of California, where it is known by the incorrect name of rock-trout.
It is a well-known food-fish, reaching a length of eighteen inches.

The sexes are quite unlike in color, the males anteriorly with blue spots, the females speckled with red or brown.

Hexagrammos octogrammus, the common greenfish of Alaska, and the greenling *Hexagrammos stelleri*, are also well-known species   Close to the latter species is the *Abura ainame*, or

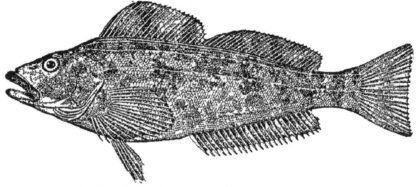

FIG 548 —Greenling, *Hexagrammos decagrammus* (Pallas)   Sitka

fat cod, *Hexagrammos otaku*, common throughout Japan   The red rock-trout, *Hexagrammos superciliosus*, is beautifully variegated with red, the color being extremely variable   Other species are found in Japan and Kamchatka. *Agrammus agram-*

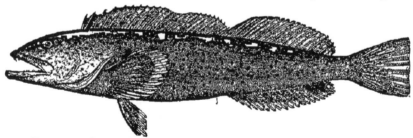

FIG 549 —Cultus Cod, *Ophiodon elongatus* (Girard)   Sitka, Alaska

mus of Japan differs in the possession of but one lateral line. *Ophiodon elongatus*, the blue cod, cultus cod, or Buffalo cod of California, is a large fish of moderate value as food, much resembling a codfish, but with larger mouth and longer teeth   The flesh and bones are deeply tinged with bluish green   *Cultus* is the Chinook name for worthless *Zaniolepis latipinnis* is a singular-looking fish, very rough, dry, and bony, occasionally taken on the California coast   *Oxylebius pictus* is a small, handsome, and very active little fish, whitish with black bands, com-

mon among rocks and algæ on the California coast It is,
however, rarely brought into the markets, as it shows great
skill in escaping the nets

No fossil *Hexagrammidæ* are known

The Flatheads or Kochi: Platycephalidæ.—The family of *Platycephalidæ* consists of spindle-shaped fishes, with flattened,
rough heads and the body covered with small, rough scales
About fifty species occur in the East Indian region, where the
larger ones are much valued as food The most abundant
species and usually the largest in size is *Platycephalus insidiator*,
the kochi of the Japanese The genus *Insidiator* contains smaller
species with larger scales In all these the head is very much
depressed, a feature which separates them from all the *Scorpænidæ* *Hoplichthys langsdorfi*, the nezupo or rat-tail of Japan,
is the type of a separate family, *Hoplichthyidæ*, characterized by
a bony armature of rough plates *Bembras japonicus*, another
little Japanese fish, with the ventrals advanced in position and
the skin with rough plates, is the type of the family of
Bembradidæ

The Sculpins: Cottidæ.—The great family of *Cottidæ* or sculpins is one especially characteristic of the northern seas, where
a great variety of species is found These differ in general
from the *Scorpænidæ*, from which they are perhaps derived,
in the greater number of vertebræ and in the relative feeble-
ness or degeneration of the spinous dorsal, the ventrals, and
the scales In all these regards great variation exists. In
the most primitive genus, *Jordania*, the body is well scaled,
the spinous dorsal well developed, and the ventral rays 1, 5 In
Hemitripterus a large number of dorsal spines remains, but the
structure in other regards is highly modified In the most
degraded types, *Cottunculus*, *Psychrolutes*, *Gilbertidia*, which
are also among the most specialized, there is little trace of
spinous dorsal, the scales are wholly lost, and the ventral fin
is incomplete Most of the species of *Cottidæ* live on the bottom in shallow seas. Some are found in deep water and a few
swarm in the rivers All are arctic or subarctic, none being
found to the south of Italy, Virginia, California, and Japan.
None are valued as food, being coarse and tough. Scarcely
any is found foss.l

Of the multitude of genera of *Cottidæ* we notice a few of the most prominent. *Jordania zonope*, a pretty little fish of Puget Sound, is the most primitive in its characters, being closely allied to the *Hexagrammidæ*

Scorpænichthys marmoratus, the great sculpin, or cabezon, of California reaches a length of 2½ feet. It has the ventral rays

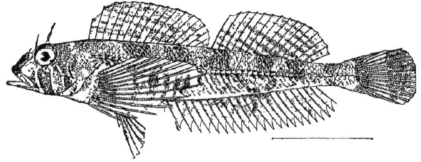

Fig 550 —*Jordania zonope* Starks   Puget Sound

1, 5, although almost in all the other sculpins the rays are reduced to 1, 3 or 1, 4   The flesh has the livid blue color seen in the cultus cod, *Ophiodon elongatus*

To *Icelinus*, *Artedius*, *Hemilepidotus*, *Astrolytes*, and related genera belong many species with the body partly scaled   These

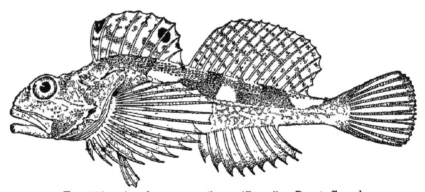

Fig 551 —*Astrolytes notospilotus* (Girard)   Puget Sound

are characteristic of the North Pacific, in which they drop to a considerable depth   *Icelus*, *Triglops*, and *Artediellus* are found also in the North Atlantic, the Arctic fauna of which is derived almost entirely from Pacific sources.   The genus *Hemilepidotus* contains coarse species, with bands of scales   The "Irish lord," *Hemilepidotus jordani*, a familiar and fantastic

inhabitant of Bering Sea, is much valued by the Aleuts as a
food-fish, although the flesh is rather tough and without much

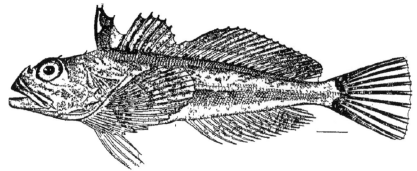

FIG 552 —Irish Lord, *Hemilepidotus jordani* Bean   Unalaska

flavor   Almost equally common in Bering Sea is the red sculpin, *Hemilepidotus hemilepidotus*, and the still rougher *Cera-*

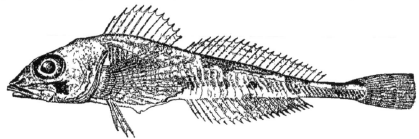

FIG 553 —*Triglops pingeli* Kroyer   Cheburto, Canada

tocottus diceraus   The stone-sculpin, or buffalo-sculpin, *Enophrys
bison*, with bony plates on the side and rough horns on the preo-

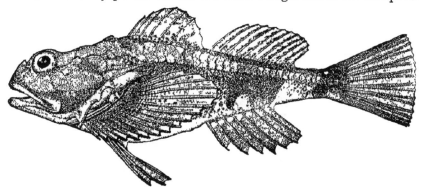

FIG 554.--Buffalo Sculpin, *Enophrys bison* (Girard).   Puget Sound.

percle, is found about Puget Sound and southward.   In all
these large rough species from the North Pacific the preopercle

is armed with long spines which are erected when the fish is disturbed. This makes it almost impossible for any larger fish to swallow them

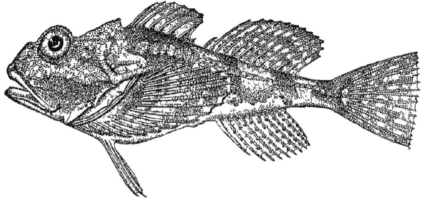

FIG. 555 —*Ceratocottus diceraus* (Cuv & Val)   Tolstoi Bay, Alaska

The genera *Cottus* and *Uranidea* include the miller's thumbs, also called in America, blob and muffle-jaws, of the Northern

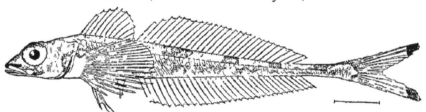

FIG 556.—*Elanura forficata* Gilbert   Bering Sea

rivers.   These little fishes are found in Europe, Asia, and America wherever trout are found   They lurk under weeds and stones,

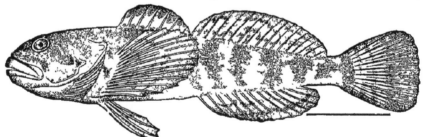

FIG 557.—Yellowstone Miller's Thumb, *Cottus punctulatus* (Gill)
Yellowstone River

moving with the greatest swiftness when disturbed   They are found in every cold stream of the region north of Virginia, and they vie with the sticklebacks in their destruction of the eggs and fry of salmon and trout   *Cottus gobio* is the commonest species of Europe   *Cottus ictalops* is the most abundant of the several species of the eastern United States, and *Cottus asper* in streams of the Pacific Coast, though very many other species

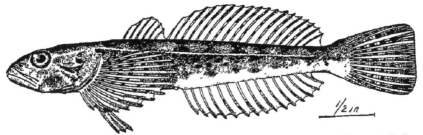

Fig   558 —Miller's Thumb, *Uranidea tenuis* Evermann & Meek   Klamath Falls

exist in each of these regions   The genus *Uranidea* is found in America   It is composed of smaller species with fewer teeth and fin-rays, the ventrals 1, 3   *Uranidea gracilis* is the commonest of these, the miller's thumb of New England *Rheopresbe fujiyamæ* is a large river sculpin in Japan.

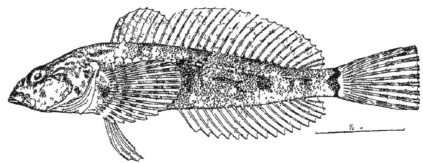

Fig   559 —*Cottus evermanni* Gilbert   Lost River, Oregon

Trachidermus ansatus is another river species, the "mountain-witch" (yama-no-kami) of Japan, remarkable for a scarlet brand on its cheek, conspicuous in life

The chief genus of Atlantic sculpins is *Myoxocephalus*, containing large marine species, in structure much like the species of *Cottus*   *Myoxocephalus bubalis* is the European fatherlasher, or proach, the European sculpin is *Myoxocephalus scorpius* The very similar daddy sculpin of New England is *Myoxocephalus grœnlandicus*   This species swarms everywhere from Cape Cod northward

According to Fabricius, *Myoxocephalus grœnlandicus* is "abundant in all the bays and inlets of Greenland, but prefers a stony coast clothed with seaweed   It approaches the shore in

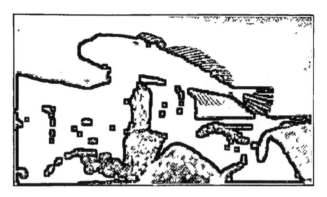

FIG 560 —California Miller's Thumb, *Cottus gulosus* Girard   McCloud River, Cal
(Photograph by Cloudsley Rutter)

spring and departs in winter   It is very voracious, preying on everything that comes in its way and pursuing incessantly the smaller fish, not sparing the young of its own species, and devouring crustacea and worms   It is very active and bold, but does not come to the surface unless it be led thither in pursuit of

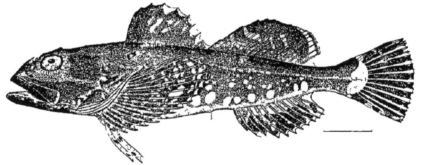

FIG 561 —Pribilof Sculpin, *Myoxocephalus niger* (Bean)   St Paul Island,
Bering Sea

other fish   It spawns in December and January and deposits its red-colored roe on the seaweed   It is easily taken with a bait, and constitutes the daily food of the Greenlanders, who are very fond of it   They eat the roe raw "

The little sculpin, or grubby, of the New England coast is *Myoxocephalus æneus,* and the larger eighteen-spined sculpin is *Myoxocephalus octodecimspinosus*   Still more numerous and varied are the sculpins of the North Pacific, *Myoxocephalus polyacanthocephalus* being the best known and most widely diffused *Oncocottus quadricornis* is the long-horned sculpin of Arctic Europe, entering the lakes of · Russia and British

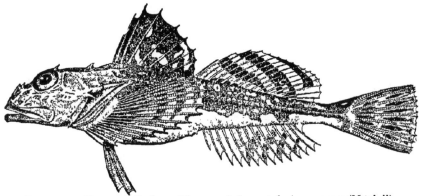

Fɪɢ 562 —18-spined Sculpin, *Myoxocephalus octodecimspinosus* (Mitchill) Beasley Point, N J

America *Triglopsis thompsoni* of the depths in our own Great Lakes seems to be a dwarfed and degenerate descendant of *Oncocottus*

The genus *Zesticelus* contains small soft-bodied sculpins from the depths of the North Pacific *Zesticelus profundorum* was

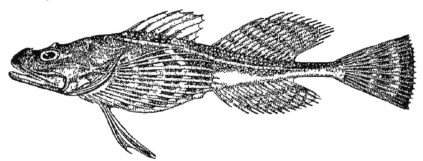

Fɪɢ 563 —*Oncocottus quadricornis* (L) St Michael, Alaska

taken in 664 fathoms off Bogoslof Island and *Zesticelus bathybius* off Japan   In this genus the body is very soft and the skeleton feeble, the result of deep-sea life   Another deep-water genus less degraded is *Cottunculus*, from which by gradual loss of fins the still more degraded *Psychrolutes* (*paradoxus*) and *Gilbertidia* (*sigolutes*) are perhaps descended   In sculpins of this type the liparids, or sea-snails, may have had their origin. Among the

remaining genera *Gymnocanthus* (*tricuspis*, etc) has no vomerine teeth   *Leptocottus* (*armatus*) and *Clinocottus* (*analis*) abound
on the coast of California, and *Pseudoblennius* (*percoides*) is

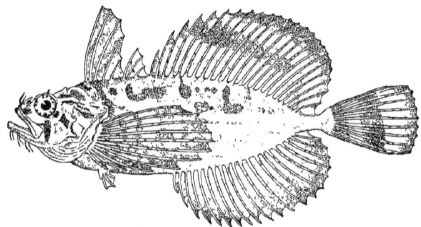

FIG 564 —*Blepsias cirrhosus* Pallas   Straits of Fuca

found everywhere along the shores of Japan   *Velhtor centropomus* of Japan is remarkable among sculpins for its compressed
body and long snout   *Dialarchus snyderi* of the California rock-

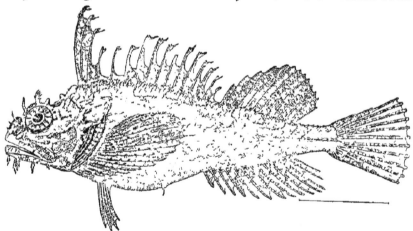

FIG 565 —Sea raven, *Hemitripterus americanus* (Gmelin)   Halifax, Nova Scotia

pools is perhaps the smallest species of sculpin, *Blepsias* (*cirrhosus*), *Nautichthys* (*oculofasciatus*), and *Hemitripterus* (*americanus*), the sea-raven, among the most fantastic   In the last-
named genus the spinous dorsal is many-rayed, as in *Scorpænidæ*, a fact which has led to its separation by Dr Gill as a dis-

tinct family   But the dorsal spines are equally numerous in *Jordania*, which stands at the opposite extreme of the cottoid seires

In *Ascelichthys (rhodorus)*, a pretty sculpin of the rock-pools of the Oregon region, the ventral fins are wholly lost   *Ereunias grallator*, a deep-water sculpin from Japan, without ventrals and

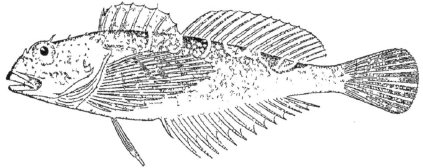

Fig 566 —*Oligocottus maculosus* Girard.   Sitka

with free rays below its pectorals, should perhaps represent a distinct family, *Ereuniidæ*

The degeneration of the spinous dorsal in *Psychrolutes* and *Gilbertidia* of the North Pacific has been already noticed   These genera seem to lead directly from *Cottunculus* to *Liparis*

Fossil *Cottidæ* are few   *Eocottus veronensis*, from the Eocene of Monte Bolca, is completely scaled, with the ventral rays 1, 5 It is apparently related to *Jordania*, but is still more primitive *Lepidocottus* (*aries* and numerous other species, mostly from the Miocene) is covered with scales, but apparently has fewer than five soft rays in the ventrals   Remains of *Oncocottus*, *Icelus*, and *Cottus* are found in Arctic Pleistocene rocks   The family as a whole is evidently of recent date

The *Rhamphocottidæ* consist of a single little sculpin with a large bony and singularly formed head, found on the Pacific Coast from Sitka to Monterey   The species is called *Rhamphocottus richardsoni*

The Sea-poachers: Agonidæ.—The sea-poachers or alligatorfishes, *Agonidæ*, are sculpins inclosed in a coat of mail made by a series of overlying plates, much like those of the sea-horses or the catfishes of the family *Loricariidæ*   So far as structure goes, these singular fishes are essentially like the *Cottidæ*, but

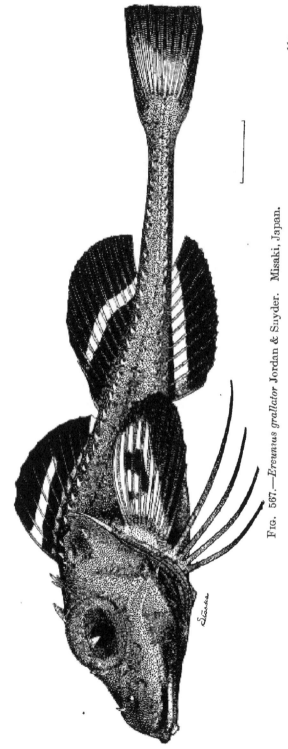

FIG. 567.—*Ereunias grallator* Jordan & Snyder. Misaki, Japan.

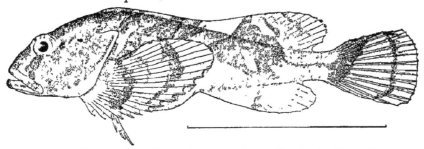

Fig. 568—Sleek Sculpin, *Psychrolutes paradoxus* (Gunther)   Puget Sound

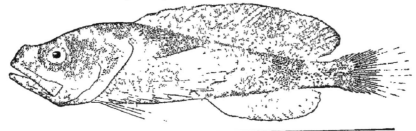

Fig 569—*Gilbertidia sigolutes* (Jordan).   Puget Sound.

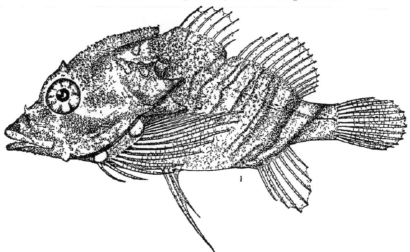

Fig 570—Richardson's Sculpin, *Rhamphocottus richardsoni* (Gunther).
Puget Sound

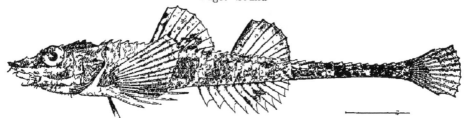

Fig 571—*Stelgis vulsus* (Jordan & Gilbert)   Point Reyes, Cal

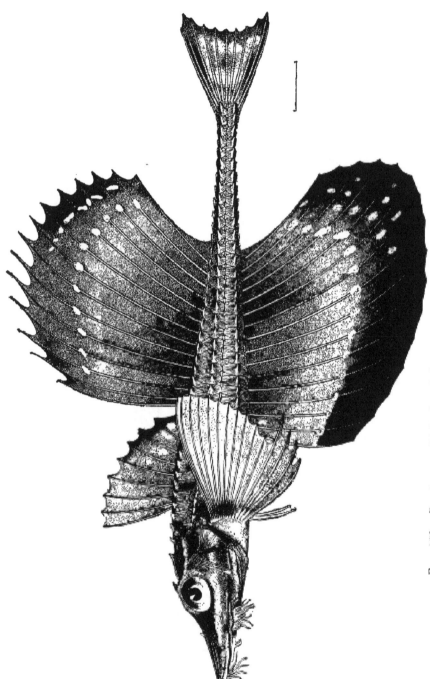

FIG. 572.—*Draciscus sachi* Jordan & Snyder. Family *Agonidæ*. Aomori, Japan.

663

with a different and more perfect armature   The many species belong chiefly to the North Pacific, a few in the Atlantic and on the coast of Patagonia   Some are found in considerable depth of water   All are too small to have value as food and some have

Fig 573 —Agonoid-fish, *Pallasina barbata* (Steindachner)   Port Mulgrave, Alaska

most fantastic forms   Only a few of the most prominent need be noticed   The largest and most peculiar species is *Percis japonicus* of the Kurile Islands   Still more fantastic is ·the Japanese *Draciscus sachi* with sail-like dorsal and anal   *Agonus cataphractus*, the sea-poacher, is the only European species   *Podothecus acipenserinus*, the alligator-fish, is the commonest species of the North Pacific   *Pallasina barbata* is as slender as

Fig 574 —*Aspidophoroides monopterygius* (Bloch)   Halifax

a pipefish, with a short beard at the chin   *Aspidophoroides monopterygius* of the Atlantic and other similar species of the Pacific lack the spinous dorsal fin

No fossil *Agonidæ* are known

The Lump-suckers. Cyclopteridæ. — The lump-suckers, *Cyclopteridæ*, are structurally very similar to the *Cottidæ*, but of very different habit, the body being clumsy and the movements very slow   The ventral fins are united to form a sucking disk by which these sluggish fishes hold fast to rocks   The skeleton is feebly ossified, the spinous dorsal fin wholly or partly lost, the skin smooth or covered with bony warts   The slender suborbital stay indicates the relation of these fishes with the *Cottidæ*   The species are chiefly Arctic, the common lump-fish or "cock and hen paddle," *Cyclopterus lumpus*, abounding on both shores of the North Atlantic   It reaches a length of twenty inches, spawning in eel-grass where the male is left to

watch the eggs. *Cyclopterichthys ventricosus* is a large species
with smooth skin from the North Pacific.

The Sea-snails: Liparididæ. — The sea-snails, *Liparididæ* are
closely related to the lumpfishes, but the body is more elongate,

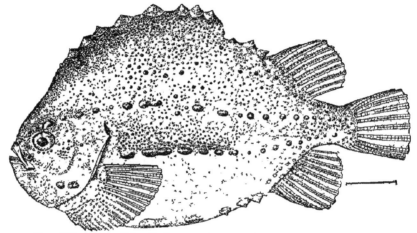

FIG 575 —Lumpfish, *Cyclopterus lumpus* (Linnæus)   Eastport, Me

tadpole shaped, covered with very lax skin, like the " wrinkled
skin on scalded milk " In structure the liparids are still more
degenerate than the lumpfishes Even the characteristic ven-

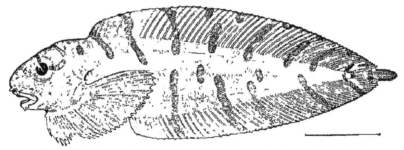

FIG 576 —Liparid, *Crystallias matsushimæ* (Jordan and Snyder)
Family *Liparididæ*   Matsushima Bay, Japan

tral disk is lost in some species (*Paraliparis, Amitra*) and in
numerous others the tail is drawn out into a point (leptocercal),
a character almost always a result of degradation The dorsal
spines are wanting or imbedded in the loose skin, and all trace
of spines on the head is lost, but the characteristic suborbital
stay is well developed The numerous species are all small,
three to twelve inches in length They live in Arctic waters,

often descending to great depths, in which case the body is very soft   One genus, *Enantioliparis*, is found in the Antarctic.   In the principal genus, *Liparis*, the ventral disk is well developed, and the spinous dorsal obsolete   *Liparis liparis* is found on both shores of the North Atlantic, and is subject to large variations in color   *Liparis agassizi* is abundant in Japan and northward, and *Liparis pulchellus* in California   In the most primitive genus, *Neoliparis*, a notch in the fin indicates the separation of the spinous dorsal   *Neoliparis montagui* is common in Europe, replaced in New England by *Neoliparis atlanticus*.   *Careproctus*, with numerous elongate species, inhabits depths of the North Pacific.   In *Paraliparis* (or *Hilgendorfia*) *ulochir*, the ventral

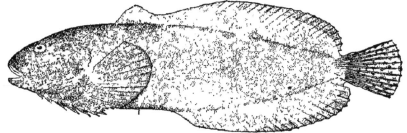

Fig 577 —Snailfish, *Neoliparis mucosus* (Ayres). San Francisco

disk is gone and the lowest stage of degradation of the Loricate or *Scorpæna-Cottus* type of fishes is reached   No fossil lump-suckers or liparids are recorded, although remains of *Cyclopterus lumpus* are found in nodules of glacial clay in Canada

The Baikal Cods: Comephoridæ.—The family of *Comephoridæ* includes *Comephorus baikalensis*, a large fresh-water fish of Lake Baikal in Siberia, having no near affinities with any other existing fish, but now known to be a mail-cheek fish related to the *Cottidæ*.   The body is elongate, naked, with soft flesh and feeble skeleton   The mouth is large, with small teeth, and the skull has a cavernous structure   There are no ventral fins   The spinous dorsal is short and low, the second dorsal and anal many-rayed, and the pectoral fins are excessively long, almost wing-like, the vertebræ number 8 +35 =43, and unlike most fresh-water fishes, the species has no air-bladder   Little is known of the habits of this singular fish   Another genus is recently described under the name of *Cottocomephorus*

Suborder Craniomi: the Gurnards, Triglidæ.—A remarkable offshoot from the *Pareioplitæ* is the suborder of gurnards, known as *Craniomi* (κράνιον, skull, ὦμος, shoulder). In these fishes the suborbital stay is highly developed, much as in the *Agonidæ*, bony externally and covering the cheeks The shoulder-girdle is distorted, the post-temporal being solidly united to the cranium, while the postero-temporal is crowded out of place by the side of the proscapula. In other regards these fishes resemble the other mail-cheek forms, their affinities being perhaps closest with the *Agonidæ* or certain aberrant *Cottidæ* as *Ereunias*.

In the true gurnards or *Triglidæ* the head is rough and bony, the body covered with rough scales and below the pectoral fin are three free rays used as feelers by the fish as it creeps along the bottom. These free rays are used in turning over stones, exploring shells and otherwise searching for food The numerous species are found in the warm seas In Europe,

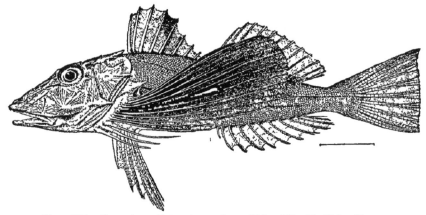

FIG 578 —Sea-robin, *Prionotus evolans* (L). Wood's Hole, Mass.

the genus *Trigla*, without palatine teeth and with the lateral line armed, is represented by numerous well-known species *Trigla cuculus* is a common form of the Mediterranean   *Chelidonichthys*, similar to *Trigla* but larger and less fully armed, is found in Asia as well as in Europe Several species occur in the Mediterranean *Chelidonichthys kumu* is a common species in Japan, a large fish with pectorals of a very brilliant variegated blue, like the wings of certain butterflies

Lepidotrigla, with larger scales, has many species on the coasts of Europe as well as in China and Japan. *Lepidotrigla*

alata, a red fish with a peculiar bony, forked snout, is common in Japan   The American species of gurnards, having teeth on the palatine, belong to the genus *Prionotus*   Northward these fishes, known as sea-robins, live along the shores in

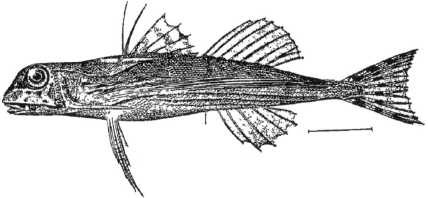

FIG 579 —Flying Gurnard, *Cephalacanthus volitans* (L)   Virginia

shallow water   In the tropics they descend to deeper water, assuming a red color   *Prionotus carolinus* is the commonest species in New England   *Prionotus strigatus*, the striped sea-robin, and *Prionotus tribulus*, the rough-headed sea-robin, are common species along the Carolina coast   None has much value as food, being dry and bony. Numerous fossil species

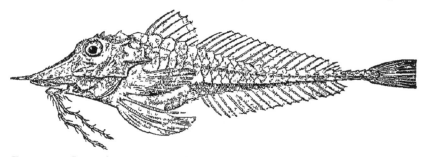

FIG 580 —*Peristedion miniatum* Goode & Bean   Depths of the Gulf Stream

referred to Trigla are found in the Miocene   *Podopteryx*, from the Italian Miocene, with small pectorals and very large ventrals, perhaps belongs also to this family, but its real affinities are unknown

The Peristediidæ. — The *Peristediidæ* are deep-water sea-robins, much depressed, with flat heads, a bony coat of mail,

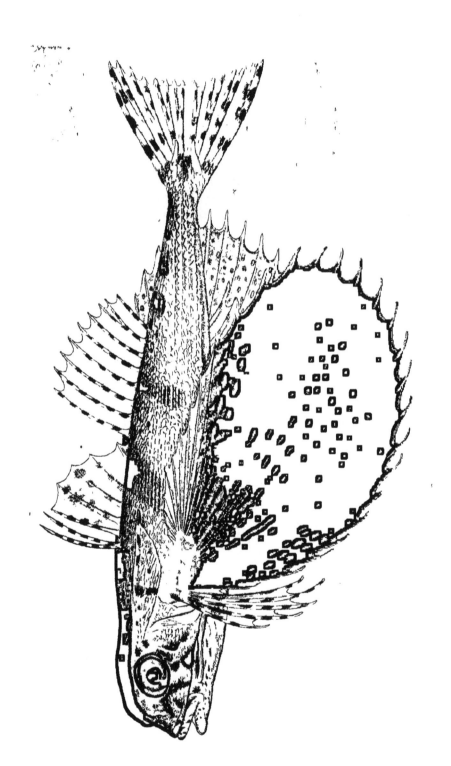

FLYING GURNARD BAT FISH
CEPHAI ACANTHUS VOLITANS (LINNÆUS)
ABOUT TWO-THIRDS NATURAL SIZE

and two free feelers on the pectoral fin instead of three   The species of *Peristedion* are occasionally taken with the dredge. *Peristedion cataphractum* is rather common in Europe   The extinct *Peristedion urcianense* is described from the Pliocene of Orciano, Tuscany

The Flying Gurnards· Cephalacanthidæ. — The flying gurnards, *Cephalacanthidæ*, differ in numerous respects and are among the most fantastic inhabitants of the sea   The head is short and bony, the body covered with firm scales, and the very long, wing-like pectoral fin is divided into two parts, the posterior and larger almost as long as the rest of the body. This fin is beautifully colored with blue and brownish red   The first spine of the dorsal fin is free from the others and more or less prolonged   The few species of flying gurnard are much alike, ranging widely in the tropical seas, and having a slight power of flight   The flying robin, or batfish, called in Spanish volador or murcielago, *Cephalacanthus volitans*, is common on both coasts of the Atlantic, reaching a length of eighteen inches   *Cephalacanthus peterseni* is found in Japan and *Cephalacanthus orientalis* in the East Indies, Japan, and Hawaii   The immature fishes have the pectoral fins much shorter than in the adult, and differ in other regards   *Cephalacanthus pliocenicus* occurs in the Lower Pliocene of Orciano, Tuscany

Petalopteryx syriacus, an extinct flying gurnard found in the Cretaceous of Mount Lebanon, is an ally of *Cephalacanthus* The body is covered with four-angled bony plates, and the first (free) spine of the dorsal is enlarged.

CHAPTER XLI

GOBIOIDEI, DISCOCEPHALI, AND TÆNIOSOMI

UBORDER Gobioidei, the Gobies Gobiidæ.—The great family of *Gobiidæ*, having no near relations among the spiny-rayed fishes, may be here treated as forming a distinct suborder

The chief characteristics of the family are the following The ventral fins are thoracic in position, each having one spine and five soft rays, in some cases reduced to four, but never wanting The ventral fins are inserted very close together, the inner rays the longest, and in most cases the two fins are completely joined, forming a single roundish fin, which may be used as a sucking-disk in clinging to rocks The shoulder-girdle is essentially perch-like in form, the cranium is usually depressed, the bones being without serrature There is no lateral line, the gill-openings are restricted to the sides, and the spinous dorsal is always small, of feeble spines, and is sometimes altogether wanting There is no bony stay to the preopercle The small pharyngeals are separate, and the vertebræ usually in normal number, 10 + 14 = 24

The species are excessively numerous in the tropics and temperate zones, being found in lakes, brooks, swamps, and bays, never far out in the sea, and usually in shallow water Many of them burrow in the mud between or below tide-marks Others live in swift waters like the darters, which they much resemble A few reach a length of a foot or two, but most of the species rarely exceed three inches, and some of them are mature at half an inch

The largest species, *Philypnus dormitor*, the guavina de rio, is found in the rivers of Mexico and the West Indies It reaches a length of nearly two feet and is valued as food Unlike most of the others, in this species there are teeth on the vomer Other related forms of the subfamily of *Eleotrinæ*, having the ventral fins separate, are *Eleotris pisonis*, a common river-fish everywhere in tropical America, *Eleotris fusca*, a river-fish abounding from Tahiti and Samoa

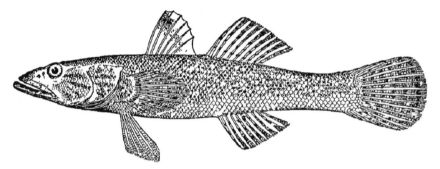

FIG 581 —Guavina de Rio, *Philypnus dormitor* (Bloch & Schneider) Puerto Rico

to Hindostan, *Dormitator maculatus*, the stout-bodied guavina-mapo of the West Indian regions, with the form of a small carp *Guavina guavina* of Cuba is another species of this type, and numerous other species having separate ventrals are found in the East Indies, the West Indies, and in the islands of Polynesia. Some species, as *Valenciennesia strigata* of the East

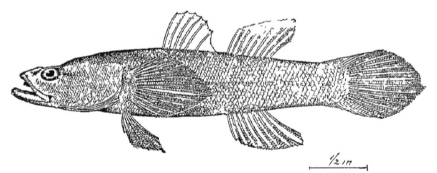

FIG 582 —Dormeur, *Eleotris pisonis* Gmelin Tortugas, Fla

Indies and *Vireosa hanæ* of Japan, are very gracefully colored One genus, *Eviota*, is composed of numerous species, all minute, less than an inch in length These abound in the crevices in coral-heads *Eviota epiphanes* is found in Hawaii, the others farther south *Hypseleotris guntheri*, of the rivers and springs of Polynesia, swims freely in the water, like a minnow, never hugging the bottom as usual among gobies

Of the typical gobies having the ventrals united we can mention but a few of the myriad forms, different species being

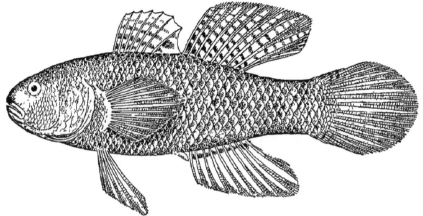

Fig 583—Guavina mapo, *Dormitator maculatus* (Schneider)   Puerto Rico

abundant alike in fresh and salt waters in all warm regions. In Europe *Gobius jozo*, *Gobius ophiocephalus*, and many others

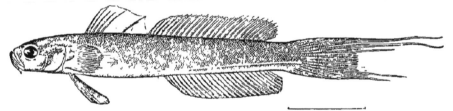

Fig 584—*Vireosa hanæ* Jordan & Snyder   Misaki, Japan

are common species. The typical genus *Gobius* is known by its united ventrals and by the presence of silken free rays on

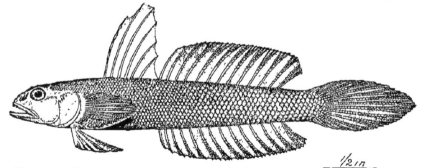

Fig 585—Esmeralda de Mar, *Gobionellus oceanicus* (Pallas)   Puerto Rico.

the upper part of the pectoral fin. *Mapo soporator* swarms about coral reefs in both Indies. *Gobionellus oceanicus*, the esmeralda or emerald-fish, is notable for its slender body and the green spot over its tongue *Gobiosoma alepidotum* and other species are scaleless. *Barbulifer ceuthæcus* lives in the cavities of sponges *Coryphopterus similis*, a small goby, swarms in almost every brook of Japan. The species of *Ptero-*

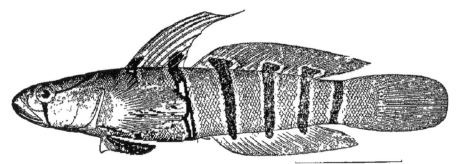

Fig 586 —*Pterogobius daimio* Jordan & Snyder   Misaki, Japan

gobius are beautifully colored, banded with white or black, or striped with red or blue *Pterogobius virgo* and *Pterogobius daimio* of Japan are the most attractive species Species of *Cryptocentrus* are also very prettily colored

Of the species burrowing in mud the most interesting is the long-jawed goby, *Gillichthys mirabilis* In this species

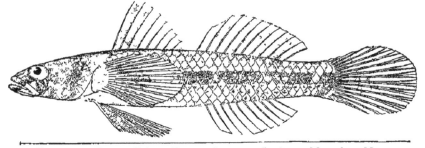

Fig 587 —Darter Goby, *Aboma etheostoma* Jordan   Mazatlan, Mex

the upper jaw is greatly prolonged, longer than the head, as in *Opisthognathus* and *Neoclinus* In the "American Naturalist" for August, 1877, Mr W N Lockington says of the long-jawed goby.

"I call it the long-jawed goby, as its chief peculiarity consists in its tremendous length of jaw A garpike has a long jaw, and so has an alligator, and it is not unlikely that the title will call up in the minds of some who read this the idea of a terrible mouth, armed with a bristling row of teeth. This would be a great mistake, for our little fish has no teeth worth bragging about, and does not open his mouth any wider than a well-behaved fish should do The great difference between his long jaws and those of a garpike is that the latter's project forward, while those of our goby are prolonged backward immensely.

"The long-jawed goby was discovered by Dr J. G Cooper in the Bay of San Diego, among seaweed growing on small stones at the wharf, and in such position that it must have been out of the water from three to six hours daily, though kept moist by the seaweed

"On a recent occasion a single *Gillichthys*, much larger than any of the original types, was presented by a gentleman who said that the fish, which was new to him, was abundant upon his ranch in Richardson's Bay, in the northern part of the Bay of San Francisco, that the Chinamen dug them up and ate them, and that he had had about eleven specimens cooked,

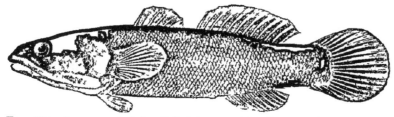

FIG 588—Long-jawed Goby *Gillichthys mirabilis* Cooper Santa Barbara

and found them good, tasting, he thought, something like eels The twelfth specimen he had preserved in alcohol, in the interest of natural science This gentleman had the opportunity of observing something of the mode of life of these fishes, and informed us that their holes, excavated in the muddy banks of tidal creeks, increase in size as they go downward, so that the lower portion is below the water-level, or at least sufficiently low to be kept wet by the percolation from the surrounding mud

"When the various specimens now acquired were placed side by side, the difference in the relative length of their jaws was very conspicuous, for while in the smallest it was about one-fifth of the total length, in the largest it exceeded one-third

"As the fish had now been found in two places in the bay,

I thought I would try to find it also, and to this end sallied out one morning, armed with a spade, and commenced prospecting in a marsh at Berkeley, not far from the State University For a long time I was unsuccessful, as I did not know by what outward signs their habitations could be distinguished, and the extent of mud-bank left bare by the retreating tide was, as compared with my powers of delving, practically limitless.

"At last, toward evening, while digging in the bend of a small creek, in a stratum of soft, bluish mud, and at a depth of about a foot below a small puddle, I found five small fishes, which at first I believed to belong to an undescribed species, so little did they resemble the typical *G. mirabilis*, but which proved, upon a closer examination, to be the young of that species There was the depressed, broad head, the funnel-shaped ventral 'disk' formed by the union of the two ventral fins, and the compressed tail of the long-jawed goby, but where were the long jaws? The jaws were, of course, in their usual place, but their prolongations had only just begun to grow along the sides of the head, and were not noticeable unless looked for A comparison of the various specimens proved conclusively that the strange-looking appendage is developed during the growth of the fish, as will be seen by the following measurements of four individuals

"In the smallest specimen the maxillary expansion extends beyond the orbit for a distance about equal to that which intervenes between the anterior margin of the orbit and the tip of the snout, in No 2 it reaches to the posterior margin of the preoperculum, in No 3 it ends level with the gill-opening; while in the largest individual it passes the origin of the pectoral and ventral fins.

"What can be the use of this long fold of skin and cartilage, which is not attached to the head except where it joins the mouth, and which, from its gradual development and ultimate large dimensions, must certainly serve some useful purpose?

"Do not understand that I mean that every part of a creature is of use to it in its present mode of life, for, as all naturalists know, there are in structural anatomy, just as in social life, cases of *survival,* remains of organs which were at some former time more developed, parallel in their nature to such survivals in costume as the two buttons on the back of a man's coat, once useful for the attachment of a sword-belt But in this fish we have no case of survival, but one of unusual development, the family (*Gobiidæ*) to which it belongs presents no similar case, although its members have somewhat similar habits, and the conviction grows upon us, as we consider the subject, that the long jaws serve some useful purpose in the economy of the creature In view of the half-terrestrial life led by this fish, I am inclined to suspect that the expansion of the upper jaw may serve for the retention of a small quantity of water, which, slowly trickling downward into the mouth and gills, keeps the latter moist when, from an unusually low tide or a dry season, the waters of its native creek fail, perhaps for several hours, to reach the holes in which the fishes dwell It may be objected to this view that, were such an appendage necessary or even useful, other species of *Gobiidæ*, whose habits are similar, would show traces of a similar adaptation This, however, by no means follows Nature has many ways of working out the same end, and it must be remembered that every real species, when thoroughly known, differs somewhat in habits from its congeners, or at least from its family friends To take an illustration from the mammalia The chimpanzee and the spider-monkey are both quadrumanous and both arboreal, yet the end which is attained in the former by its more perfect hands is reached in the latter by its prehensile tail

"Why may not the extremely long channel formed by the jaw of this rather abnormal member of the goby family be another mode of provision for the requirements of respiration?"

Of the Asiatic genera, *Periophthalmus* and *Bolcophthalmus* are especially notable In these mud-skippers the eyes are raised on a short stalk, the fins are strong, and the animal has the power of skipping along over the wet sands and mud, even skimming with great speed over the surface of the water It chases its insect prey among rocks, leaves, and weeds, and out of the water is as agile as a lizard Several species of these mud-skippers are known on the coasts of Asia and Polynesia, *Periophthalmus barbarus* and *Bolcophthalmus chinensis* being the best known *Awaous crassilabris* is the common oopu, or river goby, of the Hawaiian streams, and *Lentipes stimpsoni* is the mountain oopu, capable of clinging to the rocks in the

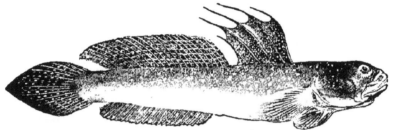

FIG. 589.—Pond-skipper, *Boleophthalmus chinensis* (Osbeck). Bay of Tokyo, Japan. (Eye-stalks sunken in preservation.)

rush of torrents. *Paragobiodon echinocephalus* is a short thick-set goby with very large head, found in crevices of coral reefs of Polynesia.

FIG. 590.—Mud-skippy, *Periophthalmus oarbarus* (L.). Mouth of Vaisigono River, Apia, Samoa.

In numerous interesting species the first dorsal fin is wanting or much reduced. The crystal goby, *Crystallogobius nilssoni*, of Europe is one of this type, with the body translucent. Equally translucent is the little Japanese shiro-uwo, or whitefish, *Leuco-psarion petersi*. *Mistichthys luzonius* of the Philippine Islands, another diaphanous goby, is said to be the smallest of all verte-brates, being mature at half an inch in length   This minute fish is so very abundant as to become an important article of food in Luzon.   The rank of "smallest-known vertebrate" has been claimed in turn for the lancelet (*Asymmetron lucayanum*), the top minnow, *Heterandria formosa*, and the dwarf sunfish (*Elassoma zonatum*)   *Mistichthys luzonius* is smaller than any of these, but the diminutive gobies, called *Eviota*, found in interstices of coral rocks are equally small, and there are several brilliant but minute forms in the reefs of Samoa   The snake-like *Eutænuichthys gilli* of Japanese rivers is scarcely larger, though over an inch long   *Typhlogobius californiensis*, "the blindfish of Point Loma," is a small goby, colorless and blind, found clinging in dark crevices of rock about Point Loma and Dead Man's Island in southern California

Its eyes are represented by mere rudiments, their loss being evidently associated with the peculiar habit of the species,

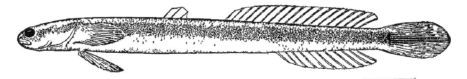

Fig 591—*Eutænuichthys gilli* Jordan & Snyder   Tokyo, Japan

which clings to the under side of stones in relative darkness, though in very shallow water   The flesh is also colorless, the animal appearing pink in life

In the Japanese species *Luciogobius guttatus*, common under stones and along the coast, the spinous dorsal, weak in numer-ous other species, finally vanishes altogether   Other gobies are band-shaped or eel-shaped, the dorsal spines being continu-ous with the soft rays   Among these are the barreto of Cuba, *Gobioides broussoneti*, and in Japan *Tænioides lacepedei* and *Trypauchen wakæ*, the latter species remarkable for its strong canines   Fossil gobies are practically unknown   A few frag-ments, otoliths, and partial skeletons in southern Europe have been referred to *Gobius*, but no other genus is represented

The family of *Oxudercidæ* contains one species, *Oxuderces dentatus*, a small goby-like fish from China   It is an elongate fish, without ventral fins, and with very short dorsal and anal.

Suborder Discocephali, the Shark-suckers: Echeneididæ.—Next to the gobies, for want of a better place, we may mention the singular group of *Discocephali* (δίσκος, disk, κεφηλή, head) In this group the first dorsal fin is transformed into a peculiar laminated sucking-disk, which covers the whole top of the head and the nape   In other respects the structure does not diverge very widely from the percoid type, there being a remarkable resemblance in external characters to the Scombroid genus *Rachycentron*   But the skeleton shows no special affinity to *Rachycentron* or to any perciform fish   The basis of the cranium is

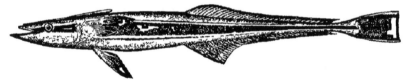

FIG 592 —Sucking-fish, or Pegador, *Leptecheneis naucrates* (Linnæus) Virginia.

simple, and in the depression of the head with associated modifications the *Discocephali* approach the gobies and blennies rather than the mackerel-like forms

The *Discocephali* comprise the single family of shark-suckers or remoras, the *Echeneididæ*   All the species of this group are pelagic fishes, widely diffused in the warm seas   All cling by their cephalic disks to sharks, barracudas, and other free-swimming fishes, and are carried about the seas by these   They do not harm the shark except by slightly impeding its movement   They are carnivorous fishes, feeding on sardines, young herring, and the like   When a shark, taken on the hook, is drawn out of the water the sucking-fish leaves it instantly, and is capable of much speed in swimming on its own account. These fishes are all dusky in color, the belly as dark as the back, so as to form little contrast to the color of the shark

The commonest species, *Leptecheneis naucrates*, called pega-pega or pegador in Cuba, reaches a length of about two feet and is almost cosmopolitan in its range, being found exclusively on the larger sharks, notably on *Carcharias lamia*   It has

20 to 22 plates in its disk, and the sides are marked by a dusky lateral band

Almost equally widely distributed is the smaller remora, or shark-sucker (*Echeneis remora*), with a stouter body and about 18 plates in the cephalic disk This species is found in Europe, on the coast of New York, in the West Indies, in California, and in Japan, but is nowhere abundant Another widely distributed species is *Remorina albescens* with 13 plates in its disk *Remoropsis brachyptera*, with 15 plates and a long soft dorsal, is also occasionally taken *Rhombochirus osteochir* is a rare species of the Atlantic with 18 plates, having the pec-

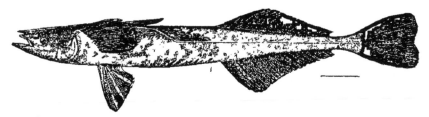

Fig 593 —*Rhombochirus osteochir* (Cuv & Val) Wood's Hole, Mass

toral rays all enlarged and stiff The louse-fish (*Phthirichthys lineatus*) is a small and slender remora having but 10 plates in its disk It is found attached, not to sharks, but to barracudas and spearfishes

A fossil remora is described from the Oligocene shales in Glarus, Switzerland, under the name of *Opisthomyzon glaronensis* It is characterized by the small disk posteriorly inserted Its vertebræ are $10 + 13 = 24$ only Dr Storms gives the following account of this species

"A careful comparison of the proportion of all the parts of the skeleton of the fossil *Echeneis* with those of the living forms, such as *Echeneis naucrates* or *Echeneis remora*, shows that the fossil differs nearly equally from both, and that it was a more normally shaped fish than either of these forms The head was narrower and less flattened, the preoperculum wider, but its two jaws had nearly the same length The ribs, as also the neural and hæmal spines, were longer, the tail more forked, and the soft dorsal fin much longer In fact it was a more compressed type, probably a far better swimmer than its living congeners, as might be expected if the smallness of the adhesive disk is taken into account"

Concerning the relations of the *Discocephali* Dr Gill has the following pertinent remarks

"The family of *Scomberoides* was constituted by Cuvier for certain forms of known organization, among which were fishes evidently related to *Caranx*, but which had free dorsal spines Dr Gunther conceived the idea of disintegrating this family because, *inter alias*, the typical *Scomberoides* (family *Scombridæ*) have more than 24 vertebræ and others (family *Carangidæ*) had just 24   The assumption of Cuvier as to the relationship of *Elacate* (*Rachycentron*) was repeated, but inasmuch as it had 'more than 24 vertebræ' (it had $25 = 12 + 13$) it was severed from the free-spined *Carangidæ* and associated with the *Scombridæ*. *Elacate* has an elongated body, flattened head, and a longitudinal lateral band, therefore *Echeneis* was considered to be next allied to *Elacate* and to belong to the same family   The very numerous differences in structure between the two were entirely ignored, and the reference of the *Echeneis* to the *Scombridæ* is simply due to assumption piled on assumption   The collocation need not, therefore, longer detain us   The possession by *Echeneis* of the anterior oval cephalic disk in place of a spinous dorsal fin would alone necessitate the isolation of the genus as a peculiar family   But that difference is associated with almost innumerable other peculiarities of the skeleton and other parts, and in a logical system it must be removed far from the *Scombridæ*, and probably be endowed with subordinal distinction   In all essential respects it departs greatly from the type of structure manifested in the *Scombridæ* and rather approximates—but very distantly—the *Gobioidea* and *Blennioidea*   In those types we have in some a tendency to flattening of the head, of anterior development of the dorsal fin, a simple basis cranii, etc   Nevertheless there is no close affinity, nor even tendency to the extreme modification of the spinous dorsal exhibited by *Echeneis*   In view of all these facts *Echeneis*, with its subdivisions, may be regarded as constituting not only a family but a suborder   Who can consistently object to the proposition to segregate the *Echeneididæ* as a suborder of teleocephalous fishes?   Not those who consider that the development of three or four inarticulate rays (or even less) in the front of the dorsal fin is sufficient to ordinarily differentiate a given form from another with only one or two such   Certainly the difference between the constituents of a disk and any rays or spines is much greater than the mere development or atrophy of articulations   Not those who consider that the manner of depression of spines, whether directly over the following, or to the right or left alternately, are of cardinal importance, for such differences, again, are manifestly of less morphological significance than the factors of a suctorial disk   Nevertheless there are doubtless many who will passively resist the proposition because of a conservative spirit, and who will vaguely refer to the development of the disk as being a 'teleological modification,' and as if it were not an actual fact and a development correlated with radical modifications of all parts of the skeleton at least   But whatever may be the closest relations of *Echeneis*, or the systematic value of its peculiarities, it is certain that it is not allied to *Elacate* any more than to hosts of scombroid, percoid, and kindred fishes, and that it differs *in toto* from it notwithstanding the claims that have been made otherwise   It is true that there is a striking resemblance, especially between the young—almost as great, for example, as that between the placental mouse and the marsupial *Antechinomys*—but the likeness is entirely superficial, and the scientific ichthyologist should be no more misled than would be the scientific therologist by the likeness of the marsupial and placental mammals ''

Suborder Tæniosomi, the Ribbon-fishes.—The suborder *Tæniosomi* (ταινία, ribbon, σῶμα, body), or ribbon-fishes, is made up of strange inhabitants of the open seas, perhaps aberrant derivatives of the mackerel stock   The body is greatly elongate, much compressed, extremely fragile, covered with shining silvery skin   The ribbon-fishes live in the open sea, probably at no very great depth, but are almost never taken by collectors except when thrown on shore in storms or when attacked by other fishes and dragged above or below their depth   When found they are usually reported as sea-serpents, and although perfectly harmless, they are usually at once destroyed by their ignorant captors   The whole body is exceedingly fragile;

the bones are porous, thin, and light, containing scarcely any calcareous matter.   In the *Tæniosomi* the ventral fins are thoracic, formed of one or a few soft rays.   More remarkable is the character of the caudal fin, which is always distorted and usually not in line with the rest of the body.   The teeth are small   The general structure is not very different from that of the cutlass-fishes, *Trichiuridæ*, and other degraded off-shoots from the scombroid group   The species are few and, from the nature of things, very imperfectly known   Scarcely any specimens are perfectly preserved   When dried the body almost disappears, both flesh and bones being composed chiefly of water.

The Oarfishes: Regalecidæ.— The *Regalecidæ*, or oarfishes, have the caudal fin obsolete and the ventrals reduced to long filaments, thickened at the tip   The species reach a length of twenty or thirty feet, and from their great size, slender forms, and sinuous motion have been almost everywhere regarded as sea-serpents.   The very long anterior spines of the dorsal fin are tipped with red, and the fish is often and not untruthfully described as a sea-serpent "having a horse's head with a flaming red mane "

The great oarfish, *Regalecus glesne* (see Fig 113), was long known to the common people of Norway as king of the herrings, it being thought that to harm it would be to drive the herring to some other coast.   The name "king of the herrings" went into science as *Regalecus*, from *rex*, king, and *halec*, herring   The Japanese fancy, which runs in a different line, calls the creature "Dugunonuatatori," which means the "cock of the palace under the sea "

The Atlantic oarfish is named *Regalecus glesne*, from the Norwegian farm of Glesnæs, where the first recorded specimen, described by Ascanius, was taken 130 years ago   Since then the species has been many times found on the shores of Great Britain and Norway, and once at Bermuda, and also twice in Florida.

In this species the body is half-transparent, almost jelly-like, light blue in color, with some darker cross-stripes, and the head has a long jaw and a high forehead, suggesting the head of a horse   The dorsal fin begins on the head, and the first

few spines are very long, each having a red tuft on the end
When the animal is alive these spines stand up like a red
mane

The creature is harmless, weak in muscle as well as feeble
in mind   It lives in the deep seas, all over the world   After
great storms it sometimes comes ashore   Perhaps this is
because for some reason it has risen above its depth and so
lost control of itself   When a deep-water fish rises to the surface
the change of pressure greatly affects it   Reduction of pressure
bursts its blood-vessels, its swim-bladder swells, if it has one,
and turns its stomach inside out   If a deep-water fish gets
above its depth it is lost, just as surely as a surface fish is when
it gets sunk to the depth of half a mile

Sometimes, again, these deep-sea fishes rush to the shore
to escape from parasites, crustaceans that torture their soft
flesh or sharks that would tear it

Numerous specimens have been found in the Pacific, and
to these several names have been given, but the species are
not at all clearly made out   The oldest name is that of *Regalecus
russelli*, for the naturalist Patrick Russell, who took a specimen
at Vizagapatam in 1788   I have seen two large examples of
Regalecus in the museum at Tokio, and several young ones
have recently been stranded on the Island of Santa Catalina
in southern California   A specimen twenty-two feet long lately
came ashore at Newport in Orange County, California.   The
story of its capture is thus told by Mr Horatio J Forgy, of
Santa Ana, California

"On the 22d of February, 1901, a Mexican Indian reported
at Newport Beach that about one mile up the coast he had
landed a sea-serpent, and as proof showed four tentacles and
a strip of flesh about six feet long   A crowd went up to see
it, and they said it was about twenty feet long and like a fish
in some respects and like a snake in others   Mr Remsberg
and I, on the following day, went up to see it, and in a short
time we gathered a crowd and with the assistance of Mr. Pea-
body prepared the fish and took the picture you have received

"It measured twenty-one feet and some inches in length,
and weighed about 500 or 600 pounds

"The Indian, when he reported his discovery, said it was

alive and in the shallow water, and that he had landed it himself

"This I very much doubt, but when it was first landed it was in a fine state of preservation and could have easily been shipped to you, but he had cut it to such an extent that shipment or preservation seemed out of the question when we first saw it

"At the time it came ashore an unusual number of peculiar fishes and sharks were found   Among others, I found a small oarfish about three feet long in a bad state of preservation in a piece of kelp.   One side of it was nearly torn off and the other side was decayed "

Mr C F Holder gives this account of the capture of oarfishes in southern California

"From a zoological point of view the island of Santa Catalina, which lies eighteen miles off the coast of Los Angeles County, southern California, is very interesting, many rare animals being found there   Every winter the dwellers of the island find numbers of argonaut-shells, and several living specimens have been secured, one for a time living in the aquarium which is maintained here for the benefit of students and the entertainment of visitors   A number of rare and interesting fishes wander inshore from time to time   Several years ago I found various Scopeloid fishes, which up to that time had been considered rare, and during the past few years I have seen one oarfish (*Regalecus russelli*) alive, while another was brought to me dead   From reports I judge that a number of these very rare fishes have been observed here   The first was of small size, not over two feet in length, and was discovered swimming in shallow water along the beach of Avalon Bay I had an opportunity to observe the radiant creature before it died.   Its 'topknot'—it can be compared to nothing else— was a vivid red or scarlet mass of seeming plumes—the dorsal fins, which merged into a long dorsal fin, extending to the tail The color of the body was a brilliant silver sheen splashed with equally vivid black zebra-like stripes, which gave the fish a most striking appearance.

" The fish was a fragile and delicate creature, a very ghost of a fish, which swam along where the water gently lapped the sands with an undulatory motion, looking like one of its names—the ribbon-fish. The fortunate finder of this specimen could not be persuaded to give it up or sell it, and it was its fate to be pasted upon a piece of board, dried in the sun as a 'curio,' where, as if in retaliation at the desecration of so rare a specimen, it soon disappeared

"This apparently was the first oarfish ever seen in the United States, so at least Dr G Brown Goode wrote me at the time that it had not been reported   In 1899 another oarfish was brought to me, evidently having been washed in after a storm and found within a few yards of the former at Avalon   The discoverer of this specimen also refused to allow it to be properly preserved, or to donate or sell it to any one who would have sent it to some museum, but, believing it valuable as a 'curio,' also impaled it, the delicate creature evaporating under the strong heat of the semitropic sun

"This, as stated, was the second fish discovered, and during the past winter (1900) a fine large specimen came in at Newport Beach, being reported by H J. Forgy, of Santa Ana   The newspapers announced that a Mexican had found a young sea-serpent at Newport, and investigation showed that, as in hundreds of similar instances, the man had found a valuable prize without being aware of it   According to the account, the discoverer first saw the fish alive in the surf and hauled it ashore   Being ignorant of its value, he cut it up, bringing in a part of the scarlet fins and a slice of the flesh   This he showed to some men, and led the way to where lay the mutilated remains of one of the finest oar- or ribbon-fishes ever seen   The specimen was twenty-one feet in length, and its weight estimated at five hundred pounds   The finder had so mutilated it that the fish was ruined for almost any purpose   If he had packed it in salt, the specimen would have returned him the equivalent of several months' labor.   Apparently the man had cut it up in wanton amusement

"This recalls a similar incident.   I was on one occasion excavating at San Clemente Island, and had remarked that it was a singular fact that all the fine stone ollas were broken 'Nothing strange about that,' said a half-breed, one of the party   'I used to herd sheep here, and we smashed mortars and ollas to pass away time '"

The Dealfishes: Trachypteridæ. — The family of *Trachypteridæ* comprises the dealfishes, creatures of fantastic form and silvery coloration, smaller than the oarfishes and more common, but of similar habit.

Just as in Norway the fantastic oarfish was believed to be the king of the herrings and cherished as such, so among the Indians of Puget Sound another freak fish is held sacred as the king of the salmon. The people about Cape Flattery believe that if one does any harm to this fish the salmon will at once leave the shores. This fable led the naturalists who first discovered this fish to give it its name of *Trachypterus rex-salmonorum*

In Europe a similar species (*Trachypterus atlanticus*) has long been known by the name of dealfish, or vogmar, neither of these names having any evident propriety

The dealfish is one of the most singular of all the strange creatures of the sea. It reaches a length of three or four feet Its body is thin as a knife and would be transparent were it not covered over with a shining white pigment which gives to the animal the luster of burnished silver On this white surface is a large black blotch or two, but no other colors The head is something like that of the oarfish, to which animal the dealfish bears a close relationship Both have small teeth and neither could bite if it would, and neither wants to, for they are creatures of the most inoffensive sort On the head of the dealfish, where the oarfish has its mane, is a long, streamer-like fin. At the end of the tail, instead of the ordinary caudal fin, is a long, slim fin which projects directly upwards at right angles to the direction of the back-bone No other fish shows this strange peculiarity.

The dealfish swims in the open sea close to the surface of the water It does not often come near shore, but it is occasionally blown on the beach by storms *Trachypterus rex-salmonorum* has been recorded two or three times from Puget Sound and twice from California The finest specimen known, the one from which our figure is taken, was secured off the Farallones in 1895 by a fisherman named W C Knox, and by him sent to Stanford University The specimen is perfect in all its parts, a condition rare with these fragile creatures, and its picture gives a good idea of the mysterious king of the salmon.

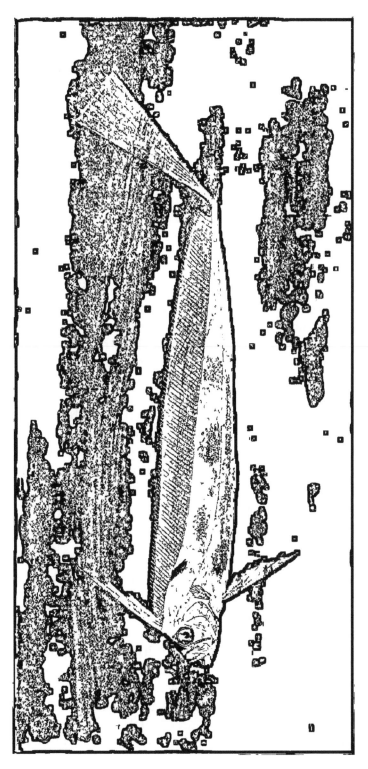

Fig. 594—Dealfish, or King of the Salmon, *Trachypterus rex-salmonorum* Jordan & Gilbert   Family *Trachypteridæ*
(From a specimen taken off the Farallones)

Four of these fishes have been obtained on the coast of Japan, and have been described and figured by the present writer in the annals of the Imperial University of Tokyo   These are different from the California species and are named *Trachypterus ishikawæ*, but they show the same bright silver color and the same streamers on the head and tail   Probably they, too, in Japan are kings of something or other, or perhaps silver swans from the submarine palace, for along such lines the Japanese fancy is more likely to run.

The young of the dealfish has the caudal symmetrical, and the dorsal spines and ventral rays produced in very long streamers

According to Goode and Bean, the dealfishes are "true deep-sea fishes, which live at very great depths, and are only found when floating dead on the surface or washed ashore by the waves   Almost nothing is known of their habits except through Nilsson's observations in the far north   This naturalist, as well as Olafson, appears to have had the opportunity of observing them in life   They say that they approach the shore at flood-tide on sandy, shelving bottoms, and are often left by the retreating waves   Nilsson's opinion is that its habits resemble those of the flatfishes, and that they move with one side turned obliquely upward, the other toward the ground, and he says that they have been seen on the bottom in two or three fathoms of water, where the fishermen hook them up with the implements employed to raise dead seals, and that they are slow swimmers   This is not necessarily the case, however, for the removal of pressure and the rough treatment by which they were probably washed ashore would be demoralizing, to say the least. *Trichiurus*, a fish similar in form, is a very strong, swift swimmer, and so is *Regalecus*   Whether or not the habits of *Trachypterus arcticus*, on which these observations were made, are a safe guide in regard to the other forms is a matter of some doubt, but it is certain that they live far from the surface, except near the arctic circle, and that they only come ashore accidentally   They have never been taken by the deep-sea dredge or trawl-net, and indeed perfect specimens are very rare, the bodies being very soft and brittle, the bones and fin-rays exceedingly fragile   A considerable number of species have been described, but in most instances each was based on one or two specimens   It is probable that future studies may be as fruitful as that of Emery, who, by means of a series of twenty-three specimens, succeeded in uniting at least three of the Mediterranean species which for half a century or more had been regarded as distinct   The common species of the eastern Atlantic, *Trachypterus atlanticus*, is not rare, one or more specimens, according to Gunther, being secured along the coast of northern Europe after almost every severe gale   We desire to quote the recommendation of Dr Gunther, and to strongly urge upon any one who may be so fortunate as to secure one of these fishes that no attempt should be made to keep it entire, but that it should be cut into short lengths and preserved in the strongest spirits, each piece wrapped separately in muslin ''

The family of *Stylephoridæ* is known from a single specimen of the species, *Stylephorus chordatus*, taken off Cuba in 1790 In this form the tail ends in a long, whip-like appendage, twice as long as the head

No fossil dealfishes or oarfishes are known.

CHAPTER XLII

SUBORDER HETEROSOMATA

THE **Flatfishes.**—Perhaps the most remarkable offshoot from the order of spiny-rayed fishes is the great group of flounders and soles, called by Bonaparte *Heterosomata* (ἔτερός, differing, σῶμα, body). The essential character of this group is found in the twisting of the anterior part of the cranium, an arrangement which brings both eyes on the same side of the head. This is accompanied by a great compression of the body, as a result of which the flounders swim horizontally or lie flat on the sand. On the side which is uppermost both eyes are placed, this side being colored, brown or gray or mottled. The lower side is usually plain white. In certain genera the right side is uppermost, in others the left. In a very few, confined to the coast of California, the eyes are on the right or left side indifferently.

The process of the twisting of the head has been already described (see p 75). The very young have the body translucent and symmetrical, standing upright in the water. Soon the tendency to rest on the bottom sets in, the body leans to left or right, and the lower eye gradually traverses the front of the head to the other side. This movement is best seen in the species of *Platophrys*, in which the final arrangement of the eyes is a highly specialized one.

In some or all of the soles it is perhaps true that the eye turns over and pierces the cranium instead of passing across it. This opinion needs verification, and the process should be studied in detail in as many species as possible. The present writer has seen it in species of *Platophrys* only, the same genus in which it was carefully studied by Dr Carlo F Emery of Bologna. In the halibut, and in the more primitive flounders

691

generally, the process takes place at an earlier stage than in *Platophrys*

Optic Nerves of Flounders.—In the Bulletin of the Museum of Comparative Zoology (Vol XL, No 5) Professor George H Parker discusses the relations of the optic nerves in the group of flounders or flatfishes

In the bony fishes the optic nerves pass to the optic lobes of the brain, the one passing to the lobes of the opposite side simply lying over the other, without intermingling of fibers, such as takes place in the higher vertebrates and in the more primitive fishes

According to Parker's observations, in ordinary bony fishes the right nerve may be indifferently above or below the other In 1000 specimens of ten common species, 486 have the left nerve uppermost and 514 the right nerve In most individual species the numbers are practically equal Thus, in the haddock, 48 have the left nerve uppermost and 52 the right nerve

In the unsymmetrical teleosts or flounders, and soles, this condition no longer obtains In those species of flounder with the eyes on the right side 236 individuals, representing sixteen species, had the left nerve uppermost in all cases

Of flounders with the eyes on the left side, 131 individuals, representing nine species, all have the right nerve uppermost

There are a few species of flounders in which reversed examples are so common that the species may be described as having the eyes on the right or left side indifferently In all these species, however, whether dextral or sinistral, the relation of the nerves conforms to the type and is not influenced by

Fig 595 — Young Flounder, just hatched, with symmetrical eyes (After S R Williams)

the individual deviation Thus the starry flounder (*Platichthys*) belongs to the dextral group In 50 normal specimens, the eyes on the right have the left nerve dorsal, while the left nerve is also uppermost in 50 reversed examples with eyes on the left In 15 examples of the California bastard halibut (*Paralichthys californicus*), normally sinistral, the right eye is always uppermost It is uppermost in 11 reversed examples

Among the soles this uniformity or monomorphism no

longer obtains.   In 49 individuals of four species of dextral soles, the left nerve is uppermost in 24, the right nerve in 25. Among sinistral soles, or tonguefishes, in 18 individuals of two species, the left nerve is uppermost in 13, the right nerve in 5.

Professor Parker concludes from this evidence that soles are not degenerate flounders, but rather descended from primitive flounders which still retain the dimorphic condition as to the position of the optic nerves, a condition prevalent in all bony fishes except the flounders.

The lack of symmetry among the flounders lies, therefore, deeper than the matter of the migration of the eye.   The asymmetry of the mouth is an independent trait, but, like the migration of the eye, is an adaptation to swimming on the side.   Each of the various traits of asymmetry may appear independently of the others.

The development of the monomorphic arrangement in flounders Professor Parker thinks can be accounted for by the

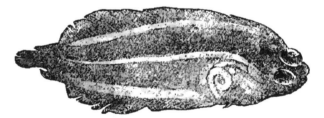

FIG. 596.—Larval Flounder, *Pseudopleuronectes americanus.*
(After S. R. Williams.)

principle of natural selection.   In a side-swimming fish the fixity of this trait has a mechanical advantage.   The unmetamorphosed young of the flounder are not strictly symmetrical, for they possess the monomorphic position of the optic nerve. The reversed examples of various species of flounders (these, by the way, chiefly confined to the California fauna) afford "striking examples of discontinuous variation."

A very curious feature among the flounders is the possession in nine of the California-Alaskan species of an accessory half-lateral line.   This is found in two different groups, while near relatives in other waters lack the character.   One species in Japan has this trait, which is not found in any Atlantic species, or in any other flounders outside the fauna of northern California, Oregon, and Alaska

Ancestry of Flounders. — The ancestry of the flounders is wholly uncertain. Because, like the codfishes, the flounders lack all fin-spines, they have been placed by some authors after the *Anacanthini*, or codfishes, and a common descent has been assumed. Some writers declare that the flounder is only a codfish with distorted cranium

A little study of the osteology of the flounder shows that this supposition is without foundation. The flounders have

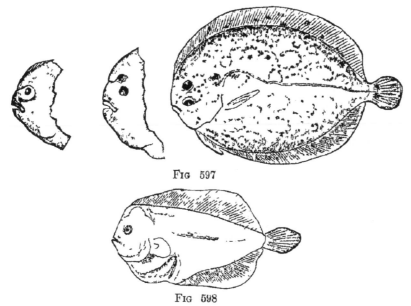

Fig 597

Fig 598

Figs. 597 and 598 —Larval stages of *Platophrys podas*, a flounder of the Mediterranean, showing the migration of the eye   (After Emery)

thoracic ventrals, not jugular as in the cod   The tail is homocercal, ending in a large hypural plate, never isocercal, except in degraded soles in which it is rather leptocercal   The shoulder-girdle, with its perforate hypercoracoid, has the normal perch-like form   The ventral fins have about six rays, as in the perch, although the first ray is never spinous   Pseudobranchiæ are developed, these structures being obsolete in the codfishes   The gills and pharyngeals are essentially as in the perch

It is fairly certain that the *Heterosomata* have diverged from the early spiny-rayed forms, *Zeoidei*, *Berycoidei*, or *Scombroidei* of the Jurassic or Cretaceous, and that their origin is prior to the development of the great perch stock.

If one were to guess at the nearest relationships of the group, it would be to regard them as allies of the deep-bodied mackerel-like forms, as the *Stromateidæ*, or perhaps with extinct Berycoid forms, as *Platycormus*, having the ventral fins wider than in the mackerel. Still more plausible is the recent suggestion of Dr. Boulenger that the extinct genus *Amphistium* resembles the primitive flounder. But there is little direct proof of such relation, and the resemblance of larval flounders to the ribbon-fishes may have equal significance. But the ribbon-fishes themselves may be degenerate Scombroids. In any case both ribbon-fishes and

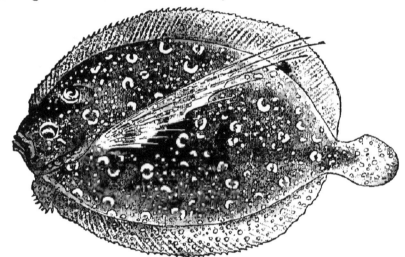

Fig. ·599.—*Platophrys lunatus* (Linnæus), the Peacock Flounder. Family *Pleuronectidæ*. Cuba. (From nature by Mrs. H. C. Nash.)

flounders find their nearest living relatives among the *Berycoidei* or *Zeoidei*, and have no affinity whatever with the isocercal codfish or with other members of the group called *Anacanthini*.

The *Heterosomata* are found in all seas, always close to the bottom and swimming with a swift, undulatory motion. They are usually placed in a single family, but the degraded types known as soles may be regarded as forming a second family.

The Flounders: Pleuronectidæ.—In the flounders, or *Pleuronectidæ*, the membrane-bones of the head are distinct, the eyes large and well separated, the mouth not greatly contracted, and the jaws

always provided with teeth   Among the 500 species of flounders
is found the greatest variation in size, ranging in weight from
an ounce to 500 pounds   The species found in arctic regions
are most degenerate and these have the largest number of vertebræ and of fin-rays   The halibut has 50 vertebræ (16 +34),
the craig-flounder 58, while in *Etropus* and other tropical forms
the number is but 34 (10 +24)   The common flounders of
intermediate geographical range (*Paralichthys dentatus*, etc) show
intermediate numbers as 40 (10 +30)

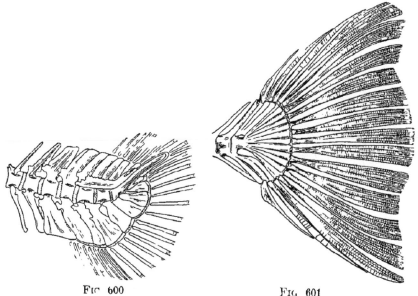

FIG 600   FIG 601

FIG 600 —Heterocercal tail of young Trout, *Salmo fario* Linnæus   (After Parker
    & Haswell)
FIG 601 —Homocercal tail of a Flounder, *Paralichthys californicus*

It is, perhaps, related to the greater pressure of natural selection
in the tropics, showing itself in the better differentiation of the
bones and consequently smaller number of the vertebræ

Fossil flounders are very few and give no clue as to the origin
of the group   In the Eocene and Miocene are remains which
have been referred to *Bothus* (*Rhombus*). *Bothus minimus* is
the oldest species known, described by Agassiz from the Eocene
of Monte Bolca   In the Miocene are numerous other species of
Bothus, as also tubercles referable to *Scophthalmus*

On the testimony of fossils alone the genus *Bothus*, or one

of its allies, would be the most primitive of the group If it be
so, the simpler structure of the halibut and its relatives is due
to degeneration, which is probable, although their structure has
the suggestion of primitive simplicity, especially in the greater
approach to symmetry in the head and the symmetry in the
insertion of the ventral fins

Soles have been found in the later Tertiary rocks *Solea
kirchbergiana* of the Miocene is not very different from species

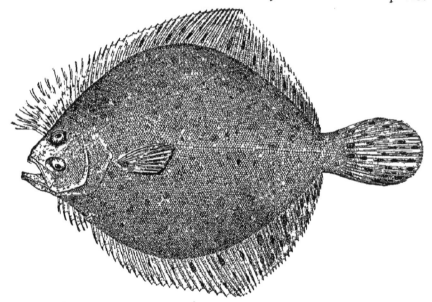

FIG 602—Window-pane, *Lophopsetta maculata.* Virginia

now extant in southern Europe No remains referable to
allies of the halibut or plaice are found in Tertiary rocks, and
these relatively simple types must be regarded as of recent origin

The Turbot Tribe: Bothinæ.—The turbot tribe have the mouth
large, the eyes and color on the left side, and the ventral
fins unlike, that of the left side being extended along the ridge
of the abdomen   The species are found in the warm seas only
They are deeper in body than the halibut and plaice, and some
of them are the smallest of all flounders   It is probable that
these approach most nearly of existing flounders to the original
ancestors of the group

Perhaps the most primitive genus is *Bothus*, species of
which genus are found in Italian Miocene. The European

brill, *Bothus rhombus*, is a common fish of southern Europe, deep-bodied and covered with smooth scales.

Very similar but much smaller in size is the half translucent speckled flounder of our Atlantic coast (*Lophopsetta maculata*), popularly known as window-pane   This species is too small to have much value as food   Another species, similar to the brill in technical characters but very different in appearance, is the turbot, *Scophthalmus maximus*, of Europe.   This large flounder has a very broad body, scaleless but covered with warty tubercles   It reaches a weight of seventy pounds and has a high value as a food-fish.   There is but one species of turbot and it is found in Europe only, on sandy bottoms from

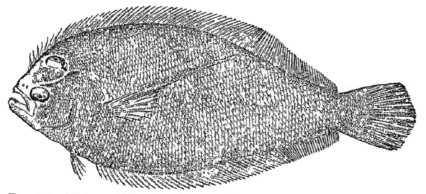

FIG. 603 —Wide-eyed Flounder, *Syacium papillosum* Linnæus.   Pensacola, Fla

Norway to Italy   In a turbot of twenty-three pounds weight Buckland found a roe of five pounds nine ounces, with 14,311,260 eggs.   The young retains its symmetrical condition for a relatively long period   No true turbot is found in America and none in the Pacific   Other European flounders allied to the turbot and brill are *Zeugopterus punctatus*, the European whiff, *Lepidorhombus whiff-jagonis*, the topknot, *Phrynorhombus regius*, the lantern-flounder, *Arnoglossus laterna*, and the tongue-fish, *Eucitharus linguatula*, the last two of small size and feeble flesh

In the wide-eyed or peacock flounders, *Platophrys podas* in Europe, *Platophrys lunatus*, etc , in America, *Platophrys mancus* in Polynesia, the eyes in the old males are very far apart, and the changes due to age and sex are greater than in any other genera   The species of this group are highly variegated and lie on the sand in the tropical seas   Numerous small species allied to these abound in the West Indies, known in a general way as whiffs The most widely distributed of these are *Citharichthys spilopterus* of the West Indies, *Citharichthys gilberti* and *Azevia panamensis* of Panama, *Orthopsetta sordida* of California, and especially the common small-mouthed *Etropus crossotus* found throughout tropical America. Numerous other genera and species of the turbot tribe are found on the coasts of tropical Asia and Africa, most of them of small size and weak structure

Samaris cristatus of Asia is the type of another tribe of flounders and the peculiar hook-jawed *Oncopterus darwini* of Patagonia represents still another tribe

The Halibut Tribe: Hippoglossinæ —In the great halibut tribe 7 the mouth is large and the ventral fins symmetrical The arctic and subarctic species have the eyes and color on the

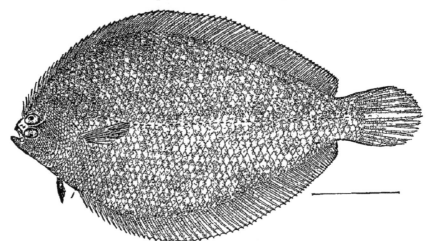

FIG 604 —*Etropus crossotus* Jordan & Gilbert Cedar Keys, Fla

right Those of the warmer regions (bastard halibut) have the eyes and color on the left These grow progressively smaller in size to the southward, the mouth being smaller and more feebly armed in southern species

The largest of the family, and the one commercially of far greatest importance, is the halibut (*Hippoglossus hippoglossus*). This species is found on both shores of both oceans, north of about the latitude of Paris, Boston, Cape Mendocino, and Matsushima Bay in Japan Its preference is for offshore banks of no great depth, and in very many localities it exists in great abundance, reaching a length of 6 to 8 feet and a weight of 600 pounds It sometimes ranges well out to sea and enters deeper waters than the cod The flesh is firm, white, and of good quality, although none of the flatfishes have much flavor, the muscles being mostly destitute of oil Small halibut, called "chicken halibut," are highly esteemed

Dr Goode states that the "history of the halibut fishery has been a peculiar one At the beginning of the present century these fishes were exceedingly abundant on George's Banks, since 1850 they have partially disappeared from this region, and the fishermen have since been following them to other banks, and since 1874 out into deeper and deeper water, and the fisheries are now carried on almost exclusively in the gullies between the offshore banks and on the outer edges of the banks, in water 100 to 350 fathoms in depth

"The halibut with its large mouth is naturally a voracious fish, and probably would disdain few objects in the way of fresh meat it would come across It is said, however, to feed more especially upon crabs and mollusks in addition to fish These fish 'they waylay lying upon the bottom, invisible by reason of their flat bodies, colored to correspond to the general color of the sand or mud upon which they rest When in pursuit of their prey they are active and often come quite to the surface, especially when in summer they follow the capelin to the shoal water near the land They feed upon skates, cod, haddock, menhaden, mackerel, herring, lobsters, flounders, sculpins, grenadiers, turbot, Norway haddock, bank-clams, and anything else that is eatable and can be found in the same waters ' Frequently halibut may be seen chasing flatfish over the bottom of the water About Cape Sable their favorite food seems to be haddock and cusk A very singular mode of attacking a cod has been recorded by Captain Collins, an experienced fisherman and good observer They often kill their prey by blows of the tail, a fact which is quite novel and interesting He has described an instance which occurred on a voyage home from Sable Island in 1877 'The man at the wheel sang out that he saw a halibut flapping its tail about a quarter of a mile off our starboard quarter. I looked through the spy-glass and his statement was soon verified by the second appearance of the tail We hove out a dory, and two men went with her, taking with them a pair of gaff-hooks They soon returned, bringing not only the halibut, which was a fine one of about seventy pounds weight, but a small codfish which it had been trying to kill by striking it with its tail The codfish was quite exhausted by the repeated blows and did not attempt to escape after its enemy had been captured The halibut was so completely engaged in the pursuit of the codfish that it paid no attention to the dory and was easily captured '

" The females become heavy with roe near the middle of the year, and about July and August are ready to spawn, although 'some fishermen say that they spawn at Christmas' or 'in the month of January, when they are on the shoals' The roe of a large halibut which weighed 356 pounds weighed 44 pounds, and indeed the 'ovaries of a large fish are too heavy to be lifted by a man without considerable exertion, being often 2 feet or more in length' A portion of the roe 'representing a fair average of the eggs, was weighed and found to contain 2185 eggs,' and the entire number would be 2,182,773 "

Closely allied to the halibut are numerous smaller forms with more elongate body The Greenland halibut, *Reinhardtius hippoglossoides*, and the closely related species in Japan, *Reinhardtius matsuuræ*, differ from the halibut most obviously in the straight lateral line The arrow-toothed halibut, *Atheresthes stomias*, lives in deeper waters in the North Pacific Its flesh is soft, the mouth very large, armed with arrow-shaped teeth The head in this species is less distorted than in any of the others, the upper eye being on the edge of the disk in front of the dorsal fin For this reason it has been supposed to be the most primitive of the living species, but these traits are doubtless elusive and a result of degeneration

Eopsetta jordani is a smaller halibut-like fish, common on the coast of California, an excellent food-fish, with firm white flesh, sold in San Francisco restaurants under the very erroneous name of "English sole" Large numbers are dried by the Chinese for export to China A similar species, *Hippoglossoides platessoides*, known as the "sand-dab," is common on both shores of the North Atlantic, and several related species are found in the North Pacific *Verasper variegatus* of Japan is notable for its bright coloration, the lower side being largely orange-red

In the bastard halibuts, *Paralichthys*, the eyes and color are on the left side These much resemble the true halibut, but are smaller and inferior as food, besides differing in details of structure. The Monterey halibut (*Paralichthys californicus*) is the largest of these, reaching a weight of sixty pounds This species and one other from California (*Xystreurys liolepis*), normally left-sided, differ from all the other flounders in having

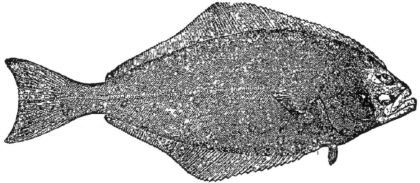

FIG 605—Halibut, *Hippoglossus hippoglossus* Linnæus   Marmot I , Alaska

the eyes almost as often on the right side as on the left side, as usual or normal in their type   The summer flounder (*Paralichthys dentatus*) replaces the Monterey halibut on the Atlantic Coast, where it is a common food-fish   Farther south it gives way to the Southern flounder (*Paralichthys lethostigma*) and the Gulf flounder, *Paralichthys albigutta*.   In Japan *Paralichthys olivaceus* is equally common, and in western Mexico *Paralichthys sinaloæ*.   The four-spotted flounder of New England, *Paralichthys oblongus*, belongs to this group Similar species constituting the genus *Pseudorhombus* abound in India and Japan

The Plaice Tribe: Pleuronectinæ —The plaice tribe pass gradually into the halibut tribe, from which they differ in the small mouth, in which the blunt teeth are mostly on the blind side The eyes are on the right side, the vertebræ are numerous, and the species live only in the cold seas, none being found in the tropics. In most of the Pacific species the lateral line has an accessory branch along the dorsal fin. The genus *Pleuronichthys*, or frog-flounders, has the teeth in bands *Pleuronichthys cornutus* is common in Japan and three species, *Pleuronichthys cænosus* being the most abundant, are found on the coast of California Closely related to these is the diamond-flounder, *Hypsopsetta guttulata* of California *Parophrys vetulus* is a small flounder of California, so abundant as to have considerable economic value *Lepidopsetta bilineata*, larger and rougher, is almost equally common It is similar to the mud-dab (*Limanda limanda*) of northern Europe and the rusty-dab (*Limanda ferruginea*) of New England

The plaice, *Pleuronectes platessa*, is the best known of the European species of this type, being common in most parts of Europe and valued as food Closely related to the plaice is a second species of southern Europe also of small size, *Flesus*

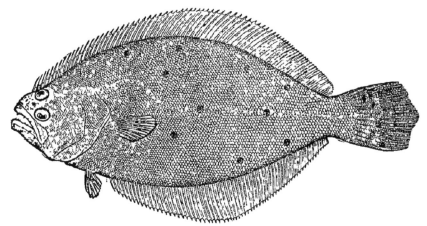

Fig 606 —Wide mouthed Flounder, *Paralichthys dentatus* (L.). St George I , Md.

flesus, to which the name flounder is in England especially applied The common winter flounder of New England, *Pseudopleuronectes americanus*, is also very much like the plaice, but with more uniform scales It is an important food-fish, the most abundant of the family about Cape Cod The eel-back flounder, *Liopsetta putnami*, also of New England, is frequently seen in the markets The males of this species have scattered rough scales, while the females are smooth. The great starry flounder of Alaska, *Platichthys stellatus*, is the largest of the small-mouthed flounders and in its region the most abundant. On the Pacific coast from Monterey to Alaska and across to northern Japan it constitutes half the catch of flounders. The body is covered with rough scattered scales, the fins are barred with black. It reaches a weight of twenty pounds. Living in shallow waters, it ascends all the larger rivers.

An allied species in Japan is *Kareius bicoloratus*, with scattered scales. *Clidoderma asperrimum*, also of northern Japan, has the body covered with series of warts.

In deeper water are found the elongate forms known as smear-dab and flukes. The smear-dab of Europe (*Micro-*

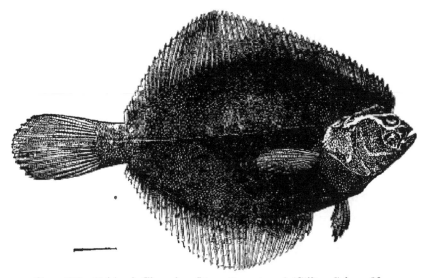

FIG. 607.—Eel-back Flounder, *Liopsetta putnami* (Gill). Salem, Mass.

stomus kitt) is rather common in deep water. Its skin is very slimy, but the flesh is excellent. The same is true of the slippery sole, *Microstomus pacificus*, of California and Alaska, and of other species found in Japan. *Glyptocephalus cynoglossus*, the craig-fluke, or pole-flounder, of the North Atlantic, is taken in great numbers in rather deep water on both coasts. Its flesh is much like that of the sole. A similar species (*Glyptocephalus zachirus*) with a very long pectoral on the right scale is found in California, and *Microstomus kitaharæ* in Japan.

The Soles: Soleidæ.—The soles (*Soleidæ*) are degraded flounders, the typical forms bearing a close relation to the plaice tribe, from which they may be derived   There are three very different groups or tribes of soles, and some writers have thought that these are independently derived from different groups of flounders   This fact has been urged as an argument against the recognition of the *Soleidæ* as a family separate from the flounders   If clearly proved, the soles should either be joined with the flounders in one family or else they should be divided into two or three, according to their supposed origin

The soles as a whole differ from the flounders in having the bones of the head obscurely outlined, their edges covered by scales   The gill-openings are much reduced, the eyes small and close together, the ventral fins often much reduced, and sometimes the pectoral or caudal also   The mouth is very small, much twisted, and with few teeth

The species of sole, about 150 in number, abound on sandy

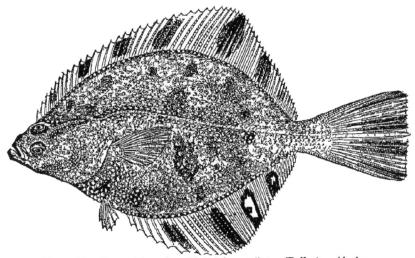

Fig 608 —Starry Flounder, *Platichthys stellatus* (Pallas)   Alaska

bottoms in the warm seas along the continents, very few being found about the Oceanic Islands   The three subfamilies, or tribes, may be designated as broad soles, true soles, and tongue-fishes

The Broad Soles: Achirinæ.—The American soles (*Achirinæ*), or broad soles, resemble the smaller members of the turbot tribe of flounders, having the ventral fin of the eyed side extended along the ridge of the abdomen. The eyes and color are, however, on the right side. The eyes are separated by a narrow interorbital ridge. In most of these forms the body is broad and covered with rough scales. The species are mostly less than six inches long, and nearly all are confined to the warmer parts of America, many of them ascending the rivers. A very few (*Aseraggodes*, *Pardachirus*) are found in Japan and China. Some are scaleless and some have but a single small gill-opening on the blind side. The principal genus is *Achirus*. *Achirus fasciatus*, the common American sole, or hog-choker, is abundant from Boston to Galveston. *Achirus lineatus* and other species are found in the West Indies and on the west coast of Mexico. Almost all the species of *Achirus* are banded with black and the pectorals are very small or wanting altogether. All these species are practically useless as food from their very small size.

Fig. 609.—Hog-choker Sole, *Achirus lineatus* (L.).   Potomac River.

The European Soles (Soleinæ).—The European soles are more elongate in form, with the ventral fins narrow and not extended along the ridge of the abdomen. The eyes are on the right side with no bony ridge between them. No species of this type is

certainly known from American waters, although numerous in
Europe and Asia The species have much in common with
the plaice tribe of flounders and may be derived from the same
stock. One species, as above noted, is found in the Miocene.

The common sole of Europe, *Solea solea*, is one of the best
of food-fishes, reaching a length, according to Dr Gill, of twenty-
six inches and a weight of nine pounds As usually seen in
the markets it rarely exceeds a pound It is found from Norway to Italy, and when properly cooked is very tender and
delicate, superior to any of the flounders According to Dr
Francis Day, it appears to prefer sandy or gravelly shores,
but is rather uncertain in its migrations, for, although mostly
appearing at certain spots almost at a given time, and usually
decreasing in numbers by degrees, in other seasons they disappear at once, as suddenly as they arrive Along the British
seacoast they retire to the deep as frosts set in, revisiting the
shallows about May if the weather is warm, their migrations
being influenced by temperature The food of the sole is to a
considerable extent molluscous, but it is also said to eat the
eggs and fry of other fishes and sea-urchins

The spawning season is late in the year and during the
spring months. The ova are in moderate number, a sole of
one pound weight has, according to Buckland, about 134,000
eggs. The newly hatched, according to Dr Day, do not appear
to be commonly found so far out at sea as some other species
They enter into shallow water at the edge of the tide and are
very numerous in favorable localities.

As is well known, the sole is one of the most esteemed
of European fishes In the words of Dr. Day, " the flesh of this
fish is white, firm, and of excellent flavor, those from the deepest
waters being generally preferred. Those on the west coast
and to the south are larger, as a rule, than those towards the
north of the British islands. In addition to its use as food,
it is available for another purpose. The skin is used for fining
coffee, being a good substitute for isinglass, and also as a
material for artificial baits

"The markets are generally supplied by the trawl The
principal English trawling-ground lies from Dover to Devonshire
They may be taken by spillers, but are not commonly captured

with hooks, it is suggested that one reason may be that spillers
are mostly used by day, whereas the sole is a night feeder.
They are sometimes angled for with the hook, baited with
crabs, worms, or mollusks, the most favorable time for fishing
is at night, after a blow, when the water is thick, while a land
breeze answers better than a sea breeze "

Several smaller species of sole are found in Europe. In
Japan *Zebrias zebra*, black-banded, and *Usinosita japonica*,
known as *Usinôshita*, or cow's tongue, are common. Farther
south are numerous species of *Synaptura* and other genera peculiar
to the Indian and Australian regions

The Tongue-fishes: Cynoglossinæ.—The tongue-fishes are soles
having the eyes on the left side not separated by a bony ridge,
the two being very small and apparently in the same socket.
The body is lanceolate, covered usually with rough scales,
and as often with two or three lateral lines as with one   The
species are mostly Asiatic   *Cynoglossus robustus* and other species are found in Japan, and in India are many others belonging to *Cynoglossus* and related genera   The larger species are
valued as food   The single European species *Symphurus nigres-
cens*, common in the Mediterranean, is too small to have any
value   *Symphurus plagiusa*, the tongue-fish of our coast, is

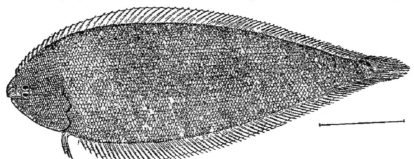

Fig 610 —*Symphurus plagiusa* (L) Beaufort, N C

common on our sandy shores from Cape Hatteras southward.
Symphurus plagusia, scarcely different, replaces it in the West
Indies *Symphurus atricaudus* is found in San Diego Bay, and
numerous other species of no economic importance find their
place farther south.

CHAPTER XLIII

SUBORDER JUGULARES

THE **Jugular-fishes.**—In all the families of spiny-rayed fishes, as ranged in order in the present work, from the *Berycidæ* to the *Soleidæ*, the ventrals are thoracic in position, the pelvis, if present, being joined to the shoulder-girdle behind the symphysis of the clavicles so that the ventral fin falls below or behind the pectoral fin To this arrangement the families of *Bembradidæ* and *Pinguipedidæ* offer perhaps the only exceptions

In all the families which precede the *Berycidæ* in the linear series adopted in this work, the ventral fins when present are abdominal, the pelvis lying behind the clavicles and free from them as in the sharks, the reptiles, and all higher vertebrates

In all the families remaining for discussion, the ventrals are brought still farther forward to a point distinctly before the pectorals. This position is called jugular (Lat *jugulum*, throat).

The fishes with jugular ventrals we here divide into six groups, orders, and suborders *Jugulares, Haplodoci, Xenopterygii, Anacanthini, Opisthomi*, and *Pediculati*. The last two groups, and perhaps the *Anacanthini* also, may well be considered as distinct orders, being more aberrant than the others

For the most primitive and at the same time most obscurely defined of these groups we may retain the term applied by Linnæus to all of them, the name *Jugulares*. This group includes those jugular-fishes in which the position of the gills, the structure of the skull, and the form of the tail are essentially as in ordinary fishes It is an extremely diversified and perhaps unnatural group, some of its members resembling *Opisthognathidæ* and *Malacanthidæ*, others suggesting the mailed-cheek

709

fishes, and still others more degenerate The fishes having the fins thus placed were long ago set apart by Linnæus, under the name of "Jugulares," *Callionymus* being the genus first placed by him in this group Besides their anterior insertion, the ventrals in the *Jugulares* are more or less reduced in size, the rays being usually but not always less than I, 5 in number and more often reduced to one or two, or even wholly lost

In general, the jugular fishes are degenerate as compared with the perch-like forms, but in certain regards they are often highly specialized The groups showing this character are probably related one to another, but in some cases this fact is not clearly shown In most of the jugular-fishes the shoulder-girdle shows some change or distortion The usual foramen in the hypercoracoid is often wanting or relegated to the interspace between the coracoids, and the arrangement of the actinosts often deviates from that seen in the perciform fishes

The Weevers: Trachinidæ. — Of the various families the group of weevers, *Trachinidæ*, most approaches the type of ordinary fishes In the words of Dr Gill, these fishes are known by "an elongated body attenuated backward from the head, compressed, oblong head, with the snout very short, a deeply cleft, oblique mouth, and a long spine projecting backward from each operculum and strengthened by extension on the surface of the operculum, as a keel. The dorsal fins are distinct, the first composed of strong, pungent spines radiating from a short base and about six or seven in number. The second dorsal and anal are very long The pectorals have the lower rays unbranched, and the ventrals are in advance of the pectorals, and have each a spine and five rays. The species of this family are mostly found along the European and western African coast, but singularly enough a species closely related to the Old World form is found on the coast of Chile None have been obtained from the intermediate regions or from the American coast Two species are found in England, and are known under the name of the greater weever (*Trachinus draco*), about twelve inches long, and the lesser weever (*Trachinus vipera*), about six inches long They are perhaps the most dreaded of the smaller English fishes. The formidable opercular spines are weapons of defense, and when seized by the fisherman the fish is apt to throw its head in the direction of the hand and lance a spine into it   The pungent dorsal spines are also defensive   Although without a poison gland, such as some fishes distantly related have at the base of the spines, they cause very severe wounds, and death may occur from tetanus   They are therefore divested of both opercular and dorsal spines before being exposed for sale   The various popular names which the weevers enjoy, in addition to their general designation, mostly refer to the armature of the spines, or are the result of the armature; such are adder-fish, sting-fish, and sting-bull "

No species of *Trachinidæ* is known from North America or from Asia. In these fishes, as Dr Boulenger has lately shown, the hypercoracoid is without foramen, the usual perforation lying between this bone and the hypercoracoid   A similar condition exists in the *Anacanthini*, or codfishes, but it seems to have been developed independently in the two groups   In the relatives of the *Trachinidæ* the position of this foramen changes gradually, moving by degrees from its usual place to the lower margin of the hypercoracoid   Species referred to *Trachinus* are recorded from the Miocene as well as *Trachinus*.

The extinct group of *Callipterygidæ* found in the Eocene of Monte Bolca seems allied to the *Trachinidæ*   It has the dorsal fin continuous, the spines small, the soft rays high, the scales are very small or wanting   *Callipteryx speciosus* and *C. recticandus* are the known species

The Nototheniidæ.—In the family of *Nototheniidæ* the foramen is also wanting or confluent with the suture between the coracoids   To this family belong many species of the Antarctic region   These are elongate fishes with ctenoid scales and a general resemblance to small *Hexagrammidæ*   In most of the genera there is more than one lateral line   These species are the antipodes of the *Cottidæ* and *Hexagrammidæ*, although lacking the bony stay of the latter, they show several analogical resemblances and have very similar habits

The *Harpagiferidæ*, naked, with the opercle armed with spines, and resemble sculpins even more closely than do the *Nototheniidæ*   *Harpagifer* is found in Antarctic seas, and the three species of

Diaconetta in the deeper waters of the North Atlantic and Pacific
These little fishes resemble *Callionymus*, but the opercle, in-
stead of the preopercle, bears spines   The *Bovichthyidæ* of New
Zealand are also sculpin-like and perhaps belong to the same
family   Dr Boulenger places all these Antarctic forms with the
foramen outside the hypercoracoid in one family, *Notothenidæ*
Several deep-sea fishes of this type have been lately described
by Dr Louis Dollo and others from the Patagonian region
One of these forms, *Macrias amissus*, lately named by Gill and
Townsend, is five feet long, perhaps the largest deep-sea fish
known   The family of *Percophidæ*, from Chile, is also closely

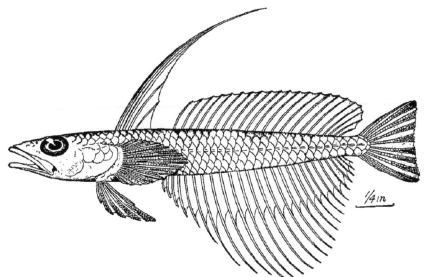

Fig 611 —*Pteropsaron evolans* Jordan & Snyder   Sagami Bay, Japan

allied to these forms, the single species differing in slight respects
of osteology

Closely related to the family of *Notothenidæ* and perhaps
scarcely distinct from it is the small family of *Pteropsaridæ*,
which differs in having but one lateral line and the foramen
just above the lower edge of the hypercoracoid   The numerous species inhabit the middle Pacific, and are prettily colored
fishes, looking like gobies   *Pteropsaron* is a Japanese genus,
with high dorsal and anal fins, *Parapercis* is more widely diffused.
Osurus schauinslandi is one of the neatest of the small fishes of
Hawaii   Several species of *Parapercis* and *Neopercis* occur in

Japan and numerous others in the waters of Polynesia *Pseudeleginus majori* of the Italian Miocene must belong near *Parapercis.*

The *Bathymasteridæ*, or ronquils, are perhaps allied to the *Nototheniidæ*, they resemble the *Opisthognathidæ*, but the jaws are shorter and they have a large number of vertebræ as befits their northern distribution *Ronquilus jordani* is found in Puget Sound and *Bathymaster signatus* in Alaska The ventral rays are I, 5, and the many-rayed dorsal has a few slender spines in front

The Leptoscopidæ.—The *Leptoscopidæ* of New Zealand resemble the weevers and star-gazers, but the head is unarmed, covered by thin skin

The Star-gazers: Uranoscopidæ. —The *Uranoscopidæ*, or star-

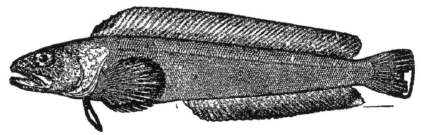

FIG 612 —*Bathymaster signatus* Cope   Shumagin Is , Alaska

gazers, have the head cuboid, mostly bony above, the mouth almost vertical, the lips usually fringed, and the eyes on the flat upper surface of the head   The spinous dorsal is short and may be wanting   The hypercoracoid has a foramen, and the body is naked or covered with small scales   The appearance is eccentric, like that of some of the *Scorpænidæ*, but the anatomy differs in several ways from that of the mailed-cheek fishes

The species inhabit warm seas, and the larger ones are food-fishes of some importance   One species, *Uranoscopus scaber*, abounds in the Mediterranean   *Uranoscopus japonicus* and other species are found in Japan   *Astroscopus y-græcum* is the commonest species on our Atlantic coast   The bare spaces on the top of the head in this species yield vigorous electric shocks   Another American species is *Astroscopus guttatus*   In Japan and the East Indies the forms are more numerous and varied   *Ichthyscopus lebeck*, with a single dorsal, is a fantastic inhabitant of the seas of Japan, and *Anema monopterygium* in New Zealand

Uranoscopus peruzzii, an extinct star-gazer, has been described from the Pliocene of Tuscany

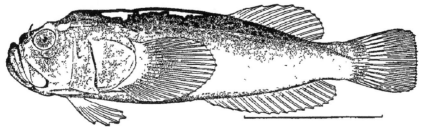

FIG 613 —A Star-gazer *Ariscopus iburius* Jordan & Snyder   Iburi, Japan

The Dragonets. Callionymidæ.—Remotely allied to the *Uranoscopidæ* is the interesting family of dragonets, or *Callionymidæ* These are small scaleless fishes with flat heads, the preopercle armed with a strong spine, the body bearing a general resemblance to the smaller and smoother *Cottidæ* The gill-openings are very small, the ventral fins wide apart The colors are highly variegated, the fins are high, often filamentous, and the sexes differ much in coloration and in the development of the fins The species are especially numerous on the shores of Japan, where *Callionymus valenciennesi, Callionymus beniteguri,* and *Calliurichthys japonicus* are food-fishes of some slight importance. Others are found in the East Indies, and several large and handsome forms are taken in the Mediterranean. *Callionymus draco,* the dragonet, or "sculpin," reaches the coast of England In America but three species have been taken These are dredged in deep water in the East Indies In other parts of the world these fantastic little creatures are shore-fishes, creeping about in the shallow bays. Species of *Synchiropus,* colored like the coral sands, abound in the Polynesian coral reefs.

A fossil species of *Callionymus (C macrocephalus)* are found in the Miocene of Croatia

The family of *Rhyacichthyidæ* is a small group of Asiatic fishes allied to the *Callionymidæ,* but less elongate and differing in minor details They are found not in the sea, but in mountain streams *Rhyacichthys* (formerly called by the preoccupied name *Platyptera*) is the principal genus

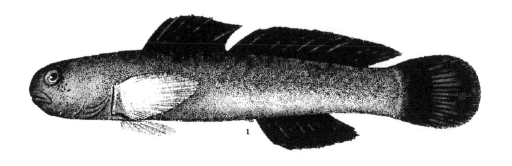

1 KELLOGGELLA CARDINALIS JORDAN & SEALE. TYPE. (FAMILY GOBIIDÆ)
2 SYNCHIROPUS LILI JORDAN & SEALE. TYPE. (FAMILY CALLIONYMIDÆ)
3 PETROSCIRTES ATRODORSALIS GÜNTHER. (FAMILY BLENNIIDÆ)

FISHES OF THE CORAL REEFS, SAMOA

FIG. 614.—Star-gazer, *Astroscopus guttatus* Abbott (From life by Dr R W Shufeldt) 715

The *Trichonotidæ*, with wide gill-openings and cycloid scales, are also related to the *Callionymidæ*. The species are few, small, and confined to the Indian and Australian seas Another small family closely related to this is the group of *Hemerocœtidæ* of the same region

The Dactyloscopidæ. —In this and the preceding families of jugular fishes the ventral rays remain 1, 5, as in the typical thoracic forms In most of the families yet to be described the number is I, 3, a character which separates the little fishes of the family of *Dactyloscopidæ* from the *Uranoscopidæ* and *Leptoscopidæ Dactyloscopus tridigitatus* is a small fish of the coral sands of Cuba The other species of this family are found mostly in the West Indies and on the west coast of Mexico Several genera, *Myxodagnus, Gillellus, Dactylagnus,* etc , are recognized In the structure of the shoulder-girdle these species diverge from the star-gazers, approaching the blennies, and their position is intermediate between *Trachinidæ* and *Blenniidæ*

CHAPTER XLIV

THE BLENNIES: BLENNIIDÆ

THE great family of blennies, *Blenniidæ*, contains a vast number of species with elongate body, numerous dorsal spines, without suborbital stay or sucking-disk, and the ventrals jugular, where present, and of one spine and less than five soft rays   Most of them are of small size, living about rocks on the sea-shores of all regions.   In general they are active fishes, of handsome but dark coloration, and in the different parts of the group is found great variety of structure. The tropical forms differ from those of arctic regions in the much shorter bodies and fewer vertebræ   These forms are most like ordinary fishes in appearance and structure and are doubtless the most primitive   Of the five hundred known species of

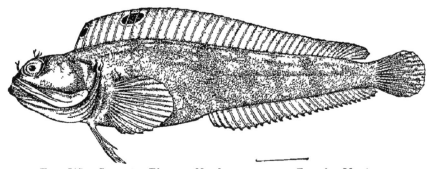

FIG 615 —Sarcastic Blenny, *Neoclinus satiricus* Girard   Monterey

blennies, we can note only a few of the most prominent.   To *Clinus* and related genera belong many species of the warm seas, scaly and ovoviviparous, at least for the most part   The largest of these is the great kelpfish of the coast of California, *Heterostichus rostratus*, a food-fish of importance, reaching the length of two feet   Others of this type scarcely exceed two inches   *Neoclinus satiricus*, also of California, is remarkable for the great length of the upper jaw, which is formed as in *Opisthognathus* Its membranes are brightly colored, being edged with bright yellow *Gibbonsia elegans* is the pretty "señorita" of the coralline-lined rock-pools of California *Leptsoma nuchipinne*, with a fringe of filaments at the nape, is very

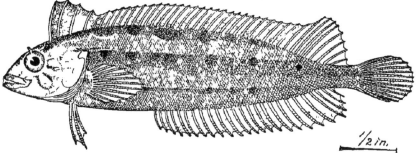

½ in.

FIG 616 —Kelp Blenny, *Gibbonsia evides* Jordan & Gilbert   San Diego

abundant in rock-pools of the West Indies   The species of *Auchenopterus* abound in the rock-pools of tropical America These are very small neatly colored fishes with but one soft ray in the long dorsal fin   Species of *Tripterygion, Myxodes, Cristiceps*, and other genera abound in the South Pacific

In *Blennius* and its relatives the body is scaleless and the slender teeth are arranged like the teeth of a comb. In most

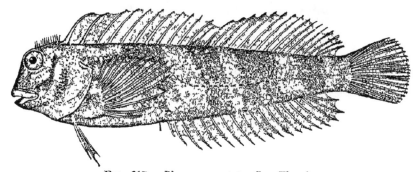

FIG 617 —*Blennius cristatus* L   Florida.

species long, fang-like posterior canines are developed in the jaws. *Blennius* is represented in Europe by many species, *Blennius galerita, ocellaris*, and *basiliscus* being among the most common   Certain species inhabit Italian lakes, having assumed a fresh-water habit   The numerous American species mostly belong to other related genera, *Chasmodes bosquianus* being most common. *Blennius yatabei* abounds in Japan. In *Petroscirtes* and its allies the gill-openings are much restricted. The

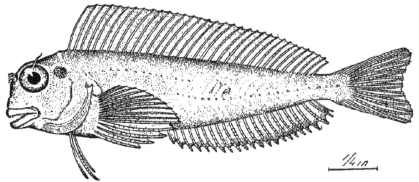

FIG. 618.—Rock-skipper, *Alticus atlanticus.* San Cristobal, Lower Cal.

FIG. 619.—Lizard-skipper, *Alticus saliens* (Forster). A blenny which lies out of water on lava rocks, leaping from one to another with great agility. From nature; specimen from Point Distress, Tutuila Island, Samoa. (About one-half size.)

species are mainly Asiatic and Polynesian and are very prettily colored. *Petroscirtes elegans* and *P. trossulus* adorn the Japanese rock-pools and others, often deep blue in color, abound in the coral reefs of Polynesia

The rock-skippers (*Salarias*, *Alticus*, etc.) are herbivorous, with serrated teeth set loosely in the jaws These live in the rock-pools of the tropics and leap from rock to rock when disturbed with the agility of lizards They are dusky or gray in color with handsome markings One of them, *Erpichthys* or *Alticus saliens* in Samoa, lives about lava rocks between tide-

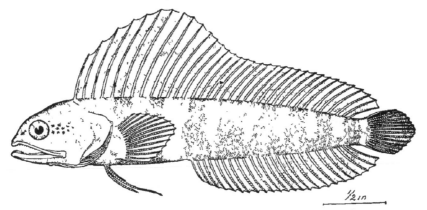

FIG 620 —*Emblemaria atlantica* Jordan. Pensacola, Fla.

marks, and at low tide remains on the rocks, over which it runs with the greatest ease and with much speed, its movements being precisely like those of *Periophthalmus* As in the species of the latter genus, otherwise wholly different, this *Alticus* has short ventral fins padded with muscle.

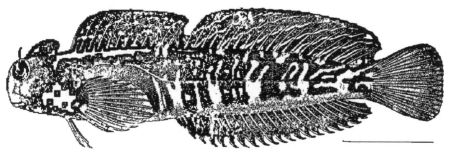

FIG 621 —*Scartichthys enosimæ* Jordan & Snyder, a fish of the rock-pools of the sacred island of Enoshima, Japan. Family *Blenniidæ*

Erpichthys atlanticus is found in abundance on both coasts of tropical America. Many species abound in Polynesia and in both Indies *Salarias enosimæ* lives in the clefts of lava rocks on the shores of Japan. *Ophioblennius* (*webbi*) is remarkable for its strong teeth, *Emblemaria* (*nivipes, Atlantica*) for its very high dorsal. Many other genera allied to *Blennius, Clinus,* and *Salarias* abound in the warm seas.

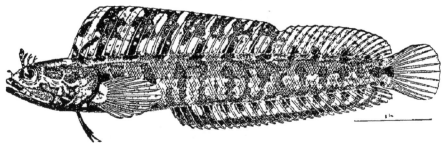

FIG 622 —*Zacalles bryope* Jordan & Snyder. Misaki, Japan.

The Northern Blennies: Xiphidiinæ, Stichæinæ, etc.—The blennies of the north temperate and arctic zones have the dorsal

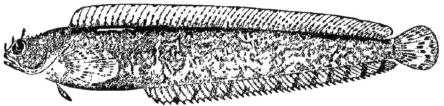

FIG 623 —*Bryostemma tarsodes* Jordan & Snyder. Unalaska

fin more elongate, the dorsal fin usually but not always composed entirely of spines. The scales are small and the ventral

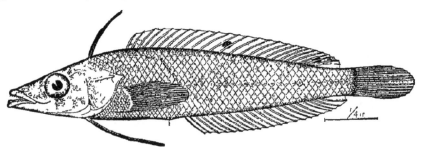

FIG 624 —*Exerpes asper* Jenkins & Evermann, Guaymas, Mexico
Family *Blenniidæ*

fins generally reduced in size. These are divided by Dr Gill into several distinct families, but the groups recognized by him are subject to intergradations.

Chirolophis (*ascanii*) of north Europe is remarkable for the tufted filaments on the head   These are still more developed in *Bryostemma* of the North Pacific, *Bryostemma polyactocephalum* and several other species being common from Puget Sound to Japan   *Apodichthys* (*flavidus*) of California is remarkable for a large quill-shaped anal spine and for the great variation in color, the hue being yellow, grass-green, or crimson, according to the color of the algæ about it   There is no evidence, however, that the individual fish can change its color, and these color forms seem to be distinct races within the species   *Xererpes fucorum* of California lies quiescent in the sea-weed (*Fucus*) after the tide recedes, its form, color, and substance seeming to correspond exactly with those of the stems of algæ   *Pholis gunnellus*

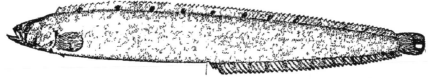

FIG 625 —Gunnel, *Pholis gunnellus* (L)   Gloucester, Mass

is the common gunnel (gunwale), or butter-fish, of both shores of the North Atlantic, with numerous allies in the North Pacific Of these, *Enedrias nebulosus*, the ginpo, or silver-tail, is especially common in Japan   *Xiphidion* and *Xiphistes* of the California coast, and *Dictyosoma* of Japan, among others, are remarkable for the great number of lateral lines, these extending crosswise

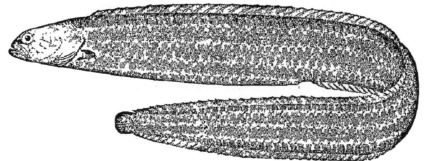

FIG 626 —*Xiph stes chirus* Jordan & Gilbert.   Amchitka I , Alaska

as well as lengthwise   *Cebedichthys violaceus*, a large blenny of California, has the posterior half of the dorsal made of soft rays *Opisthocentrus* of Siberia and north Japan has the dorsal spines flexible, only the posterior ones being short and stiff The snake-blennies (*Lumpenus*), numerous in the far North, are extremely slender, with well-developed pectorals and ventrals *Lumpenus lampetræformis* is found on both shores of the Atlantic. In *Stichæus* a lateral line is present There is none in *Lumpenus*, and in *Ernogrammus* and *Ozorthe* there are three All these are elongate fishes, of some value as food and especially characteristic of the Northern seas Fossil blennies are almost unknown *Pterygocephalus paradoxus* of the Eocene resembles

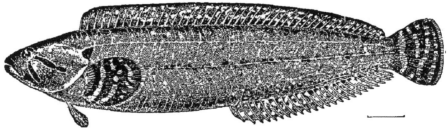

FIG 627 —*Ozorthe dictyogramma* (Hertzenstein), a Japanese blenny from Hakodate showing increased number of lateral lines, a trait characteristic of many fishes of the north Pacific

the living *Cristiceps*, a genus which differs from *Clinus* in having the first few dorsal spines detached, inserted on the head The first spine alone in *Pterygocephalus* is detached and is very strong A species called *Clinus gracilis* is described from the Miocene near Vienna, *Blennius fossilis* from the Miocene of Cro-

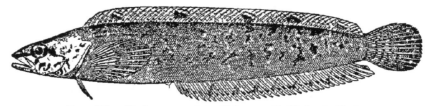

FIG 628 —*Stichæus punctatus* Fabricius St Michael, Alaska

atia, and an uncertain *Oncolepis isseli* from Monte Bolca The family is certainly one of the most recent in geologic times The family of *Blenniidæ*, as here recognized, includes a very great variety of forms and should perhaps be subdivided into several families, as Dr. Gill has suggested At present there is, however, no satisfactory basis of division known.

The Quillfishes: Ptilichthyidæ. — The *Ptilichthyidæ*, or quill-fishes, are small and slender blennies of the North Pacific, with very numerous fin-rays　　Ptilichthys goodei has 90 dorsal spines and 145 soft rays　　Another group of very slender naked blennies is the small family of Xiphasiidæ from the South Pacific

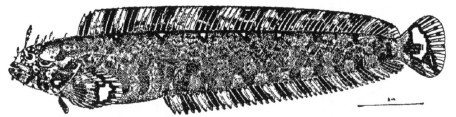

FIG 629 —*Bryostemma otohime* Jordan & Snyder　　Hakodate, Japan
Family *Blenniidæ*

The jaws have excessively long canines, there are no ventral fins　　The dorsal fin is very high and the caudal ends in a long thread

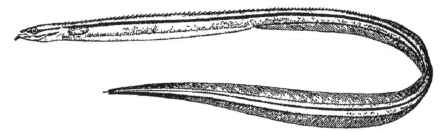

FIG 630 —Quillfish, *Ptilichthys goodei* Bean　　Unalaska

The Blochiidæ. — Of doubtful relationship is the extinct family of *Blochiidæ*　　In this group the body is elongate, covered with keeled plates imbricated like shingles. The

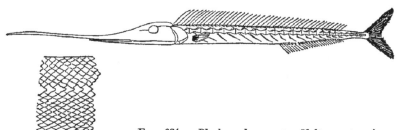

FIG 631 —*Blochius longirostris* Volta, restored
Upper Eocene of Monte Bolca　　(After Woodward)

dorsal is composed of many slender spines, and the vertebræ much elongate　　In *Blochius longirostris* (Monte Bolca Eocene)

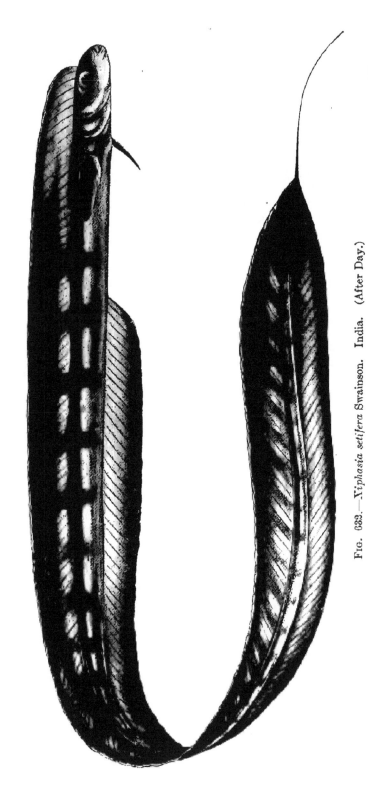

Fig. 632.—*Niphasia setifera* Swainson. India. (After Day.)

has very long jaws, lined with small teeth   Zittel regards the family as allied to the *Belonorhynchidæ*, but the prolongation of the jaws may be a character of analogy merely   Woodward places it next to the *Blennidæ*, supposing it to have small and jugular ventral fins   But as the presence of ventral fins is uncertain, the position of the family cannot be ascertained and it may really belong in the neighborhood of *Ammodytes*. The dorsal rays are figured by Woodward as simple

The Pataecidæ, etc.—The *Pataecidæ* are blenny-like fishes of Australia, having the form of *Congriopus*, the spinous dorsal being very high and inserted before the eyes, forming a crest. *Pataecus fronto* is not rare in South Australia   The *Gnathanacanthidæ* is another small group of peculiar blennies from the Pacific The *Acanthoclinidæ* are small blennies of New Zealand with numerous spines in the anal fin   *Acanthoclinus littoreus* is the only known species

The Gadopsidæ, etc.—The family of *Gadopsidæ* of the rivers of New Zealand and southern Australia consists of a single species, *Gadopsis marmoratus*, resembling the scaly blennies called *Clinus*, but with long ventrals of a single ray, and three spines in the anal fin besides other peculiarities   The species is locally very common and with various other fishes in regions where true trout are unknown, it is called "trout."

The *Cerdalidæ* are small band-shaped blennies of the Pacific

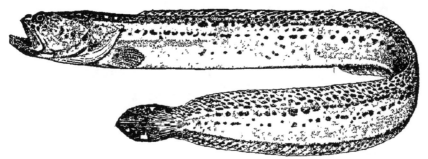

Fig 633 —Wrymouth, *Cryptacanthodes maculatus*   New York

coast of Panama   The slender dorsal spines pass gradually into soft rays   Three species are known.

The wrymouths, or *Cryptacanthodidæ*, are large blennies of the northern seas, with the mouth almost vertical and the head cuboid The wrymouth or ghostfish, *Cryptacanthodes maculatus*, is frequently taken from Long Island northward It is usually dusky in color, but sometimes pure white Other genera are found in the north Pacific

The Wolf-fishes: Anarhichadidæ.—The wolf-fishes (*Anarhichadidæ*) are large blennies of the northern seas, remarkable for their strong teeth Those in front are conical canines Those behind are coarse molars The dorsal is high, of flexible spines.

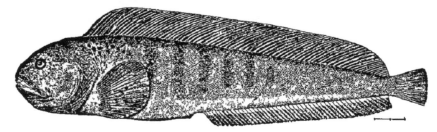

FIG 634 —Wolf-fish, *Anarhichas lupus* (L) Georges Bank

The species are large, powerful, voracious fishes, known as wolf-fishes *Anarhichas lupus* is the common wolf-fish of the north Atlantic, reaching a length of four to six feet, the body

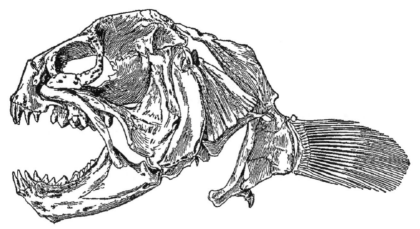

FIG 635 —Skull of *Anarrhichthys ocellatus* Ayres

marked by dark cross-bands Other similar species are found both in the north Pacific and north Atlantic *Anarhichas lepturus*, plain brown in color, is common about the Aleutian Islands.

In the wolf-eel (*Anarrhichthys ocellatus*) of the coast of California, the head is formed as in *Anarhichas* but the body is band-shaped, being drawn out into a very long and tapering tail   This species, which is often supposed to be a "sea-serpent," sometimes reaches a length of eight feet   It is used for food It feeds on sea-urchins and sand-dollars (*Echinarachinius*) which it readily crushes with its tremendous teeth

The skull of a fossil genus, *Laparus* (*aliceps*), with a resemblance to *Anarhichas*, is recorded from the Eocene of England

The Eel-pouts: Zoarcidæ.—The remaining blenny-like forms lack fin spines, agreeing in this respect with the codfishes and their allies   In all of the latter, however, the hypercoracoid is imperforate, the pseudobranchiæ are obsolete, and the tail isocercal   The forms allied to *Zoarces* and *Ophidion*, and which we may regard as degraded blennies, have homocercal (rarely leptocercal) tails, generally but not always well-developed pseudobranchiæ and the usual foramen in the hypercoracoid

The *Zoarcidæ*, or eel-pouts, have the body elongate, naked, or covered with small scales, the dorsal and anal of many soft rays and the gill-openings confined to the side   Most of the species live in rather deep water in the Arctic and Antarctic regions   *Zoarces viviparus*, the "mother of eels," is a common fish of the coasts of northern Europe   In the genus *Zoarces*,

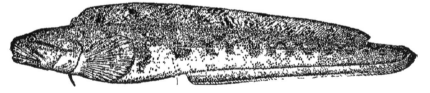

Fig 686 —Eel-pout, *Zoarces anguillaris* Peck   Eastport, Me

the last rays of the dorsal are short and stiff, like spines   The species are viviparous, the young being eel-like in form, the name "mother of eels" has naturally arisen in popular language. The American eel-pout, sometimes called mutton-fish, *Zoarces anguillaris*, is rather common north of Cape Cod, and a similar species, *Zoarces elongatus*, is found in northern Japan   *Lycodopsis pacifica*, without spines in the dorsal, replaces *Zoarces* in California   The species of *Lycodes*, without spines in the dorsal, and with teeth on the vomer and palatines, are very abundant in the northern seas, extending into deep waters farther south *Lycodes reticulatus* is the most abundant of these fishes, which are valued chiefly by the Esquimaux and

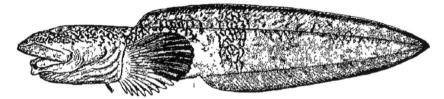

FIG. 637 —Eel-pout, *Lycodes reticulatus* Reinhardt   Banquereau.

other Arctic races of people Numerous related genera are recorded from deep-sea explorations, and several others occur about Tierra del Fuego *Gymnelis*, small, naked species brightly colored, is represented by *Gymnelis viridis* in the Arctic and by *Gymnelis pictus* about Cape Horn

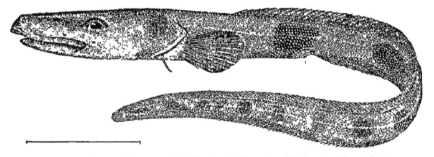

FIG 638 —*Lycenchelys verrilli* (Goode & Bean)   Chebucto, Nova Scotia.

The family of *Scytalinidæ* contains a single species, *Scytalina cerdale*, a small snake-shaped fish which lives in wet gravel between tide-marks, on Waada Island near Cape Flattery in Washington, not having yet been found elsewhere It dives

FIG 639 —*Scytalina cerdale* Jordan & Gilbert   Straits of Fuca.

among the wet stones with great celerity, and can only be taken by active digging.

To the family of *Congrogadidæ* belong several species of

eel-shaped blennies with soft rays only, found on the coasts of Asia
Another small family, *Derepodichthyidæ*, is represented by one
species, a scaleless little fish from the shores of British Columbia.

The *Xenocephalidæ* consist of a single peculiar species, *Xeno-
cephalus armatus*, from the island of New Ireland. The head
is very large, helmeted with bony plates and armed with spines.
The body is short and slender, the ventrals with five rays, the
dorsal and anal short

The Cusk-eels: Ophidiidæ. — The more important family of
Ophidiidæ, or cusk-eels, is characterized by the extremely anterior position of the ventral fins, which are inserted at the throat,
each one appearing as a long forked barbel The tail is lepto-

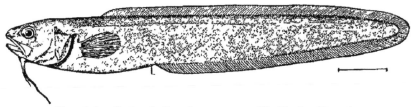

FIG 640 —Cusk-eel, *Rissola marginata* (De Kay)   Virginia

cercal, attenuate, the dorsal and anal confluent around it. *Ophidion barbatum* and *Rissola rochei* are common in southern
Europe. *Rissola marginata* is the commonest species on our
Atlantic coast, and *Chilara taylori* in California. Other species
are found farther south, and still others in deep water *Genypterus* contains numerous species of the south Pacific, some
of which reach the length of five feet, forming a commercial
substitute for cod *Genypterus capensis* is the klipvisch of the
Cape of Good Hope, and *Genypterus australis* the "Cloudy Bay
cod" or "rock ling" of New England   Another large species,

FIG 641 —*Lycodapus dermatinus* Gilbert   Lower California

Genypterus maculatus, occurs in Chile   A few fragments doubtfully referred to *Ophidion* and *Fierasfer* occur in the Eocene and
later rocks   The *Lycodapodidæ* contain a few small, scaleless
fishes (*Lycodapus*) dredged in the north Pacific.

Sand-lances · Ammodytidæ. — Near the *Ophidiidæ* are placed the small family of sand-lances (*Ammodytidæ*) This family comprises small, slender, silvery fishes, of both Arctic and tropical seas, living along shore and having the habit of burying themselves in the sand under the surf in shallow water. The jaws are toothless, the body scarcely scaly and crossed by many crossfolds of skin, the many-rayed dorsal fin is without spines, and the ventral fins when present are jugular The species of the family are very much alike From their great abundance they have sometimes much value as food, more perhaps as bait, still more as food for salmon and other fishes, from which they escape by plunging into the sand Sometimes a falling tide

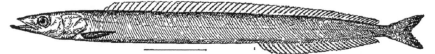

FIG. 642 —Sand-lance, *Ammodytes americanus* De Kay Nantucket

leaves a sandy beach fairly covered with living "lants" looking like a moving foam of silver. *Ammodytes tobianus* is the sand-lance or lant of northern Europe *Ammodytes americanus*, scarcely distinguishable, replaces it in America, and *Ammodytes personatus* in California, Alaska, and Japan This is a most excellent pan fish, and the Japanese, who regard little things, value it highly

In the genus *Hyperoplus* there is a large tooth on the vomer In the tropical genera there is a much smaller number of vertebræ and the body is covered with ordinary scales instead

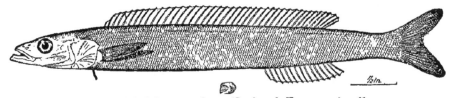

FIG 643 —*Embolichthys mitsukurii* (Jordan & Evermann) Formosa

of delicate, oblique cross-folds of skin These tropical species must probably be detached from the *Ammodytidæ* to form a distinct family, *Bleekeriidæ* *Bleekeria kallolepis* is found in India, *Bleekeria gilli* is from an unknown locality, and the most primitive species of sand-lance, *Embolichthys mitsukurii*, occurs in Formosa   In this species, alone of the sand-lances, the ventral fins are retained   These are jugular in position, as in the *Zoarcidæ*, and the rays are I, 3.   The discovery of this species makes it necessary to separate the *Ammodytidæ* and *Bleekeriidæ* widely from the *Percesoces*, and especially from the extinct families of *Crossognathidæ* and *Cobitopsidæ* with which its structure in other regards has led Woodward, Boulenger, and the present writer to associate it

Although an alleged sand-lance, *Rhynchias septipinnis*, with ventral fins abdominal, was described a century ago by Pallas, no one has since seen it, and it may not exist, or, if it exists, it may belong among the *Percesoces*   The relation of *Ammodytes* to *Embolichthys* is too close to doubt their close relationship   According to Dr. Gill the *Ammodytidæ* belong near the *Hemerocœtidæ*

The Pearlfishes: Fierasferidæ.—In the little group of pearlfishes, called *Fierasferidæ* or *Carapidæ*, the body is eel-shaped

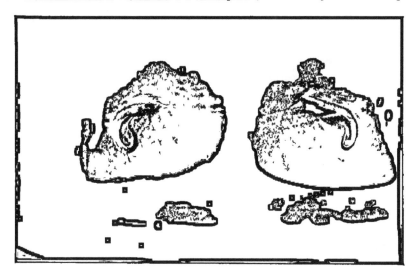

FIG. 644 —Pearlfish, *Fierasfer dubius* Putnam, embedded in a layer of mother-of-pearl La Paz, Lower California   (Photograph by Capt M. Castro)

with a rather large head, and the vent is at the throat.   Numerous species of *Fierasfer* (*Carapus*) are found in the warm seas   These little fishes enter the cavities of sea-cucumbers (Holothurians) and other animals which offer shelter, being frequently taken from the pearl-oyster   In the Museum of Comparative

Zoology, according to Professor Putnam, is "one valve of a pearl-oyster in which a specimen of *Fierasfer dubius* is beautifully inclosed in a pearly covering deposited on it by the oyster." A photograph of a similar specimen is given above. The species found in Holothurians are transparent in texture, with a bright pearly luster. Species living among lava rocks, as *Jordanicus umbratilis* of the south seas, are mottled black. Since this was written a specimen of this black species has been obtained from a Holothurian in Hilo, Hawaii, by Mr. H. W. Henshaw.

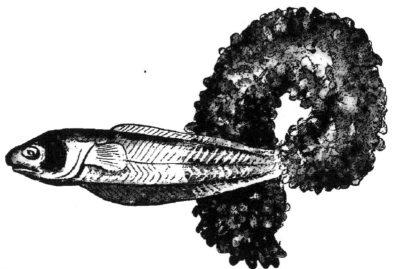

FIG. 645.—Pearlfish, *Fierasfer acus* (Linnæus), issuing from a Holothurian. Coast of Italy. (After Emery.)

The Brotulidæ.—The *Brotulidæ* constitute a large family of fishes, resembling codfishes, but differing in the character of the hypercoracoid, as well as in the form of the tail. The resemblance between the two groups is largely superficial. We may look upon the *Brotulidæ* as degraded blennies, but the *Gadidæ* have an earlier and different origin which has not yet been clearly made out. Most of the *Brotulidæ* live in deep water and are without common name or economic relations. Two species have been landlocked in cave streams in Cuba, where they have, like other cavefishes, lost their sight, a phenomenon which richly deserves careful study, and which has been recently investigated by Dr. C. H. Eigenmann. These blind

Brotulids, called Pez Ciego in Cuba, are found in different caves
in the county of San Antonio, where they reach a length of
about five inches.   As in other blindfishes, the body is translu-

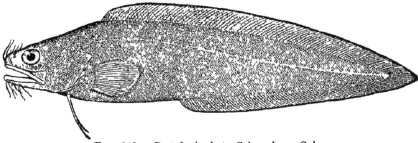

FIG 646 —*Brotula barbata* Schneider.   Cuba.

cent and colorless   These species are known as *Lucifuga subterranea* and *Stygicola dentata*   They are descended from allies
of the genera called *Brotula* and *Dinematichthys*   *Brotula barbata* is a cusk-like fish, occasionally found in the markets of

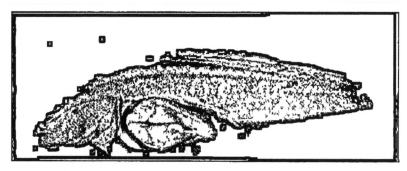

FIG 647 —Blind Brotula *Lucifuga subterranea* (Poey), showing viviparous habit
Joignan Cave, Pinar del Rio, Cuba   (Photograph by Dr Eigenmann)

Havana   Similar species, *Brotula multibarbata* and *Sirembo
inermis*, are common in Japan, and *Brosmophycis marginatus*,
beautifully red in color, is occasionally seen on the coast of
California.   Many other genera and species abound in the
depths of the sea and in crevices of coral reefs, showing much
variety in form and structure

The *Bregmacerotidæ* are small fishes, closely related to the
Brotulids, having the hypercoracoid perforate, but with several minor peculiarities, the first ray of the dorsal being free
and much elongate   They live near the surface in the open
sea   *Bregmaceros macclellandi* is widely diffused in the Pacific

Ateleopodidæ.—The small family of *Ateleopodidæ* includes long-bodied, deep-water fishes of the Pacific, resembling *Macrourus*, but with smooth scales. The group has the coracoids as in *Brotulidæ*, and the actinosts are united in an undivided plate. *Ateleopus japonicus* is the species taken in Japan

Suborder Haplodoci.—We may here place the peculiar family of *Batrachoididæ*, or toadfishes It constitutes the suborder of *Haplodoci* (ἀπλόος, simple, δόκος, shaft) from the simple form of the post-temporal This order is characterized by the undivided post-temporal bone and by the reduction of the gill-arches to three. A second bone behind the post-temporal connects the shoulder-girdle above to the vertebral column. The coracoid bones are more or less elongate, suggesting the arm seen in pediculate fishes

The single family has the general form of the *Cottidæ*, the body robust, with large head, large mouth, strong teeth, and short spinous dorsal fin The shoulder-girdle and its structures differ little from the blennioid type. There are no pseudobranchiæ and the tail is homocercal. The species are relatively few, chiefly confined to the warm seas and mostly American, none being found in Europe or Asia Some of them ascend rivers, and all are carnivorous and voracious None are valued

Fig 648 —Leopard Toadfish, *Opsanus pardus* (Goode & Bean) Pensacola

as food, being coarse-grained in flesh The group is probably nearest allied to the *Trachinidæ* or *Uranoscopidæ*.

Opsanus tau, the common toadfish, or oyster-fish, of our Atlantic coast, is very common in rocky places, the young clinging to stones by a sucking-disk on the belly, a structure which is early lost   It reaches a length of about fifteen inches. *Opsanus pardus*, the leopard toadfish, or sapo, of the Gulf coast, lives in deeper water and is prettily marked with dark-brown spots on a light yellowish ground

In *Opsanus* the body is naked and there is a large foramen, or mucous pore, in the axil of the pectoral   In the *Marcgravia cryptocentra*, a large Brazilian toadfish, this foramen is absent. In *Batrachoides*, a South American genus, the body is covered with cycloid scales   *Batrachoides surinamensis* is a common species of the West Indies   *Batrachoides pacifici* occurs at Panama   The genus *Porichthys* is remarkable for the development of series of mucous pores and luminous spots in several different lateral lines which cover the body   These luminous spots are quite unlike those found in the lantern-fishes (*Myctophidæ*) and other *Iniomi*   Their structure has been worked out in detail by Dr Charles Wilson Greene

The common midshipman, or singing fish, of the coast of California is *Porichthys notatus*   This species, named midshipman from its rows of shining spots like brass buttons, is found among rocks and kelp and makes a peculiar quivering or humming noise with its large air-bladder.

Porichthys porosissimus, the bagre sapo, is common on all coasts of the Gulf of Mexico and the Caribbean Sea. *Po-*

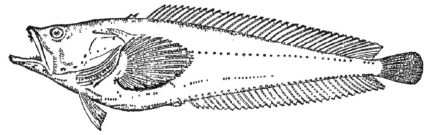

Fig 649 —Singing Fish or Bagre Sapo, *Porichthys porosissimus* (Cuv & Val) Galveston

richthys margaritatus is found about Panama and *Porichthys porosus* in Chile

The species of *Thalassophryne* and *Thalassothia*, the poison toadfishes, are found along the coasts of South America, where they sometimes ascend the rivers   In these species there is an elaborate series of venom glands connected with the hollow spines of the opercle and the dorsal spines. Dr Gunther gives the following account of this structure as shown in *Thalassophryne reticulata*, a species from Panama

"In this species I first observed and closely examined the poison organ with which the fishes of this genus are provided Its structure is as follows. (1) The opercular part The operculum is very narrow, vertically styliform and very mobile, it is armed behind with a spine, eight lines long in a specimen of 10½ inches, and of the same form as the venom fang of a snake, it is, however, somewhat less curved, being only slightly bent upward It has a longish slit at the outer side of its extremity which leads into a canal perfectly closed and running along the whole length of its interior, a bristle introduced into the canal reappears through another opening at the base of the spine, entering into a sac situated on the opercle and along the basal half of the spine, the sac is of an oblong-ovate shape and about double the size of an oat grain Though the specimen had been preserved in spirits for about nine months it still contained a whitish substance of the consistency of thick cream, which on the slightest pressure freely flowed from the opening in the extremity of the spine On the other hand, the sac could be easily filled with air or fluid from the foramen of the spine No gland could be discovered in the immediate neighborhood of the sac (2) The dorsal part is composed of the two dorsal spines, each of which is ten lines long The whole arrangement is the same as in the opercular spines, their slit is at the front side of the point, each has a separate sac, which occupies the front of the basal portion

Suborder Xenopterygii — The clingfishes, forming the suborder *Xenopterygii* (ξενός, strange, πτερυξ, fin), are, perhaps, allied to the toadfishes The ventral fins are jugular, the rays 1, 4 or 1, 5, and between them is developed an elaborate sucking-disk, not derived from modified fins, but from folds of the skin and underlying muscles

The body is formed much as in the toadfishes The skin is naked and there is no spinous dorsal fin The skeleton shows several peculiarities, there is no suborbital ring, the palatine arcade is reduced, as are the gill-arches, the opercle is reduced to a spine-like projection, and the vertebræ are numerous   The species are found in tide-pools in the warm seas, where they cling tightly to the rocks with their large ventral disks

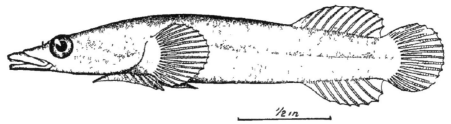

Fig 650 —*Aspasma ciconiæ* Jordan & Snyder   Wakanoura, Japan.

Several species of *Lepadogaster* and *Mirbelia* are found in the Mediterranean. *Lepadogaster gouani* is the best-known European species   *Aspasma ciconiæ* and *minima* occur about the rocks in the bays of Japan

Most of the West Indian species belong to *Gobiesox*, with entire teeth, and to *Arbaciosa*, with serrated teeth   Some of these

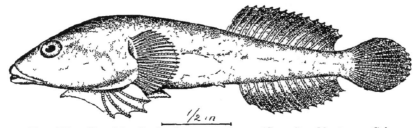

Fig 651 —Clingfish, *Caularchus mœandricus* (Girard).   Monterey, Cal

species are deep crimson in color, but most of them are dull olive   *Gobiesox virgatulus* is common on the Gulf Coast   *Caularchus mœandricus*, a very large species, reaching a length of six inches, abounds along the coast of California.   Other genera are found at the Cape of Good Hope, especially about New Zealand. *Chorisochismus dentex,* from the Cape of Good Hope, reaches the length of a foot.

CHAPTER XLV

OPISTHOMI AND ANACANTHINI

ORDER Opisthomi.—The order *Opisthomi* (ὄπισθη, behind, ὦμος, shoulder) is characterized by the general traits of the blennies and other elongate, spiny-rayed fishes, but the shoulder-girdle, as in the Apodes and the *Heteromi*, is inserted on the vertebral column well behind the skull.

The single family, *Mastacembelidæ*, is composed of eel-shaped fishes with a large mouth and projecting lower jaw, inhabiting the waters of India, Africa, and the East Indies. They are small in size and of no economic importance. The dorsal is long, with free spines in front and there are no ventral fins. Were these fins developed, they should in theory be jugular in position. There is no air-duct in *Mastacembelus* and it seems to be a true spiny-rayed fish, having no special relation to

FIG. 652 —*Mastacembelus ellipsifer* Boulenger   Congo River   (After Boulenger)

either *Notacanthus* or to the eels. Except for the separation of the shoulder-girdle from the skull, there seems to be no reason for separating them far from the Blennioid forms, and the resemblance to *Notacanthus* seems wholly fallacious

Mastacembelus armatus is a common species of India and China. In *Rhynchobdella* the nasal appendage or proboscis, conspicuous in *Mastacembelus*, is still more developed. *Rhynchobdella aculeata* is common in India

Order Anacanthini.—We may separate from the other jugular fishes the great group of codfishes and their allies,

739

retaining the name Anacanthini ($\overset{\acute{}}{\alpha}\nu\alpha\kappa\alpha\nu\theta o\varsigma$, without spine)
suggested by Johannes Muller   In this group the hyper-
coracoid is without foramen, the fenestra lying between this
bone and the hypocoracoid below it   The tail is isocercal, the
vertebræ in a right line and progressively smaller backward,
sometimes degenerate or whip-like (leptocercal) at tip   Other
characters are shown in the structure of the skull   There are
no spines in any of the fins, the ventrals are jugular, the scales
generally small, and the coloration dull or brownish.   The
numerous species live chiefly in the northern seas, some of
them descending to great depths   The resemblance of these
fishes to some of the Blennioid group is very strongly marked, but
these likenesses seem analogical only and not indicative of true
affinity   The codfishes probably represent an early offshoot from
the ancestors of the spiny-rayed fishes, and their line of evolution
is unknown, possibly from Ganoid types   Among recent fishes
there is nothing structurally nearer than the *Nototheniidæ* and
Brctulidæ, but the line of descent must branch off much farther
back than either of these.   For the present, therefore, we may regard the codfishes and their allies (*Anacanthini*) as a distinct order

The Codfishes · Gadidæ —The chief family is that of the *Gadidæ*,
or codfishes   These are characterized by a general resemblance
to the common codfish, *Gadus callarias*   This is one of the best

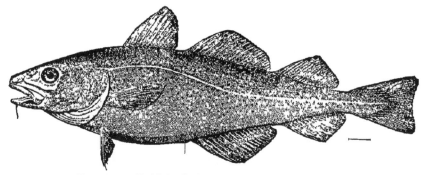

Fig 653 —Codfish, *Gadus callarias* L   Eastport, Me

known of fishes, found everywhere on the shores of the North
Atlantic, and the subject of economic fisheries of the greatest
importance   Its flesh is white, flaky, rather tasteless, but takes
salt readily, and is peculiarly well adapted for drying   The
average size of the codfish is about ten pounds, but Captain

Nathaniel Atwood of Provincetown records one with the weight of 160 pounds

"The cod ranks among the most voracious of ordinary fishes, and almost everything that is eatable, and some that is not, may find its way into its capacious maw."

"The codfish in its mode of reproduction exhibits some interesting peculiarities It does not come on the coast to spawn, as was once supposed, but its eggs are deposited in mid-sea and float to the surface, although it does really, in many cases, approach the land to do so Prof C O Sars, who has discovered its peculiarities, 'found cod at a distance of twenty to thirty Norwegian miles from the shore and at a depth of from one hundred to one hundred and fifty fathoms' The eggs thus confided to the mercy of the waves are very numerous, as many as 9,100,000 have been calculated in a seventy-five-pound fish 'When the eggs are first seen in the fish they are so small as to be hardly distinguishable, but they continue to increase in size until maturity, and after impregnation have a diameter depending upon the size of the parent, varying from one-nineteenth to one-seventeenth of an inch. A five-to eight-pound fish has eggs of the smaller size, while a twenty-five-pound one has them between an eighteenth and a seventeenth.' There are about 190,000 eggs of the smaller size to a pound avoirdupois They are matured and ejected from September to November "

Unlike most fishes, the cod spawns in cooling water, a trait also found in the salmon family

The liver of the cod yields an easily digested oil of great value in the medical treatment of diseases causing emaciation

The Alaska cod, *Gadus macrocephalus*, is equally abundant with the Atlantic species, from which it differs very slightly, the air-bladder or sounds being smaller, according to the fishermen, and the head being somewhat larger This species is found from Cape Flattery to Hakodate in Japan, and is very abundant about the Aleutian Islands and especially in the Okhotsk Sea With equal markets it would be as important commercially as the Atlantic cod In the codfish (*Gadus*) and related genera there are three dorsal and two anal fins In the codfish the lateral line is pale and the lower jaw shorter than the upper

The haddock (*Melanogrammus æglifinus*) closely resembles the cod and is of similar quality as food   It is known at sight by the black lateral line   It is found on both shores of the Atlantic and when smoked is the "finnan haddie" of commerce

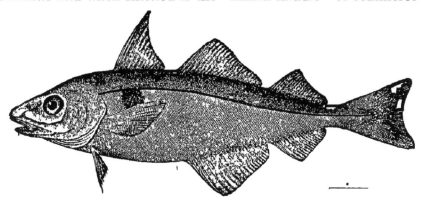

FIG 654 —Haddock, *Melanogrammus æglifinus* (L).   Eastport, Me

The pollack, coalfish, or green cod (*Pollachius carbonarius*) is also common on both shores of the north Atlantic.   It is darker than the cod and more lustrous, and the lower jaw is longer, with a smaller barbel at tip   It is especially excellent when fresh

The whiting (*Merlangus merlangus*) is a pollack-like fish common on the British coasts, but not reaching the American shores.

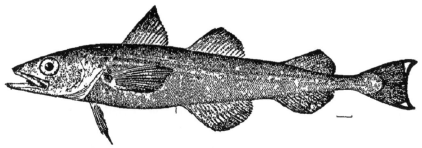

FIG 655 —Pollock, *Theragra chalcogramma* (Pallas)   Shumagin I , Alaska

It is found in large schools in sandy bays   The Alaska pollack (*Theragra chalcogramma*) is a large fish with projecting lower jaw, widely diffused in the north Pacific and useful as a food-fish to the Aleutian peoples   It furnishes a large part of the food of the fur-seal (*Callorhinus alascanus* and *C ursinus*) during its migrations   The fur-seal rarely catches the true codfish, which swims near the bottom The wall-eyed pollack (*Theragra fucensis*) is found about Puget Sound Smaller codfishes of this type are the wachna cod (*Eleginus navaga*) of Siberia and the Arctic codling (*Boreogadus saida*), both common about Kamchatka, the latter crossing to Greenland

Several dwarf codfishes having, like the true cod, three dorsal fins and a barbel at the chin are also recorded Among these are the tomcod, or frostfish, of the Atlantic (*Microgadus tomcod*), the California tomcod (*Microgadus proximus*), and *Micromesistius poutassou* of the Mediterranean These little cods are valued as pan fishes, but the flesh is soft and without much flavor

Other cod-like fishes have but two dorsals and one anal fin. Many of these occur in deep water Among those living near shore, and therefore having economic value, we may mention a few of the more prominent The codlings (*Urophycis*) are represented by numerous species on both shores of the Atlantic.

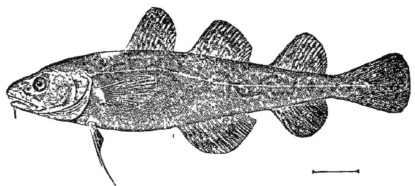

FIG 656 —Tomcod, *Microgadus tomcod* (Walbaum)   Woods Hole, Mass

Urophycis blennoides is common in the Mediterranean. *Urophycis regius*, on our South Atlantic coast, is said to exhibit electric powers in life, a statement that needs verification In the Gulf of Mexico *Urophycis floridanus* is common Farther north are the more important species *Urophycis tenuis*, called the white hake, and *Urophycis chuss*, the squirrel-hake The ling (*Molva molva*) is found in deep water about the North Sea.

A related genus, *Lota*, the burbot, called also ling and, in America, the lawyer, is found in fresh waters This genus contains the only fresh-water members of the group of *Anacanthini*.

The European burbot, *Lota lota*, is common in the streams and lakes of northern Europe and Siberia. It is a bottom fish, coarse in flesh and rather tasteless, eaten sometimes when boiled and soaked in vinegar or made into salad It is dark olive in color, thickly marbled with blackish

The American burbot, or lawyer (*Lota maculosa*), is very much like the European species It is found from New England throughout the Great Lakes to the Yukon It reaches a length of usually two or three feet and is little valued as food in the United States, but rises much in esteem farther north The liver and roe are said to be delicious In Siberia its skin is used instead of glass for windows In Alaska, according to Dr Dall, it reaches a length of six feet and a weight of sixty pounds

FIG 657 —Burbot, *Lota maculosa* (Le Sueur) New York

The rocklings (*Gaidropsarus* and *Enchelyopus*) have the first dorsal composed of a band of fringes preceded by a single ray The species are small and slender, abounding chiefly in the Mediterranean and the North Atlantic The young have been

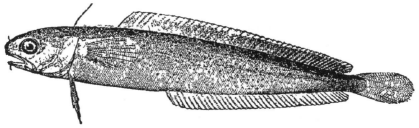

FIG 658 —Four-bearded Rockling, *Enchelyopus cimbrius* (Linnæus) Nahant, Mass

called "mackerel-midges" Our commonest species is *Enchelyopus cimbrius*, found also in Great Britain.

The cusk, or torsk, *Brosme brosme*, has a single dorsal fin only. It is a large fish found on both shores of the North Atlantic, but rather rare on our coasts

Fossil codfishes are not numerous Fragments thought to belong to this family are found in English Eocene rocks.

Nemopteryx troscheli, from the Oligocene of Glarus, has three dorsal fins and a lunate caudal fin Other forms have been referred with more or less doubt to *Gadus, Brosmius, Strinsia,* and *Melanogrammus*

Gill separates the "three-forked hake" (*Raniceps trifurcus*) of northern Europe as a distinct family, *Ranicipitidæ*. In this species the head is very large, broad and depressed, differing in this regard from the codlings and hakes, which have also two dorsal fins The deep-water genus, *Bathyonus,* is also regarded as a distinct family, *Bathyonidæ*

The Hakes: Merlucidæ.—Better defined than these families

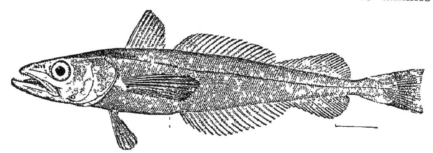

FIG 659 —California Hake, *Merluccius productus* (Ayres) Seattle

is the family of hakes, *Merlucidæ* These pike-like codfishes have the skull peculiarly formed, the frontal bones being paired, excavated above, with diverging crests continuous forward from the forked occipital crest The species are large fishes, very voracious, without barbels, with the skeleton papery and the flesh generally soft The various species are all very much alike, large, ill-favored fishes with strong teeth and a ragged appearance, the flesh of fair quality. *Merluccius merluccius,* the hake or stock-fish, is common in Europe, *Merluccius bilinearis,* the silver hake, is common in New England, *Merluccius productus* in California, and *Merluccius gayi* in Chile

The Grenadiers: Macrouridæ. — The large family of grenadiers, or rat-tails, *Macrouridæ* is confined entirely to the oceanic depths, especially of the north Atlantic and Pacific   The head is formed much as in the codfishes, with usually a barbel at the chin. There are two dorsals, the second like the anal being low, but the leptocercal tail is very long and tapering, ending in a fila-

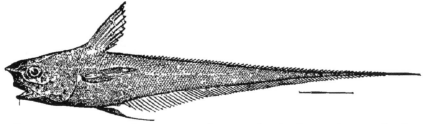

Fig 660 —*Coryphænoides carapinus* (Goode & Bean), showing leptoceral tail Gulf Stream

ment without caudal fin.   The scales are usually rough and spinous   The species are usually large in size, and dull gray or black in color

The best-known genus is *Macrourus*.   *Macrourus berglax* is found on both shores of the north Atlantic.   *Macrourus*

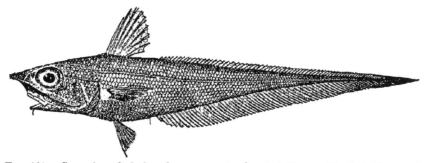

Fig 661 —Grenadier, *Cælorhynchus carminatus* Goode & Bean   Martha's Vineyard.

bairdi is abundant in off-shore dredgings from Cape Cod to Cuba *Macrourus cinereus*, the pop-eye grenadier, outnumbers all other fishes in the depths of Bering Sea   *Cælorhynchus japonicus* is often taken by fishermen in Japan   *Coryphænoides rupestris* is common in the north Atlantic   *Bogoslovius clarki* and *Albatrossia pectoralis* were dredged by the *Albatross* about the volcanic island of Bogoslof.   *Trachyrhynchus trachyrhynchus* is characteristic of the Mediterranean   *Nematonurus goodei* is common in the Gulf Stream, and *Dolloa longifilis* is found off

Japan   Other prominent genera are *Bathygadus*, *Gadomus*, *Regania*, and *Steindachnerella*

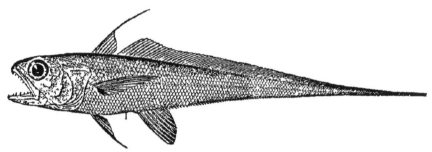

Fɪɢ. 662 —*Steindachnerella argentea* (Goode & Bean)   Gulf Stream.

The *Murænolepidæ* are deep-sea fishes, with minute eel-like scales, and no caudal fin.   The ventrals are five-rayed and there are 10 pterygials

CHAPTER XLVI

ORDER PEDICULATI: THE ANGLERS

THE Angler-fishes.—The few remaining fishes possess also jugular ventral fins, but in other regards they show so many peculiarities of structure that we may well consider them as forming a distinct order, *Pediculati* (*pedicula*, a foot-stalk), although the relation of these forms to the *Batrachoididæ* seems a very close one.

The most salient character of the group is the reduction and backward insertion of the gill-opening, which is behind the pectoral fins, not in front of them as in all other fishes The hypocoracoid and hypercoracoid are much elongate and greatly changed in form, so that the pectoral fin is borne on the end of a sort of arm The large ventrals are similarly more or less exserted The spinous dorsal is much reduced, the first spine being modified to form a so-called fishing-rod, projecting over the mouth with a fleshy pad, lure, or bait at its tip The form of the body varies much in the different families. The scales are lost or changed to prickles and the whole aspect is very singular, and in many cases distinctly frog-like The species are mostly tropical, some living in tide-pools and about coral reefs, some on sandy shores, others in the oceanic abysses

The nearest allies of the Pediculates among normal fishes are probably the *Batrachoididæ* One species of *Lophiidæ* is recorded among the fossils, *Lophius brachysomus*, from the Eocene of Monte Bolca. No fossil *Antennariidæ* are known Fossil teeth from the Cretaceous of Patagonia are doubtfully named "*Lophius patagonicus*"

The Fishing-frogs: Lophiidæ.—In the most generalized family, that of the fishing-frogs (*Lophiidæ*), the body is very much depressed, the head the largest part of it. The mouth is excessively wide, with strong jaw-muscles, and strong sharp teeth.

748

The skin is smooth, with dermal flaps about the head   Over the mouth, like a fishing-rod, hangs the first dorsal spine with a lure at the tip   The fishes lie flat on the bottom with sluggish movements except for the convulsive snap of the jaws. It has been denied that the bait serves to attract small fishes to their destruction, but the current belief that it does so is certainly plausible

Mr Saville Kent recently expressed doubt as to whether the fishing-frogs really use the first spine for purposes of angling In no other group, however, is the coloring more distinctly that of the rocks and algæ among which the fishes lurk

The great fishing-frog of the North Atlantic, *Lophius piscatorius*, is also known as angler, monkfish, goosefish, allmouth,

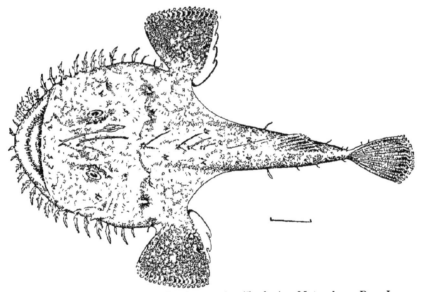

Fig 663 —Anko or Fishing-frog, *Lophius litulon* (Jordan)   Matsushima Bay, Japan

wide-gape, kettleman, and bellows-fish   It is common in shallow water both in America and Europe, ranging southward to Cape Hatteras and to the Mediterranean   It reaches a length of three feet or more   A fisherman told Mr Goode that "he once saw a struggle in the water, and found that a goosefish had swallowed the head and neck of a large loon, which had pulled it to the surface and was trying to escape   There is authentic record of seven wild ducks having been taken from the stomach of one of them   Slyly approaching from below, they seize birds as they float upon the surface "

The genus *Lophius* of northern range has a vertebral column of about thirty vertebræ   *Lophius litulon* occurs in Japan. In the North Pacific is found *Lophiomus*, similar in appearance but smaller in size, ranging southward to the equator, a southern fish having but eighteen vertebræ.   *Lophiomus setigerus* is the common anko of Japan, and other species are recorded from Hawaii and the Galapagos

The Sea-devils: Ceratiidæ.—The sea-devils, or *Ceratiidæ*, are degenerate anglers of various forms, found in the depths of the arctic seas   The body is compressed, the mouth vertical; the substance is very soft, and the color uniform black   Dr. Gunther thus speaks of them

"The bathybial sea-devils are degraded forms of *Lophius,* they descend to the greatest depths of the ocean.   Their bones

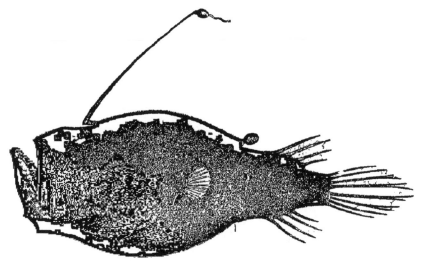

FIG 664 —*Cryptopsaras couesi* Gill   Gulf Stream

are of an extremely light and thin texture, and frequently other parts of their organization, their integuments, muscles, and intestines, are equally loose in texture when the specimens are brought to the surface   In their habits they probably do not differ in any degree from their surface representative, *Lophius* The number of the dorsal spines is always reduced, and at the end of the series of these species only one spine remains, with a simple, very small lamella at the extremity (*Melanocetus john-sonii, Melanocetus murrayi*). In other forms sometimes a

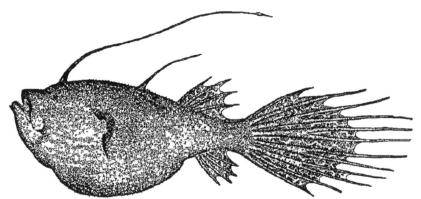

FIG 665 —Deep-sea Angler, *Ceratias holbolli* Kroyer   Greenland.

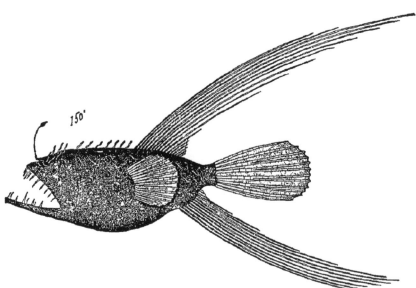

FIG. 666 —*Caulophryne jordani* Goode & Bean   Gulf Stream   Family *Ceratiidæ*

second cephalic spine, sometimes a spine on the back of the trunk, is preserved   The first cephalic spine always retains the original function of a lure for other marine creatures, but to render it more effective a special luminous organ is sometimes developed in connection with the filaments with which its extremity is provided (*Ceratias bispinosus, Oneirodes eschrichtii*). So far as known at present these complicated tentacles attain to the highest degree of development in *Himantolophus* and *Ægæonichthys* In other species very peculiar dermal appendages are developed, either accompanying the spine on the back or replacing it They may be paired or form a group of three, are pear-shaped, covered with common skin, and perforated at the top, a delicate tentacle sometimes issuing from the foramen."

Of the fifteen or twenty species of *Ceratiidæ* described, none

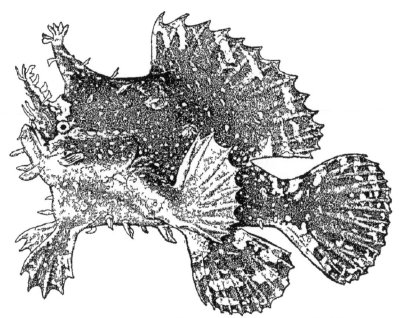

FIG 667 —Sargassum-fish, *Pterophryne tumida* (Osbeck), Florida
Family *Antennariidæ*

are common and all are rare catches of the deep-sea dredge. *Caulophryne jordani* is remarkable for its large fins and the luminous filaments, *Linophryne lucifer* for its large head, and *Corynolophus reinhardti* for its luminous fishing-bulb.

The Frogfishes: Antennariidæ —The frogfishes, *Antennariidæ*, belong to the tropical seas and rarely descend far below the surface. Most of them abound about sand-banks or coral reefs, especially along the shores of the East and West Indies, where they creep along the rocks like toads Some are pelagic, drifting

about in floating masses of seaweed   All are fantastic in form
and color, usually closely imitating the objects about them.
The body is compressed, the mouth nearly vertical, and the skin
either prickly or provided with fleshy slips

The species of *Pterophryne* live in the open sea, drifting with
the currents in masses of sargassum   Two species, *Pterophryne
tumida* and *Pterophryne gibba*, are found in the West Indies and
Gulf Stream   Two others very similar, *Pterophryne histrio* and
Pterophryne ranina, live in the East Indies and drift in the Kuro

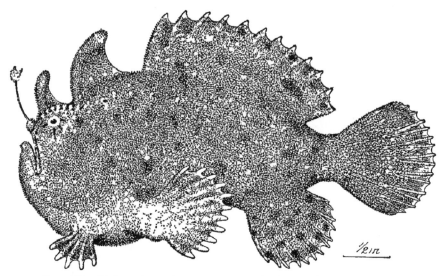

FIG 668 —Fishing-frog, *Antennarius nox* Jordan   Wakanoura, Japan

Shiwo of Japan   All these are light olive-brown with fantastic
black markings

The genus *Antennarius* contains species of the shoals and
reefs, with markings which correspond to the colors of the rocks
These fishes are firm in texture with a velvety skin, and the prevailing color is brown and red   There are many species wherever reefs are found   *Antennarius ocellatus*, the pescador, is
the commonest West Indian species. *Antennarius multiocel-
latus*, with many ocellated spots, is the Martin Pescador of Cuba,
also common

On the Pacific coast of Mexico the commonest species is
Antennarius strigatus   In Japan, *Antennarius tridens* abounds
everywhere on the muddy bottoms of the bays   *Antennarius*

nox is a jet-black species of the Japanese reefs, and *Antennarius sanguifluus* is spotted with blood-red in imitation of coralline patches　Many other species abound in the East Indies and in

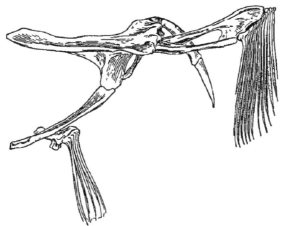

[FIG. 669 —Shoulder-girdle of a Batfish, *Ogcocephalus radiatus* (Mitchill).

Polynesia.　The genus *Chaunax* is represented by several deep-water species of the West Indies, Japan, etc.

The *Gigactinidæ* of the deep seas differ from the *Ogcocephalidæ*, according to Boulenger, in the absence of ventrals.

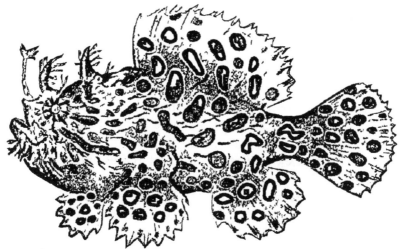

FIG 670.—Frogfish, *Antennarus scaber* (Cuvier)　Puerto Rico.

The Batfishes: Ogcocephalidæ.—The batfishes, *Ogcocephalidæ*, are anglers with the body depressed and covered with hard bony warts.　The mouth is small and the bony bases of the pectoral and ventral fins are longer than in any other of the anglers The species live in the warm seas, some in very shallow water, others descending to great depths, the deep-sea forms being small and more or less degenerate These walk along like toads on the sea-bottoms, the ventrals, being jugular, act as fore legs and the pectorals extend behind them as hind legs

The common sea-bat, or diablo, of the West Indies, *Ogcocephalus vespertilio*, is dusky in color with the belly coppery red It reaches the length of a foot. The angling spine is very short, hidden under the long stiff process of the snout Farther north

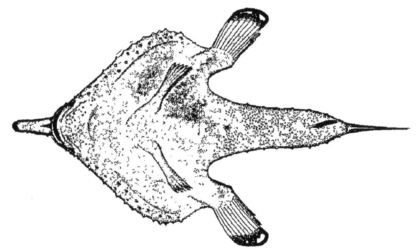

Fig 671.—*Ogcocephalus vespertilio* (L) Florida

occurs the short-nosed batfish, *Ogcocephalus radiatus*, very similar, but with the nostril process, or snout, blunt and short. *Zalieutes elater*, with a large black eye-like spot on each side of the back, is found on the west coast of Mexico In deeper water are species of *Halieutichthys* in the West Indies and of *Halieutæa* in Japan *Dibranchus atlanticus* has the gills reduced to two pairs *Malthopsis* consists of small species, with the rostrum prominent, like a bishop's miter Two species are found in the Pacific, *Malthopsis mitrata* in Hawaii and *Malthopsis tiarella* in Japan.

And with these dainty freaks of the sea, the results of centuries on centuries of specialization, degeneration, and adaptation, we close the long roll-call of the fishes, living and dead

And in their long genealogy is enfolded the genealogy of men and beasts and birds and reptiles and of all other back-boned animals of whom the fish-like forms are at once the ancestors, the cousins, and the younger brothers   When the fishes of the Devonian age came out upon the land, the potentiality of the

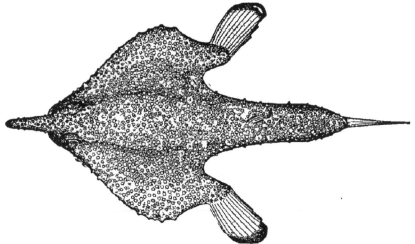

Fig 672 —Batfish, *Ogcocephalus vespertilio* (L)   Florida

higher methods of life first became manifest   With the new conditions, more varied and more exacting, higher and more varied specialization was demanded, and, in response to these new conditions, from a fish-like stock have arisen all the birds and beasts and men that have dwelt upon the earth

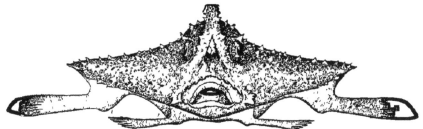

Fig 673 —Batfish, *Ogcocephalus vespertilio* (Linnæus)   Carolina Coast.

THE END.

RÉSUMÉ OF THE CLASSIFICATION OF FISHES AND FISH-LIKE VERTEBRATES

We here present a résumé of the classification of the families and higher groups of fishes and of the other aquatic Chordata, as adopted in this volume, a few slight changes being made in certain groups   The names of extinct families are printed in italics

Branch or Phylum CHORDATA
   Division PROTOCHORDATA
     Class ENTEROPNEUSTA
         Order ADELOCHORDATA
            Harrimaniidæ
            Glandicepitidæ
            Balanoglossidæ
     Class TUNICATA
         Order LARVACEA
            Appendiculariidæ
         Order ASCIDIACEA
            Ascidiidæ
            Cynthiidæ
            Clavellinidæ
            Molgulidæ
            Botryllidæ
            Polystyelidæ
            Didemnidæ
            Distomidæ
            Polyclinidæ
            Pyrosomidæ
         Order THALIACEA
            Salpidæ
   Division VERTEBRATA
     Class LEPTOCARDII
            Branchiostomidæ (Lancelets)
     Class CYCLOSTOMI
         Order HYPEROTRETA
            Eptatretidæ (Borers)
            Myxinidæ (Hagfishes)

757

Order HYPEROARTIA
    Petromyzonidæ (Lampreys)
    Mordaciidæ

Class ELASMOBRANCHII
  Subclass SELACHII
    Order *PLEUROPTERYGII*
      Cladoselachidæ
    Order *ACANTHODEI*
      Acanthoessidæ
      Diplacanthidæ
      Ischnacanthidæ
    Order *ICHTHYOTOMI*
      Pleuracanthidæ
    Order NOTIDANI
      Hexanchidæ (Cow-sharks)
      Chlamydoselachidæ (Frill-sharks)
    Order CESTRACIONTES
      Cochliodontidæ
      Hybodontidæ
      Orodontidæ
      Heterodontidæ (Bull-head Sharks)
      Psammodontidæ
      Tamiobatidæ
    Order ASTEROSPONDYLI (GALEOIDEI)
      Scylliorhinidæ (Cat-sharks)
      Hemiscylliidæ
      Orectolobidæ
      Ginglymostomidæ (Nurse-sharks)
      Odontaspididæ (Sand-sharks)
      Mitsukurinidæ (Goblin-sharks)
      Alopiidæ (Threshers)
      Pseudotriakidæ
      Lamnidæ (Man-eater Sharks)
      Cetorhinidæ (Basking-sharks)
      Rhineodontidæ
      Carchariidæ (Common Sharks)
      Sphyrnidæ (Hammer-head Sharks)
    Order TECTOSPONDYLI (SQUALOIDEI)
      Squalidæ (Dog-fishes)
      Dalatiidæ
      Echinorhinidæ (Bramble-sharks)

Order TECTOSPONDYLI (SQUALOIDEI)—*Continued*
 Squatinidæ (Angel-sharks)
 Pristiophoridæ (Saw-sharks)
Order BATOIDEI (HYPOTREMA)
 Pristidæ (Sawfishes)
 Rhinobatidæ (Guitar-fishes)
 Rajidæ (Skates)
 Narcobatidʌ (Torpedoes)
 Petalodontidæ
 Pristodontidæ
 Dasyatidæ (Sting-rays)
 Aetobatidæ (Eagle-rays)
 Psammodontidæ
 Mobulidæ (Devil-rays)
Subclass HOLOCEPHALI
 Order CHIMÆROIDEI
  Chimæridæ (Chimæras)
  Rhinochimæridæ
  Callorhynchidæ (Bottle-nose Chimæras)
  Ptyctodontidæ
  Squalorajidæ
  Myriacanthidæ
Class OSTRACOPHORI
 Order *HETEROSTRACI*
  Thelodontidæ
  Psammosteidæ
  Drepanaspidæ
  Pteraspidæ
 Order *OSTEOSTRACI*
  Cephalaspidæ
  Thyestidæ
  Odontodontidæ
 Order ANTIARCHA
  Asterolepidæ
 Order ANASPIDA
  Birkeniidæ
Class TELEOSTOMI
 Subclass CROSSOPTERYGII
  Order *HAPLISTIA*
   Tarrassiidæ

Order *RHIPIDISTIA*
    Holoptychidæ
    Megalichthyidæ
    Osteolepidæ
    Onychodontidæ
Order *ACTINISTIA*
    Cælacanthidæ
Order CLADISTIA
    Polypteridæ (Bichirs)
Subclass DIPNEUSTI
  Series SIRENOIDEA
    Order *CTENODIPTERINI*
        Uronemidæ
        Dipteridæ
        Ctenodontidæ
    Order SIRENOIDEI
        Ceratodontidæ (Barramundas)
        Lepidosirenidæ (Loalaches)
  Series ARTHRODIRA
    Order *STEGOPHTHALAMI*
        Macropetalichthyidæ
        Asterosteidæ
    Order *TEMNOTHORACI*
        Chelonichthyidæ
    Order *ARTHROTHORACI*
        Coccosteidæ
        Dinichthyidæ
        Titanichthyidæ
        Mylostomidæ
        Selenosteidæ
    Order *CYCLIÆ*
        Palæospondylidæ
Subclass ACTINOPTERI
  Series GANOIDEI
    Order *LYSOPTERI*
        Palæoniscidæ
        Platysomidæ
        Dorypteridæ
        Dictyopygidæ
    Order CHONDROSTEI
        Chondrosteidæ

Order CHONDROSTEI—*Continued*
  Belonorhynchidæ
  Acipenseridæ (Sturgeons)
Order SELACHOSTOMI
  Polyondontidæ (Paddle-fishes)
Order *PYCNODONTI*
  Pycnodontidæ
Order HOLOSTEI (RHOMBOGANOIDEA)
  Semionotidæ
  Lepidotidæ
  Isopholidæ
  Macrosemiidæ
  Aspidorhynchidæ
Order GINGLYMODI
  Lepisosteidæ (Garpikes)
Order HALECOMORPHI (CYCLOGANOIDEI)
  Pachycormidæ
  Protosphyrænidæ
  Liodesmidæ
  Amiatidæ (Bowfins)
Series TELEOSTEI
Order ISOSPONDYLI
  Pholidophoridæ
  Archæomænidæ
  Oligopleuridæ
  Leptolepidæ
  Elopidæ (Ten-pounders)
  Megalopidæ (Tarpons)
  Spaniodontidæ
  Pachyrhizodontidæ
  Albulidæ (Lady-fishes)
  Thryptodontidæ
  Chanidæ (Milk-fishes)
  Pterothrissidæ
  Hiodontidæ (Moon-eyes)
  Chirocentridæ (Dorabs)
  Ichthyodectidæ
  Ctenothrissidæ
  Phractolæmidæ
  Notopteridæ
  Clupeidæ (Herrings)

Order ISOSPONDYLI—*Continued*
    Engraulidæ (Anchovies)
    Dorosomidæ (Gizzard-shads)
    Osteoglossidæ
    Phareodontidæ
    Pantodontidæ
    Alepocephalidæ
    Gonorhynchidæ
    Cromeriidæ
    Salmonidæ (Salmon and Trout)
    Thymallidæ (Graylings)
    Argentinidæ (Smelts)
    Microstomidæ
    Salangidæ (Ice-fishes)
    Stomiatidæ
    Astronesthidæ
    Malacosteidæ
    Chauliodontidæ
    Gonostomatidæ
    Aulopidæ
    Synodontidæ (Lizard-fishes)
    Benthosauridæ
    Bathypteroidæ
    Ipnopidæ
    Rondeletiidæ
    Cetomimidæ
    Myctophidæ (Lantern-fishes)
    Chirothricidæ
    Rhinellidæ
    Exocoetoididæ
    Maurolicidæ
    Plagyodontidæ (Lancet-fishes)
    Evermannellidæ
    Paralepidæ
    Sternoptychidæ
    Idiacanthidæ
    Enchodontidæ
    Dercetidæ
    Stratodontidæ
Order LYOPOMI
    Halosauridæ

Order SYMBRANCHIA
  Suborder ICHTHYOCEPHALI
    Monopteridæ (Rice-eels)
  Suborder HOLOSTOMI
    Symbranchidæ
    Amphipnoidæ
    Chilobranchidæ
Order APODES
  Suborder ARCHENCHELI
    Urenchelyidæ
  Suborder ENCHELYCEPHALI
    Anguillidæ (Eels)
    Simenchelyidæ (Pug-nosed Eels)
    Synaphobranchidæ
    Leptocephalidæ (Conger-eels)
    Murænesocidæ
    Ilyophidæ
    Heterocongridæ
    Myridæ
    Dysommidæ
    Ophichthyidæ (Snake-eels)
    Nettastomidæ (Duck-billed Eels)
    Nemichthyidæ (Snake-eels)
  Suborder COLOCEPHALI
    Murænidæ (Morays)
    Myrocongridæ
    Moringuidæ
Order CARENCHELI
    Derichthyidæ
Order LYOMERI
    Eurypharyngidæ (Gulpers)
    Saccopharyngidæ
Order HETEROMI
    Pronotacanthidæ
    Notacanthidæ (Spring-eels)
    Lipogenyidæ
Order OSTARIOPHYSI
  Suborder HETEROGNATHI
    Characidæ (Characins)
    Erythrinidæ

Suborder EVENTOGNATHI
    Cyprinidæ (Carp and Minnows)
    Catostomidæ (Suckers)
    Cobitidæ (Loaches)
    Homalopteridæ
    Kneriidæ
Suborder NEMATOGNATHI
    Diplomystidæ
    Siluridæ (Catfishes)
    Sisoridæ
    Bunocephalidæ
    Plotosidæ
    Chacidæ
    Clariidæ
    Hypophthalmidæ
    Pygidiidæ
    Argidæ
    Loricariidæ
    Callichthyidæ
Suborder GYMNONOTI
    Electrophoridæ (Electric Eels)
    Gymnotidæ (Carapos)
Order SCYPHOPHORI
    Mormyridæ
    Gymnarchidæ
    Haplochitonidæ
    Galaxiidæ (New Zealand Trout)
Order HAPLOMI
    Esocidæ (Pikes)
    Umbridæ (Mud-minnows)
    Pœciliidæ (Killifishes)
    Amblyopsidæ (Cave Blindfishes)
    Crossognathidæ
    Cobitopsidæ
Order XENOMI
    Dalliidæ (Blackfishes)
Order ACANTHOPTERI
Suborder SYNENTOGNATHI
    Belonidæ (Garfishes)
    Exocœtidæ (Flying-fishes)

Suborder PERCESOCES
    Atherinidæ (Silversides)
    Mugilidæ (Mullets)
    Sphyrænidæ (Barracudas)
Suborder RHEGNOPTERI
    Polynemidæ (Thread-fins)
Suborder HEMIBRANCHII
    Gasterosteidæ (Sticklebacks)
    Aulorhynchidæ
    Protosyngnathidæ
    Fistularidæ (Cornet-fishes)
    Aulostomidæ (Trumpet-fishes)
    Macrorhamphosidæ (Snipe-fishes)
    Urosphenidæ
    Rhamphosidæ
    Centriscidæ (Shrimp-fishes)
Suborder LOPHOBRANCHII
    Solenostomidæ
    Syngnathidæ (Pipefishes and Sea-horses)
Suborder HYPOSTOMIDES
    Pegasidæ (Sea-moths)
Suborder SALMOPERCÆ
    Percopsidæ (Trout-perch)
    Erismatopteridæ
Suborder SELENICHTHYES
    Lampridæ (Opahs)
    Semiophoridæ
Suborder ZEOIDEA
    Amphistiidæ
    Zeidæ (John-dories)
    Grammicolepidæ
Suborder BERYCOIDEA
    Berycidæ (Alfonsinos)
    Trachichthyidæ
    Holocentridæ (Soldier-fishes)
    Polymixiidæ
    Monocentridæ (Pine-cone Fishes)
    Stephanoberycidæ
Suborder PERCOMORPHI
    Group SCOMBROIDEA
        Scombridæ (Mackerels)

Group SCOMBROIDEA—*Continued*
    Gempylidæ (Escolars)
    Lepidopidæ (Frost-fishes)
    Trichiuridæ (Cutlass-fishes)
    Palæorhynchidæ
    Istiophoridæ (Sailfishes)
    Xiphiidæ (Swordfishes)
    Carangidæ (Cavallas)
    Nematistiidæ (Papagallos)
    Vomeropsidæ
    Cheilodipteridæ (Pomatomidæ) (Bluefishes)
    Rachycentridæ (Sergeant-fishes)
    Stromateidæ (Harvest-fishes)
    Icosteidæ (Ragfishes)
    Acrotidæ
    Zaproridæ
    Bramidæ (Pomfrets)
    Steinegeriidæ
    Pteraclidæ
    Coryphænidæ (Dolphins)
    Equulidæ
    Lactaridæ
    Menidæ
    Luvaridæ (Louvars)
    Pempheridæ
    Bathyclupeidæ
    Tetragonuridæ
Group PERCOIDEA
    Centrarchidæ (Sunfishes)
    Aphredoderidæ (Pirate-perches)
    Kuhliidæ (Seseles)
    Elassomidæ (Pygmy-perches)
    Oxylabracidæ (Centropomidæ) (Robalos)
    Percidæ (Perches and Darters)
    Apogonidæ (Apogonichthyidæ) (Cardinal-fishes)
    Ambassidæ (Parambassidæ)
    Scombropidæ
    Acropomidæ
    Enoplosidæ
    Anomalopidæ
    Astneopidæ

Group PERCOIDEA—*Continued*

    Serranidæ (Basses and Groupers)
    Lobotidæ (Flashers)
    Priacanthidæ (Big-eyes)
    Histiopteridæ
    Lutianidæ (Snappers)
    Cæsionidæ
    Hæmulidæ (Grunts)
    Scorpidæ
    Sparidæ (Porgies)
    Mænidæ (Picarels)
    Gerridæ (Mojarras)
    Kyphosidæ (Rudder-fishes)
    Mullidæ (Goat-fishes)
    Sciænidæ (Croakers)
    Sillaginidæ
    Oplegnathidæ (Stone-wall Fishes)
    Nandidæ
    Polycentridæ
    Pseudochromidæ
    Opisthognathidæ (Jawfishes)
    Trichodontidæ (Sand-fishes)
    Chiasmodontidæ (Swallowers)
    Champsodontidæ
    Malacanthidæ (Matajuelos)
    Latilidæ (Blanquillos)
    Pinguipedidæ
    Cepolidæ (Ribbon-fishes)
    Cirrhitidæ (Hawk-fishes)
    Latrididæ (Trumpeters)
    Aplodactylidæ

Suborder KURTOIDEA
    Kurtidæ

Suborder LABYRINTHICI
    Anabantidæ (Climbing-fishes)
    Osphromenidæ (Gouramies)
    Helostomidæ
    Luciocephalidæ
    Ophicephalidæ (Snakefishes)

Suborder HOLCONOTI
    Embiotocidæ (Surf-fishes)

Suborder CHROMIDES
     Cichlidæ (Cichlids)
     Pomacentridæ (Demoiselles)
Suborder PHARYNGOGNATHI
     Labridæ (Wrasses)
     Scaridæ (Scarichthyidæ) (Parrot-fishes)
     Odacidæ
     Siphonognathidæ
Suborder SQUAMIPINNES
     Antigoniidæ (Boarfishes)
     Toxotidæ (Archers)
     Ephippidæ
     Ilarchidæ (Spadefishes)
     Drepanidæ
     Platacidæ (Batfishes)
     Chætodontidæ (Butterfly-fishes)
     Zanclidæ (Moorish idols)
     Acanthuridæ (Surgeons)
Suborder AMPHACANTHI
     Siganidæ
Suborder SCLERODERMI *
     Triacanthidæ
     Balistidæ (Trigger-fishes)
     Monacanthidæ (Filefishes)
     Spinacanthidæ
Suborder OSTRACODERMI *
     Ostracidæ (Trunkfishes)
Suborder GYMDODONTES *
     Triodontidæ (Pursefishes)
     Chonerhinidæ
     Tetraodontidæ (Puffers)
     Diodontidæ (Rabbit-fishes)
     Heptadiodontidæ
     Molidæ (Headfishes)
Suborder GOBIOIDEA
     Gobiidæ (Gobies)
     Oxudercidæ
Suborder DISCOCEPHALI
     Echeneidæ (Remoras)

* These three suborders constitute the series called Plectognathi

Suborder SCLEROPAREI
  Scorpænidæ (Rockfishes)
  Caracanthidæ
  Anoplopomatidæ (Skil-fishes)
  Ophiodontidæ (Blue Cods)
  Oxylebidæ
  Zaniolepidæ
  Hexagrammidæ (Greenlings)
  Platycephalidæ
  Hoplichthyidæ
  Bembridæ
  Cottidæ (Sculpins)
  Ereuniidæ
  Rhamphocottidæ
  Comephoridæ (Baikal-fishes)
  Agonidæ (Sea-poachers)
  Cyclopteridæ (Lumpfishes)
  Liparidæ (Snailfishes)
Suborder CRANIOMI
  Triglidæ (Gurnards)
  Peristediidæ
  Cephalacanthidæ (Flying Gurnards)
Suborder TÆNIOSOMI
  Lophotidæ
  Regalecidæ (Oarfishes)
  Trachypteridæ (Dealfishes)
  Stylephoridæ
Suborder HETEROSOMATA
  Pleuronectidæ (Flounders)
  Soleidæ (Soles)
Suborder JUGULARES
  Trachinidæ (Weevers)
  Callipterygidæ
  Nototheniidæ
  Harpagiferidæ
  Bovichthyidæ
  Percophidæ
  Pteropsaridæ
  Bathymasteridæ (Ronquils)
  Leptoscopidæ
  Uranoscopidæ (Star-gazers)

Suborder JUGULARES—*Continued*
    Dactyloscopidæ
    Callionymidæ (Dragonets)
    Rhyacicnthyidæ
    Trichonotidæ
    Hemerocœtidæ
    Blenniidæ (Blennies)
    Xiphidiidæ (Gunnels)
    Ptilichthyidæ (Quillfishes)
    Xiphasiidæ
    Patæcidæ
    Blochiidæ
    Gnathanacanthidæ
    Acanthoclinidæ
    Gadopsidæ
    Cerdalidæ
    Anarrhichadidæ (Wolf-fishes)
    Cryptacanthodidæ (Wry-mouths)
    Zoarcidæ (Eel-pouts)
    Scytalinidæ
    Congrogadidæ
    Derepodichthyidæ
    Xenocephalidæ
    Ophidiidæ (Cusk-eels)
    Lycodapodidæ
    Ammodytidæ (Sand-lances)
    Bleekeriidæ
    Fierasferidæ (Pearlfishes)
    Brotulidæ (Brotulas)
    Bregmacerotidæ
Suborder HAPLODOCI
    Batrachoididæ (Toadfishes)
Suborder XENOPTERYGII
    Gobiesocidæ (Clingfishes)
Suborder OPISTHOMI
    Mastacembelidæ
Suborder ANACANTHINI
    Gadidæ (Codfishes)
    Ranicipitidæ
    Bathyonidæ
    Merluciidæ (Hakes)

Suborder ANACANTHINI—*Continued*
    Macruridæ (Grenadiers)
    Ateleopodidæ
    Murænolepidæ
Order PEDICULATI
    Lophiidæ (Fishing-frogs)
    Ceratiidæ
    Antennariidæ (Frogfishes)
    Gigantactinidæ
    Ogcocephalidæ (Sea-bats)

INDEX

INDEX

(Illustrations are indicated by an asterisk)

THE AMERICAN NATURE SERIES

The fortunate increase in the attention paid by the American people to Nature study, has led to the publication of many popular books on the subject, some of which are good, and some not. In the hope of doing something toward furnishing a series where the seeker will surely find a readable book of high authority, the publishers of the American Science Series have begun the publication of the American Nature Series. It is the intention that in its own way, the new series shall stand on a par with its famous predecessor.

The primary object of the new series is to answer questions—those (outside of the domain of philosophy) which the contemplation of Nature is constantly arousing in the mind of the unscientific intelligent person. But a collateral object will be to give some intelligent notion of the " causes of things "

The books will be under the guarantee of American experts, and from the American point of view, and where material crowds space, preference will be given to American facts over others of not more than equal interest

The series will be in five divisions

GROUP I. CLASSIFICATION OF NATURE

This division will consist of three sections

Section A. A large popular Natural History in several volumes, with the topics treated in due proportion, by authors of unquestioned authority. There is no existing Natural History which does not fall short in some one of these particulars. Possibly the Natural History in the American Nature Series may not be kept ideal regarding all of them, but if it is not, the fault will not be due to carelessness or apathy on the part of the publishers.

The books so far arranged for in this section are

FISHES, by David Starr Jordan, President of the Leland Stanford University

INSECTS, by Vernon L. Kellogg, Professor in the Leland Stanford Junior University. $5.00 net, carriage, 35 cents.

TREES, by N. L. Britton, Director of the New York Botanical Garden.

WILD MAMMALS OF NORTH AMERICA, by C. Hart Merriam, Chief of the United States Biological Survey.

BIRDS OF THE WORLD. A popular account by Frank H. Knowlton, M.S., Ph.D., Member American Ornithologists Union, President Biological Society of Washington, etc., etc., with Chapter on Anatomy of Birds by Frederick A. Lucas, Chief Curator Brooklyn Academy Arts and Sciences, and edited by Robert Ridgway, Curator of Birds, U.S. National Museum

Section B. A Shorter Natural History by the authors of Section A, preserving its popular character, its proportional treatment and its authority so far as that can be preserved without its fullness.

Section C. Identification Books—"How to Know," brief and in portable shape. By the authors of the larger treatises.

GROUP II. FUNCTIONS OF NATURE

These books will treat of the relation of facts to causes and effects—of heredity in organic Nature, and of the environment in all Nature In treating of Inorganic Nature, the physical and chemical relations will be specially expounded, and in treating of organized creatures, the relations to food and climate, with the peculiarities of their functions—internal and external

THE BIRD· ITS FORM AND FUNCTION, by C W Beebe, Curator of Birds in the New York Zoological Park. 8vo, 496 pp $3 50 net, by mail, $3 80.

GROUP III. REALMS OF NATURE

Detailed treatment of various departments in a literary and popular way

Already published

FERNS, by Campbell E Waters, of Johns Hopkins University. 8vo, pp xi+362. Price $3 00 net, by mail, $3 30.

GROUP IV. WORKING WITH NATURE

How to propagate, develop and care for the plants and animals
Published in this division is

NATURE AND HEALTH, by Edward Curtis, Professor Emeritus in the College of Physicians and Surgeons 12mo, $1 25 net, by mail, $1 37.

Arranged for are

CHEMISTRY OF DAILY LIFE, by Henry P Talbot, Professor of Chemistry in the Massachusetts Institute of Technology.

DOMESTIC ANIMALS, by William H Brewer, Professor Emeritus in Yale University

THE CARE OF TREES IN LAWN, STREET AND PARK, by B E Fernow, Late Head of the Cornell School of Forestry

GROUP V. DIVERSIONS FROM NATURE

This division will include a wide range of writings not rigidly systematic or formal, but written only by authorities of standing

FISH STORIES, by David Starr Jordan, President of the Leland Stanford Junior University

HORSE TALK, by William H Brewer, Professor Emeritus in Yale University

BIRD NOTES, by C W Beebe, Curator of Birds in the New York Zoological Park

HENRY HOLT AND COMPANY, Publishers
29 WEST TWENTY-THIRD STREET, NEW YORK

Lightning Source UK Ltd.
Milton Keynes UK
UKHW030848250321
380972UK00006BA/443